JESUS AMONG THE GODS

Early Christology in the Greco-Roman World

Michael F. Bird

BAYLOR UNIVERSITY PRESS

© 2022 by Baylor University Press
Waco, Texas 76798

All Rights Reserved. No part of this publication may be reproduced, stored in a retrieval system, or transmitted, in any form or by any means, electronic, mechanical, photocopying, recording, or otherwise, without the prior permission in writing of Baylor University Press.

Cover and book design by Kasey McBeath
Cover art: The Holy Face (tempera & gold on panel), Novgorod School (12th century) / Russian, Tretyakov Gallery, Moscow, Russia, © Bridgeman Images

The Library of Congress has cataloged this book under ISBN 978-1-4813-1675-0.
Library of Congress Control Number: 2022940713

For David Capes, fellow scribe of the kingdom.

Contents

Preface ix

    Introduction 1

I   Jesus and Ancient Divinity

    1 Problematizing Jesus' Divinity 9

    2 The Search for Divine Ontology 41

II   Jesus and Intermediary Figures

    3 Putting Jesus in His Place 87
       Scholarship on Early Christology and Intermediary Figures

    4 Jesus and the "In-Betweeners" 115
       Comparing Early Christologies and Intermediary Figures

    5 Setting Jesus apart from Demiurges, Deities,
       Daemons, and Divi 381

Bibliography 413
Index of Modern Authors 445
Index of Ancient Authors 453
Index of Ancient Sources 455

Preface

In my research about Jesus and early Christianity, I've covered several areas: the historical Jesus and the origins of the Gentile mission, the historical Jesus as a messianic claimant, the messianic texture of the Gospels, the beginnings of divine Christology in dialogue with Bart Ehrman, and the late origins of adoptionist Christology. This book, however, is my attempt to make a contribution to the study of early Christology by making two original claims.

First, I give renewed attention to divine ontology—what a god is—in relation to literary representations of Jesus. In other words, I'm asking: What is a god, what are the types of gods of antiquity, and what type of god was Jesus presented as being? This is important because most studies of early Christology focus on christological titles, divine functions, divine identity, and types of worship. The subject of "ontology" is considered something that happened in the second and third centuries as the early church engaged in a flamboyant Platonic interpretation of Jesus. My rejoinder is to say no: divine ontology was there from the beginning, and a comparison of first-century authors like Philo, Paul, and Plutarch proves it so. The upshot is that I think I can show that belief in Jesus as an absolute, eternal, true, and unbegotten deity goes back to the first century.

Second, much is made of comparisons between Jesus and intermediary figures, earthly beings promoted to heaven, or heavenly beings who visit earth. Some consider these intermediary figures to be the key to understanding how Jesus became divine, while for others such comparative enterprises are a bland instance of "this" is really "that" and commit the fallacy of equivocation called parallelomania. My rejoinder is to say yes and no. Yes, Jesus is similar in some respects to some intermediary figures. However, when we look at the aggregate differences between Jesus and these intermediary figures, they show that what is distinctive of Jesus appears to be demonstrably Jewish, in which case, Jesus resembles a Jewish deity, or, more properly, he is a revelation and embodiment of the Jewish deity. Thus, in whatever ways Jesus resembles the intermediary figures of Greco-Roman religions and Second Temple Judaism, he remains a close analogue of the God of Israel.

The idea for this book came after spending a week in Bellingham in Washington state, United States, at the invitation of the Faithlife Corporation. It was there, in a charming local bookstore, that I came across a second-hand copy of Plutarch's *Isis and Osiris*, which I devoured and wondered why the language sounded like a cross between Paul, Philo, and Athanasius, thoughts which eventually began to crystallize in my 2020 Leon Morris Lecture at Ridley College on Jesus and divine ontology. Otherwise, this book was enabled by Ridley College's generous provision of study leave, the Australian College of Theology making me a senior research fellow, and the support of Ridley librarians Ruth Weatherlake, Alison Foster, and Harriet Sabarez, as well as bibliographical assistance by James Darlack from Vanguard University. I received generous help searching for some Coptic texts from Francis Watson and Christian Askeland, for which I remain most grateful.

Many friends and colleagues read segments of this book and offered important feedback, including Jonathan Lookadoo, David Runia, Laszlo Gallusz, Jörg Frey, Ruben Bühner, Chris Tilling, and M. David Litwa. Brandon Smith read portions, too. Also, his PhD thesis on the Trinity and the book of Revelation was a rewarding read that introduced me to important things in patristic literature and discussions in Revelation scholarship. Theron Clay Mock generously shared with me a forthcoming SBL paper that was full of terrific insights.

The COVID pandemic, with libraries closed to visitors, made it harder to access so many primary and secondary source materials, which meant sometimes relying on Google Books and websites like Perseus for original sources. I know I speak for many when I say that conducting tertiary education on Zoom and attempting to homeschool children, as well as do original research, was an utterly miserable affair. God be praised that it is over. Thankfully, I was able to work through it and produce what I hope will be known as my COVID monograph.

I'm grateful too to the wonderful editorial staff at Baylor University Press, especially Cade Jarrell, who received this project with enthusiasm and was incredibly supportive as it was guided into publication.

On a sadder note, while this book was being written, two giant scholars in the study of early Christology passed away, Larry Hurtado and Jimmy Dunn. As I was writing this volume, I was constantly wondering to myself what they might say in reply, or whether I would have convinced them. I stand on their shoulders and remain in their debt as much as in deep appreciation of their scholarship. That is a conversation that I hope to take up with them in a more luminous and everlasting environment. Until then, may they both rest in peace and rise in glory.

Finally, this book is dedicated to my dear friend David Capes, a wonderful scholar, teacher, administrator, and churchman. David has been a generous host and a great dialogue partner. He has made his own contribution to the study of divine Christology, and he has blessed me with his friendship.

Rev. Dr. Michael F. Bird
Academic Dean and Lecturer in New Testament at Ridley College
Senior Research Fellow with the Australian College of Theology
December 1, 2021

Introduction

Studies on Christology in the last one hundred years have usually focused on one of the following approaches: explaining how Jesus went from being regarded as a Jewish prophet to becoming a Gentile God; documenting the various christological titles attributed to Jesus; mapping the impact of Hellenistic influences on an earlier Jewish Christology; expositing Jesus' functional divinity; looking at how Jesus fits into a strict Jewish monotheism (dovetailing with the debates as to whether monotheism was actually strict and whether monotheism was an actual thing back then); explaining Jesus' divinity as based on either devotional practices or divine identity; analyzing how Old Testament Yahweh texts were applied to Jesus in the New Testament; searching for the closest parallel among ancient intermediary beings to describe Jesus as a semi-divine figure. Those are the debates that we have had and are still having up to this point.[1] While I will touch upon some of these debates, many of which are now stale and stagnated, I have no intention of rehearsing them or fully solving them. Instead, this book is an attempt to open a new front in the study of early Christology—a new front that I hope partly retrieves some neglected

---

[1] See Andrew Chester, "High Christology—Whence, When and Why?" *EC* 2 (2011): 22–50; Jörg Frey, "Eine neue religionsgeschichtliche Perspektive: Larry W. Hurtados *Lord Jesus Christ* und die Herausbildung der frühen Christologie," in *Reflections on the Early Christian History of Religion—Erwägungen zur frühchristlichen Religionsgeschichte*, ed. Cilliers Breytenbach and Jörg Frey (AJEC 81; Leiden: Brill, 2013), 115–69; Crispin Fletcher-Louis, *Jesus Monotheism*, vol. 1: *Christological Origins: The Emerging Consensus and Beyond* (Eugene, Ore.: Wipf & Stock, 2015); Brandon Smith, "What Christ Does, God Does: Surveying Recent Scholarship on Christological Monotheism," *CBR* 17 (2019): 184–208; and Matthew V. Novenson, "Introduction," in *Monotheism and Christology in Greco-Roman Antiquity*, ed. Matthew V. Novenson (Leiden: Brill, 2020), 1–31.

wisdom of older generations while at the same time combining it with the very best of *Religionsgeschichte Ansätze* in its twenty-first-century permutation. Hopefully this new front will be more like Eisenhower in France than Churchill in Gallipoli, but reviewers will have to decide that for themselves.

I am endeavoring to do two things. First, I aim to demonstrate that ancient notions of divine ontology have been sidelined for too long in academic discussions of early Christology and it is time to retrieve them. Second, I want to engage in a comparative analysis of Jesus and ancient intermediary figures with a view to showing what is distinctive about Jesus' divinity in early Christian discourse. The argument can be broken down further.

First of all, I endeavor to show that there were two metrics of divinity in antiquity, the absolute (i.e., ontological) and the euergetic (i.e., honorific, relative, and relational). In other words, gods were either eternal and unbegotten (uncreated) or deified and begotten (created). This is the taxonomy that is used with remarkable consistency by Greek, Roman, Jewish, and Christian authors over several centuries. So, which one is relevant to the Jesus of early Christianity? The answer is both! Some envisaged Jesus as a begotten deity, whether an angelic creature inhabiting a human or a human being adopted as God's son (i.e., Ebionites, Theodotians, etc.). Some envisaged Jesus as divine in an unbegotten sense (i.e., Hebrews, Gospel of John, Ignatius of Antioch, Gospel of Truth, perhaps the apostle Paul). In addition, two authors roughly contemporary with the beginnings of Christianity, Philo and Plutarch, both use ontological language for God/gods. Philo decries Caligula's pretention to deity on the grounds that he does not have the *ousia* of divinity. Plutarch says his native country worships Apollos as an unbegotten rather than begotten deity. If we analyze early Christology in light of this unbegotten/begotten distinction and read Christian texts beside Philo and Plutarch, then ontological language for Jesus would seem normal and natural.

Even so, the secondary literature on ancient religion and Christology tells us ad nauseam that (1) Greco-Roman religions were about ritual, not theology; (2) early Christology was functional or devotional and all that ontological language only arrives in the second century; and (3) the Creed of Nicaea in 325 CE represents the triumph of a Platonic eisegesis in patristic exegesis with talk of a divine nature. Yet I map out a significant amount of explicit ontological language for describing Jesus in the New Testament and by proto-orthodox and heterodox authors of the second century. Now, I never assert that the New Testament and Nicaea are saying the precise same thing about Christ's nature, but I do contend that an ontological dimension to Christology is not a *novum* introduced by a Platonic big bang in the second and third centuries that crystallized into Nicene Christology. Divine ontology was part of the environment and manifests itself in early Christologies in various ways.

Second, I attempt to demonstrate that intermediary figures are genuinely illuminating for early Christology, but they are neither a negative foil nor a template for explaining the origins of early divine Christology. The intermediary figures we find described in Jewish and Greco-Roman texts, such as demiurges, principal angels, exalted patriarchs, or deified emperors, are not a hermeneutical key for explaining the origins of Jesus' divinity, but neither are they irrelevant for how early Christian authors described Jesus as a divine being. There are clear similarities and dissimilarities between accounts of Jesus and these various intermediary figures. This is where David Litwa's maxim is helpful: "To focus on pure similarity is parallelomania; to focus on difference is apologetics."[2] Consequently, I map these similarities and differences at length. Moreover, I argue that the similarities show that the first Christians participated in Greco-Roman discourse about the divine realm and its interaction with the world; and when we analyze the various dissimilarities they are striking because they accentuate specifically Jewish traits in early christological discourse. Thus, while the Jesus of early Christianity is in many respects a Greco-Roman deity (i.e., akin to a Greek demigod, a principal angel, a deified emperor, or a demiurge), when we parse the distinctive features (i.e., both the unique and the characteristic), Jesus appears more and more like the God of the Judeans. Jesus is, then, a bit like a Jewish Hercules, an apotheosized Augustus, or an archangel, but he is a lot like the Jewish deity Yahweh.

I happily identify with the new *religionsgeschichtliche Schule* of scholars who have given primacy to the Jewish context and shaping of early Christology, scholars such as Martin Hengel, Larry Hurtado, Richard Bauckham, William Horbury, N. T. Wright, David Capes, and Crispin Fletcher-Louis.[3] However, I believe it necessary to take a step toward scholars like Luke Timothy Johnson, Adela Collins, Michael Peppard, and David Litwa, who have majored in the importance of Greco-Roman culture because of the complex interface between Judaism and Hellenism, because of Christianity's parity with

---

[2] M. David Litwa, *Iesus Deus: The Early Christian Depiction of Jesus as a Mediterranean God* (Minneapolis: Fortress, 2014), 33.

[3] Larry Hurtado, "The New *religionsgeschichtliche Schule* at Thirty," in *Monotheism and Christology in Greco-Roman Antiquity*, ed. Matthew V. Novenson (Leiden: Brill, 2020), 7–31; Frey, "Eine neue religionsgeschichtliche Perspektive," 117–70; and Jarl Fossum, "The New Religionsgeschichtliche Schule: The Quest for Jewish Christology," in *SBL Seminar Papers 1991*, ed. Eugene H. Lovering (Atlanta: Scholars Press, 1991), 638–46.

aspects of Greco-Roman "theology," and because we can only understand how Christianity was dissimilar to Greco-Roman religions after we have seen how they are similar. Becoming a Christian in antiquity might have required one to be cut off from Greco-Roman cults, but it did not cut one off completely from Greco-Roman culture. In fact, literary representations of Jesus suggest that Greco-Roman culture played a major part in shaping early Christology.[4] As Luke Timothy Johnson puts it: "Insisting that Christianity derives from Judaism does not itself answer the question of how Greco-Roman religious sensibilities may have been among the elements of the symbolic world that Christians recatalyzed in light of their own experience."[5]

As for a methodology, I am convinced that in order to explore early Christology one must look wider than the New Testament and beyond the first century. Early Christology has to be examined up to at least Irenaeus, perhaps up to the time of Origen, and maybe as late as the entire Nicene era. We must explore the first and second centuries together because the New Testament writings were composed, collected, and edited into discrete collections during the apostolic period (pre-70 CE), sub-apostolic period (70–130 CE), and early patristic period (130–200 CE). Notwithstanding debates about authenticity and dating, many early Christian writings, both proto-orthodox and heterodox, were probably composed before some later New Testament texts were written.[6] The transition between apostolic and post-apostolic is not hard and fast, but fuzzy and imprecise. The categories of proto-orthodox and heterodox, even when viewed retrospectively, are flexible and permeable (the *Epistula Apostolorum* is an anti-Gnostic text with a Christology that has a certain affinity with Gnostic texts!). Therefore, one must look beyond canonical texts and look at para- and post-canonical texts irrespective of whether they are works of the apostolic fathers, "other" Gospels, apologetic writings, various *Acts*, letters, textual fragments, or come from proto-orthodox or heterodox groups. In other words, I am attempting to study early Christology in light of Greco-Roman literature and religion, Second Temple Judaism, New Testament exegesis, Christian origins, patristic studies, and early Christian thought. A bold undertaking, but one that I believe allows for a robust diachronic and synchronic analysis that recovers some neglected factors and offers some fresh insights into early Christology.

---

[4] Litwa, *Iesus Deus*, 218.

[5] Luke Timothy Johnson, *Among the Gentiles: Greco-Roman Religion and Christianity* (New Haven, Conn.: Yale University Press, 2009), 30.

[6] Many scholars would date 2 Peter, the Pastoral Epistles, Acts of the Apostles, Revelation, James, and Jude in the second century.

In the first section concerning the nature of divinity in relation to Christology, we have chapter 1, "Problematizing Jesus' Divinity," which examines the problem of Jesus as a divine being. What do we mean by "god," and how is Jesus "divine"? I give several examples from ancient Judaism and Greco-Roman religions and philosophy to explain the conundrum. Next, chapter 2, "The Search for Divine Ontology," establishes the two ancient metrics for divinity, the absolute and the euergetic, and reapproaches the question of how Jesus is divine in light of that taxonomy. The result is to show that many writers, perhaps as early as the apostle Paul, conceived of Jesus as an absolute deity.

In the second section focus turns to Jesus vis-à-vis intermediary figures. Accordingly, chapter 3 is entitled "Putting Jesus in His Place: Scholarship on Early Christology and Intermediary Figures," and surveys scholarly perspectives on Jesus and intermediary figures, including those who make much of them, and those who suppose they have only tangential relevance. Then comes chapter 4, "Jesus and the 'In-Betweeners': Comparing Early Christologies and Intermediary Figures," which is a lengthy, dense, and detailed discussion of Jesus in relation to (1) demiurge, logos, and wisdom; (2) angels; (3) exalted patriarchs; and (4) ancient ruler cults. In this mega-chapter, I set out the various intermediary figures, show points of parallel with Christian literary representations of Jesus, and then attempt to identify points of differentiation. Then finally, chapter 5, "Setting Jesus apart from Demiurges, Deities, Daemons, and Divi," is where I make some inferences about the preceding analysis between intermediary figures and early Christologies. It is true that Jesus resembles Jewish and Greco-Roman intermediary figures in some respects. However, if we examine the distinctiveness of Jesus vis-à-vis various intermediary figures, then it is apparent that those distinctive elements appear to be amplifying specifically Jewish traits. In other words, Jesus generally resembles a Mediterranean deity, a Greek hero, or Roman *divus*, but more specifically, he is a close analogue to the God of Israel and this God's mode of activity in creation and on behalf of his people Israel. Such a conclusion is controversial and requires some brief comments on whether anything in Judaism can be distinctive from Greco-Roman antiquity in relation to divinity, whether my thesis perpetuates the alleged Judaism vs. Hellenism divide, and whether I am merely pursuing an apologetic quest for Jesus' uniqueness.

In sum, I am arguing that in order to understand in what sense Jesus was divine for the earliest churches we must consider ancient categories of divinity and how Jesus maps against them. The result is that positing Jesus as absolutely divine—a true, living, and uncreated God—did not first happen with the christological debates of the fourth century, but took place in the first century.

Beyond that, I claim that early Christologies need to be located in the context of the Judaism of the Greco-Roman world. That is because the influence of Greco-Roman religions and philosophy is part of the explanation as to why and how early Christologies made the various literary representations of Jesus that they did. However, when it comes to the genetic origins and first moments of divine Christology and the features that make Jesus stand out among the gods of antiquity, primacy must be given to the particularities of Jewish divine discourse.

I
Jesus and Ancient Divinity

1

Problematizing Jesus' Divinity

> The effort to arrive at the Truth, and especially the truth about the gods, is a longing for the divine.
>
> Plutarch, *Is. Os.* 2.

> The christological question, as to whether the statement "Jesus is God" is true, and if so in what sense, is often asked as though "God" were the known and "Jesus" the unknown; this, I suggest, is manifestly mistaken. If anything, the matter stands the other way round.
>
> N. T. Wright, *The New Testament and the People of God*

The fourth-century Nicene-Constantinopolitan Creed states that Jesus is "God from God, light from light, true God from true God, begotten, not made, of the same substance as the Father." This is the classic and creedal affirmation of Jesus' full and equal deity with God the Father as professed among the Catholic, Greek Orthodox, Oriental Orthodox, and Protestant churches. Yet strong affirmations of Jesus' deity precede the fourth century and go back to earlier centuries. Eusebius stated, "All the Psalms and hymns which were written by faithful Christians from the beginning sing of Christ as the Logos of God and treat him as God" (*Hist. eccl.* 5.28.5–6). Bishop Melito of Sardis wrote: "For he was born a son, and led as a lamb, and slaughtered as a sheep, and buried as a man, and rose from the dead as God, being God by his nature and a man" (*Peri Pascha* 8). In the Christian additions to the eighth book of the *Sibylline Oracles*, from the late second century, Jesus is proclaimed this way: "This is our God, now proclaimed in acrostics [i.e., *icthys*], the king, the immortal savior, who suffered for us" (*Sib. Or.* 8.249–50). The second-century apologist Justin Martyr (ca. 155 CE) was typical of proto-orthodox Christology when he described Christ as "Lord and God the Son of God" who is "deserving to be worshipped as God and as Christ" (*Dial.* 63.5; 128.1). Indeed, analogous affirmations of Jesus as "God" go back as far as *2 Clement*, with its opening statement: "Brothers and sisters, we ought to think of Jesus Christ as we do of God" (*2 Clem.* 1.1). Or else, bishop Ignatius of Antioch in the first quarter of the second century could also say of Jesus: "There is only one physician, who is both flesh and spirit, born and unborn, God in man, true life in death, both from Mary and from God, first subject to suffering and then beyond it, Jesus Christ our Lord" (Ign. *Eph.* 7.2), and to Polycarp he wrote, "I bid you farewell always in our God Jesus Christ" (*Pol.* 8.3). Pliny the Younger, when he was governor of Bithynia in the early second century, learned that Christians would sing hymns to Christ "as to a god" (*Ep.* 10.97.6). Later, Celsus observed that Christians "worship to an extravagant degree this man who appeared recently" (*Cels.* 8.12). I take it as uncontroversial to claim that the church fathers regarded Jesus as "God," a divine being, and offered him cultus-like worship. This was a conclusion largely arrived at by virtue of their use of several texts and traditions, including those that eventually became the New Testament.

The inference of Jesus' deity is hardly illegitimate, considering explicit New Testament affirmations about Jesus. In the Gospel of John, Jesus is the "Word" who was "with God," "was God," and "became flesh" (John 1.1–2, 14), the divine Son who makes himself "equal with God" (John 5.18), who declares that everyone should "honor the Son just as they honor the Father" (John 5.23), and in his resurrected body is hailed by Thomas as "my Lord and my God" (John 20.28). Looking at the Pauline corpus, Jesus is called "our great God and Savior" (Titus 2.13), and—assuming some grammar—the subject of acclamation as "the Messiah, who is God over all, forever praised! Amen" (Rom 9.5). We could add to these various Yahweh texts from the Old Testament that are applied to Jesus by Paul (e.g., Deut 6.4 in 1 Cor 8.4–6; Isa 45.23 in Phil 2.9–11) and the nature miracles attributed to Jesus by the Evangelists, where he exhibits theophanic qualities like walking on water (Mark 6.45–53). It is far more likely than not that the New Testament corpus as a whole identifies Jesus as a divine being and ascribes the qualities of divinity to him.[1]

---

[1] This specifically undermines the claims of James Dunn (*Christology in the Making: A New Testament Inquiry into the Origins of the Doctrine of the Incarnation* [2nd ed.; Grand Rapids: Eerdmans, 1989], 259) and Maurice Casey (*From Jewish Prophet to Gentile God*

Nonetheless there is a real riddle associated with Jesus' ascribed divinity. When the apostolic and post-apostolic generations called Jesus "God," what did they mean by that? What is a god? What are the substance and attributes of deity? Who is the God of Israel? How does Jesus' apparent divinity relate to the identity, nature, and functions of God the Father's divinity? The church's contentious debates across the second to fourth centuries were not about the fact of Christ's divinity, whether or not he was God; rather, the torrid debates were concerned with the quest for a scripturally sound and philosophically coherent account of Christ as divine beside God the Father. Precisely how is Christ "God" beside "God" the Father without compromising monotheism?[2] As Origen explained to Heraclides: "But as our brothers take offence at the statement that there are two gods, we must formulate the doctrine carefully, and show in what sense they are two and in what sense the two are one God" (*Dial.* 1).

To this end, manifold options were explored in the search for a Christian doctrine of God that could incorporate a divine Jesus. Was Jesus divine in the sense of a supreme angel, the firstborn within the cosmos, yet subordinated to the Father in nature and rank (Arianism)? Was Jesus divine in the sense that he was a manifestation of the Father in a new mode of existence (Sabellianism)? Was Jesus divine in the sense of a human being who had become inhabited by an angel (Ebionites) or a human being who had been deified upon his resurrection (Theodotians)? Was Jesus divine in the sense of being an inferior yet perfect aeon sent from the heavenly pleroma to give humans true knowledge of the Father (Valentinians)? Was Jesus divine in the sense of being the eternal Son who possessed the same divine substance as God the Father, equal to God in being, eternally begotten of the Father, but a different person who was subordinated only during the incarnation (Nicene)? All these views affirm Jesus' divinity, but they differ over how he

---

[Louisville, Ky.: Westminster John Knox, 1991], 37) that it is only with the Gospel of John that Jesus is unambiguously divine.

[2] Posed this way, it renders superfluous the questions about whether early Christology was "high" or "low," whether early Christology was influenced by Jewish and pagan concepts, or whether early Christology emerged immediately or gradually. In all accounts, Jesus is divine, whether he is inhabited by an angel, deified upon his resurrection, identified with divine Wisdom, or venerated as a messianic ruler. Ideally, the focus must be upon the *sense* in which and how *intensely* he is identified with the God of Israel. Cf. Wesley Hill, *Paul and the Trinity: Persons, Relations, and the Pauline Letters* (Grand Rapids: Eerdmans, 2015), 23–25; and April D. DeConick, "How We Talk about Christology Matters," in *Israel's God and Rebecca's Children: Christology and Community in Early Judaism and Christianity*, ed. David B. Capes, April D. DeConick, Helen K. Bond, and Troy A. Miller (Waco, Tex.: Baylor University Press, 2007), 1–4.

acquired it, how it manifests itself in Jesus' life and the economy of redemption, and how it relates to the divinity of God the Father.

Thus, to assert that Jesus is divine might appear to end one argument, but it merely erupts with several others. The question remains: How, or in what sense, is Jesus divine?[3] Or, in the words of Richard Hanson: "How can an unyielding monotheism accommodate the worship of Jesus Christ as divine? This was the question which had been with the church since the second century or perhaps earlier and which came to a head in the fourth."[4] This is a

---

[3] On the meaning of "God" and "divinity" in the ancient world, see Ramsay MacMullen, *Paganism in the Roman Empire* (New Haven, Conn.: Yale University Press, 1981), 88; S. R. F. Price, "Gods and Emperors: The Greek Language of the Roman Imperial Cult," *JHS* 104 (1984): 79–95; N. T. Wright, *The New Testament and the People of God* (COQG 1; London: SPCK, 1992), xv; Charles Gieschen, *Angelomorphic Christology: Antecedents and Early Evidence* (AGAJU 42; Leiden: Brill, 1998), 31–33; Marianne Meye Thompson, *The God of the Gospel of John* (Grand Rapids: Eerdmans, 2001), 17–48; Adela Y. Collins, "'How on Earth Did Jesus Become a God?': A Reply," in *Israel's God and Rebecca's Children: Christology and Community in Early Judaism and Christianity*, ed. David B. Capes, April D. DeConick, Helen K. Bond, and Troy A. Miller (Waco, Tex.: Baylor University Press, 2007), 57–61; James D. G. Dunn, *Did the First Christians Worship Jesus? The New Testament Evidence* (London: SPCK, 2010), 132–36; Bart D. Ehrman, *How Jesus Became God: The Exaltation of a Jewish Preacher from Galilee* (New York: HarperOne, 2014), 40–45; Matthias Reinhard Hoffmann, *The Destroyer and the Lamb: The Relationship between Angelomorphic and Lamb Christology in the Book of Revelation* (WUNT 2.203; Tübingen: Mohr Siebeck, 2005), 21–26; Ruben Bühner, *Messianic High Christology: New Testament Variants of Second Temple Judaism* (Waco, Tex.: Baylor University Press, 2021), 10–20; and Gabriele Boccaccini, "How Jesus Became Uncreated," in *Sibyls, Scriptures, and Scrolls*, ed. Joel Baden, Hindy Nayman, and Eibert Tigchelaar (JSPSup 175; Leiden: Brill, 2016), 1:186–88. Richard Bauckham (*Jesus and the God of Israel* [Milton Keynes, U.K.: Paternoster, 2008], 4) sums it up best when he observes that in studies of Jewish monotheism what "really counts as 'divine' . . . is rarely faced with clarity," and discussions about intermediary figures "tend to apply a variety of unexamined criteria for drawing the boundary between God and what is not God or between the divine and the non-divine." Resultantly, "it is also unclear what the attribution of divinity to Jesus in early Christology would really imply."

[4] R. P. C. Hanson, *The Search for the Christian Doctrine of God* (Edinburgh: T&T Clark, 1988), 874. Or, as John J. Collins puts it ("Jewish Monotheism and Christian Theology," in *Aspects of Monotheism: How God Is One*, ed. Hershel Shanks and Jack Meinhardt [Washington, D.C.: Biblical Archaeological Society, 1997], 82): "The question is, How was it possible for first-century C.E. Jews to accept this man Jesus as the pre-existent Son of God and still believe, as they surely did, that they were not violating traditional Jewish monotheism? How did this development come about?" Larry Hurtado (*One God, One Lord: Early Christian Devotion and Ancient Jewish Monotheism* [3rd ed.; London: T&T Clark, 2015], 2) asks much the same: "How did the early Jewish Christians accommodate the veneration of the exalted Jesus alongside God while continuing to see themselves as loyal to the fundamental emphasis of their ancestral tradition on one God, and without the benefit of the succeeding

question which, as we will see, has various problematic layers that need to be peeled back. Moreover, it is a question that requires giving attention to Greco-Roman and Hebrew religions, the Old Testament and its reception in Second Temple literature, and establishing a conversation between New Testament exegesis and patristic interpretation.

Ancient Discourses of Divinity

The word "god" means different things in different cultures, in different religions, and in different discourses about deity. To discuss the meaning of "god" with a modern Hindu is quite different from reading about what it meant to an ancient Hebrew. The referent, significance, and consequences of god or gods will be wildly variable depending on the religious environment that one inhabits and the religious grammar that one has inherited. In the case of the early church, the two formative backgrounds for their discourses of deity were the Greco-Roman and Jewish cultures of antiquity.

Greco-Roman Mythologies and Theologies

Christian discourses about deity belong incontrovertibly in the Greco-Roman context because it provided the cultural encyclopedia that, in diverse ways, shaped the early church's christological conceptuality and vocabulary. Numerous philosophies, frameworks, and precedents about a deity background the early church's intellectual world.

(1) Intermediary beings.

In ancient religion, the cosmic realm was characterized by a hierarchy of heavenly beings with ontological distinctions, so that between the supreme gods of the pantheon and humans was a class of in-between beings. These included the *stoicheia*, who are elemental powers or cosmic bodies; *daemons* (*daimōn/paredros*), who are spirits or angels; demigods (*hēmitheos*), who are either divine progeny or else deified humans; and heroes (*hērōs*), who are humans

---

four centuries of Christian theological discussion which led to the Christian doctrine of the Trinity?" Or else, Christopher B. Kaiser (*Seeing the Lord's Glory: Kyriocentric Visions and the Dilemma of Early Christology* [Minneapolis: Fortress, 2014], 1) writes: "How could deity Christology arise from pious Jews whose tradition consistently opposed the exaltation of any living human being to equality with God?" Jörg Frey ("Between Jewish Monotheism and Proto-trinitarian Tradition Relations: The Making and Character of Johannine Christology," in *Monotheism and Christology in Greco-Roman Antiquity*, ed. Matthew V. Novenson [Leiden: Brill, 2020], 190) notes too: "How did the *Jewish* Jesus became a God? And—to be clear—not a 'Gentile God,' but 'a Jewish God'" (italics original).

of super ability—ranging from soldiers to athletes to poets to healers to city founders (Plato, *Leg.* 4.717A–B; Plutarch, *Def. orac.* 11).

According to Plato, between the heavens and the world are *daimones*, who are "interpreting and ministering human things to the gods and divine things to men; offering entreaties and sacrifices from below, and ordinances and requitals from above, being midway between, it takes each to supplement the other, so that the whole is combined in one. Through it are conveyed all divination and priestcraft concerning sacrifice and ritual" (*Symp.* 202E). In Ps.-Plato there are five tiers of divinity beginning with stars and celestial bodies, daemons, water-beings, and demigods, and finally Zeus and Hera and all the Olympian gods (*Epin.* 984d–985c). For Plutarch, the category of "demigods" refers to those who are "stronger than men and in their might, greatly surpassing our nature, yet not possessing the divine quality unmixed and uncontaminated, but with a share also in the nature of the soul and in the perceptive faculties of the body, and with a susceptibility to pleasure and pain and to whatever other experience is incidental to these mutations" (*Is. Os.* 25). He also refers to various elements as rulers (*archontes*) and celestial bodies as managers (*dioikētai*) and rulers (*prytaneis*; *Mor.* 601A).

Christian apologist Athenagoras (*Leg.* 10.5) wrote: "We also say that there is a host of angels and ministers whom God, the Maker and Artificer of the world, set in their place through the Word that issues from him and whom he commanded to be concerned with the elements, the heavens, and the world with all that is in it and the good order of all that is in it." Later Tertullian (*Apol.* 24.2) noted, "The common way is to apportion deity, giving an imperial and supreme domination to one, while its offices are put into the hands of many, as Plato describes great Jupiter in the heavens, surrounded by an array at once of deities and demons. It behoves us, therefore, to show equal respect to the procurators, prefects, and governors of the divine empire." Divinity then was a heavenly hierarchy filled out with tiers of deities, ranks of angels, various heroes, demigods, spirits, and deified rulers.[5]

The ability of human beings to enter this in-between realm by attaining divine honors, to become "gods" by accomplishment, adoption, accession, or apotheosis, means that divine and human existences are compatible and interpenetrable. The gods, according to Heraclitus, were immortal humans, while humans are mortal Gods (Lucian, *Vit. auct.* 14). This observation has created the impression among many scholars that ancient accounts of divinity were

---

[5] Cf. n. 43 below.

not ontological, but rather a pyramid, spectrum, or gradient.⁶ Toynbee thus suggests: "To the Greeks and Romans, men and gods were not on two completely separate and differentiated levels. . . . They occupied either end, as it were, of a sliding scale," and for Manfred Clauss, "Deities are immortal people. Human beings are therefore mortal deities, which means that the boundary between the two could be crossed."⁷ As such, what distinguished worshippers from their deities was not divine substance but divine status.⁸

Moreover, that status was capable of gradation based on perceptions of power and experiences of patronage. Feats of deliverance and benefaction were reciprocated with varying degrees of divine worship toward the god, whether it was a traditional god, a demigod, a hero, a local god, a living emperor, or a deified emperor. Plutarch, following Hesiod, saw the spectrum in ascending order consisting of humans → heroes → demigods/immortals → eternals (*Def. orac.* 10). Plutarch (*Is. Os.* 27) wrote that Osiris, Herakles, and Dionysus are among those who were "promoted from daemons into gods" (*ek daimonōn . . . eis theous metabalontes*) with souls that are "purified" and "share completely the divine nature" (*Def. orac.* 10). Accordingly, if divinity is a spectrum of status, if various tiers of intermediary figures populate the heavenly sphere, if it is

---

⁶ On the pyramid/scale/spectrum/hierarchy of divinity, see J. M. C. Toynbee, "Ruler-Apotheosis in Ancient Rome," *Numismatics Chronicle* 7 (1947): 126–27; MacMullen, *Paganism in the Roman Empire*; Duncan Fishwick, *The Imperial Cult in the Latin West* (3 vols.; Leiden: Brill, 1987–2004), 1:33; Mary Beard, John North, and Simon Price, *Religions of Rome* (2 vols.; Cambridge: Cambridge University Press, 1998), 1:141; William Horbury, *Jewish Messianism and the Cult of Christ* (London: SCM Press, 1998), 70; Manfred Clauss, *Kaiser und Gott: Herrscherkult im römischen Reich* (Berlin: K. G. Saur, 1999); Ittai Gradel, *Emperor Worship and Roman Religion* (Oxford: Clarendon, 2002), 25–32, 71–72, 101–3, 321–36, 349–56; Paula Fredriksen, "What Does Jesus Have to Do with Christ? What Does Knowledge Have to Do with Faith? What Does History Have to Do with Theology?" in *Christology: Memory, Inquiry, Practice*, ed. A. M. Clifford and A. J. Godzieba (Maryknoll, N.Y.: Orbis, 2003), 10; Michael Peppard, *The Son of God in the Roman World: Divine Sonship in Its Social and Political Context* (Oxford: Oxford University Press, 2012), 31–36; Ehrman, *How Jesus Became God*, 40; and Emma Wasserman, *Apocalypse as Holy War: Divine Politics and Polemics in the Letters of Paul* (New Haven, Conn.: Yale University Press, 2018), 59–107.

⁷ Toynbee, "Ruler-Apotheosis," 126; and Clauss, *Kaiser und Gott*, 30–31 ("Gottheiten sind unsterbliche Menschen. Menschen sind demnach sterbliche Gottheiten, was sagen will, dass die Grenze zwischen beiden durchaus überschreitbar war").

⁸ Gradel, *Emperor Worship*, 26, 29. He puts it well: "If we see divinity and divine honours, in pagan terms as primarily concerned with status rather than nature, ruler cult will begin to make sense. In terms of the traditional republican social hierarchy there could be little doubt. Augustus had burst out of the top of the social structure into the level of the gods, his power was divine, that is, absolute in his sphere of control. Divine cult would be, and was, the traditional response to this new situation; and the higher the emperor was placed on the social ladder, the higher also was the possible place of his worshippers" (101–2).

possible to be promoted into and within this divine realm, then where on the spectrum of divinity should Jesus be situated?

(2) Comparative mythology.

The whole industry of "parallelomania," which consists of mapping the similarities between Greco-Roman myths/religions and Christianity, often mistakes superficial semblances for genetic relationships and requires critical sifting. The parallels are often illuminating, but not always explanatory for the origins of the text and its underlying tradition. The single greatest failure of the old *religionsgeschichtliche Schule*, at least as it applied to Christology, was forgetting the axiom that analogy does not entail genealogy.[9] Nonetheless, comparisons between the Christian accounts of Jesus and other Mediterranean deities were made by early Christian theologians and pointed out by pagan critics such as Celsus and Porphyry. Whether it was the virgin birth, Jesus' miracles, his atoning death, resurrection, and ascension into heaven—these all have parallels to some degree or another with Greco-Roman myths and stories about deities and semi-divine beings.[10] That Christ adopted the "form" or "likeness" of a human (Phil 2.7) is not much different than Zeus adopting a human guise to appear in public (Acts 14.11-12). Justin Martyr can admit that Jesus originated like Hermes, who was the angelic word of God, he was born of a virgin like Perseus, he healed the sick like Asclepius, he was begotten of God similar to how Zeus begat Athena, and he suffered like the sons of Zeus (Justin, *1 Apol.* 21.1-22.3; 64.5; *Dial.* 69.1-3). Arnobius too accepted the parity of the promotion of Minerva, Asclepius, and Herakles as gods for their achievements with an a fortiori argument for Christ's divinity (*Adversus gentes* 1.38).

In modern scholarship, some genuinely interesting parallels do get pointed out: for instance, George H. van Kooten describes how John the Evangelist affirms that Jesus is the incarnation of the only begotten Son of God, much like how Athena is the only begotten daughter of Zeus (*Orphic Hymns* 32.1; Aelius Aristides, *Orations* 37). John identifies Jesus as the hermeneutical and

---

[9] See criticism in Martin Hengel, *The Son of God: The Origin of Christology and the History of Jewish Hellenistic Religion* (Minneapolis: Fortress, 1976), 17-56; and Hurtado, *One God, One Lord*, 48.

[10] See, e.g., Wilhelm Bousset, *Kyrios Christos* (Waco, Tex.: Baylor University Press, 2013 [1970]); Casey, *From Jewish Prophet*; Dieter Zeller, "Die Menschwerdung des Sohnes Gottes im Neuen Testament und die antike Religionsgeschichichte," in *Menschwerdung Gottes—Vergöttlichung von Menschen* (Göttingen: Vandenhoeck & Ruprecht, 1988), 141-76; idem, "New Testament Christology in Its Hellenistic Reception," *NTS* 46 (2001): 312-33; and M. David Litwa, *Iesus Deus: The Early Christian Depiction of Jesus as a Mediterranean God* (Minneapolis: Fortress, 2014).

cosmological Logos of God, much like how Hermes is identified as a cosmic principle (Heraclitus, *All.* 28.2, 55.1, 72.4–5; Porphyry, *Agalm.* 8.103–6).[11] He also points out that Jesus exegetes or explains God (John 1.18) in a manner reminiscent of how Socrates carried the daemon of Apollo, who is the definitive interpreter of the Athenian ancestral religion (Plato, *Rep.* 427C).[12] I would add that John's prologue has a poetic and almost hymnic quality, and with its focus on the Logos it is similar to Cleanthes' *Hymn to Zeus*, whereby God reigns over all things through his Logos, which pervades everything as a kind of natural law (Strobaeus, *Ecl.* 1.1.12).

In some cases, the similarities between Greco-Roman deities and Jesus were deliberately forged by Christians themselves. Whereas Jupiter was the "*princeps* of the gods," Christ was depicted in artwork as a new Jupiter and described under the title "Christ Imperatorus" in Italy before the middle of the third century.[13] Some Christ-devotees wanted to show that the new God had some semblance with the old ones![14] There is, then, something to be said for Elisabeth Schüssler Fiorenza's account of "reflective mythology" so that Christology emerged from the appropriation of mythical language, materials, and patterns pertaining to intermediary figures who stand between God and the world.[15]

(3) Ruler cults.

Ancient Near Eastern and Greco-Roman ruler cults have also merited comparison with early Christian views of Jesus.[16] Alexander the Great was proclaimed as

---

[11] George H. van Kooten, "The Last Days of Socrates and Christ: *Euthyphro, Apology, Crito*, and *Phaedo* Read in Counterpoint with John's Gospel," in *Religio-philosophical Discourses in the Mediterranean World: From Plato, through Jesus, to Late Antiquity*, ed. Anders Klostergaard Petersen and George van Kooten (Leiden: Brill, 2017), 230. According to the Stoic Cornutus, "Hermes, son of Zeus and Maia, is the Logos which the gods have sent us from heaven," cited from Hengel, *Son of God*, 35.

[12] George H. van Kooten, "The Sign of Socrates, the Sign of Apollo, and the Signs of Christ: Hiding and Sharing Religious Knowledge in the Gospel of John; A Contrapuntal Reading of John's Gospel and Plato's Dialogues," in *Sharing and Hiding Religious Knowledge in Early Judaism, Christianity, and Islam*, ed. M. Popovic, L. R. Lanzillotta, and C. Wilde (Berlin: de Gruyter, 2018), 155–56.

[13] MacMullen, *Paganism in the Roman Empire*, 81–82.

[14] See Robin M. Jensen, "The Emperor Cult and Christian Iconography," in *Rome and Religion: A Cross-Disciplinary Dialogue on the Imperial Cult*, ed. Jeffrey Brodd and Jonathan L. Reed (Atlanta: SBL, 2011), 153–71.

[15] Elisabeth Schüssler Fiorenza, "Wisdom Mythology and the Christological Hymns of the New Testament," in *Aspects of Wisdom in Judaism and Early Christianity*, ed. Robert L. Wilken (Notre Dame, Ind.: University of Notre Dame Press, 1975), 29.

[16] See, e.g., Ernst Lohmeyer, *Christuskult und Kaiserkult* (Tübingen: Mohr Siebeck, 1919); David E. Aune, "The Influence of Roman Imperial Court Ceremonial on the

divine during his life by his subjects. Although the cult of Alexander developed after his death, already during his lifetime, under Egyptian and Persian influence, Alexander allegedly instituted a cult complete with coinage, altars, statues, shrines, and sacrifices, a priesthood, civic tribes, and prostration (Arrian, *Anab.* 4.10–12; 7.23.2; Plutarch, *Alex.* 27.8–28.6; 33.1; 54.1–55.1; 74.2–3).[17] Alexander's cult was continued by the Ptolemaic and Seleucid dynasties and persisted even into the Roman period. Julius Caesar despaired of his own meagre accomplishments after seeing a statue of Alexander in Spain (Suetonius, *Jul.* 7.1–2). Augustus paid homage to Alexander at a shrine after defeating Cleopatra IV and Mark Anthony (Suetonius, *Aug.* 18.1). Trajan made a sacrifice to Alexander in Babylon after defeating the Parthians in the second century CE (Cassius Dio 68.29.1–30.1).

The Romans adopted the practice of worshipping and then deifying rulers, albeit with some degree of hesitation.[18] Rome did not originally have a ruler cult because it had no ruler: it was a republic, the kings had long been expelled, and there was supposed to be no king but Jupiter.[19] Even so, during the imperial period, political pragmatics and propaganda required divine honors for the emperor. The Roman conquest of Egypt by Julius Caesar and its annexation by Augustus meant that the Roman ruler was a de facto god, as the Egyptian monarch was by custom designated as a living god or image of a god. Also, the "Roman imperial cult in Asia Minor provided an ideal forum for

---

Apocalypse of John," *BR* 28 (1983): 5–26; Hans-Josef Klauck, "Das Sendschreiben nach Pergamon und der Kaiserkult in der Johannes Offenbarung," *Bib* 73 (1992): 153–82; Horbury, *Jewish Messianism*; Adela Y. Collins, "The Worship of Jesus and the Imperial Cult," in *The Jewish Roots of Christological Monotheism: Papers from the St. Andrews Conference on the Historical Origins of the Worship of Jesus*, ed. Carey C. Newman, James R. Davila, and Gladys S. Lewis (JSJSup 63; Leiden: Brill, 1999), 234–57; idem, "Mark and His Readers: The Son of God among Jews," *HTR* 92 (1999): 393–408; and idem, "How on Earth," 55–66.

[17] See Hans-Josef Klauck, *Religious Context of Early Christianity: A Guide to Graeco-Roman Religions* (Edinburgh: T&T Clark, 2000), 266–74; Angela Chaniotis, "The Divinity of Hellenistic Rulers," in *A Companion to the Hellenistic World*, ed. A. Erskine (Oxford: Blackwell, 2003), 434–35; Tyson L. Putthoff, *God and Humans in the Ancient Near East* (Cambridge: Cambridge University Press, 2020), 161–67; Joseph D. Fantin, *The Lord of the Entire World: Lord Jesus, a Challenge to Lord Caesar?* (NTM 31; Sheffield: Sheffield Phoenix, 2011), 103–5; and E. Badian, "Alexander the Great between Two Thrones and Heaven: Variations on an Old Theme," in *Subject and Ruler: The Cult of the Ruling Power in Classical Antiquity* (Ann Arbor: University of Michigan Press, 1996), 11–26.

[18] See Beard, North, and Price, *Religions of Rome*, 1:140–49; Gradel, *Emperor Worship*, 261–371; Michael Koortbojian, *The Divinization of Caesar and Augustus: Precedents, Consequences, Implications* (Cambridge: Cambridge University Press, 2013); and Spencer Cole, *Cicero and the Rise of Deification at Rome* (Cambridge: Cambridge University Press, 2013).

[19] Livy, *Hist.* 1.53; Cicero, *Phil.* 2.34; 3.5; Suetonius, *Jul.* 79.2; Cassius Dio, *Hist.* 44.11.3. See Gradel, *Emperor Worship*, 30.

disseminating Rome's ideological counter-response to the Parthian claims of Achaemenid legitimacy."[20] Imperial regimes had to manage divine honors and cults with respect for the traditional deities, the ambition of the princeps, and the need for *moderatio* in the face of eastern enthusiasm for ruler worship.[21] Romulus' deification was something of a legitimizing precedent for the deification of Roman emperors, which was normalized by Augustus' deification of Julius Caesar.[22] That said, emperors often resisted state-sanctioned divine honors during their lifetime, especially Tiberius and Claudius (Suetonius, *Tib.* 26.1; *Claud.* 12.1; P. Lond. 1912 46–51), plus the deification of emperors was never automatic—Tiberius, Caligula, Nero, and Domitian were not deified.[23]

---

[20] Benjamin B. Rubin, *(Re)presenting Empire: The Roman Imperial Cult in Asia Minor, 31 BC–AD 68* (PhD diss., University of Michigan, 2008), 26.

[21] Augustus had criticized Mark Antony for styling himself as an eastern god-king, i.e., neo-Dionysus (Plutarch, *Ant.* 60.3; 75.4), while Augustus himself later accepted divine honors from his eastern subjects. Augustus had to tread a fine line between not claiming too many honors and titles for himself, yet not appearing ungrateful to his subjects, who wanted to bestow divine honors upon him. Mary Beard (*The Roman Triumph* [Cambridge, Mass.: Belknap, 2007], 234) puts it well: "Emperors drew back from claiming the role and privileges of gods as enthusiastically as they basked in divine worship. The dividing line between mortality and immortality could be as carefully respected as it was triumphantly crossed. Nonetheless, divine power and status were a measure against which to judge its human equivalents, and a potential goal and ambition for the super-successful."

[22] On Romulus, see Livy, *Ab urbe cond.* 1.16; Cicero, *Nat. d.* 2.62. Other contributing factors were the cult of the dead and the temporary epiphanic nature of the triumphator during a triumphal celebration. Note too that Scipio Africanus identified himself with Jupiter (Aulus Gellius, *Noct. att.* 6.1.6). Greek cities in Asia responded to Rome's liberation/conquest by erecting temples to the city of Rome in the form of its goddess *Roma*, as Smyrna boasted of doing (Tacitus, *Ann.* 4.56.1), and some of the first proconsuls sent to the region received cultic honors, such as Titus Quinctius Flamininius, who was granted a cult ca. 191 BCE for his benefactions to the city of Chalcis that persisted into the second century CE (Plutarch, *Flam.* 16.3-4). From the Roman populace, the Gracchi brothers (Plutarch, *C. Gracch.* 18) received posthumous cultic honors ca. 111 BCE, and Marius received ceremonial food and libations along with the gods while still alive in ca. 85 BCE (Plutarch, *Mar.* 27.5). Cicero's *Pro Lege Manilia* curates an image of Pompey as a quasi-divine deliver, while in *Pro Marcello* he attempts to presage Caesar's divinity as something to be awarded posthumously. Cicero, it seems, combined the individual immortality of the soul with a merit-based divinity (*Leg.* 2.27-28). Appian (*Bell. civ.* 2.148) sees the main shift in Octavius' deification of Caesar: "From this example the Romans now pay like honors to each emperor at his death if he has not reigned in a tyrannical manner or made himself odious." See Cole, *Cicero and the Rise*, 185–86.

[23] Deification reached something of a summit with the emperor Hadrian, who deified family members and even his teenage lover Antinous. Between Augustus and Constantine, thirty-six of sixty emperors were deified and twenty-seven people from imperial families were deified; see Fantin, *Lord of the Entire World*, 118.

By the first century the various imperial cults (i.e., the diverse forms of worship of living and deceased emperors) were among the most significant aspects of the Mediterranean religious landscape. The imperial cult became a civic instrument to bind together the emperor, local elites, and the people. To this end, the empire was saturated with temples, altars, images, inscriptions, and coins honoring the emperors and their families. For example, an Egyptian papyrus dated to 1 CE describes priests offering sacrifices and libations to Augustus as "the god and lord emperor" (P. Oxy. 1143.4). Tacitus reports that all the great houses of Rome contained worshippers of Augustus (*Ann.* 1.73). We know too that wealthy freedman in Italy formed societies of *Augustales*, a cult association from which its members engaged in public benefactions.[24] A temple in Campania to Augustus' two sons, Gaius and Lucius, contained an inscription: "When time shall demand you as a god, Caesar, and you shall take your seat in heaven, whence you will rule the world, may it be these who in your stead hold sway here on earth and rule us by their felicitous vows."[25] In Asia Minor, Pergamum won the right to host the temple of Augustus (Cassius Dio 51.20.6–8; cf. Rev 2.13), Tiberius gave permission for his temple to be built in Smyrna after something of a tendering process (Tacitus, *Ann.* 4.55), Caligula ordered one to be erected in Miletus (Cassius Dio 59.28.1), and Domitian had the Flavian dynastic temple built in Ephesus. A Greek decree reciprocates Caligula's benefactions with a remark that "the greatness of his immortality should be in every matter all the more splendid" (*IGRR* 4.145), and a Cypriot priesthood was devoted to "The Immortality of the Sebastoi."[26]

First-century Judea was literally surrounded by cities that featured imperial temples and altars, including Caesarea Maritima, Caesarea Philippi, Sebaste, the Decapolis, and Petra.[27] The imperial cult was then something that Jews and Christians could not but fail to see and engage. The book of Revelation depicts the imperial cult, symbolized as the "false prophet," as the number one enemy of

[24] On the Augustales, see Fishwick, *Imperial Cult*, 2:1.609–16.
[25] *CIL* 10.3757, cited from Gradel, *Emperor Worship*, 269.
[26] Cited from Price, "Gods and Emperors," 88.
[27] See Monika Bernett, "Der Kaiserkult in Judäa unter herodischer und römischer Herrschaft: Zu Herausbildung und Herausforderung neuer Konzepte jüdischer Herrschaftslegitimation," in *Jewish Identity in the Greco-Roman World*, ed. Jörg Frey, Daniel R. Schwartz, and Stephanie Gripentrog (AJEC 71; Leiden: Brill, 2007), 205–51; Samuel Rocca, *Herod's Judaea: A Mediterranean State in the Classical World* (TSAJ 122; Tübingen: Mohr Siebeck, 2008), 315–16; and Andreas Kropp, "King-Caesar-God: Roman Imperial Cult among Near Eastern 'Client' Kings," in *Lokale Identität im Römischen Nahen Osten*, ed. Michael Blömer, Margherita Facella, and Engelbert Winter (Stuttgart: Franz Steiner, 2009), 99–150.

the Christian people (Rev 14.9–10). At the same time, one can easily imagine Christians attempting to subvert the imperial cult's claims for the emperor as a divine *kyrios* ("Lord") and *sōtēr* ("savior") by deliberately parodying its language and applying it to Jesus, the true *kyrios* and the one *sōtēr* (see Luke 2.11; Phil 3.20; 2 Pet 1.11; 2.20; 3.2, 18; Pol. *Phil.* 1.1; *Mart. Pol.* 19.2).[28] In view of this imperial context, Jesus could be said to be divine much in the same way that some Roman emperors were worshipped and deified as part of the divine honors afforded in the imperial cults.

(4) Philosophy.

Christian theology was immersed in the philosophical currents of the ancient world with its conception of how the divine and terrestrial realms interfaced. Greco-Roman philosophy had its own theologies about the nature of divinity and the divinity of nature. Discussion encompassed God (singular) and gods (plural), their bodies, abode, and interest—or not—in the affairs of human beings. Greco-Roman categories for divine nature, dialogues about a demiurge, descriptions of daemons, and state rituals for deification are the environment in which discourses about Jesus' deity crystallized. For a case in point, John the Evangelist, Justin Martyr, Clement of Alexandria, Origen, and Athanasius applied Heraclitus' category of the Logos, a cosmic intermediary principle, to describe Jesus as the eternal Word of the Father made flesh. Similarly, Plato's demiurge, a divine principle who generated terrestrial matter, was associated with God and Jesus by many Christian intellectuals in the second century. Also, Hellenistic philosophy possessed a suite of "prepositional metaphysics" whereby intermediary agents were associated with various types of causality in creation and distinguished by what came from, in, through, or for them. These causal/prepositional distinctions fostered a grammar of agency which Christians (Rom 11.36; 1 Cor 8.6; 11.12; Col 1.15–20; Heb 1.2; 2.10; John 1.3, 10) inherited from Hellenistic Judaism (e.g, Philo, *Leg. all.* 1.41; *Cher.* 124–27; *QG* 1.58) if not directly from pagan sources (e.g., Seneca, *Ep.* 65.7–10).[29] The result is that the New Testament and early Christian literature contain "a fusion of these Platonized Jewish traditions with Christian eschatological convictions."[30]

---

[28] See discussion in Michael F. Bird, *An Anomalous Jew: Paul among Jews, Greeks, and Romans* (Grand Rapids: Eerdmans, 2016), 205–55, for a qualified argument that Christianity's apocalyptic and messianic narrative was a deliberate counterpoint to the imperial cults. Recommended also is the studious research of Fantin, *Lord of the Entire World*.

[29] Gregory Sterling, "Prepositional Metaphysics in Jewish Wisdom Speculation and Early Christian Liturgical Texts," *Studio Philonica Annual* 9 (1997): 219–38.

[30] Ronald Cox, *By the Same Word: Creation and Salvation in Hellenistic Judaism and Early Christianity* (Berlin: de Gruyter, 1997), 354.

On the upside, Hellenistic philosophy bequeathed to the first Christian theologians a toolbox of categories for speaking about deity vis-à-vis the world. On the downside, this indigenizing of philosophy in Christian thought also facilitated several problems that required a solution. How to reconcile God's ontological permanence with the story of a God-man who was born, suffered, died, and returned to heaven was a philosophical problem. Was God simple or complex? Can a God's being involve any becoming? The fourth-century debates on whether Jesus was begotten vs. made or whether the one who begets is superior to what is begotten are pieces of the jigsaw puzzle over the nature of deity that the church had to work out.

One should not imagine what took place was a gradual and corrupting Hellenization of the church. Rather, Hellenistic philosophy, particularly Middle Platonism, became the conceptual toolbox that helped the church attain clarity, coherence, and consensus on the doctrine of God. For every Tertullian who denounced "Athens," there was a Clement of Alexandria and an Origen who were setting up a department of Christian philosophy within it. The success of Christianity in the intellectually competitive environment of the Greco-Roman world was only possible because Christianity was able to participate in the main discourses of ancient religion and philosophy and hold its own weight.[31] One could say that early Christian philosophy contributed a clarifying logos to the church's devotion to its *theos*, so that, as Eric Osborn noted, "An extended treatment of the earliest Christian philosophy showed that, with all its Platonism and Stoicism, it ended on the claim Jesus was God."[32]

(5) Summary.

In sum, whatever differences there are between Christianity's Son of God and the Roman Son of the Divine Augustus, between Jesus and Jupiter, or between a messiah cult and a mystery cult, those differences can only be pronounced once we have first grappled with the many similarities between Christianity and Greco-Roman myths and religious devotion. Thus, for external observers of Christianity as much as for its internal practitioners, the Jesus written about

---

[31] Udo Schnelle, "Philosophische Interpretation des Johannesevangeliums: Voraussetzungen, Methoden und Perspektiven," in *The Prologue of the Gospel of John: Its Literary, Theological, and Philosophical Contexts*, ed. Jan G. van der Watt, R. Alan Culpepper, and Udo Schnelle (WUNT 359; Tübingen: Mohr Siebeck, 2016), 174.

[32] Eric F. Osborn, *The Emergence of Christian Theology* (Cambridge: Cambridge University Press, 1993), 4.

and worshipped by Christians was, in many respects, a Greco-Roman deity who was described with the language of Greco-Roman religions.[33]

Jewish Monotheism

Christian discourses about deity are also deeply embedded within the Jewish context of Second Temple Judaism. Therefore, Jewish sacred texts, the Jerusalem cultus, and the Jewish encounter with Hellenism provide a key backdrop upon which christological claims should be mapped.

Ancient Judaism—which I take to be a mixture of shared ethnicity, custom, and cultus—was the soil in which Christianity took root and sprouted. The Jews were distinctive in the relative peculiarity and homogeneity of their national way of life. Judaism was, or at least became in the post-Maccabean era, a form of cultural resistance to Hellenism, even as Hellenism influenced all expressions of Judaism in some way or other, in both Judea and the Diaspora. On the one hand, the Jewish devotion to one deity, ordinarily called "monotheism," was not unique to the Jews, as pagan versions of monotheism were extant in antiquity.[34] But on the other hand, Jewish monotheism certainly

---

[33] Note the words of Charles H. Talbert (*The Development of Christology during the First Hundred Years: And Other Essays on Early Christology* [Leiden: Brill, 2011], 41): "The earliest followers of Jesus had a distinct constitutive core, experientially grounded, that gave them the ability to sift and sort through language and concepts from their surroundings to express what the Christ-event meant to them in terms of their past, present, and future. There was no alien invasion of pagan culture into the pure faith. Rather, there was a sovereign use of the general culture for self-understanding and evangelization insofar as it could be adopted to the constitutive, soteriological core." Similar is Marinus de Jonge, *Christology in Context: The Earliest Christian Responses to Jesus* (Philadelphia: Westminster, 1988), 189–90.

[34] See M. P. Nilsson, "The High God and the Mediator," *HTR* 56 (1963): 101–20; Javier Teixidor, *The Pagan God: Popular Religion in the Graeco-Roman Near East* (Princeton, N.J.: Princeton University Press, 1977), 13–17; MacMullen, *Paganism in the Roman Empire*, 83–89; Barbara N. Porter, ed., *One God or Many? Concepts of Divinity in the Ancient World* (Chebeague, Maine: Casco Bay Assyriological Institute, 2000); Manfred Krebernick and Jürgen van Oorschot, eds., *Polytheismus und Monotheismus in den Religionen des Vorderen Orients* (Münster: Ugarit-Verlag, 2002); Reinhard G. Kratz and Hermann Spieckermann, eds., *Götterbilder, Gottesbilder, Weltbilder: Polytheismus and Monotheismus in der Welt der Antike* (Tübingen: Mohr Siebeck, 2006); Alfons Fürst, "Pagan und christlicher 'Monotheismus': Zur Hermeneutik eines antiken Diskurses," *JAC* 51 (2008): 5–24; Polymnia Athanassiadi and Michael Frede, eds., *Pagan Monotheism in Late Antiquity* (Oxford: Clarendon, 2008); Stephen Mitchell and Peter van Nuffelen, eds., *One God: Pagan Monotheism in the Roman Empire* (Cambridge: Cambridge University Press, 2010); and idem, eds., *Monotheism between Pagans and Christians in Late Antiquity* (Leuven: Peeters, 2010). The key differences between pagan monotheism and Jewish monotheism are that the former often engaged in polyonomy, where a supreme deity could have many names like Yahweh, Dios, and Baal; there was no restriction

stood out in antiquity and had to be carefully negotiated by Jewish communities living in a world saturated with images and idols, guilds who had patron deities, civic cults, and state temples. Judaism, then, was tied to certain fixtures concerning God's oneness and exclusive worship, Israel's exodus and election, the covenant and calendar, Torah and temple, land, and variegated hopes for the future. It was around these Jewish fixtures that Christian thought, including its Christology, crystallized.

Jewish monotheism and scriptural intermediary figures provided the primary categories and boundaries in which the first Christians spoke about Jesus as both God's chief agent and a divine being. Before proceeding any further, we must pause and presage two umbilical topics, namely, whether the Jews were in fact monotheists and whether Jewish monotheism was exclusive or inclusive of other beings.

(1) Were the Jews actually monotheists?

What we call "monotheism," defined as the belief in the existence of only one God who is metaphysically distinct from mortals and matter, is simply one of the many "isms" that derived from the eighteenth century. Such a view is a product of modern rationalist and romantic ideas of one sole God that was projected onto the ancient Jews and their beliefs pertaining to their national deity.[35] In addition, it is widely recognized that ancient Israelite religion was not originally, or perhaps not ever, a monotheistic religion whereby Israel's deity was the only deity thought to exist or the only deity worshipped by Israelite tribes. During the monarchial period, several cults existed in Judea beside Yahweh worship, notably those pertaining to Asherah and Baal (e.g., 1 Kgs 18.19; 2 Kgs 17.16; 21.3; 23.4). During the Persian and Hellenistic period, evidence from papyri shows that the Judean garrison at Elephantine in upper Egypt worshipped several deities beside Yahweh, including Yahu, Anat-Yahu, Bethel, Anat-Bethel, Eshem, Eshem-Bethel, Herem, and Herem-Bethel. The

---

of worship to the supreme deity; the supreme deity was to some degree unknown; and the supreme deity was not tethered to a particular ethno-territorial group. See N. Clayton Croy, "A God by Any Other Name: Polyonymy in Greco-Roman Antiquity and Early Christianity," *BBR* 24 (2014): 27–43; and Larry Hurtado, "First-Century Jewish Monotheism," in *Ancient Jewish Monotheism and Early Christian Jesus-Devotion: The Context and Character of Christological Faith* (Waco, Tex.: Baylor University Press, 2017), 132–35.

[35] Nathan MacDonald, *Deuteronomy and the Meaning of "Monotheism"* (FZAT 2.1; Tübingen: Mohr Siebeck, 2012), 5–58. MacDonald (5–7) says that "monotheism" was first coined by the Cambridge Platonist Henry More (1614–87) in 1660. N. T. Wright (*Paul and the Faithfulness of God* [COQG 4; London: SPCK, 2014], 632) complains that "It is precisely the dry Enlightenment Deism, not first-century Jewish monotheism, that scooped up all other non-spatio-temporal existence into the oneness of 'monotheism.'"

Elephantine temples imply that Yahwism did not require monotheism or monolatry.³⁶ Although there were pre-exilic (e.g., Ps 29; 68; 89) and exilic (e.g., Isa 40) manifestations of Yahweh-alone worship, it was not until the post-exilic period, especially in the face of imperial pressures to Hellenize the Jerusalem cultus, that the Yahweh-alone party came to predominate in Judea. Even then the Judeans could still acknowledge the existence of deities that belonged to different tribes and territories, and certain indigenous cults persisted in post-exilic Judea.³⁷ According to many scholars, the important detail in what we call "Old Testament religion" was that Yahweh was Israel's God, the God of the patriarchs, the God of the exodus and election, the God of Israel's heritage and hope. Whoever or whatever the other gods are, they are not in relationship with the Israelites.³⁸

The ancient Jews could then on some accounts be categorized not as abstract and absolute monotheists, but as *henotheists*, loyal to one specific deity above other divine beings, and characterized by an *aniconic monolatry*, exclusive and imageless worship of this one deity. This is evident from how

---

³⁶ James S. Anderson, *Monotheism and Yahweh's Appropriation of Baal* (London: T&T Clark, 2015), 32–33.

³⁷ See Bernhard Lang, "The Yahweh-Alone Movement and the Making of Jewish Monotheism," in *Monotheism and the Prophetic Minority: An Essay in Biblical History and Sociology* (Sheffield: Almond, 1983), 13–59; idem, "Zur Entstehung des biblischen Monotheismus," *ThQS* 166 (1985): 135–42; Robert K. Gnuse, *No Other Gods: Emergent Monotheism in Israel* (JSOTSup 242; Sheffield: Sheffield Academic Press, 1997); Susan Akerman, *Under Every Green Tree: Popular Religion in Sixth-Century Judah* (Winona Lake, Ind.: Eisenbrauns, 2001); Mark S. Smith, *The Origins of Biblical Monotheism: Israel's Polytheistic Background and the Ugaritic Texts* (Oxford: Oxford University Press, 2001); and William G. Dever, *Did God Have a Wife? Archaeology and Folk Religion in Ancient Israel* (Grand Rapids: Eerdmans, 2005). In a minority report, Benjamin D. Sommer (*The Bodies of God and the World of Ancient Israel* [New York: Cambridge University Press, 2009], 145) writes: "Another group of scholars, however, argue that the exclusive worship of Yhwh as the only true deity was widespread in ancient Israel well before the exile, perhaps even well before the rise of the monarchy." Of course, this does not mean that everybody in the ancient Israelite religion was a monotheist/monolatrist, hence Sommer quips (*Bodies of God*, 149): "A depressingly large amount of scholarly writing on this subject consists of an attempt to debunk the Bible by demonstrating something the Bible itself asserts—indeed, something the Bible repeatedly emphasizes: that Israelites before the exile worshipped many gods."

³⁸ MacDonald (*Monotheism*, 96, 180, 207, 215) argues that Deuteronomic monotheism was confessional and soteriological, not ontological. It was about God's relationship vis-à-vis Israel. Jan Assman (*Exodus: Die Revolution der Alten Welt* [Munich: C. H. Beck, 2015], 112) sums this up as a "monotheism of loyalty" (*Monotheismus der Treue*) as opposed to a "monotheism of truth" (*Monotheismus der Wahrheit*). In support, note how Abraham in *Jub.* 12.19–20 prays, "My God, the Most High God, you alone are God to me." Even Paul's christological monotheism highlights the relational aspect for, despite the "many gods and lords—yet *for us* there is one God, the Father" (1 Cor 8.5–6).

the Hebrew Bible recognizes that Yahweh presides over the "hosts" of heaven, proving that other deities are out there.[39] Even the naked pronouncements in Deutero-Isaiah that "besides me there is no god,"[40] are "more like a rhetorical moment than a religious revolution" toward absolute monotheism in the post-exilic period.[41] This explains why Paul can say that there are "many gods and many lords" (1 Cor 8.5), and refer to the "god of this age" (2 Cor 4.4), the "rulers of this age" (1 Cor 2.8), and various cosmic "powers" (Rom 8.38; Col 1.16; 2.15; Eph 6.12).[42] The early church recognized a class of intermediary angels and ministering spirits around God's throne, hostile powers in rebellion against God, and for Gnostic cosmologies there were various emanations, aeons, and archons.[43] Jews, Christians, and sometimes "pagans" recognized a single God as presiding over a "celestial monarchy."[44] Consequently, modern ideas of an absolute metaphysical monotheism, where God is the single and solitary divine being, do not correspond to ancient Jewish or Christian beliefs of their God among other "gods."[45]

---

[39] Presumably angels (1 Sam 1.3; 1 Kgs 22.19–23; Ps 24.10 [23.10 LXX]; 29.1; 82.1; 79.5, 8, 15, 20 [LXX]; 89.7; Job 1.6; 38.7; Isa 1.24; Neh 9.6; Dan 4.35; 1 Esdr 9.46), but including too the "gods" of the nations (Exod 12.12; 15.11; 18.11; Deut 10.17; 32.8, 43; 33.3, 27; Josh 22.22; Ps 22.18; 29.1–3; 47.8; 82.8; 84.7; 86.8; 89.5–8; 95.3; 97.7, 9; 103.19–22; 135.5; 136.2; 138.1; Isa 24.21; Dan 2.47).

[40] Isa 44.6, 8; 45.5, 6, 14, 18, 22; 46.9; cf. Deut 4.35, 39; 7.9; 1 Kgs 8.60.

[41] Matthew J. Lynch, "Mapping Monotheism: Modes of Monotheistic Rhetoric in the Hebrew Bible," *VT* 64 (2014): 48.

[42] MacDonald (*Monotheism*, 96) says, "Paul, it can be argued, is breathing the same spirit as Deuteronomy 32. Other gods exist, but in another sense they are 'no-gods' and 'demons.' It is only YHWH that is 'God.'"

[43] See Rev 5.1–14; *Ascen. Isa.* 10–11; Justin, *Dial.* 56.2; Athenagoras, *Leg.* 10.5; Irenaeus, *Haer.* 1.2.6; 3.6.5; *Epid.* 9; Minucius Felix, *Oct.* 18; Tertullian, *Apol.* 24.2; *Prax.* 3; Clement, *Strom.* 5.14.125; Origen, *Cels.* 8.35; *Gos. Truth* 19.7–10; 41.15–42.10; *Ap. John* 3–14; *Tri. Trac.* 63.30–35; 105.1–3. According to *Ap. John* 13.5–13, Yaldabaoth's statement that "I am a jealous God" implies the existence of angels, because "if there were no other one, of whom would he be jealous?" While in *Gos. Truth* 18.32–19.10, the Father could not be jealous because he did not give his perfection to the totality of aeons; instead, he occasionally and conditionally grants perfection to them.

[44] MacMullen, *Paganism in the Roman Empire*, 86.

[45] Peter Hayman, "Monotheism—A Misused Word in Jewish Studies?" *JJS* 42 (1991): 1–15; Paula Fredriksen, "Mandatory Retirement: Ideas in the Study of Christian Origins Whose Time Has Come to Go," in *Israel's God and Rebecca's Children: Christology and Community in Early Judaism and Christianity*, ed. David B. Capes, April D. DeConick, Helen K. Bond, and Troy A. Miller (Waco, Tex.: Baylor University Press, 2007), 35–38; idem, "How High Can Early Christology Be?" in *Monotheism and Christology in Greco-Roman Antiquity*, ed. Matthew V. Novenson (Leiden: Brill, 2020),

However, even if Jewish theism was not an absolute metaphysical monotheism, I am not convinced we should rush to dispense with the term "monotheism"[46] and label ancient Israelite religion as "henotheism" just because Yahweh exists beside other gods, angels, spirits, and daemons.[47] The existence of other supernatural entities was not a problem for Jewish/Christian theism unless these gods were attributed independence, exercised comparable omnipotence, or possessed the attributes of being uncreated and autonomous.[48] For those Israelites committed to the exclusive worship of Yahweh, their worship was based on more than a single redemptive event; it was premised on Yahweh as creator of all things in heaven and earth, and it

---

295–99; Michael S. Heiser, "Monotheism, Polytheism, Monolatry, or Henotheism? Toward an Understanding of Divine Plurality in the Hebrew Bible," *BBR* 18 (2008): 1–30; and Jens-André P. Herbener, "On the Term 'Monotheism,'" *Numen* 60 (2013): 616–48.

[46] Joachim Schaper (*Media and Monotheism: Presence, Representation, and Abstraction in Ancient Judah* [ORA 33; Tübingen: Mohr Siebeck, 2019], 41) retorts that "the fact that the category of 'monotheism' is indeed a 'creation of the modern world' does not preclude the possibility that it might be a helpful analytical tool for the historian of religion and the biblical exegete and might rightfully be used in the reconstruction of the history of the Yahwistic religion from the late pre-exilic period onwards."

[47] Note the summaries of Shaye J. D. Cohen (*From the Maccabees to the Mishnah* [Philadelphia: Westminster, 1987], 78–79): "The Jewish monotheism of antiquity did not exclude belief in many and diverse supernatural beings aside from God. Precisely because the deity had grown so in power and prestige, a need was felt during Second Temple times to populate this intermediate world with beings of all sorts, notably angels. . . . The impulse to believe that myriads of angels serve the Lord both in this world and in the world above was apparently the belief in God's cosmic majesty. The more exalted God became, the more he required retainers to sing his glory and intermediaries to communicate with the world." Wright (*Paul and the Faithfulness of God*, 626, 632) is similar: "It is simply wrong-headed to suggest that such 'monotheism' might be compromised by a recognition of the existence of non-human powers or intelligences, whether good (angels) or evil (demons); it was no part of second-Temple monotheism to suggest that Israel's God was the only non-human intelligence in the cosmos. . . . In second-Temple monotheism, the fact that there was one God, utterly supreme, the only creator and governor of all, did not rule out the possibility of other inhabitants of the heavenly realm, but actually tended to entail that possibility."

[48] Cohen, *From the Maccabees to the Mishnah*, 80. Bauckham (*Jesus and the God of Israel*, 87–88) notes that the existence of other heavenly beings besides Yahweh is not at stake in monotheism, but the nature and status of such beings. Similarly, Sommer (*Bodies of God*, 146–47) wonders what the problem is with "monotheism" since Christianity, Judaism, and Islam are monotheistic even while they believe in angels, supernatural beings, and even venerated saints, but we do not call their adherents henotheists or polytheists.

was about creation as much as covenant.⁴⁹ Yahweh was set apart from other gods in several respects.⁵⁰

To begin with, God is one (Deut 6.4; Neh 9.6; Mark 12.29; Rom 3.30; Gal 3.20; Josephus, *Ant.* 1.155; 4.201), he revealed himself with the unique name Yahweh (Exod 3.14–16), and God is especially known as Israel's deliverer (Exod 20.2; Deut 5.6) and so established the particular identity of Israel's deity.⁵¹ These views were not necessarily unanimous in ancient Israelite religion, but they do crystallize and become ubiquitous in the Hellenistic period. Philo gives a very crisp and clear definition of Jewish monotheism: "Therefore, of first importance, let us inscribe in ourselves this first commandment as the holiest of all commandments, to think that there is but one God, the Most High, and to honor him alone; and do not permit polytheistic doctrine to even touch the ears of any person who is accustomed to seek after the truth, with a clean and pure heart" (*Dec.* 65). Ps-Philo sums up Jewish faith as "We know the one LORD, and him we worship" (*LAB* 6.4). Josephus restates the first commandment in light of the *shema*: "The first word teaches us that God is one and he only must be worshipped" (*Ant.* 3.91). Josephus later makes monotheism axiomatic and assumes that "to recognize God as one is common to all the Hebrews" (*Ant.* 5.112). Equally forthright is the Jewish Sibyl: "There is one God, sole ruler, ineffable, who dwells in heaven, unbegotten, invisible, who himself sees all things. No sculptor's hand did make him, nor does a cast of gold or ivory reveal him, by the crafts of man, but himself, eternal, revealed himself as existing now, and formerly and again in the future" (*Sib. Or.* 3.11–16).

Most important of all, Israel's God was identified as the incomparable, unrivaled, uncreated Creator of heaven and earth and everything in them.⁵²

---

⁴⁹ Bauckham (*Jesus and the God of Israel*, 67–68) rightly adds: "Given Israel can *recognize* YHWH's uniqueness only from what YHWH does for Israel, it does not follow that this uniqueness cannot include what YHWH objectively is even independently of Israel" (italics original). Similar is Heiser ("Monotheism," 29): "Israel did not believe that Yahweh should be viewed as the supreme god *only* because of his deeds on behalf of Israel. The canonical authors considered Yahweh to be in a class by himself. He was 'species unique'" (italics original).

⁵⁰ Samuel Vollenweider ("Zwischen Monotheismus und Engelchristologie: Überlegungen zur Frühgeschichte des Christusglaubens," *ZTK* 99 [2002]: 23–25) sees a "steep monotheism" (steilen monotheismus) based around: (1) God's name; (2) God as Creator; (3) God as ruler; (4) God as deliverer; and (5) God as objection of cultic devotion.

⁵¹ Exod 8.10; 15.11; Deut 3.24; 4.35, 39; 6.4; 32.39; 33.26–27; 1 Sam 2.2; 2 Sam 7.22; 1 Kgs 8.6; Ps 86.8; 89.6–8; 95.3–4; Jer 10.10; Isa 43–46; Joel 2.27; Wis 12.13; Sir 36.5; Pr Azar 22; 2 Macc 1.24–25; 7.28–29, 35–38; *2 En.* 33.4.

⁵² Cf., e.g., Exod 20.11; Ps 96.4–5; 115.15; Isa 40.28; 44.24; Jer 10.11; Neh 9.6; *Jub.* 2.2; 1QHᵃ 15.26–33; 18.8–12; Philo, *Opif.* 170–71; *Conf.* 170; *Mos.* 2.100; *Leg. all.* 3.82; *Mut.* 22;

Yahweh was maker of all things; whether heavenly or terrestrial, angels or archons, principalities or powers, these were part of the created order that owed its existence to him.[53] Yahweh, then, had categorical superiority and supreme unlikeness in his dominion over earthly creatures and heavenly councils (see

Legat. 115; Rom 1.18–25; Acts 4.24; 14.15; 17.24; Rev 14.7. A similar view is attributed to the Socratic philosopher Antisthenes (ca. 446–366 BCE), who reportedly taught that there are "popularly many gods, but only one god according to nature, the creator of the whole universe" (according to Lactantius, *Div. Inst.* 1.5.18), and Sophocles (497–406 BCE) allegedly wrote, "There is one God, in truth there is but one, who made the heavens, and the broad earth beneath" (according to Athenagoras, *Leg.* 5.2). Generally, however, it was more typical of Near Eastern deities, such as Marduk (Babylon) and Amun-Re (Egypt), to associate a chief god with the action of creation.

[53] If God is the ontological source of all other gods, angels, and powers, I do not think it is quite right to say that "ancient monotheists were polytheists" (Fredriksen, "Mandatory Retirement," 37). Of course, Fredriksen ("How High Can Early Christology Be?" 300–301) thinks we should be agnostic on whether God created the gods, as such an act is more "assumed or inferred" by scholars. These "gods and angels . . . are just there," she claims. I consider God as maker of the gods, angels, and hosts valid for several reasons: (1) many texts do distinguish God as Creator from other gods, angels, and heavenly beings (e.g., Exod 15.11; Ps 89.5–8; 95.3; 97.7–9; 148.1–13; Isa 37.16; Neh 9.6; 3 Macc 2.2–3; *1 En.* 9.5; Athanasius, *Cont. Ar.* 2.21); (2) references to God creating the world without assistants (Isa 44.24; Sir 42.31; *2 En.* 33.4; *4 Ezra* 3.4; 6.6; Josephus, *Ag. Ap.* 2.192; Philo, *Opif.* 23; Justin, *Dial.* 56.3); (3) angels do not assist in creation but rejoice/bask over God as creator (Ps 148.2; Job 38.7; *Jub.* 2.3; 11Q5 26.12; Pr Azar 37); (4) God creates the angels/gods implicitly with the language "all things . . . apart from him . . . nothing" (e.g., 1QS 11.11; 1QH^a 9.20; John 1.3; *Odes Sol.* 16.18) and in mention of God making the heavens "and all that is in them" (e.g., Exod 20.11; Ps 148.1–5; Neh 9.6; Jas 1.17; Rev 10.6); (5) God explicitly makes ranks of angels, spirits, and godlike beings in Jewish and Christian literature (*Jub.* 2.2; *1 En.* 9.4–5; *2 En.* 29.1–3; *3 En.* 4.1; 4Q403 I 1.35; 1QS 3.13–26; 1QM 13.9–13; *Herm.* 12.1; 58.3; Justin, *Dial.* 128.3; Irenaeus, *Epid.* 8; Ps.-Clem. *Rec.* 2.42); (6) Gnostic interpretation of Gen 1.1–2 arguably understood the scriptural creator-god to be ignorant because he thought he was the only deity who created in solitary (Irenaeus, *Haer.* 1.5.3–4; 1.30.6; *Ap. John* 11.20–22; 13.5–13; *Gos. Eg.* 58.25–59.9); (7) the Son makes the angels to be ministering spirits according to Heb 1.7; (8) I should add that God as exclusive Creator does not require *creatio ex nihilo* since Philo and Justin distinguish God from gods and creation yet believe in *creatio ex matera*. Gen 1.1–2 does not necessitate *creatio ex nihilo*; however, such a view is implicit in Jewish literature at Qumran (1QS 3.15–16; 11.11, 17–18), apocalypses (*4 Ezra* 3.4; 6.38; *2 Bar* 21.4; *2 En.* 24.2), and rabbinic writings (*b.Ber.* 32b; *b.Ḥag.* 14a), and expressed implicitly or explicitly in Christian writings (Rom 4.17; Col 1.16; Heb 11.3; John 1.3; *Herm. Mand.* 26.1; Theophilus, *Autol.* 2.13; Irenaeus, *Haer.* 3.10.3). What authors stress is "creation's comprehensive and absolute contingency on the Creator while at the same time affirming his unlimited sovereignty and freedom" (Markus Bockmuehl, "The Idea of Creation out of Nothing: From Qumran to *Genesis Rabbah*," in *Visualising Jews through the Ages: Literary and Material Representation of Jewishness and Judaism*, ed. Hannah Ewence and Helen Spurling [New York: Routledge, 2015], 27).

1QH^a 15.26–33 and 18.8–12 modulating Exod 15.11).[54] Yahweh was separate from the world as its creator, whereas the Near Eastern and Greco-Roman gods, in the majority of cases, were the mightiest powers within the world and did not stand outside of it. The world already existed before the gods came to power and persisted long after their departure.[55] It was with respect to being the creator, without equal or competitor, that Yahweh was distinct from gods, angels, and daemons.[56] Ancient Jews intuited a divide between their God, Yahweh, and the gods of the nations, as well as angels, spirits, and daemons. There could be occasional blurriness when it came to the role of heavenly powers as God's agents in creation (e.g., the Angel of the Lord, Wisdom, Logos, etc.). Nonetheless, there was a strong and consistent pattern of insisting that Yahweh was God of gods, and, while not solitarily divine, Yahweh was uniquely species divine by virtue of his identity as creator of "all things."

Such a view of Israel's God as the unrivaled and uncreated Creator becomes predominant during the Hellenistic period. Josephus attributes to Abraham the view that "God, the Creator of the universe, is one; if any other being contributed anything to man's welfare, each did so by his command and not from its own inherent power" (*Ant.* 1.155). Philo states that there is "no created Lord,

[54] Lynch, "Mapping Monotheism," 50. See Sommer (*Bodies of God*, 163), who differentiates Israelite monotheism from pagan monotheism by comparing American and British systems of government: "One can imagine two models of divine kingship: a monotheistic one, in which members of a divine retinue praise the one God and carry out that God's wishes; and a polytheistic one, in which the king is first among equals, mightiest to be sure, but in control of the universe neither automatically nor permanently. Conceptually, the difference between a monotheistic council and a pagan pantheon is clear: The divine retinue of the monotheistic god might be compared to the American cabinet, where secretaries of various departments carry out the president's policies and serve at the president's whim. The polytheistic pantheon resembles the British cabinet, where each minister may have an independent power base and in which all cabinet members, the prime minister included, may be dismissed at the whim of lower politicians in Parliament or (at least in theory) of a higher and more august, if otiose, authority."

[55] Arnaldo Momigliano, "Roman Religion: The Imperial Period," in *On Pagans, Jews, and Christians* (Middletown, Conn.: Wesleyan University Press, 1987), 181; James J. O'Donnell, *Pagans: The End of Traditional Religion and the Rise of Christianity* (New York: Ecco, 2016), 67. Cf. Sommer (*Bodies of God*, 169): "The gods in charge of the world (including even a creator god like Marduk) are part of creation rather than older than it, for all these gods had a moment of origin; the world once existed without them. Similarly, the gods who had once been in charge have a moment of departure; the world now exists without them."

[56] Rightly, Wright, *New Testament and the People of God*, 248–51; Bauckham, *Jesus and the God of Israel*, 3–5, 8–13; Hurtado, "First-Century Jewish Monotheism," 121–24; Sommer, *Bodies of God*, 166–71; Boccaccini, "How Jesus Became Uncreated," 188–89; and idem, "From Jewish Prophet to Jewish God," in *Reading the Gospel of John's Christology as Jewish Messianism*, ed. Benjamin Reynolds and Gabriele Boccaccini (AJEC 106; Leiden: Brill, 2018), 338–42.

not even shall a king extend his authority and spread it from the edge of the world to its end, except the only uncreated God" (*Mut.* 22). Philo knows that Israel's God is the "highest God," and "first God" over various powers (*Sacr.* 60; *Mos.* 2.205; *Dec.* 65), yet Phinehas had zeal for the "first and only God" (*Post.* 183), and "only" applies not in the sense of solitary existence but as the "only true and living God" (e.g., *Abr.* 143; *Mos.* 2.100; *Dec.* 81). Philo is aware that there are "subordinate powers," yet they do not compromise God's oneness nor compete with his sovereignty, self-existence, and authorship of creation.[57] Philo deploys the hierarchy of heavenly powers as a teaching device to persuade his readers to seek a more elevated understanding of God and to recognize the ineffable nature of God.[58] In sum, the picture before us is that God is "ontologically (and not merely practically) superior to the gods of the nations," encompassing ontological priority and absolute ontological uniqueness.[59]

The practical result of the creator-creation distinction was that Yahweh alone was to be worshipped, which is why the cultic worship of angels, idols, mortals, and other gods was strictly prohibited.[60] Yahweh's position as Creator and Sovereign of the universe meant that other gods are created, demoted, dethroned, denied, die, or are consigned to servitude before Yahweh's supremacy (see esp. Deut 32.17, 21, 37–39).[61] They are somewhere between nonexistence and insignificance! Philo chastises Jethro for saying that "now I know that the Lord is great beyond all gods" (Num 18.11) because "no one, then,

---

[57] *Opif.* 170–72; *Sacr.* 60; *Conf.* 170–75, 179–81; *Dec.* 65; *Spec. leg.* 1.13–19; *Leg. all.* 1.49; 2.1; *Imm.* 110; *Virt.* 65, 172; *Fug.* 68–70; *Somn.* 1.70, 227–39; *Abr.* 143–45; *Legat.* 6; *Her.* 206; *QE* 2.68. It is interesting too that Philo (*Conf.* 170) and Caligula (according to Suetonius, *Cal.* 22) both cite *Il.* 2.204–5, where Agamemnon said to Achilles, "Let there be one lord, one king," to underscore the unrivaled authority of either Yahweh or Caligula himself. This line was also used by Aristotle (*Metaph.* 12.1076a.3) in relation to theology. Cicero wrote that Jupiter is the "lord of the universe, ruling all things by his nod" (*Nat. d.* 2.2).

[58] Hurtado, *One God, One Lord*, 48.

[59] Wright, *New Testament and the People of God*, 249, contra James F. McGrath, *The Only True God: Early Christian Monotheism in Its Jewish Context* (Urbana: University of Illinois Press, 2009), 18.

[60] Exod 20.2–3; 23.13, 24, 32; 34.14; Deut 5.7; 6.13–14; 7.3–4; 8.19–20; 11.16, 28; 13.1–15; 17.2–6; 18.20; 28.14; 28.26; 30.17–18; 31.18–20; Isa 40.18–20; 41.21–24; 44.6; 45.20–21; 46.5–7; *Ep. Arist.* 134–39; Tob 12.16–22; *Jos. & Asen.* 11.7–9; *Ascen. Isa.* 7.21–23; 8.5; *Apoc. Zeph.* 6.11–15; Philo, *Legat.* 116; *Dec.* 52–65; Josephus, *Ant.* 3.91; 1.155–56; Add Esth 13.12–14; Acts 10.25–26; 14.11–15; Col 2.18; Rev 19.10; 22.8–9; Tacitus, *Hist.* 5.3; *2 En.* 2.2; *3 En.* 16.1–5; Justin, *Dial.* 55.1–2.

[61] On this point, see Lynch, "Mapping Monotheism." According to Werner H. Schmidt (*The Faith of the Old Testament* [Oxford: Blackwell, 1983], 279), the Old Testament "regarded the gods not as nothing, but as good for nothing; it does not deny their existence but their power and effectiveness."

could have the boldness to compare the true God with those falsely so called, if he had any knowledge of him which was free but falsehood. But your ignorance of the One produced your opinion of the existence of the many whereas in real truth they had no existence" (*Ebr.* 45). Justin's Jewish interlocutor Trypho acknowledged that Deut 10.17 speaks of Yahweh as God of gods, but only to emphasize that "the true God, the Creator of all, is the sole Lord of all those who are falsely regarded as gods and lords" (*Dial.* 55.2). This emphasis on God as one, distinct from both creation and intermediary beings, and alone to be worshipped is carried over into the New Testament and early Christian literature, where it becomes programmatic for divine discourse.[62]

This qualified sense—what I would call creational and monarchial monotheism[63]—was apparent to external pagan observers since the Jews believed that there is "only one God" and they were instructed by Moses to "worship the one Almighty God over all creation" (*Ep. Arist.* 132; 139). In the case of Tacitus, the Jews were distinguished in that they "acknowledge one God only and conceive of him by the mind alone" (*Hist.* 5.3). Celsus censured the goatherds and shepherds of Israel, "who were deluded by Moses" into "thinking there was only one God . . . [and] abandoned the worship of many gods" in favor of "one God called the Most High, or Adonai, or the Heavenly One, or Sabaoth, or however they like to call this word; and they acknowledge nothing more" (Origen, *Cels.* 1.23–24).

---

[62] See, e.g., Mark 10.29; Rom 3.30; 16.27; 1 Cor 8.4–6; Gal 3.20; Eph 4.6; 1 Tim 2.5; Jas 2.19; John 5.44; 17.3; Jude 25; *1 Clem.* 43.6; 46.6; Ignatius, *Magn.* 8.2; Aristides, *Apol.* 1.

[63] By "monarchical monotheism" I mean the belief in one God as the sole cosmic potentate over a heavenly hierarchy; see Theodore Ludwig, "Monotheism," in *The Encyclopedia of Religion*, ed. Lindsay Jones (Detroit: MacMillan, 2005), 9:6159. Bauckham (*Jesus and the God of Israel*, 10) finds in the Hebrew Bible that "the dominant image is of God as the great emperor ruling the cosmos as his kingdom, and employing, like a human emperor, vast numbers of servants who do his will throughout his empire." April D. DeConick ("The One God Is No Simple Matter," in *Monotheism and Christology in Greco-Roman Antiquity*, ed. Matthew V. Novenson [Leiden: Brill, 2020], 263–92) offers her own taxonomy of monotheisms including "hypertheism" as "belief in a superior God who created and rules the universe" (269). M. David Litwa (*We Are Being Transformed: Deification in Paul's Soteriology* [Berlin: de Gruyter, 2012], 239–45) follows Eric Voegelin's model of "summodeism," where Yahweh is "the imperial 'high God,' who shares his divine power with the hierarchically subordinate Gods below him" (239) and "summodeism assumes a divine world with more than one grade and shade of divinity" (240). See further Bauckham, *Jesus and the God of Israel*, 82–94; McGrath, *Only True God*, 3–4, 12–13, 26–29, 35–37; Larry Hurtado, "Principal Angels and the Background of Christology," in *Ancient Jewish Monotheism and Early Christian Jesus-Devotion: The Context and Character of Christological Faith* (Waco, Tex.: Baylor University Press, 2017), 167–68; Schaper, *Media and Monotheism*, 38–51; and Bühner, *Messianic High Christology*, 12.

Thus, notwithstanding debates concerning the origins of Yahweh-only theism in ancient Israelite religion, and even allowing for incidents of apostasy, syncretism, and degrees of civic participation in pagan customs by Jews,[64] common Judaism was monotheistic to the extent that Yahweh was regarded as the source and sovereign of the heavenly and earthly realms and was the exclusive recipient of Israel's cultic worship through the temple.[65]

(2) Was Jewish monotheism exclusive or inclusive?

Even if the common Judaism of the Second Temple period was broadly "monotheistic," was it guarded in its account of God's uniqueness, or was it inclusive with other beings, heavenly or human, able to share in divine functions and divine worship? Israel's sacred literature often describes God's direct intervention in human affairs (e.g., Deut 33.26–29; Isa 66.18–19; Ezek 5.8; 21.3; Tob 13.1–5; *1 En.* 1.3–8). In other places, God acts through special agents such as Wisdom, Word, Spirit, the Angel of the Lord, named angels like Michael and Metatron, Daniel's "one like a son of man" (Dan 7.13), Israel's king, the high priest, and patriarchs Enoch and Moses. Sometimes these agents exercise divine functions, and on some occasions they even receive types of reverence/obeisance. Were these figures a personification of God? Were they angelic creatures deputized into divinity by God? Were they exalted patriarchs given a share in divine glory who then became angels? Or were they subordinated beings existing in an inferior mode of divinity? James McGrath points out that "numerous Jewish texts allow for the existence of a 'second figure' alongside God—of high rank and at times almost blending into God, yet at other times clearly subordinate and distinct."[66] Similarly, Ruben Bühner concludes that there is "an impressive panorama" with respect to "concrete motifs in early Jewish messianic discourses, independent of the early Jesus movement, about an eschatological figure of deliverance who could be placed in close proximity

---

[64] See Michael F. Bird, *Crossing over Sea and Land: Jewish Missionary Activity in the Second Temple Period* (Peabody, Mass.: Hendrickson, 2010), 77–83. There were also several ways that Jews could negotiate Hellenism by assimilation, convergence, or antagonism; see John M. G. Barclay, *Jews in the Ancient Mediterranean Diaspora: From Alexander to Trajan (323 BCE—117 CE)* (Edinburgh: T&T Clark, 1996).

[65] See Hurtado, "First-Century Jewish Monotheism," 115–35; idem, "Monotheism," in *The Eerdmans Dictionary of Early Judaism*, ed. John J. Collins and Daniel C. Harlow (Grand Rapids: Eerdmans, 2010), 961–64; idem, "'Ancient Jewish Monotheism' in the Hellenistic and Roman Periods," *Journal of Ancient Judaism* 4 (2013): 379–400; and idem, "Observations on the 'Monotheism' Affirmed in the New Testament," in *The Bible and Early Trinitarian Theology*, ed. Christopher A. Beeley and Mark E. Weedman (Washington, D.C.: Catholic University of America Press, 2018), 50–68.

[66] McGrath, *Only True God*, 16.

to God." Further, he notes that in "some messianic discourses the boundary between people, God, and various 'divine beings' is by no means clear in qualitative and functional terms as is often assumed."[67] None of these figures are necessarily on par with Israel's God; even so, they "indicate that the line separating the human from the divine in ancient Judaism was not absolute as is sometimes supposed."[68] That brings us to the primary issue under consideration. Was Jesus considered divine in the same way that these intermediary figures were divine? That is very much the heart of the debates about Jewish monotheism and early Christology!

(3) Jesus as a God . . . like Moses?

A good example for the potentially inclusive nature of Jewish monotheism is the portrayal of Moses in biblical and postbiblical literature as a god. In the book of Exodus, Moses is ordered by Yahweh to keep confronting Pharaoh despite his feelings of inadequacy. Moses is encouraged with the promise that he will have godlike power and Aaron will be his prophet.

> And the LORD said to Moses, "See, I've made you like God to Pharaoh; and your brother Aaron shall be your prophet" (Exod 7.1 [CEB]; cf. 4.16).

Given that the Pentateuch contains strong monotheistic convictions, the mention of Moses like a "god" (Hebrew: *Elohim*; Greek: *Theos*) is unusual. It is unusual precisely because it attributes comparative divinity to Moses, complete with his own prophetic servant in his brother Aaron. One would think that such an attribution is excluded by the stringent, on-pain-of-death prohibition of following other gods or by the general Jewish aversion to human deification.[69] For some commentators this text means no more than Moses "is to function

---

[67] Ruben A. Bühner, *Hohe Messianologie: Übermenschliche Aspekte eschatologischer Heilsgestalten im Frühjudentum* (WUNT 2.523; Tübingen: Mohr Siebeck, 2020), 330 ("ein beeindruckendes Panorama dessen, wie sehr und unter Zuhilfenahme welcher konkreten Motive in frühjüdischen messianischen Diskursen unabhängig von der frühen Jesusbewegung bereits eine eschatologische Heilsgestalt in starker Nähe zu Gott gezeichnet werden konnte. . . . in manchen messianischen Diskursen die Grenze zwischen Menschen, Gott und verschiedenen 'divine beings' in qualitativer wie funktionaler Hinsicht keineswegs so eindeutig ist, wie dies häufig angenommen wird").

[68] Collins, "Jewish Monotheism," 88.

[69] Interestingly, translations of Exod 7.1 for people groups living within Islamic-majority contexts, such as the Pattanai Malay translation, translate this as "I will cause you to be my voice to Pharaoh" to avoid offending Islamic sensitivities. See David J. Clark, "Linguistic and Cultural Influences on Interpretation in Bible Translations," in *The Oxford Handbook on the Reception History of the Bible*, ed. Michael Lieb, Emma Mason, and Jonathan Roberts (Oxford: Oxford University Press, 2011), 211.

with divine authority before Pharaoh, and like God, make known his word through his prophet."[70] Or else, Moses is god in a parodic sense to rival the so-called god-Pharaoh, with Aaron as a counterpart to the Egyptian magicians.[71] But more concretely, Ambrose of Milan believed that Moses was called god by virtue of the "in-dwelling of the Godhead within him," an intensification of the divine presence resting upon him, though he explicitly denies that this is on par with the mode of Christ's own divinity.[72] In any case, Moses is stated to be godlike, above a human being like Pharaoh, while below Yahweh. When combined with the later description of Moses as "the finger of God" (Exod 8.19), Moses is portrayed as a figure possessing divine power and exercising divine agency! Thus, Exod 7.1 can be interpreted as depicting Moses as a supernatural being with quasi-divine qualities even if he is still subordinated to Yahweh. Moses is, on some level, in some way, a god!

The reception history of Exod 7.1 indicates authors wrestling with Moses and monotheism. Ben Sirach venerates Moses' memory by saying that God made Moses "equal in glory to the holy ones, and made him great, to the terror of his enemies" and "glorified him in the presence of kings" (Sir 45.2–3). According to the *Testament of Moses*, Moses was appointed "from the beginning of the world, to be the mediator of the covenant" (*T. Mos.* 1.14) and he is venerated as "that sacred spirit, worthy of the Lord" (*T. Mos.* 11.16). In Ps.-Philo, Moses was miraculously born already circumcised (*LAB* 9.13). In the Qumran scrolls, Moses is called "a god over the mighty" (4Q374 II 2.6). Philo alludes to Exod 7.1 to imagine Moses as a god in the sense of one who rules over his own body and mind as part of the cultivation of virtue towards divinity (Philo, *Sacr.* 8–10). His virtue reached such heights that he was granted a participation in God's own nature that is quietude (*Post.* 28). Elsewhere Philo says that some speculated whether Moses possessed a "divine intellect" (*Mos.* 1.27), and Moses was designated as "god and king of the whole nation" because of his unique communion with God and because he was granted dominion by God over the created order (*Mos.* 1.155–58).[73] Josephus narrates that Moses was, because of his great virtue, assumed up into heaven in a cloud (*Ant.* 4.326). Also, the Essenes venerated Moses as

---

[70] Brevard S. Childs, *Exodus: A Commentary* (OTL; London: SCM Press, 1974), 118.

[71] Thomas Römer, "From the Call of Moses to the Parting of the Sea: Reflections on the Priestly Version of the Exodus Narrative," in *The Book of Exodus: Composition, Reception, and Interpretation*, ed. Thomas Dozeman, Craig A. Evans, and Joel N. Lohr (Leiden: Brill, 2014), 143.

[72] Ambrose, *On the Christian Faith* 5.1.23.

[73] Philo also mentions Exod 7.1 in *Leg. all.* 1.40–41; *Pot.* 160–61; *Migr.* 84; *Mut.* 19, 125–29; *Somn.* 2.189; *Sacr.* 8–9; *QE* 2.6.

second only to God and considered anything spoken against Moses as blasphemy (*War* 2.145). The Alexandrian Jewish historian Artapanus stated that Moses was "deemed worthy of godlike honor by the priests and called Hermes [Thoth], on account of the interpretation of sacred letters": noticeably, Moses is equal to God in honor and is assimilated to a Greek deity (Eusebius, *Praep. ev.* 9.27.6).

Another important text for the deification of Moses is *Ezekiel the Tragedian*, otherwise known as the *Exagōgē*, a Hellenistic drama retelling the Exodus narrative. In the drama, Moses has a dream where it is reported that

> On Sinai's peak, I saw what seemed a throne
> so great in size it touched the clouds of heaven.
> Upon it sat a man of noble mien,
> becrowned, and with a scepter in one hand
> while with the other he did beckon me.
> I made approach and stood before the throne.
> He handed o'er the scepter and he bade
> me mount the throne, and gave to me the crown;
> Then he himself withdrew from off the throne.
> I gazed upon the whole earth round about;
> things under it, and high above the skies.
> Then at my feet a multitude of stars
> fell down, and I their number reckoned up.
> They passed by me like armed ranks of men.
> Then I in terror wakened from the dream. (*Ezek. Trag.* 68–82)

This dream indicates Moses' greatness in an extraordinary and unprecedented manner, for it depicts Moses not only invited onto God's throne, but also God vacating the throne for Moses, after which stars parade before Moses like an army under review by its king. The arresting scene portrays Moses arrayed with cosmic majesty and divine sovereignty. The description of Moses on the throne and God's seeming abdication imply for some commentators Moses' deification,[74] his appointment as God's vice-regent,[75] or his becoming a heavenly counterpart to God.[76]

---

[74] Pieter W. van der Horst, "Moses' Throne Vision in Ezekiel the Dramatist," *JJS* 34 (1983): 25.

[75] Wayne A. Meeks, *The Prophet-King: Moses Traditions and the Johannine Christology* (NovTSup 14; Leiden: Brill, 1967), 148–49.

[76] Andrei A. Orlov, *The Enoch-Metatron Tradition* (TSAJ 107; Tübingen: Mohr Siebeck, 2005), 266–68.

Taken together, the depictions of Moses as a god, as god and king of the Israelites, and as sitting on God's throne in God's place raise questions whether ancient monotheism was strict and exclusive. If Moses can be called a "god," exercise sovereignty over the earth, and occupy the divine throne with celestial honors, does this not demonstrate that monotheism was malleable and flexible enough to include a human subject within the honors and functions attributed to the God of Israel? Much like the Greco-Roman world, then, Judaism has its own pyramid of deities. In which case, Jesus could be "god" in a Jewish sense, the same sense as Moses, a human figure imagined and portrayed as "god" next to Israel's "God." One could pursue peculiar analogies for the exaltation and deification of Jesus in the realms of apocalyptic, mystical, or Hellenistic Judaism, especially among angels and the patriarchs elevated to a heavenly position.[77]

Recapitulation of the Problem

Thus far I have attempted to problematize Jesus' divinity. To recap, the problem is *how* is Jesus a divine being? Jesus' divinity can be explained with recourse to placing him along an ancient spectrum of divinity, pointing to parallels in Greco-Roman mythology, comparing devotion to Jesus with ancient ruler cults, or finding analogies for divine agents in Greco-Roman philosophy. Alternatively, if one prefers a Jewish setting for early Christology, we could aver that Jewish monotheism was inclusive since we have the example of Moses, a human figure who was portrayed as a god, becoming a divine intermediary agent situated between Israel's God and the Israelites. Beyond that, there are principal angels, divine personifications of Word and Wisdom, and exalted patriarchs to consider as analogues too. Against this backdrop, Jesus is not divine in any unique or unprecedented manner, nor in a way that transgresses the absolute divinity of God. On this scenario, the challenge is to identify which myth, mighty ruler, or intermediary figure provides the closest analogue to how Jesus was divine for the early church. The origins of divine Christology become the quest for the "missing link" or precursory "parallel"![78]

If that is the case, then the implication would be that the Nicene account of Jesus as "true God from true God," "begotten not made," and "of one substance with the Father" is a philosophical world away from how the early church constructed and described Jesus as a divine figure. Therefore, it is frequently alleged that the Christology of the New Testament

---

[77] Vollenweider, "Zwischen Monotheismus und Engelchristologie," 25.

[78] Cf. similarly Timo Eskola, *Messiah and the Throne* (WUNT 2.142; Tübingen: Mohr Siebeck, 2001), 383; and Bühner, *Hohe Messianologie*, 339.

is functional and subordinationist, whereas later pro-Nicene Christology was given to an excess of philosophical speculation and blatant eisegesis about a so-called divine nature.[79] The underlying premise is that early Christology had no inherent ontology,[80] no sense of ontic divine equality between Father and Son, nor a view of Jesus' divinity as a species of "being" or "substance." The concepts of a divine nature and divine reality were perhaps true for elites immersed in Platonic thought, yet not part of everyday *religio*. As a result, fourth-century Nicene categories should not be anachronistically projected into the initial phases of christological formulation when mapping the origins of divine Christology. Pro-Nicene christological reasonings, whatever their utilities and merits, were unmoored from New Testament Christology.[81] We have, then, an abrupt rupture between the

---

[79] Oscar Cullmann (*The Christology of the New Testament* [2nd ed.; London: SCM Press, 1963], 3-4) influenced many when he wrote, "When it is asked in the New Testament 'Who is Christ?', the question never means exclusively, or even primarily, 'What is his nature?', but first of all, 'What is his function?' Therefore, the various answers given to the question in the New Testament . . . visualize both Christ's person and his work." Raymond E. Brown (*Introduction to New Testament Christology* [New York: Paulist, 1994], 171) referred to a transition from the New Testament's "functional approach" to the church fathers' "ontological approach." Geza Vermes (*Christian Beginnings: From Nazareth to Nicaea* [New Haven, Conn.: Yale University Press, 2012], 225) asserted: "Ever since the New Testament era and throughout the next two centuries, equivocation about the divinity of Christ was standard, yet one point was certain. The Son was not recognized as having *quite* the same dignity and standing as God the Father, and the same judgment was applied *a fortiori* to the Holy Spirit" (italics original). Even more brutal is Ulrich Mauser ("One God and Trinitarian Language in the Letters of Paul," *HBT* 20 [1998]: 100): "The historically trained New Testament scholar will today proceed with the task of interpretation without wasting a minute on the suspicion that the Trinitarian confessions of later centuries might be rooted in the New Testament itself, and that the Trinitarian creeds might continue to function as valuable hermeneutical signposts for modern understanding." For Adela Yarbro Collins and John J. Collins (*King and Messiah as Son of God: Divine, Human, and Angelic Messianic Figures in Biblical and Related Literature* [Grand Rapids: Eerdmans, 2008], 174, 192, 203, 208, 211), divinity has different degrees, so that Jesus is divine in a sense, mostly a functional sense, as a preexistent emanation or principal angel, and the language is not philosophical. In contrast, Chris Tilling (*Paul's Divine Christology* [Grand Rapids: Eerdmans, 2012], 249, 265-70) argues that understanding Christ's divinity as relational requires one to move beyond the ontological vs. functional dichotomy.

[80] I should say that by "ontology" I mean that branch of metaphysics that pertains to the nature of being, exploring the what-ness of an existing being.

[81] R. P. C. Hanson (*Search for the Christian Doctrine of God*) recognizes that pro-Nicene argumentation was intensely exegetical, yet he remains critical of its biblical exegesis. Although figures like Athanasius had a "firm grasp of the ultimate drive or burden of the New Testament," there still remained a "great gulf which divides him and virtually all his contemporaries of whatever ecclesiastical complexion, from the moderns in his methods of

Catholic christological dogma of the fourth century, with its philosophical recasting of Jesus, set against the functional and subordinationist Christology of the primitive church, where Jesus' divinity was a mutation based on existing schemes of (semi-)divinity drawn from either the Greco-Roman or Jewish spheres.

But what if divine ontology was not an alien Platonic intrusion into the church's christological discourse? What if ancient religion believed something about the nature of the gods? What if ontological convictions about God are indeed traceable among Jews and Christians long before the council of Nicaea?[82] This would open a whole new front in comparisons between Greco-Roman religion, Second Temple Judaism, and early Christianity. It would also mean that the relationship between New Testament and patristic Christologies is far more complex than a functional and subordinationist Christology[83] giving way to a more philosophical and platonizing variety. To this we now turn.

---

handling and presuppositions in approaching the text of the Bible" (843). He adds that "the expounders of the text of the Bible [in the fourth century] are incompetent and ill-prepared to expound it," as "the presuppositions with which they approached the Biblical text that clouded their perceptions, the tendency to treat the Bible in an 'atomic' way as if each verse or set of verses was capable of giving direct information about Christian doctrine apart from its context, the 'oracular' concept of the nature of the Bible, the incapacity with a few exceptions to take serious account of the background and circumstances and period of the writers" (848–49). Maurice Casey (*From Jewish Prophet*, 163) believed "Patristic exegesis was extraordinarily free in distorting the meaning of texts in the interests of dogma." Of course, one could dispute whether patristic exegesis was quite so myopic, just as one could argue that pre-critical exegesis is far more coherent and enduring than the fragmentation and faddishness that has characterized modern critical exegesis since the eighteenth century. See Craig A. Carter, *Interpreting Scripture with the Great Tradition* (Grand Rapids: Baker, 2018).

[82] See C. F. D. Moule, "The Borderlands of Ontology in the New Testament," in *The Philosophical Frontiers of Christian Theology*, ed. Brian Hebblethwaite and Stewart Sutherland (Cambridge: Cambridge University Press, 1977), 1–11.

[83] As Vollenweider ("Vom israelitischen zum christologischen Monotheismus. Überlegungen zum Verhältnis zwischen dem Glauben an den einen Gott und dem Glauben an Jesus Christus," in *Antike und Urchristentum: Studien zur neutestamentlichen Theologie in ihren Kontexten und Rezeptionen* [WUNT 436; Tübingen: Mohr Siebeck, 2020], 131) puts it: "Later theological-historical categories such as 'subordinationism' do not do proper justice to this complex relationship between Christocentrism and Theocentrism" ("Spätere theologiegeschichtliche Kategorien wie 'Subordinatianismus' werden diesem komplexen Beziehungsgefüge zwischen Christozentrik und Theozentrik nicht hinreichend Gerecht"). Cf. Wolfgang Schrage, *Unterwegs zur Einheit und Einzigkeit Gottes: Zum "Monotheismus" des Paulus und seiner alttestamentlich-frühjüdischen Tradition* (Neukirchen-Vluyn: Neukirchener, 2002), 158, n. 360 on differentiating a subordination of order under God from later dogmatic accounts of subordinationism in patristic literature.

The Search for Divine Ontology

2

"The more you know you're a man, the more you become a god."

Plutarch, *Pomp.* 27 reporting Graffiti in Athens about Pompey

"As for myself, Conscript Fathers, [I know] that I am mortal, that my functions are the functions of men, and that I hold it enough if I fill the foremost place among them."

Tiberius according to Tacitus, *Ann.* 4.38.1

The standard story of the development of Christology is that the early church, as reflected in the New Testament, did not regard Jesus as possessing a divine nature per se. His divinity was functional not ontological, and he remained subordinated to the authority and divinity of God the Father. Jesus was regarded as being on the divine spectrum, somehow and somewhere, perhaps like a deified ruler or as a demigod, yet he was still beneath the Father just as a deified emperor was still beneath Jupiter. The attempt to make Jesus part of God the Father's own being belongs either to a gradual evolution of language or perhaps to a Platonic revolution of conception that postulated Jesus as sharing one divine substance with God the Father.

Michael Peppard is one who prefers to construe early Christology within the matrix of a gradation of divinity, where Jesus' status is "as high as humanly possible," and he thus rejects the "Nicene Approach" with its "Platonic epistemology and ontology."[1] Even among those with an admittedly "early high Christology," there is still an allergy to thinking that the early church had any

---

[1] Michael Peppard, *The Son of God in the Roman World: Divine Sonship in Its Social and Political Context* (Oxford: Oxford University Press, 2012), 5, 10–12, 29–30, 32–36.

firm ontological commitments in mind about Jesus' divine nature or his shared being with God the Father. Larry Hurtado provided something of a virtual memo when he wrote on his blog, "The so-called 'ontological' categories are simply the products of one particular historical discourse and philosophical development, whereas the NT writings are largely shaped by the categories and concepts that derive from the biblical and ancient Jewish tradition. So, for example, NT writers tend to refer to God's name, glory, throne, and role as creator and sovereign over all, instead of God's 'being' or 'essence.'"[2] Richard Bauckham seeks to go beyond the functional and ontic distinction by a Christology of "divine identity," which focuses on *who* God is, not on *what* God is. On this measure, Jesus is part of what makes God unique as Creator and Sovereign of the cosmos. Jesus is part of the identity of God, and this christological monotheism was intended to be revealed as an eschatological monotheism in the coming consummation. Thus, Bauckham believes that the ontological categories of Greek metaphysics did not influence Christian theological tradition until "the period after the New Testament."[3] Chris Tilling too rejects the static being of Aristotelian categories in favor of relational and epistemological aspects that express God's uniqueness.[4]

In this chapter, I shall argue that divine ontology has been sidelined for too long in discussions of early Christology. Ontological concerns do not belong exclusively in the patristic period with its purported penchant for Platonic

[2] Larry Hurtado, "Chronology and Ontology," *Larry Hurtado's Blog*, September 26, 2016, https://larryhurtado.wordpress.com/2016/09/26/chronology-and-ontology/. Andrew Chester (*Messiah and Exaltation* [WUNT 207; Tübingen: Mohr Siebeck, 2007], 380–81) rightly pushes back on Hurtado on this point: "His constant emphasis on functional categories . . . involves a failure to raise the corresponding question of whether functional attributes necessarily preclude ontological status. They can hardly be mutually incompatible, presumably, since they are combined in New Testament portrayals of Jesus," and "It is indeed precisely in the context of Christological debate in the last few decades that the point has been emphatically made that no firm dividing line can be drawn between what is 'functional' and what is 'ontological.' Hence to insist on limiting the discussion exclusively to functional analysis, in the way that Hurtado does, is unsatisfactory; the question of the ontological implications of his functional analysis, and the corresponding ontological status of the figures he discusses needs to be raised again."

[3] Richard Bauckham, *Jesus and the God of Israel* (Milton Keynes, U.K.: Paternoster, 2008), 7, 30–31, 235. Chester (*Messiah and Exaltation*, 20–21) suggests that Bauckham has bought into Karl Barth's critique of the ontological tradition (i.e., Aristotle and Aquinas) and its replacement with the notion that God's being is defined by divine actions. I suggest that might be true, but perhaps due to influence from Jürgen Moltmann.

[4] Chris Tilling, *Paul's Divine Christology* (Grand Rapids: Eerdmans, 2012), esp. 40–41, 71, 264–70. I suspect that Tilling regards ontological categories as permissive with the caveat they only have utility to describe the type of being that underlies the relational ecosystem that the divine person expresses within himself and toward other persons.

eisegesis of the New Testament.⁵ Instead, ontological concerns and language were part of the theological discussions and religious grammar of the ancient world among Jews, Greeks, Romans, and Christians. Ontology is not a magical key that explains all the complexities, developments, and backgrounds of early christological discourse, but it must be included as a contributing factor to how the early church regarded Jesus as a divine being.

To be clear, I am not going to deny the palpable differences in terminology and texture between first- and fourth-century christologizing. Even so, I think it is wrong to play off the New Testament's christological discourses against Nicaeano-Constantinopolitan dogma, with the former characterized as a variation of the Greco-Roman spectrum of divinity and the latter regarded as an extravagant (mis)reading of the New Testament driven by Hellenistic philosophies of ontology. I will hopefully show that ontological commitments about deity are part of the religious ambience of antiquity, that early Christian authors make tacit and overt ontological statements about Jesus as divine, and that patristic exegesis needs to be better appreciated as a fusion of various scriptural, philosophical, and religious dimensions.

Two Classes of Divinity in the Ancient World

The first point of order is to dismantle the widespread assumption that ontologies of divinity were something that popped up in christological discourse sometime in the second and third centuries. Well, the truth is that Greeks and Romans had thought long and hard about the nature of a God and gods, to the point that there were generally thought to be two types of divinity: a divinity by nature and a divinity by merit. It is the failure to distinguish these two classes of divinity that for my mind creates some of the confusion about divinity in relation to Greco-Roman mythology, Jewish monotheism, intermediary figures, and the Christology of the early church. As we will see, this distinction proves to be illuminating for christological discourses in early Christianity.⁶

---

⁵   On patristic exegesis, see *inter alia* John C. Murray, *The Problem of God: Yesterday and Today* (New Haven, Conn.: Yale University Press, 1964), 45–46; R. P. C. Hanson, *The Search for the Christian Doctrine of God* (Edinburgh: T&T Clark, 1988), 824–49; Lewis Ayres, *Nicaea and Its Legacy: An Approach to Fourth-Century Trinitarian Theology* (Oxford: Oxford University Press, 2004), 31–40; idem, "Scripture in Trinitarian Controversies," in *The Oxford Handbook of Early Christian Biblical Interpretation*, ed. Paul M. Blowers and Peter W. Martens (Oxford: Oxford University Press, 2019), 439–54; and Stephen R. Holmes, *The Quest for the Trinity: The Doctrine of God in Scripture, History, and Modernity* (Downers Grove, Ill.: InterVarsity, 2012), 33–55.

⁶   Among the few scholars who recognize the relevance of this classification are Charles H. Talbert, "The Concept of Immortals in Mediterranean Antiquity," *JBL* 94 (1975): 419–36; idem, *The Development of Christology during the First Hundred Years: And Other Essays on*

The ancient historian Herodotus (ca. 484–425 BCE) observed two types of worship of Herakles, as an Olympian god and as a deified mortal: "And further, those Greeks, I think, are most in the right, who have established and practice two worships of Heracles, sacrificing to one Heracles as to an immortal [*athanatō*], and calling him the Olympian, but to the other bringing offerings as to a dead hero [*hērōi enagizousi*]" (*Hist.* 2.44). Plato (ca. 428–348 BCE) defined absolute divinity as those who exist "beyond being in surpassing honour and power" (*epeikeina tēs ousias presbeia kai dumanei hyperchontas*), who are "not generated in [themselves]" (*ou genesin auton onta*) but give others "generation and growth and nurture" (*genesin kai auxēn kai trophēn*; *Rep.* 6.509b). The Greek Stoic philosopher Chrysippus (ca. 279–206 BCE) wrote that gods are "subject to generation, but Zeus is everlasting" (Plutarch, *Stoic rep.* 1052A). Diodorus Siculus (ca. 90–30 BCE) referred to this bipartite classification of deities: "As regards the gods, men of ancient times have handed down to later generations two different conceptions. Certain of the gods, they say, are eternal and imperishable ... for each of these genesis and duration are from everlasting to everlasting. But the other gods, we are told, were terrestrial beings who attained to immortal honors and fame because of their benefactions to mankind, such as Heracles, Dionysus, Aristaeus, and the others who were like them" (*Lib.* 6.1.2). He said the same is particularly true for how the Ethiopians conceive of the divine realm: "The Ethiopians entertain two opinions. They believe that some of them ... have a nature which is eternal and imperishable, but others of them, they think, share a mortal nature and have come to receive immortal honors because of their virtue and the benefactions which they have bestowed on all mankind" (*Lib.* 3.9.1). Cicero (106–43 BCE) refers to gods who have always lived in heaven and to those installed in the heavens by merit (*Leg.* 2.19; *Nat. d.* 2.62). Cicero was involved in a senatorial delegation to determine if Amphiaraus was a god and his shrine in Boetia entitled to tax-exempt status. Amphiaraus was a hero of Greek mythology who was swallowed by the earth and allegedly transformed into a god. His shrine was subsequently associated with the healing god Asclepius. The senators decided that Amphiaraus was a god, despite the local *publicani* complaining that "anyone who had at one time been mortal was not immortal" (*SIG* 747; Cicero, *Nat. d.* 3.49; *Div.* 1.88). The

---

Early Christology (Leiden: Brill, 2011), 17; William Horbury, *Jewish Messianism and the Cult of Christ* (London: SCM Press, 1998), 70; Jerome H. Neyrey, *Render to God: New Testament Understandings of the Divine* (Minneapolis: Fortress, 2004), 228–42; Bart D. Ehrman, *How Jesus Became God: The Exaltation of a Jewish Preacher from Galilee* (New York: HarperOne, 2014), 31; and Paula Fredriksen, "How High Can Early Christology Be?" in *Monotheism and Christology in Greco-Roman Antiquity*, ed. Matthew V. Novenson (Leiden: Brill, 2020), 299–303.

Roman orator Quintilian (ca. 35–100 CE) declared: "Some [gods] . . . may be praised because they were born immortal, others because they won immortality by their valour, a theme which the piety of our sovereign [emperor Domitian] has made the glory of these present times" (*Inst.* 3.7.9). Quintilian divided gods into those who exist in immortality as the Olympian gods and those who have been deified on account of their amazing exploits, like Roman emperors since Julius Caesar. Plutarch (ca. 46–119 CE) contrasted the god Apollo with deified mortals: "My native tradition removes this god [Apollo] from among those deities who were changed from mortals into immortals, like Heracles and Dionysus, whose virtues enabled them to cast off mortality and suffering; but he is one of those deities who are eternal and unbegotten" (*aidiōn kai agennētōn*; *Pel.* 16.5).⁷

Importantly, the difference between these two types of divinity is one of kind, not merely of degree; it is a difference of intrinsic and extrinsic divinity.⁸ For an analogy we might compare it to the two types of peerages in the United Kingdom, where one can be a "Lord" by descent or become a "Lord" by meritorious appointment. Both Lords are real and true, even if they obtain and exercise their lordship in a different way, with different relationships to their peers and people.⁹

The significance of this distinction for contemporary christological debates can hardly be understated. It shifts attention from debates about the strictness (or not) of Jewish monotheism, the search for christological parallels with intermediary figures, and whether divinity is about hierarchy, identity, worship, or functionality. None of that is irrelevant per se. Those topics each have their part to play in the story of the making of Christology and for explaining when, how, and why Jesus was considered to be divine. But none of them explain what precisely makes someone a god rather than the God. The answer is, as Boccaccini puts it: "While 'being divine' and 'being worshiped' were a matter of power, and created beings could share some degrees of 'divinity' and devotion, being 'the one God' meant essentially to be 'uncreated.'"¹⁰ Or else, "Ancient Jews saw God not only at the top of a hierarchical pyramid, but also

---

⁷ Herakles could be worshipped as both a hero and a god; see Pausanias 2.20.1; Herodotus, *Hist.* 2.44.

⁸ Contra Ittai Gradel, *Emperor Worship and Roman Religion* (Oxford: Clarendon, 2002), 25–26, 29–30, 148; followed by Joseph D. Fantin, *The Lord of the Entire World: Lord Jesus, a Challenge to Lord Caesar?* (NTM 31; Sheffield: Sheffield Phoenix, 2011), 120.

⁹ I owe this analogy to a conversation with N. T. Wright.

¹⁰ Gabriele Boccaccini, "How Jesus Became Uncreated," in *Sibyls, Scriptures, and Scrolls*, ed. Joel Baden, Hindy Nayman, and Eibert Tigchelaar (JSPSup 175; Leiden: Brill, 2016), 1:188.

as belonging to a different dimension. What defined God was not as much that God was the most divine being and the worthiest of honor and veneration. The decisive factor was that God was the only creator of all. It was God's uncreated status, what made God 'God,' and defined God's uniqueness."[11] The differences between being Deity and lesser divinity were attributes such as eternality and uncreatedness that were predicated of a subject.[12]

Some will complain that this distinction between absolute and relative gods theologizes Greco-Roman religion and that such classifications were far from the minds of ancient religious practitioners. However, even while ancient *religio* was concerned with ritual rather than dogma, it was not ideationally vacuous, as the rituals reified what was believed about the gods and the benefits conferred upon worshippers. Ritual was how one conceptualized the divine world and expressed convictions about it.[13] The dichotomy of ritual vs. belief is overstated.[14] There was a *theologos* enfaced in visual representation in

---

[11] Gabriele Boccaccini, "From Jewish Prophet to Jewish God," in *Reading the Gospel of John's Christology as Jewish Messianism*, ed. Benjamin Reynolds and Gabriele Boccaccini (AJEC 106; Leiden: Brill, 2018), 338.

[12] Ruben Bühner (*Messianic High Christology: New Testament Variants of Second Temple Judaism* [Waco, Tex.: Baylor University Press, 2021], 156) mostly agrees, though he cautions that we should not treat "someone's status as created or uncreated as the *only* and *universal* criterion for Jewish monotheism" (italics original).

[13] S. R. F. Price, *Rituals and Power: The Roman Imperial Cult in Asia Minor* (Cambridge: Cambridge University Press, 1984), 7.

[14] Note the words of Michael Frede, "The Case for Pagan Monotheism," in *One God: Pagan Monotheism in the Roman Empire*, ed. Stephen Mitchell and Peter van Nuffelen (Cambridge: Cambridge University Press, 2010), 81: "In conclusion I want to say that ancient religion is not just a matter of cult and ritual, but that ancient religious thought and writing are a crucial part of it, especially if these themselves are regarded as religious activities." Similar is D. S. Levene, "Defining the Divine in Rome," *TAPhA* 142 (2012): 42, n. 1: "While 'belief' was not the primary criterion by which Romans assessed the correctness or otherwise of religious behavior, Roman writings on religion, as on other topics, constantly present, explicitly or implicitly, accounts of the conceptual assumptions underlying religious practices and narratives, and indeed it is often hard to make sense of those practices and narratives without taking into account the underlying assumptions." James B. Rives (*Religion in the Roman Empire* [Oxford: Blackwell, 2007], 48) notes Pliny, *Nat. Hist.* 2.26 on the importance of religious beliefs, surmising that "beliefs about the divine world were left implicit, embedded in cult acts and myth and art.... What distinguishes the Graeco-Roman religious tradition from Christianity is thus the absence not of religious beliefs, but of pressures to define and scrutinize those beliefs." See also Charles King, "The Organization of Roman Religious Beliefs," *Classical Antiquity* 22 (2003): 275–31, esp. on belief as it pertains to prayer and piety; and Julia Kindt, "The Story of Theology and the Theology of the Story," in *Theologies of Ancient Greek Religion*, ed. Esther Eidinow, Julia Kindt, and Robin Osborne (Cambridge: Cambridge University Press, 2016), 12–34. Finally, the word *theologia* goes as far back as Plato (*Rep.* 2.378d–e; 4.493d), even if it was not freighted with specific Christian metaphysical

monuments, carried in the parading of statues at a festival, and executed in the sacrifice of animals. The uttering of prayers, the singing of hymns, the reading of poetry, the watching of tragedies, while no less ritual or performance, are explicitly theological insofar as they instantiate the story, status, power, and nature of the god that make them worthy of veneration.

Peppard notes that a divine ontology can even be constructed by rituals. He writes: "When continuous benefactions led to continuous honors, that process could admittedly lead to a kind of ontology—a status solidified because of a god's perpetual benefactions."[15] That rings true particularly in the imperial cults because the performance of sacrifices to the emperor indicated that the subjects were dependent on the emperor as on other gods. The rituals denoted a special relationship with the emperor and connoted a certain type of divine reality at work.[16] Rituals, art, hymns, poems, and decrees were discursive acts that attempted to manufacture the reality of what it proclaimed, namely, that the emperor had somehow, and to some degree, traversed the ontic mortal-immortal distinction. We should not forget that Tiberius allegedly rejected divine honors because he was "mortal," which is an ontological rationale for its rejection (Tacitus, *Ann.* 4.38.1). Rituals and decrees were the attempt to get around that limitation. Further proof is that there was a recognized difference between being declared a god, being honored as a god, and being made a god.[17] Tiberius, we are told, "consecrated his father [Augustus] not by imperial decree, but by divine worship; he did not simply call him a god, but made him a god" (*sed fecit deum*; Velleius Paterculus, 2.126.1). The rituals for divine honors and deification aspired to create what they celebrated in the minds of practitioners. It was sometimes a case of divine honors seeking ontological legitimacy.

Concerning ruler cults, the distinction between relative and absolute deity was how civilizations negotiated the relationship between divinity, power, and being while remaining respectful of traditional deities and the exceptional accomplishment of leaders. Ruler cults were diverse across the Mediterranean and Near East since "a ruler who was viewed as having achieved an elevated *status* in one location could easily have been viewed as having obtained a share in the divine *nature* in

---

assumptions; see the discussion in Gerd Van Riel, "Theology and Religiosity in the Greek Pagan Tradition," in *The Origins of New Testament Theology*, ed. Rainer Hirsch-Luipold and Robert Matthew Calhoun (WUNT 440; Tübingen: Mohr Siebeck, 2020), 93–118.

[15] Peppard, *Son of God*, 35.

[16] S. R. F. Price, "Gods and Emperors: The Greek Language of the Roman Imperial Cult," *JHS* 104 (1984): 89.

[17] Michael Koortbojian, *The Divinization of Caesar and Augustus: Precedents, Consequences, Implications* (Cambridge: Cambridge University Press, 2013), 21–23.

another location."[18] Yet it was possible to migrate from the former sphere to the latter sphere, and this is where rituals and performances come in. In other words, rulers can not only be honored as divine but can even be made divine.

In instances where the living emperors are assimilated to gods, especially Jupiter/Zeus/Dios, in statues, inscriptions, and decrees, "making divine" does not mean an incarnation of a god, but rather a public association of the emperor with a supreme deity (Virgil, *Ecl.* 4.1–10; Horace, *Carm.* 1.2.1–46). So, despite their mortal appearance, the emperors were thought to manifest the reality of an immortal god. Furthermore, the miraculous birth stories of Alexander (Plutarch, *Alex.* 2.2–3.9) and Augustus (Suetonius, *Aug.* 94.4; Cassius Dio, 1.1–2.4; Virgil, *Ecl.* 4) whereby their mothers were impregnated by gods were an attempt to connect their deity to something genealogically if not biologically divine (i.e., divine by birth or nature). Egyptian texts presage the divine begottenness of Augustus, calling him, literally, "god from god" (*theou ek theou*) in several sources (P. Oxy. 1453.10–11; *OGIS* 655.1–2). The continued worship of emperors was justified precisely because they were said to have metamorphosed into an astral entity at death, which grounded the bestowal of divine honor in a proposed transformation into a divine form (see Ovid, *Met.* 14.284–85; 15.844–48; Suetonius, *Jul.* 88; Pliny, *Nat. Hist.* 2.93–94 on Julius Caesar's transformation; while Plutarch, *Rom.* 28.8 rejects the idea of "sending the bodies of good men with their souls to heaven").[19] The combination of *consecratio* and continuous cultus was designed to make someone a god by effecting the transformation of the subject venerated from a mortal nature into an immortal being. Hellenistic city-cults seem to have had no religious problem with cultic worship of a king or liberator *as* an Olympian deity. However, pan-polis and postmortem worship of a monarch did seem to have required some kind of "religious theory" to justify the continued cultus and to make an even stronger identification of the king with a deity. The Ptolemaic court poetry about rulers *carried* off to the gods and Roman *consecratio* ceremonies seem to have filled this gap.[20]

The imperial cults were not, then, an ontology-free zone. In fact, literature and rituals were often trying to announce the ontological alteration of the emperor to justify the honors bestowed upon him. This deliberately blurs the absolute and honorific modes of divinity, but only because it admits that the

---

[18] Tyson L. Putthoff, *God and Humans in the Ancient Near East* (Cambridge: Cambridge University Press, 2020), 160–61 (italics original).

[19] See Levene, "Defining the Divine in Rome," 63–66, for the physical transformations that take place in apotheosis.

[20] Christian Habicht, *Divine Honors for Mortal Men in Greek City States: The Early Cases* (Ann Arbor: Michigan Classical Press, 2017), 144–45.

two modes exist in the first place; there is a tangible difference between the two, and to transition from one to another takes some convincing.[21]

In addition, the *theologia tripartita* distinguished the metaphysical theology of philosophers, the mythical theology of poets, and the political theology of civic rites, but the presence or absence of ontology was not the mark of distinction.[22] The distinctions were the religious genre, social function, and type of divine nature elaborated in each of the *theologia*. Differences were whether the deity was characterized by impassible stativity, anthropomorphism, or a magnification of human power. In each case, ontological assumptions pervade and distinguish all three *theologia*. This is why Plutarch wrote that among the poets, lawgivers, and philosophers "all agree that there are gods; but concerning their number, their order, their essence and power, they vastly differ one among another" (*einai theos omoiōs tithemenoi, plēthous de, peri kai taxeōs autōn ousias te kai dunameōs megala diapheromenoi pros allēlous*; Amat. 18). Note these are differences of species, not merely differences of status!

From all this, D. S. Levene concludes that "many Roman [and Greek] literary texts assume a boundary between the divine and human not unlike that postulated by Judaism and Christianity."[23] While some might accuse Levene of simply rehearsing the Christianized view of deity that has been bequeathed to us by Christendom, I would aver that he is totally correct, as the ancient sources reiterate this distinction repeatedly.

In the *Epistle to Diognetus* (ca. 150–200 CE) we have a prime example of these two classifications of absolute and relative divinity being used side by side.

---

[21] Gradel (*Emperor Worship*, 270) rightly speaks of rituals as "actually constructing social reality" but adds that the emperor's "exact nature, man or god, appears to have been without relevance to the establishment and workings of his cults, which merely formulated his status in the hierarchy of the world." I would aver that the rituals were trying to construct or declare something about the ontology of the emperor, at least in the minds of some participants and observers.

[22] Varro, *Antiquitates rerum divinarum*, in Augustine, *Civ.* 6.5, 12 (cf. 4.27; 6.5); see explanation in Jan Assman, "Monotheism and Polytheism," in *Religions of the Ancient World: A Guide*, ed. Sarah Illes Johnston (Cambridge, Mass.: Belknap, 2004), 17–20; and Rives, *Religion*, 21–23.

[23] Levene, "Defining the Divine in Rome," 44. He concludes, contra Gradel (*Emperor Worship*, 50, 72): "The evidence strongly supports the assertion of humans and gods being conceived by the Romans as being in separate categories. . . . It was commonplace at Rome to conceive of divinity as an absolute rather than relative category. Gods were conceived as having a nature which was fundamentally distinct from humans, and which was associated with a group of properties which were, if not unique to the divine, at any rate typically associated with a high degree of irregularity [i.e., immortality, physical form, spatial location, and unusual powers]."

First, there is an ontological divinity attributed to the divine Son when the author says that the omnipotent Creator did not establish truth and holiness among humans by sending "some subordinate, or angel, or ruler or one of those who manage earthly matters, or those entrusted with the administration of things in heaven." Instead "the Designer and Creator of the universe" sent his Son "in gentleness and meekness, as a king might send his son who is a king; he sent him as God; he sent him as a human to humans" (*alla en epieikeia kai prautēti hōs basileus pempōn huion basilea empempsen, hōs theon epempsen, hōs anthrōpon pros anthrōpon epempsen*; *Diogn.* 7.2–4). This is a statement that is remarkable for its presentation of Jesus "as God" and as "human" in the same way that the son of a king is a king. In an analogy similar to "the son of a duck is a duck," there is a strong affirmation of the Father's divine being shared with the Son.[24]

Second, a relative or relational sense of divinity is created by benefaction given to the less fortunate. The author exhorts his audience to the imitation of God. "No one is able to imitate God in these matters [goodness]; on the contrary, these things are alien to his [a normal person's] greatness. But one who takes up a neighbor's burden, one who wishes to benefit someone who is worse off in something in which one is oneself better off, one who provides to those in need things that one has received from God, and thus becomes a god [*theos ginetai*] to those who receive them—this one is an imitator of God" (*Diogn.* 10.5–6). Here goodness to one's neighbor is not only an imitation of God,[25] but also means, relationally, becoming a god by exercising divine-like benevolence in human benefaction toward others.

In *Diognetus*, God is uniquely Almighty and his son is sent to humans not as a lesser subordinate being: he comes "as" God and "as" a human being, language which speaks to his divine and human natures, a dual

---

[24] According to Clayton N. Jefford (*The* Epistle to Diognetus [*with the* Fragment of Quadratus]: *Introduction, Text, and Commentary* [OAF; Oxford: Oxford University Press, 2013], 230), "The portrayal of the Word with positive attributes that follows is somewhat muddled without a clear distinction between whether the author intends a description of God or instead of the Word."

[25] The imitation of God is a well-known Platonic theme; see Plato, *Phaed.* 252DE: "And so it is with the follower of each of the other gods; he lives, so far as he is able, honoring and imitating that god, so long as he is uncorrupted, and is living his first life on earth, and in that way he behaves and conducts himself toward his beloved and toward all others. Now each one chooses his love from the ranks of the beautiful according to his character, and he fashions him and adorns him, like a statue, as though he were his god, to honor and worship him. The followers of Zeus desire that the soul of him whom they love be like Zeus; so they seek for one of philosophical and lordly nature, and when they find him and love him, they do all they can to give him such a character." The motif was incorporated into Hellenistic Judaism (e.g., Philo, *Virt.* 168; *Mut.* 129; *Dec.* 111) and early Christianity (e.g., Eph 5.1).

consubstantiality. At the same time, acts of benefaction to one's own neighbor are an imitation of God's goodness and make the benefactor a god, relatively speaking, to the supplicant.

Jerome Neyrey sketches out these two different types of divinity, which he calls "true gods" and "divinized benefactor-heroes."[26]

True Gods	Divinized Benefactor-Heroes
Ancient	Recent, new
Celestial	Terrestrial
Without a beginning and ungenerated	Came into being and born in time
Imperishable	Died, translated in death
Eternal	Made immortal

It is worth expounding these two divisions of divinity more fully to understand them singularly and in juxtaposition.

True Gods: God by Nature

Ancient Definitions of God's Divine Nature

In ancient philosophy and religion there was a category of gods who were regarded as eternals in the sense of being uncreated (*agenētos*), ungenerated (*agennētos*), everlasting (*aidios*), imperishable (*aphthartos*), and immortal (*athanatos*).[27] Among Greco-Roman authors, a good example is Diogenes Laertius, who quoted Zeno on the eternal nature of God as "indestructible and ingenerable" (*Vit. Phil.* 7.1.137). Plutarch placed Isis and Osiris among the gods who have "no begetting and shall have no end" (*agennētoi mēd aphthartoi*; *Is. Os.* 21). For Plutarch, the Delphic maxim "Know thyself" demands the refrain "Thou art," because Apollo is "the true, unfeigned and sole appellation of being, as suitable to him alone." Plutarch contrasts those who possess a mortal nature, who exist between "generation and corruption," with those who possess a mode of being that is "eternal, unbegotten, incorruptible, which time does not change" (*E. Delph.* 17–19).

In the Jewish sphere, Philo repeatedly describes Jewish worshippers as devoted to the "uncreated and eternal" God (*Spec. leg.* 2.166), the "Father of all things, the unbegotten God, begetter of everything" (*Cher.* 44), the "uncreated, and immortal, and everlasting God, who is in need of nothing and who is the

---

[26] Neyrey, *Render to God*, 237.
[27] Largely following Neyrey, *Render to God*, 228–42. Another way to put it would be that gods have birthdays, while God does not!

maker of the universe, and the benefactor and King of kings, and God of gods" (*Dec.* 41), the "one true God" (*Somn.* 1.229; *Post.* 66; *Ios.* 254; *Mos.* 2.171; *Leg. all.* 2.68; *Legat.* 347, 366). Philo's view of deity is one that neither begets nor is begotten (*Opif.* 100). Josephus declares that Moses taught "one, uncreated and immutable [deity] to all eternity" (*Ag. Ap.* 2.167). The prologue to the *Sibylline Oracles* indicates a similar view: "One God, who alone rules, exceedingly great unbegotten but God alone, one highest of all, who made heaven and sun and stars and moon and fruitful earth and waves of water of sea, who alone is God, abiding as indomitable creator" (*Sib. Or.* Prologue 94–98). The *Apocalypse of Abraham* acclaims God as "Eternal one, Mighty one, Holy El, God autocrat, self-originate, incorruptible, immaculate, unbegotten, spotless, immortal, self-perfected, self-devised, without mother, without fear, ungenerated" (*Apoc. Ab.* 17.8–11).[28]

In the New Testament, descriptions of God's attributes are remarkably terse and restrained, with the focus instead on God's character, covenant-history, and revelation in Jesus Christ. Even so, Luke recounts speeches that refer to the "living God, who made the heaven and the earth and the sea and all that is in them" (Acts 14.15) and "the God who made the world and everything in it, he who is Lord of heaven and earth, does not live in shrines made by human hands, nor is he served by human hands, as though he needed anything, since he himself gives to all mortals life and breath and all things" (Acts 17.24–25). Paul refers to "the living and true God" (1 Thess 1.9) as well as God's "eternal power and divine nature" (Rom 1.20). Hebrews proclaims "the living God" (Heb 3.12; 12.22). In the Johannine writings, God is un-seeable and unknowable and God is Spirit (John 1.18; 4.24; 1 John 4.12; 3 John 11). God is one, the author of creation, ontologically "other," but principally covenantor with Israel and the Father of Jesus the Son.

Later Christian writings accent God's ingenerate and incomparable nature. Clement of Rome claimed that Moses desired to glorify "the name of the true and only God" (*1 Clem.* 43.6). Aristides began his apology with a definition of true deity: "God is not born, not made, an ever-abiding nature without beginning and without end, immortal, perfect, and

---

[28] Bauckham (*Jesus and the God of Israel*, 7, 31) is aware that Jewish authors used metaphysical language for God; however, he strangely plays off the Jewish context against patristic discourse because the latter was overtly metaphysical, which proves to be a false dichotomy. For Hellenistic Jews as much as for patristic authors, God's identity cannot be and was not described apart from God's being as eternal, unchangeable, and immortal. The sources cited above prove that the who and what of God are not mutual exclusives. On the relative parity between Jewish and Neo-Platonic accounts of deity, see Tarmo Toom, *Classical Trinitarian Theology: A Textbook* (London: T&T Clark, 2007), 13–14.

incomprehensible" (*Apol.* 1). Justin Martyr referred to the God "who is most true" (*1 Apol.* 6.1), the "unchangeable and eternal God" who is "good and unbegotten," the "unbegotten and impassible God" (*1 Apol.* 13.4; 14.2; 25), and "God alone is unbegotten and incorruptible" (*Dial.* 5.4; *2 Apol.* 5.1). Theophilus of Antioch said of the Christian God: "He has no beginning because he is unbegotten; he is immutable because he is immortal. . . . He is Lord because he is master of the universe, Father because he is before the universe, Demiurge and Maker because he is creator and maker of the universe, Most High because he is above everything, Almighty because he controls and surrounds everything" (*Autol.* 1.4). Athenagoras distinguished God from the physical realm because "the divine is unbegotten and eternal" whereas matter is created and perishable (*Leg.* 4.1; 15.1–16.4). Further to that, he cites Plato as an example of belief that God the Creator is unbegotten and eternal in contradistinction to the cosmic elements, who are gods derived from the Creator (*Leg.* 6.2). Christians, he says, acknowledge "one God, unbegotten, eternal, invisible, impassible, incomprehensible, and infinite," unlike "the gods" in pagan poetry, who are "no better than men" (*Leg.* 10.1–2).

The *Kerygma Petrou* piles up adjectives to describe God as "incomprehensible, perpetual, incorruptible, uncreated, who made all things by the word of his power" (*Keryg. Pet.* 2). Irenaeus declares that humans owe their existence, not to angels or to a distant power, but to "the true God" (*Haer.* 4.20.1), who "was not made by anyone, but everything was made by him . . . God, the Father, uncreated, uncontainable, invisible, one God, the Creator of all" (*Epid.* 4, 6). The Christian redaction of the eighth book of the *Sibylline Oracles* defines God as "self-begotten, undefiled, everlasting, eternal, master of heaven in might, measuring the fiery breath" (*Sib. Or.* 8.429–30). According to Tertullian, Christians saw themselves as engaging in the "true religion of the true God" (*Apol.* 24). Clement of Alexandria declares "God is one, indestructible, unbegotten," possessing "an existence true and eternal" (*Protr.* 6), who is "the highest essence of all beings" (*Protr.* 117). Ptolemy offered a gloss on 1 Cor 8.6 to refer to the "unbegotten Father" contrasted with the begotten and inferior demiurge-lawgiver (*Flor.* 33.7.6). The *Apocryphon of John* includes a section outlining how the divine monad is a monarch superior in rank and essence to the aeons (*Ap. John* 2.27–4.10). In the *Gospel of Truth*, "the Father is ungendered, he alone is the one who begot him for himself as a name, before he brought forth the aeons" (*Gos. Truth* 38.33–36). There is a lengthy description of the Father's ineffable and incomparable divine nature in the *Tripartite Tractate* as the "unbegotten Father and the complete perfect one" who is "unbegotten and immortal, just as he had no beginning and no end as he is, he is unattainable in his greatness, inscrutable in his wisdom, incomprehensible in his power and unfathomable in his sweetness" (*Tri. Trac.* 51.6–57.8).

Ancient Critiques of Deification

God's absolute deity and his incommunicable nature were at the heart of Greco-Roman, Jewish, and Christian critiques of human deification.

Among Greeks and Romans, the concept of deification, especially of emperors, was complex and contested.[29] That said, the worship and deification of emperors should not be thought of as political fiction or top-down propaganda masquerading as religion, as per A. D. Nock's description of divine honors as "an expression of gratitude which did not involve any theological implications."[30] The ruler cult was a real religion.[31] The divinity attributed to emperors, living or deceased, was real, at least real within the chain of benefactor-client relationships and amid the symbolic nexus of divine pantheon and earthly power that constituted the imperium.

Nonetheless, for all the compatibility and interpenetration of the divine and human realms, the gods were still "other."[32] As such, deification was occasionally sneered at, not only for its pretentiousness, but even for its alleged impiety. Homer has the god Apollo tell Diomedes: "Never think yourself the gods' equal—since there can be no likeness ever between the race of immortal gods and men who walk on the ground" (*Il.* 5.440–42). Xenophanes of Colophon had a well-known saying about deceased mortals who were worshipped

---

[29] See esp. Spencer Cole, *Cicero and the Rise of Deification at Rome* (Cambridge: Cambridge University Press, 2013), and Koortbojian, *Divinization of Caesar and Augustus*; cf. Michael F. Bird, *Jesus the Eternal Son: Answering Adoptionist Christology* (Grand Rapids: Eerdmans, 2017), 38–49. Mary Beard, John North, and Simon Price (*Religions of Rome* [2 vols.; Cambridge: Cambridge University Press, 1998], 1:148–49) comment that "Every narrative of Roman apotheosis tells, at the same time, a story of uncertainty, challenge, debate and mixed motives," and this "complicated and conflicted *set* of myths opens up each time the uncertainty of any human claim to be, or to have become, a god—or, for that matter to have witnessed that 'becoming'. It asserts deification as a process that involved fraud *and* piety, tradition *and* contrived novelty, political advantage *and* religious truth: for the Romans, as for us" (italics original). Horbury (*Jewish Messianism*, 77) notes that ruler cults "presented a vigorous challenge to traditional Greek and Roman piety, but they also had a capacity for integration with it."

[30] A. D. Nock, *Cambridge History: 10, Augustan Empire 44 B.C.–A.D. 70*, ed. F. E. Adcock, J. B. Bury, M. P. Charlesworth, N. H. Baynes, and S. A. Cook (Cambridge: Cambridge University Press, 1934), 481.

[31] Horbury, *Jewish Messianism*, 69–70; and Price, *Rituals and Power*, 14–16.

[32] Cf. summary in M. David Litwa, *We Are Being Transformed: Deification in Paul's Soteriology* (Berlin: de Gruyter, 2012), 89–92.

as deities: "If they are gods, do not mourn them; if they are mortals, *do not sacrifice* to them" (Plutarch, *Is. Os.* 70; *Amat.* 18.12; *Sup.* 13; Clement of Alexandria, *Protr.* 2.24.3). Arrian had an account of Callisthenes, who debated Anaxarchus over Alexander the Great's alleged divinity and request for prostration.[33] For Callisthenes "there is no honour which Alexander is unworthy to receive, provided that it is consistent with his being human." That is because

> Men have made distinctions between those honours which are due to men, and those due to gods, in many different ways, as for instance by the building of temples and by the erection of statues. Moreover, for the gods sacred enclosures are selected, to them sacrifice is offered, and to them libations are made. Hymns also are composed in honour of the gods, and eulogies for men. But the greatest distinction is made by the custom of prostration. For it is the practice that men should be kissed by those who salute them; but because the deity is located somewhere above, it is not lawful even to touch him, and this is the reason no doubt why he is honoured by prostration. Bands of choral dancers are also appointed for the gods, and paeans are sung in their honour. And this is not at all wonderful, seeing that certain honours are specially assigned to some of the gods and certain others to other gods, and, by Zeus, quite different ones again are assigned to heroes, which are very distinct from those paid to the deities. It is not therefore reasonable to confound all these distinctions without discrimination, exalting men to a rank above their condition by extravagant accumulation of honours, and debasing the gods, as far as lies in human power, to an unseemly level, by paying them honours only equal to those paid to men. (*Ann.* 4.11.1–4)

In Cicero's treatise, *On the Nature of Gods*, the philosopher Cotta attacked "those who teach that brave or famous or powerful men have been deified after death, and that it is these who are the real objects of the worship, prayers, and adoration to which we are accustomed to offer" (*Nat. d.* 1.119). Or else, deification is a problem, because if humans, animals, islands, virtues, and planetary objects are divine, then divinity becomes so widespread that it loses its currency. Divinity then has little differentiation from ordinary existence (Cicero, *Nat. d.* 3.39–50).

---

[33] Note the conclusion of Putthoff about Alexander (*God and Humans*, 189): "It seems likely that he viewed himself as having a share in the divine nature. But even if he did not, he certainly wanted others to think of him in that way. It is likely that he was understood according to the local conceptions of rulers in different regions of his empire. In Egypt and in Persia in particular, he declared himself as a god king on par with the pharaohs and Achaemenid kings."

The system of deification was already sufficiently established to be satirized by Seneca on the death of Claudius in his famous book about the "pumpkinification" of Claudius. The story mocks the deification of Claudius, with the gods debating whether Claudius should be admitted to their company and then deciding against it. In the satire, Janus complains, "At one time, it was a great thing to be made a god, but now you have made the distinction a farce. So that my remarks do not seem to be directed at a particular individual, rather than the issue, I propose that from this day onwards no one shall be made a god from those who eat the fruits of the earth or whom the fruitful earth nourishes" (*Apoc.* 9). Seneca is not against apotheosis per se, but he certainly objects with sardonic taunts the implausibility of Claudius' deification.[34] Ittai Gradel grasps the barb of the story: "Humans can, according to Seneca, elevate a man to heaven; only the gods, however, decide if he will actually be admitted."[35]

Seneca's satire dovetails with Plutarch's oblique criticism of deification, using Romulus as the example but probably having in mind contemporary Roman practices. Truth and right reason, urges Plutarch, demand that one is not made a god by civic pronouncement, but a virtuous soul may evolve from human to hero to demigod and, after purification, into a god in a true sense (*Rom.* 28.8).[36] In addition, those who presume "to be called gods and to have temples dedicated in their honour," whose glory is fleeting and whose pretentiousness is now exposed as "vain-glory and imposture," are "like fugitive slaves without claim to protection, they have been dragged from their shrines and altars, and have nothing left to them save only their monuments and their tombs" (*Is. Os.* 24). In his treatise on boasting, Plutarch accepts the fittingness of certain honors for rulers, such as "Philadelphus or Philometor or Euergetesor or Theophiles," but he deems inappropriate accepting the titles of "god or son of a god" (*De laude* 12). Plutarch then can embrace divinity as the terminus of the soul in its journey toward virtue; anything other than that, however, is vanity.

---

[34] Cf. Price, *Rituals and Power*, 115; and Christoph Heilig, *Hidden Criticism? The Methodology and Plausibility of the Search for a Counter-Imperial Subtext in Paul* (Minneapolis: Fortress, 2017), 83–84.

[35] Gradel, *Emperor Worship*, 329. Gradel admits (327) that Seneca's point is that Claudius does not possess "absolute divinity," which for my mind undermines his central premise that divinity was only about honorific status. Gradel's concession is that absolute divinity did not matter, and that only relative divinity was important in regard to the Roman state.

[36] Similar interpretations of deification are given by Philo, *Sacr.* 9–10; *Legat.* 91; *Prob.* 42–44; and Justin, *1 Apol.* 21.4.

In the end, deification had meaning within the symbolic world of the imperium, but it was also a contested process: the divinity of the deified was sometimes ridiculed (Seneca), reinterpreted (Plutarch), or rejected (Cicero's Cotta).

There was a long and rich Jewish tradition of attacking ruler worship.[37] Philo drew from this tradition in his vigorous critique of Caligula's pretentions to divinity. For Philo, God was not a divine being somewhat further along the divinity spectrum than others. It was more the case that there was an ontological chasm that existed between the eternal and imperishable God and created, perishable creatures, between the immortal and the mortal. He declared, "There is no created being who is truly God [*genētos gar oudeis alētheia theos*], but such a one is so only in appearance and opinion, being destitute of that most indispensable quality in God, namely, eternity" (*Virt.* 65). No man should "dare to compare himself to the all-blessed one" (*Somn.* 2.130). He censured those who think of themselves as neither human beings nor demigods but as "complete deity" (*holon daimona*), which was affronting, as it overstepped the boundaries of "human nature" (*anthrōpinēs physeōs*; *Virt.* 172). Importantly, the ontological distinction between God and humans was at the heart of Philo's critique of Caligula's "godless deification" (*atheōtatēn ektheōsin*; *Legat.* 77; cf. Josephus, *Ant.* 18.256–61; 19.4; *Ag. Ap.* 2.75–76; Suetonius, *Cal.* 22). Philo wrote that "the form of God is not a thing which is capable of being imitated by an inferior form, as good currency is not replicated by counterfeit coinage" (*Legat.* 110), and Caligula, though he pranced around like Ares, resembled Ares in neither "rumour" (*metheuō*) nor "nature" (*physis*; *Legat.* 112).[38] Caligula "should not be likened to any god, not even to any demigod, since he has neither the same nature, nor the same essence [*mēte physeōs, mēte ousias*], nor even the same wishes and intentions as any one of them" (*Legat.* 114). The Jews, said Philo, "believe that there was but one God, their Father and the Creator of the world" (*Legat.* 115), so Caligula's attempt to put a statue of himself in the Jerusalem temple was affronting because it meant "deifying the created and perishable nature of a man, as far as appearance go, into the uncreated and imperishable nature of God, which is the very summit of impiety" (*Legat.* 118). Philo abruptly added a pointed parenthetical remark that both divine incarnation and human deification are out of the realms of

---

[37] See Bird, *Jesus the Eternal Son*, 38–62; idem, *An Anomalous Jew: Paul among Jews, Greeks, and Romans* (Grand Rapids: Eerdmans, 2016), 227–28. Note other Jewish critiques of ruler worship in 2 Chr 24.17; Isa 14.13; Ezek 28.2; 29.3; Dan 3.1–30; 11.36–39; 2 Macc 9.5–12; Wis 7.1–6; 14.17–21; Jdt 3.8; 6.2–4; *Sib. Or.* 3.545–49; 5.33–55, 137–54, 214–21.

[38] Cf. Philo, *Legat.* 93–118, 278. On Caligula dressing as various gods, see Suetonius, *Cal.* 52; Cassius Dio 59.7.1.

possibility: "Sooner could God change into a man than a man into a god" (*Legat.* 118).³⁹ Philo regarded the whole concept of demigods to be "worthy of ridicule" (*chleuēs axion*), because it was impossible for the same man be "both immortal and mortal" (*athanatos te kai thnētos*; *Contempl.* 6).⁴⁰ Importantly, Philo did not attack the imperial cult per se; in fact, he composed a panegyric to Augustus including the fitness of his divine honors (*Legat.* 143–53). His assault on Caligula's divinity ingratiated him to the Claudian regime, which muted attempts at divine worship (Suetonius, *Claud.* 11.1–12.1). Philo's primary concern was Jewish freedom from charges of *maiestas* (i.e., insulting the emperor's honor) because of their national way of life.

Christians intensified the criticisms of deification, the apotheosis of emperors, and ruler cults as inappropriate and impious. Luke exhibited a clear distaste for the citizens of Tyre and Sidon fawning over Herod Agrippa I and saying that he spoke with "the voice of a god, and not of a man!" (Acts 12.20–23). Aristides critiqued the mistaken belief of "those who believed that some of the men of the past were gods" on the grounds that finite mortals do not have the nature of true deity, which "is uncreated and imperishable" (*1 Apol.* 7). Justin referred to the deification of the emperors and the emperor Hadrian's teenage lover Antinous, who was worshipped as a god despite everyone knowing his origins (Justin, *1 Apol.* 21.3; 29.4; *Dial.* 69.3; and Tatian, *Orat.* 10.3). Athenagoras noted that a being who is born and dies is not on the same plane as the "unbegotten God [who] alone is eternal" (*Leg.* 30.3). Theophilus pointed out that Christians worship the "living and true God," not the emperor, for the emperor is not a god but a man appointed by God, so he should be obeyed but not worshipped (*Autol.* 1.11). The apologist Minucius Felix recognized that the deifications of Romulus and Juba were a matter of reputation rather than

---

³⁹ Philo elsewhere accentuated the God-human incomparability in *Opif.* 69: "Let no one represent the [divine] likeness as one to bodily form; for neither is God in human form, nor is the human body God-like." See also Trypho according to Justin Martyr (*Dial.* 68.1): "You are attempting to prove what is incredible and practically impossible, namely, that God deigned to be born and to become man." What is interesting is that Jewish authors object to the divinity of Jesus, but never on the grounds that it compromises monotheism; see Oskar Skarsaune, "Is Christianity Monotheistic? Patristic Perspectives on a Jewish/Christian Debate," *Patristic Studies* 29 (1997): 355. Skarsaune adds: "Seen from a Jewish perspective the Christians were doing one of two things. Either they deified a man of purely human origin—which was blasphemy plain and simple. Or, if the Christian claims about Jesus were true, that he was divine from the beginning, Christology raised the whole question of divine suffering, the suffering of God" (362).

⁴⁰ Plutarch (*Is. Os.* 26) notes that daemons "have a complex and inconsistent nature and purpose."

realism, because they were venerated "not on account of belief in their divinity, but in honor of the power that they exercised" (*Oct.* 23). He added a lament for its apparent fiction, saying "miserable indeed" are those whose hope is in mortal men like princes and kings, for "to invoke their deity" and to worship them with sacrifices is "a false flattery" (*Oct.* 29). Tertullian rejected the veracity of so-called witnesses who claimed to have seen an emperor ascend into heaven alongside Jupiter (*Spect.* 30). A rejection of human deification is something that Celsus and Origen agreed upon (*Cels.* 3.22).

In the later church, arguments based on Christ's divine nature were deployed to rule out that his divinity was a matter of deification or a granting of divine honors. Cyril of Alexandria wrote: "For there are many anointed ones by grace, who have attained the rank of adoption [as sons], but [there is] only one who is by nature the Son of God" (*Frag.* 190). John Chrysostom made a similar statement: "Christ did not become god from human advancement—perish the thought.... We preach not a human made into god, but confess a god made human."[41] Augustine critiqued Varro's "civil theology" with divinized benefactors as vanity and spectacle (*Civ.* 6.6–7). For a significant part of the early church, divinity is such that humans cannot and should not be deified—and Christ is not a deified man.

Absolute Deity Ascribed to Christ

If early Christology developed out of identifying Jesus with certain intermediary figures, or focused on Jesus' divine functions rather than any divine nature, then when and why did various wings of the nascent churches suddenly start describing Jesus in philosophical categories? If descriptions of Jesus as divine by nature were a late Platonic import, when did this Platonic "big bang" of christological ontology happen?[42] Not until the second or third century? Far more likely, an awareness of and concern about divine ontology was part of early Christian discourse from very early on in its discussion of Israel's God, Jesus, and other spiritual entities.

To begin with, Jewish language for God made much of a distinction between the one God and "all things," which is based on an ontological distinction of Creator and creation that found its way into the New Testament

---

[41] John Chrysostom, *PG* 61.697, 38–42, cited in M. David Litwa, *Iesus Deus: The Early Christian Depiction of Jesus as a Mediterranean God* (Minneapolis: Fortress, 2014), 2.

[42] Levene ("Defining the Divine in Rome," 45) points out that those who posit divinity exclusively as a spectrum struggle "to explain how the notion of an absolute division appeared so readily and so widely in different philosophical schools if it did not come from a standard part of the Roman thought-world."

(1 Cor 8.6; Rom 11.36; Heb 1.2–3; 2.10; Col 1.16–17; John 1.3).⁴³ Paul does not consider Greco-Roman deities/daemons to have a "nature" (*physis*) or "being" (*ousin*) comparable to God (1 Cor 8.4; 10.20; Gal 4.8). He contrasts idols with the "true and living God" (1 Thess 1.9; 2 Cor 6.16) and the images of mortal humans and animals with the "immortal God" (Rom 1.24; cf. 1 Tim 1.17).

In addition, Paul makes what are effectively ontological claims about Jesus by stating that Jesus exists in the "form of God" and is "equal to God" (Phil 2.6).⁴⁴ Udo Schnelle believes such a text marks "the beginnings of thinking of God and Christ as equals."⁴⁵ Adela Collins takes Phil 2.6 to "mean that he [Christ] was god-like in appearance or nature, that is, a heavenly being as opposed to a human being."⁴⁶ Put differently, Jesus exhibits the outward display of God's being and glory, which itself expresses the inner reality of God's nature.⁴⁷ Or, in Plutarchian language, the divine offspring is an image (*eikōn*) and copy (*mimēma*) of the divine being (*ousia/ontos*).⁴⁸ Josephus (*Ag. Ap.* 2.190–91, 248) connects God's form (*morphē*) with God's "nature" (*physis*) and "magnitude" (*megethos*). Philo and Justin believed that the "form of God" expresses the divine nature,

---

⁴³ Richard Bauckham, "The 'Most High' God and the Nature of Early Jewish Monotheism," in *Israel's God and Rebecca's Children: Christology and Community in Early Judaism and Christianity*, ed. David B. Capes, April D. DeConick, Helen K. Bond, and Troy A. Miller (Waco, Tex.: Baylor University Press, 2007), 39–53.

⁴⁴ Contra Marinus de Jonge (*Christology in Context: The Earliest Christian Responses to Jesus* [Philadelphia: Westminster, 1988], 197), who thinks the hymnic language "does not allow for metaphysical or systematic theological conclusions."

⁴⁵ Udo Schnelle, *Apostle Paul: His Life and Theology* (Grand Rapids: Baker, 2005), 396.

⁴⁶ Adela Y. Collins, "'How on Earth Did Jesus Become a God?': A Reply," in *Israel's God and Rebecca's Children: Christology and Community in Early Judaism and Christianity*, ed. David B. Capes, April D. DeConick, Helen K. Bond, and Troy A. Miller (Waco, Tex.: Baylor University Press, 2007), 57.

⁴⁷ Cf. Gordon D. Fee, *Pauline Christology: An Exegetical-Theological Study* (Peabody, Mass.: Hendrickson, 2007), 378–79; Andrew Ter Ern Loke, *The Origin of Divine Christology* (SNTSMS 169; Cambridge: Cambridge University Press, 2017), 14, 35–36; and Michael Wade Martin and Bryan A. Nash, "Philippians 2.6–11 as Subversive *Hymnos*: A Study in the Light of Ancient Rhetorical Theory," *JTS* 66 (2015): 116–17. See in contrast Carolyn Osiek (*Philippians, Philemon* [Nashville: Abingdon, 2000], 61): "when applied to persons in this very status-conscious culture, it [*isos*] is more likely to mean equality of status or importance in a hierarchical order. It is not likely to mean what modern interpreters would want to read into the hymn, namely, equality of nature or substance with God. In other words, it is not a metaphysical but a social statement." Also, Joseph H. Hellerman ("Μορφῇ θεοῦ as a Signifier of Social Status in Philippians 2.6," *JETS* 52 [2009]: 784) sees this as entirely honorific, referring "to visible appearance, with no indication, one way or another, of any corresponding inward quality." His view is refuted by Crispin H. T. Fletcher-Louis, "'The Being That Is in a Manner Equal with God' (Phil 2:6c): A Self-Transforming, Incarnational, Divine Ontology," *JTS* 96 (2020): 581–627.

⁴⁸ Plutarch, *Is. Os.* 53, talking about Isis and her creation.

which makes human deification and idol worship utterly inappropriate (Philo, *Legat.* 80, 95, 97, 110–11; Justin, *1 Apol.* 9.1). It should be remembered that across Phil 2.6–11 is a combined affirmation of Christ's preexistence, his divine being in terms of possessing the "form" and "equality" of God,[49] and inclusion of Christ within the monotheistic rhetoric of Isa 45.23. That Jesus exercises divine functions and receives a form of worship is merely the window dressing to the more astonishing claim that he shares in what sets Yahweh apart from other gods and creation: he shares in the divine name and exclusive monotheistic devotion. There is a *Verbindungsidentität* (shared identity)[50] between God and Jesus only because there is also a *Verbindungswesen* (shared being). In fact, the Nicene description of Jesus as *homoousios* ("same substance") with the Father is a theological explication of Pauline judgments about Jesus sharing the form, equality, glory, and name of the Father in language that ruled out Arian and semi-Arian duplicity on the subject.[51]

As an addendum here, Paul declares that Christ is the "image of God" (2 Cor 4.4; Col 1.15), which can refer to Jesus as an Adamic figure (Gen 1.27), God's Wisdom (Wis 7.26),[52] or else, like Philo's Logos, a mediator between the uncreated God and the created realm after whom humanity

---

[49] N. T. Wright (*The Climax of the Covenant: Christ and the Law in Pauline Theology* [Edinburgh: T&T Clark, 1991], 83) rightly takes "equality" as an epexegetical reference back to "form of God" and suggests that "the stronger translation 'this divine equality'" operates best.

[50] This term comes from C. Kavin Rowe, *Early Narrative Christology: The Lord in the Gospel of Luke* (Berlin: de Gruyter, 2006), 201.

[51] David S. Yeago, "The New Testament and the Nicene Dogma: A Contribution to the Recovery of Theological Exegesis," *STR* 45 (2002): 379–80; cf. Martin Hengel, *The Son of God: The Origin of Christology and the History of Jewish Hellenistic Religion* (Minneapolis: Fortress, 1976), 76; and Bauckham, *Jesus and the God of Israel*, 59. Clement of Alexandria saw in Phil 2.6 "the merciful God exerting himself to save humankind" (*Protr.* 1). Basil (*Adv. Eunomium* I.18) regarded the *morphē* of God as equivalent to the *ousia* of God. St. Bernard of Clairvaux wrote, "How beautiful you appear to the angels, Lord Jesus, in the form of God, eternal, begotten before the daystar amid the splendours of heaven, the radiant light of God's glory and the perfect copy of his nature, the unchanging and untarnished brightness of eternal life!" (cited from Markus Bockmuehl, "'The Form of God' [Phil. 2.6]: Variations on a Theme of Jewish Mysticism," *JTS* 48 [1997]: 23). According to George Hunsinger (*Philippians* [BTCB; Grand Rapids: Brazos, 2020], 38): "The idea of 'the form of God' (*morphē theou*) anticipates the later idea of God's 'being' (*ousia*). From this point of view, the divine *morphē* is a conceptual precursor for the idea of divine essence or substance."

[52] Eckhard Schnabel (*Law and Wisdom from Ben Sira to Paul* [WUNT 2.16; Tübingen: Mohr Siebeck, 1985], 261–62) believes that Paul's affirmation that Christ "is" God's wisdom should be understood in "ontological respects," as it implies "pre-existence" and it evokes "trinitarian questions."

is patterned (Philo, *QG* 2.62; *Her.* 205–6).⁵³ Paul writes too that in Jesus the "fullness of deity dwells in him bodily" (Col 2.9), which marks Jesus as inhabited by more than divine power, but by the abundance of a divine substance.⁵⁴

An absolute sense of divinity seems present in other parts of the New Testament and early Christian literature.⁵⁵ John the Elder refers to Jesus Christ as "true God and eternal life" (1 John 5.20), which postulates Jesus as possessing an absolute form of divinity. The terminology of "true God" came to influence the later church, for whom "true God" designated absolute deity apart from demons and lesser deities (see Justin, *Dial.* 55.2; *1 Apol.* 6.1; 13.3; 53.6; Irenaeus, *Haer.* 3.8.1; 4.20.1; Minucius Felix, *Oct.* 26; Athanasius, *Inc.* 16.1; 45.4; 47.3; 55.5).⁵⁶ The author of Hebrews delves into ontological categories with his vivid description of the Son as "the reflection of God's glory and the exact imprint of God's very being" (Heb 1.3). Jesus is ontologically different from the angels as one who is above them as a divine being while also below them as a human being (Heb 1–2). The author later declares that "Jesus Christ is the same yesterday and today and forever" (Heb 13.8; cf. 1.8–12), and this amounts to language about the future eternity of a true God.⁵⁷ If the language of divine sonship and begottenness (Heb 1.2, 5, 8; 4.14; 5.5) is combined with preexistence and eternality (Heb 1.1–14; 7.3, 28; 13.8), it yields something analogous to eternal generation.⁵⁸

⁵³ Note Otfried Hofius ("Christus als Schöpfungsmittler und Erlösungsmittler: Das Bekenntnis 1Kor 8,6 im Kontext der paulinischen Theologie," in *Paulinische Christologie: Exegetische Beiträge*, ed. Udo Schnelle and Thomas Söding [Göttingen: Vandenhoeck & Ruprecht, 2000], 58): "It is *one thing* to speak of God's 'Wisdom' or 'logos' as the highest powers of God, whether as hypostatizations or personifications, and to ascribe a cosmological or soteriological function to them, but *another thing entirely* to make these statements about a historical human figure, and one who had been crucified" ("Denn *eines* ist es, von Gottes 'Weisheit' oder Gottes 'Logos' zu reden und ihnen als den höchsten Kräften Gottes, mögen sie auch hypostasiert oder gar personifiziert gedacht sein, eine kosmologische und soteriologische Funktion zuzuschreiben, ein *anderes* aber, eben dieses von einem geschichtlichen Menschen auszusagen, der dazu noch am Kreuz hingerichtet worden ist!").

⁵⁴ Schnelle (*Apostle Paul*, 398) sums up Paul's divine Christology this way: "Paul's understanding of the relation of Jesus Christ to God can best be expressed by saying that they belong to the same category. Jesus Christ is at the same time subordinate to the Father and fully incorporated into his essence and status."

⁵⁵ See similarly Loke, *Origin of Divine Christology*, 13–17, and Chester, *Messiah and Exaltation*, 380–81, for a concern to rehabilitate ontology for early Christology.

⁵⁶ Ayres, *Nicaea and Its Legacy*, 14.

⁵⁷ Moule, "Borderlands," 5; Neyrey, *Render to God*, 234; Talbert, *Development of Christology*, 34; and Bauckham, *Jesus and the God of Israel*, 243.

⁵⁸ Cf. Bauckham, *Jesus and the God of Israel*, 251–52; Madison N. Pierce, "Hebrews 1 and the Son Begotten 'Today,'" in *Retrieving Eternal Generation*, ed. F. Sanders and S. R.

John the Evangelist portrays Jesus as the preexistent Word (John 1.1–2; 17.4–5), set apart from "all things" as the instrument of creation (1.3), sent by the Father (5.36–37; 8.16–18), from heaven (3.13; 6.33, 38, 50–51), who takes on human flesh (1.14), becoming the "son of Joseph of Nazareth" (1.45), who is "one" with the Father to the point of mutual indwelling (10.30, 38; 14.8–11, 20; 17.11, 21–23), equal to God (5.18), possesses "life in himself" (5.26), makes himself God (10.33–34), who returns to the "glory" that he had with the Father before the creation of the world (17.5, 24; 20.17), who is honored as the Father (5.23), worshipped by a supplicant (9.38), and confessed by Thomas with the honorific acclamation of "my Lord and my God" (John 20.28). True, the accent falls on an economic Christology whereby the "only true God" is known exclusively in the mediatorship of the "only begotten" Son (1.14, 18; 17.3), who is the nexus between heaven and earth (1.51; 3.13), with emphasis on Jesus as the agent of revelation (1.18; 15.15; 17.6, 26) and salvation (3.16; 4.42; 5.24, 34; 12.47) par excellence. However, the journey from divine *archē* to inhabiting flesh in the world, and then going back to heaven is couched as a narrative of messianic revelation as much of ontological transformation of a divine being into human existence. Indeed, the jarring Johannine combination of divine oneness, creator-creature distinction, preexistence, perichoresis, begottenness, messianic testimony, incarnation-glorification, receiving worship, divine functions of judging and saving, presses into a theological and ontological direction that makes the Johannine Jesus' divinity absolute if one is to describe who Jesus is and how he is divine.[59] According to Frey, the language describes "the Logos/Son sharing in the 'quality' and 'divinity' of the one God"[60] and the Logos possesses "divinity in the sense that the Logos clearly belongs to the realm of the creator, uncreated. He is *divine* in the sense that he is uncreated."[61] Or, as Ruben Bühner puts it, "the first two verses of the Gospel of John deal with Beginning *before* beginning. The

---

Swain (Grand Rapids: Zondervan, 2017), 117–31; and Sigurd Grindheim, "Eternal Generation of the Son in Heb 1,5," *Bib* 102 (2021): 97–105.

[59] Jörg Frey, "Between Jewish Monotheism and Proto-trinitarian Tradition Relations: The Making and Character of Johannine Christology," in *Monotheism and Christology in Greco-Roman Antiquity*, ed. Matthew V. Novenson (Leiden: Brill, 2020), 198.

[60] Jörg Frey, "The Johannine Logos and the Reference to the Creation of the World in Its Second Century Receptions," in *Les Judaïsmes dans tours leurs états aux Ier-IIIe siècles (les Judéens des synagogues, les chrétiens et les rabbins)*, ed. C. Clivaz (Turnhout: Brepols, 2015), 231.

[61] Frey, "Between Jewish Monotheism," 209 (italics original).

Logos itself thus appears separate from the works of creation, as absolutely pre-existing, that is, as uncreated."[62]

Unfortunately many detect in John's Gospel no interest in divine ontology; no interest in *what* God is, or *what* God, Jesus, and the Spirit are, seeing John's Gospel concerned primarily with divine identity or believing epistemology.[63] In contrast, Troels Engberg-Pedersen argues that John's Logos is indebted to Stoic philosophy, with all the ontological entailments that accompany it.[64] While I demur from Engberg-Pedersen on several points,[65] even so, the Stoic differentiation between the *endiathetos logos* (word in mind) and *prophorikos logos* (word displayed) may well express the transition from the preexistent Word to the incarnate Word that John introduces in his prologue. Several later authors arguably understood the incarnation this way (Ignatius, *Eph.* 3.2; Justin, *Dial.* 61.1; Athenagoras, *Leg.* 10.2, 3, 5; 24.2; Theophilus, *Autol.* 2.10, 22). Thus, Stoic philosophy, beside the Septuagint and Hellenistic Judaism, constitutes a useful framework in which the Johannine Logos could be understood, and it demonstrates that divine ontology can be read as native to the Johannine Gospel.[66]

[62] Ruben A. Bühner, "Die theologischen Implikationen der Präexistenzchristologie in Joh 1,1–3," in *Perspektiven zur Präexistenz im Frühjudentum und frühen Christentum*, ed. Jörg Frey, Friederike Kunath, and Jens Schröter (Tübingen: Mohr Siebeck, 2021), 189. Also in Bühner, *Messianic High Christology*, 152–53.

[63] Cf., e.g., Bauckham, *Jesus and the God of Israel*, 31; Harold W. Attridge, *History, Theology and Narrative Rhetoric in the Fourth Gospel* (Milwaukee, Wis.: Marquette University Press, 2019), 71; and Frey, "Between Jewish Monotheism," 198.

[64] Troels Engberg-Pedersen, "Logos and Pneuma in the Fourth Gospel," in *Greco-Roman Culture and the New Testament*, ed. David E. Aune and Frederick E. Brenk (Leiden: Brill, 2012), 27–48; and idem, *John and Philosophy: A New Reading of the Fourth Gospel* (Oxford: Oxford University Press, 2017), esp. 110–12.

[65] In the end, Engberg-Pedersen opts for a kind of Spirit-Christology whereby the Logos inhabits Jesus in the form of the *pneuma* at his baptism (John 1.32–34; see conflation of Spirit and Logos in Hippolytus, *Ref.* 6.35; Justin, *1 Apol.* 33.6; 46.5; *2 Clem.* 9.5, where a variant swaps *pneuma* for *logos* concerning what Christ originally was), a proposition I do not think represents the Johannine position. That is because John depicts the Spirit with its own personhood and prerogatives related to but apart from Jesus (esp. in John 14–16), plus Jesus has a prehistory prior to his public ministry in the testimony of John the Baptist (John 1.26–30). For a better account of the Logos and the Spirit, see Myk Habets, *The Anointed Son: A Trinitarian Spirit Christology* (Eugene, Ore.: Pickwick, 2010), esp. 53–88. I think Engberg-Pedersen is wrong then on the precise proposal, but right to be thinking how the Johannine prologue works or sounds in a Stoic key. For a further critique, see Jörg Frey, "Review of *John and Philosophy*, by Troels Engberg-Pedersen," *EC* 10 (2019): 225–36 (esp. 229–35).

[66] See, similarly, for reading John's prologue in light of Stoicism, Udo Schnelle, "Philosophische Interpretation des Johannesevangeliums. Voraussetzungen, Methoden und

The Search for Divine Ontology   65

John the Seer's apocalypse contains two strategically placed announcements where the Lord God says of himself, "I am the Alpha and the Omega," the one "who is and who was and who is to come, the Almighty," and "the beginning and the end" (Rev 1.8; 21.6). Quite amazingly Jesus later refers to himself with the same theophanic language, saying "I am the Alpha and the Omega, the first and the last, the beginning and the end" (Rev 1.17; 22.13). This is allusive of Isaianic monotheistic rhetoric, such as "I am the first and the last; besides me there is no god" (Isa 44.6; cf. 41.6; 48.12). Similar sentiments were extant in Hellenistic Judaism, where God "is the beginning and end of all things" (Josephus, *Ant.* 8.280; *Ag. Ap.* 2.190; Philo, *Plant.* 93). It is reminiscent too of the Derveni papyrus (ca. 350 BCE) containing a poem declaring that "Zeus is the beginning, Zeus is the middle, all things are filled by Zeus," and Plato's remark that "God . . . holds the beginning and the middle and the end of all things" (Plato, *Leg.* 4.715e; cf. Irenaeus, *Haer.* 3.25.5; Hippolytus, *Ref.* 19.6; Clement of Alexandria, *Strom.* 2.22; Origen, *Cels.* 6.15; *Sib. Or.* 8.375-76).[67] By using these words, the Seer stresses the absolute sovereignty and power of both God and the risen Jesus,[68] but also identifies Jesus with the God "who transcends time [and] guides the entire course of history because he stands as sovereign over its beginning and its end."[69]

We might note too Ignatius' letter to the Ephesians, where Jesus is described as "begotten" (*gennētos*) with respect to his humanity and "unbegotten" (*agenētos*) with respect to his divinity, a major terminological shift that signals absolute deity (*Eph.* 7.2; cf. *Pol.* 3.2).[70] This continues into a later period with

---

Perspektiven," in *The Prologue of the Gospel of John: Its Literary, Theological, and Philosophical Contexts*, ed. Jan G. van der Watt, R. Alan Culpepper, and Udo Schnelle (WUNT 359; Tübingen: Mohr Siebeck, 2016), 174–80; Jörg Frey, "Between Torah and Stoa: How Could Readers Have Understood the Johannine Logos?" in *The Prologue of the Gospel of John*, ed. Jan G. van der Watt, R. Alan Culpepper, and Udo Schnelle (WUNT 359; Tübingen: Mohr Siebeck, 2016), 202–9; and idem, "Jewish Monotheism," 207.

[67] David E. Aune, *Revelation* (3 vols.; WBC; Dallas: Word, 1997), 3:1126.
[68] Aune, *Revelation*, 3:1126.
[69] Greg K. Beale, *The Book of Revelation* (NIGTC; Grand Rapids: Eerdmans, 1999), 199.
[70] See the defense of Ignatius' language by Athanasius, *Syn.* 47. The problem was that the Father was commonly regarded as unbegotten/uncreated/ingenerate (see Justin, *1 Apol.* 14.1; one should follow "the only unbegotten God through the Son"), and to make Jesus unbegotten was, in the mind of some, risking the error of creating two gods or two sources of divinity. The Ps.-Clementine Homilies contain a debate between Simon Peter and Simon Magus with Peter arguing that the Father is unbegotten divinity and the Son is an inferior begotten divinity, implying that Jesus is not God, but the Son of God (*Ps.-Clem. Hom.* 16.15–16). Later, Arius' *Thalia* (3) would maintain in its opening stanza a marked difference between the Father's unbegottenness and the Son's begottenness: "We call him

the *Epistula Apostolorum* designation of Jesus "being unborn yet born among humans" (ⲛⲓⲙ· ⲉⲉⲓϩⲟⲟⲡ ⲛ̄ⲁⲧⲧⲣⲉⲡⲟ ⲉⲁⲩⲧⲣⲉⲡⲁⲓ̈ ϩⲛ ⲛ̄ⲣⲱ-; *Ep. Ap.* 21.2) and Origen, who calls the Son "the unborn first-born" (*ton agenētov prōtotokon*; *Cels.* 6.17). Justin accepted that God's nature is "indivisible and inseparable" and there can be no division in the "essence of the Father," yet Christ is neither an excision of the divine nature nor a created angel, but properly "begotten from the Father" as "fires kindled from fire": "distinct" and yet "remain[ing] the same" (*Dial.* 61.2; 128.3–4; cf. Tatian, *Or.* 5). Irenaeus provided a strong defense of the incarnation as different from an emanation and an inhabitation, with the imperishable and immortal Word becoming human (*Haer.* 3.19.1–3). Clement of Alexandria described the human Jesus as the "divine word" who was "truly most manifest deity . . . made equal to the Lord of the universe, because he was his Son, and the Word was in God" (*Protr.* 10).

Among the apologists Athenagoras systematically thinks through God's ingenerate nature, God's distinction from creation, including from various gods and angels, with the Son and Spirit concomitantly united with God in his being. He identifies the Logos as God's eternal mind, with the Father and Son mutually indwelling in each "by a powerful unity of Spirit" while "distinct in order," and carefully distinguished from the multitude of angels and ministering spirits (*Leg.* 10.2, 5; 24.2). Some gods are made by the bestowal of honor, or else they are demigods born through begetting. In either case they are no different to matter, because they are created (*Leg.* 18.1–19.3). Similarly, in the *Epistle to Diognetus*, the author highlights the Son's absolute divinity in contradistinction to various intermediary figures. The author declares that God the Creator did not send "some subordinate, or angel, or ruler or one of those who manage earthly matters, or those entrusted with the administration of things in heaven." Instead "the Designer and Creator of the universe" sent the one

> by whom he created the heavens, by whom he enclosed the sea within its proper bounds, whose mysteries all the elements faithfully observe, from whom the sun has received the measure of the daily courses to keep, whom the moon obeys as he commands it to shine by night, whom the stars obey as they follow the course of the moon, by whom all things have been ordered and determined and placed in subjection, including the heavens and the things in the heavens, the earth and the things in the earth, the sea and the things in the sea, fire, air, abyss, the things in

---

unbegotten, in contrast to him who by nature is begotten." In a letter to Eusebius of Nicomedia, Arius quoted a formula of Eusebius of Caesarea: "God exists before the Son without beginning. . . . Before the Son was begotten, created, determined, or established, he was not. He was not unbegotten" (*Urk.* 1.6).

the heights, the things in the depths, the things in between—this one he sent to them! But perhaps he sent him as one might suppose to rule by tyranny, fear, and terror? Certainly not! On the contrary, he sent him in gentleness and meekness, as a king might send his son who is a king; he sent him as God; he sent him as a human to humans [*alla en epieikeia kai prautēti hōs basileus pempōn huion basilea empempsen, hōs theon epempsen, hōs anthrōpon pros anthrōpon epempsen*]. (*Diogn.* 7.2-4)

Then, in the homily, the Word is clearly identified as an eternal deity: "the Eternal One, today considered to be a Son" (*Diogn.* 11.5).

These statements are perhaps the most densely packed precursor to Nicene Christology in all Christian literature pre-325 CE. They refer to God's incomparability; the Son is not an intermediary nor part of creation, but he is the divine instrument for creation. He comes "as" God and "as" human, an eternal Son, which sounds very much like creedal formulas of Jesus' dual consubstantiality in deity and humanity (i.e., *vere deus et vere homo*—or "Gottheit und Menschheit vereinen," as a famous German hymn says). An identical sentiment occurs in Irenaeus, who likewise differentiates the Word from intermediary figures (*Haer.* 1.22.1; 3.11.1-2; 4.7.4; 5.18.1) and identifies the Logos as "true God and true man" (*Haer.* 3.19.1-3; 4.6.7). The Father and Son share in the lordship and divine being because "that which [is] begotten of God is God" (*Epid.* 47). Athenagoras, Irenaeus, and Diognetus make explicit what is implicit in the New Testament, namely, that the Son is an absolutely divine intermediary who is not divine in the sense of other intermediaries (Phil 2.9-11; 1 Cor 8.6; Col 1.15-20; Heb 1.1-4; 2.10; John 1.1-3; Rev 5.1-14).[71] For the apologists, while God remains transcendent and the source of all, the Logos is the immanent aspect of the divine manifested in the created order, a heavenly agent of creation, revelation, and redemption, "whose very being derived from the one, true God."[72] Or, in the language of Athanasius, Jesus is the "true Son of the Father" who is "true God, *homoousios* with the true Father" (*Or. adv. Ar.* 1.9).

---

[71] I think this answers Chester's question (*Messiah and Exaltation*, 45) as to "how conscious the earliest Christians were of this absolute distinction" between Christ and these intermediary figures. Christ sits on the Creator side of the Creator-creature distinction, and Christ is the object of creation's worship beside God the Father. The evidence is that "all things" can be said to be "through him," with the "him" as either God (Heb 2.10; Rom 11.36) or Jesus/Son (John 1.3; Heb 1.2; 1 Cor 8.6; Col 1.16).

[72] Frances M. Young, "Monotheism and Christology," in *The Cambridge History of Christianity: Origins to Constantine*, ed. Margaret M. Mitchell and Frances M. Young (Cambridge: Cambridge University Press, 2006), 455.

Ontological commitments to Christology were also prominent in "other" Christianities outside the proto-orthodox churches. In the late first and early second centuries, adherents to docetic Christologies, which denied Jesus came in the flesh (1 John 4.2–3; 2 John 7; Ignatius, *Trall.* 10.1; *Smyrn.* 2.1; 3.1–3; 4.2; 5.2; 7.1; 12.2; Irenaeus, *Haer.* 1.24.2; Tertullian, *Carn. Chr.* 24), as well as separatist Christologies, which distinguished the divine Christ from the man Jesus (Irenaeus, *Haer.* 1.26.1; 1.30.13; 3.9.3; 3.11.7), were arguably trying to insulate Jesus' absolute "divinity" from either matter or suffering.[73] They did this by denying Jesus' physical body or else by erecting a buffer between a divine Christ and a human Jesus.[74] On these views, the humanity of Jesus raises a significant problem for the divine nature of the Christ, yielding docetic interpretations. Irenaeus alleged that Saturninus of Antioch said the Savior was "unbegotten, incorporeal, and shapeless" and "was seen only as a man in appearance" (*Haer.* 1.24.1).

Irenaeus attributed to the Valentinians the view that the unbegotten Father begat Monogenes, who is "similar and equal to him who had produced him" (Irenaeus, *Haer.* 1.1.1). Monogenes in turn produced Christ, who, like the aeons, is "a being of most perfect beauty, the very star of the Pleroma, and the perfect fruit of it," and who shares the same nature as the angels (Irenaeus, *Haer.* 1.2.5–6). Jesus is, on this scheme, the perfection of the divinity within the pleroma, even if inferior to the divinity of the unbegotten and incomprehensible Father. Clement of Alexandria recorded *Excerpts* of the Valentinian teacher Theodotus that constitute an intense account of Christ's divinity. He stressed that the Logos of God is the same as the Logos of Christ, so that the "essential Logos is God in God [*ton en tautotēti logon theon en theō*], who is also said to be 'in the bosom of the Father,' without separation or division, one God" (*Exc.* 8.1). The Son who descended is the same as the Son who ascended (*Exc.* 7.3–4). The incarnation was a divine-human conjunction, not an admixing, so that the divine nature is not divided or denigrated by its union with humanity (*Exc.* 17.4).

In the Valentinian *Gospel of Truth*[75] the author appears to invest ontological meaning in Jesus possessing the "name" of the Father (perhaps amplifying

---

[73] Celsus' charge against Christians is that they degraded the pure and holy Logos by associating him with a man who was scourged and crucified; he found the idea of a God changing into human form unimaginable (Origen, *Cels.* 2.31; 4.18).

[74] See discussion in Michael F. Bird and N. T. Wright, *The New Testament in Its World* (London: SPCK, 2019), 791–95; and esp. Jens Schröter, Reimund Bieringer, Joseph Verheyden, and Ines Jäger, eds., *Docetism in the Early Church* (Tübingen: Mohr Siebeck, 2018).

[75] Known to Irenaeus, *Haer.* 3.11.9.

the emphasis on a divine "name" in John 1.12; 3.18; 17.6, 11–12, 26; cf. *Ap. John* 7.27–29). The Son bears the name of the Father, which came forth from the Father (*Gos. Truth* 38.7–14; cf. *Gos. Phil.* 54.5–10), and the Son functions as the name of the Father (*Gos. Truth* 30.24–26; 40.26). The Son bearing a divine name (e.g., Acts 2.38; 1 Cor 6.11; Phil 2.10–11; 1 John 3.23) and Jesus revealing the Father (Matt 11.27; Luke 10.22; John 15.15) are common enough in the New Testament. Yet between the familiarity of the concept and the obscurity of the language, Harold Attridge picks up on the christological significance: "On the one hand, the name is external to the thing named. Hence, the Son, as name, is distinct from the Father whom he names. On the other hand, the name is the essence of the thing named and is thus identical with it. Hence, the Son, as name, is identical with the Father. . . . The two contrary affirmations about the status or function of the Son as name are simply ways of speaking about the intimate relation of Father and son." Accordingly, "The Son is the name of the Father in the first sense (i.e., the visible pointed to the invisible reality of the Father) because he does indeed 'come forth.'" But more significantly: "The Son is the name of the Father in the second sense (i.e., is the essence of the Father), because that which comes forth from the Father is the Father himself. In the language of later Christological dogma, the Son is *homoousios* (i.e., one in being) with the Father."[76]

A similar view of the consubstantiality of the Father and Son appears in the *Tripartite Tractate*, where the self-begotten Father begets "a Son, who subsists in him" (*Tri. Trac.* 56.23–24). The uniqueness of the Son among other intermediaries is made clear: the Son as "firstborn" has no one who exists before him and as "only son" has no one who exists after him (*Tri. Trac.* 57.19–22). The Son too is "unbegotten and without beginning" (*Tri. Trac.* 58.7–8). Finally, in the Sethian scheme, Christ is the preexisting and self-existing son of Barbelo (*Ap. John* 6.10–8.28).

Thus, whatever differences there were between proto-orthodox and heterodox Christologies, it was not over functional vs. ontological Christology; rather, it was mostly over competing species of divine ontological Christology and its entailments.

In each of the instances examined above, the language of being, eternity, authenticity, immortality, and unbegottenness indicate that an absolute ascription of deity, often distinguished from other heavenly beings, is attributed to Jesus. In my mind, this blows apart the notion that divinity in the Roman world "was not an essence or nature, but a concept of *status and power* in a

---

[76] Harold W. Attridge, *Essays on John and Hebrews* (Grand Rapids: Baker, 2010), 186–87.

cosmic spectrum that had no absolute dividing lines"—that is demonstrably false.[77] As I will show below, divinity was relative, but only to the point of absoluteness![78] The idea of an absolute deity was well known and forms the background to Jewish and Christian discourse. More importantly, absolute divinity was attributed to Jesus. The significance of this is spelled out by Boccaccini: "The crossing of the boundary between the 'created' and the 'uncreated' distinctively set the Christian messiah apart and brought Jesus to an unprecedented level of exaltation, from an inferior divine being to a Jewish God."[79]

Divine Benefactors: God by Relative Relationship and Reciprocation

Euergetic Divinity

In the Greco-Roman world, deity was sometimes relative to a relationship and plottable along a spectrum. Divinity was about honor, status, and power, relative to asymmetrical relationships, and divine status was ascribed as a reciprocal response to benefaction. We might call this euergetic divinity, where the chasm between the divine and human was traversable for those who achieved great things in military exploits or even in civic patronage. The traditional deities were conceived as archetypical benefactors of cities, so that the granting of a cult to a ruler who had used his power for the benefit of the city was a logical development of the culture of euergetism. Philo is crisp and clear on this point: "The chief characteristic of a god is to be a benefactor" (*Mut.* 129), in which case, human benefactions can be equated with divine prerogatives.[80]

---

[77] Contra Peppard, *Son of God*, 31; against also Paula Fredriksen ("What Does Jesus Have to Do with Christ? What Does Knowledge Have to Do with Faith? What Does History Have to Do with Theology?" in *Christology: Memory, Inquiry, Practice*, ed. A. M. Clifford and A. J. Godzieba [Maryknoll, N.Y.: Orbis, 2003], 10): "Divinity did not imply ontological identity"; and Fantin (*Lord of the Entire World*, 12): "The Roman concept of divinity was relative. The notion of deity in an absolute sense appears to be foreign to Roman religious practice."

[78] Cf. Bauckham (*Jesus and the God of Israel*, 179), who argues against a "continuous spectrum of reality through which a developing Christology could gradually move until eventually he [Jesus] shared the divine identity."

[79] Boccaccini, "How Jesus Became Uncreated," 208. Where I disagree with Boccaccini is that he thinks that this uncreatedness is only first attributed to Jesus in the Gospel of John, where Jesus the Logos is the uncreated God. I am inclined to think that some people are already thinking this way much earlier, depending on how one understands passages like 1 Cor 8.6 and Phil 2.5–11.

[80] This is why M. P. Charlesworth ("Einige Beobachtungen zum Herrscherkult, besonders in Rom," in *Römischer Kaiserkult*, ed. Antonie Wlosok [Darmstadt: Wissenschaftliche Buchgesellschaft, 1978], 168) prefers to speak of a cult of benefactors rather than a cult of rulers.

These human objects of veneration are not "divine" in the same sense as Jupiter or Dios,[81] but they are elevated into divine honors as an act of gratitude for their accomplishments.[82]

Aristotle laid out the basis for the euergetic forms of divinity:

> But if there is any one man so greatly distinguished in outstanding virtue, or more than one but not enough to be able to make up a complete state, so that the virtue of all the rest and their political ability is not comparable with that of the men mentioned, if they are several, or if one, with his alone, it is no longer proper to count these exceptional men a part of the state; for they will be treated unjustly if deemed worthy of equal status, being so widely unequal in virtue and in their political ability: since such a man will naturally be as a god among men. (*Pol.* 3.13)

Accordingly, great men have great honor and deserve to be honored with the highest venerations possible: "Honor is a token of a reputation for doing good; and those who have already done good are justly and above all honored ... the components of honor are sacrifices, memorials in verse and prose, privileges, grants of land, front seats, public burial, State maintenance, and among the barbarians, prostration and giving acclamations, and all gifts which are highly prized in each country" (*Rhet.* 1.5.9). Cicero explained, "Human experience and widespread custom have accepted that men providing outstanding benefits were raised to the sky by their reputation and our gratitude" (*Nat. d.* 2.62). Pliny the Elder also equated divinity with service to a people: "To assist man is to be a god; this is the path to eternal glory. This is the path which the Roman nobles formerly pursued, and this is the path which is now pursued by the greatest ruler of our age, Vespasian Augustus, he who has come to the relief of an exhausted empire, as well as by his sons. This was the ancient mode of remunerating those who deserved it, to regard them as gods" (*Nat. Hist.* 2.14). In a third-century CE martyrology, the proconsul Africanus berates St. Phocus for denying the divinity of Trajan: "Is this the Phocas who denies the existence of the gods and that the emperor Trajan is a god? Come now, has not every bellicose race been destroyed by his hands? Who then can he be but a god?"[83]

---

[81] Erik M. Heen, "Phil 2:6–11 and Resistance to Local Timocratic Rule," in *Paul and the Roman Imperial Order*, ed. Richard A. Horsley (Harrisburg, Penn.: Trinity Press International, 2004), 131. Habicht (*Divine Honors*, 143) states: "Divinity that depends on human judgment cannot be absolute as the divinity of the Olympians is. Such divinity is not immanent, but rather reveals itself only at certain places and certain moments and therefore is neither universal nor eternal."

[82] Gradel, *Emperor Worship*, 25–26, 267.

[83] Cited in Price, *Rituals and Power*, 125.

72 Jesus among the gods

A second-century CE papyrus asks: "What is a god? Exercising power. What is a king? One who is equal to God" (P. Heid. 1716.5).

The ruler was a god who manifested godlike power and who embodied the essential qualities of a god like Jupiter or Dionysus in relation to his subjects.[84] Thus, if beneficial power is divinity, then gratitude must be worship. The act of saving a province from barbarian invasion, tyrannical rule, famine, civil war, or such could meet with a response of divine worship from a city with the building of temples, altars, priesthood, and offering sacrifices. Offering worship implied an obligation of benefaction incumbent upon a ruler in the form of tax relief, the promise of security, the hosting of games, and the like. Benefaction resulted in worship, and continuous benefaction resulted in continuous worship.[85] John White sums it up well: "Good rulers were divinized for the same reason that gods were worshiped: they were acknowledged as saviors of the social order."[86]

Imperial Cults as Euergetic Divinity

We see clear examples of euergetic divinity in reference to the emperors. Julius Caesar, who had already been honored with temples, statues, and altars during his life,[87] was deified by Augustus with "all divine and human honors" because of his victories and achievements (Suetonius, *Jul.* 76.1–3; 84.2; Cassius Dio, *Hist. rom.* 51.20.6). This, of course, conveniently made Augustus "Imperator Caesar, son of god, god" (*Autokratōr Kaisar theō huiō theō*; IGRR 4.975) and "god from god" (*theos ek theou*; P. Oxy. 1453.10–11). In the early principate, divine honors and accolades became normalized. Virgil wrote that Augustus was "a god who wrought for us this peace—for a god he shall ever be to me; often shall a tender lamb from our folds stain his altar" (*Ecl.* 1.6–8). In a similar vein, Horace said of Augustus: "Thunder in heaven confirms our faith—Jove rules there; but here on earth Augustus shall be hailed as god also, when he

---

[84] Litwa, *We Are Being Transformed*, 84.
[85] Peppard, *Son of God*, 40.
[86] John L. White, *The Apostle of God: Paul and the Promise of Abraham* (Peabody, Mass.: Hendrickson, 1999), 99.
[87] See Cicero, *Phil.* 2.110; Cassius Dio, 44.4.4–5; Suetonius, *Jul.* 76.1; Appian, *Bell. civ.* 2.106. In Cassius Dio (43.14.6; 43.45.3), it is narrated that after several victories Caesar had an ivory statue of him, and later a chariot paraded in the games at the Circus together with the statues of the other gods, calling him a *hēmitheos* (half-god; maybe *deo Caesari* in original Latin), and later still statues of him were also set up in the temple of Quirinius and in the Capitol with the inscription *Theō anikētō/Deo Invicto* (unconquered god). On early veneration of Caesar as divine, see Manfred Clauss, *Kaiser und Gott: Herrscherkult im römischen Reich* (Berlin: K. G. Saur, 1999), 48–51; and Koortbojian, *Divinization of Caesar and Augustus*, 84–91.

makes new subjects of the Britons and the dour Parthians" (*Carm.* 3.5). After Augustus resolved a diplomatic issue with the Parthians, mainly relating to the recovery of Roman standards and establishing Armenia as a Roman client kingdom, the senate "arranged that his name should be included in their hymns equally with those of the gods" (Cassius Dio, 51.20.1). A first-century BCE inscription from Mytilene acclaims the emperor Augustus with divine honors and offers to deify him further if any reasons can be found: "We reckon on his magnanimity to see that those who have attained celestial glory, and divine superiority and might, can never stand on the same level with what is humbler by both fortune and nature. However, if something more honoring should be discovered in the time to come, the city's willingness and piety will omit nothing that could contribute more effectively to his deification" (*OGIS* 456). The city offered to level up Augustus' divinity if reason should merit further deification. Some did indeed level up Augustus' divine honor, declaring it to be equal to that of the Olympian gods. In one inscription, Augustus is "son of God" who "has by his benefaction to all people outdone even the Olympian Gods" (*I. Olympia* 53), and Philo observes that "the whole inhabited world granted honors to him [Augustus] equal to that of the Olympian gods" (*Legat.* 149). Augustus is, then, a good example of the sliding scale of divinity and the euergetic nature of divine honors.

The origin story behind Augustus' divinity gets a few different treatments. Augustus could be regarded as a son of Apollo by a legend about the impregnation of his mother, Atia, while his legal father dreamed that his son would one day be arraigned in the power and majesty of Jupiter (Suetonius, *Aug.* 94.4–6); he was an appearance of Apollo descending to earth to establish peace (Virgil, *Ecl.* 4.1–10); or else he was described as an epiphany of Mercury sent by Jupiter (Horace, *Carm.* 1.2.1–46). At Augustus' funeral, and in a moment that was perhaps staged, the former praetor Numerius Atticus swore that during Augustus' cremation he had seen Augustus ascend to the heavens in the manner of Romulus (Suetonius, *Aug.* 94.4; Cassius Dio, 56.46). In any case, Augustus is a great god—whether by destiny, descent, procreation, epiphany, adoption, or apotheosis—because he does great things for the people, to which worship is the most fitting response.

Cassius Dio is often quoted as saying that Augustus allowed temples to *Roma* and Julius Caesar to be built in Ephesus and Nicaea, to himself in Pergamum and Nicomedia for native Greeks, but otherwise he forbade worship of himself as a god in Italy (Cassius Dio 51.20.6–8; cf. Suetonius, *Aug.* 51.1). That restriction only applied to the official state cult in Rome; Augustus otherwise permitted or even cultivated divine honors in neighborhood shrines among various associations and municipal elites, so much so that Tacitus complained, "No honor was left for the gods when Augustus allowed himself to be worshipped with temples and statues of deities and flamens and priests" (Tacitus, *Ann.* 1.10.6). Early on in his life the young Octavian said that he "aspired to the honors of his father [Julius Caesar]" (Cicero, *Ad. Att.* 16.15.13). There is evidence not only for the worship of Augustus' *genius* and *numen* in Italy during his lifetime, but also various temples and altars were built in his honor.[88] One vignette illustrates that Augustus took his divine honors with a modicum of seriousness. The people of Tarraco in Spain built an altar to Augustus, and a delegation later told Augustus that a palm tree had miraculously sprung out of it. In response Augustus sarcastically quipped that they obviously didn't light fires on it very often (Quintilian 6.3.77)! Divine honors were serious, as much for piety as for statecraft.

Importantly, bestowing divine honors and deification was not propaganda masquerading as piety—the divinity was real within the bounds of a relative relationship, and real within the symbolic world of Rome and its hierarchies of power. Ovid lauded Julius Caesar as a deity towards Rome: "Caesar is a god in his own city. He was a man of importance in armour and toga, but it is no less thanks to the wars which he brought to a triumphal conclusion of victory that he has become a star with a blazing tail" (*Met.* 15.745–50). This is why Tiberius, at Augustus' funeral, gave a speech where he noted what the verdict of the Roman people was about Augustus: "It was for all this, therefore, that you, with good reason, made him your leader and a father of the people, that you honoured him with many marks of esteem and with ever so many consulships, and that you finally made him a demigod and declared him to be immortal. Hence it is fitting also that we should not mourn for him, but that, while we now at last give his body back to Nature, we should glorify his spirit, as that of a god, for ever" (Cassius Dio, 56.41.9). Slightly later, Seneca, who would lampoon Claudius' deification, said of Augustus: "We believe him to be a god, but *not* because we are ordered to do so," but because "we declare that Augustus was a good emperor" (*Clem.* 1.10.3). Pliny's panegyric contrasts Trajan's piety with that of his predecessors: "You gave your father [Nerva] his place among the stars with no thought of terrorizing your subjects, of bringing the gods into disrepute, or of gaining reflected glory, but simply because you thought he was a god" (*Pan.* 11.2). What is clear is that living and deified gods are real gods for

---

[88] Lily Ross Taylor, *The Divinity of the Roman Emperor* (New York: Arno, 1975), 190-91; and corrections to Taylor's view by Gradel, *Emperor Worship*, 73-108, 271-82. See too Beard, North, and Price, *Religions of Rome*, 1:206-10; and esp. Duncan Fishwick, *The Imperial Cult in the Latin West* (3 vols.; Leiden: Brill, 1987-2004), 1:76.

those who pay them homage.[89] It is incorrect to see this process as making the emperor a god in a fictive sense; rather, as Fantin observes, "it granted divine status and honor to an individual *in relation to* the worshippers."[90] The aim was the creation of a unique religious and political reality for the populace, *salus* in exchange for *pietas*, not merely a marketable metaphor for the empire.[91]

It could be argued that civic worship to the point of deification and ongoing cultus meant that someone had entered the divine spectrum. Perhaps, but this was still an inferior position compared to the eternal gods.[92] The distinction between eternal gods and deified humans was fundamental to the cultic devotion offered to the deity and the benefits given by the deity in return. Thus, while Jupiter and Julius Caesar were not worshipped because of their divine nature but because of their divine power,[93] the species of god they were determined the type of benefit a supplicant might expect from them. This is precisely why sacrifices for eternal gods were different from those offered to deified emperors. According to Michael Koortbojian, "while the performance of these rites may well have required merely a sense of 'relative' power distinctions, their success and the *beneficia* they brought forth were predicated on the 'absolute' power of those gods to whom the rites appealed."[94] This is why deceased emperors were ranked last of all in quality of sacrifices they were offered, behind the traditional gods and even behind the living emperor. The sacrifices made by the Arval Brothers, a college of Roman priests, to both traditional gods and the imperial family indicate the ranking of deities. A major sacrifice consisting of a bull was made to the *genius* of the living emperor and to major male gods (e.g., Jupiter, Mars, Apollo), while a cow was offered to female divinities (e.g., Juno, Minerva), and a minor sacrifice consisting of a castrated steer was offered to a *divus*, or deified emperor. The deities were ranked, and

---

[89] Gradel, *Emperor Worship*, 270; Peppard, *Son of God*, 35, 43–44; and Fantin, *Lord of the Entire World*, 121.

[90] Fantin, *Lord of the Entire World*, 117 (italics original); cf. Gradel, *Emperor Worship*, 323.

[91] Christian Habicht writes ("Die augusteische Zeit und das Jahrhundert nach Christi Geburt," in *Le culte des souverains dans l'empire romain* [Geneva: Fondation Hardt, 1973], 70), "It can therefore be assumed that the following consecration did not create a god of the empire, but a *divi* for the Roman community" ("Daher ist davon auszugehen, dass auch die folgenden Konsekration nicht Götter des Reiches, sondern *divi* der römischen Bürgergemeinde geschaffen haben").

[92] See Price, *Rituals and Power*, 231–33; and criticism from Gradel, *Emperor Worship*, 28–29 and Steven J. Friesen, *Twice Neokoros: Ephesus, Asia, and the Cult of the Imperial Family* (Leiden: Brill, 1993), 150–52.

[93] Rightly Gradel, *Emperor Worship*, 28, 32.

[94] Koortbojian, *Divinization of Caesar and Augustus*, 23–24.

that ranking was expressed in sacrifice and ritual.⁹⁵ Even the Mytilene imperial cult, which was unique in the intensity of honors afforded to the *sebastoi*, offered a white victim to the Olympian deities and a mottled one to the emperors, indicative of doubts about the Olympian nature of Augustus.⁹⁶ Although the *divi* were divine and received sacrifice, they were not on par with the traditional gods in terms of absolute power and status, a difference translatable into one of nature, which is why the *divi* received a lesser sacrifice.⁹⁷ As S. R. F. Price notes, "Language sometimes assimilated the emperor to a god, but ritual held it back."⁹⁸

The divine emperors were still intermediaries between the eternal gods and the people. While the emperor was honored with titles as venerable as "lord" and "god," he was still *pontifex maximus*, high priest of the empire's deities. Julius Caesar and later emperors all held multiple priestly offices, with Augustus declaring in his list of accomplishments: "I have been pontifex maximus, augur, a member of the fifteen commissioners for performing sacred rites, one of the seven for sacred feasts, an Arval brother, a sodalis Titius, a fetial priest" (*Res Gestae* [*RG*] § 7).⁹⁹ The worship of the emperor, living or deified, was embedded within the constellation of temples and cults, placed among the gods, and often subordinate to them. This is why an inscription from Eresos refers to "The priest and high priest of the Sebastoi and all of the other gods and goddesses for life" (*IGRR* 4.18).¹⁰⁰ Pliny modulates his veneration of Trajan as one who had power "equal to that of the gods," but also moderates it, as one does "not address him with the flattering title of a god or divinity; for we speak not of a tyrant, but of a fellow citizen; not of a master, but of a father. He boasts that he is one of us; nor does he forget that he is only a man, though the ruler of men" (*Pan.* 1, 4). Pliny lauds Trajan's piety for rejecting statues of himself to be erected and instead requiring that thanksgiving sacrifices be directed towards Jupiter (*Pan.* 52.6). The author of a speculative treatise sums up the situation well: "the emperor

---

⁹⁵ Gradel, *Emperor Worship*, 275–76; Koortbojian, *Divinization of Caesar and Augustus*, 126; and John Scheid, "Hierarchy and Structure in Roman Polytheism: Roman Methods of Conceiving Action," in *Roman Religion*, ed. Clifford Ando (Edinburgh: Edinburgh University Press, 2003), 164–89.

⁹⁶ Price, *Rituals and Power*, 218.

⁹⁷ Scheid ("Hierarchy and Structure," 173–74) notes that the Arval Brothers ranked deities in descending order as: (1) Mars and Dia; (2) deities between Janus and Vesta; (3) Adolenda Conmolenda Deferunda; (4) the imperial *genius*; and (5) the various *divi*.

⁹⁸ Price, *Rituals and Power*, 213.

⁹⁹ Fantin, *Lord of the Entire World*, 90, 97.

¹⁰⁰ To give a similar and earlier example, King Attalos III of Pergamum (138–33 BCE) had his statue placed in the temple of Asclepius as a "temple companion of the god" (*OGIS* 332).

is the last of the other gods, but the first of men; as long as he is on earth, he is removed from true divinity, but among men has something exceptional, which is like the divine" (*Corp. herm.*, frag. 24.3).[101] Thus, the living emperor is divine, but only up to a certain point! Price rightly concludes: "The predication of *theos* placed the emperor within the traditional religious system. He was located in an ambivalent position, higher than mortals but not fully the equal of the gods. The cult he received was described as *isotheoi timai*, and the *eusebeia* which the cult displayed was compatible with honours not fully divine."[102]

Other Expressions of Euergetic Divinity

Euergetic and relational accounts of divinity were not limited to emperors. There are several good examples of relational divinity in human interactions. The Roman playwright Plautus, in his *Asinaria*, provides a scene where the slave Libanus acquired money so that his master's son Argyrippus could buy his beloved Philaenium. But before handing over the money, Libanus relishes in the opportunity to taunt his master, commanding him to sacrifice to him as a god before: "Only if you also erect a statue and an altar and sacrifice an ox to me as a god—for I am now your Salvation" (Plautus, *Asinaria* 712–13).[103] This is an ironic and comical scene where the language of deliverance and reciprocation enables a slave to hold godlike power over his master. Looking at the first century BCE, in Ovid's *Metamorphoses*, Aeneas offers to worship the Sibyl for her assistance because, whether she is a goddess or one chosen by the gods, "You will always be the equivalent of a god for me, and I will confess myself bound to your service . . . I will establish temples to you, and will repay to you the honor of incense." To which she sighs and replies, "I am not a goddess, and nor should you reward a human person with the honor of sacred incense, nor ignorantly fall into error" (*Met.* 14.123–39). Aeneas offers the Sibyl euergetic divinity, and she rebuffs it as an insult to true divinity! Also, when Herod Agrippa I was reconciled to the people of Tyre and Sidon and promised to assist them with the provision of bread, the assembled body shouted that he had "the voice of a god, not of a man" (Acts 12.20–23; Josephus, *Ant.* 19.343–50). Herod's benefaction was rewarded with divine acclamation. It is a transaction where deliverance is reciprocated with divine honor.

I suggest that it is a similar relational dynamic that enables the Israelite king to be heralded with the words "Your throne, O God, will last forever" in a royal psalm (Ps 45.6) and Hezekiah's heir to be labeled "Mighty God"

---

[101] Cited from Rives, *Religion*, 155.
[102] Price, "Gods and Emperors," 94.
[103] I was alerted to this by reading Gradel, *Emperor Worship*, 45–46.

in a prophetic promise (Isa 9.6). This language mimics Ancient Near Eastern throne rhetoric for monarchs and accents their godlike power over their subjects. Further, in a psalm of judgment, Yahweh's declaration—"I said, 'You are gods; you are all sons of the Most High'"—indicates that Israel's judges can execute godlike power in the courts and therefore must execute justice (Ps 82.6). Notably, in these three instances, there is still recognition that Israel's God is supreme over these kings and judges since he has anointed the king (Ps 45.7), presides over the lesser gods (Ps 82.1), and is the sovereign over the gods and nations (Isa 10.23–24).

The honorific mode of divinity elucidates the previously mentioned texts that described Moses as a "god." Accordingly, in Exod 7.1, Moses is like a god over Pharaoh because Moses possesses great power, brings deliverance, and enacts judgment in a manner analogous to a deity, albeit on a lesser scale. Moses is not the God or even a god; rather, Moses has analogous godlike power in terms of the asymmetrical power he will exercise in relationship to Pharaoh. This is not a question of divine ontology or even divine function, but a matter of divinity equated with powers of deliverance and judgment. It is more than Moses being Yahweh's agent to Pharaoh—true though that is. Instead, Moses will be analogous to a powerful deity opposing Pharaoh. Moses is metaphorically and relatively a god like Yahweh in relation to Pharaoh.

Philo makes much of Exod 7.1 (*Sacr.* 9–10) and calls Moses "god and king of the nation" (*Mos.* 1.156), but he never describes Moses' deification into a god's power and status. Philo, even with his elastic application of *theoi* to angels and powers, still has a strict monotheism based on a divine ontology that separates God from creation and rules out incarnation and deification.[104] So, when Philo calls Moses a "god" it should be taken in a relational and relative sense. It is Moses' kingship that defines the sense in which he is a god.[105] Moses has godlike authority over Pharaoh and the Israelites, but he does not infringe on God's being or prerogatives. The proof is that Philo explicitly says that Moses "is not God" in either "truth or being" (*alētheian kai to einai*), but is a man of God who is godlike over a foolish man (Philo, *Det.* 161–62).[106] Also, "though, indeed, [Moses is] a god to men, not to different parts of nature, thus leaving to the Father of all the place of king and God of gods" (*Prob.* 43). This

---

[104] D. T. Runia, "God and Man in Philo of Alexandria," *JTS* 39 (1988): 67: "The distance between God and man is expressed first, by the ontological gap between model and copy (or origin and derivative), and secondly by the fact that man is not directly imaged on God, but on the Logos which is posterior to him."

[105] Runia, "God and Man," 54.

[106] Cf. exposition by Runia, "God and Man," 61.

is hardly surprising, given that Philo believes that questioning divine promises is to make oneself a divine judge of divine faithfulness, which is "to declare the created uncreated, the mortal immortal, the destructible indestructible, and, if it is not blasphemy to say this man [is] God" (*Mut.* 181). Philo is careful to avoid any suggestion that Moses was a being on par with God, even if he thinks he is elevated far and above mere mortals.[107] Thus, Philo's employment of Exod 7.1 is governed by the conviction that it is impious and improper for a human being to be acclaimed as truly and ostensibly god.[108]

For Philo, Moses had progressed in his journey towards God, so that while he himself was not God, he was far beyond mortal limitations, existing "between the uncreated and the perishable nature" (*Somn.* 2.234–35, based on Num 16.48). Philo sees Moses as godlike "in the sense that Moses was blessed with a special measure of the divine qualities such as true tranquility and with special knowledge of God's nature and purposes."[109] Philo regards Moses as one who has escaped slavery to one's passions; his so-called divinity is purely of an ethical and allegorical nature. Philo's Moses is honored with a divine title but remains a mediating figure, communicating divine blessings. Moses is neither a heavenly being nor a hypostatized divine power, but the quintessential sage who is "god and king" (Diogn. Laert. 7.117–20).[110] Philo labels Moses a god in the sense of his proximity to God, his piety, power, freedom from passions, and possession of earthly domains. This still elevates Moses to a mighty position where he is, as Wayne Meeks said, "the intermediary *par excellence* between the divine and the human."[111]

Similarly, in the dream sequence in *Ezekiel the Tragedian*, Moses sits on God's throne—yet it is with a certain degree of hyperbole precisely because it is a dream, just like Joseph's dream about the sun, moon, and stars bowing down to him as his brothers one day would (Gen 37.9–10).[112] In fact, Jethro's interpretation of the dream makes it clear that this dream speaks not to Moses sharing in

---

[107] John Lierman, *The New Testament Moses: Christian Perceptions of Moses and Israel in the Setting of Jewish Religion* (WUNT 2.173; Tübingen: Mohr Siebeck, 2004), 194.

[108] See Carl R. Holladay, *Theios Aner in Hellenistic Judaism* (Missoula, Mont.: Scholars Press, 1977), 108–55.

[109] Larry Hurtado, *One God, One Lord: Early Christian Devotion and Ancient Jewish Monotheism* (3rd ed.; London: T&T Clark, 2015), 64.

[110] Runia, "God and Man," 60–62.

[111] Wayne A. Meeks, "The Divine Agent and His Counterfeit in Philo and the Fourth Gospel," in *Aspects of Religious Propaganda in Judaism and Early Christianity*, ed. Elisabeth Schüssler Fiorenza (Notre Dame, Ind.: University of Notre Dame Press, 1976), 47 (italics original). Cf. too Runia, "God and Man," 61.

[112] Bauckham, *Jesus and the God of Israel*, 16n34, 168.

God's sovereignty and sphere, but rather it means that "You shall cause a mighty throne to rise and you yourself shall rule and govern men. As for beholding all the peopled earth, and things below and things above God's realm: things present, past and future you shall see" (*Ezek. Trag.* 85–89). In other words, the dream is a symbolic description of how Moses will help establish the Israelite kingdom, have total authority over people, and will see future events—a benign conclusion for a dramatic dream about occupying God's throne. The rest of the narrative makes clear that Moses is God's very human servant who leads Israel out of Egypt.[113]

A further example is the fifth-century archbishop of Ravenna, Peter Chrysologus, who understood Moses as a god by virtue of his military success, supernatural deeds, lawgiving, and provisions of food and drink for the Israelites.[114] Moses' benefactions and power made him "god" relative to the Israelites. There was no compromise of monotheism, no inclusion of Moses within God's unique identity, functions, or being; rather, Moses is god or godlike in his superlative sovereign power over Pharaoh and Israel as relative to his relation to them.[115] Thus, when Moses is called "god," it is in an honorific sense,

---

[113] Cf. John J. Collins ("A Throne in the Heavens: Apotheosis in Pre-Christian Judaism," in *Death, Ecstasy, and Otherworldly Journeys*, ed. John J. Collins and Michael Fishbane [Albany, N.Y.: State University of New York Press, 1995], 51): "This dream occurs in a self-conscious literary work. There is no question of a reflection of an actual experience of ascent. In fact, what is described is not really an ascent in any case. Moses sees the throne on top of Mount Sinai, not in the heavens." Pierluigi Lanfranchi (*L'Exagoge d'Ezéchiel le Tragique* [Leiden: Brill, 2006], 194) notes: "The semantics of the dream are revealed on the basis of the criterion according to which the vertical plane of Moses's celestial enthronement is brought back to a horizontal, historical, and earthly dimension. In other words, Moses's divinization is conceived as a metaphor of his earthly kingship, in the same way that his contemplation of the three parts of the universe declares his knowledge of the past, of the present, and of the future" (citation and translation by Joshua Leim, "Theological Hermeneutics, Exegesis, and J. R. Daniel Kirk's *A Man Attested by God*," *JTI* 15 [2021]: 33).

[114] Peter Chrysologus, *Sermon* 43, cited in J. T. Lienhard and R. J. Rombs, eds., *Exodus, Leviticus, Numbers, Deuteronomy* (ACCS; Downers Grove, Ill.: InterVarsity, 2001), 39.

[115] Other ancient interpreters could see in Moses a parable of someone who was "God" not by nature, but by grace, in the sense of persons "made worthy to be sons of God," with an equating of "divinity" with "adoption" (Jerome, *Hom. Ps.* 14). Or else holy people are likened to "lords and kings" who "have ruled over and dominated sufferings and because they have kept undebased the likeness of the divine image to which they were made—for the image of the king is also called a king" and are "united to God and [by] receiving him as a dweller within themselves have through association with him become by grace what he is by nature" (John of Damascus, *de Fid. Orth.* 4.15). Note how John explicitly relates this god-ness to a type of kingship in sanctification and grace, which is explicitly contrasted with god-ness by nature. Cited in Lienhard and Rombs, *Exodus*, 39.

not a sharing in the divine nature, and not transgressing that which made the God of the Israelites unique and set apart from creation.

In sum, to call a being "God" is not necessarily to absolutize them into a divine ontology. In some cases, divinity is a relative and honorific status (i.e., euergetic divinity.) Accordingly, in the Jewish tradition, to be "god" speaks to someone's special relationship with God and their special relationship with others in exercising godlike power without transgressing the absolute divinity of Yahweh.[116]

Christ as Euergetic Divinity

It would be entirely expected that this euergetic and relational mode of divinity was used by some Christians to postulate Jesus as divine. A late second-century group known to heresiologists as the Theodotians seem to have held to an adoptionist Christology whereby Jesus became divine upon his resurrection, and they were arguably influenced by Roman traditions of apotheosis.[117] I would concede to Peppard that while Mark's Gospel does not intend Jesus' baptism to signify a moment of deification, some readers immersed in Roman culture might well have understood it that way.[118] As it turned out, Justin Martyr considered the deification of emperors to be a demonic imitation of Christ's divinity, which of course implies a genuine resemblance between the two (*1 Apol.* 21.1–6). Celsus too allegedly thought it was odd of Christians to reject the deification of Hercules, Asclepius, and Dionysus while worshipping the risen and exalted Jesus (Origen, *Cels.* 3.22). The aggravated denunciations of human deification by Justin, Athenagoras, Theophilus, and Minucius Felix were occasioned precisely because it was possible to explain Jesus' divinity on those terms. For some Christians, Jesus was divine within the ancient spectrum of divinity without transgressing the supreme divinity of Israel's God.

Conclusion

In the last chapter, I began by considering the problem of how Jesus was considered divine in the early church. I then pointed out that Christian groups conceived of Jesus as divine in numerous ways. The diverse modes of divinity attributed to Jesus were due to the many types of divine discourse within which Jesus' deity could be articulated. To this end, I observed the relevance of

---

[116] See Marianne Meye Thompson, *The God of the Gospel of John* (Grand Rapids: Eerdmans, 2001), 42, 47–48.

[117] Peppard, *Son of God*, 147; and Bird, *Jesus the Eternal Son*, 120–22.

[118] Peppard, *Son of God*, 26–28; Dieter Zeller, "New Testament Christology in Its Hellenistic Reception," *NTS* 46 (2001): 312–33; cf. critique in Bird, *Jesus the Eternal Son*, 73–76.

Greco-Roman taxonomies of divinity with pyramids of intermediary beings, mythologies, ruler cults, and philosophies. I concluded that divinity was a kind of spectrum where accession to the divine realm and promotion within it was possible. I noted too that ancient Judaism is best characterized as a monarchical monotheism with an aniconic monolatry. Even so, Israel's God was regarded as superior to lesser gods and powers because Israel's God was the creator of all things in heaven and earth and was alone worthy of Israel's cultic devotion. Israel's religion was monotheistic to the extent that it delineated God from created beings and regarded God as a deity of incomparable attributes and worthy of exclusive veneration. Yet this monotheism may not have been strict since Second Temple Judaism envisaged various intermediary figures, beings who moved between heaven and earth, who exercised divine functions, received types of veneration, and were given the appellation "God"—Moses being a case in point. As a result, this brief analysis of ancient theaters of theology could indicate that Jesus was divine in the sense that he was a deified human being placed on a spectrum of divinity (like an emperor) or else divine like an intermediary figure (like Moses). It could also mean that Nicene constructions of Jesus' divinity, with its ontological language and allegedly labored scriptural exposition, are a world away from how the early church initially constructed Jesus' divinity as largely functional or honorific.

In this chapter, I have pointed out the problem of considering Jesus as a divine figure in the early church purely within a spectrum of escalating honors. To the contrary, I argued that ancient religion and philosophy, whether Greco-Roman or Jewish, cannot be insulated from ontological commitments in its accounts of deity. Ontology was a regular and reliable part of ancient discourses about deities. I mapped out two parallel indices of divinity according to ancient authors, the absolute (i.e., ontological) and the euergetic (i.e., relative to a relationship, and based on benefaction). I noted how Jews and Christians identified God as an absolute deity, that is, eternal, immortal, imperishable, uncreated, and unbegotten. What is more, Christian authors in some instances began to identify Jesus with the characteristics of absolute deity. Thus, I would argue that early Christology fits naturally between the divine discourses of Philo and Plutarch, where ontological commitments were part of the theological repertoire when discussing divine beings and their natures. What we find in early Christianity is, I think, a burgeoning ontology combined with intertextual argumentation, devotional patterns, eschatological narratives, and a mutually interpreting loop of redefinition between Israel's God and his Messiah.[119]

[119] On how "God" defines "Jesus" and "Jesus" redefines "God," see C. K. Barrett, *The Gospel according to St. John* (2nd ed.; London: SPCK, 1978), 98–99; Larry J. Kreitzer, *Jesus and God in Paul's Eschatology* (Sheffield: Sheffield Academic Press, 1987), 165; Marinus

The qualifying point to this thesis—and may book reviewers underline this sentence—is that identifying Jesus with absolute divinity was not necessarily immediate or universal. We can countenance development and diversity as a ubiquitous feature of early christological discourse. It is no contradiction or concession to affirm that some Christ-believing groups clearly thought of Jesus as euergetically divine because his humanity and suffering were an obstacle to ascribing absolute divinity to him. Neither did I insinuate that the apostle Paul, Athenagoras, or Athanasius are all saying the same thing about divine Christology; they are not, as there are tangible differences in the context and content of their Christologies. Apostolic authors narrated God's oneness with Jesus nested between divine agency and co-regency. Gnostics postulated God and the Son/Savior within a pleromatic hierarchy that made the Son an expression of the unbegotten Father yet somehow inferior to him. Proto-orthodox authors struggled and even floundered in espousing the Father and the Son's ontic sameness in tandem with the Son's economic subordination. The divine ontologies ascribed to God and the Son varied based on the creational framework (Platonist cosmos or Jewish creation myth), preferred analogies (such as thought-mind or fire-heat), exegetical analyses (from Prov 8.22 and Ps 110.1 to Col 1.15 and John 1.1), assumptions about the divine nature (as impassible, invisible, and indivisible, etc.), and the metaphysics of begetting (whether the one begotten remains equal or inferior to the begetter, whether begetting is eternal or temporal, etc.). For cases in point, John, Justin, Valentinus, and Origen develop and decant diverse appropriations of the Logos, with Jesus' divine nature expressed differently vis-à-vis the Father, angels, and the cosmos.

Nonetheless, even taking those diversities on board, it is salient that a consistent trajectory of ontological language for Jesus is either intimated or else explicit in Paul's letters, post-apostolic authors, and the apologists, and among Gnostic groups. There could never be a discourse on divine economy without some, even if only tacit, convictions pertaining to divine ontology (and vice versa). This should be totally unsurprising if we locate the apostolic and post-apostolic authors at the intersection of Judaism and Hellenism, which were

---

de Jonge, *God's Final Envoy: Early Christology and Jesus' Own View of His Mission* (Grand Rapids: Eerdmans, 1998), 130; N. T. Wright, *Paul and the Faithfulness of God* (COQG 4; London: SPCK, 2014), 655, 666; Wesley Hill, *Paul and the Trinity: Persons, Relations, and the Pauline Letters* (Grand Rapids: Eerdmans, 2015), 49, 78, 81; John Barclay, *Paul: A Very Brief History* (London: SPCK, 2018), 27; and Samuel Vollenweider, "Vom israelitischen zum christologischen Monotheismus. Überlegungen zum Verhältnis zwischen dem Glauben an den einen Gott und dem Glauben an Jesus Christus," in *Antike und Urchristentum: Studien zur neutestamentlichen Theologie in ihren Kontexten und Rezeptionen* (WUNT 436; Tübingen: Mohr Siebeck, 2020), 129–32.

equally adept at drawing on myths, sacred texts, rituals, devotional praxes, and adjectives to describe the divine being with an absolute nature. It is further unsurprising that absolute divinity was soon attributed to Jesus as one who was not only personal and preexistent, but also eternal and equal with God. Thus, the dichotomy between the New Testament's supposedly "functional Christology" and the "Platonic/ontological Christology" of the patristic period is, if not patently false, in serious need of recalibration. Accordingly, irrespective of the different ways in which Jesus was accorded divinity, the proto-orthodox and pro-Nicene conception of Jesus as "true God" was not the product of a late Platonic big bang; rather, ontological commitments in Christology were early, explicit, and explicable within first-century religious environs, and proved to be enduring.[120]

---

[120] Against Fredriksen ("How High Can Early Christology Be?" 317), who believes that if Paul equated or identified God with Jesus, then "the next several centuries of theological development [are] all but incomprehensible.... Why, if Paul provides the Christological Big Bang, do we have this big lag?" I just do not see a big lag, since divine prerogatives, divine being, creator-creation distinction, and differentiation from intermediary figures are increasingly attributed to Jesus by John, Hebrews, Ignatius, Justin, Valentinus, Diognetus, Athenagoras, and Irenaeus. Areas still being worked out are monotheism and messianism, experiments with subordinationism and modalism, and the search for a glossary and grammar that are biblically rooted yet philosophically coherent, then wrestling with further questions that are generated.

II
Jesus and Intermediary Figures

3

Putting Jesus in His Place

Scholarship on Early Christology and Intermediary Figures

> For the figure of a son-deity suffering and dying and raised again to life is also known to the mystery religions, and Gnosticism above all is aware of the notion of the Son of God become man—of the heavenly redeemer become man.
>
> Rudolf Bultmann

> Earliest christology has quite an original stamp, and is ultimately rooted in the contingent event of the activity of Jesus, his death and resurrection appearances. A history-of-religions comparison can only explain the derivation of individual themes, traditions, phrases and functions, and not the phenomenon of the origin of christology as a whole.
>
> Martin Hengel

In the previous chapter I argued that Jesus was identified as divine in both the absolute and euergetic senses, depending on the reasonings behind a given instance of christological discourse. More specifically, I maintained that parts of the New Testament and segments of early Christian literature appear to describe Jesus as tacitly or even explicitly divine in an absolute degree. Such a conclusion would seem to marginalize the significance of various intermediary figures and semi-divine beings to explicate how Jesus is simultaneously divine while also a human figure. However, these intermediary figures remain especially relevant because Jesus is described as a divine agent, and there are genuine analogies between portrayals of Jesus and these various in-between entities that operate between heaven and earth according to ancient cosmologies.

In early Christian literature of the first two centuries, Jesus' mission, titles, saving work, and status are overtly identified with intermediary figures that were extant in the Greco-Roman world. In this period, we find the portrayal of Jesus as a preexistent heavenly person sent by God to earth; he is Israel's Messiah with royal and priestly roles; he is given the titles Son of Man and Son of God; he undertakes divine functions of ruling, saving, and judging; he is positioned upon or beside God's heavenly throne. In places there are descriptions of him taking on angelic form or performing angelic roles; he is identified with the Stoic Logos; he embodies the cosmic pleroma; the man Jesus is possessed by the heavenly Christ; he can be conceived as a divine emanation; he is adopted as God's son at his baptism or resurrection; and there is the identification of Jesus as God's Wisdom.

In all these accounts, Jesus is a divine agent of extraordinary significance and status. Thus, I take it as given that early Christian authors, even as they acutely identified Jesus with God's own identity and activity, nonetheless asserted that Jesus was a divine agent acting on behalf of God. As such, Christians of all stripes explored Israel's Scriptures and interrogated Jewish traditions, looking for figures and agents that explained Jesus' close relationship to Israel's God and his extraordinary role as God's definitive mode of self-expression and saving power. That is even without considering the wider cultural encyclopedia of semi-divine entities and human heroes to whom Jesus bears some resemblance as one who descends to earth, embodies divine power, works miracles, and ascends to the heavens. As a result, when someone read the Lucan accounts of the ascension of Jesus into heaven, they could legitimately think of the assumptions of Enoch and Elijah into heaven, the apotheosis of Herakles, or the consecration of Julius Caesar as a god—interpretations that would depend upon what tropes were familiar in a given religious setting. Jesus is therefore a divine agent who is frequently described in titles and roles that resemble Jewish intermediary figures and Greco-Roman semi-divine beings.

The real question to be explored is how is Jesus different from these intermediary figures? I am particularly interested in how the New Testament, with its influence in proto-orthodox communities, generated accounts of Jesus as an absolutely *divine* divine agent that crystallized into Nicaeano-Constantinopolitan dogma. Proto-orthodox and pro-Nicene authors were under pressure to explain how Jesus was divine in an absolute sense even while he was clearly a divine agent, personally separate from the Father, economically subordinate to the Father, with a human life that suffered, died, rose, and returned to heaven. Their answer was, in the end, a Christology of incarnation and hypostatic union. That said, there is no doubt that among diverse Christian groups of the first through fourth centuries this question of Jesus vis-à-vis intermediary figures would have been answered differently. For some groups, Christ was effectively and fully identical to these intermediary figures, as a heavenly being who took on angelic form (*Ascension of Isaiah*; *Epistula Apostolorum*; *Pistis Sophia*), an antitype to the demiurge (Sethianism), or the created Wisdom of God begotten into human flesh (Arianism). Yet those options and others were resisted by the proto-orthodox and pro-Nicenes based on a particular set of christological commitments and interpretive conventions that derive, I would argue, from the New Testament itself.

As the opening quotes from Bultmann and Hengel show, scholarship on this topic is hardly of a united mind on whether the chief influences on Christology were Greco-Roman or Jewish, and what role if any intermediary figures played in the origins and development of early Christology. The divisions are between those who attach tremendous weight to these intermediary figures for mapping christological origins, those who posit some relevance but find the main impetus elsewhere, and those who see little familiarity between these intermediary figures and the primitive church's christological commitments. Therefore, in this chapter I will engage in a brief survey of scholarly opinion on the relevance of Jewish intermediary beings for Christology by laying out the options, positions, and general state of the debate. Then, in the following two chapters, I will undertake a comparative and juxtaposing analysis of intermediary figures with a view to identifying how they do and do not explicate early Christology.

Scholarly Perspectives on Christology and Intermediary Figures: Negative Evaluations

For many researchers, the intermediary figures of Jewish and Greco-Roman literature are not relevant precursors or sufficient explanations for the early church's attribution of divinity to Jesus Christ. The significance of intermediary figures is denied or marginalized in favor of other formative factors shaping the early church's christological discourse.

James D. G. Dunn

James D. G. Dunn made significant contributions to debates about the making of early Christology with his own distinctive construal of the gradual development of a doctrine of incarnation. Dunn did not think intermediary figures explain the origins of incarnational Christology because New Testament Christology does not bear the influence of popular pagan myths of gods taking human form; there is no evidence for a myth about a preexistent heavenly redeemer; Jesus was not identified as a figure like Elijah or Enoch ascending to heaven; there was no notion of an angel becoming human in order to redeem humans; and the "speculation" about the exalted Christ as an angel was strongly rejected by leading voices in the communities, while elsewhere it was not considered at all.[1]

Dunn pointed out that while Spirit, Wisdom, and Word are commonly called "intermediary figures," this is improper because "they never really reach the status of divine beings independent of God in Jewish thought." Instead, they "remain in the literature of our period (Philo included) ways of speaking of God's powerful interaction with his world and his people, God's experienced immanence through nature and revelation, in Torah, prophet and saving act, which yet did not infringe his transcendence. Their pre-existence is the pre-existence of God, of God's purpose to create and redeem."[2] Even while Jewish authors conceived of Wisdom in ways analogous to pagan polytheistic categories, they never "regarded Wisdom in the same way as worshippers of Isis regarded Isis."[3] As a result, Dunn concluded, "In short, *we have found nothing in pre-Christian Judaism or the wider religious thought of the Hellenistic world which provides sufficient explanation of the origins of the doctrine of incarnation, no way of speaking about the gods, or intermediary beings which so far as we can tell would have given birth to this doctrine apart from Christianity*."[4]

On the actual development of Christology, Dunn sketched out a view that (1) the historical Jesus had a strong sense of divine sonship, but not a belief in his own divinity, let alone incarnation; (2) the earliest generation of believers inferred from Jesus' resurrection that he was the locus of God's personal presence and saving power—God's clearest self-expression, God's last word; and (3) Paul accented previous tradition with its Adamic Christology that presented Jesus in solidarity with fallen humanity (i.e., the first Adam) and as the prototype of redeemed and glorified humanity (i.e., the last Adam). In addition, Paul innovatively applied Jewish Wisdom categories to Jesus in order to designate Jesus as the climactic embodiment of God's own actions on behalf of humanity: (4) the post-Pauline letters of Colossians and Ephesians deploy the language of "mystery" to describe Christ as the fulfillment of God's eschatological purposes from the beginning of the world; and (5) a doctrine of incarnation emerges

---

[1] James D. G. Dunn, *Christology in the Making: A New Testament Inquiry into the Origins of the Doctrine of the Incarnation* (2nd ed.; Grand Rapids: Eerdmans, 1989), 251–52, 258–59.

[2] Dunn, *Christology in the Making*, 252–53.

[3] Dunn, *Christology in the Making*, 253.

[4] Dunn, *Christology in the Making*, 253 (italics original).

in second-generation Christianity with the author of Hebrews combining a polemic against angel Christology with a positive wisdom Christology; and with the Fourth Evangelist using the Logos speculation of Alexandrian Judaism to herald Jesus as God's creative and revelatory word become flesh.

Dunn attempted to do for first-century Christianity what Walter Baeur had done for second-century Christianity, to identify and work through the assortments of diversities and developments. Concerning Christology, much is commendable here, but Dunn's rejection of the relevance of intermediary figures for divine Christology is somewhat mistaken.

(1) Dunn equated incarnation with divinity and then quested to find the cause of incarnational doctrine. To this end, he found nothing among these intermediary figures that could cause belief in the incarnation by appropriation and application to Jesus. Perhaps he was right, but the problem is that he was operating with an erroneous scheme of cause and effect. The cause of belief in Jesus' "divinity" was not a doctrine of incarnation; more probably it was the experience of the earthly and exalted Jesus by his disciples, belief in his resurrection, the expectation for him to return in divine power, and exegesis of key texts like Pss 2, 8, 110 from Israel's sacred traditions that made the early church conceive of Jesus as a divine being. The narratives and arguments in early Christian literature that we designate as incarnation, exaltation, and angelomorphism were attempts to explain *how* Jesus was divine, and they appear *throughout* Christian literature of the first two centuries. They did not cause belief in Jesus' divinity—that was already presumed. Rather, they were trying to explain how Jesus was divine. Mapping the origins of incarnational Christology does not explain the emergence of a divine Christology; it is the other way around. Incarnational Christology came to be a compelling explanation for a divine Christology! Dunn's conclusion in the end yielded weak claims about the Christology in the New Testament: Jesus is a twofold mediator who mediates God to humans and humans to God; Jesus sums up and embodies the divine presence; and Jesus was not worshipped but was the instrument by whom God was worshipped.[5]

(2) Dunn stated with striding confidence that neither descending angels nor exalted patriarchs were the stimulus for an incarnational Christology. The problem with that naked denial is that it is premised on the assumption that "the Hellenistic Judaism out of which the first Christians drew the christological categories which concern us had no room for such heavenly beings independent of God in their scheme of things—apart, that is, from angels,

---

[5] James D. G. Dunn, *Did the First Christians Worship Jesus? The New Testament Evidence* (London: SPCK, 2010), 146–51.

and it was precisely the option of identifying Christ with or as an angel which the first-century Christians either ignored completely or rejected so emphatically."[6] I detect a few problems here.

First, the primitive and patristic church did indeed make connections between Jesus and angels, and this cannot be glossed over as Dunn did. For a start, the description of the risen Jesus in Rev 1.12–20 resembles the angelic figure described in Dan 10.2–9, and Justin refers to Christians worshipping God, the Son, and "other" angels (*1 Apol.* 6.2). Furthermore, the energetic contrast of Jesus and angels (Heb 1–2) as well as the rejection of the worship of angels (Col 2.18; Rev 19.10; 22.9) is prima facie proof that many early Christians strove to differentiate Christ devotion from types of veneration of angels precisely because of some level of similarity. Indeed, as I will show later, angel Christology was the most catholic and ecumenical of Christologies as it could be affirmed, in various ways, by proto-orthodox, Jewish, and Valentinian Christianities.

Second, the category of "independent" intermediary figures such as angels is problematic. Philo (*Opif.* 46) stated that "[God] has no need of his heavenly offspring on which he bestowed powers but not independence: for, like a charioteer grasping the reins or a pilot the tiller, he guides all things in what direction he pleases as law and right demand, standing in need of no one besides: for all things are possible to God." Ultimately no intermediary figures in the Jewish cosmos are truly independent of God, not even Yahoel or Metatron; they remain created and subordinated beings. Even Philo's Logos is a hypostatic representation of God spliced with angelic creatureliness to become a genuine in-between entity. It is precisely because Judaism lacked independent figures beside God that the emergence of an intense divine Christology, where Jesus was regarded as co-eternal and co-equal with God, was as radical as it was potentially problematic. What is more, independent or not, nothing precludes that christological discourses were shaped by descriptions of various Jewish intermediary figures.

(3) If a doctrine of incarnation emerged relatively late, only really crystallizing in the Fourth Gospel, then the possibility of Greco-Roman influence becomes far more likely.[7]

(4) Dunn was reliant on Christian deployment of Jewish wisdom traditions—especially in Paul's letters, Hebrews, and the Fourth Gospel—to do the heavy lifting in the development of a doctrine of incarnation. However,

---

[6] Dunn, *Christology in the Making*, 258–59.

[7] Larry Hurtado, *One God, One Lord: Early Christian Devotion and Ancient Jewish Monotheism* (3rd ed.; London: T&T Clark, 2015), 6–7.

while wisdom traditions undoubtedly contributed to early Christology in terms of postulating Jesus as identifiable with God and God's activity in creation, even so, wisdom traditions alone cannot yield an incarnational Christology. First, other traditions and texts must factor in as well (i.e., those associated with God's Word, angels, Son of David, Daniel's Son of Man, etc.). Second, wisdom Christology can be taken in several different directions. For a case in point, while second-century authors pointed to Wisdom in Prov 8.22–23 to explain the incarnation, they did that beside appeals to other texts like Exod 23.20, Isa 9.6, and Col 1.15. Accordingly, while Paul, John, Justin, Valentinus, and Arius all believed that Jesus was the "Wisdom of God," they understood that claim to point to different ways of being divine![8] Wisdom traditions are part of the explanation for the spectrum of divine Christologies, but not necessarily the explanation for a divine Christology of incarnation.

Richard Bauckham

Richard Bauckham is one of the most erudite and compelling authorities on early Christology. I regard his account of "christological monotheism," blending as it does monotheism, eschatology, and Christology, to be mostly persuasive.[9] Christian authors such as Paul and John identified Jesus as part of God's own identity (i.e., part of what set God apart from all other reality, as the creator of and sovereign over the cosmos, recipient of Israel's worship, and bearer of the divine Name Yahweh). It is Bauckham's opinion that Jesus was identified "directly with the one God of Israel" in a way that was "largely unprecedented in Jewish theology."[10]

Accordingly, Bauckham maintains that Jesus cannot be fitted into divinity by appealing to semi-divine Jewish intermediary figures on account of the strictness of ancient Jewish monotheism that separated God from all other created reality, whether heavenly or earthly. "The concern of early Christology,"

---

[8] The fourth-century debates between the pro-Arians and pro-Nicenes about Prov 8.22–23 are proof of this very point!

[9] See positive affirmations of Bauckham's approach in Simon J. Gathercole, *The Preexistent Son: Recovering the Christologies of Matthew, Mark, and Luke* (Grand Rapids: Eerdmans, 2006), 69–70, 76; N. T. Wright, *Paul and the Faithfulness of God* (COQG 4; London: SPCK, 2014), 624, 629–30, 633, 651–53; Richard B. Hays, *Reading Backwards: Figural Christology and the Fourfold Gospel Witness* (Waco, Tex.: Baylor University Press, 2014), 369, n. 14; Nina Henrichs-Tarasenkova, *Luke's Christology of Divine Identity* (LNTS 542; London: T&T Clark, 2016), 26–88; David B. Capes, *The Divine Christ: Paul, the Lord Jesus, and the Scriptures of Israel* (ASBT; Grand Rapids: Baker, 2018), 122, 162–64; and Ruben A. Bühner, *Hohe Messianologie: Übermenschliche Aspekte eschatologischer Heilsgestalten im Frühjudentum* (WUNT 2.523; Tübingen: Mohr Siebeck, 2020), 339–40.

[10] Richard Bauckham, *Jesus and the God of Israel* (Milton Keynes, U.K.: Paternoster, 2008), 3–4.

he argues, "was not to conform Jesus to some pre-existing model of an intermediary figure subordinate to God."[11] The intermediary figures do not "blur or bridge the line of absolute distinction which Jewish monotheism maintained between God and all other reality"[12] because "What Jewish monotheism could not accommodate were precisely semi-divine figures, subordinate deities, divinity by delegation and participation."[13]

Bauckham divides intermediary figures into two categories: First, principal angels and exalted patriarchs, figures who fall outside of God's unique identity, and irrespective of how mighty and glorious they might be, they do not infringe upon God's unique identity (which is why they are not ordinarily portrayed as sharing God's throne or receiving cultic worship). Second, God's Word and Wisdom, who are personifications or hypostatizations of God himself, expressing God's mind and will in relation to the world. The first category is excluded from God's unique identity, while the second is included within it.[14] As such, the

> so-called intermediary figures were not ambiguous semi-divinities straddling the boundary between God and creation. Some were understood as aspects of the one God's own unique reality. Most were regarded as unambiguously creatures, exalted servants of God whom the literature often takes pains to distinguish clearly from the truly divine reality of the one and only God. Therefore . . . I do not think such intermediary figures are of any decisive importance for the study of early Christology. While not denying some relevance, I think the intensive interest in them as the key to understanding the Jewishness of early Christology has been misleading. The real continuity between Jewish monotheism and New Testament Christology is not to be found in intermediary figures.[15]

The implication for early Christology is that "the key way in which Jewish monotheism and high Christology were compatible in the early Christian movement is not the claim that Jewish monotheism left room for ambiguous semi-divinities, but the recognition that its understanding of the unique identity of the one God left room for the inclusion of Jesus in that identity."[16]

---

[11] Bauckham, *Jesus and the God of Israel*, 176.
[12] Bauckham, *Jesus and the God of Israel*, 18.
[13] Bauckham, *Jesus and the God of Israel*, 20.
[14] Bauckham, *Jesus and the God of Israel*, 15–17, 158–61.
[15] Bauckham, *Jesus and the God of Israel*, 182.
[16] Bauckham, *Jesus and the God of Israel*, 20.

Unlike some critics, I am not averse to Bauckham's language of "divine identity," as I do not believe that it runs the risk of modalism (i.e., Jesus is still a distinct person within the one divine identity, with a distinct set of relationships and characteristics, just as family members do not forfeit their individuality by existing in one collective family identity); nor does it displace a concept of divine personhood (i.e., identity and personhood are not the same thing—someone can have multiple identities related to gender, family relationships, ethnicity, and profession, while remaining the same fundamental person with constant personality traits).[17] More contentious is whether exercising divine functions such as ruling means that an agent participates in a divine identity.[18]

There are of course still some points of contention with Bauckham's account of divine identity and its construal of intermediary figures.

(1) As stated in the last chapter, I am concerned with Bauckham's dismissal of metaphysical categories and ontic relationships in favor of divine identity. Many expressions of Jewish monotheism either presupposed or presented God as ontologically distinct from creation/creatures. I do not think it possible to separate God's identity, functions, and being, as ancient Jews and Christians evidently did not do so.[19]

(2) Bauckham's construal of divine identity is still inferred from several functions (i.e., creating and ruling). In that case, one must wonder whether divine identity is truly an alternative to functional divinity or whether divine identity is simply an inference drawn from divine functions. And therein lies the problem. For, if other intermediary figures, whether human or angelic, exercise creative and ruling functions, then they too can be identified with God in some way. For instance, I would argue that what *equates* God's reign (Rev 11.17; 19.6) with Jesus' (co-)reign (1 Cor 15.25; Rev 11.15) and what *separates*

---

[17] Contra Dunn, *Did the First Christians?* 141–44; and Matthew Bates, *The Birth of the Trinity* (Oxford: Oxford University Press, 2015), 24–25, 91–92.

[18] For instance, Crispin H. T. Fletcher-Louis, *Jesus Monotheism*, vol. 1: *Christological Origins: The Emerging Consensus and Beyond* (Eugene, Ore.: Wipf & Stock, 2015), 14, states: "Time and again we find divine *action* or *functions* ascribed to Christ in a way that now makes sense if Christ belongs within the divine identity and if he fully participates in the divine nature" (italics original). Alternatively, J. R. Daniel Kirk (*A Man Attested by God: The Human Jesus of the Synoptic Gospels* [Grand Rapids: Eerdmans, 2016], 17–23, 174), warns that being identified *with* God is not the same as being identified *as* God. Jewish writings are filled with ideal human figures identified with God in the sense of ruling with or on behalf of him but without encroaching upon God's unique identity.

[19] Cf. similarly Bates, *Birth of the Trinity*, 24–25; and Samuel Vollenweider, "Zwischen Monotheismus und Engelchristologie: Überlegungen zur Frühgeschichte des Christusglaubens," *ZTK* 99 (2002): 42.

Jesus' reign from the co-reign of humans over (new) creation (Ps 8.4; Rev 1.6; 5.10; 20.4–6; 22.5; 2 Tim 2.12) is that Jesus is not part of the created order! It is the Creator-creature distinction which is paramount (with Bauckham), and that distinction is not only functional, but ontological and relational (contra Bauckham).

(3) I think Bauckham is generally correct that intermediary figures can normally be divided into two categories: divine personifications and divine agents, who are part of the created order. I think that particularly rings true in early Christian texts. The problem is the niggling exceptions to this taxonomy, as some agents can be put into either category.[20]

The most obvious is Philo's account of the Logos, who appears in some ways as an intermediate divine hypostasis operating between God and the world, described as a divine helmsman of the universe or the substance of a divine intellect (e.g., *Deus* 83; *Fug.* 101; *Cher.* 36; *Her.* 235–36). The Logos is also divisible into God's creative and royal powers. Philo calls the creative aspect "God" and the reigning aspect "Lord," while both are aspects of the "one true God" (*Fug.* 95, 103; cf. *Mos.* 2.99–100; *Her.* 166; *Abr.* 121; *QG* 2.16; *QE* 2.62, 68). Yet elsewhere the Logos is portrayed more creaturely as a "Son of God," "his firstborn word," "the elder angel," "an archangel," who "is called the 'authority,' the name 'God' and 'Word' and 'man according to God's image who sees God'" (*Conf.* 146; *Somn.* 1.215). Most significantly, the Logos is "neither uncreated as God, nor created as you [mortals], but exists between the two extremities" (*oute agenētos hōs ho theos ōn oute genētos hōs hymeis, alla mestos tōn akrōn*; *Her.* 205–6). Looking at it one way, Philo's Logos is both a divine personification and an angelic creature; but looking at it another way, the Logos is neither, and is something totally in between God's metaphysics and the material world.[21]

In addition, there is no consistent view of God's Wisdom. For instance, in Prov 8.22–31, a text which became the epicenter of Arian exegesis in the fourth century, Wisdom is portrayed as the first-created being, who then functions as a divine assistant in the work of creation. Elsewhere, Wisdom is a created agent (Sir 24.3, 8–9), part of the heavenly council (Sir 24.2), with her "throne

---

[20] Andrew Chester (*Messiah and Exaltation* [WUNT 207; Tübingen: Mohr Siebeck, 2007], 22) thinks Bauckham works in "neat, watertight and absolute categories," which he finds problematic since "the distinction between at least some of these figures and God could appear very blurred, and the portrayal of the heavenly world could be extremely difficult to distinguish divine from non-divine (or semi-divine) categories."

[21] Philo's Logos is then similar to Ptolemy's demiurgical deity, who also has an intermediary essence between the perfect God and the Devil (*Flor.* 33.7.5–7).

in a pillar of cloud." She is sovereign over the sea, earth, peoples, and nations (Sir 24.4, 6). Wisdom dwells among Israel and Zion, and even in the Torah (Sir 24.10–12, 23). In addition, Wisdom is the "breath of the power of God, and a pure emanation of the glory of the Almighty" and "a reflection of eternal light, a spotless mirror of the working of God, and an image of his goodness" (Wis 7.25–26). Wisdom participates in creation as the "fashioner of all things" (Wis 7.22), the one by whom God "formed humankind" (Wis 9.2) and who rules "by your throne" (Wis 9.4, 10; cf. *1 En.* 84.2–3). Notably Wisdom has creative and ruling functions even as there is variation as to whether Wisdom is a divine personification or a created entity.[22]

Chris Tilling

Chris Tilling is part of a new generation of scholars addressing the problems and perplexities of divine Christology. Tilling tries to open up a new front in the discussion by focusing on the Yahweh-relation pattern in Israel's Scriptures and the Christ-relation pattern in Paul's letters. According to Tilling, in ancient Judaism, God's uniqueness was expressed relationally, in terms of God's presence, activity, and sovereignty. For Tilling, Paul discourses about "the relation between believers and the risen Lord, and he does so by using the sort of language and themes which Second Temple Judaism used to speak of the relation between Israel and YHWH."[23] While God-relations and Christ-relations are distinguished in several ways, what Tilling finds striking are the many overlaps in terms of divine faithfulness, slavery to a deity, devotion to a deity, divine presence while physically absent, and divine communications in terms of prayer.[24] This supports his claim that Second Temple Judaism knew God as unique through the God-relation pattern, a pattern deployed by Paul to express the Christ-relation to believers. The central fixture here is the blend of epistemology and relationality, God known in a specific relationship. Christ is known and experienced as divine by the manner in which Paul relates him to himself and to other believers.

When it comes to intermediary figures, Tilling examines the figures often thought to blur the God-creature distinction and who receive types of worship,

---

[22] It may well be possible to integrate Bauckham's view of divine identity with intermediary figures. As Larry Hurtado ("Worship and Divine Identity: Richard Bauckham's Christological Pilgrimage," in *Ancient Jewish Monotheism and Early Christian Jesus-Devotion: The Context and Character of Christological Faith* [Waco, Tex.: Baylor University Press, 2017], 105) notes: "In short, it seems to me that Jesus is included within the 'divine identity' specifically as God's unique chief agent!"

[23] Chris Tilling, *Paul's Divine Christology* (Grand Rapids: Eerdmans, 2012), 72.

[24] Tilling, *Paul's Divine Christology*, 234–39.

notably the high priest Simon ben Oniad (Sirach), Adam (*Life of Adam and Eve*), and the Son of Man (*1 Enoch*). He acknowledges the exalted status and forms of veneration attributed to these figures but also observes the absence of Yahweh-relations between these intermediaries and humans. Compared to Sirach 44–50, Paul's Christ-devotion language more properly mirrors the relationship God has with Israel rather than with anything attributed to Simon ben Oniad or to the Israelite ancestors. Similarly, in the *Life of Adam and Eve*, the worship given to Adam does not appear to provide a paradigm for Paul's infrequent references to Christ's worship. What is more, Christ is depicted by Paul far more like God than Adam in these texts as far as relationality goes. Concerning the Son of Man in *1 Enoch*, Tilling is quite aware that matters here are murky. He acknowledges that the Enochic Son of Man is preexistent, is given exalted titles, is worshipped, exercises judgment, carries a revelatory name, and even has scriptural Yahweh texts applied to him, so there are palpable parallels with Paul's Christology. Even so, Tilling lists some sixteen points of differentiation: the most compelling for my mind are that the Enochic Son of Man's position is cast as an unrealized eschatological future, not a current relational reality; the obeisance offered to the Son of Man is not on par with divine cultic worship; and Paul's Christ relates to creation and creatures far more like the Enochic Lord of Spirits than the Enochic Son of Man.[25] Tilling thus contends that while such texts "use exalted language of figures other than God, the God-relation pattern of data remains descriptive of the deity alone."[26]

Tilling has opened a new front in discussions on Paul's divine Christology, moving us away from concentration on intermediary parallels, divine identity, and divine worship, by focusing on God-relations and Christ-relations. Here is where one might demur: (1) Questioning whether Christ-relations entail Christ's divinity or are merely compatible with it. For instance, if we found literary testimony to angels who exercised some similar Yahweh-relationship, would that make them necessarily divine?[27] (2) Pressing that point further, we perhaps need a more complex synthesis of divine relationships, functions, and ontology whereby relationship is intrinsic to divinity but not sufficient grounds for it.

Scholarly Perspectives on Christology and Intermediary Figures: Positive Evaluations

Several scholars have been far more positive in terms of the influence or analogies between intermediary figures and portrayals of Jesus: views

---

[25] Tilling, *Paul's Divine Christology*, 212–30.
[26] Tilling, *Paul's Divine Christology*, 72.
[27] Matthew V. Novenson, "A Novel Argument for the Divinity of Christ in Paul," *ExpT* 124 (2013): 619.

range from those who see one particular figure, like the Angel of the Lord, or the Enochic Son of Man, as the definitive pattern after which early Christologies were modeled; or else, these figures are partial explanations for the types of ways that Jesus was considered divine by the early church; or again, the intermediary agents fed into a process of christological development that was formed and framed by a unique range of experiences and exegeses.

Martin Hengel

Martin Hengel made several seminal contributions to discussions on the origins of early Christology. In sum, Hengel argued with acumen that early Christology developed largely within Palestinian and Diaspora Judaism rather than owing its impetus to pagan influences. Hengel provided a heavily qualified yes to the application of Jewish intermediary figures to Jesus.

Hengel was aware of the presenting issue: "The confession of the exaltation of Jesus as Son of Man and Son of God in the resurrection and his appointment as God's eschatological plenipotentiary immediately posed for earliest Christianity the question of the relationship of Jesus to other intermediary figures, whether the supreme angels or Wisdom-Torah, which was at least partially thought of as a personification."[28] In search of an answer, Hengel dismissed the view that the Christian notion of a divine son is indebted to "a syncretistic paganization of primitive Christianity" whereby Jesus was divine according to the categories of pagan mythic heroes, Gnosticism, or mystery religions.[29] He did not think ruler cults, divine men, or Gnostic redeemer myths exerted any substantive influence on early Christology. "As far as I can see," commented Hengel, "there are only a few parallels in the Graeco-Roman world to the sending of a pre-existent divine redeemer into the world, and these are remote."[30]

Hengel prioritized the impact of the earthly activity of Jesus as well as Jesus' death and resurrection appearances upon primitive Christology. He concurrently posited a Palestinian rather than pagan setting for acclamation of Jesus as "Son of God" and "Lord." Crucial for Hengel was that belief in Jesus' preexistence emerged through an eschatological Christology, which required a protological prequel. In effect, the exalted Jesus' eschatological status was retrojected backwards into God's ancient plan, so that the Messiah was a preexistent figure, at least in God's purposes. This accorded with Jewish texts that describe the Messiah as someone whom God knows and someone whom God

---

[28] Martin Hengel, *The Son of God: The Origin of Christology and the History of Jewish Hellenistic Religion* (Minneapolis: Fortress, 1976), 67.
[29] Hengel, *Son of God*, 18.
[30] Hengel, *Son of God*, 34.

reveals, explaining the application of preexistence to Jesus. Thereafter, Hengel argued that Hellenistic Jewish wisdom traditions explicated the sending and mission of the preexistent Son from heaven and were extended to include the notion of the Son as the mediator of creation. Thus, "all the functions of Wisdom were transferred to Jesus."[31]

Concerning Jewish intermediary figures, these mediators and redeemers "were differentiated from God and yet closely connected with him," and "acquired special significance in the final eschatological events." Hengel found in these intermediary beings a mixture of "analogies" and "fundamental differences" with early Christology.[32] The analogies pertain to how Jesus was the "mediator of revelation and salvation," "God's eschatological messianic ambassador" with a "unique connection with the Father."[33] This is why Hengel could admit similarities between Jesus and God's Wisdom and the Enochic Son of Man. On the differences, this was principally in the scandal of the cross, the folly of a crucified man as the *messias designatus* and chief agent of creation, revelation, and redemption.

Hengel is undoubtedly the most formidable critic of the older *religionsgeschichtliche Schule* and its attempt to explain Christology by way of pagan influences. Nonetheless, he did envisage a role for intermediary figures, especially Jewish Hellenistic wisdom traditions, in shaping divine Christology. That said, we might note two questionable aspects of Hengel's scheme:

(1) Hengel's approach required reestablishing the divide between Judaism and Hellenism that he had formerly disassembled. On the one hand, Hengel was highly successful in arguing that all of Judaism in the first century was Hellenistic Judaism, so that the erroneous divide between Jewish Christianity and Hellenistic Christianity had to be dismantled.[34] On the other hand, Hengel insisted that early Christology was not shaped by pagan or Hellenistic influences, but by Jewish sources, albeit within a Hellenistic Judaism. Hengel treated Hellenistic Judaism as something of a buffer, or even a bodyguard, protecting Jewish Christianity from direct pagan influences. Any pagan similarities are either sanitized or else deflected by Hellenistic Judaism.[35] For a case in point, Hengel saw incarnational

---

[31] Hengel, *Son of God*, 72.
[32] Hengel, *Son of God*, 89.
[33] Hengel, *Son of God*, 90.
[34] Martin Hengel, *Judaism and Hellenism: Studies in the Encounter in Palestine during the Early Hellenistic Period* (2 vols.; Philadelphia: Fortress, 1974).
[35] M. David Litwa, *Iesus Deus: The Early Christian Depiction of Jesus as a Mediterranean God* (Minneapolis: Fortress, 2014), 16–18; and John J. Collins, "Judaism as *Praeparatio Evangelica* in the Work of Martin Hengel," *RelSRev* 15 (1989): 226–28. Luke Timothy

Christology as shaped by Jewish wisdom traditions rather than by the Stoic idea of the Logos.³⁶ Hengel reduced Palestinian Judaism to a *praeparatio evangelium* and Hellenistic Judaism to the *Cohors Praetoria* to keep pagan influence away from Christology.

(2) Hengel was circumspect on the influence of ruler cults on Christology, regarding it as "at best a negative stimulus, not a model" for Christology.³⁷ Even if a conflict between Christology and imperial worship only happened later during the reigns of Nero and Domitian, the conflicts were due to the similarities in language and claims between the two religious conceptualities. Hengel's dismissal of ruler cults is even more incongruent given that he admits a "certain formal analogy" between Matthew and Luke's risen Jesus and the apotheosis of Romulus and how ancient rulers could be considered hidden epiphanies of the gods.³⁸ Furthermore, Palestine itself was literally surrounded with imperial temples, cults, and media, which often incited nearby Judeans to fits of violent religious protest. If Christology emerged principally in a Palestinian context, then it should be remembered that the cult of the princeps was no less Palestinian.

Maurice Casey

Maurice Casey's approach had several distinct features. First, he divided up christological development into three categories:³⁹ (1) Jewish Christianity within Judaism; (2) Jewish Christianity receiving numerous Gentile converts; and (3) Gentile Christianity as a non-Jewish religion. Second, he categorized intermediary figures who parallel early Christology into two types: (1) static parallels, discrete items of Jewish belief found during the time of Jesus, defined by titles such as "Lord," "Messiah," and "Son of God"; (2) dynamic parallels pertaining to a figure who increases in status, or function—the Enochic Son of Man and Hellenistic notions of Wisdom being the most obvious examples.⁴⁰ In his view, Paul and others had an elevated view of Jesus, but Jesus is only divine or incarnate in the Gospel of John.⁴¹

Johnson calls this the "Hengel sidestep," whereby any possible influence of Greco-Roman culture on the New Testament is systematically filtered through Hellenistic Judaism, which presumably renders it nontoxic for Christianity. See his review of *No One Seeks for God: An Exegetical and Theological Study of Romans 1:18–3:20* by Richard H. Bell, *RBL* (1999).

36 Hengel, *Son of God*, 35–36.
37 Hengel, *Son of God*, 30.
38 Hengel, *Son of God*, 38–39.
39 Maurice Casey, *From Jewish Prophet to Gentile God* (Louisville, Ky.: Westminster John Knox, 1991), 17, 97.
40 Casey, *From Jewish Prophet*, 78–96.
41 Casey, *From Jewish Prophet*, 114–16, 169.

Casey's approach was commendable in trying to hold together the constraint of monotheism, exploring how conceptions of intermediary figures and Christology intersect with the sociology of group identity, and offering an explanatory model for precisely when and how divine Christology emerged. In terms of what is lacking:

(1) On Jewish monotheism, Casey believed that among most Second Temple Jews, even Philo of Alexandria, there is a strict monotheism in operation, so that there is no second deity on par with the God of Israel. As such, he thinks it impossible for Jesus to be "God" in a Jewish Christianity that is still under the auspices of Jewish monotheism: "You could not both generate belief in the deity of Jesus and remain within the Jewish community."[42] But, as we will see, the questions are, how flexible was that strict monotheism, and when do the edges blur into polytheism? If we accept Casey's definition of Jewish monotheism, then Jesus is only truly divine in John's Gospel and John becomes in effect a bi-theist! Yet John's christological account posits an intensely divine Jesus constructed in association with an affirmation of monotheism. John's Gospel is a Jewish text, not a polytheistic one! Accordingly, I do not think it possible to justify the statement "This Gentile self-identification [in the Gospel of John] was a necessary cause of belief in the deity of Jesus, a belief which could not be held as long as the Christian community was primarily Jewish."[43]

Casey repeatedly appealed to monotheism to shut down any suggestion that Jesus might be divine, especially in Paul's letters.[44] In some places, Casey offered a question-begging argument that Paul was a monotheist and therefore he could not have posited Jesus as divine irrespective of what titles or roles were attributed to him.[45] Casey was reluctant to see Jesus worshipped even in Revelation because John the Seer is still within a mixed-Jewish community that only worships the one God. But this defies what pretty much every

---

[42] Casey, *From Jewish Prophet*, 169.
[43] Casey, *From Jewish Prophet*, 38, 158–59, 162.
[44] For a case in point, Casey (*From Jewish Prophet*, 110) says that the confessions "Our Lord, come" and "Jesus is Lord" make Jesus a "superior heavenly being, and a central figure of identity and authority to whom the church was subject," but they did not "equate him with God." But what is the difference, and what is the criterion for the difference? If the church is subject to Jesus, as to Yahweh, is Jesus not equated with Yahweh on some relational level (see Chris Tilling above!)? Or else, Casey says that in Phil 2.6–11 Jesus is "on the verge of deity," and even the quotation of Isa 45.23 does not mean "Jesus was God" due to the constraint on monotheism. But does not the Isaiah quote show the constraint being broken or at least flexibly transgressed?
[45] Casey, *From Jewish Prophet*, 169.

observer of the text says is attributed to the exalted Jesus: divine worship.[46] The problem here is that there is no evidence that the Gentilization of a community was the sine qua non for a divine Jesus, as Jesus can be god or God in a very Jewish sense. Jewish scholars like Daniel Boyarin believe that the Danielic Son of Man and its various interpretations among Jewish and Christian authors were espousing a divine intermediary agent beside God with unusual proximity and participation in God.[47] This amounts to a very Jewish way of envisaging Jesus as a god or God. Casey's definitions of monotheism and what is possible within the aegis of monotheism are the Achilles' heel of his argument.

(2) On his three-tiered development of Christology, there are serious shortcomings with Casey's taxonomy. For a start, whether the Pauline or Johannine networks can be definitively classified as "Jewish" or "Gentile" puts too much freight in what remains a contentious debate about the ethnic makeup of these networks. Paul is a Jewish apostle working among Gentile-majority churches. The Gospel of John is a sectarian Jewish text largely devoid of explicit theologizing about Gentile assemblies attempting to justify their socio-religious distance from Judaism. On top of that, Casey assumed insularity between the three stages rather than any kind of "interactive diversity."[48] But that will not do, because social groupings tend to be far messier with cross-pollination and internal diversities.[49] A figure like Barnabas was a Cypriot Jew who was part of the Jerusalem church (Acts 4.36), a leader of the Antiochene church (Acts 11.22–25; Gal 2.1), and engaged in the Gentile mission in partnership with Paul (Acts 13–15; 1 Cor 9.6; Gal 2.1–10) and then independently of Paul (Gal 2.12–14; Acts 15.37–39). Barnabas traverses the three divisions, and yet we have no indication that this required his Christology to evolve in the course of entering these three different settings.

(3) Casey buttressed his reconstruction of christological origins with appeals to the dubious category of Jewish orthodoxy. If by Jewish orthodoxy Casey meant something like the homogenous ideational traits and practices of a common Judaism, then maybe so. But the language of orthodoxy and the way Casey used it sound somewhat anachronistic and perhaps more fitting for the post-135

---

[46] Casey, *From Jewish Prophet*, 142–43.
[47] Daniel Boyarin, *The Jewish Gospels: The Story of the Jewish Christ* (New York: New Press, 2013).
[48] Larry Hurtado, "Interactive Diversity: A Proposed Model of Christian Origins," *JTS* 64 (2013): 445–62.
[49] Cf. Marinus de Jonge, *Christology in Context: The Earliest Christian Responses to Jesus* (Philadelphia: Westminster, 1988), 19.

CE rabbinic period. It renders questionable his judgment that the Enochic Judaism of the *Similitudes* did not belong to the "orthodox wing of Judaism."[50]

(4) While the relevance of sociology should never be understated, one does wonder if Casey is guilty of reducing early Christology and intermediary figures to a social epiphenomenon. This yields two problems. First, whether his sociology is right, is it truly the case that the sociological drive towards Jesus' divinization was based on the Gentilization of Christian faith rather than an internal reconfiguring of Jewish discourse about God and intermediary figures within Jewish communities? Second, considerations must also be given to the impact that the historical Jesus had upon his followers, the psychology of apocalypticism, religious experience, and rereading sacred texts in light of one's situation and wider cultural context.

Larry Hurtado

Larry Hurtado also represented a sharp move away from the old *religionsgeschichtliche Schule* by explaining the origins of divine Christology without reference to pagan influences, as well as moving beyond the banal method of exploring Christology through the titles applied to Christ. His primary thesis was that there are linguistic parallels between the way the exalted Jesus is described in the New Testament and personified divine attributes, exalted patriarchs, and principal angels. Hurtado surmised that Jesus was initially identified as an intermediary figure, a divine agent of some variety, until religious experience in the form of visions caused a "mutation" that propelled members of the early Palestinian church to offer the same type of cultic devotion offered to Yahweh to the exalted Jesus in a binitarian mode of worship. Jesus was given cultic worship even while the worshippers maintained that they were worshipping the one God of Israel.

For Hurtado, "Jewish belief in the uniqueness of God was able to accommodate surprising kinds of reverence for and interest in other heavenly figures such as chief angels and exalted patriarchs as well as personified attributes or powers of God. Interest in the role of these divine agents was apparently widespread and probably of some importance in understanding how early Jewish Christians were able to accommodate the exalted Jesus without feeling that they had violated the uniqueness of God."[51] In the Aramaic-speaking church there was, said Hurtado, an "unprecedented reshaping of monotheistic piety to include a second object of devotion alongside God, a figure seen in a position of God's chief agent, happening among a group that continued to consider itself firmly

---

[50] Casey, *From Jewish Prophet*, 88.
[51] Hurtado, *One God, One Lord*, 8–9.

committed to 'one God'"⁵² whereby "the risen Christ came to share in some of the devotional and cultic attention normally reserved for God."⁵³ The cause of this mutation in Jewism monotheism was "visions and other experiences that communicated the risen and exalted Christ and presented him in such unprecedented and superlative divine glory that they felt compelled to respond devotionally as they did."⁵⁴ In short, "early Christians seem to have drawn upon a wide array of traditions, attributing to Jesus multiple honorific categories to an extent that seems without real precedent or parallel."⁵⁵ This occurred, he added, without "a clumsy crossbreeding of Jewish monotheism and pagan polytheism under the influence of gentile Christians too ill-informed about the Jewish heritage to preserve its character." Rather, "we have a significantly new but essentially internal development within the Jewish monotheistic tradition, a mutation within that species of religious devotion."⁵⁶ As such, the religious heritage of the first Jewish Christians furnished them with the resources for accommodating the exalted Jesus with their devotion to the one God *as well as* engaging in cultic devotion to Jesus as part of their worship of the one God. This cultic worship is highly significant because it is the "decisive criterion" by which the Jews maintained the uniqueness of God over and against idols, rulers, and angels.⁵⁷

Most responses have taken issue with Hurtado on his account of ancient Jewish monotheism, his disregard for pagan influences on early Christology, and his precise definition of cultic and divine worship. The main points of contention are over the exclusivity of Jewish cultic worship of Yahweh and the substance of Christ devotion in the early church in relation to Jesus' divine status.

(1) Even Richard Bauckham, who did much to show how early Christian worship of Jesus as divine was very early, thinks that divine worship needs to be integrated with a wider account of monotheism and Christology (i.e., Jesus' inclusion in a divine identity).⁵⁸ Bauckham points out that exclusive worship of the God of

⁵² Hurtado, *One God, One Lord*, 104.
⁵³ Hurtado, *One God, One Lord*, 129.
⁵⁴ Hurtado, *One God, One Lord*, 126.
⁵⁵ Larry Hurtado, "Principal Angels and the Background of Christology," in *Ancient Jewish Monotheism and Early Christian Jesus-Devotion: The Context and Character of Christological Faith* (Waco, Tex.: Baylor University Press, 2017), 183.
⁵⁶ Hurtado, *One God, One Lord*, 105.
⁵⁷ Larry Hurtado, "First-Century Jewish Monotheism," in *Ancient Jewish Monotheism and Early Christian Jesus-Devotion: The Context and Character of Christological Faith* (Waco, Tex.: Baylor University Press, 2017), 131.
⁵⁸ Richard Bauckham, "The Worship of Jesus in Apocalyptic Christianity," NTS 27 (1981): 322–41; republished as "The Worship of Jesus," in *The Climax of Prophecy: Studies on the Book of Revelation* (Edinburgh: T&T Clark, 1993), 118–49; idem, "Jesus, Worship of," ABD 3:812–19; republished in *Jesus and the God of Israel*, 127–51.

Israel was premised on a recognition and response to God's unique identity as creator and covenantor.[59] In other words, the divine worship of Jesus is a corollary of the inclusion of Jesus within the divine identity, precisely what Bauckham claims is depicted in Phil 2.9–11 and Rev 5.1–14. It is, then, divine identity rather than divine worship that is paramount for the divinity of both God and Jesus.[60]

(2) The primary points of contention against Hurtado are whether Jews worshipped figures other than the one God, and whether the worship afforded to Jesus was genuinely cultic. Whereas Hurtado argued that Jews were generally exclusive in their cultic worship of their one God and included Jesus in forms of cultic worship, both propositions are disputed.[61] One could point out that the Jews in the Elephantine community in upper Egypt in the fifth century BCE worshipped Yahweh at their own temple and worshipped multiple other deities such as Anath, Banit, and Nabu.[62] Although none of these other deities were necessarily conceived as Yahweh's deputy, many members of the Jewish garrison were obviously not monolatrous. The Elephantine Jews might be considered an outlier or exception if it were not for the fact that we have epigraphic evidence of Jews paying homage to various gods at various shrines and temples for healing or thanks for a safe journey.[63] Furthermore, it is true that angel veneration or homage to a divinely appointed king is not necessarily a mode of cultic worship that mirrors or transgresses the cultic worship of Yahweh. That said, the worship of a penultimate and plenipotentiary divine figure, like a superhuman messiah or an archangel, can be conceived as a type of divine worship because it venerates the divine agent whom God stands behind and whose veneration redounds towards God.[64] Thus, for those Jews for whom

---

[59] Bauckham, *Jesus and the God of Israel*, 25.

[60] Bauckham, *Jesus and the God of Israel*, 11–13, 25; contested by Hurtado, "Worship and Divine Identity," 108–9.

[61] See James F. McGrath, *The Only True God: Early Christian Monotheism in Its Jewish Context* (Urbana: University of Illinois Press, 2009), 23–37; Dunn, *Did the First Christians?*; and Maurice Casey, "Monotheism, Worship and Christological Developments in the Pauline Churches," in *The Jewish Roots of Christological Monotheism: Papers from the St. Andrews Conference on the Historical Origins of the Worship of Jesus*, ed. Carey C. Newman, James R. Davila, and Gladys S. Lewis (JSJSup 63; Leiden: Brill, 1999), 214–33.

[62] Allen Kerkeslager, "Jewish Pilgrimage and Jewish Identity in Hellenistic and Early Roman Egypt," in *Pilgrimage and Holy Space in Late Antique Egypt*, ed. David Frankfurter (Leiden: Brill, 1998), 110.

[63] Stephen G. Wilson, *Leaving the Fold: Apostates and Defectors in Antiquity* (Minneapolis: Fortress, 2004), 52–65.

[64] Theron Clay Mock III, "'New Testament Christology': A Critique of Larry Hurtado's Influence," unpublished paper presented at the Redescribing Christian Origins Seminar, Society of Biblical Literature (San Antonio, Tex., November 21, 2021), 65–66.

the exclusive, aniconic worship of Yahweh was strict, the inclusion of Jesus within such worship would require a mutation of monotheistic convictions to remain coherent. Alternatively, for those Jews who did not share in exclusive worship of Yahweh, the worship of Jesus in association with Yahweh or beside Yahweh would have been unproblematic and did not require an elevation of Jesus to the same level as Yahweh in a divine hierarchy.

In favor of Hurtado, it is true that we have no evidence of an organized cult for the worship of a second figure besides Yahweh in Second Temple Judaism, and it is also true that early Christianity appears to spring from that species of Judaism committed to God's unique identity and exclusive worship. However, attempting to define monotheism by the restriction of cultic worship to Yahweh, or else insisting on a sharp contrast between cultic worship and general venerative practices, runs the risk of dying the death of a thousand cuts from a thousand exceptions.

Andrew Chester

Andrew Chester's work in early Christology and intermediary figures is perhaps the most underrated contribution to the debate. Even though I disagree with him on several points, he presents something of a minority report that does the grit and grind of textual analysis rather than recycling rehearsed opinions or trading in overgeneralizations.

Against Bauckham and Hurtado, Chester detects many angelic and human figures exalted in places and in language normally reserved for Yahweh. He finds that angels are exceedingly close with and even confused with Yahweh, such as Yahoel in the *Apocalypse of Abraham* and the angel who receives worship in *Joseph and Aseneth*. In addition, concerning venerated human figures, Abel is given exalted status and sits on a throne of judgment in *Testament of Abraham*, while Adam receives worship as the image of God in the *Life of Adam and Eve*. Chester asserts that we are faced with the prospect that angelic and exalted figures can be seen as "identical in being, role or function" and perhaps "represent a challenge or complement to God's sole rule and supreme position."[65]

For Chester, it is not the case that "New Testament writers fit Christ into an existing category of 'semi-divine intermediary figures,'" as much as the portrayal of such figures within Jewish tradition "helps these very Christian authors towards expressing and articulating what they want to say about Christ."[66] These angelic and exalted figures were not ready-made models that were picked up and used to explain Christ. Rather, they were either the "least

[65] Chester, *Messiah and Exaltation*, 379.
[66] Chester, *Messiah and Exaltation*, 25–26.

inadequate way" of capturing the extraordinary nature of their experience of Christ or were part of how Christ was variously understood by Christians even as they affirmed that he is "utterly different, and unique altogether in his own being and in relation to God, and as 'part' of God."[67]

Chester claims that Christology emerged with early Christian visionary experiences of a transformed Jesus who embodied divine glory, bore the divine image, possessed the divine name, and was seated at God's right hand. Yet those visions needed categories for Jesus to be considered "divine," as the experiences alone would not furnish Jesus' exalted status. As such, Jewish intermediary figures constituted a central and integral part of the context where Jesus was experienced and explained as a divine being. That is not to say, however, that earliest Christology can be simply correlated with any of these figures, nor that there is a causal connection from these Jewish figures to the portrayal of the exalted Christ. Their main contribution is that they show that mediating and moving between the heavenly and earthly realms, between divine and human spheres, was possible. Thus, authors like Paul regarded Jesus as a messianic and angelic figure who was part of the heavenly world, who had a limited time on earth, who returned to heaven, with various angelological, wisdom, and exalted human traditions utilized to explain this narrative. Yet it remained truly remarkable that a figure who had been crucified, raised from the dead, and transformed into a mode of existence alongside God in the heavenly world shared in the divine rule.[68]

The strength of Chester's account is his refusal to find one key that unlocks the door to the beginnings of divine Christology, whether that is divine worship or divine identity; instead, he postulates a process of experience, exegesis, and extended Jewish categories to account for the emergence of divine Christology. He is also open to ontological categories rather than relying purely on divine functions that are then correlated with divinity. Chester is wise to contend that while Jesus is undoubtedly different to Jewish intermediary figures, he is not entirely unique either. Thus, unlike Bauckham, he sees the intermediary figures as immensely relevant; unlike Hurtado, he does not require the idea of a mutation in the theology of intermediary figures in order to make Jesus "divine" since intermediary figures were identified closely and intimately with God's being and functions.

Where one can push back on Chester is in his reading of several texts as to whether they really do show these intermediary figures being worshipped and afforded divine status. In several cases, I suspect that Chester is incorrect, and

[67] Chester, *Messiah and Exaltation*, 26, 44–45.
[68] Chester, *Messiah and Exaltation*, 119–21, 394–95.

there are more differences between early Christology and the intermediary figures than he acknowledges.

Adela Collins

Adela Collins' distinguished academic career has included comparative studies of the New Testament's Christology vis-à-vis its Jewish and Greco-Roman context. Collins has shown particular interest in how the Gospel of Mark, Paul's epistles, and the book of Revelation mesh with the messianism, angelology, wisdom traditions, and spectrums of divinity found in antiquity.

Collins grounds early Christology and the worship of Jesus in Jewish messianism and ancient ruler cults, so that Jesus was indeed a messianic agent for the primitive church in general and for Paul in particular.[69] It was the "prior cultural experiences" and the "cultural situation" of Christians in the Greco-Roman world that shaped and interpreted christological beliefs.[70] Given the presence of the Greco-Roman culture and religion in Palestine, including the imperial cult, Collins asserts that we "should take seriously the likelihood that non-Jewish Hellenistic and Roman traditions, as well as Jewish traditions, shaped the religious experiences, ideas and writings of especially the Greek-speaking Jewish followers of Jesus in the period immediately following his death." She finds it plausible that such traditions were "deliberately and consciously" adapted to construct a meaningful system of belief, though she thinks it possible that such borrowing of ideas was also unconscious.[71] Collins' thesis is that a combination of visions of the risen Jesus and the influence of the Roman imperial cult was the catalyst for the worship of Jesus.

According to Collins, the apostle Paul, in passages like 1 Cor 8.5–6 and 2 Cor 4.4–6, identifies the preexistent Christ with God's Wisdom, God's agent in creation as per Prov 8.22–31 and Wis 7.22–8.1.[72] In the Philippian "Christ hymn," Christ is a preexistent being of sorts, but concerning the phrase "equal

---

[69] Adela Yarbro Collins, "The Worship of Jesus and the Imperial Cult," in *The Jewish Roots of Christological Monotheism: Papers from the St. Andrews Conference on the Historical Origins of the Worship of Jesus*, ed. Carey C. Newman, James R. Davila, and Gladys S. Lewis (JSJSup 63; Leiden: Brill, 1999), 234–57; idem, "Psalms, Philippians 2:6–11, and the Origins of Christology," *BibInt* 11 (2002): 361–72; and idem, "'How on Earth Did Jesus Become a God?': A Reply," in *Israel's God and Rebecca's Children: Christology and Community in Early Judaism and Christianity*, ed. David B. Capes, April D. DeConick, Helen K. Bond, and Troy A. Miller (Waco, Tex.: Baylor University Press, 2007), 55–66.

[70] Collins, "Worship of Jesus and the Imperial Cult," 235, 241.

[71] Collins, "Worship of Jesus and the Imperial Cult," 242.

[72] Adela Yarbro Collins and John J. Collins, *King and Messiah as Son of God: Divine, Human, and Angelic Messianic Figures in Biblical and Related Literature* (Grand Rapids: Eerdmans, 2008), 111–12, 147, 207–8.

with God," she doubts this refers to something that Jesus already possessed but is rather something he did not violently try to usurp. Further, given the negative connotations of human beings seeking equality with God (e.g., 2 Macc 9.12), Jesus is portrayed as the opposite of the arrogant ruler who tries to claim divine honors. Instead, Christ's elevation to the rank of *kyrios* marks his installation as messiah or universal king. Phil 2.6–11 is, for Collins, laced with political rhetoric and is a simultaneous critique and parody of the imperial cult, where the emperor was lauded as a divine *kyrios* (e.g., Acts 25.26). In addition, Collins regards the narration of Jesus' service, suffering, and super-exaltation in the hymn as closer to myths surrounding Herakles than to anything in the Jewish tradition.[73] Collins argues that Paul, much like the portrayal of the Enochic Son of Man (*1 En.* 48.2–3, 6), explicates the preexistent messiah in terms of preexistent and personified divine Wisdom.[74]

Collins also argues for the importance and influence of Daniel's phrase "one like a Son of Man" on Jesus and the early church. Whereas Jesus was an apocalyptic prophet who looked forward to the advent of the kingdom and the revelation of a heavenly messiah (Mark 13.26–27), after Jesus' death, his followers had visions of him as raised to life and exalted to heaven, and they then identified him with the "coming Son of Man" of Dan 7.13 and the kingly warrior of Ps 110.1 (e.g., 1 Thess 4.16–17).[75] In the case of the Gospel of Mark,[76] Jesus' miracle-working abilities meant that he was a "heroic figure analogous to the great poets and sages of Greek tradition," while the acclamation of Jesus as a/the "Son of God" by the centurion (Mark 15.39) would have entailed that "members of the audience of Mark familiar with the imperial cult would understand that the centurion recognized Jesus as the true ruler of the known world, rather than the emperor."[77] Mark defines Jesus' messiahship around several royal and apocalyptic motifs, so that "the picture of the messiah that emerges is a cosmic ruler, a heavenly being who mediates the blessing and rule of God to all creation."[78]

Moving into the Johannine materials, Collins contends that John's prologue incorporates the idea of a divine *Logos*, an explanatory principle in Hellenistic

---

[73] Collins, "Worship of Jesus and the Imperial Cult," 246–47; and idem, "Psalms, Philippians 2:6–11," 366–67.

[74] Collins and Collins, *King and Messiah*, 114–16, 148, 174, 208–9.

[75] Collins and Collins, *King and Messiah*, 168–74.

[76] Adela Y. Collins, "Mark and His Readers: The Son of God among Greeks and Romans," *HTR* 93 (2000): 85–100.

[77] Collins, "Son of God among Greeks and Romans," 88.

[78] Adela Y. Collins, "Mark and His Readers: The Son of God among Jews," *HTR* 92 (1999): 408.

philosophy for how a transcendent and incorporeal God could also be the creator of the material world. That is combined with Jewish traditions of a personified Wisdom associated with God's life and light (Sir 4.12; Wis 7.10, 26) so that Jesus is likened to preexistent Wisdom, who becomes incarnate. The Johannine blend of a royal and Davidic messiah (i.e., Son of God) with Jewish wisdom traditions (i.e., the Word) uses Hellenistic Jewish speculation to portray Jesus as "preexistent and divine in the sense of being an emanation of God or being 'a god.'"[79] Collins judges the book of Revelation to be indirectly messianic by building on several royal and Davidic images for Jesus (Gen 49.9; Ps 2.8–9; Rev 5.5; 12.5). At the same time, the risen Jesus is portrayed in angelomorphic terms, with Rev 1.13–16 arguably adapted from the angelic figure in Dan 10.5–9 with echoes of imagery from Ezek 1.26–28; 8.2. In addition, the description of Jesus as "the first and the last" (Rev 1.17; 22.13) resembles wisdom traditions so that Jesus is the first creature of God in creation and the agent of God for the new creation, consistent with the view of Jesus as either a divine emanation or a principal angel.[80] Collins concludes: "The Gospel and Revelation both present Jesus as preexistent and as divine in some sense. In the Gospel, he is either an emanation of God or God's first creature, namely, the only-begotten god. In Revelation, the evidence suggests that he is God's first creature, namely, the principal angel."[81]

Collins has majored on comparative studies between early Christology and Jewish wisdom tradition, Hellenistic philosophy, ruler cults, the influence of Daniel's "Son of Man," and principal angels. In her conclusion, Jesus' divinity was not monolithic, but diversified, and could be expounded in a variety of ways, none of which implied Jesus' parity with God's being, attributes, or identity. Three things give me doubts about Collins' proposal:

(1) While Collins' comparative exegesis of Jesus with intermediary figures is normally compelling, her comparisons do not extend to Jesus and God. For instance, she does not countenance the fact that Paul's identification of Jesus as the "Lord of glory" (1 Cor 2.8) is similar to the Enochic "Lord of glory" (*1 En.* 22.14; 25.3, 7; 27.3, 5; 36.4; 63.2; 83.8). Or else, she breezes over the observation that in Revelation Jesus is called "first and last" (Rev 1.17; 22.13), and John the Seer says the same thing of God the Father (Rev 1.8; 21.6).[82] Collins thus downplays the similarities between God and Jesus in Christian literature.

---

[79] Collins and Collins, *King and Messiah*, 175–81, 209–10 (quote from 181).
[80] Collins and Collins, *King and Messiah*, 187–94.
[81] Collins and Collins, *King and Messiah*, 203.
[82] Collins and Collins, *King and Messiah*, 111, 193.

(2) Collins seems unduly to favor Greco-Roman analogues to Jewish ones. The problem is that the Philippian "Christ hymn," with its explicit quotation of Isa 45.23 (LXX), allusiveness to stories of patriarchs, prophets, or people exalted to heavenly positions (e.g., Gen 5.24; Sir 44.16; 49.14; Heb 11.5; 1 Kgs 2.11–12; 1 Macc 2.58; Ps 8.5–6), and plausible echoes of wisdom traditions (Wis 2.23–34), seems far closer to Jewish traditions than to Greco-Roman literature and legends about Herakles. The language of being "equal with God" is certainly part of Hellenistic regal rhetoric, just as is the Jewish opposition towards it (2 Macc 9.12; Philo, *Conf.* 170).

(3) Whereas Collins admits that Jesus is divine in some undetermined sense, mostly functional and not metaphysical, I would be more inclined to see New Testament statements like "form of God," "equal with God," (Phil 2.6), "only begotten" (John 1.18; 3.16, 18), "The Father and I are one" (John 10.30), "true God" (1 John 5.20), and "imprint of God's very being" (Heb 1.3) as tacitly ontological even if ontological concerns are not the center of gravity in a specific instance of christological discourse.

Emma Wasserman

Emma Wasserman has argued that ancient Jewish apocalypses were not characterized by an equilibrated dualism between the good and evil powers of the universe, who engaged in a cosmic conflict for control of the heavens. Rather, God is consistently portrayed as the all-powerful monarch of the heavenly order, and the lesser deities are normally depicted as "relatively powerless competitors who are foolishly arrayed against heaven, not as rebels or usurpers who threaten the established order."[83] As such, Paul's letters presuppose a "world constituted as a single, unified political hierarchy that required a plurality of divine beings who organize, shape, and rule it."[84] According to Wasserman, Paul's Christ is an eschatological warrior figure in this cosmo-political ecosystem. Paul in turn "develops a distinctive myth that celebrates Christ's noncompetition and heroic submission" to God in passages such as 1 Cor 15.23–28 and Phil 2.6–9. Wasserman's Paul identifies Christ as the agent of the end-time scenario, ushering in not a dissolution to the space-time universe, but the purification and perfection of the existing social and political order.[85]

What this means in terms of Christology is that Christ is presented as one of the lower deities who, because of his submission and service, is

---

[83] Emma Wasserman, *Apocalypse as Holy War: Divine Politics and Polemics in the Letters of Paul* (New Haven, Conn.: Yale University Press, 2018), 107.
[84] Wasserman, *Apocalypse as Holy War*, 3.
[85] Wasserman, *Apocalypse as Holy War*, 15, 108–9.

elevated in the heavenly hierarchy, above where he was, but still below God the Father. Wasserman argues that Paul's mythmaking in 1 Cor 15.23–28 depicts no parricide, coup, or conflict as per other Jewish literature, but Christ appears as an obedient general who defeats the powers and hands the kingdom back to the Father, highlighting Christ's noncompetitive relationship with God the Father.[86] Moving to the "Christ hymn" in Phil 2.6–11, Wasserman says that the text emphasizes Christ's heroic obedience and non-rivalry with the supreme deity. She prefers a *res rapienda* interpretation of Phil 2.6 whereby Christ did not seize/grasp after equality with God by force. In addition, Jesus is in the "form of God," or a god, in the same sense that Melchizedek is called a "god" in the Qumran scrolls (11QMelch 2.10). So Paul's innovative myth celebrates how "Christ was originally a lesser divine being, probably a member of the heavenly entourage," an "intermediary being who does not 'seek equality with God as something to be grasped by force' and then willingly assumes a much lower rank, remaining obedient to the point of death," and thereafter is promoted within the divine hierarchy as a reward.[87] The narrative is not V-shaped, with God's equal descending from heaven, taking human form and dying a slave's death, and then returning to a position of glory and honor. Her narrative is more of a √-shape where a heavenly being descends from heaven, takes human form and dies a slave's death, and is then super-exalted above other gods but remains below the supreme god. "As a result," Wasserman concludes, "Christ now becomes the object of acclamation, reverence, and submission (not the supreme God), and the adoring hosts emerge as those 'in heaven and on earth and under the earth.'"[88]

Wasserman is surely correct to identify the heavenly hierarchy as part of the background to Paul's Christology. Where one might contest her view is whether Phil 2.6 portrays Christ as a lower deity in that hierarchy, who descends to earth, ascends to heaven, and is exalted further in the heavenly hierarchy. For my mind, Christ's preexistence combined with the parallel possession of the "form of God" and "equality with God" arguably puts Christ closer to God in the heavenly hierarchy than to any intermediary figure. Thereafter, Christ does not ascend in heavenly honors or morph into a higher deity; rather, he becomes a recipient of Yahweh-cultic worship from heavenly and human creatures as defined by Isa 45.23.

---

[86] Wasserman, *Apocalypse as Holy War*, 122–25.
[87] Wasserman, *Apocalypse as Holy War*, 132–35.
[88] Wasserman, *Apocalypse as Holy War*, 137.

Conclusion

The preceding survey has by no means been exhaustive. More specific studies about divine Wisdom, angelology, heavenly thrones, messianism, ruler cults, and Son of Man figures could have been incorporated in the taxonomy of scholarly perspectives.[89] Nevertheless, the review has provided a useful sample of the debate over the utility of appealing to intermediary beings for mapping the origins of divine Christology, discussions over which intermediary figures are the most salient for early Christology, and precisely when, in the development of Christology, influences from sources pertaining to intermediary figures occurred. What remains to be done is to plot the precise similarities and differences between early Christologies and the many intermediary figures. We are interested in more than "Is intermediary figure X divine or human?" followed by "How is Jesus like X?" We need to examine a mediator's physical characteristics, morphological transformations, spatial location in heaven or earth and traversing the two; whether it is created or made, its relationship to creation, role in salvation; whether it is a recipient of worship or veneration, its superhuman traits, and its relation to God and to other heavenly figures.[90] Such a comparative project will enable us to (1) identify the continuities and discontinuities between early Christologies and these intermediary figures; (2) determine if the figures are partial analogies or explanatory genealogies for the emergence of divine Christology; and (3) identify anything characteristic and/or unique about the divine status, nature, and functions attributed to Jesus. That arduous exercise of comparison and juxtaposition is what lies ahead.

---

[89] See Andrew Chester, "High Christology—Whence, When, and Why?" *EC* 2 (2011): 22–50; and Brandon D. Smith, "What Christ Does, God Does: Surveying Recent Scholarship on Christological Monotheism," *CBR* 17 (2019): 184–208.

[90] See the helpful list of questions compiled by Bühner, *Hohe Messianologie*, 19–20.

4

Jesus and the "In-Betweeners"

Comparing Early Christologies and Intermediary Figures

> To his Word, his chief messenger, highest in age and honour, the Father of all has given the special prerogative, to stand on the border and separate the creature from the Creator. The same Word both pleads with the immortal as supplicant for afflicted mortality and acts as ambassador of the ruler to the subject. He glories in the prerogative and proudly describes it in these words, "and I stood between the Lord and you" (Dt. 5.5), that is neither uncreated as God, nor created as you, but midway between the two extremes.
>
> Philo, *Who Is the Heir?* 205–6

> The lawgiver is the craftsman and maker of the universe and of all things within it. Since he is different from the essences of the other two (i.e., God and the Devil) and exists in a state intermediate between them, he would rightly be described by the term intermediateness.
>
> Ptolemy, *Letter to Flora* 33.7.4

Larry Kreitzer opened his PhD thesis with a good question: "Do any of the New Testament writers call Jesus 'God' or identify Jesus with God ontologically?"[1] His own answer, at least in relation to Paul, is: "I would like to assert that he [Paul] stops short of asserting absolute equality between Jesus the Messiah and God. Yet at the same time, for Paul, Jesus' identification with God is such that he cannot be fully explained or comprehended via human categories

---

[1] Larry J. Kreitzer, *Jesus and God in Paul's Eschatology* (Sheffield: Sheffield Academic Press, 1987), 15.

alone. Nor can Jesus' significance be assessed as simply another expression of the phenomenon of intermediary figures populating Jewish apocalyptic literature of the time. Within Paul's thought, Jesus transcends the boundaries of such categories without, at the same time, entirely usurping the position of God."[2] Kreitzer adroitly asks about divine ontology in Christology and opts for a "no, but . . ." answer. After that he finds an intense and close connection between God and Jesus, without equating the two, while remaining unconvinced of the relevance of intermediary figures to explain Jesus vis-à-vis God.

As should be clear, I disagree with Kreitzer on both points. To begin with, I think New Testament authors do in places, implicitly and explicitly, incorporate Jesus into a divine ontology—even if they primarily focus on the story of Jesus' mission and exaltation, the place of Jesus in an eschatological narrative, and Jesus' relationship to believers via the Spirit. In addition, the similarities between Jesus and the various intermediary figures are quite palpable, if only for the fact that authors are drawing on the same suite of texts, like Ps 110.1 and Dan 7.13, to talk about an eschatological deliverer who traverses the heavenly and earthly realms. I find it hard to deny that Jewish and Greco-Roman readers of the New Testament thought of Jesus as related to these intermediary figures—the reception history of the New Testament proves this beyond all doubt.[3] One must be conscious too of the theological proclivity of some researchers wanting both to find something that intrinsically separates God from intermediary figures and to attribute this intrinsic divine quality to Jesus as the root of divine Christology. Early "high" Christology may well have some precedents and is none the worse for it![4]

Of course, whether these intermediary figures are factors explaining the origins of divine Christology or merely analogues that were "in the air," so to speak, is an open question for my mind. As Charles Darwin said, "analogy may be a deceitful guide" when it comes to origins![5] Consequently, whether the early Christians were deliberately explaining their experience and expectations of the exalted Jesus by depicting him like the Angel of the Lord, the assumption of Elijah, a deified emperor, the Enochic Son of Man, Qumran's Melchizedek, or

[2] Kreitzer, *Jesus and God in Paul's Eschatology*, 16.
[3] Cf. Jörg Frey, "Between Torah and Stoa: How Could Readers Have Understood the Johannine Logos?" in *The Prologue of the Gospel of John*, ed. Jan G. van der Watt, R. Alan Culpepper, and Udo Schnelle (WUNT 359; Tübingen: Mohr Siebeck, 2016), 196, 219-31.
[4] Cf. Ruben A. Bühner, *Hohe Messianologie: Übermenschliche Aspekte eschatologischer Heilsgestalten im Frühjudentum* (WUNT 2.523; Tübingen: Mohr Siebeck, 2020), 335.
[5] Quoted in Yii-Jan Lin, *The Erotic Life of Manuscripts: New Testament Textual Criticism and the Biological Sciences* (New York: Oxford University Press, 2016), 149. I was alerted to this quote by Dr. Robert Turnbull.

the apotheosis of Herakles—or whether the similarities were mere happenstance because Christians were breathing the same intermediary air—is moot.

Besides that, maybe we should not rule out something genuinely innovative about certain aspects of emerging Christology. It would be wrong to say that all early Christology is merely recycled traditions and tropes and the only new aspect is telescoping it into the man Jesus.[6] Paul is a master at polemical improvisation and scriptural reimagination. Mark provides a distinctive achievement by marrying the Jesus tradition to the *bios* genre. John achieves something of a watershed in his incarnational Christology of the Logos, while Justin and the Gnostics were trying to reconcile the Gospels with Hellenistic philosophy—all things considered, something fresh and inventive should be expected. Notwithstanding the fact that Christian authors were hardly cutting and pasting ideas into their texts, we do well to remember that every rehearsal of a script always creates a new performance. Of course, any uniqueness will be qualified or relative, still "within reach" of Jewish tradition,[7] but the human capacity for innovation and creative synthesis should not be underestimated.

Accordingly, my contention is that we can only understand how articulations of a divine Jesus are different from the intermediary figures after we have first seen how they are similar. Then, we can offer analysis to see what, if anything, is distinctive or even (dare I say) exceptional about the early church's christological discourses. I am quite cognizant that to inquire as to how Christian portrayals of Jesus as a human agent correlate with Jewish and Greco-Roman intermediary figures is to open a box of perilous parallelomania whose contents are practically infinite. In other words, one could engage in a detailed drudgery of comparative analysis as to how Jesus resembles or diverges from these heroes, immortals, demigods, exalted patriarchs, chief angels, and divine hypostatizations until the Son of Man returns to put all exegesis to rights. Thus, an exhaustive survey is impossible, but some salient highlights are indicative of patterns of similarity and differentiation that we should take note of if we are interested in the characteristics of early christological discourses in their eastern Mediterranean context.[8]

---

[6] Contra Daniel Boyarin, "Enoch, Ezra, and the Jewishness of 'High Christology,'" in *Fourth Ezra and Second Baruch: Reconstruction after the Fall*, ed. Matthias Henze and Gabriele Boccaccini (JSJSup 164; Leiden: Brill, 2013), 353.

[7] Bühner, *Hohe Messianologie*, 339 ("in Reichweite"); and idem, *Messianic High Christology: New Testament Variants of Second Temple Judaism* (Waco, Tex.: Baylor University Press, 2021), 4, 63, 94.

[8] See surveys in Frances Young, "Two Roots or a Tangled Mess?" in *The Myth of God Incarnate*, ed. John Hick (Philadelphia: Westminster, 1977), 117–18; Nils A. Dahl, *Jesus the Christ: The Historical Origins of Christological Doctrine* (Minneapolis: Fortress, 1991), 113–36; Andrew Chester, *Messiah and Exaltation* (WUNT 207; Tübingen: Mohr Siebeck,

In what follows, the approach I take in each subsection consists of three moves: first, describing the intermediary figures or agents as they appear in our sources; second, analyzing the ways in which early Christologies resemble or rehearse said intermediary figures; third, engaging in a comparative analysis to sort out what precisely is similar and different between christological discourses and the intermediary figures under examination. This admittedly detailed and dense analysis will be followed up with a subsequent chapter that tries to pan back, look at the evidence globally, and try to make sense of the aggregate similarities and differences.

Demiurge, Logos, and Wisdom

Jewish and Christian views of God and creation are not monolithic; they developed over time, and moved in different directions. The beginning of this process is observable in the transition from Gen 1 to Gen 2 in the Hebrew Scriptures, all the way through to Basil of Caesara's *Hexaemeron* and Augustine's *The Literal Meaning of Genesis*. Nonetheless, when it comes to Gen 1.1 and God's creation of the world, many questions arose for interpreters: *creatio ex nihilo* vs. *creatio ex matera*, the prospect of *creatio continua*, and the origins of evil, as well as the issue of agency in the act of creation itself. On this last point, Miguel Herrero de Jáuregui notes the tension in the topic:

> A lively debate surrounds these verses [Gen 1–2] in both Jewish and Christian circles from the Hellenistic age well into the fifth century. The problem was adapting the biblical idea of God's absolute primacy and transcendence with respect to the material universe He created, an idea made explicit both in these verses and in many other passages in both Testaments, to the categories of Greek philosophy. The principal problem

---

2007), 45–80, 363–82; Bart D. Ehrman, *How Jesus Became God: The Exaltation of a Jewish Preacher from Galilee* (New York: HarperOne, 2014), 47–84; John J. Collins, "Jewish Monotheism and Christian Theology," in *Aspects of Monotheism: How God Is One*, ed. Hershel Shanks and Jack Meinhardt (Washington, D.C.: Biblical Archaeological Society, 1997), 82–94; Larry Hurtado, "Monotheism, Principal Angels, and the Background of Christology," in *The Oxford Handbook of the Dead Sea Scrolls*, ed. Timothy H. Lim and John J. Collins (Oxford: Oxford University Press, 2010), 546–64; Sigurd Grindheim, *God's Equal: What Can We Know about Jesus' Self-Understanding in the Synoptic Gospels?* (LNTS 446; London: T&T Clark, 2011), 134–67; Charles H. Talbert, *The Development of Christology during the First Hundred Years: And Other Essays on Early Christology* (Leiden: Brill, 2011), 3–26; Michael F. Bird, "Of Gods, Angels, and Men," in *How God Became Jesus: The Real Origins of Belief in Jesus' Divine Nature*, ed. Michael F. Bird (Grand Rapids: Zondervan, 2014), 22–44; and Andrew Ter Ern Loke, *The Origin of Divine Christology* (SNTSMS 169; Cambridge: Cambridge University Press, 2017), 48–78.

rested in the matter with which God creates the heaven, the earth, and the other elements of the cosmos. If it is preexistent, there is a risk of creating an entity independent of God and shattering the monism that is fundamental to Jewish-Christian theology. If it is conceived of as proceeding (or emanating) from God Himself, however, God's transcendence and the creator's independence with respect to His creation come into question, and the field opens for the infinite problems of theodicy.[9]

Many ancients tried to conceive as to how Reason, Mind, the First Principle, an unmoved Mover, or God created the material world while remaining distinct from that world. What was apparently required was an intermediary entity within the heavenly hierarchy to act as God's agent either to create matter or bring order to chaos. An influential answer to this problem was Plato's demiurge, as expounded in the central sections of his *Timaeus*, where the demiurge assumes the role of a cosmic craftsman. The Platonic demiurge soon generated a rich and variegated reception history among Middle and Neo-Platonists, and it found expression in the Logos of Stoic philosophy. Furthermore, there are Jewish wisdom traditions of Hebraic and Hellenistic origins which attribute a demiurgical function to Wisdom, and of course in early Christianity there are demiurgical roles attributed to Jesus Christ in creation and new creation. On the whole, Christian statements about Jesus as the agent, unity, and goal of creation fit precisely into this domain of discourse about God's creative-crafting agent.[10] Below I explore these creative agent roles in a taxonomy of demiurge, Logos, and Wisdom.

The Demiurge

The demiurge was a divine figure in Greco-Roman, Jewish, and Christian cosmologies and creation stories who was responsible, in diverse ways, for the formation of the physical world. The concept and language of demiurgy was to prove very salient in proto-orthodox and Gnostic schemes, so that Christ was either co-demiurge with God the Father, or else removed altogether from the demiurgical role in fashioning the created realm.

(1) Greco-Roman philosophy.

One of Plato's revolutionary ideas expounded in *Timaeus* was the postulation of the demiurge (*dēmiourgos*), a cosmic craftsman, a maker and Father, who

---

[9] Miguel Herrero de Jáuregui, *Orphism and Christianity in Late Antiquity* (Berlin: de Gruyter, 2010), 300–301.
[10] See, e.g., 1 Cor 8.6; Col 1.15–18; John 1.3; Heb 1.2; *Keryg. Pet.* 2; *Herm.* 3.4; 91.5; *Diogn.* 7.2; Justin, *2 Apol.* 6.3; Minucius Felix, *Oct.* 18; Theophilus, *Autol.* 1.7; 2.10, 22; Athenagoras, *Leg.* 4.2; 6.2; 10.1, 5; 18.2; Irenaeus, *Haer.* 1.22.1; 3.11.8; 4.20.1–4.

was responsible for the origins of the universe as well as the creation of human souls (Plato, *Tim.* 28A–C; 41C). Plato was a monistic idealist, and *Timaeus* was his attempt to provide a teleological explanation for the universe wrapped in an intricate synthesis of metaphysics, myth, and math.[11] In such a project, the demiurge is somewhere between a cosmic intelligence and an ideal Zeus, the father of the cosmos, who creates, or more often than not, orders a world from preexisting materials that mirrors the world of Forms (*Tim.* 29B). The demiurge does this by contemplating that which is good, by fashioning human souls, and by delegating the formation of matter and human bodies to subordinate entities, the young gods (*Tim.* 40D–41B; 42D–43A; 68E–69D). The demiurge is also the artificer of the World-Soul, a divine intellect immanent within the cosmos—comprised of Sameness, Otherness, and Being (*Tim.* 30B; 35A–B). The demiurge discharges the supervision of the universe to the World-Soul. Thus, while the demiurge fashioned the world, it is the World-Soul who sustains it.[12] And so begins the demiurgic tradition, and here it is useful to note the definition of demiurgy offered by Carl Séan O'Brien:

> Demiurgy can be described as world-generation via the ordering of preexistent matter by an entity, sometimes represented as endowed with only limited abilities, according to some sort of model, so that the activity is generally regarded as intellective, as opposed to the *creatio ex nihilo* envisaged in the Judaeo-Christian concept of creation, where God creates simply by willing it to happen.[13]

Plato's demiurge was an agent or metaphor that proved useful for a variety of theo-cosmological schemes when it came to the interface between the divine, noetic, and cosmic realms. As such, there emerged a variety of demiurgic patterns in Platonic, Middle Platonic, Neo-Platonic, Stoic, Philonic, Gnostic, Hermetic, and Christian systems.[14] When it comes to the position of the demiurge in a heavenly hierarchy, for Plato the demiurge is "an intermediary between the higher, noetic world and the sublunar, material realm" or "an intermediary

---

[11] R. G. Bury, trans., *Plato: Timaeus, Critias, Cleitophon, Menexenus, Epistles* (LCL; Cambridge, Mass.: Harvard University Press, 1929), 5, 13. On Plato's theology, see Max J. Lee, *Moral Transformation in Greco-Roman Philosophy of Mind* (WUNT 2.515; Tübingen: Mohr Siebeck, 2020), 129–33.

[12] Herb Gruning, *How in the World Does God Act?* (Lanham, Md.: University of America Press, 2000), 1–2.

[13] Carl Séan O'Brien, *The Demiurge in Ancient Thought: Secondary Gods and Divine Mediators* (Cambridge: Cambridge University Press, 2015), 2.

[14] On which, see O'Brien, *Demiurge*.

entity, midway between matter and the Forms."[15] In later platonizing schemes, "authors of Middle Platonism developed one hierarchically ordered theology, at the head of which was a first, absolutely transcendent deity, followed by a second god endowed with the properties and functions of the demiurge, and finally a third god, usually identified with the cosmos or its soul," writes Franco Ferrari.[16] A complicating factor is that some Platonists considered the demiurge to be the first god (e.g., Xenocrates, Plutarch, Atticus), while the tendency of Neo-Platonism was to demote the demiurge to a much inferior position (e.g., Numenius, Plotinus, Porphyry). In which case, the arguments between proto-orthodox, Sabellian, and Gnostic authors in the second through third centuries were perhaps an intra-platonizing debate about the status of the demiurge.[17]

(2) Philo.

In Second Temple Judaism, Philo is the most obvious proponent of a platonized Judaism.[18] Philo depicts God as the supreme demiurge (*Opif.* 10; *Her.* 133–43, 156; *Cher.* 126–27), who demiurges through the Logos (*Sacr.* 8), while incorporeal powers called Forms help things take shape, much like Plato's young gods (*Spec. leg.* 1.329). Philo is sometimes charged as the "Cro-Magnon Man of Gnosticism" by his linking together biblical exegesis with Platonic demiurgism.[19] He is quite comfortable with the idea of dual powers within the Logos and various inferior powers generated by the Logos (*Fug.* 95, 103; cf. *QG* 2.16; *QE* 2.62, 68; *Her.* 166; *Mos.* 2.99–100; *Abr.* 121). We see that when Philo says that

---

[15] O'Brien, *Demiurge*, 4, 11.

[16] Franco Ferrari, "Der Gott Plutarchs und der Gott Platons," in *Gott und die Götter bei Plutarch: Götterbilder—Gottesbilder—Weltbilder*, ed. Rainer Hirsch-Luipold (RVV 54; Berlin: de Gruyter, 2005), 18 ("Autoren des mittleren Platonismus eine hierarchisch geordnete Theologie, an deren Spitze eine erste, absolut transzendente Gottheit stand, gefolgt von einem zweiten Gott, der mit den Eigenschaften und Funktionen des Demiurgen ausgestattet war, und schließlich einem dritten Gott, der gewöhnlich mit dem Kosmos oder seiner Seele gleichgesetzt wurde").

[17] Jan Opsomer, "Demiurges in Early Imperial Platonism," in *Gott und die Götter bei Plutarch: Götterbilder—Gottesbilder—Weltbilder*, ed. Rainer Hirsch-Luipold (RVV 54; Berlin: de Gruyter, 2005), 52–56.

[18] See David T. Runia, *Philo of Alexandria and the* Timaeus *of Plato* (Leiden: Brill, 1986); and Masanobu Endo, *Creation and Christology: A Study of the Johannine Prologue in Light of Early Jewish Creation Accounts* (WUNT 2.146; Tübingen: Mohr Siebeck, 2002), 167–70.

[19] O'Brien, *Demiurge*, 38. Cf. C. K. Barrett (*The Gospel according to St. John* [2nd ed.; London: SPCK, 1978], 155), who said Philo "must be reckoned among the witnesses to an early form of gnosis, which developed into gnosticism as primitive Christianity was added to the syncretism of Hellenism with Judaism and other oriental movements."

although God alone made the heavens,[20] nonetheless, he needed the assistance of inferior subordinates to create something as inferior as humans (*Opif.* 72–76; *Leg. all.* 1.41; *Fug.* 70; *Conf.* 175; *Abr.* 143; *Legat.* 6), even while their creative work was never entirely independent of divine direction (*Spec. leg.* 1.13–20). In addition, Philo's Logos resembles a Gnostic demiurge when he declares that the Logos "is called a god by those of us with imperfect knowledge, while the wise and perfect know the first God" (*Leg. all.* 3.207), yet that is because some persons cannot differentiate God's being from the copy of God (*Somn.* 1.234–49). Also, what mitigates against the charge of being a proto-Gnostic is how Philo maintains that God is one; God is the good Creator and Ruler; creation itself is good; and demiurgical assistants are not opposed to God (esp. *Opif.* 100; *Conf.* 171; *Leg. all.* 3.96; *Cher.* 125; *Migr.* 6; *Spec. leg.* 1.81).[21] Philo deploys Jewish scriptural interpretation with Platonic and Stoic frames to stress the unity of God and to exposit God's relationship with the world through subordinate figures who possess demiurgical qualities.

(3) Proto-orthodox authors.

All forms of early Christianity were demiurgical—whether Pauline, Johannine, proto-orthodox, Valentinian, Sethian, or Marcionite—as they all postulated an intermediary entity who (co-)created the world, whether that was Christ or some other figure. Christian demiurgisms were largely shaped by Jewish Wisdom traditions, Middle Platonic developments of Plato's cosmic hierarchy, and the Stoic notion of the Logos. What is of immediate relevance are (1) the explicit identifications of God and Christ as a type of *dēmiourgos*, (2) the identity of who performed the work of *dēmiourgia*, and (3) other demiurgical figures apart from God and Christ (all translations below are my own!).

In the New Testament, the writer to the Hebrews describes God as the "architect and demiurge" (*technitēs kai dēmiourgos*) of the heavenly Jerusalem (Heb 11.10). Among the proto-orthodox theologians, God as demiurge appears in Clement of Rome, who, at the end of the first century, wrote how the "great Demiurge and Master [*ho megas dēmiourgos and despotēs*] of the universe ordered [all things] to exist in peace and harmony" (*1 Clem.* 20.11; cf. 26.1; 33.2; 35.3; 38.3; 59.2). Justin referred to "God the Father and demiurge [*dēmiourgos*] of all" (*1 Apol.* 8.2) and argued that Greek writers such as Plato borrowed from Moses' words in Gen 1.1 about how God "fashioned" or

---

[20] Cf. e.g., *Opif.* 7; 23; 29; 74; *Conf.* 170; *Leg. all.* 1.18; 2.3; *Mos.* 1.100; Josephus also (*Ag. Ap.* 2.192) asserts that God created without any assistance or cooperation. See also Trypho, who says that next to "the Creator of the world ... no other God or Lord exists" (*Dial.* 56.3).

[21] O'Brien, *Demiurge*, 38.

"demiurged" (*edēmiourgēsen*) the world in the beginning (*1 Apol.* 59.1). Irenaeus defined God as "the Creator, who is, in respect of his love, the Father; but in respect of his power, he is Lord; and in respect of his wisdom, our Maker and Demiurge" (*Haer.* 5.17.1), who has "created and fashioned all things" (*Epid.* 4). Theophilus of Antioch labels God the "Maker and Demiurge of all things" (*Autol.* 2.34). In the *Epistle to Diognetus*, God is the "Master and Demiurge of all things" out of his goodness (*Diogn.* 8.7).

Authors explain how God's demiurgical work takes place explicitly through the Logos or Son. Aristides designated God as the "the creator and demiurge of all things through the only-begotten Son and the Holy Spirit" (*Apol.* 15 [Gk]). Athenagoras referred to God as the "demiurge of the universe" who "demiurged all things by the Logos" (*Leg.* 6.2). Irenaeus described the "uncreated God—the Father planning everything well and giving his commands, the Son carrying these into execution and performing the work of demiurging, and the Spirit nourishing and increasing what is made" (*Haer.* 4.38.3; cf. 1.15.5; 2.1.1). Tatian declared the Logos as "begotten in the beginning, who begat in turn our world, having first demiurged for himself the necessary matter" (*Orat.* 5). In the *Epistle to Diognetus*, God is the "Master and Demiurge" (8.7), but the Word too is the "Designer and Demiurge of the universe" by whom God created and sustains all things (*Diogn.* 7.2).

Origen responded to Celsus' objection that the world was created over six days by saying that the Word/Son of God is the "the immediate demiurge [*prosechōs dēmiourgon*], and, as it were, very maker of the world," whereas "the Father of the Word, by commanding his own Son—the Word—to create the world, is the *first* demiurge [*prōtōs dēmiourgon*]" (*Cels.* 6.60).

There are other mentions of Christ as the demiurge as well. Tatian claimed that the Logos was the "demiurge of angels" (*Orat.* 7). Clement of Alexandria surmised that "the Word, who in the beginning bestowed on us life as demiurge [*hōs dēmiourgos*] when he formed us, taught us to live well when he appeared as our teacher; that as God he might afterwards conduct us to the life which never ends" (*Protr.* 1). Origen predicates the title demiurge to Christ on account of him being God's generated Wisdom (*sophia*) and the beginning/principle (*archē*) of the universe: "Christ is, in a certain sense, a demiurge, since the Father said to him, 'Let there be light,' 'Let there be a heaven.' It is as principle that Christ is the demiurge, insofar as he is Wisdom, it is because he is Wisdom that he is called a principle" (*Comm. Jo.* 1.110–11). For the proto-orthodox, God is indeed the Creator and demiurge, fashioning by his Logos, but there is no other god involved in creation, and no other god or sequence of entities above them (Irenaeus, *Haer.* 1.10.3; 1.16.3; 1.22.1; 2.1.2; 3.3.3; 3.7.1; 3.16.8; *Epid.* 5; 99).

(4) Heterodox authors.

The most formative factor for the construction of the theo-cosmogeny of Gnostic systems was the influence of Plato's demiurgism and its reception in Middle Platonic philosophy.

Firstly, Gnostics[22] adopted Plato's crowded cosmos with its multiple ranks of heavenly entities who are delegated different roles in cosmic production (*Tim.* 27C–34B; 40D–41E). In Plato's theology, the demiurge and young gods exist within a divine hierarchy, and they generate mortal elements and lesser souls. Some Middle Platonists posited a thick distinction between the First Principle and the demiurge, while some Neo-Platonists postulated multiple demiurges functioning within cosmic triads. These platonizing schemes, where aspects of creation are attributed to a collaboration of intermediaries of various ontological states with demarcated roles, parallel the Gnostic systems of populating the pleroma and spiritual world with a dizzying array of entities.[23]

Secondly, Plato's demiurge became a central actor for Gnostic cosmology, theology, Christology, and theodicy. Plato's demiurge was good and aimed for good, but it was constrained by the nature of matter itself (*Tim.* 28A–E; 29A; 68E).[24] In contrast, Gnostic thinkers often proposed that the demiurge was less

---

[22] There are intense debates about the origins and definition of Gnosticism: (1) the genealogical definitions of heresiologists (Irenaeus; Eusebius); (2) an acute Hellenization of Christianity (Harnack); (3) an eclectic oriental religion of Iranian origin (Bultmann); (4) a type of theology with certain characteristics (Markschies); (5) biblical demiurgism (Williams); (6) a nebulous category that is broad to the point of being meaningless (King); and (7) a self-identifying group of Sethians (Brakke). I regard Gnosticism as one type of Christian appropriation of Middle Platonism generally typified by a negative evaluation of the material realm and the demiurge. For all the ambiguities and problems surrounding "Gnostics," we do well to remember that the second-century Christian bishop Irenaeus and the third-century Neo-Platonist philosopher Plotinus both refer to Gnostics as a discernible group to be refuted. I will continue to use the term "Gnosticism" in this broad sense, but where possible I will specify the groups referred to (e.g., Valentinian, Sethian, Marcionite, etc.). O'Brien (*Demiurge*, 205) notes: "'Gnosticism' is still a convenient 'label' to present an anti-cosmic tradition in which the Platonic Demiurge undergoes a radical transformation and in which the separation between the First Principle and the demiurgic one appears to reach its most extreme." See also Christoph Markschies, "Gnosis/Gnostizismus," in *RGG* (Tübingen: Mohr Siebeck, 2000), 3:1045.

[23] Philo (*QE* 2.68) sees a heavenly hierarchy with the uncreated God, the Logos, then other unnumbered and unnamed powers besides. Note too the creation of archons and angels in the Sethian *Ap. John* 10.20–12.13; 19.2–3; and critiques of the multiplication of entities in Irenaeus' account of Valentinianism in *Haer.* 1.11.1–5; 1.20.1; 3.16.8; 3.18.3; 3.24.2, and Plotinus in *Enn.* II 9 [33] 6.29–31. O'Brien, *Demiurge*, 28, 207.

[24] Precisely what Irenaeus (*Haer.* 3.25.5) points out by noting that Plato believed that God the creator was good and just.

than benevolent.[25] In fact, in some Gnostic systems, the demiurge's weakness was reconceived as nothing to do with material constraint or even negligence, and more to do with a moral deficit. Accordingly, Gnostic antipathy for the demiurge was based on the belief that the demiurge mistakenly thought that he was the First Principle, who created the world by himself and was ignorant about what he had created (Irenaeus, *Haer.* 1.5.1–6; 1.30.6; *Ap. John* 11.15–22; *Gos. Eg.* 58.25–59.9), or he was ignorant about the Father and he created the world in error (*Ap. John* 24.12; *Gos. Truth* 17.5–20; *Tri. Trac.* 105.19, 29–35). Or, in some cases, the demiurge was a wicked principality (Irenaeus, *Haer.* 1.27.2; Tertullian, *Marc.* 1.2; *Ap. John* 24.8–25).[26] The creator of the world was the "fruit of ignorance" (Irenaeus, *Haer.* 2.1.1; 5.18.1).

The demiurgism of Gnostic systems manifests itself in several different ways. For instance, Irenaeus described the views of Cerinthus: "Cerinthus... taught that the world was not made by the primary God, but by a certain Power far separated from him, and at a distance from that Principality who is supreme over the universe, and ignorant of him who is above all" (*Haer.* 1.26.1). In the Sethian *Apocryphon of John*, Sophia conceives without the consent of the Spirit, bringing forth Yaltabaoth, a demiurgical figure who makes the earth and Adam in collaboration with the archons and angels (*Ap. John* 9.25–19.33). The role of Jesus is to break the slavery of ignorance, evil spirits, and death introduced by Yaltabaoth (*Ap. John* 30.11–31.31). In the Valentinian *Gospel of Truth*, an emanation known as the "Error" or the "Oblivion of Error" is the demiurge who "became powerful" and "worked on its own matter foolishly, not having known the truth" (*Gos. Truth* 17.1–37). The Error/Oblivion came not from the Father, but because of the Father. It emerged due to ignorance about the Father, for when the Father is known, the Error/Oblivion is then extinguished. The role of Jesus Christ is to "enlighten those who were in darkness through oblivion" (*Gos. Truth* 17.37–18.19; 24.28–25.2). In the *Tripartite Tractate*, a revised Valentinian text, the Logos produces a chief archon known among other names as the demiurge, who with his angelic servants makes the world and Adam (*Tri. Trac.* 80.30–81.7; 100.19–35; 104.30–106.5). The Logos also produces the Savior, who reveals the Father to everyone inside and outside of the pleroma (*Tri. Trac.* 108.13–138.27). Heracleon, according to Origen (*Comm. Jo.* 2.8), believed that the aeons (i.e., pleroma) existed prior to the formation of the world, and the Logos was merely the commissioning

---

[25] See O'Brien, *Demiurge*, 140–41, 205–6.
[26] This was not universal, and Michael A. Williams (*Rethinking "Gnosticism": An Argument for Dismantling a Dubious Category* [Princeton, N.J.: Princeton University Press, 1999], 99–100) notes traditions where the demiurge is not necessarily evil.

agent who charged the demiurge to make "all things," which did not include the aeons (John 1.3).

That said, Gnostic systems did ascribe a demiurgical role to Christ at least as it pertained to the pleroma and the aeonic realm. Valentinus made Christ a heavenly demiurge as opposed to a creational one. Christ brought order back to the *pleroma* (Irenaeus, Haer. 1.4.5; 1.8.5), while it is stressed that Sophia produced the Demiurge, who made the world (Irenaeus, Haer. 1.5.1–2). In Clement of Alexandria's *Excerpts of Theodotus* (*Exc.* 45.1–3; 47.1–2), based on Valentinian sources, the Savior is the first demiurge of the outer world, while Wisdom is the second demiurge. Wisdom generated the "Father," the god through whom she then crafted heaven and earth. In *Ap. John* 7.30–8.27, Christ created the aeonic realm as structured around the four luminaries, but was uninvolved in the creation of lower realm that originated through Sophia. Similarly, in *Trim. Prot.* 38.7–12, the First Thought declared that "it is through me that the All took shape," which pertains to the aeons and their realm. Many Gnostic systems can be characterized as holding together both anti-demiurgical creationism and pro-demiurgical pleromatism.

The Valentinian teacher Ptolemy in his letter to Flora differentiated four beings: (1) the perfect God, (2) the demiurgical god of creation who gave the spiritual legislation of the decalogue, (3) the Devil, and (4) the Savior. Ptolemy cited John 1.3 to prove that God's demiurge is not the Devil since "the craftsmanship is that of a god who is just and hates evil" (*Flor.* 33.3.6; cf. Irenaeus, Haer. 1.8.5). The perfect part of the law—not the bits which are from Moses or from the elders—derives neither from the perfect God, nor from the Devil, but from the lawgiver. This lawgiver is "The craftsman and maker of the universe or world and the things within it. Since he is different from the essence of the other two [i.e., God and the Devil] and rather is in a state intermediate between them, he would rightfully be described by the name intermediateness [*mesostētos onoma*]" (*Flor.* 33.7.4). Importantly, the god/demiurge/lawgiver is neither good nor evil, but is just (*Flor.* 33.7.5). Concerning divine ontology, Ptolemy's perfect God is "one unbegotten Father, from whom are all things" (*Flor.* 33.7.6). The demiurge is begotten—he has an essence distinct from the Father and the Devil, he is inferior to the Father but is superior to the Devil, and he is the image of the better god. The Devil, then, is inferior to both the Father and the demiurge; his essence is "corruption" and "darkness" and is "material and divided into many parts" (*Flor.* 33.7.6–7). Where the Savior (i.e., Jesus) fits into this cosmological scheme and ontological division is not stated.

Marcion's view of the demiurge is notoriously hard to pin down, coming to us secondhand from the heresiologists, who perhaps misunderstood Marcion or else conflated him with other dissenting groups. According to heresiologists, Marcion believed in two demiurgic principles, one good and one evil (Irenaeus, *Haer.* 3.25.3; Hippolytus, *Ref.* 7.29–30). Tertullian (*Marc.* 1.2–2.1) claimed that Marcion found license for this dualism in Luke 6.43 about trees that bear good and bad fruit, respectively, and the statement in Isa 45.7 where Yahweh claims to "make weal and woe" (Isa 45.7).[27] Irrespective of whether Marcion thought the Creator or creation was the source of evil,[28] his Christ introduced "a new and foreign divinity" who was different in character and origin to the Creator (Tertullian, *Marc.* 2.1; cf. Ps.-Clem. *Hom.* 3.38). Certain Marcionites might be among the "thoughtless people" whom Ptolemy criticized for attributing creation to a "pernicious" demiurge rather than to a just one (*Flor.* 33.3.6).[29]

(5) Comparative analysis.

In terms of a comparative analysis between demiurgical and christological discourses, we can conclude the following about Christian notions of the demiurge: (1) God the Father and Christ are identified as dual demiurgical figures (i.e., cosmic craftsmen). (2) Whereas the Platonic First Principle does not cooperate or co-opt the demiurge to create/fashion the world, there is a close relationship in proto-orthodox discourse between God and the Logos/Son in the crafting of creation. Often, God "demiurges" through the Logos/Son. (3) Unlike Platonic and Gnostic demiurgical systems, the apostolic and proto-orthodox Christ does not generate other lesser entities to accomplish or manage the work of creation.[30] (4) Christ is explicitly differentiated from

---

[27] Such views were clearly in the air, as Plutarch (*Is. Os.* 46) testifies: "The great majority of the wisest of men hold this opinion: they believe that there are two gods, rivals as it were, the one the Artificer of good and the other the demiurge of evil. There are also those who call the better one a god and the other a daemon, as, for example, Zoroaster the sage."

[28] See Judith M. Lieu, *Marcion and the Making of a Heretic: God and Scripture in the Second Century* (Cambridge: Cambridge University Press, 2015), 348–57.

[29] It is interesting that both Ptolemy (from the Valentinians [*Flor.* 33.3.5–6]) and Irenaeus (from the proto-orthodox [*Haer.* 3.11.1–2]) both appeal to the Johannine prologue to refute Marcion. See Tuomas Rasimus, "Ptolemaeus and the Valentinian Exegesis of John's Prologue," in *The Legacy of John: Second-Century Reception of the Fourth Gospel*, ed. Tuomas Rasimus (NovTSup 132; Leiden: Brill, 2010), 153: "both Irenaeus and Ptolemy have utilized an already established anti-Marcionite use of the prologue."

[30] Hence John 1.3, "*without him* nothing came into being," from which Barrett (*St. John*, 156) comments: "There was no other demiurge"; similar was Rudolf Bultmann (*The Gospel of John: A Commentary* [Philadelphia: Westminster, 1971], 29): "The figure of the Logos stands alone between God and the world." Also, note Jörg Frey ("The Johannine Logos and the Reference to the Creation of the World in Its Second Century Receptions," in *Les Judaïsmes dans tours leurs états aux Ier-IIIe siècles [les Judéens des synagogues, les chrétiens et les rabbins]*, ed. C. Clivaz [Turnhout: Brepols, 2015], 231): "This means that any distinction

the creational demiurge in Gnostic systems because the demiurge is normally ignorant, inferior, or insidious even if sometimes repentant and righteous. (5) In Gnostic schemes, Christ does appear as the creator, curator, and purifier of the pleroma and aeonic orders, but always distinguished from material creation.

Some Christian authors positively employed the image of the demiurge to describe both God the Father and the divine Son as the cosmic craftsmen who formed the universe. Here, the demiurgical role was admittedly shorn of its Platonic framework, but demiurgy was positively utilized as a fitting image in a biblical exposition of the divine work of creation. Quite strikingly, the Platonic gap between the First Principle and the demiurge is functionally flattened by attributing creation, or at least different aspects of it, to the Father and Son even as they remained distinct personal entities. In Christian appropriations, the demiurgical role indicates the god-ness of the Son by making the Son co-crafter with the Father (esp. in the *Epistle to Diognetus*, Athenagoras, and Clement of Alexandria). John the Evangelist, Justin, and other apologists rehearse a Stoic interpretation of the demiurge in their identification of the Son as the Logos, the intermediary intelligence of creation, which evinces a different suite of operations and nuances (see below). Gnostic authors were naturally resistant to ascribing demiurgical roles to Jesus since Jesus was a Savior sent by the supreme God and not creation's progenitor. In Gnostic treatments, Jesus is an intermediary, but not a demiurge.

Logos

The *Logos* was originally developed as a philosophical concept about a rational principle that mediated between the transcendent and material worlds. The concept of the Logos developed in Stoic and platonizing systems of thought, it was reinterpreted in light of religious traditions by both Philo and Plutarch, and it was given a thorough Christianization by John the Evangelist and several authors in the second century. As a result, Logos Christology would become one of the primary modes of discourse in Christianity for espousing Jesus' intense identification with the God of Israel and his involvement in the divine world of the pleroma.

(1) Greco-Roman philosophy.

In ancient philosophy an entity called the Logos could be postulated in discussions related to math, grammar, logic, rhetoric, psychology, anthropology,

---

between the true God and another deity or creator is precluded. The Logos is not another God, nor a minor 'demiurge.' Thus, the later readings of the prologue that try to insert a division between the true God and the Logos, are obviously in contrast with the intention not only of John 1:1–2 but of the whole gospel."

ethics, cosmology, and theology.³¹ Logos discourses are usually connected with the notions of universal rational thought as well as the underlying basis for the metaphysics of reality.³² The pre-Socratic philosopher Heraclitus (ca. 500 BCE) identified the Logos as a principle of cosmic order (i.e., the rational aspect of the universe). It was "reason" (i.e., Logos), Heraclitus taught, that "guides all the world everywhere" (Diogenes Laertius, *Liv.* 9.1.1). Added to that, for Heraclitus, a supreme deity was the sum of dualities between day/night, summer/winter, and war/peace, etc. In which case, it was a short step from identifying an all-pervasive and immanent deity as the Logos.³³ This is probably why Heraclitus' Logos was incorporated into Stoic philosophy with an application to cosmology and theology. Among the Stoa, the creative principle that made the universe rationally intelligible went under several names, including Logos, Zeus, Pronoia, Fate, etc. (Diogenes Laertius, *Liv.* 7.134, 136). The Logos can be materially manifest as fire or pneuma and seeded into matter.³⁴ "In the monistic system of the Stoics," writes Udo Schnelle, "the Logos is the power that penetrates all bodies. In the conception of the *logoi spermatikoi*, the Stoics develop the basic idea of the ubiquitous presence of the divine that 'passed through matter like honey passing through honeycombs' (*SVP* 1.42, 1–3). According to the Stoic conception there was, is, and will be nothing in the world without the Logos."³⁵

One example of the Stoic Logos is well illustrated by Cleanthes' *Hymn to Zeus* (third century BCE):³⁶

---

³¹ See introductions in Thomas H. Tobin, "Logos," *ABD* 4:348–56; idem, "Logos," in *The Eerdmans Dictionary of Early Judaism*, ed. John J. Collins and Daniel C. Harlow (Grand Rapids: Eerdmans, 2010), 894–96; David T. Runia, "Logos," in *Dictionary of Deities and Demons in the Bible*, ed. Karel van der Toorn, Bob Becking, and Pieter W. van der Horst (Grand Rapids: Eerdmans, 1999), 525–31; Benjamin E. Reynolds, "Logos," in *Dictionary of Jesus and the Gospels*, ed. J. B. Green, J. K. Brown, and N. Perrin (Downers Grove, Ill.: InterVarsity, 2013), 523–26; and Frey, "Between Torah and Stoa," 202–19.

³² Frey, "Between Torah and Stoa," 203.

³³ Runia, "Logos," 526.

³⁴ Runia, "Logos," 526.

³⁵ Udo Schnelle, "Philosophische Interpretation des Johannesevangeliums: Voraussetzungen, Methoden und Perspektiven," in *The Prologue of the Gospel of John: Its Literary, Theological, and Philosophical Contexts*, ed. Jan G. van der Watt, R. Alan Culpepper, and Udo Schnelle (WUNT 359; Tübingen: Mohr Siebeck, 2016), 177: "Im monistischen System der Stoa ist der Logos die alle Körper durchdringende Kraft. In der Vorstellung der *logoi spermatikoi* entfaltet die Stoa den Grundgedanken der ubiquitären Answesenheit des Göttlichen in der durch die Materie 'hindurchgegangen wie der Honig durch die Waben' (SP 1:42, 1–3). Nach stoischer Vorstellung war, ist und wird in der Welt nichts seine ohne den Logos."

³⁶ See Johan C. Thom, *Cleanthes' Hymn to Zeus: Text, Translation, and Commentary* (Tübingen: Mohr Siebeck, 2005).

Noblest of immortals, many-named, always all-powerful
Zeus, first cause and ruler of nature, governing everything with your law,
Greetings! For it is right for all mortals to address you:
for we have our origin in you, bearing a likeness to God,
we, alone of all that live and move as mortal creatures on earth.
Therefore I shall praise you constantly; indeed I always sing of your rule.
This whole universe, spinning around the earth, truly
obeys you wherever you lead, and is readily ruled by you;
such a servant do you have between your unconquerable hands,
the two-edged, fiery, ever-living thunderbolt.
For by its stroke all works of nature <are guided>.
With it you direct the universal reason, which permeates
everything, mingling with the great and the small lights.
Because of this you are so great, the highest king for ever.
Not a single deed takes place on earth without you, God,
nor in the divine celestial sphere nor in the sea,
except what bad people do in their folly.
But you know how to make the uneven even
and to put into order the disorderly; even the unloved is dear to you.
For you have thus joined everything into one, the good with the bad,
that there comes to be one ever-existing rational order for everything.
This all mortals that are bad flee and avoid,
the wretched, who though always desiring to acquire good things,
neither see nor hear God's universal law,
obeying which they could have a good life with understanding.
But they on the contrary rush without regard to the good, each after
    different things,
some with a belligerent eagerness for glory,
others without discipline intent on profits,
others yet on indulgence and the pleasurable actions of the body.
<They desire the good,> but they are borne now to this, then to that,
while striving eagerly that the complete opposite of these things happen.
But all-bountiful Zeus, cloud-wrapped ruler of the thunderbolt,
deliver human beings from their destructive ignorance;
disperse it from their souls; grant that they obtain
the insight on which you rely when governing everything with justice;
so that we, having been honored, may honor you in return,
constantly praising your works, as befits
one who is mortal. For there is no other greater privilege for mortals
or for gods than always to praise the universal law in justice.
   (Strobaeus, *Anth.* 1.1.12 [trans. J. C. Thom]).

Minucius Felix summarized Cleanthes as teaching that God is "a mind, now of a soul, now of air, but for the most part of reason" (*Oct.* 19). That observation comports with the theological distinctive of Stoicism, where "God" was entirely immanent within nature as the substance constituting the one divine reality, a reality unified by the Logos as the rationale principle or law of the universe. In some cases, an actual physical element, like air or fire, guided or illuminated all things. As God is one with the world, so God's rationality permeates all things. It is to this end that Cleanthes depicted Zeus as the governor of the world, as well as its integrating point and very fullness. Similarly, in the second/third century CE, the Stoic philosopher Diogenes Laertius considered God as one with "Reason, Fate, and Zeus," and this polyonomous Logos constituted the "seminal reason of the universe" (*Liv.* 7.135–36). In the Stoic sphere, the Logos was the ubiquity of divine rationality that holds all things together.

Many Middle Platonists adopted the Stoic Logos into their systems to describe God's creative reasoning that was active in forming the world and something embedded in human noetic faculties. But Middle Platonists did not generally embrace the monism of the Stoics; instead, they were dualists, postulating two divine realities: a primary reality of God that was an immaterial and noetic realm, and a secondary reality governed by the demiurge and its subordinates, who were responsible for the ordering of the material world. Middle Platonists were able to move beyond regarding the Logos as purely a divine rationality immanent within the universe by combining it with a notion of a divine hypostasis instantiated in a deity. Two good examples come from the first century of Middle Platonists discoursing on the Logos. Plutarch described the Logos as the one rationality that binds the universe together, and he identified it with the Egyptian deity Osiris (*Is. Os.* 67). Plutarch also regarded Hermes as the Logos, who testifies to Nature's creation of the world (*Is. Os.* 54; cf. Plato, *Crat.* 407e–408b). Similarly, Cornutus wrote about how "Hermes represents the Logos, whom the gods sent down to us from heaven, when they made man alone of all living creatures on earth as a rational creature, a characteristic which they themselves regarded as superior to others."[37]

(2) Jewish tradition.

In Jewish tradition God's word (Hebrew: *dābār*; Aramaic: *memra*; Greek: *Logos*) functioned as the divine instrument in the world, specifically associated with creation, revelation, instruction, and salvation. The Jewish Scriptures portray God creating the world by creative fiat: "God *said*, 'Let there be light'; and there was light" (Gen 1.3; cf. 1.6, 9, 11, 14, 20, 24, 26). God's verbal power was later

---

[37] Cited in Runia, "Logos," 527.

identified as the instrumental force behind the divine work of creation. For example, "By the word of the LORD the heavens were made" (Ps 33.6); "God of my ancestors and Lord of mercy, who have made all things by your word" (Wis 9.1); "By the word of the Lord his works are made" (Sir 42.15); "He himself made these things with a word, and all came to be" (*Sib. Or.* 1.19; 3.20); "He made heaven and earth, and by the word of his mouth" (4Q381 I 3); and "O Lord, you spoke at the beginning of creation, and said on the first day, 'Let heaven and earth be made,' and your word accomplished the work" (*4 Ezra* 6.38). There are similar remarks about God's word going forth in redemption and judgment so that God's word brings about the events of which it speaks about (e.g., Ps 107.20; 147.15, 18; Isa 9.8; 55.10–11; Hab 3.5 [LXX]; Wis 18.14–16). Philo, as we will see, is a clear example of someone who found it possible to marry together the Logos of philosophy with the Logos of the Septuagint.

Closely related is the importance of Wisdom for understanding Logos Christology. In Jewish and Christian literature, the roles attributed to God's Word and Wisdom are often set in parallel (e.g., Wis 7.26; 9.1–2, 18.15; *2 En.* 33.4; Col 3.16; Justin, *Dial.* 129.3–4; Athenagoras, *Leg.* 10.3–4; Theophilus, *Autol.* 2.15; Irenaeus, *Haer.* 4.20.1). Unsurprisingly, John's testimony to the Logos closely mirrors Jewish wisdom traditions, especially the association of Wisdom with a divine craftsman, light, life, and tabernacling (Prov 8.22–23, 30; Wis 7.26, 29; 8.6; 9.9; Sir 4.12; 24.8; 43.26; *1 En.* 42.2). John's prologue fuses Jewish wisdom traditions with a suite of christological commitments to declare that God's Wisdom or Word becomes the fully human Jesus. Furthermore, in the Aramaic Targumim, God's *memra* sometimes becomes a circumlocution for God. In the case of the Targum Onqelos, whereas the Hebrew of Gen 3.8 says, "They heard the sound of the Lord," in the targum this is transformed into "They heard the voice of the *memra* of the Lord God."[38] Rabbinic literature also engages in a frequent personification of God's Torah as God's partner and even a spouse for Israel.[39] Several commentators see in these targumim and rabbinic writings the closest parallels to John's Logos Christology.[40]

---

[38] Cited from Barrett, *St. John*, 153.

[39] Craig S. Keener, *The Gospel of John* (2 vols.; Grand Rapids: Baker, 2010), 1:359–60.

[40] See Daniel Boyarin, "The Gospel of the *Memra*: Jewish Binitarianism and the Prologue to John," *HTR* 94 (2001): 243–84. According to Boyarin (270–71): "They are not the formal model for the Prologue to John, but, as the intertext for the Logos midrash of the Prologue to John, they do provide us with access to a pre-Christian world of ideas in which Wisdom was personified and characterized in ways that are very similar to the Logos of Logos theology." Sean M. McDonough (*Christ as Creator: Origins of a New Testament Doctrine* [Oxford: Oxford University Press, 2009], 77) is more circumspect: "The specific influence of *Memra* theology on the New Testament can only remain an intriguing possibility."

For the most part what we find in Israel's sacred literature is not so much a clear depiction of God's word as a divine hypostasis but more of a metaphorical way of describing God's action and immanence. That language, to be fair, was certainly open to wider philosophical interpretation, as Philo, the targumim, and rabbinic corpora demonstrate. All in all, the Johannine Logos is unimaginable and unintelligible apart from prior Jewish texts and traditions about God's word in creation and redemption.[41]

(3) Philo.

Philo was certainly aware of the association between God's word and God's creative action. He noted at one point, "God spoke and at the same time acted, . . . this word was deed" (*Sacr.* 65). Yet Philo exceeded that assertion as he attributed a variety of functions and forms to the Logos that have various degrees of affinity with the Platonic demiurge, Stoic Logos, and Jewish wisdom traditions. The problem, as Darrell Hannah points out, is that "neither in Platonism, Stoicism nor Aristotelian thought do we find the kind of significance that the concept has for Philo, nor the range of meanings that he gives to the term *logos*." Resultantly, Philo "appears to be dependent upon a tradition in Alexandrian Judaism which was attributing a certain independence to God's word."[42] Yet that is exactly the matter in dispute, precisely how "independent" from God is the Logos for Philo. Philo's Logos is many things—a divine mind, a divine image, a divine hypostasis—but can also be understood as a subordinate or second power in the heavens, an intermediate figure between the transcendent, immaterial God and the material, terrestrial realm. The principal functions of Philo's Logos are typological, cosmological, and intermediatory.[43]

First, on the typological side, Philo's Logos is an archetype for God, the blueprint for creation, the image for humanity, and a priestly pattern.

---

[41] Cf., e.g., C. H. Dodd, *The Interpretation of the Fourth Gospel* (Cambridge: Cambridge University Press, 1963), 272; Craig A. Evans, *Word and Glory: On the Exegetical and Theological Background of John's Prologue* (JSNTSup 89: Sheffield: JSOT Press, 1993), 77–99, 113–45; James D. G. Dunn, *Christology in the Making: A New Testament Inquiry into the Origins of the Doctrine of the Incarnation* (2nd ed.; Grand Rapids: Eerdmans, 1989), 217–20; Keener, *Gospel of John*, 1:350–62; Frey, "Between Torah and Stoa"; Larry Hurtado, *Lord Jesus Christ: Devotion to Jesus in Earliest Christianity* (Grand Rapids: Eerdmans, 2003), 366–67; and Endo, *Creation and Christology*. Against Wilhelm Bousset, *Kyrios Christos* (Waco, Tex.: Baylor University Press, 2013 [1970]), who practically ignores Jewish precedents in his account of the Logos.

[42] Darrell D. Hannah, *Michael and Christ: Michael Traditions and Angel Christology in Early Christianity* (WUNT 2.109; Tübingen: Mohr Siebeck, 1999), 80.

[43] My taxonomy here varies slightly from Tobin ("Logos," 4:350–52), who prefers the division of cosmological, anthropological, and anagogical.

In relation to God, Philo says the "divine word" is the "image of God" and "chiefest of all beings," alone proximate to the truly existent One (*Fug.* 101). God's image in creation and humanity are not direct impressions, but patterned after the Logos. Concerning the cosmos, the whole of creation is a copy of the "divine image," which is the Logos of God, the sum and substance of the noumenal realm reflecting into the phenomenal world (*Opif.* 24–25, 29–31, 36). The Logos is the "rising one" of Zech 6.12, not a human person but a kind of noetic progeny, who is the reflection of the "divine image," and who shaped things according to "archetypal patterns which the Father supplied" (*Conf.* 60–63; cf. *Mos.* 2.127–29).

Humans reflect the image of God, a divine rationality resident in the soul, an image provided by the Logos (*Opif.* 24–25; *Conf.* 147; *Det.* 83; *Her.* 230–35; *Somn.* 1.75). It is striking how the anti-polytheistic Philo calls the Logos a second god as part of his explanation of Gen 9.6 (LXX). The rationale is that while God's image in humanity is indeed a God-image, it is nonetheless mediated via the Logos: "For nothing mortal can be made in the likeness of the most High One and Father of the universe but only in that of the second god [*ton deuteron theon*], who is his Logos. For it was right that the rational part of the human soul should be formed as an impression by the divine Logos, since the pre-Logos God [*ho pro tou logou theou*] is superior to every rational nature" (*QG* 2.62).

Further, the Logos is a type of priestly mediator, which is why the Logos is the high priest of creation who is typologically represented in the high priest of the Jerusalem cultus:

> For there are, as is evident, two temples of God: one of them this universe, in which there is also as High Priest his firstborn, the divine Word, and the other the rational soul, whose priest is the real man; the outward and invisible image of whom is he who offers the prayers and sacrifices handed down from our fathers, to whom it was been committed to wear the aforesaid tunic, which is a copy and replicate of the whole heaven, the intention of this being that the universe may join with man in the holy rites and man with the universe. (*Somn.* 1.215)

Consequently, the high priest of the Jerusalem cultus is—allegorically interpreting Lev 16.17 LXX—"not a man, but the word of God" (*Fug.* 108). In fact, the high priest, when presiding in judgment, disrupts the "boundary between God and human nature, as one less than God but greater than man," even though this applies only in name, just as Moses the chief prophet was a god to Pharaoh as per Exod 7.1 (*Somn.* 2.188–89).

The Logos is, then, a kind of divine noetic fullness that is reflected in the created order, a divine intelligence that corresponds to the human soul and mind (i.e., *imago dei*), and even God's priestly mediation to the world is mirrored in the Jerusalem cultus. Philo's typological imagery contends that not only is God the archetype of the Logos and the Logos is the image of God, but also the Logos provides the pattern for creation, humanity, and the Jerusalem priesthood.

Second, Philo's Logos is cosmological as the creative instrument by which the world was ordered. The "image of God" is not only typological but also is demiurgical as "the Word through whom the whole universe was framed [*dēmiourgeito*]" (*Spec. leg.* 1.81; cf. *Leg. all.* 3.96).[44] Philo declares God to be the "cause" of the universe, while the instrument is the "word of God through which it was framed, and the final cause of the building is the goodness of the architect [*dēmiourgou*]" (*Cher.* 127). The Logos is even a "glue and a bond and fills up all things with his essence" (*Her.* 187; *Fug.* 112; *Plant.* 8–10; *Somn.* 1.241; cf. Sir 43.26), which has affinity with the Christian Logos as sustaining the universe (Col 1.17; Heb 1.3; *Herm.* 91.5; *Diogn.* 7.2). According to O'Brien, Philo's Logos "is a mediating entity which functions as a co-Creator and plays an active role in the universe after genesis, although it does not compromise God's unity."[45]

Third, Philo's Logos is an intermediary figure described with a rich array of roles in Philo's combination of metaphysical speculation and biblical exposition.

On the one hand, the Logos is a divine personification, God's personalized thought, Wisdom, and power operating between God and humans. To know God truly is to know his Word, who brings one towards God (*Sacr.* 8; *Somn.* 1.65–69; *Post.* 16–20). God and God's Logos are divisible into two aspects, namely, God's creative and reigning powers (*Fug.* 95, 103; *Mos.* 2.99–100; *Her.* 166; *Abr.* 121; *QG* 2.16; *QE* 2.62, 68; cf. *Cher.* 27–29, where the Logos unites God's goodness and sovereignty). Philo calls the creative aspect "God" and the sovereign aspect "Lord," while both are facets of the "one true God" (*Mos.* 2.99–100).[46]

On the other hand, the Logos is a divine agent, separate from God and inferior to God, but with a supremacy over the heavenly hierarchy of subordinate beings.[47] We see this in Philo's designation of the Logos as the "charioteer

---

[44] See *Leg. all.* 3.96; *Migr.* 6; *Her.* 119; *Spec. leg.* 1.81; *Cher.* 127; *Sacr.* 8.

[45] O'Brien, *Demiurge*, 45.

[46] Larry Hurtado (*One God, One Lord: Early Christian Devotion and Ancient Jewish Monotheism* [3rd ed.; London: T&T Clark, 2015], 49) is correct to the point that divine personifications such as God's Word, Wisdom, Name, or other divine attributes never received their own veneration or cultic devotion in Greco-Roman Judaism, which is proof that they did not compromise God's uniqueness or oneness. Cf. Runia ("Logos," 527), who adds that unlike personified gods such as *Dikē* and *Tychē*, the Logos "is not personified as an independent deity, and is not the object of cultic worship in the form of statues or altars."

[47] Marian Hillar (*From Logos to Trinity: The Evolution of Religious Belief from Pythagoras to Tertullian* [Cambridge: Cambridge University Press, 2012], 58) comments: "The

of the powers," who holds the "reins of the universe" (*Fug.* 101). We observe that the Logos is the "divine reason, the ruler and steersman of all" (*Cher.* 35). While God is the king and shepherd over the elements, mortals, and deities, he sets over it "his true Word and firstborn Son who shall take upon him its government like some viceroy of a great king" (*Agr.* 51). While not everyone is yet learned enough to be considered "sons of God" (Deut 14.1), even so, Philo avers that everyone with a soul set on the pursuit of moral beauty can take their place under "God's firstborn, the Word, who holds the eldership among the angels, their ruler as it were. And many names are his, for he is called, 'the Beginning,' and the 'Name of God,' and 'his Word,' and 'the Man after his image,' and 'he that sees,' that is Israel. . . . For if we have not yet become fit to be thought sons of God yet we may be sons of his invisible image, the most holy Word. For the Word is the eldest-born image of God" (*Conf.* 146–47). Much like Zeus in the Stoic tradition, Philo's Logos goes by many names. The Logos is an "archangel" (*Her.* 205; *Conf.* 146), the "high priest of the cosmos" (*Fug.* 108; *Somn.* 1.215), the "Firstborn" (*Agr.* 51; *Conf.* 146; *Somn.* 1.215, 241), "God" (*Somn.* 1.230), "God's man," and the "Word of the Eternal" (*Conf.* 41). The angel of the Lord is God seeming to appear as an angel to who those who cannot see the "true God," appearing as "the angel of his Logos" (*Somn.* 1.238–39; *Fug.* 5). Even if the Logos is a "second God" (*QG* 2.62), it is "a god" differentiated from the "one true God" (*Somn.* 1.229–30).[48] For Philo the Logos is a mediator who stands "on the border to separate the creature from

---

Logos is more than a quality, power, or characteristic of God; it is an entity eternally generated as an extension, to which Philo ascribes many names and functions." This would seem to rule out the common idea that Philo's Logos is merely a divine personification, *pace* H.-F. Weiss, *Untersuchungen zur Kosmologie des hellenistischen und palästinischen Judentums* (Berlin: Akademie Verlag, 1966), 318–31; Dunn, *Christianity in the Making*, 220–30; Maurice Casey, *From Jewish Prophet to Gentile God* (Louisville, Ky.: Westminster John Knox, 1991), 84; Aquila H. I. Lee, *From Messiah to Preexistent Son: Jesus' Self-Consciousness and Early Christian Exegesis of Messianic Psalms* (Eugene, Ore.: Wipf & Stock, 2005), 72; Peter R. Carrell, *Jesus and the Angels: Angelology and the Christology of the Apocalypse of John* (SNTSMS 95; Cambridge: Cambridge University Press, 1997), 94; Richard Bauckham, *Jesus and the God of Israel* (Milton Keynes, U.K.: Paternoster, 2008), 16–17; and Hurtado, *One God, One Lord*, 41–49. This does not make the Logos an entirely independent entity, but more like a second power strangely within and beside God—almost like God's executive self, who can be spoken of in the third person. The Logos is somewhere between an aspect of God and an angel of God. See discussion in David T. Runia, "God and Man in Philo of Alexandria," *JTS* 39 (1988): 72–73, for the tension in Philo's thought on this point.

48 Cf. Casey (*From Jewish Prophet*, 93): "There is . . . no doubt that Philo was fully monotheistic in the strict sense." See further David Runia, "Philo, *Quaestiones in Genesim* 2.62 and the Problem of Deutero-theology," in *Armenian, Hittite and Indo-European Studies*, ed. U. Bläsing, J. Dum-Tragut, and T. M. van Lint (Leuven: Peeters, 2019), 259–69.

the Creator"; he is "neither uncreated as God, nor created as you [mortals], but midway between the two extremes" (*Her.* 205–6).⁴⁹

The hypostatic and agential roles attributed to the Logos in Philo's theological cosmology are united in the intermediate role that the Logos plays between the transcendent God and the rest of the universe. Philo, like other Middle Platonists, deploys the Logos as the intermediate metaphysical instrument through which the universe was originally crafted and continues to be sustained. The Logos shielded the transcendence of God and guarded the divine coherence at the core of the universe even as it imaged and mediated on God's behalf.⁵⁰

(4) Gospel of John.

The prologue to the Gospel of John is one of the Rubik's Cubes of biblical studies: a set of puzzles, riddles, and questions that challenge interpreters.⁵¹ Everything, literally everything about the prologue is disputed: religious background, origins, redaction, structure, intertextuality, literary analysis, narrative function, theology, and reception. I have no intention to explore them all. Suffice to say that John the Evangelist's opening stichs about the Logos are pregnant with a cosmos of theological significance. The notable words are, of course, John 1.1–5, 14: "In the beginning was the Word, and the Word was with God, and the Word was God. He was in the beginning with God. All things came into being through him, and without him not one thing came into being. What has come into being in him was life, and the life was the light of all people. The light shines in the darkness, and the darkness did not overcome it. . . . And the Word became flesh and lived among us, and we have seen his glory, the glory as of a father's only son, full of grace and truth."

In brief, John's prologue is a feat of christological midrash on Gen 1.1, intentionally merged with scriptural witness to God's creative speech-acts, primitive confessions of the preexistent Son of God, Jewish Hellenistic wisdom

---

⁴⁹ Also Chester (*Messiah and Exaltation*, 49): "Thus Philo cannot allow God to come into any direct contact with the world whatever; hence he uses the Logos as one of the many ways he has of expressing divine agency, and specifically activity, within the world, and portraying the active divine reason. Yet at the same time, the Logos is an intermediary figure and a person distinct from God; he moves between God and the human world, and is in some sense similar to both, yet is also distinct from both as well." Note that Origen can say that the Son is the same substance and nature of the Father (*Princ.* 1.2.6); he elsewhere says that Christ is an "intermediate between the nature of the uncreated and that of all created things" (*Cels.* 6.34).

⁵⁰ Tobin, "Logos," 4:350–51.

⁵¹ See Jan G. van der Watt, R. Alan Culpepper, and Udo Schnelle, eds., *The Prologue of the Gospel of John: Its Literary, Theological, and Philosophical Contexts* (WUNT 359; Tübingen: Mohr Siebeck, 2016); and Paul Anderson, *The Riddles of the Fourth Gospel* (Minneapolis: Fortress, 2011), 26–28.

traditions, and messianic discourse, and fashioned in such a way as to deliberately resonate with tropes in Greco-Roman philosophy.⁵² In effect, John takes the Logos, a malleable yet popular concept in Greco-Roman philosophy for cosmic rationality, and he baptizes it in Jewish wisdom traditions and re-codes it with christological meaning. The assertion is astounding, as Schnelle notes: "John is expressing a universal claim: the Logos Jesus Christ has come forth from his original unity with God, he is God's own creative power, he is the origin and goal of all being, and in the Logos Jesus Christ the religious and intellectual history of antiquity reaches its goal."⁵³

In Johannine testimony, the Word is more than an intermediary with unusual proximity to God; rather, the Word is intrinsic to God's self-revelation, shares in God's God-ness, demonstrates God's participation in humanity, and participates in God's unique identity as creator.

First, the statement that God has in the *archē*, eternity past, always had a Word, indicates God's intrinsic self-communicative nature and that God's self-communication consists of his Logos. The Logos emerges in vv. 1–5 from divine transcendence, even hiddenness, to bring illumination to those mired in noetic falsehood and moral darkness. The repeated imagery of "light" (*phōs*) in vv. 4–9 is indicative of the Logos as source and subject of a saving revelation analogous to Jewish depictions of Wisdom or the giving of the Torah.⁵⁴ In addition, the provocative point behind v. 18 is that no one sees God without seeing his Word, just as no one can understand the things of heaven except for the Son of Man, who came down from heaven (3.11–13), just as no one can hear God's voice, see his form, or harbor his word without believing in the Son (5.37–38), just as no one can come to the Father apart from him (14.6). The Logos is the sine qua non of revelation. After the prologue, the Logos Christology does not recede; it is, rather, modulated in the unfolding drama

---

⁵² Cf. Thomas H. Tobin, "The Prologue of John in Hellenistic Jewish Speculation," *CBQ* 52 (1990): 252–69; Martin Hengel, *The Son of God: The Origin of Christology and the History of Jewish Hellenistic Religion* (Minneapolis: Fortress, 1976), 73; Dunn, *Christology in the Making*, 213–14; Jörg Frey, "Between Jewish Monotheism and Proto-trinitarian Tradition Relations: The Making and Character of Johannine Christology," in *Monotheism and Christology in Greco-Roman Antiquity*, ed. Matthew V. Novenson (Leiden: Brill, 2020), 207; and Bühner, *Messianic High Christology*, 150–51.

⁵³ Schnelle, "Philosophische Interpretation des Johannesevangeliums," 179–80: "Johannes . . . drückt er einen universalen Anspruch aus: Der Logos Jesus Christus ist aus der ursprünglichen Einheit mit Gott hervorgegangen, er ist Gottes schöpferische Kraft, er ist der Ursprung und das Ziel allen Seins, und im Logos Jesus Christus findet die antike Religions- und Geistesgeschichte ihr Ziel."

⁵⁴ Cf. Endo, *Creation and Christology*, 217–20.

of the revelation of God's messianic savior. This is evident in the stress placed on Jesus' *logoi*, where the Word is expressed in the very words of Jesus.[55] Jesus' words focus on explaining the themes of life, light, truth, and knowing, with a particular emphasis too on the Father-Son relationship, which at least partly validates Bultmann's observation that the Johannine Jesus is the revealed *Revealer*.[56] The "one true God" (17.4), then, is "exegeted" (1.18) and made known (17.4–8, 26) in Jesus the Christ (20.31). God reveals himself as creator and savior only as God reveals, creates, and saves in, by, and through his Word. The Logos is, then, God in his revelation.[57]

Second, the prologue intimates what will be a key christological motif of the Fourth Gospel, namely, Jesus' preexistence. "The topic of pre-existence is gradually developed in the course of the Gospel," says Friederike Kunath, "and it climaxes in Jesus's farewell prayer, in connection with his departure and his glorification."[58] Whereas Mark introduces Jesus with the beginning of the gospel of God (Mark 1.1–15), John introduces his Gospel with the Logos at the center of the beginning of creation (John 1.1–3). John's prologue and the wider Gospel indicate far more than the Word's ideal or relative preexistence,

---

[55] See esp. Robert H. Gundry, *Jesus the Word according to John the Sectarian: A Paleofundamentalist Manifesto for Contemporary Evangelicalism, Especially Its Elites, in North America* (Grand Rapids: Eerdmans, 2002), 1–50. Oscar Cullmann (*The Christology of the New Testament* [2nd ed.; London: SCM Press, 1963], 259) wrote: "The word of Jesus—the word he preached—plays such an important part in the whole Gospel of John that one can hardly assume the evangelist did not think also of this 'word' when in the prologue he identified Jesus himself as the Logos.... [H]e brings the word, because he is the Word." Keener (*Gospel of John*, 1:334) notes: "The Logos theme actually does pervade the Fourth Gospel, if it is understood as portraying Jesus as the embodiment of Torah ... a theme presented in a variety of images throughout the Gospel." Also, Dodd, *Interpretation of the Fourth Gospel*, 265–67; Bultmann, *John*, 29, 83; Endo, *Creation and Christology*, 230–48; and Adele Reinhartz, "'And the Word Was God': John's Christology and Jesus' Discourse in Jewish Context," in *Reading the Gospel of John's Christology as Jewish Messianism*, ed. Benjamin Reynolds and Gabriele Boccaccini (AJEC 106; Leiden: Brill, 2018), 77–78.

[56] Bultmann, *John*, 34–35. But note Aloys Grillmeier's qualification (*Christ in Christian Tradition* [2 vols.; 2nd ed.; London: Mowbrays, 1975], 1:28): "Essential as the idea of the revealer is for the Logos, it does not exhaust it."

[57] Cullmann, *Christology*, 265: "The Logos is the self-revealing, self-giving God—God in action" (266).

[58] See Friederike Kunath, *Die Präexistenz Jesu im Johannesevangelium: Struktur und Theologie eines johanneischen Motivs* (BZNW 212; Berlin: de Gruyter, 2016), 266: "Das Thema der Präexistenz wird sukzessive, im Verlauf des Evangeliums entwickelt und es kommt im Abschiedsgebet Jesu, im Zusammenhang mit seinem Weggang und seiner Verherrlichung, zum Höhepunkt."

as if the Word were an idea or plan that God hatched in eternity past.[59] More concretely, what we find is what Ruben Bühner calls "the Johannine maximal preexistent christological assertions," where the Logos has the attributes of "uncreatedness" and "participates in the essence of the one God."[60] This maximal and personal preexistence is implied by the Word's intense proximity with God and agency in creation (1.1–3), then filled out with Jesus identifying himself with God's name as the one who "is" from Exod 3.14 (8.58), his heavenly origins (1.15, 30; 3.13, 31; 6.32–58, 62; 8.23, 42; 16.27–28), scriptural imagery that makes him the nexus between heaven and earth (1.51), and his sharing in divine glory prior to creation (17.5, 24). The accent on preexistence means that John describes the heavenly descent of a personal divine agent who is enfleshed as a human being.

Third, the Word is more than "towards" or "close" to God, as the Word "was God" and is therefore in an intrinsic unity with God (John 1.1–2, 18). John does not say that the Word is adjectively *theios* ("divine-like") as a lesser divine being, yet neither does John say that the Word is absolutely *ho theos* ("the God"), which would conflate God and the Word. Rather, John predicates *theos* of the Word so that Jesus is one with God although distinct in the Father-Son relationship and enactment of his mission.[61] What is striking is that this Word comes forth from a unity with God. John sets forth neither bi-theism nor modalism, neither the epiphany of an angel nor the metamorphosis of an Olympian god, nor the emanation of a lesser heavenly power.[62] Rather, the

[59] Of course, one should note the caveat of Nils A. Dahl ("Christ, Creation, and the Church," in *The Background of the New Testament and Its Eschatology*, ed. William D. Davies and David Daube [Cambridge: Cambridge University Press, 1954], 422–43): "The distinction between 'real' and 'ideal' pre-existence is often fluid, and so is also the distinction between existence from the foundation of the world, pre-creational or eternal existence." On the diverse modes of preexistence, see Gottfried Schimanowski, *Weisheit und Messias. Die jüdischen Voraussetzungen der urchristlichen Präexistenzchristologie* (WUNT 2.17; Tübingen: Mohr Siebeck, 1985).

[60] Ruben A. Bühner, "Die theologischen Implikationen der Präexistenzchristologie in Joh 1,1–3," in *Perspektiven zur Präexistenz im Frühjudentum und frühen Christentum*, ed. Jörg Frey, Friederike Kunath, and Jens Schröter (Tübingen: Mohr Siebeck, 2021), 207–8 (". . . die johanneische Maximierung christologischer Präexistenzaussagen . . . Attribut der Ungeschaffenheit . . . die Partizipation des Logos am Wesen des einen Gottes Israels").

[61] Bühner, *Messianic High Christology*, 152–53.

[62] Contra Adela Yarbro Collins and John J. Collins, *King and Messiah as Son of God: Divine, Human, and Angelic Messianic Figures in Biblical and Related Literature* (Grand Rapids: Eerdmans, 2008), 181. See rather Bultmann, *John*, 32–33; and Jörg Frey, "The Incarnation of the Logos and the Dwelling of God in Jesus Christ," in *The Glory of the Crucified One: Christology and Theology in the Gospel of John* (Waco, Tex.: Baylor University Press, 2018), 268–72.

Word's human existence witnesses to a figure who in the course of the narrative is declared to be equal to God (5.18; 10.33–34), to be one with God (10.30), to mutually interpenetrate him (10.38; 14.8–11, 20; 17.11, 21–23),[63] to be worshipped beside God the Father (5.23), and to share in God's eternity, glory, love, judgment, and deliverance (4.42; 5.22, 27, 30; 8.58; 12.47; 17.24, 26).[64] The relationship of the Word with God is never expressed as creation, emanation, or adoption, but in terms of begottenness (1.14, 18; 3.16, 18). The genus of sonship makes explicable the one-ness and sent-ness (8.29; 10.36; 13.16–20; 17.20–23) as well as equality and subordination (5.18; 14.28).[65] The opening words of the prologue intend a simple yet fundamental claim: God has an eternal Word, a Word that is interior to God and intrinsically God, as that which is true of God is also true of his Word.[66] The Word is not a "depotentiated divinity" but is to be understood as part of a "divine self-distinction."[67] The Word is not an "intermediate being" but part of "God's self-expression."[68]

Fourth, God's own Word enters into human existence and draws God into the experience of human life. At one level, there is nothing in vv. 1–5 that a Hellenistic Jew like Philo or the author of the Wisdom of Solomon would find

---

[63] This perichoresis, coinherence, or mutual interpenetration cannot be underestimated. Whereas many see an overriding christological subordination in John, Feldmeier contends that "reciprocal immanence trumps the subordination" (Reinhard Feldmeier and Hermann Spieckermann, *God Becoming Human: Incarnation in the Christian Bible* [Waco, Tex.: Baylor University Press, 2021], 333).

[64] Hengel (*Son of God*, 73) comments: "The christological climaxes of the Fourth Gospel, like 1.1: '... and the Word was with God and the Word was God,' or 10.30: 'I and the Father are one,' mark the goal and consummation of New Testament christology." Aloys Grillmeier (*Christ in Christian Tradition*, 1:26) is similar: "The climax in the New Testament development of christological thought is reached in John. His prologue to the Fourth Gospel is the most penetrating description of the career of Jesus Christ that has been written. It was not without reason that the christological formula of John 1:14 could increasingly become the most influential New Testament text in the history of dogma."

[65] Bousset (*Kyrios Christos*, 215) noted that in John "the concepts 'Sonship to God' and 'deity' move very close together." Grillmeier (*Christ in Christian Tradition*, 1:28) observed: "True, the two concepts Logos and Son are not to be equated formally. But in fact *logos*, *theos*, *monogenēs* at least imply the one and the same subject who is to be understood as pre-existent, beyond time and beyond the world."

[66] According to Grillmeier (*Christ in Christian Tradition*, 1:28): "The Logos is God in God, mediator of creation and bringer of revelation—and this in the full sense by virtue of his appearance in the flesh. He 'is' the Word of God in the flesh."

[67] Feldmeier and Spieckermann, *God Becoming Human*, 313–14.

[68] Michael Theobald, *Fleischwerdung des Logos: Studien zum Verhältnis des Johannesprologus zum Corpus des Evangeliums und zu 1 Joh* (Münster: Ascendorff, 1988), 491–92 ("Ein Zwischenwesen ist ihm der Logos nicht.... {aber} sein Selbst-Ausdruck").

remotely objectionable. That God's creative Word or Wisdom was involved in creation is a legitimate reading of Gen 1.1 in light of Ps 33.6 or Prov 8.22–23. All is good until one gets to vv. 14, 18 and rereads vv. 1–5 in light of John's provocative christological claims made therein. Greco-Roman "theology" was allergic to the idea of the gods taking on a true human form; they could only have a quasi-body and quasi-blood (Cicero, *Nat. d.* 1.18). Similarly, Jewish tradition could say that God's Wisdom came forth or God's word was revealed, but never that they became flesh; this takes us beyond the range of Jewish ideas of divine speech-acts, Wisdom's immanence, and the Word's efficacy.[69] What would be startling is the particularity (v. 14) and exclusivity (v. 18) of the Christology (i.e., God's divine Logos has become a human being who reveals God in a way that surpasses Moses, the prophets, and the sages). The language of John 1.14 riffs off Jewish wisdom tradition to make a striking claim about Jesus as God's Word in human flesh: "And the Word became flesh and lived [lit., 'tabernacled'] among us [*kai ho logos sarx egeneto kai eskēvōsen en hēmin*], and we have seen his glory, the glory as of a father's only son, full of grace and truth." It is notable that the metaphor of the body as a "tent" (*skēvos*) was known to Jewish and Christian tradition (Wis 9.15; 2 Cor 5.4; *Diogn.* 6.8; 2 Pet 1.13, 14). The tabernacling language too is significant as it is allusive to: (a) the tabernacle as the place for divine speech (Exod 33.9) and the presence of divine glory (Exod 40.34); (b) the prophetic promise that God would tabernacle among his people during Israel's restoration from exile (Ezek 37.27; Joel 3.17; Zech 2.14–15 [LXX]; *Jub.* 1.17; 11Q19–20 29.7–8); and (c) Wisdom coming forth from God and pitching her tent in Israel in the form of the Torah (Sir 24.1–23), or the "angel of God," who "tabernacled among men" in Jacob-Israel (*Pr. Jos.* A 4).[70] Thus, the tabernacling of the Logos is the dwelling of God's speech, Wisdom, and glory in the human life of Jesus, which is simultaneously the engrafting of humanity into the life of God.

Fifth, the Word shares in what made God unique as creator. Beyond the surprising idea that the Word is identifiable with Jesus the son of Joseph from Nazareth (1.45; 4.5; 6.42), equally striking is John's assertion that Jesus the Logos shares in the creator-creature division that separates God from the cosmic order. John declares that God makes himself known in the Logos enfleshed in the very cosmos that God brought into being through this very same Logos (1.1–3, 10, 14, 18). The Logos might even a cryptograph for the divine name,

---

[69] Dodd, *Interpretation of the Fourth Gospel*, 272–76.
[70] Cf. Craig R. Koester, *The Dwelling of God: The Tabernacle in the Old Testament, Intertestamental Jewish Literature, and the New Testament* (Washington, D.C.: Catholic Biblical Association of America, 1989), 102–4.

suggested by usage in *Jub.* 36.7, which mentions "the name . . . which created the heavens and the earth and all things together."[71] The implication is that Jesus the Logos is on the God-side of the creator-creature distinction. The Word is divine in the sense of being the uncreated instrument of creation.[72] This is expressed in the statement that "apart from him nothing came into being" (1.3), which underscores a lack of superior, inferior, and parallel figures who assisted in the creative act—it is God who creates by his Word alone.[73] The same language—"apart from him is nothing done"—is attributed to Yahweh in 1QS 11.11 and 1QH^a 9.20, and this language of "apart from him" was to have salient significance in proto-orthodox and Gnostic cosmologies to distance the Logos from other intermediary figures.[74] Bauckham offer a sagacious summary: "The opening five verses of John's Prologue, therefore, read in light of the later statement in 1.14 that the Word became flesh and lived among us as Jesus Christ, include Jesus in the unique divine identity by identifying him with the Word that was with God in the beginning and was God's agent in the creation of all things." Resultantly: "The statements place Jesus unequivocally on the divine side of the absolute distinction between the one Creator and all other things. By identifying Jesus with an entity intrinsic to the divine identity—that is, with God's Word—they include Jesus in that identity without infringing monotheism. The Word 'was with God,' but it was not another besides God—for it 'was God' (1.1)." Bauckham concludes: "Thus, the Gospel begins by engaging with one of the most important ways in which Jews defined

[71] Reinhartz, "'And the Word Was God,'" 80.
[72] Gabriele Boccaccini, "From Jewish Prophet to Jewish God," in *Reading the Gospel of John's Christology as Jewish Messianism*, ed. Benjamin Reynolds and Gabriele Boccaccini (AJEC 106; Leiden: Brill, 2018), 351–52; and Bühner, *Messianic High Christology*, 155–57.
[73] On God having no assistants in creation, see Isa 44.24; Sir 42.21; *2 En.* 33.4; *4 Ezra* 3.4; 6.6; Josephus, *Ag. Ap.* 2.192; Philo, *Opif.* 23; Justin, *Dial.* 56.3.
[74] See, e.g., *Odes Sol.* 16.18; *Keryg. Pet.* 2; *Gos. Truth* 37.21; *Flor.* 33.3.6; Justin, *2 Apol.* 6.9; Tatian, *Or.* 19; Athenagoras, *Leg.* 4.2; 6.2; 10.2; Theophilus, *Autol.* 2.10; Irenaeus, *Haer.* 3.11.1–2; 3.21.10; *Epid.* 43; *Diogn.* 7.2; Origen, *Comm. Jo.* 2.8. The theme of all things by God, without him nothing being done, is common in ancient hymnic literature; see Eduard Norden, *Agnostos Theos: Untersuchungen zur Formengeschichte religiöser Rede* (Leipzig: Teubner, 1923), 157–69, 349–50. But I am not so sure. The language of God making "all things" in the heavens and on earth "and all that is in him" is common in the Hebrew Bible and other writings (e.g., Exod 20.11; Ps 148.1–5; Neh 9.6; Jas 1.17; Rev 10.6). When combined with "apart from him . . . nothing" found in John and Qumran, the implications are even clearer. Admittedly, in Gnostic writings, the production of the pleroma and its aeons could be siloed from the creation of the material realm by a demiurgical figure. The question is whether that division was normal and widespread in Jewish writings and other expressions of Christianity.

the uniqueness of the one God—that is, as the sole Creator of all things—and uses this way of understanding the unique identity of God in order to include Jesus within it."[75] John's Logos is "God" and shares in a key attribute that makes God unique, namely, not being part of the heavenly cast or terrestrial creation.[76]

The Johannine prologue, then, functions like an operatic overture, a foreshadowing of the musical motifs still to come: Jesus as God's word-of-revelation, only begotten Son, light, life, testimony, truth, knowledge, glory, and even his rejection. Jesus is God's Wisdom and Word, demiurge and deliverer, made one with human flesh.

(5) Post-apostolic church.

The Johannine Logos had a momentous impact on the christological discourses of the early church, but it was more than mere repetition, as diverse *Logoi* emerged among proto-orthodox and heterodox groups. Of course, the influence of John's Gospel in the second and third centuries is deeply contested.[77] Many scholars regard the developing Logos Christologies of the apologists and Gnostic groups as altogether independent of the Johannine Gospel and more indebted to Middle Platonism, Stoicism, and Hellenistic Jewish wisdom speculation.[78] My intuition is that John's Logos was looming largely but sometimes quietly behind a lot of the Christology of the early church. This is supported by the observation that there is reasonable manuscript attestation for John's Gospel as early as the second/third centuries (P^{52}, P^{45}, P^{66}, P^{75}, P^{90}), and one can detect citations and allusions to John's Gospel in a wide variety of locations and literature that cuts across theological divisions well before the late second century (i.e., Papias, Ignatius of Antioch, *Epistle of Barnabas*, longer ending of Mark, *Epistula Apostolorum, Gospel of Thomas, Gospel of Peter, Gospel of Truth, Kerygma*

---

[75] Richard Bauckham, "Monotheism and Christology in the Gospel of John," in *Contours of Christology in the New Testament*, ed. Richard N. Longenecker (Grand Rapids: Eerdmans, 2005), 151.

[76] Cf. too Frey, "Between Jewish Monotheism," 209.

[77] Joseph N. Sanders, *The Fourth Gospel in the Early Church: Its Origin and Influence on Christian Theology up to Irenaeus* (Cambridge: Cambridge University Press, 1943); Martin Hengel, *The Johannine Question* (London: SCM Press, 1989), 1–23; Charles E. Hill, *The Johannine Corpus in the Early Church* (Oxford: Oxford University Press, 2004); Bernhard Mutschler, *Das Corpus Johanneum bei Irenäus von Lyon: Studien und Kommentar zum dritten Buch von Adversus Haereses* (Tübingen: Mohr Siebeck, 2006); Tuomas Rasimus, ed., *The Legacy of John: Second-Century Reception of the Fourth Gospel* (NovTSup 132; Leiden: Brill, 2010); Lorne R. Zelyck, *John among the Other Gospels: The Reception of the Fourth Gospel in the Extra-canonical Gospels* (WUNT 2.347; Tübingen: Mohr Siebeck, 2013); and Frey, "Johannine Logos," 221–44.

[78] Cf., e.g., Sanders, *Fourth Gospel*, 27; and Tobin, "Logos," 4:355–56.

Petrou, Basilides, Valentinus, Ptolemy, Heracleon, Justin Martyr, Tatian, Melito of Sardis, Montanus, P. Oxy. 840, P. Eg. 2). In other words, we have no reason to deny or doubt the widespread influence of John's Gospel.

The most immediate echo of the Johannine Logos Christology is within the Johannine network itself. Assuming the Johannine letters post-date the Johannine Gospel, there is a reflection of the Logos in 1 John 1.1–4 concerning the "Word of life" that was revealed by the Father and testified to by John the Elder. That is combined with emphasis on his messianic identity against apostates who returned to Judaism (1 John 2.2; 5.1) and his participation in human flesh against attempts by secessionists to insulate God's impassibility and immutability from material contamination by denying the enfleshing of the Logos (1 John 4.2–3; 2 John 7). Similarly, in the apocalypse of John the Seer, the parousia of the warrior messiah is described as the "Word of God," who brings divine vengeance on the persecutors of the saints (Rev 19.13). That is concurrent with an angelomorphic Christology reminiscent of Dan 10.5–6 (Rev 1.12–16) and an intensified vision of Jesus sharing God's throne and receiving divine cultic worship (Rev 5.1–14). In Johannine idiom, Jesus the Word is the incarnation of divine life, the worshipped Almighty, and the harbinger of divine judgment.

Turning to the apostolic fathers, the fact and extent of the influence of John's Gospel is disputed, but we do have tacit allusions to John's Logos at certain points. There is a possible echo of John 1.14 in the *Epistle of Barnabas* and *2 Clement*, where it is stressed that Jesus came "in the flesh," but the allusion is hardly overwhelming and the Christology of these texts does not appear to move in distinctly Johannine groves (*Barn.* 5.10–11; 6.14; *2 Clem.* 9.5).[79] More promising is that Ignatius of Antioch has a genuine incarnational Christology with Jesus as "God" in an absolute sense who came in the "flesh" (*Eph.* 7.2; 18.2; *Rom.* 3.3; *Smyrn.* 1.1; *Pol.* 3.2; 8.3). Ignatius' reference to Jesus as the "mind of the Father" (*Eph.* 3.2) is probably more indebted to a general Stoic notion of the *logos endiathetos* than to direct Johannine influence. However, Ignatius does underscore Jesus' origins and oneness with the Father, which has a very

---

[79] In the *Shepherd of Hermas* there is a reference to Jesus' preexistence: "The Son of God is far older than all his creation, with the result that he was the Father's counsellor in his creation" (89.2). However, we should resist attributing all mentions of the Son's preexistence to the influence of the Fourth Gospel. Also, in Aristides' apology, we read: "It is said that God came down from heaven, and from a Hebrew virgin assumed and clothed himself with flesh; and the Son of God lived in a daughter of man" (*Apol.* 2 [Syr]), but the mention of "flesh" cannot be taken as proof of Johannine influence. In *Mart. Pol.* 20.2 there is a doxology to "his only-begotten Son, Jesus Christ," which more closely aligns with Johannine idiom.

Johannine ring to it (*Magn.* 7.2 = John 10.30; 16.28; 17.11, 21–22). Furthermore, Ignatius makes an explicit reference to the Logos coming forth from God like a sound as the living reverberation of God's self-revelation (*Magn.* 8.2). To this Allen Brent comments: "Ignatius' references to becoming manifest in the flesh, to the Logos proceeding from God's silence,[80] to Jesus coming from and returning to God are unmistakably Johannine [*Magn.* 7.2; 8.2]."[81] Ignatius reiterates the Johannine network's emphasis on Jesus as a revealer expresses an absolute divine Christology that is clearly influenced by Johannine idiom.

In the sub-apostolic era, several writings convey the influence of John's Logos on their divine Christology. The *Odes of Solomon* is a Syrian text from the first quarter of the second century, reading something like a cross between the Qumran Hodayot (1QH) and the Gospel of John, Jewish in ambience, but hardly Gnostic as once thought.[82] The Odist's "Lord Messiah" (*Odes Sol.* 17.17; 24.1; 29.6; 39.11) is one who existed "before anything came to be" (*Odes Sol.* 16.18 = John 1.1), "before the foundations of the world" (*Odes Sol.* 41.15 = John 17.24), and "worlds" were created "by his Word" (*Odes Sol.* 16.19 = John 1.3). Further, the stich stating that "the dwelling place of the Word is man, and his truth is love" (*Odes Sol.* 12.10) is not a strict rehearsal of John 1.14 since there is no mention of the Word becoming "flesh"; rather, the Word inhabits people as a type of knowledge manifested as truth and love. While the Odist's Christology is slightly ambiguous on Jesus' humanity, the language of *Odes Sol.* 7.4—"He became like me . . . In form he was considered like me"—is no more docetic than Rom 8.3 or Phil 2.7. In addition, Christ is the preexistent Son of Man and Son of God, who was already worshipped by the holy ones (*Odes Sol.* 36.3–4), who humbled himself in his appearance (*Odes Sol.* 41.12–13), and who was exalted to lordship (*Odes Sol.* 29.6). The Odist also combines a trinitarian milk metaphor with the incarnation through Mary (*Odes Sol.* 19.1–11; cf. *Gos. Truth* 24.9–14). The *Odes* attest to how Johannine Logos Christology

---

[80] On Jesus deriving from divine silence, see also Irenaeus, *Haer.* 1.11.1, where he describes a Valentinian scheme that gave the name Sigē to the aeonic consort of Arrhetos, who together generated the Logos, Zoē, Anthropos, and Ecclēsia.

[81] Allen Brent, "Ignatius and Polycarp: The Transformation of New Testament Traditions in the Context of Mystery Cults," in *The New Testament and the Apostolic Fathers*, ed. Andrew Gregory and Christopher Tuckett (2 vols.; Oxford: Oxford University Press, 2006), 2:329. Unconvinced of Johannine usage by Ignatius is Paul Foster, "The Epistles of Ignatius of Antioch and the Writings That Later Formed the New Testament," in *The New Testament and the Apostolic Fathers*, ed. Andrew Gregory and Christopher Tuckett (2 vols.; Oxford: Oxford University Press, 2006), 1:183–84.

[82] Cf. Michael Lattke, *The Odes of Solomon* (Hermeneia; Minneapolis: Fortress, 2009), 12–14.

provided the scaffolding for an eclectic synthesis of materials that were eagerly consumed by proto-orthodox and Gnostic authors alike, who amplified the notion of the Word as the divinely revealed divine redeemer.

The *Epistula Apostolorum* is an epistle recounting a post-resurrection dialogue between Jesus and the disciples; it can be dated as early to the mid-second century, and arguably has a provenance in Asia Minor.[83] The document is ostensibly anti-Gnostic, with its denunciation of Simon Magus and Cerinthus as false apostles (*Ep. Ap.* 1.2; 7.1–4). The epistle rehearses an exceeding amount of early Christian literature, quite conspicuously John's Gospel. Johannine Logos Christology is discernible in its *regula Christi*:

> This we declare, that our Lord and Saviour Jesus Christ is God, the Son of God, who was sent from God, ruler of the whole world, maker of every name that is named; who is above all authorities, Lord of lords and King of kings, Power of the heavenly powers; who sits above the Cherubim at the right hand of the throne of the Father; who by his word commanded the heavens and founded the earth and what is in it, and established the sea, and it did not cross its boundary, and depths and springs to gush forth and flow into the earth day and night; who established the sun and moon and stars in heaven; who separated light and darkness; who summoned Gehenna, and summons rain in the twinkling of an eye for the winter time, and mist and frost and hail, and the days each in its time; who shakes and makes firm; who made humankind in his image and likeness; who spoke with the forefathers and prophets in parables and in truth; whom the apostles preached and the disciples touched. And God the Son of God do we confess, the Word who became flesh of Mary, carried in her womb through the Holy Spirit. And not by the desire of the flesh but by the will of God was he born; and he was swaddled in Bethlehem and manifested and nourished and grew up, as we saw. (*Ep. Ap.* 3.1–15 [trans. F. Watson])

Added to that is an account of the incarnation where Mary is impregnated by the word: "I, the Word, went into her and became flesh" (*Ep. Ap.* 14.6 [Eth.]). There is a constant repetition of phrasing tantamount to "I am in the Father and the Father in me" (*Ep. Ap.* 17.4, 8; 19.16). Plus another first-person self-description: "I the Word who became flesh and suffered" (*Ep. Ap.* 39.12). Yet the incarnation of the Logos in *Epistula Apostolorum* is explained in terms of an angelomorphic Christology: "It came to pass that when I came from

---

[83] Charles E. Hill, "The *Epistula Apostolorum*: An Asian Tract from the Time of Polycarp," *JECS* 7 (1999): 1–53; and Francis Watson, *An Apostolic Gospel: The "Epistula Apostolorum" in Literary Context* (SNTS 179; Cambridge: Cambridge University Press, 2021), 7–8.

the Father of all and passed through the heavens, I put on the wisdom of the Father and clothed myself in the power of his might. I was in the heavens, and archangels and angels I passed in their likeness as though I were one of them" (*Ep. Ap.* 13.1–2). The *Epistula Apostolorum* is proof that while John's Logos could be read as absolute divinity (Ignatius), much like the book of Revelation (Rev 1.12–16), it was possible to hold it in tandem with an angelomorphic Christology, a judgment explicable in light of Philo's identification of the Logos as an (arch)angel (*Conf.* 146; *Her.* 205; *Mut.* 87; *Fug.* 5; *Leg. all.* 3.177; *Imm.* 182; *Somn.* 1.239).

Among the noncanonical Gospels, the *Gospel of Thomas* alludes to the Johannine prologue: "Jesus said, 'I took my place in the midst of the world, and I appeared to them in flesh. I found all of them intoxicated; I found none of them thirsty'" (*Gos. Thom.* 28). The *Gospel of Philip* likewise declares: "the Logos went out from that place [i.e., heaven]" (*Gos. Phil.* 58.33). In both cases, the Logos is a revealer of truths outside or in contradiction to the errors of the proto-orthodox churches.

Valentinians engaged in a pleromatic exegesis of the Johannine prologue.[84] Such a move is understandable enough given the theological and cosmic terminology found in John 1.1–5 and the philosophical atmospherics of the second century. For a start, Plato had long argued that the First Principle was characterized by an irreducible plurality even with its inherent unity. A second-century reader steeped in Hellenistic metaphysics could be forgiven for reading John 1.1–3 and thinking of a universe filled with a First Principle and its many emanations and dyads. In addition, Aristotle listed six possible meanings of *archē* and concluded that it referred to a first principle, the first point from which something comes to be or is known by, a combination of thought, will, and essence (*Metaph.*1013a).[85] For most interpreters, the *archē* in John 1.1, understood in light of Gen 1.1 (LXX), means "beginning," the start of temporal sequence. Alternatively, "Beginning" could be a title for the Logos (Philo, *Conf.* 146) and Jesus as the Logos (Col 1.18; Rev 3.14; Justin, *Dial.* 61.1; 62.4; Tatian, *Or.* 5; Theophilus, *Autol.* 2.13, 20; Clement, *Eclog.* 4.1; *Strom.* 7.1; Origen, *Hom. Gen.* 1.1; *Comm. Jo.* 1.19). Understandably some Valentinians regarded Beginning, sometimes combined with Monogenes, as a cosmic principle who existed within a cosmic triad of God, Beginning, and

---

[84] Irenaeus, *Haer.* 1.8.5; 1.11.1; 1.12.1–4; Ptolemy, *Flor.* 33.3.6, 33.7.4; Clement, *Exc.* 6.1–4; 19.1; 45.3; Hippolytus, *Ref.* 6.42.2; Origen, *Comm. Jo.* 2.8.

[85] On Hellenistic philosophy about a First Principle, see Eric F. Osborn, *The Emergence of Christian Theology* (Cambridge: Cambridge University Press, 1993), 39–68.

Logos (Irenaeus, *Haer.* 1.8.5; 1.18.1; Clement, *Exc.* 6.1–4).[86] Accordingly, some Valentinians identified Christ as the sum of perfections within the pleroma, a hybrid aeon and angel (*Exc.* 23.1), who was inferior to the ingenerate Father, even to Beginning/Monogenes, and it was Christ's purpose to rescue spiritual beings trapped in error and the material world (Irenaeus, *Haer.* 1.1.1; 1.2.1–6; 1.11.1; 1.18.1). The Son took on "flesh" not as a "substance" (*ousia*) but as a "sketch" (*perigraphē*) of fleshly form, no different from his appearance to the prophets (*Exc.* 19.1).

The *Gospel of Truth* likewise engages in a pleromatic exegesis of the Johannine prologue (*Gos. Truth* 26.4–7; 31.4–6 = John 1.14; *Gos. Truth* 16.31–17.4; 18.11–21; 30.27–31 = John 1.1, 5, 9; *Gos. Truth* 37.20–24 = John 1.3).[87] However, in the *Gospel of Truth*, Jesus is not one of many aeons within the pleroma; rather, he is the Logos who came forth from the pleroma, the "thought" and "mind" of the Father (*Gos. Truth* 16.31–17.4; 37.1–38.6), the fruit of the Father's heart and the impression of his will (*Gos. Truth* 23.33–24.2), "by means of fleshly form" (*Gos. Truth* 31.5–6), the "Son" who bears the name of the Father (*Gos. Truth* 38.7–39.28). The Logos has a unique relationship to the Father, which is far more parallel to the role attributed to Beginning/Monogenes in other Valentinian cosmogonies as the only aeon capable of communicating the knowledge of the Father (*Gos. Truth* 23.19–24.10; 30.32–31.12; Irenaeus, *Haer.* 1.1.1; 1.2.5).[88] In which case, the *Gospel of Truth* "views the preexistent Word/Logos in a similar way to John as being equal to and one with God the Father."[89] The *Gospel of Truth* plays the Johannine Logos in a Valentinian key whereby the Father is uniquely revealed in the Son/Logos because the Son/Logos is a unique expression of the Father's own being.

(6) Apologists.

There is an intensification of Logos Christology among the early apologists, including Justin Martyr, Theophilus of Antioch, Athenagoras, and *Epistle to Diognetus*.

Justin makes no explicit mention of the Fourth Gospel, but it is far more likely than not that he knows of it and alludes to it,[90] as his Logos theology

---

[86] Cf. Rasimus, "Ptolemaeus and the Valentinian Exegesis of John's Prologue," 160.
[87] Cf. Rasimus, "Ptolemaeus and the Valentinian Exegesis of John's Prologue," 158–69.
[88] Peter C. Johnson, *The Gospel of Truth: Christology, Deification and the Kingdom of God* (PhD diss., University of New England, 2015), 47.
[89] Johnson, *Gospel of Truth*, 58.
[90] The reference to "new birth" and entering the "kingdom of heaven" in *1 Apol.* 61.4–5 is far more likely derived from John 3.5 than from an independent baptismal liturgy or general tradition.

is best understood in light of its Johannine heritage.[91] Justin's Logos is God's instrument of revelation to humans (*Dial.* 128.2). The whole world came into being by a "Word of God" (*Dial.* 84.2; *1 Apol.* 59.5; 64.5; *2 Apol.* 6.3).[92] The Logos goes under various names from Scripture such as "Glory of the Lord," "Son," "Wisdom," "Angel," "God," "Lord," "Logos," and "Commander" (*Dial.* 61.1; cf. 126.1; 128.1). The Logos is the seed of reason[93] by which philosophers and barbarians were able to know the truth (*1 Apol.* 5.4; 44.10; 46.1–6; *2 Apol.* 13.3–6). The "divine Logos" moved the prophets to prophesy (*1 Apol.* 36.1). Jesus as the Logos is, then, that "rational power" (*Dial.* 61.1) or "rational principle" (*2 Apol.* 10.1), who "acquired physical form and became a human being" (*1 Apol.* 5.4; 23.2; 63.10) by taking on "flesh" (*1 Apol.* 32.10; 66.2; *Dial.* 45.4; 84.2; 100.2).[94] Trypho sums up Justin's view of God become human: "You say that this Christ existed as God before the ages, then that he submitted to be born and become man" (*Dial.* 48.1). Justin writes that Christ was "born from God ... as Logos of God" (*1 Apol.* 22.2), born in a special manner from a virgin (*Dial.* 63–70; *1 Apol.* 21.1–2; 22.2; 23.2; 32.10–33.9; 46.5; 63.16).

The center of gravity in Justin's Christology is to argue for a God beside God the Father, a first Power, the firstborn and only begotten Son of the unbegotten Father, the Logos who is Christ (*Dial.* 61.1–3; *1 Apol.* 13.3; 21.1; 22.1–2; 23.2; 32.10; 46.2; 53.2; 60.7; 63.4, 10, 15; *2 Apol.* 10.3, 8). To that end, we can detect a very strong sense of divinity attributed to the Logos. The "Logos is divine" ([*ho logos theios*] *1 Apol.* 10.6; 36.1); he was preexistent before creation and "already existed as God" (*Dial.* 61.1; 62.1–4; 87.2; 129.3; *2 Apol.* 6.3). The Logos is "the son of the true God" (*1 Apol.* 13.3) and is worshipped (*Dial.* 38.1; *1 Apol.* 6.2; 13.3–4; *2 Apol.* 13.4). Even so, the Son is not the Father, but the "first-born Logos of God, is also God" (*logos prōtotokos ōn tou theou kai theos hyparchei*; *1 Apol.* 63.15). Justin's analogies for Christ's divinity vis-à-vis God the Father are like a thought from a mind or a fire

---

[91] Hengel (*Johannine Question*, 13) wrote that Justin's Logos Christology "is inconceivable without the prologue of John." For Hill (*Johannine Corpus*, 318), Justin's notion of Christ as "God's only Son, begotten in a peculiar manner is more or less simply a repackaging of John's notion of the pre-existent, divine Word, the monogenes of the Father." One would still have to admit that Justin augments the Johannine Logos with the "firstborn" of Col 1.15, marries it with the Synoptic infancy narratives, and identifies Christ with angelic traits. More circumspect is Frey ("Between Torah and Stoa," 199): "John could inspire all these ideas, but they are also easily developed from Philo and the Bible, in the context of Greek philosophy, and in dispute with contemporary Jewish views."

[92] Of course, Justin might mean "Word" here like Ps 33.6 rather than John 1.1–3.

[93] A clear allusion to the *logos spermatikos* of Stoic thought.

[94] Justin's favorite word here is the participle *sarkopoētheis* for "making flesh."

kindling fire. Jesus is begotten from the Father, not an excision (*apotome*) of his essence (*ousia*; *Dial.* 61.2; 128.3–4). Jesus is distinct in number, but not in substance (*Dial.* 56.11; 128.4; 129.3). Eric Osborn summarizes Justin's thought well enough: "The word is God's first-born, God himself, second to him in number, but one with him in essence."[95]

Yet Justin also implies a certain subordination because God is unbegotten and everything after him is begotten and corruptive (*Dial.* 5.4), and the Son holds "second place" with the prophetic spirit "in the third rank" (*1 Apol.* 13.3–4; 60.7).[96] Justin argues that the Logos is "another God and Lord under the Creator of all things, who is also called an Angel, because he proclaims to man whatever the Creator of the world—above whom there is no other God—wishes to reveal to them" (*Dial.* 56.4; cf. 55.1; 56.17; 61.1; 128.4; 129.4). This angel "called God, is distinct from God, the Creator; distinct, that is, in number, but not in mind" (*Dial.* 56.11). A God beneath God is supported by way of citations to Ps 45.6–7 and 110.1 (*Dial.* 56.14). Justin identifies God with the Angel of the Lord, and this Angel with the pre-incarnate Christ, who appeared to Moses in the fire (*Dial.* 57–60; 127.4; *1 Apol.* 62.3–4; 63.7–8, 17).[97]

Athenagoras of Athens wrote his *Embassy* ca. 177–76 CE as a defense of Christianity addressed to emperors Marcus Aurelius and Lucius Commodus. Athenagoras utilized the Hellenistic philosophical tradition to argue for the unity and aseity of God, a rejection of both polytheism and pantheism, and rebuffed the charges of atheism against Christians. He complained, "Now if Plato is no atheist when he understands the Creator of all things to be the one uncreated God, neither are we atheists when we acknowledge him by whose Logos all things were created and upheld by his Spirit and assert that he is God" (*Leg.* 6.2; cf. 4.2; 10.1, 5; 18.2). Importantly, he defended the idea of God having a Son, the "Logos of the Father, in ideal form and in operation; for in his likeness and through him all things came into existence, which

---

[95] Eric F. Osborn, *Justin Martyr* (BZHT 47; Tübingen: Mohr Siebeck, 1973), 28. Cf. Bousset (*Kyrios Christos*, 401), who summarized the apologists this way: "The Christians do not worship a man but the incarnate Logos, who belongs altogether to the very essence of deity."

[96] L. W. Barnard (*Justin Martyr: His Life and Thought* [Cambridge: Cambridge University Press, 1967], 100) points out: "It was inevitable that his unsystematised language about the derivative nature of the logos should later be capable of an Arian interpretation. Yet it is equally clear that Justin believed in the full Divinity of the Son." Grillmeier (*Christ in Christian Tradition*, 1:110) sees Justin's subordination in far more stark terms: "There is a *deus inferior* subordinate to the *theos hypsistos*" (italics original).

[97] Justin frequently cites Gen 19.24 (LXX): "The Lord rained down fire from the Lord out of heaven," in *Dial.* 56.23; 60.5; 127.5; 129.1.

presupposes that the Father and the Son are one" (*Leg.* 10.2). If God is "mind" (*nous*), then the Logos is his eternal reason (*logikos*), one with God, not created, but proceeding from him in a manner like Wisdom in Prov 8.22 (*Leg.* 10.3–4). Between God, the Son/Logos, and Spirit, Athenagoras refers to their "powerful unity in spirit," a "power in unity and diversity in order," and "unity in power yet distinguished in order" (*Legat.* 10.2, 5; 24.2). He said that those who are prepared for judgment know the oneness, communion, oneness, and variety in unity between the Father, Son, and Spirit (*Leg.* 12.3).

Athenagoras also used analogies to buttress the unity in the Godhead: "We say that there is God and the Son, his Logos, and the Holy Spirit, united in power yet distinguished in order as the Father, the Son, and the Spirit, since the Son is mind, Logos, and wisdom of the Father, the Spirit an effluence like light from fire" (*Leg.* 24.2). Notable is that Athenagoras differentiates the true, uncreated, and eternal God from the created order and posits the Son and Spirit on the God-side of that distinction (*Leg.* 6.2; 10.1, 5; 15.1; 18.1–19.3). In his argument, the divinity of God is not that of angels, a deified man, a daemon, or a created deity, so that the Son shares in God's unique, unitary, and uncreated divine nature (*Leg.* 10.5; 24.2–5; 27.1–30.6). Athenagoras, then, identifies God as the uncreated Demiurge with the Son/Logos as his chief agent, and describes their unity in being through psychological and pyrological metaphors. John's Logos Christology is undoubtedly constitutive for the incipient trinitarianism of Athenagoras, and he intensifies the shared divinity between the two. According to Frey, the interweaving of Johannine texts (i.e., John 1.2, 10.30, 14.10) means that Athenagoras "does not focus on the creatorship of the one God, but on the co-creatorship of the Logos" combined with "a deliberate stress on the unity between God and the Logos, against any idea of a plurality of divine beings or a split between God and Christ."[98]

Bishop Theophilus of Antioch wrote to his pagan friend *Autolycus* to convince him of the truth of the Christian religion ca. 180 CE. Among other things, like critiques of human deification and idolatry, he explains the divinity of the Logos: "Therefore God, having his own Logos innate in his own bowels, generated him together with his own Sophia, vomiting him forth before everything else. He used this Logos as his servant in the things created by him, and through him, he made all things. He is called Beginning because he leads and dominates everything fashioned through him." It was also the "Logos of God" speaking through Moses that caused Moses to write about the creative work of the Logos in Gen 1.1 (*Autol.* 2.10). In regards to reconciling God's

---

[98] Frey, "Johannine Logos," 241.

omnipresence with anthropomorphic descriptions of God walking in paradise, Theophilus retorted:

> The God and Father of the universe is unconfined and is not present in a place, for there is no place of his rest. But his Logos, through whom he made all things, who is his power and wisdom, assuming the role of the Father and Lord of the universe, was present in paradise in the role of God and conversed with Adam. For the divine scripture itself teaches us that Adam said that he "heard the voice." What is the "voice" but the Logos of God, who is also his Son—not as the poets and mythographers describe sons of gods begotten of sexual union, but as the truth describes the Logos, always innate in the heart of God. (*Autol.* 2.22)

Theophilus then explains the Logos' divinity using the mind-thought metaphor: "For before anything came into existence he had this as his Counsellor, his own Mind and Intelligence. When God wished to make what he had planned to make, he generated this Logos, making him external, as the firstborn of all creation. He did not deprive himself of the Logos but generated the Logos and constantly converses with his Logos." What immediately follows is a citation of John 1.1–3, to which Theophilus explains: "Since the Logos is God and derived his nature from God, whenever the Father of the universe wills to do so he sends him into some place where he is present and is heard and seen" (*Autol.* 2.22). Theophilus offers an instance of exegesis of John 1.1–3 that accents the ontological unity between God and his Logos.

The *Epistle to Diognetus* is ordinarily placed among the apostolic fathers even though it is generically closer to the apologists, while the homiletical additions in chapters 11–12 resemble the interpretive style of *2 Clement*, Melito of Sardis, and Hippolytus of Rome. Dating the epistle is notoriously difficult, though most commentators prefer a date in the late second century.[99] At one point, the unknown author explains that the Creator "established among humans the truth and the holy, incomprehensible word from heaven and fixed it firmly in their hearts, not, as one might imagine, by sending them some subordinate, or angel, or ruler or one of those who manage earthly matters, or those entrusted with the administration of things in heaven." Instead, he sent them the one by whom he created the world, sustains its operations, and commands its obedience, namely, the Son (*Diogn.* 7.2). It could be the case that the "word" is brought by being taught by the

---

[99] Michael F. Bird and Kirsten Mackerras, "The Epistle to Diognetus and the Fragment of Quadratus," in *The Cambridge Companion to the Apostolic Fathers*, ed. Michael F. Bird and Scott Harrower (Cambridge: Cambridge University Press, 2021), 312.

Son rather than by an angel or another intermediary figure. But more likely, the true, holy, and incomprehensible word is none other than the Logos conceived as God's instrumental, integrative, and sustaining force over creation, and the Logos too is God's supreme agent in redemption (*Diogn.* 7.3–5). The acute point of Johannine influence is that no one else apart from the Logos/Son is involved in creation and the Logos/Son is explicitly differentiated from other intermediary figures.

The final two chapters of *Diognetus*, most likely secondary to the work, include a homily on the Word. The author claims that love for the "Word" emerges from knowledge of the "Word to the disciples." For it was to the disciples that "the Word appeared and revealed these things" (*Diogn.* 11.2). The Word, though "dishonored by the chosen people," was still "preached by apostles and believed in by Gentiles," and thus through apostolic proclamation the Word "appeared to the world" (*Diogn.* 11.3). This Word has its origins "from the beginning," and, though ancient, it is always new when born in the hearts of saints. Further: "This is the Eternal One, who today is accounted a Son, through whom the church is enriched and grace is unfolded and multiplied among the saints" (*Diogn.* 11.4–5). The commanding Word makes his instruction known through his disciples and their disciples, and those who accept it will receive its grace and increase in love for it (*Diogn.* 11.7–9). In the church's liturgical and catechetical life "the Word rejoices as he teaches the saints, the Word through whom the Father is glorified" (*Diogn.* 12.9). The author interweaves the apostolic word of Christ with the story of the Word as revealer of the mysteries of the Father and the conduit of divine grace.

The apologists stand out as those who engaged in philosophical exposition of the divine Logos as part of their theological explication of God's Word in the Jewish Scriptures and in Johannine prologue. Justin refers to the Stoic idea of the *logikos spermatikos* for the implanting of God's word in human hearts, which is none other than the germinal roots of the truth about Christ. Further, Justin, Athenagoras, and Theophilus all make a clear use of the Stoic distinction between *logos endiathetos* (word in mind) and *logos prophorikos* (word expressed) to explain the relationship of God the Father to the Logos. That said, the Word-Mind analogy can be explained in modalist, Arian, or pro-Nicene senses.[100] The author of *Diognetus* and Athenagoras differentiate the Logos/Son from other intermediary figures

---

[100] Tarmo Toom, *Classical Trinitarian Theology: A Textbook* (London: T&T Clark, 2007), 62–63.

of the heavenly hierarchy.[101] One detects too an explicit engagement with philosophy apparent in the citations of Plato, Aristotle, and others, as well as a creative interaction with scriptural traditions about God's own Wisdom, Word, and Law.[102] The apologists enterprisingly identified Christ with God's Logos and amplified the Johannine tradition by accenting the unity of God with his Logos.

(7) *Trimorphic Protennoia*.

One document that has excited energetic debate about its relationship to John's Logos is the *Trimorphic Protennoia* (*Three Forms of First Thought*) from the Nag Hammadi Codices.[103] The *Trim. Prot.* narrates the origins of the Protennoia, the divine First Thought, and its triple descent into the world in the form of Voice, Speech, and Word. There are affinities with the Sethian *Apocryphon of John* (30.11–31.25) and Irenaeus' account of the Barbeloites scheme (*Haer.* 1.29.1–4), which also describe a triple descent of Pronoia into the world. Most striking are the affinities with the Johannine prologue.[104]

John's Prologue	*Trimorphic Protennoia*
In the beginning	35.1–6, 33–34; 46.10
Word revealed	37.4–20; 40.29–41.1
Word	37.4–5; 46.5–6, 14–16, 30; 47.15
All things through him	38.12–13; 46.24–25
Light and life	35.12–13; 36.5; 37.7–8, 13–14; 41.16
Word became flesh	47.15–16
Word pitched tent	47.13–18
Only begotten Son	38.22–23; 39.6, 12–13

The third descent of the Logos drips with Johannine resonances, especially with John 1.14: "The third time I revealed myself to them in their tents as

---

[101] As does Irenaeus, *Haer.* 1.22.1.

[102] See Mark J. Edwards, "Justin's Logos and the Word of God," *JECS* 3 (1995): 261–80.

[103] On Gnostic exegesis of John's prologue more broadly, see Elaine Pagels, *The Johannine Gospel in Gnostic Exegesis: Heracleon's Commentary on John* (SBLMS 17; Nashville: Abingdon, 1973), 1–50.

[104] See Craig A. Evans, "On the Prologue of John and the Trimorphic Protennoia," *NTS* 27 (1981): 397; idem, *Word and Glory*, 50–53; and Paul-Hubert Poirier, "The *Trimorphic Protennoia* (NHC XIII,I) and the Johannine Prologue: A Reconsideration," in *The Legacy of John: Second-Century Reception of the Fourth Gospel*, ed. Tuomas Rasimus (NovTSup 132; Leiden: Brill, 2010), 97–99.

Word and I revealed myself in the likeness of their shape. And I wore everyone's garment and hid myself within them" (*Trim. Prot.* 47.14–18).[105]

Unsurprisingly, the *Trim. Prot.* has been treated as the Holy Grail of the pre-Christian Gnostic redeemer myth. Many commentators detected among its sources a preexisting Gnostic scheme that had been independently Christianized by John the Evangelist in his prologue.[106] However, the *Trim. Prot.* in its extant form is a third-century CE Gnostic text that has probably undergone a complex yet indeterminable composition history, including a genetic relationship with the *Apocryphon of John*, Gospel of John, and other Christian writings, most likely in terms of dependence upon them.[107] There is no evidence that *Trim. Prot.* is based on a pre-Christian myth of a Gnostic redeemer who descends to earth simply because no such myth existed as far as the evidence allows.[108] More likely, the Johannine prologue and the *Trim. Prot.* represent adaptations of Jewish wisdom traditions, with *Trim. Prot.* incorporating the Johannine prologue at some stage in its composition history.

The Logos of the *Trim. Prot.* appears in partial human form in "their tents as Word," the "likeness of their shape" (47.15–16), in partial angelic form in the "likeness" of angels (49.16), differentiated from the "Jesus" who was cursed on the wood of the cross (50.12–14). The Logos pervades all intermediary figures and inhabits all matter (47.19–25). But the Logos is not recognized by those who worship (48.15–35), and the archons mistake the Logos for "their Christ" (47.6–8). The Logos becomes the "beloved" of the archons, having disguised herself as Son of the Archigenetor, appearing too in angelic likeness to angels, and as a son of man among the sons of men, though she is in reality the Father of everyone (49.6–20). The chief functions of the *Trim. Prot.* Logos are revelation and illumination, bringing true Gnosis to true disciples about the tripartite story of the First Thought. In *Trim. Prot.* the author rejects the claim of the Johannine prologue that "In the beginning was the Logos" on the grounds that what existed in the beginning

---

[105] Cf. *Ap. John* 31.3–4: "I entered into the midst of their prison which is the prison of the body."

[106] James Robinson, "Sethians and Johannine Thought: The Trimorphic Protennoia and the Prologue of the Gospel of John," in *The Rediscovery of Gnosticism: Proceedings of the International Conference on Gnosticism at Yale, New Haven, Connecticut, March 28–31, 1978*, vol. 2: *Sethian Gnosticism*, ed. Bentley Layton (Leiden: Brill, 1981), 660–62.

[107] I concur with Evans (*Word and Glory*, 54) that "the burden of proof rests heavily on those who maintain that the Trimorphic Protennoia has not been significantly influenced by distinctively Christian ideas."

[108] Charles H. Talbert, "The Myth of a Descending-Ascending Redeemer in Mediterranean Antiquity," *NTS* 22 (1976): 418–40; and Hengel, *Son of God*, 33–35.

was not the Logos, but rather the silent divine First Thought, which was only later manifested as the Logos in her third descent. This Logos inhabited Jesus and all heavenly intermediaries; she rescued Jesus from his cross, then exalted him to the Father's dwelling place. Yet she was not recognized by the Christian assemblies, who foolishly supposed that Christ was the son of the world-creator.[109] In other words, the Logos is the docetic deliverer of Jesus and his ignorant worshippers. The result is a "polemical reinterpretation of the Johannine prologue" with a view to "devaluing the Johannine, and purely Christian, Logos and of elevating the Gnostic Logos."[110]

(8) Proto-orthodox theologians.

Early theologians represent another stage in the development of Logos Christology before Origen's contribution and the debris that followed in his trail, which was only gradually resolved in the tumultuous christological debates of the fourth century.[111]

Tatian's *Oratio* demonstrates a strong interest in the Johannine prologue for its cosmology and Christology. Tatian glosses John 1.1: "God 'was in the beginning' and we have received the tradition that the beginning was the power of the Logos." The Lord was alone in the beginning, and the Logos sprang forth from the Father as his "firstborn," a procession from within the divine power (*Or.* 5). Like Justin (*Dial.* 128.4) and Tertullian (*Prax.* 8), Tatian adds that the Logos emerged by "partition" (*kata merismon*), not by "excision" (*kata apokopēn*), the difference being that "what is cut off is separated from the original substance, but that which comes by partition, exercises a distinctive function and does not diminish the source from which whom it is taken." Tatian explains further: "For, just as from one fire many fires are lit, while the light of the first fire is not lessened by the igniting of many fires, so too the Logos, coming forth from the Logos-power of the Father, has not diminished the Logos-power of him who begat him" (*Or.* 5). Later, Tatian says of the "one God" that "all things were made by him and without him nothing has been made," a remark that either misreads the subject of *ginomai* from John 1.3, or else designates Jesus as "God" (*Or.* 19). Tatian presents a scheme whereby God is the incomparable creator (*Or.* 4), who generates the Logos from the same

---

[109] John D. Turner, "The Johannine Legacy: The Gospel and *Apocryphon* of John," in *The Legacy of John: Second-Century Reception of the Fourth Gospel*, ed. Tuomas Rasimus (NovTSup 132; Leiden: Brill, 2010), 123–24.

[110] Poirier, "The *Trimorphic Protennoia*," 94, 102.

[111] In addition to what is cited below, one can detect hints of a Logos Christology with a strong sense of Jesus' divinity in *Sib. Or.* 8.445–46, 469–73; *Keryg. Pet.* 1; Hippolytus, *C. Noet.* 16.

divine substance to be coauthor of creation (*Or.* 5; 19), who is set apart from intermediaries as one who was alone with the Lord in the beginning and is also the author of the angels (*Or.* 5; 7; 19). Tatian, writing during the 170s, during his pre-heterodox phase, affirms the Logos' same divinity with the Lord and the Logos' superiority to the angels as a restatement of the tradition that he has received.

Irenaeus was arguably the first great biblical theologian of the church, who deployed his unique synthesis of Greek philosophy with Matthean, Pauline, and especially Johannine thought to confront the Marcionite and Gnostic heresies of his own day. It is true to say that in Irenaeus "Athens and Jerusalem meet at Patmos."[112] Given the largely Johannine texture of his discourse,[113] it is no surprise that more than one-third of Irenaeus' references to John come from the Johannine prologue and that the Logos expectantly looms large.[114]

Irenaeus attributes preexistence to the Logos in Israel's sacred history, in either angelic or typological form, as well as in the prophecies of his incarnation (*Haer.* 3.11.8; 3.21.1; 4.20.5; 4.22.1–23.2; *Epid.* 5; 10; 30–31; 43–66). He rejects that Christ was a mere man born of normal procreation (*Haer.* 1.25.1; 1.26.1; 3.19.1). Nor did he pass through Mary like water passing through a pipe without acquiring her humanity (3.11.3; 3.22.2). Irenaeus repeats John 1.14 that the Logos "became flesh" (*Haer.* 3.11.3; 3.16.2; 3.19.1; 4.20.2; *Dem.* 31; 37; 39; 84; 94). The one who is Word of God, Son of God, and Lord became the Son of Man as the son of Mary, who was tested as a man and glorified as the Word (*Haer.* 3.19.3). In his human life he recapitulates Adam, drawing humanity from Mary, so that he could draw humanity towards God (*Haer.* 3.21.9; 4.6.2).

Irenaeus asserts that "God makes, [while] man is made" (*Haer.* 4.11.1), and he places the Word on the God-side of the creator-creature distinction. He cites John 1.3 (and Ps 33.2) to the effect that God creates nothing without the Word and the Spirit. No other angel or power shared in this creative and governing work. The Word and Wisdom are God's co-eternal collaborators in creation (*Haer.* 1.22.1; 3.11.1–2; 3.21.10; 4.7.4; 4.20.1–5; 4.24.1; 5.18.2–3; *Epid.* 5; 43). Irenaeus refers to Christ's "primal, powerful and glorious generation from

---

[112] Eric Osborn, *Irenaeus of Lyons* (Cambridge: Cambridge University Press, 2001), xi.

[113] Cf. Hill, *Johannine Corpus*, 96–102; Bernhard Mutschler, *Irenäus als johannischer Theologe: Studien zur Schriftauslegung bei Irenäus von Lyon* (Tübingen: Mohr Siebeck, 2004); idem, *Das Corpus Johanneum*.

[114] Mutschler, *Irenäus als johannischer Theologe*, 192; idem, "John and His Gospel in the Mirror of Irenaeus of Lyons: Perspectives of Recent Research," in *The Legacy of John: Second-Century Reception of the Fourth Gospel*, ed. Tuomas Rasimus (NovTSup 132; Leiden: Brill, 2010), 331.

the Father" (*Haer.* 3.11.8), the "pure generation of the Word of God . . . who became man" (*Haer.* 3.19.1). Elsewhere, citing John 1.18, he declares that the Word made the invisible and inexpressible Father known to all since the Son is the revealer of the Father from the beginning (*Haer.* 3.11.6; 4.20.6–7).

The Logos is united with God and with creation and so unites God with creation. To begin with, Irenaeus' Son and Father share a oneness in being and redemption: "The Father is Lord and the Son is Lord, and the Father is God and the Son is God; since he who is born of God is God (*to gar ek theou gennethen theos estin*), and in this way, according to his being (*hypostasis*) and power and essence (*ousia*), one God is demonstrated; but according to the economy of our salvation, there is both Father and Son" (*Epid.* 47). The Logos is united with the Father and with the man Christ Jesus as "true God and true man." This entails a unity in deity, dispensation, and deliverance with "one God, the Father, and one Word, and one Son, and one Spirit, and one salvation to all who believe in him" (*Haer.* 4.6.7). The operating premise is that Christ, the Son of God before all the world, is with the Father and one with the Father, and close enough to commune with humanity (*Epid.* 52–53). This establishes a "communion of God and man" as "the Word became flesh, that by means of the flesh which sin had mastered and seized and dominated" (*Epid.* 31). As a result, by becoming incarnate, the Word united "imperishability and immortality" with humanity so that humanity might become imperishable and immortal (*Haer.* 3.19.1). The economic unity of the Word's incarnation, revelation, and salvation is found in Irenaeus' aphorism that combines Johannine and Matthean language: "For the glory of God is a living man, and the life of man is the vision of God. If the revelation of God by the creation already gives life to all the beings living on earth, how much more does the manifestation of the Father by the Word give life to those who see God" (*Haer.* 4.20.7).

In distinction to the apologists, Irenaeus rejected the Mind-Word analogy (1) because it was deployed in Gnostic schemes to multiple entities, (2) because of divine simplicity whereby God is "all Mind and all Logos," (3) because God's generation of his Logos is different to the human mind's generation of words (appealing to Isa 53.8), and (4) because the result would be a type of subordination and inferiority on the part of the Logos to God himself, which is unacceptable since the Logos is God (*Haer.* 2.13.2–8; 2.28.4–5). In addition, Irenaeus identified the Son as God's Word and the Spirit as God's Wisdom, and likened them with the angelic orders of Cherubim and Seraphim (*Epid.* 10). This falls into line with wider trends of associating John's Logos with angelic characteristics.

In the end, Irenaeus is easily the most comprehensive and systematic exegete of the Johannine Gospel prior to Origen, even without writing a commentary on the Gospel.¹¹⁵ For Irenaeus, a truly divine Christology is paramount, as it is the point at which protology, eschatology, theology, soteriology, and cosmology all intersect. How one interprets John 1.3, 14 proves to be a shibboleth for apostolic Christianity as opposed to its allegedly unwholesome deviations.¹¹⁶ That is because Irenaeus takes John 1.1–3, 14, 18 to be definitive proof for God's unity with the world, that the Logos is united with the Father, the Logos made the world, and the Logos was himself made flesh in order to recapitulate and sum up all things in himself for a salvation that makes mortals partakers of immortality (esp. *Haer.* 3.11.1–6; 3.19.1–20.2; 4.20.1–7; *Epid.* 5; 10; 47; 52).

Clement of Alexandria tethers his theology of the incarnation to the Logos: "This Logos, who alone is both God and man, the cause of all our good, appeared but lately in his own person to men" (*Protr.* 7). He frequently refers to "the divine Logos" (*ho theios logos*) and equates him with God's divinity in an absolute sense: "The Lord . . . is the real Purifier, Saviour and Gracious One, the divine Logos, the truly most manifest God [*ho phanerōtatos ontōs theos*], who is made equal to the Master of the universe [*ho tō despotē tōn holōn exisōtheis*], because he was his Son, 'and the Word was in God'" (*Protr.* 110). Clement thus argues for the unity of the preexistent Logos with the man Christ Jesus and the ontological unity of the incarnate Logos with the divine being of the Father.¹¹⁷

(9) Comparative analysis.

Do we have to imagine that the Greco-Roman Logos is mediated to John only via Hellenistic Judaism? That is not necessarily the case! Heraclitus' description of the Logos as true reason and a metaphysical principle has some parity with the Johannine Logos.¹¹⁸ The Logoi of Heraclitus and John are similar, at least when it comes to ascriptions of eternity, divinity, association with light, creative work, universal presence, the need for it to be followed, and how it

---

¹¹⁵ Mutschler, "John and His Gospel," 332.
¹¹⁶ Mutschler, *Irenäus als johanneischer Theologe*, 263.
¹¹⁷ Henny Fiskå Hägg, *Clement of Alexandria and the Beginnings of Christian Apophaticism* (OECS; Oxford: Oxford University Press, 2006), 197–201.
¹¹⁸ Walther Kranz ("Der Logos Heraklits und der Logos des Johannes," *Rheinisches Museum für Philologie* 93 [1950]: 88) wrote: "If we now compare the Prooemium of John with the Heraclitic, it becomes evident that it is to be understood as a Christian doctrine of the Logos, which consciously imitates the great pagan thinker, yet at the same time honors and attacks him; because the concepts are parallel" ("Wenn wir nun das Prooimion des Iohannes mit dem Heraklitischen vergleichen, so wird offenbar, dass es zu verstehen ist als eine christliche Logoslehre, welche die des grossen Heiden bewusst nachbildend zugleich ehrt und bekämpft; denn ihr Gedankengang ist parallel").

Jesus and the "In-Betweeners" 161

experienced rejection by people.[119] Plus, subsequent readers we come across were reminded of the Logos of Heraclitus when discoursing about the Logos themselves. The Jewish Philo and the Christian Justin both appealed directly and positively to Heraclitus concerning the Logos (Philo, *Her.* 213–14; *Leg. all.* 1.105–8; Justin, *1 Apol.* 46.3; *2 Apol.* 7.1). Augustine noticed that John's Logos was similar to the Neo-Platonists, not in language but in effect, as both pertain to a revelatory and mediating Reason. For Augustine, the distinction was evangelical, as the Word came to his own people to give them the power to attain divine sonship (*Conf.* 7.9.13; cf. *Civ.* 10.29). At a bare minimum, John shares with Greco-Roman philosophers an interest in the Logos as a mode of cosmic intermediation and the interpenetration of the divine in the material world. So, it is not out the question that John the Evangelist may have been directly aware of Heraclitus' philosophy or a Stoic adaptation of it.

But that is not the end of the matter. First, John's Logos, whatever its philosophical heritage, is primarily shaped by Jewish tradition concerning God's Word and Wisdom. These parallels are the most prevalent and most powerful influences on John's Logos Christology (esp. Sirach 24). Second, John's Logos departs from philosophical schemes that characterize the Logos with intense immanence, whether that is cosmic regularity, universal law, or a rational seed. John's Logos exists in the beginning with God, not in the world, not in the human mind, and not in the constitution of Hellenistic city-states. Third, it is equally clear that John's Logos was not regarded merely as a divine abstraction or divine personification in its reception history as much as it was reinterpreted by Christian authors in light of Platonic cosmology, Stoic distinctions, and wider scriptural texts such as Prov 8.22–23 and Col 1.15. The philosophical exegesis of the Johannine prologue functioned primarily to differentiate Jesus from other intermediary figures and to clarify the divinity of the Son in relation to the Father. This explains why the apologists resource the Stoic distinction between the *logos endiathetos* (word as mind) and *logos prophorikos* (word as speech) and utilize the notion of *logos spermatikos* (the organic seed for rationality) in their explanation of Jesus as the Father's thought, who at the same time is spoken into the world.[120] Or else, for the Valentinians, the Savior is either the ultimate aeon of the pleroma, or at least the one charged with the most significant role in bringing salvation to psychic beings in the lower depths who are open to new insights. There is, then, no Hellenistic influence on John's Logos without simultaneous influence from Jewish

---

[119] Ed L. Miller, "The Logos of Heraclitus: Updating the Report," *HTR* 74 (1980): 174–75.
[120] See similarly Philo, *Her.* 119; *Fug.* 191; *Abr.* 29, 83; *Mos.* 2.127; *Mut.* 208; *Det.* 39.

wisdom traditions. Added to that, the reception history shows not a thick line being drawn between Heraclitus and John, but a tendency to try to explain John's Logos in light of Hellenistic categories in order to make the concept more palatable and persuasive to readers.

There are clear analogies too with the role attributed to the Logos in the Stoic philosopher Cleanthes' *Hymn to Zeus*. Not least, the blending of Zeus with the "universal law" at the very end of the hymn resembles the correlation between God and the Word in John 1.1. Yet what is truly striking is that John's Logos more closely resembles God/Zeus—as the one without whom creation would not exist, who is associated with cosmic unity, who dispels ignorance, who rules with justice, and who is worthy of worship—than the Logos, who constitutes a type of universal law and ubiquitous reason.

Closer to the first century, John's Logos has a genuine analogue in the "logos-ization" of Osiris by Plutarch and of Hermes by Cornutus.[121] The key similarity is that an intermediate divine figure is identified as the supreme mediating principle between the transcendent and material realms. That was quite appropriate for Hermes as the messenger of the gods and entirely comprehensible by Plutarch's allegorical interpretation of Osiris as the locus of cosmic rationality. The key difference, however, is that John identified the Logos with a figure of history, not a figure of mythology. John historicizes the Logos by portraying him as "becoming" human in the midst of Judean history as the man Jesus of Nazareth, in whom the one true God is revealed. John's Logos is not a temporary epiphany of a god in human *morphē*,[122] but God's Word *sarx egeneto*,

---

[121] Justin (*1 Apol.* 21.2) explicitly compares Jesus to Hermes as the Logos. Bousset (*Kyrios Christos*, 391–99) notes the similarities of depictions of Hermes, Thoth, and Mercury with the Logos of the apologists, but he invests far too much in the Oriental-Egyptian mythologizing as a forerunner of the Christian Logoi.

[122] Cf. Euripides, *Bacchae* 1–5: "I, the son of Zeus, have come to this land of the Thebans—Dionysus, whom once Semele, Kadmos' daughter, bore, delivered by a lightning-bearing flame. And having taken a mortal form instead of a god's, I am here at the fountains of Dirke and the water of Ismenus." See Michael B. Cover, "The Death of Tragedy: The Form of God in Euripides's *Bacchae* and Paul's *Carmen Christi*," *HTR* 111 (2018): 66–89. Hengel (*Son of God*, 40) points out: "These examples [from pagan mythology] do not mention sending, nor does God take upon himself human fate and death. True, the Greek gods are born and have human pleasures (sometimes even with human beings), but they can never die. Their bodily form is only 'show', and their immortality distinguishes them even more fundamentally from transitory 'mortals.'" Frey ("Incarnation of the Logos," 281) adds: "The history-of-religion parallels of the temporary transformation of gods into human or animal form precisely do not match what is intended here [in John]."

"become flesh," with participation in the full suite of human experiences from birth to death.[123]

John, like the Stoics and Middle Platonists, identifies the Logos as a creative agent, a power from God and beside God, but without reflecting a world of forms and without any assistance from a World-Soul or young gods. John's Logos does not guard the true God from creation; rather, he unites them in his own person—precisely what proved intolerable for Gnostic interpreters, who had to remove the Logos from this creative role and sometimes from full humanity. Similarly, John's Logos does not share the Stoic story of successive worlds climaxing in conflagration or dissipate into God's universal immanence with all things. Clearly then, as Christopher Atkins says, John does not operate "in anachronistic isolation but in creative participation in the discourses of philosophical antiquity, including the cosmogonic discourses of Middle-Platonism." That is because John "departs from and innovates within the philosophical discourse of cosmogony and divine intermediaries" by refusing to limit the aegis of the Logos "to the domain of metaphysics and cosmogony" and incorporating it within a Jewish and christological "model of human access to and relationship with the divine."[124]

Dunn asked whether "the original readers of the Johannine prologue, familiar with the literature of Hellenistic Judaism as many of them presumably would be, [would] have identified the Logos of John 1.1–18 as a divine hypostasis or intermediary being between God and man?"[125] In answer, far

---

[123] Dodd (*Interpretation of the Fourth Gospel*, 284 [italics original]) said: "The Logos did not merely descend upon Jesus, enter into Him, or abide in Him. The Logos *became* the *sarx* or human nature which He bore. The life of Jesus *is* the true history of the Logos, as incarnate, and this must be, upon the stage of limited time, the same thing as the history of the Logos in perpetual relations with man and world." Jörg Frey ("Review of *John and Philosophy*, by Troels Engberg-Pedersen," *EC* 10 [2019]: 232) adds: "John does not simply say that the Logos went into a human body, thus creating a composite being, a 'duality.' Nor does he claim that the Logos adopted or empowered a human being, elevating him to a new status, authority, or messianity, to be the 'Christ' Jesus. Such ideas and understandings of the Logos come dangerously close to those which were considered already in the early church but ultimately dismissed as insufficient. They fail as soon as we ask, for example, with which part of that duality Jesus did his miracles, spoke his words, suffered, or died." John McHugh (*John 1–4* [ICC; London: Bloomsbury, 2014], 53) commented: "The purpose . . . is to emphasize that the Logos did not just 'dwell in' human flesh, did not just 'have' a human body in order to speak his part for one or more performances, like a Greek actor walking on stage with a particular mask."

[124] Christopher S. Atkins, "Rethinking John 1:1: The Word Was Godward," *NovT* 63 (2021): 62.

[125] Dunn, *Christology in the Making*, 216.

more likely than not! John is undoubtedly aware of the wisdom traditions of Proverbs, Wisdom of Solomon, and Sirach with their representations of Wisdom—the parallels with John's prologue are overwhelming. Similarly, a comparison between Philo and John demonstrates how John is clearly working with the hermeneutical and philosophical tools of Hellenistic Judaism and its account of divine intermediary figures. The problem is that Philo's Logos is not merely a divine personification nor merely an angelic power; it is a complex array of several things: divine mind, divine image, divine hypostasis, pattern of creation and priesthood, image of the heavenly man, (arch)angel, demiurge, and Wisdom. Christian Logoi can never represent the entire array of Philonic images for the Logos. Comparing and contrasting the Logoi of Philo and John is a difficult though worthwhile task as it enables us to observe how John christologizes the Logos within Hellenistic Judaism.[126]

Concerning the similarities between the Philonic and Johannine Logoi, we can say the following:

(a) *Eternal and preexistent*. The Logos is co-eternal with God and preexists the created realm. Philo makes this clear with the Logos sharing in the immortality and eternality of God (*Conf.* 41). John accents preexistence at several points by placing the Logos with God in the beginning (John 1.1–2), with Jesus sharing in God's own name and self-existence (John 5.26; 8.58), and possessing a glory before the creation of the world (John 17.4).

(b) *Heightened proximity*. The Logos is close to God in a way that no other intermediary figure is ever described. Philo declared the Logos to be the divine image and therefore the nearest one to God with no intervening figure between them (*Fug.* 101), which corresponds to John's remark that the Word was with/towards God with nothing between or beside (John 1.1, 18).

(c) *God and with God*. The Logos is part of the divine executive yet distinguishable from God. Both Logoi are identified with God and God's actions, yet they never act independently of God, and they do not compromise God's unity and oneness. Philo declared there to be "one true God," and the Logos can appear in his place because the title "God" is given to his "chief Word" (*Somn.* 1.229–30). Philo contends that the "God" and "Lord" whom Abraham saw at Mamre (Gen 18.1) was none other than the "Holy Logos" (*Abr.* 70–71; *Mut.* 16–17). That corresponds with the Johannine Jesus' remark that Abraham had a vision of his own day and even of him, precisely because Jesus is the "I am" who was before Abraham (John 8.56–58). John thus claims that Abraham

[126] Cf. A. W. Argyle, "Philo and the Fourth Gospel," *ExpT* 63 (1951–1952): 385–86; Robert McL. Wilson, "Philo and the Fourth Gospel," *ExpT* 65 (1953–1954): 47–49; Dodd, *Interpretation of the Fourth Gospel*, 71–73, 276–70; and Evans, *Word and Glory*, 100–112.

encountered a heavenly being, the divine Logos, whom Moses also encountered as a heavenly figure bearing the divine name, and with whom Jesus is identified.[127] Philo also says that Moses calls the Logos "God" as the divine creative power (*Fug.* 97; QE 2.62, 68), and he even labels it a "second God" (*QG* 2.62). John designates the Logos as "God" in a strong sense and attaches the title to the risen Jesus too (John 1.1; 20.28). In fact, Thomas' attribution of the titles "Lord" and "God" to the risen Jesus is parallel to Philo dividing the Logos into two parts, the creative (God) and sovereign powers (Lord) within the one true God (*Fug.* 95; 103; cf. QG 2.16; QE 2.62, 68; *Abr.* 121; *Mos.* 2.99–100; *Her.* 165–66). Justin too identifies the Logos as "another God and Lord under the Creator of all things" (*Dial.* 56.4), and Origen is also comfortable with describing Jesus as "a second God" even though he qualifies it (*Cels.* 5.39; 6.61; 7.57). Philo, John, Justin, and Origen all have a strong belief in one God and maintain that the Logos is not an independent deity; nonetheless, they do struggle for conceptual clarity in how to precisely explain that the Logos is intrinsic to God's being while functionally distinct and derivative.

(d) *Demiurge.* The Logos is God's instrument of creation. Philo and John both identify God as the Creator, yet the act of creation is undertaken through the Logos, even though neither of them applies the term *dēmiourgos* to the Logos (*Sacr.* 8; *Cher.* 127; *Fug.* 95, 97; *Opif.* 20; 24; *Migr.* 6; QE 2.68; *Leg. all.* 3.96; *Her.* 119; *Spec. leg.* 1.81). John is clear that God creates "all things" through the Logos and nothing "apart from him" (John 1.3). This Johannine language meant very different things, as the debates between the proto-orthodox and Gnostics illustrate. For the former, this meant that the Logos was not part of creation and not an ordinary intermediary; for the latter, the Logos was at best the curator of the pleroma.

(e) *Light and life.* God's creative work through the Logos abounds in life and light. Philo says as much in his narration of the creation story (*Opif.* 24, 30, 33). John's Logos is the bearer of life and light for all people (John 1.4) and so John associates the Logos with God's role as life-giver and revealer in creation.[128]

(f) *Adoption.* The Logos makes people children of God. Philo identifies the Logos as the agent of adoption, for while not everyone is learned enough to be considered "sons of God" (Deut 14.1), even so, he contends that everyone willing to put aside polytheism and pleasures can take their place under "God's

---

[127] Harold W. Attridge, "Stoic and Platonic Reflections on Naming in Early Christian Circles: Or, What's in a Name?" in *From Stoicism to Platonism: The Development of Philosophy, 100 BCE–100 CE*, ed. Troels Engberg-Pedersen (Cambridge: Cambridge University Press, 2017), 286–87.

[128] Endo, *Creation and Christology*, 216–19, 251.

firstborn, the Word . . . For if we have not yet become fit to be thought sons of God yet we may be sons of his invisible image, the most holy Word" (*Conf.* 146–47). John is analogous in his claim that receiving the Word, believing in him, gives one the power to become children of God, begotten of God and not of human procreative process (John 1.12–13).

(g) *The Logos with and in human beings.* The Logos comprises the heavenly archetype of human existence. In regard to Gen 1.27, "Let us make man in our image," Philo discerns in the plural pronoun "us" not an angelic assembly, but God and his Logos. He argues, "nothing mortal can be made in the likeness of the most high One and Father of the universe but only in that of the second God, who is his Logos" (*QG* 2.62). Humans were created according to an archetypal seal, which corresponds to the divine image, which is the Word of God (*Opif.* 24–25; *Conf.* 147; *Leg. all.* 3.96; *QG* 1.4). The Logos is, then, the archetype of humanity, with the titles "man according to the image of God" (*Conf.* 146) and "the true man" (*Somn.* 1.215). Philo does make the interesting allegorical interpretation of Lev 16.17 with the high priest offering sacrifices as "not a man, but the word of God" (*Fug.* 108).[129] John's testimony is far stronger than this with the Word becoming flesh and identifying with the human life of the man Jesus of Nazareth (John 1.14).

(h) *Exclusive mediator.* Philo believes that the Logos fulfills a role like Moses in Deut 5.5 (LXX): "I stood between the Lord and you." The Logos is the "chief messenger" who "pleads with the immortal as supplicant for afflicted mortality and acts as ambassador of the ruler to the subjects" (*Her.* 205–6). In regard to Exod 23.20–21, the angel whom God sends before the Hebrews is the Logos who is "judge and mediator" (*QE* 2.13) or "mediator and arbitrator" (*QE* 2.68). The Logos is also the "interpreter and prophet" of the divine will (*Deus* 138). God's transcendence is such that none can see God in his essence, but only his Word as he dispatches it, the "angel of his Logos" (*Somn.* 1.65–69, 239). Matching this is a strong emphasis on the Logos as the exclusive revelation of God (*Somn.* 1.18; 3.13; 8.19; 14.7–9; 16.3; 17.24) and a special mediator (*Somn.* 1.51; 14.6; 15.5), which parallels similar Johannine assertions (John 1.18; 3.13; 14.6; 17.3).

(i) *Philo and Christian tradition.* Philo describes the Logos with terms that were to have currency in Christian circles (esp. *Conf.* 146). Labeling the Logos as "son of God" coalesces with early Christian tradition, particularly acute in John, where Jesus is the Son of God par excellence with a messianic vocation and unique filial relationship to God the Father. Likewise, his designation of

[129] Otherwise, the next best analogy is where Philo says that Moses "was made in a likeness and imitation of the Word, when the Divine Breath was breathed into his face" (*Opif.* 139).

the Logos as "firstborn" corresponds to Col 1.15, which was frequently married to Johannine christological discourse in the second century. Even the titles "Beginning" and "name of God" popped up in Gnostic and proto-orthodox narratives for Jesus as well. In addition, it was very common among a diverse range of authors to describe the Logos as an angel, as Philo does at several points. Philo anticipates in his Logos many of the christological titles that were to be used in apostolic and sub-apostolic Christology, and he intimates the Platonic possibilities that emerge when the Logos is situated as the primary actor in a hierarchy of subordinate powers where God is supreme, but kept at arm's length from creation.

The Philonic and Johannine Logoi intersect most acutely at the point of postulating a supreme cosmological and intermediary agent who traverses the universal and the particular of creation and revelation.[130] They demonstrate how philosophical traditions could be interrogated and applied to biblical exegesis in such a way as to cogently explain God's movement towards the world without forfeiting divine transcendence. They both exposit God's revelation in his creation with a view to attaining true knowledge of God's being through the Logos.[131]

Yet, for all the many similarities between Philo and John on the Logos, it is the differences that remain stark.

(a) *God, Logos, and creation*. To put it simply, Philo's Logos explains creation, whereas John's Logos explains God.[132] Unlike Philo, John's Logos is not a divine form, intellect, archetype, or imprint impressed upon creation and creatures; rather, it belongs intrinsically to the one God and is sent into creation. Philo separates the invisible and visible worlds via the Logos, whereas John unites them in the Logos. Philo's Logos is imprinted upon the physical world, whereas John's Logos enters the physical world and is the Savior of the world. Philo's Logos begets a cosmos and other powers, as do some Gnostic Logoi. But in Johannine and proto-orthodox discourse, the Logos does not generate anything; instead, the cosmos is addressed by the Logos rather than expressed within it.[133]

---

[130] Harold W. Attridge, *Essays on John and Hebrews* (Grand Rapids: Baker, 2010), 46–59.

[131] Jutta Leonhardt-Balzer, "Der Logos und die Schöpfung: Streiflichter bei Philo (Op. 20–5) und im Johannesprolog (Joh 1:1–18)," in *Kontexte des Johannesevangeliums: Das vierte Evangelium in religions- und traditionsgeschichtlicher Perspektive*, ed. Jörg Frey and Udo Schnelle (WUNT 175; Tübingen: Mohr Siebeck, 2004), 317.

[132] Leonhardt-Balzer, "Der Logos und die Schöpfung," 317.

[133] Folker Siegert, "Der Logos, 'älterer Sohn' des Schöpfers und 'zweiter Gott': Philons Logos und der Johannesprolog," in *Kontexte des Johannesevangeliums: Das vierte*

(b) *Relationship with God.* Philo's Logos is close to God, as close as any entity can get, between a divine hypostasis and an archangel. The Logos constitutes God's creative and sovereign power in heavens of which there is an equality with God (*Her.* 166), and no other being can be equal in honor with God (*Conf.* 170). Similarly, John accents the Logos' parity with God as cocreator and Jesus' own oneness and equality with God (John 5.18; 10.30). Even so, while Philo and John both attribute to the Logos a sense of subordination (*QG* 2.62; John 14.28), Philo's subordination is premised on a cosmic Platonic hierarchy, whereas the Johannine Jesus' subordination is rooted in his messianic obedience to the Father's redemptive will. In addition, even though Philo and John both call the Logos "God," there are more features of divine sovereignty attributed to John's Logos in the prologue and to Jesus in the narrative, not the least in the receipt of worship and divine prerogatives in salvation and judgment.[134]

(c) *Mediation without participation.* Philo's Logos is explicitly described as a "mediator," even a cosmic priest, because it is neither "uncreated" as God nor "created" as humanity (*Her.* 206; *Fug.* 101; *Somn.* 1.215; *QE* 2.13, 68). It exists genuinely between both types of being and operates between the two realms. In contrast, John's Logos participates in God's God-ness and in the form and flesh of humanity. The Johannine Logos is a mediator and priest precisely because he participates in God's being and human nature. Philo's Logos might better be understood as a cipher or conduit between the noumenal and phenomenal horizons rather than comprising an actual mediator.[135]

(d) *Incarnation.* Philo regards the Logos as the archetype of humanity, sometimes a divine personification, otherwise a supreme angelic figure, but nothing here is analogous to incarnation nor even conducive to it. In fact, Philo stresses much the opposite: "Let no one represent the [divine] likeness as one to bodily form; for neither is God in human form, nor is the human body God-like" (*Opif.* 69). If that is not enough, regarding Caligula's divine pretentiousness to deity, he charges, "Sooner could God change into a man than a man into a god" (*Legat.* 118). Elsewhere, he says "to declare the created uncreated, the mortal immortal, the destructible indestructible" is "blasphemy" as it tries to make "man" into "God" (*Mut.* 181). In which case, John 1.14 would be blasphemous to Philo because the unbegotten God cannot himself ever be begotten without forfeiting his immutable and impassible essence. Celsus, in fact, made the very same

---

Evangelium in religions- und traditionsgeschichtlicher Perspektive, ed. Jörg Frey and Udo Schnelle (WUNT 175; Tübingen: Mohr Siebeck, 2004), 293.

[134] Leonhardt-Balzer, "Der Logos und die Schöpfung," 317.
[135] Cf. Carrell, *Jesus*, 93–94.

objections (*Cels.* 4.14, 18). True, Philo would agree with John that "no one has ever seen God," but he would either balk or treat as blasphemous the following claim that "it is God the only Son, who is close to the Father's heart, who has made him known" (John 1.18).[136] For John, the ineffable and imperceptible divine being *becomes* knowable and perceptible *exclusively* in the Word/Son. Thus, despite some minor terminological affinities, "in Philo, the Logos is never fully personal, certainly never incarnate, and never the object of faith and love."[137]

Finally, what should also be taken into account is how the Johannine Logos was diversely appropriated and augmented by Christian authors. John the Seer accents the worshipability of Jesus the Word and his proximity to God the Father even as he engages in an angelomorphic Christology. The *Epistula Apostolorum* similarly describes the Logos as divine but amiable to adopting angelic form. Justin deploys angelic types from the Septuagint to explain the Logos' preexistence in Israel's sacred history. Irenaeus can offer a robust intensification of Johannine Logos Christology even as he identifies Christ with one of the cherubim. Justin and Origen define the Logos as definitively divine, but still subordinate to the Father. Athenagoras, Theophilus of Antioch, Tatian, and the author of *Diognetus* consider Jesus to be God's Word, the instrument of creation, who sits on the divine side of the God-creature dichotomy, and is set apart from other intermediaries. Many Gnostics distinguished the Logos of God from the Logos of creation. Indeed, there were considerable variations within Gnostic schemes as to the Savior's proximity to God the Father within the cosmic pleroma. The Johannine Logos was generally interpreted by Gnostics cosmologically, that is, in light of a stark separation between the true God and the pleroma contrasted with the demiurge and his creation.[138] The overall

---

[136] Attridge, "Stoic and Platonic Reflections," 284.

[137] McHugh, *John 1–4*, 94. Cf. Evans, *Word and Glory*, 104; and Frey, "Between Jewish Monotheism," 207. According to Dunn (*Christology in the Making*, 243 [italics original]), John "has taken language which any thoughtful Jew would recognize to be the language of personification and has *identified* it with a particular person, *as* a particular person, that would be so astonishing: the manifestation of God become man! God's utterance not merely come through a particular individual, but actually become that one person, Jesus of Nazareth!" Boyarin ("Gospel of the *Memra*," 261) notes: "I would like to propose that what marks the Fourth Gospel as a new departure in the history of Judaism is not to be found in its Logos theology at all but in its incarnational Christology, and that that very historical departure, or rather advent, is iconically symbolized in the narrative itself. When the text announces in v. 14 that 'the Word became flesh,' that announcement is an iconic representation of the moment that the Christian narrative begins to diverge from the Jewish Koine and form its own nascent Christian kerygma."

[138] Frey, "Between Torah and Stoa," 192–93; and idem, "Johannine Logos," 243.

impression is that John's Logos generated diverse yet intensified identifications of Jesus as a divine figure by the proto-orthodox and heterodox alike.

To conclude, the Logos Christology of the early church, beginning with the evangelist John, was significant in several respects: (1) It demonstrates a convergence between Jewish discourses about divine Wisdom and a messiah with a Christian Son of God tradition in a way that resources and resonates with Middle Platonic and Stoic philosophy. John's Logos has affinities with Heraclitus, Cornutus, Philo, or Plutarch. Yet John's identification of the Logos as becoming the man Jesus is without parallel, and his Christology is of such a character as to imply that Jesus is one with the God of Israel and he is an "uncreated" deity.[139] (2) Logos Christology in all its varieties, often combined with angelomorphism or pleromatic exegesis, attempted to offer a conceptually coherent account of how God is to be identified with the man Jesus of Nazareth by identifying Jesus with the preexistent Logos. (3) Notwithstanding the questions that Logos Christology threw up for interpreters, such as whether the Logos was 100 percent divine or only 99.9 percent divine, Logos Christology represented the most serious and sublime effort of the church to know its own mind and to explain its own kerygma to itself. Logos Christology was the attempt to explain what it meant to say that "God sent his Son" (Gal 4.4; Rom 8.3), that "God was in Christ" (2 Cor 5.19), and that the Son is "the reflection of God's glory and the exact imprint of God's very being" (Heb 1.3).[140]

Wisdom

The final part of the trilogy of God's creative-crafting agents is the figure of Wisdom.[141] Jewish traditions concerning Wisdom exhibit clear similarities with Greco-Roman demiurgical figures but are distinct in that they possess a specific connection to Israel's monotheistic traditions as well as associations

---

[139] Gabriele Boccaccini, "How Jesus Became Uncreated," in *Sibyls, Scriptures, and Scrolls*, ed. Joel Baden, Hindy Nayman, and Eibert Tigchelaar (JSPSup 175; Leiden: Brill, 2016), 1:186–88; Bauckham, *Jesus and the God of Israel*, 185–208; and Boccaccini, "From Jewish Prophet to Jewish God." According to Frey ("Between Jewish Monotheism," 208): "This implies that the Logos is not only divine in the sense in which in Greco-Roman thought numerous superhuman figures could be called divine as having a share in some kind of divinity. He is not merely the first one of God's creatures, as is Wisdom in Prov 8:22, but—in the line of further 'elevation' of Wisdom in the wisdom tradition—the *logos* is 'uncreated.'" See too Bühner, *Messianic High Christology*, 146–51.

[140] Cf. Dunn, *Christology in the Making*, 213.

[141] In what follows I use "Wisdom" as personification of God and "wisdom" as an attribute or quality. For discussion of the differences between divine personification and divine hypostasis, see Lee, *From Messiah to Preexistent Son*, 37–44.

with eschatological schemes. Wisdom, we will see, played a large part in the formation of christological narratives, especially in relation to Christ's preexistence and proximity to God.[142] The precise way that Wisdom is interwoven with other christological and cosmological discourses, from Logos to the Sophia myth, is also quite illuminating for the overall significance of the wisdom tradition in the early church's thought.

(1) Personified Wisdom in Jewish tradition.

In Israel's sacred literature, the word *ḥokmâ* in the Hebrew Scriptures and *Sophia* in the Greek Scriptures designate wisdom: the quality of intelligence, insight, and pragmatic competence, frequently predicated of God, yet shareable with human subjects. Both nouns are feminine, and Wisdom was accordingly personified as a woman, a preacher of truth, who invites the attentive to heed her instruction (Prov 8.1–11; Bar 3.9; Sir 4.11; 24.19–21; 4Q185 I–II 1.13–2.8) with the promise that those who accept her will become her children and avoid misfortune (Prov 8.32–36; Bar 3.10–14; Sir 4.12–13; 24.22). Among the earliest of Jewish wisdom texts is Job 28, which laments the lack of access humans have to Wisdom. Wisdom is portrayed as precious, yet she remains elusive, and her origins are ineffable. God either invented Wisdom or discovered Wisdom, and the human path to Wisdom is to "fear the Lord" and "depart from evil" (Job 28.27–28). Subsequent Jewish tradition made much of the Lord's relationship to Wisdom and how she took up residence among Israel largely through the Torah.

In Proverbs, Lady Wisdom is a sage in the street reproving the foolish and offering her insight (Prov 1.20–33; 8.1–11), a goddess offering life and wealth (Prov 3.18–20; 8.12–21), and a companion in God's creative work (8.22–31). In this last passage, Lady Wisdom is personified as someone "created" (*qānâ/ektisen*), "installed/established" (*nissakhti/ethemeliōsen*), and "brought forth" (*ḥolalti/genna*) in the beginning of creation but prior to the beginning of the earth. She is a "master worker" (*'amon*)[143] at God's side, rejoicing in God's creative work and delighting in humanity (Prov 8.22–31). Importantly, Wisdom here is not eternal but a created entity, nor a demiurge as she does not cooperate in the work of creation.[144] More properly, she is a something of an authenticator and audience to God's creative artistry.

---

[142] Cf., e.g., Hengel, *Son of God*, 72–76; Seyoon Kim, *The Origin of Paul's Gospel* (Eugene, Ore.: Wipf & Stock, 2007), 102–36; and Lee, *From Messiah to Preexistent Son*, 42–43.

[143] The LXX has instead *harmozousa* for "fitting together" (NETS) or "joining it" (LES).

[144] On Wisdom as a demiurgical figure, see Prov 3.19; Wis 7.22; 8.6; 9.1–2.

Baruch is a post-exilic writing that reinterprets Israel's story of exile and forthcoming restoration and along the way constructs a discourse about the relationship of Wisdom and Torah (Bar 3.9–4.4). Israel's "exile" will not fully end until she learns Wisdom from the "commandments of life" in the Torah. While Wisdom may seem inaccessible, as per Job 28, nonetheless, God has given knowledge to Israel in the form of Torah: "She appeared on earth and lived with humankind. She is the book of the commandments of God, the law that endures forever" (Bar 3.37–4.1). Wisdom is personified as a teacher given to Israel, and her revelation is described in epiphanic ("appeared," *ōphthē*) and anthropomorphic ("lived with," *synavestraphē*) language (Bar 3.38).

The book of Sirach was written by the scribal sage Yeshua ben Sira ca. 200 BCE and contains various proverbs for all sorts of circumstances and situations; it was composed originally in Hebrew but received a Greek translation by Ben Sira's grandson. Ben Sira appears to regard Wisdom as created by God before the beginning of creation and yet persisting into an eternal future (Sir 1.1, 4; 24.3, 9). Wisdom is specifically connected to the Torah as its fulfillment (Sir 15.1; 19.20; 21.11; 34.8; 39.1). At one point, Lady Wisdom narrates her journey from the Lord's mouth, the heavenly host, and God's throne to dwelling in Israel's temple through inhabitation of the Torah (Sir 24.1–23). The turning point is that she comes to dwell in Israel in a manner similar to how the *shekinah* dwelt in the temple (Exod 40.34–35; Sir 24.8–10). Then, in the climax, "All this is the book of the covenant of the Most High God, the law that Moses commanded us" (Sir 24.23).[145] The striking thing is that Ben Sira presents Wisdom as God's personified word (Sir 4.24, 24.1–2), closely associated with God's spirit (Sir 39.6; 24.3) and glory (Sir 24.1–2, 8–10, 16) and embodied in the Torah (Sir 24.23).

The Wisdom of Solomon is most probably an Alexandrian text, written either side of the turn of the eras, dependent upon Proverbs and Sirach, and represents a synthesis of Jewish sapiential traditions and Hellenism. Lady Wisdom is she who "came to be" from the "beginning of creation" (Wis 6.22), and her knowledge is "the salvation of the world" (Wis 6.24; cf. 9.18). In Solomon's encomium to wisdom, she is "the fashioner of all things" (*pantōn technitis*) with strongly immanent qualities as "all-powerful, overseeing all, and penetrating through all spirits . . . For wisdom is more mobile than any motion; because of her pureness she pervades and penetrates all things" (Wis 7.22–24). Wisdom is the personification of divine attributes that in manifold senses are generated from God: "breath of the power of God," "a pure emanation of the glory of the Almighty," "a reflection of eternal light," "a spotless mirror of the working of

---

[145] Philo links Torah not with Wisdom, but with Logos in *Migr.* 130.

God," and "an image of his goodness" (Wis 7.25–26). She has a "shared life with God," is an "initiate in the knowledge of God" and "chooses his works" (Wis 8.3–4). In addition, God made all things by his Word/Wisdom, and Wisdom "sits by your throne" (Wis 9.1–4; cf. *1 En.* 84.2–3). Wisdom is probably identical to the judgment against the firstborn of Egypt during the Passover, whereby the "all-powerful word leaped from heaven, from the royal throne into the midst of the land that was doomed, a stern warrior carrying the sharp sword of your authentic command" (Wis 18.15–16). Importantly, the presence of Hellenistic influences is discernible in that Wisdom is analogous to the pervasive nature of the Stoic Logos/Pneuma (Wis 1.7; 7.23–24; 8.1; 12.1) and the Platonic view of the Logos as an emanation from the one God (Wis 7.25–26).[146]

The Enochic tradition also contributes to the personification of Wisdom in Jewish thought. Many Jewish traditions are concerned with Wisdom's inaccessibility and absence (Job 28.12–28; Prov 30.4–5; Bar 3.14–23), which is why Wisdom must be given as a gift from the Lord (1 Kgs 4.29; 5.12; Prov 2.6; Dan 1.17; Bar 3.36–37; Sir 1.1; 39.6; 43.33; 51.17; Wis 8.21). As we have seen, Ben Sira modulates this motif with Lady Wisdom descending to dwell with Israel (Sir 24.8–10). Here we can note *1 En.* 42.1–3, from the earliest section of the Enochic parables, describing the descent of Wisdom and her experience of rejection:

> Wisdom could not find a place where she might dwell;
>   so her dwelling was in the heavens.
> Wisdom went forth to dwell among the sons of men,
>   but she did not find a dwelling.
> Wisdom returned to her place
>   and sat down in the midst of the angels.
> Then Iniquity went forth from her chambers,
>   those whom she did not seek she found,
> and she dwelt among them,
>   like rain in a desert,
>   like dew in a thirsty land.

The rejection of Wisdom is well attested enough, attributed to Adam in particular (Sir 24.28) and the wicked in general (Wis 10.8). Yet the Enochic narration of Wisdom's descent is remarkable for a few reasons. First, it retells the story of Sirach 24 but as a type of tragedy, where Wisdom finds no dwelling on earth and so returns to heaven, while Iniquity thereafter was able to take

---

[146] Other telltale signs of Hellenistic influences include an emphasis on immortality (Wis 3.4; 6.18–19; 8.138.17; 12.1; 15.3), the preexistence of souls (Wis 8.19–20), and creation out of "formless matter" (Wis 11.17).

up residence among the sons of men. Second, there is an analogue with later Gnostic accounts of the tragic descent of *Sophia* to the earth and her return to the pleroma. Third, it is reminiscent of John 1.10–11: "He was in the world, and the world came into being through him; yet the world did not know him. He came to what was his own, and his own people did not accept him." The rejection of Wisdom is translated into Christian narratives pertaining to either cosmology (Gnostic) or Christology (Johannine).

Philo's contribution to Jewish personifications of Wisdom is principally in its marriage to Platonic and Stoic concepts. Philo likens Wisdom to several things: a city or home for the virtuous man (*Leg. all.* 3.3), a tabernacle where the wise man dwells (*Leg. all.* 3.46), a tree of life (*Leg. all.* 3.52), and a fountain (*Leg. all.* 2.86–87; *Det.* 117; *Post.* 136–38; *Somn.* 2.242; *Spec. leg.* 4.75). Philo depicts Wisdom as possessing many names (*Leg. all.* 1.43), and she is the "mother of all things" (*Leg. all.* 2.49; *Det.* 54, 115–17; *Ebr.* 31, 61; *Her.* 53; *Fug.* 109; *Mut.* 137), both of which are true also of Isis (Apuleius, *Met.* 11.5; Plutarch, *Is. Os.* 53).

Philo's Wisdom relates to the Logos in several ways. First, Wisdom is God's female consort (*Cher.* 49), with whom God fashioned the universe in the tradition of Prov 3.19 and 8.22–23, 30, and so has a demiurgical role (*Fug.* 109; *Ebr.* 30–31; *Det.* 54; *Her.* 199). Second, Wisdom also has many of the same titles as the Logos, including "beginning" and "image" (*Leg. all.* 1.43). Third, Wisdom is the mother of the Logos, while Logos is the fountain of Wisdom, a motif with clear resonance to later Gnostic authors (*Fug.* 97, 108–9). Fourth, Wisdom is explicitly identified with the Logos in an allegory concerning the river that flows from Eden (*Leg. all.* 1.65; *Somn.* 2.242–45). Wisdom also has a close relationship with God, as God himself is the "fountain of wisdom," and Wisdom flows to humans through the Logos (*Leg. all.* 2.87; *Sacr.* 64; *Post.* 136, 138; *Fug.* 97; *Spec. leg.* 1.277).

In Israel's sacred traditions, Wisdom is given significant attention in relation to monarchical virtue and practical piety. Kings need her counsel, and the upright pursue her way. In addition, a common trope is that Wisdom is inaccessible and absent because she resides with God (Job 28; Bar 3.29–31). Thus, to find the divine will is to find Wisdom personified in the Torah (Bar 3.9–4.4; Sir 24.1–23). Wisdom is also the immanent feature of God's ordering of the world, hence the link with creation. Notably, Wisdom is a divine attribute evident in the work of creation (Prov 3.19) and a literary device pertaining to God's personified companion in creation (Prov 8.22–30), an associate (Wis 8.4), or advisor (*2 En.* 33.4). Generally, Wisdom is the poetically personified aspect of God's creative works and a shrewd female guide for making wholesome choices in life as directed in the Torah.[147] God's wisdom is normally not something other than God—it is not an independent entity but is God in his wisdom, a way of talking about God acting in the world.[148] The exceptions are, first, the Wisdom of Solomon, where Wisdom received a Stoic and Platonic interpretation, Wisdom is described in ways congruent with Hellenistic views of intermediation, and there are perhaps even tacit echoes of Isis traditions (i.e., a feminine figure, royal advisor, and savior).[149] Second, Philo attributes to Wisdom some demiurgical properties and treats Wisdom as the Lord's metaphorical consort with a maternal relationship to creation. In these cases, Wisdom becomes more than a poetic personification; it is a semi-independent entity, and it is a "hypostatization" in the sense of "a quasi-personification of certain attributes proper to God, occupying an intermediate position between personalities and abstract beings."[150]

(2) Wisdom in the Jesus tradition.

The associations of Jesus and Wisdom very probably began with the historical Jesus himself, or at least, with the memory of Jesus carried by tradents of the Jesus tradition.[151] The diverse corpus of Jesus literature, canonical and noncanonical texts, preserve sayings and stories that present Jesus as

---

[147] See Roland E. Murphy, "The Personification of Wisdom," in *Wisdom in Ancient Israel*, ed. John Day (Cambridge: Cambridge University Press, 1995), 222-33.

[148] James D. G. Dunn, *Theology of Paul the Apostle* (Edinburgh: T&T Clark, 1998), 271; idem, *Christology in the Making*, 176; Hurtado, *One God, One Lord*, 36-44, 50-51; N. T. Wright, *The New Testament and the People of God* (COQG 1; London: SPCK, 1992), 258-59; Bauckham, *Jesus and the God of Israel*, 16-17; and Lee, *From Messiah to Preexistent Son*, 42, 61-62.

[149] John J. Collins, *Jewish Wisdom in the Hellenistic Age* (OTL; Philadelphia: Westminster John Knox, 1997), 203-4.

[150] W. O. E. Oesterley and G. H. Box, *The Religion and Worship of the Synagogue* (London: Pitman, 1911), 195, cited in Dunn, *Christology in the Making*, 168. Commendable too is Lee's differentiation between divine personification and divine hypostasis: "By 'personified divine attribute' we mean 'a quality, epithet, attribute, manifestation or the like of a deity which, having been subjected to a literary personification, behaves *as though* it is a distinct (if not fully independent) divine being in its own right, but still remains within the literary realm.' By 'divine hypostasis' we mean 'a quality, epithet, attribute, manifestation or the like of a deity, which through a process of personification, concretization, or differentiation, has become a distinct (if not fully independent) divine being in its own right.' While the former still remains within the literary realm, the latter has already crossed over the boundary of the literary world to encompass a concrete, actual, divine being alongside a deity" (*From Messiah to Preexistent Son*, 39, emphasis original).

[151] Cf. Hengel (*Son of God*, 74): "The connection between Jesus and Wisdom had been prepared for by Jesus' own preaching during his ministry, the form of which was very much in the wisdom tradition." Dunn (*Christology in the Making*, 206): "In other words, if Jesus thought of himself at all in relation to wisdom it was as Wisdom's (eschatological) messenger."

something of a messianic sage. Ben Witherington observes, "Those who collected, edited, and passed on the Jesus tradition also seem to have gone out of their way to emphasize the Wisdom element in Jesus' teaching, for no other literary type receives anywhere near the representation in the teaching material in the Synoptics. By even a conservative estimate, at least 70% of the Jesus tradition is in the form of some sort of Wisdom utterance such as an aphorism, riddle, or parable."[152]

Jesus' teaching style mostly comprised of short, provocative, and often witty aphorisms: for example, memorable sayings about asking and receiving (Mark 11.24; Matt 21.22; John 16.24), the Father hiding things from the "wise" but revealing them to "babes" (Matt 11.15–30/Luke 10.21–22), the pipe-dance/dirge-cry comparison (Matt 11.16–17/Luke 7.32), the first being last and the last being first (Mark 9.35; 10.31), or a camel going through the eye of a needle (Mark 10.25). Jesus could also regard himself as a type of "wisdom" who would soon be vindicated by his actions (Matt 11.19/Luke 7.35). Jesus, like Wisdom, claims to send prophets and sages to Israel, all while knowing that they will be mistreated (Matt 23.34/Luke 11.49). The famous logion "Come to me all who are weary, and I will give you rest" (Matt 11.28–30) rehearses a similar invitation issued by Lady Wisdom herself in scriptural texts (Prov 9.3–5; Sir 24.19–22; 51.23–27). Elsewhere, Jesus compares himself to one like, or even greater than, Solomon, the paragon of the wise king (Matt 12.42). This accords with associations between a messianic figure and Wisdom in other writings. For instance, in the similitudes of *1 En.*, the "Elect One/Son of Man" is indwelt by the "spirit of wisdom" (*1 En.* 49.1–4) and himself reveals "secrets of wisdom" (*1 En.* 51.3). Let us not forget either that Josephus in his famous *Testimonium* called Jesus a "wise man" (*sophos anēr*), a benign statement that is unlikely to be a Christian interpolation (*Ant.* 18.63). In the late second century, Lucian calls Christians worshippers of a "crucified sophist" (*Pereg.* 13). The image of Jesus the sage is too ubiquitous across the various tiers of Jesus literature to be a late invention. Jesus was a teacher of wisdom to the point that he was identified as a type of Wisdom in person.[153]

---

[152] Ben Witherington, *Jesus the Sage: The Pilgrimage of Wisdom* (Minneapolis: Fortress, 1994), 155–56.

[153] But see Simon J. Gathercole, *The Pre-existent Son: Recovering the Christologies of Matthew, Mark, and Luke* (Grand Rapids: Eerdmans, 2006), 191–209; and Grant Macaskill, *Revealed Wisdom and Inaugurated Eschatology in Ancient Judaism and Early Christianity* (Leiden: Brill, 2007), 235–38, on the dangers of trying to make too much of Wisdom Christology in the Synoptic Gospels.

(3) Wisdom in Pauline Christology.

Wisdom themes loom large in Pauline discourse, often in relation to Christology.[154] In contrast to the Corinthians, for whom wisdom was a mixture of rhetorical verve, philosophical sophistry, and pneumatic pretentiousness, Paul declared that the "message of the cross," though mocked and maligned, is God's Wisdom against the world and God's power in the nadirs of defeat and death (1 Cor 1.18-21). Paul's gospel entails a radical reversal of worldly systems of calculating worth because "Christ [is] the power of God and the wisdom of God . . . who became for us wisdom from God, and righteousness and sanctification and redemption" (1 Cor 1.24, 30). Paul goes on to say that his message of "Christ crucified" is part of a mystery whereby God's Wisdom is exhibited in the cross, purposed to turn the tables on the wisdom of this age and the rulers of this age, something grasped only by the Spirit's illumination (1 Cor 2.1-10). Paul refers to a hidden wisdom that is revealed and declares that Christ "became" wisdom (1 Cor 1.30; 2.6-7), yet he is not referring to

[154] The pioneering study on Paul, wisdom, and Christ was by Hans Windisch, "Die göttliche Weisheit der Juden und die paulinische Christologie," in *Neutestamentliche Studien*, ed. Adolf Deissmann (Leipzig: Hinrichs, 1914), 220-34, followed up by André Feuillet, *Le Christ, sagesse de Dieu: d'après les épitres pauliniennes* (Paris: Lecoffre, 1966). There is debate as to whether Wisdom is an influence in Paul's Christology of preexistence (e.g., Dunn, *Theology of Paul*, 266-93) or whether it is entirely irrelevant (e.g., Aart van Roon, "The Relationship between Christ and the Wisdom of God according to Paul," *NovT* 16 [1974]: 207-39; Gordon D. Fee, *Pauline Christology: An Exegetical-Theological Study* [Peabody, Mass.: Hendrickson, 2007], 595-630). I am more circumspect about finding wisdom traditions behind texts such as 1 Cor 8.6 and Phil 2.5-11, while I find the influence of personified Wisdom in places such as 1 Cor 1.30 and Col 1.15-20 to be undeniable. McDonough (*Christ as Creator*, 70-71) complains: "The early Christians did not necessarily need a pre-existing figure like Wisdom, nor even a tradition of a preexistent Messiah, onto which they could attach Jesus. This Messiah could, as it were, preexist on his own two feet." While that is technically true, the many parallels with wisdom traditions suggest that Wisdom certainly was a contributing factor as to how (not why!) preexistence was attributed to Jesus. I fully agree with McDonough, who asserted: "If the one true God had sent Jesus the Messiah as the definitive agent of redemption, and if this redemption was at one level simply the outworking of the project of creation (a view with ample precedent in the Hebrew Bible and indeed the Ancient Near East in general), it must be that the Messiah was the agent of creation as well" (2-3; cf. 235). I only wish to add that if one is thinking about *how* Jesus is the agent of creation (i.e., *Schöpfungsmittler*), personified and hypostatic accounts of Wisdom in Scripture and Hellenistic Judaism were a ready-made model to be utilized to such an end. Wise is the judgment of Eckhard Schnabel (*Law and Wisdom from Ben Sira to Paul* [WUNT 2.16; Tübingen: Mohr Siebeck, 1985], 245-46): "It appears to be beyond doubt that Paul consciously describes Christ in wisdom language: Christ, as is divine wisdom in the Jewish sapiential theology, is the creative and salvational power and action of God which seems to be the natural consequence from his identification with wisdom [which] implies or presupposes a pre-existence christology."

Wisdom as a preexistent divine personification, nor plotting Christ's transformation from a heavenly state to an earthly existence. Rather, wisdom here is God's foreordained plan of salvation from ages past now manifested in the cross. Dunn puts it well: "*Christ* is the wisdom of God, the crucified Christ is the embodiment of God's plan of salvation and the measure and fullest expression of God's continuing wisdom and power."[155]

Paul, in a feat (or fit) of hermeneutical creativity (or anarchy), pits Lev 18.5 against a composite citation of Deut 9.4 and 30.12–14 in Rom 10.5–8:

> Moses writes concerning the righteousness that comes from the law, that "the person who does these things will live by them." But the righteousness that comes from faith says, "Do not say in your heart, 'Who will ascend into heaven?'" (that is, to bring Christ down) or "Who will descend into the abyss?" (that is, to bring Christ up from the dead). But what does it say? "The word is near you, on your lips and in your heart" (that is, the word of faith that we proclaim).

The intertextual logic is disputed and open to a wide variety of interpretations. My own view is that Paul is arguing that striving in the Torah, or waiting for someone to traverse heaven or Hades to bring salvation, is needless because the word which brings covenantal renewal is not only near but present in the message of faith that he proclaims in the gospel.[156] What is notable for our purposes is that Deut 30.12–13 is also alluded to in Prov 30.4 and Bar 3.29–30 with reference to human inaccessibility to wisdom and God's unique possession of wisdom. I doubt that Paul intended a connection with Prov 30 or Bar 3, nor did he expect his readers to pick up on it. But it is telling that Paul's narration of Christ transcending heaven and the abyss parallels the association of wisdom as something that resides uniquely with God.

The poem in Col 1.15–20 is most probably a reworking of prior traditions, even if its final form is ostensibly Pauline. The poem is evidently rooted in a Jewish framework of monotheism, creation, and intermediaries. Looking at Col 1.15–16, the phrases "image of the invisible God," "firstborn of creation," and "beginning," when combined with creative instrumentality (i.e., "all things were created in him"), bear a remarkable resemblance to descriptions

---

[155] Dunn, *Christology in the Making*, 179 (italics original). See R. G. Hamerton-Kelly (*Pre-existence, Wisdom, and the Son of Man: A Study in the Idea of Pre-existence in the New Testament* [Cambridge: Cambridge University Press, 1973], 115–17), who concludes that the wisdom of God is not a christological title, but more of a synecdochic idiom for God's apocalyptic plan of salvation revealed in Christ.

[156] Michael F. Bird, *Romans* (SGBC; Grand Rapids: Zondervan, 2016), 352–58.

of Wisdom in Jewish literature (Prov 3.19; 8.22-23, 30; Ps 104.24; Wis 1.6-7; 7.22, 26; 8.4-6; 9.1-10; Sir 1.4; 24.9; 43.26; Philo, *Leg. all.* 1.43; *Det.* 54; *Her.* 199; *Fug.* 109; *Plant.* 18; *Virt.* 62; *Conf.* 61-63, 146-67; *QG* 4.97; 4Q415 9 5-11; 11Q5 26 14). The poem, then, identifies Christ with God's Wisdom to express Christ's priority to creation and his agency in the making of creation.[157]

The equation of Christ with God's Wisdom in Col 1.15-16 is easy enough to grasp, but it is what that means given the precise language and wider imagery that prompts dispute. Alas, however we try, we cannot forget that Col 1.15-16 was the forward edge of the battle era in the Arian debates of the fourth century as to whether Christ was a "firstborn" creature of creation or the Father's divine agent in a triune act of creation. Let me be clear, the Arian debate about Christ's alleged creatureliness was not a semantic philosophical debate; it is very much an exegetical debate concerning Wisdom and Christ in key scriptural texts. The fact is that Jewish texts oscillate between treating Wisdom as something created or begotten by God (Prov 8.22; Sir 1.4; 24.3, 9; Philo, *Fug.* 50-51) or an emanation of God (Wis 7.25-26). Accordingly, if the first strophes of the Christ poem emerged from a christological reading of Gen 1.1 and Prov 8.22-23, then, it remains possible that Christ's priority to and preeminence over creation are concurrent with his own creatureliness of some heavenly variety. Arius was not clutching at straws. Arius, given certain assumptions, by accenting certain interpretive traditions, by privileging certain texts, was well within his rights to construct his argument the way he did about Christ as a supreme angel.[158] In fact, one could argue that Arius was attempting to restore the Judeo-Christian monotheism of an earlier generation.[159]

---

[157] See N. T. Wright, *The Climax of the Covenant: Christ and the Law in Pauline Theology* (Edinburgh: T&T Clark, 1991), 112; Jeffrey S. Lamp, "Wisdom in Col 1:15-20: Contribution and Significance," *JETS* 41 (1998): 45-53; Christopher A. Beetham, *Echoes of Scripture in the Letters of Paul to the Colossians* (BIS 96; Leiden: Brill, 2008), 113-41, 135-36; Michael F. Bird, *Colossians and Philemon* (NCCS; Eugene, Ore.: Cascade, 2009), 48-53; and Kyu Seop Kim, *The Firstborn Son in Ancient Judaism and Early Christianity: A Study of Primogeniture and Christology* (BIS 171; Leiden: Brill, 2019), 182, 190-91 (who links "firstborn" to Wisdom and Israel). Others question the presence of wisdom motifs in Col. 1.15-16 including Fee, *Pauline Christology*, 601; and McDonough, *Christ as Creator*, 172-91.

[158] This is largely the thesis of Martin Werner, *The Formation of Christian Dogma* (Boston: Beacon, 1965); followed by Rudolf Lorenz, *Arius Judaizans? Untersuchungen zur dogmengeschichtlichen Einordnung des Arius* (Göttingen: Vandenhoeck & Ruprecht, 1980), 141-80; see response from Joseph Barbel, *Christos Angelos: Die Anschauung von Christus als Bote und Engel in der gelehrten und volkstümlichen Literatur des christlichen Altertums: Zugleich ein Beitrag zur Geschichte des Ursprungs und der Fortdauer des Arianismus* (Bonn: Hanstein, 1964).

[159] Bauckham, *Jesus and the God of Israel*, 149.

What mitigates against the Arian reading are several things: (1) There are better words besides *prōtotokos* that could be supplied if Paul wanted to refer to Christ as an angelic creature, such as *prōtoktistos* ("created first"),[160] *prōtoplastos* ("first formed"), *prōtogonos* ("first generated"), *prōtosystatos* ("primordial"), *prōtochronos* ("first in chronology"), or *prōtopresbyteros* ("first ancient being"). In all likelihood, Paul deploys *prōtotokos* because of its association with Israel (Exod 4.22–23; Sir 36.17) and the Messiah (Ps 89.27), to make Christ the eschatological ruler of Israel (*Jos. Asen.* 18.11; 21.4), not for a connotation of creatureliness. (2) In 1.16, Christ is not part of *ta panta* ("all things"); the poem distinguishes Christ from other angelic powers and heavenly intermediaries, the same distinction that generally separates God from creation and angels in other Jewish and Christian writings (e.g., Isa 44.24; 66.1–2; Sir 24.8; *1 En.* 9.5). (3) Two unique aspects are also attributed to Christ in the poem: first, that creation was made "for him" (1.16);[161] second, that God's "fullness" inhabits him (1.19), neither of which are attributed to lesser angelic powers as far as I am aware.[162]

In sum, the titles and roles attributed to Wisdom in Jewish literature are applied to a piece of poetic Christology.[163] As the "image of God," Christ is "an anthropomorphous hypostatic representation of God,"[164] while as "firstborn of all creation" Christ is given the mantle of God's preeminent partner and progeny in the act of creation itself. This is more than a conviction that Christ embodies or expresses the power of God in creation; more likely, it implies personal preexistence, which perhaps coalesces with a preexisting Son of God Christology.[165] Christ is slotted into the intermediary role of preexisting divine Wisdom, with a due emphasis on Christ's proximity to God, as well as his creative and sustaining agency in creation. The unique glosses made to Jewish wisdom traditions are that Christ is distinguished from other heavenly powers and angelic beings, he is the goal of creation, and he is pervaded with divine

[160] As precisely found in *Herm.* 12.1; 58.3.

[161] Contra Wolfgang Schrage, *Unterwegs zur Einheit und Einzigkeit Gottes: Zum "Monotheismus" des Paulus und seiner alttestamentlich-frühjüdischen Tradition* (Neukirchen-Vluyn: Neukirchener, 2002), 170–71, who thinks Christ is never the origin and goal of creation but only a mediator between God and creation.

[162] Cf. *Barn.* 12.7: "the glory of Jesus; for in him and to him are all things."

[163] Cf. Schnabel (*Law and Wisdom*, 258): "To sum up, the author of the hymn attributed the sapiential functions of creational and salvational mediation to Jesus Christ[,] thus portraying the pre-existent, incarnate, and exalted Christ in the light of the Jewish divine wisdom."

[164] Ian K. Smith, *Heavenly Perspective: A Study of the Apostle Paul's Response to a Jewish Mystical Movement at Colossae* (LNTS 326; London: T&T Clark, 2006), 161.

[165] Contra Dunn, *Christology in the Making*, 194, 211–12, but with Hengel, *Son of God*, 72–74; Kim, *Origin of Paul's Gospel*, 117–19, 259; and Schnabel, *Law and Wisdom*, 261.

fullness, followed in the remainder of the poem with an Adamic typology, messianic motifs, and apocalyptic eschatology.[166]

(4) Wisdom and Word in Johannine Christology.

The connections between the Johannine prologue and Jewish wisdom traditions are well known, and we have already touched upon them.[167] It suffices to note that Hellenistic Jewish wisdom speculation, which made Wisdom a divine personification and often assigned it a demiurgical role in creation, constituted something of a catalyst that could be used to expound a Son of God Christology that already identified Jesus as God's exalted vice-regent with a cosmic prehistory. Of course, rather than use the feminine *Sophia*, John utilizes the masculine title *Logos* because his subject becomes the man Jesus of Nazareth.[168] A cursory comparison shows that Wisdom corresponds to the Johannine Logos in several ways: (1) Wisdom preexists creation and is an agent of creation (e.g., Prov 8.22–23; Wis 6.22; 7.22; 8.6; 9.1–2; Sir 1.1, 4; 24.9 = John 1.1–3); Wisdom descended from heaven (Bar 3.29–30; Sir 24.3; Wis 9.10; *1 En.* 42.2 = John 1.14; 3.13); Wisdom dwells on earth (Bar 3.37; Sir 1.10; 24.8–8; *1 En.* 42.2 = John 1.14); Wisdom is uniquely loved by God (Wis 8.3 = John 1.14, 18; 3.35; 5.20); Wisdom is an expression of divine glory (Wis 7.25 = John 1.14); and Wisdom finds no positive reception on earth (Bar 3.12; Sir 24.28; *1 En.* 42.2 = John 1.10–11). More broadly, Wisdom's descent from heaven and her return provide a basic plotline for the Fourth Gospel as Jesus the Logos returns to the Father (John 3.13; 14.3; 17.5, 24; 20.17). In sum, John's prologue is an exercise in explaining how God's Wisdom is revealed in and as Jesus, albeit in light of certain kerygmatic and philosophical commitments.

(5) Christ and Wisdom in proto-orthodox Christianity.

In the proto-orthodox churches we see two basic trends in relation to Christ and Wisdom. First, some authors identify Christ as the God's Word and the Spirit

---

[166] The first strophe of the poem is clearly backgrounded in Jewish wisdom traditions and speculation, while the second strophe of the poem is an eclectic combination of Christ as new Adam, prophetic motifs, and Christian materials. See Matthew E. Gordley, *New Testament Christological Hymns: Exploring Texts, Contexts, and Significance* (Downers Grove, Ill.: InterVarsity, 2018), 129–32.

[167] Cf., e.g., J. R. Harris, *The Origin of the Prologue to St. John's Gospel* (Cambridge: Cambridge University Press, 1917); Dodd, *Interpretation of the Fourth Gospel*, 274–76; Evans, *Word and Glory*, 83–94; Harmut Gese, *Essays on Biblical Theology* (Minneapolis: Augsburg, 1981), 167–222; Keener, *Gospel of John*, 1:353; and William Loader, "Wisdom and Logos Traditions in Judaism and John's Christology," in *Reading the Gospel of John's Christology as Jewish Messianism*, ed. Benjamin Reynolds and Gabriele Boccaccini (AJEC 106; Leiden: Brill, 2018), 303–34.

[168] A point made by Origen, *Cels.* 5.39.

as God's Wisdom, especially in relation to creation. For Theophilus this yields a creative triad of God, Logos, and Sophia (*Autol.* 1.7; 2.10, 15), and for Irenaeus the Son and Spirit are the two hands of God in creation so that God made all things by his Word and adorned them by his Wisdom (*Haer.* 4.20.1–6). Second, Christ is identified as God's Wisdom in the sense that he is God's Word. The Roman *Shepherd* implies a demiurgical Christology whereby God "by his invisible and mighty power and by his great wisdom created the world, and by his glorious purpose clothed his creation with beauty, and by his mighty word fixed the heaven and set forth the earth's foundations upon the waters and by his own wisdom and providence created his holy church" (*Herm.* 3.4). Minucius Felix implies much the same: "He orders everything, whatever it is, by a word; arranges it by his wisdom; perfects it by his power" (*Oct.* 18). Athenagoras describes the Son as the "mind, word, and wisdom of the Father," while the Spirit is "an effluence like light from fire" (*Legat.* 24.2). Justin is the author who aligns Christ with God's Wisdom with an acute intensity, referring to the "Word of Wisdom, who is himself this God begotten of the Father of all things, and Word, and Wisdom, and Power, and the Glory of the Begetter" (*Dial.* 61.3). Then, in a piece of interpretation which foreshadows the coming debates of the fourth century, Justin appeals to Prov 8.22–23: "the Scripture has declared that this Offspring was begotten by the Father before all things created; and that which is begotten is numerically distinct from that which begets" (*Dial.* 129.3–5). Tertullian writing later is similar in that he says that Christ is the Word and Wisdom of the Father with an explicit appeal to Prov 8.22–23 (*Prax.* 6–7). There are some variations of this scheme. For instance, in the *Epistula Apostolorum* Christ acquires the Father's wisdom and power as he descends from heaven to earth (*Ep. Ap.* 13.1).

(6) Christ, Wisdom, and the Sophia myth.

The Jewish tradition of Wisdom's descent to earth was utilized by Hellenistic, apocalyptic, Christian, and Gnostic authors, albeit in different ways and for different ends. Concerning Gnosticism, Wisdom's descent combined with a Platonic demiurgism (*Timaeus*), coalesced with a Philonesque account of the multiplication of heavenly beings in and around the Logos (*Fug.* 95, 103; *Mos.* 2.99–100; *Her.* 166; *Abr.* 121; *QG* 2.16; *QE* 2.62, 68), and merged with the attribution to Sophia of a role like "mother of the Logos" (*Fug.* 108–9). The Sophia myth probably combined several eclectic aspects of ancient mythology, including that of a female consort to a supreme deity, but the parallels between Gnostic Sophia myths and Jewish wisdom traditions are palpable and are indicative of a genetic relationship.[169] The Gnostic Sophia myth, with numerous variations, generally runs that Sophia[170] was expelled from the pleroma, generated the demiurge, yielded something like death (*Gos. Phil.* 60.12) or corruption (*Gos. Judas* 44.4), and then penitently returned to the pleroma (e.g., Irenaeus, *Haer.* 1.2.2–5; 1.29.4; 1.30.1–14; *Ap. John* 9.25–10.7). This myth, in all its permutations, had a key role in Gnostic cosmology, theodicy, and soteriology. Importantly, Christ was not identified with Sophia; instead, he was a separate aeon, or sometimes a son or brother of Sophia (Irenaeus, *Haer.* 1.30.2, 12).

(7) Comparative analysis.

The portrayal of Wisdom as a personified divine attribute, demiurge, and divine companion, in both Scripture and Hellenistic Judaism, provided a ready-made category for Christians to use to describe Jesus as preexistent person and a divine agent of creation and revelation. Several similarities are readily apparent:

(a) *Preexistence and proximity to God.* In wisdom literature and related writings, Wisdom preexists creation and is a companion with God in the beginning of things (Prov 8.22–23, 27, 30; Wis 6.22; 8.3–4; 9.9; Sir 1.1, 4; 24.3, 9). Similarly, Jesus' preexistence is stated or implied (Col 1.15–17; Gal 4.4–5; Rom 8.3; Phil 2.6–7; 1 Cor 8.6; 2 Cor 8.9) and sometimes combined with a description of a deep connection with God the Father in eternity past (John 1.1–2, 18; 17.5, 24).

(b) *Divine expression.* Although Wisdom can be an entity made before creation or in the beginning of creation, Wisdom can also be an entity that is the personal expression of God's very being. The Wisdom of Solomon posits Wisdom as somewhere between divine attribute and divine agent: "For she is a breath of the power of God, and a pure emanation of the glory of the Almighty; therefore nothing defiled gains entrance into her. For she is a reflection of eternal light, a spotless mirror of the working of God, and an image of his goodness" (Wis 7.25–26). Philo shares the perspective of Wisdom's unique proximity to God as the rationale for its unique capacity to reveal God as the

---

[169] George W. MacRae, "The Jewish Background of the Gnostic Sophia Myth," *NovT* 12 (1970): 86–101. He notes the following similarities: (1) Sophia is personal; (2) Sophia is joined in intimate union with god; (3) Sophia was brought forth in the beginning; (4) Sophia dwells in the clouds; (5) Sophia attends God's throne; (6) Sophia is identified with the (Holy) Spirit; (7) Sophia was instrumental in the creation of the world; (8) Sophia communicates wisdom and revelations to humanity; (9) Sophia descends into the world of humanity; (10) Sophia returns to her celestial home; (11) Sophia protected and preserved Adam; (12) Sophia is a sister; (13) Sophia is part of a sevenfold cosmic structure; (14) Sophia is identified with life; and (15) Sophia is a tree of life.

[170] Sophia is sometimes known as Barbelo, Prunicus, or Achamoth.

divine "image" (*Leg. all.* 1.43). In Christian discourse, Christ images God principally as the divine Son, who shares in God's being, sovereignty, and glory (Col 1.15; 2 Cor 4.4; Heb 1.3). In a more revelatory sense, to see Jesus is to see the Father, as the Son is the image of the Father (John 14.7–10).

(c) *Agent of creation.* Although Prov 8 does not explicitly attribute a demiurgical role to Wisdom, there are scriptural statements about God making the world through his wisdom (Prov 3.19; Ps 104.24; Jer 10.12; 51.15; cf. 1QH^a 9.7, 14; 4Q415 IX 5–11; 11Q5 XXVI 14). Elsewhere there are affirmations of Wisdom as the "fashioner" of all things or the one by whom all things were made (Wis 7.22; 8.4–6; 9.1–2; Philo, *Det.* 54; *Her.* 199; *Ebr.* 30–31; *Fug.* 109; Irenaeus, *Haer.* 1.5.3). Jesus is also given a demiurgical role as the one in, through, or by whom God made all things (1 Cor 8.6; Col 1.15–18; Heb 1.2; John 1.3; Rev 3.14; *Odes Sol.* 16.19; *Keryg. Pet.* 2; *Herm.* 3.4; 91.5; *Diogn.* 7.2; Justin, *2 Apol.* 6.3; Irenaeus, *Haer.* 4.11.1) even if restricted to the noetic and spiritual planes (*Exc.* 8.2).

(d) *Dwells among people.* Wisdom comes to dwell among people, either in the Torah or in relation to the Jerusalem temple (Sir 1.10; 24.8; *1 En.* 42.2; Bar 3.37). This is the language of God's glory dwelling (Exod 25.8; 29.46) or returning to the temple during a period of restoration (Joel 3.17; Zech 2.10). Paul had spoken of Christ as the "glory of God" (2 Cor 4.4–6) and one who took on the "likeness" of human flesh and form (Rom 8.3; Phil 2.7; 1 Tim 3.16; cf. *Barn.* 6.14). Yet John exceeds this when he refers to the Word "become flesh and dwelling among us" whose flesh still conveys "his glory, the glory of the Father's only son" (John 1.14). John takes up the tradition of the preexistent Wisdom of God in Israel and God's own glory amid the people to annunciate how God's Logos was enfleshed in the human being Jesus of Nazareth.[171] These striking statements, while influenced by Wisdom traditions, far exceed what is normally attributed to Wisdom in Jewish tradition. In the end, "If John can say that the Word 'was God' (1.1 c; cf. 1.18), that Jesus claims, 'Before Abraham was, I am' (8:58), and that it is appropriate to believe in Jesus as Lord and God (20:28)," then, infers Craig Keener, "John's Jesus is more than merely divine Wisdom."[172]

(e) *Titles.* Wisdom receives many titles that designate its close relationship with God and God's actions. Proverbs says that Wisdom is "begotten" or "brought forth" (Prov 8.25), which matches the Johannine idea of the Son as God's only begotten (John 1.14, 18; 3.16, 18; cf. Justin, *1 Apol.* 12.7; 21.1; 22.2; *Dial.* 62.4; *Diogn.* 10.2). Wisdom is sometimes set in parallel to the divine Word, often in a narration of the Word launching from heaven to earth (Wis

---

[171] Frey, "Incarnation of the Logos," 282.
[172] Keener, *Gospel of John*, 1:369.

9.1–4; 18.15; cf. Sir 4.24; Philo, *Leg. all.* 1.65), which again finds expression in the Logos of the Johannine prologue (John 1.1). The notion of the Word or Wisdom as God's "firstborn" is found in Philo (*Conf.* 62–63, 146; *QG* 4.97; *Agr.* 51; *Somn.* 1.215, 241) and arguably corresponds to designations of Jesus as God's firstborn in creation and new creation (Rom 8.29; Col 1.15; Justin, *1 Apol.* 33.6; 46.2; 63.15) or else as a heavenly man (1 Cor 15.47–49).

(f) *Associations.* Wisdom is often associated with certain divine attributes or heavenly décor, which are mirrored in Christian writings. Wisdom results in life and light (Prov 8.35; Bar 4.1–2; Wis 7.29–30; 8.13), something John claims inhabits the Logos (John 1.4–5). Wisdom is at once glorious (Wis 7.25; Sir 24.17) and Jesus reflects divine glory (John 1.14; 2 Cor 4.4–6). Wisdom sits by God's throne (Wis 9.4, 10), on a throne comprised of a "pillar of cloud" (Sir 24.4), sits among angels (*1 En.* 42.2), and notwithstanding some textual conjectures is connected to God's royal throne room (*1 En.* 84.3–4). Christian authors put Jesus on a heavenly throne, God's own throne, demonstrated in citations and allusions to Ps 110.1, and specifically in the book of Revelation (Rev 3.21; 5.6; 7.17; 22.3). Finally, Wisdom is closely associated with God's Torah, inhabiting it, or else providing instruction in divine wisdom (Sir Prologue 1; Sir 1.26; 6.37; 15.1; 19.20; 24.23; 34.8; 39.8; Bar 3.9; 4.1; Wis 9.9). The Pauline binary of Christ and Torah should not obscure the fact that a variety of relationships between Christ and the Torah are posited with Christ himself embodying, like Wisdom, a new Torah. W. D. Davies detects such a view precisely in Paul, so that "Jesus Himself—in word and deed or fact is a New Torah."[173] Keener goes so far as to say that the purpose of the Johannine prologue is to identify the Logos as God's Torah in human form: "Jesus himself embodies the Torah and is its fullest revelation, and the apostolic witnesses thus deliver a revelation of greater authority than that of Moses (1:14–18; cf. 2 Cor. 3). It is rejecting Jesus, rather than obeying him, that constitutes rejection of Torah (cf. 1:11–13)."[174] In the second century, there is a remarkable constellation of views about Jesus as Torah-as-person or Torah-in-new-dispensation. In one of the Roman Shepherd's parables the "law is the Son of God, who has been proclaimed to the ends of the earth" (*Herm.* 69.2). In the *Kerygma Petrou*, the Lord is given the titles "Law and Word" (*Keryg. Pet.* 1). Justin claimed that the old law is superseded by Christ, who "is the new law, the new covenant" (*Dial.* 11.4; cf. 24.1; 43.1). For Irenaeus, Christ is the "law of liberty" and "Word of God," who was preached by the apostles throughout all the earth (*Haer.* 4.34.4).

---

[173] W. D. Davies, *Paul and Rabbinic Judaism* (Philadelphia: Fortress, 1980), 148.
[174] Keener, *Gospel of John*, 1:360.

Evidently, when Christian authors felt the need to express Jesus' prehistory conceived as his heavenly position proximate to God, his mediation in creation, his association with God's glory and goals, the category of personified Wisdom was useful to that end. Beyond that, it is possible to drill down to what is distinctive in the application of preexistent Wisdom to Jesus by looking principally at the apostle Paul and the evangelist John.

Paul, in some instances, by identifying Jesus with Wisdom, was arguably doing no more than seeing in Jesus' death and resurrection the embodiment of God's saving plan and power. Paul lays out in 1 Cor 1–2 an argument whereby Jesus' *crucifixion*, the epitome of defeat and degradation, and Jesus' *resurrection*, the unthinkable reanimation of a dead corpse, two notions that were nonsense to the sages of the ages, are where God's purposes, victory, and deliverance are wrought. Yet elsewhere, Paul rehearses traditions of Wisdom as a divine personification to identify Jesus as the agent, unity, and goal of creation. These assertions, when combined with his taking a human nature (Rom 8.3; Gal 4.4–5; Phil 2.6–7), set him apart from other intermediary figures. In addition, what is truly unique in Col 1.15–20 are the associations of personified Wisdom with a christological recasting of Gen 1, embodying divine fullness, locating the image of God supremely in Christ, making Christ a heavenly man or new Adam, describing the Messiah's reign as cosmic, and setting Christ as head of both creation and new creation. Paul narrates the story of Jesus as the coming of God's heavenly wisdom to earth as the divine Son, who fulfills in his life, death, resurrection, and exaltation Israel's messianic vocation.

In the case of the Johannine prologue, John is riffing off wisdom traditions, yet he plays them in a distinct christological chord. John, like Ben Sira, believes that Wisdom finds a home. But, unlike Ben Sira, Wisdom does not tabernacle in the Torah or set up shop in Jerusalem; rather, it becomes a human being. John, like the Wisdom of Solomon, could affirm that Wisdom is the image or effluence of God. But, unlike the Wisdom of Solomon, "This Logos does not reside here or there (cf. Wis 7.27–28); nor does it appear now in Jesus and elsewhere later . . . Rather, the Logos of John 1 is so inextricably linked with the 'I' of Jesus that it follows for the evangelist: Jesus alone is the 'incarnate' Word of God; he is the only authentic 'exegesis' of God as per v. 18."[175] John,

---

[175] Michael Theobald, *Das Evangelium nach Johannes: Kapital 1–12* (Regensburg: Friedrich Pustet, 2009), 192: "Dieser Logos nimmt nicht einmal hier, einmal dort Wohnung (vgl. Weish 7,27f. [siehe zu V. 14b]); er zeigt sich auch nicht jetzt in Jesus, später anderswo (der Logos ist nicht der Weltgeist, der in der Geschichte epiphan wird!). Vielmehr hat der Logos von Joh 1 sich mit dem 'Ich' Jesu derart unlöslich verbunden, dass für den Evangelisten gilt: Ausschließlich Jesus ist das 'Fleisch gewordene' Wort Gottes, er allein die authentische 'Exegese' Gottes, wie V. 18."

like *1 En.* 42, sees an underlying tragedy in that Wisdom comes to humanity yet is sadly turned away. But, unlike *1 En.* 42, Wisdom does not glumly saunter back to heaven and leave Lady Iniquity to takes her place; instead, Wisdom remains long enough to testify and redeem the world before returning to the Father's glory.[176] John, like Philo, conflates Wisdom and Logos and regards him as the one who truly sees God. But, unlike Philo, Wisdom does not buffer God from the world; instead, she brings God's light, life, and love to the world. In this way, John affirms Sirach's conviction of God's self-communication, but declares that divine revelation climaxes in Jesus the Christ. John shares the Wisdom of Solomon's stress on Wisdom's nearness to God and Wisdom's nearness to us, but his account of "nearness" in both instances becomes bound up with notions of divine identity and incarnation. John addresses the Enochic rejection of Wisdom, but the tragedy turns to triumph as Wisdom overcomes the darkness within the world. John would agree with Philo that Wisdom (or Logos) is a human archetype, but for John this Wisdom transgresses the creator-creation boundary so that the ideal becomes real human flesh.

John combines Jewish wisdom traditions with a reimagining of genesis in Christ. In the prologue, the "beginning" of Gen 1.1 is combined with the "word/wisdom" of creation (Ps 33.6; Prov 3.19; 4Q403 I 1.35; 4Q422 I 1.6), who was with God "in the beginning of his work" (Prov 8.22), who descended to earth (Wis 18.15; Sir 24.8–10; Bar 3.36–37). The narrative then takes a surprising twist so that what is revealed is the full humanness of the Logos (John 1.14). The climax of Gen 1 was the creation of the human being in the image of the creator (Gen 1.26–28). But here in John's new genesis, the climax is the enfleshing of the Logos, who, possessing many of the characteristics of Wisdom, is the divine image-bearer par excellence (Wis 7.26). According to Frey:

> It is the echo of Genesis in [John] 1.1—which was unmistakable for the first readers of the Gospel—that removes the talk of the Logos from its semantic openness and history-of-religion or history-of-philosophy polysemy from the outset and places it in the context of the revelation of the God of the Scriptures of Israel. It is now this divine Logos, or, more precisely, the personified creative Word, who precedes the world in creative power and stands in relation to it, about whom the *sarx egeneto* is announced and in relation to whom this extraordinary statement, i.e., *sarx egeneto*, forms an extremely great contrast.[177]

The Johannine Logos, then, is not Wisdom filling a human subject; neither does the Logos appear in human guise, nor does the Logos kenotically divest

---

[176] Wright, *New Testament and the People of God*, 415–16.
[177] Frey, "Incarnation of the Logos," 279.

itself of divine glory to become human. John, without saying how (there is no virgin birth narrative), affirms the divine Word's complete entrance into a fully orbed human life, fostering a "fullness" whereby his flesh still exhibits divine glory, grace, life, and light (John 1.4–5, 14, 16).

Angels

Angels were significant in Jewish tradition especially for conceiving of the celestial court, heavenly messengers, and divine immanence. The Jewish Scriptures, Second Temple texts, and rabbinic writings contain various accounts of angelic messengers, warriors, guardians, guides, and intercessors. The category of a supreme or principal angel, a heavenly being of high status with close proximity to God and who acts as a mediating agent, might constitute a specific divine intermediary who informed christological discourses. Indeed, as heavenly origins and a preexistence were attributed to Jesus it was natural if not inevitable that Jesus would be described either with angelic qualities (angelomorphism) or even identified as an angel (angel Christology). Principal angels have been an obvious point of comparison for describing several salient features in emerging Christologies. Various accounts of angel Christology have been proposed, and they are a good test case for the applicability of heavenly intermediaries to Christology, since some scholars resist their relevance and others treat them as the most significant influence. Therefore, this (lengthy!) section will examine how Jesus became an angel and why some thought it necessary to un-make him an angel.

(1) Angels and the heavenly council.

Angels are heavenly beings who form a divine entourage as the "host of heaven," consisting of something of a hybrid heavenly council, choir, and army (1 Kgs 22.19; Neh 9.6; Dan 4.35; Pr Man 15). Elsewhere the word "hosts" designates the gods and kings of the nations who are wrongly worshipped besides the heavenly bodies (Deut 4.19–20; 17.3; 32.8; 2 Kgs 17.16; 21.3–5; 23.4; Isa 24.21; Dan 10.13; Rev 9.11). One prominent designation is the "sons of God," which signifies angels, minor deities, and godlike men (Gen 6.2, 4; Job 1.6; 2.1; 38.7; Ps 29.1; 82.6; 89.7; Josephus, *Ant.* 1.73; Ps.-Philo, *LAB* 3.1).[178] Angels are commonly identified as "spirits" (1 Kgs 11.19–23; Judg 9.22–23; Heb 1.14; Rev 1.4; *1 En.* 15.6–11; 1QS 3.18–19, 25; CD 12.2–3; 1QH 3.21–23; 11.13; 1QM 13.2, 11–12; 14.10). Angelic beings can also be called "heavenly ones"

---

[178] Archie T. Wright, *The Origin of Evil Spirits* (Tübingen: Mohr Siebeck, 2005), 62. The LXX frequently translates the Hebrew *bene elim* (sons of god) and *elohim* (gods) as *angeloi* (see Deut 32.43; Ps 8.6; 96.7; 137.1; Job 1.6; 2.1; 38.7).

(Ps 89.5–7; Job 15.15; 1 Cor 15.48), "stars" as celestial objects (1 Kgs 22.19; Job 38.5–7), "watchers" as there are both good and wicked angels who watch over humanity (Dan 4.13, 17, 23; *Jub.* 4.15; 5.1; 4Q201 1; 4Q204 1; 1Q266 2.2; 4Q212 3; *1 En.* 6–16; *2 En.* 18.1–9), and "holy ones" reflecting a divine attribute (Deut 32.2–3; Ps 89.5; Job 5.1; Zech 14.5; Dan 4.17; 1 Thess 3.13; Jude 14). Angels commonly function as messengers and can undertake a variety of functions on behalf of God. In the post-exilic period Jewish angelology develops through to the Second Temple era until it declines in significance during the rabbinic era.[179] Several aspects of ancient angelology are applicable to developing Christologies.

(a) The Angel of the Lord and a second heavenly power.

A significant figure in the Jewish Scriptures is the "Angel of the Lord," who is an ambiguous figure because he not only delivers a message from Yahweh but also speaks for Yahweh in the first person and even stands in for Yahweh.[180] Abram's concubine Hagar names the angel as *El-roi*, or "God who sees" (Gen 16.7–13; cf. 21.17–18). Later in Genesis the angel declares to Jacob, "I am the God of Bethel" (Gen 31.13), and Jacob blesses Joseph's sons while remembering how God/the angel preserved him from evil (Gen 48.14–16). The angel appears in the burning bush to Moses and self-describes as "I am the God of your father, the God of Abraham, the God of Isaac, and the God of Jacob" (Exod 3.6). The angel who led Israel in the exodus and wilderness wanderings is associated with the pillar of cloud signifying the divine presence (Exod 14.19; 23.20–23; 32.34; 33.2–3; Num 20.16). In Judges, the angel asserts, "I brought you up out of Egypt and led you into the land I swore to give to your ancestors" (Judg 2.1). When Gideon meets the angel of the Lord he despairs and pleads for help: "Help me, Lord God (*Adonai Yahweh/kyrie mou kyrie*)! For I have seen the angel of the Lord face to face" (Judg 6.22). The pattern is repeated when the angel tells Manoah's wife that she will conceive and have a son (Judg 13.1–22). The couple despair because, "We shall surely die, for we have seen God" (Judg 13.22). The intermediary function of the angel is accented in David's vision, according to the Chronicler, where David saw the angel of the Lord "standing between heaven and earth" (1 Chr 21.16). Philo regarded the angel in Jacob's dream as

---

[179] For a useful and accessible summary of angels in the Old and New Testament, see Michael S. Heiser, *Angels: What the Bible Really Says about God's Heavenly Host* (Bellingham, Wash.: Lexham, 2018), esp. 1–27, 76–77, on terminology for angelic/heavenly beings. See also Friedrich V. Reiterer, Tobias Nicklas, and Karin Schöpflin, eds., *Angels: The Concept of Celestial Beings: Origins, Development and Reception* (Berlin: de Gruyter, 2007).

[180] Hence, why Andrew Malone (*Knowing Jesus in the Old Testament? A Fresh Look at Christophanies* [Nottingham, U.K.: InterVarsity, 2015]) treats them as straight-up theophanies.

the "archangel, the Lord himself" (*Her.* 157). Paradoxically the Angel of the Lord both *is* Yahweh and *is not* Yahweh. The angel, says Charles Gieschen, is indicative of "a delicate distinction between YHWH and his visible form" and illustrates "that a figure that has some independence from YHWH can still share in his being through the possession of the divine Name."[181] Ultimately the angel of the Lord is the subject in mysterious divine encounters that attempted to speak of Yahweh's immanence with his people without forfeiting his transcendence, precisely why Philo connected the angel to the Logos (*Abr.* 51; *Migr.* 174; *QE* 2.13).[182]

The scriptural depiction of the Angel of the Lord arguably contributed to the notion of a duality within God or else the prospect that God had a deputy deity operating as a grand vizier. As such, Christian binitarianism with the Father and Christ, Jewish *merkabah* mysticism with its enthroned angelic figures, and Gnostic theo-cosmology with a pleroma populated with aeons and angels are alleged to have emerged from "a cluster of mythologoumena about the archangelic hypostasis of God."[183] Alan Segal's influential thesis is that second-century rabbinic authorities in Palestine castigated a constellation of views as "heretical" for postulating a second heavenly power alongside God derived from biblical speculation (e.g., Exod 24.10–11; Dan 7.9–10) and ecstatic experiences (e.g., visions of Metatron on a divine throne). According to Segal, "the basic heresy involved interpreting scripture to say that a principal angelic or hypostatic manifestation in heaven was equivalent to God."[184]

The genetic origins for the two-powers heresy were scriptural theophanies that pictured God as a human being or else conflated Yahweh with an angel. Apocalyptic and mystical traditions further speculated about exalted heavenly figures who were proximate to the divine throne even as monotheism was still principally affirmed.[185] In Philo one can further

---

[181] Charles Gieschen, "The Divine Name in the Ante-Nicene Christology," *VC* 57 (2003): 122–23.

[182] Cf. Archie T. Wright ("Angels," in *The Eerdmans Dictionary of Early Judaism*, ed. John J. Collins and Daniel C. Harlow [Grand Rapids: Eerdmans, 2010], 328): "Whether the heavenly being is identified as an angelic messenger or as YHWH seems incidental; more important is that the presence of the angel of the Lord affirms the continued involvement of YHWH in the life of Israel."

[183] Gedaliahu Stroumsa, "Form(s) of God: Some Notes on Metatron and Christ," *HTR* 76 (1983): 279.

[184] Alan F. Segal, *Two Powers in Heaven: Early Rabbinic Reports about Christianity and Gnosticism* (Leiden: Brill, 1977), x. See also Andrei Orlov, *The Glory of the Invisible God: Two Powers in Heaven and Early Christology* (London: T&T Clark, 2019).

[185] Segal, *Two Powers in Heaven*, 261.

detect divine attributes and angels becoming a divine abstraction, speculation about the divine names Yahweh and Elohim, which together had the potential to foster belief in a second power beside Yahweh. Accordingly, Philo is willing to indulge the language of two gods (*QG* 2.62), explicitly applied to the Logos and Angel of the Lord, based on divine anthropomorphisms and angelophanies (e.g., Gen 31.13; Exod 23.21; 24.10–11). Even so, Philo is strident that this is not injurious to monotheism, as the Logos or Angel of the Lord is merely a visible copy of the one true God and holds no rivalry with him. Philo allows language of two gods, partly because of biblical pressure to account for the phenomena of the text, partly because the duality emerges from those who know God by intellectual reflection contrasted with those who know God by empirical perception, and partly because some cannot differentiate a copy of God from the original form of God (*Somn.* 1.227–37; *Mos.* 1.66–67, 167). Among the *tannaim*, the two-powers heresy also included the view that the creator was ignorant of a higher god and that there was a complete separation of divine mercy from divine justice, to the point of making them the properties of two different deities, thus testifying to rabbinic encounters with varieties of Gnosticism.[186]

To loosely map the origins of the two-powers tradition: (1) Already within the Hebrew Scriptures, principal angels and divine attributes could be ascribed divine powers and prerogatives. (2) Scriptural language for a humanlike figure in the midst of the divine throne who was associated with divine glory fed speculation of a supreme heavenly agent (Ezek 1.26–28; Dan 7.13). (3) Philo can regard the Logos as an archangel and even a "second god," and also allegorize parts of Israel's Scriptures to split up God's divinity into creative and kingly aspects. (4) In some texts, the divine being recedes from the apocalyptic scenery to be replaced with a divine voice and a superior angel, such as Yahoel, who stands in for God's physical presence as in the *Apocalypse of Abraham*.[187] (5) Dan 7.9 makes a reference to "thrones" plural, which Rabbi Akiba said meant one throne for Yahweh and another throne for the Davidic messiah, but Rabbi Yosi regarded this as blasphemy, and he argued instead that one throne was for the divine attribute of justice and another one for the divine attribute of mercy. (6) Rabbi Elisha ben Avuya (i.e., "Aher") had the beginning of his apostasy explained by his vision of Metatron on a throne in heaven which he erroneously took to imply that "there are two gods" (*b.Ḥag.* 15a; *3 En.* 16).

---

[186] Segal, *Two Powers in Heaven*, 205, 244–45.
[187] Orlov, *Glory of the Invisible God*, 38–53.

²⁶ And above the dome over their heads there was something like a throne, in appearance like sapphire; and seated above the likeness of a throne was something that seemed like a human form. ²⁷ Upward from what appeared like the loins I saw something like gleaming amber, something that looked like fire enclosed all around; and downward from what looked like the loins I saw something that looked like fire, and there was a splendor all around. ²⁸ Like the bow in a cloud on a rainy day, such was the appearance of the splendor all around. This was the appearance of the likeness of the glory of the LORD. When I saw it, I fell on my face, and I heard the voice of someone speaking (Ezek 1.26–28).

⁹ As I watched, thrones were set in place, and an Ancient One took his throne, his clothing was white as snow, and the hair of his head like pure wool; his throne was fiery flames, and its wheels were burning fire. ¹⁰ A stream of fire issued and flowed out from his presence. A thousand thousands served him, and ten thousand times ten thousand stood attending him. The court sat in judgment, and the books were opened (Dan 7.9–10).

One passage says: "His throne was fiery flames" (Dan. 7.9) and another passage says: "Until thrones were placed; and One that was ancient of days did sit"—there is no contradiction; One [throne] for Him, and one for David: this is the view of R. Akiba. Said R. Yosi the Galilean to him: Akiba, how long will you treat the divine presence as profane! Rather, one for justice and one for mercy. Did he accept [this explanation] from him, or did he not accept it?—come and hear: One for justice and one for mercy; this is the view of R. Akiba (*b.Ḥag.* 14a).

For nothing mortal can be made in the likeness of the most High One and Father of the universe but only in that of the second god, who is his Logos. For it was right that the rational part of the human soul should be formed as an impression by the divine Logos, since the pre-Logos God is superior to every rational nature (Philo, *QG* 2.62).

What is signified here under a figure are the two most ancient and supreme powers of the divine God, namely, his creative and his kingly power; for his creative power is called "God"; according to which he ordered, created, and adorned this universe, and his kingly power is called "Lord," by which he rules over the beings whom he has created, and governs them with justice and firmness; for he, being the one true living God, is also really the Creator of the world; since he brought things into being which had no existence into being; and he is also by nature a king, because no one can rule over things that have been created more justly than he who created them (Philo, *Mos.* 2.99–100).

Aher mutilated the shoots. Of him Scripture says: "Suffer not thy mouth to bring thy flesh into guilt" [Eccl. 5.6]. What does it refer to?—He saw that permission was granted to [the angel] Metatron to sit and write down the merits of Israel. Said he [Aher]: "It is taught as a tradition that on high there is no sitting and no emulation, and no back, and no weariness. Perhaps,— God forbend!—There are two gods!" [Thereupon] they led Metatron forth, and punished him with sixty fiery lashes, saying to him: "Why didst thou not rise before him when thou didst see him?" Permission was [then] given to him to strike out the merits of Aher. A Bath Kol went forth and said: "Return, ye backsliding children—except Aher." [Thereupon] he said: "Since I have been driven forth from yonder world, let me go forth and enjoy this world." So Aher went forth into evil courses (*b.Ḥag.* 15a).

The relevance and connections of the two-powers view to early Christology is obvious. Segal inferred that "many traditions found heretical by the rabbis in the second century were intimately connected to the apostolic understanding of Jesus," especially those related to "a manlike figure enthroned as judge next to God," who was described in epiphanic imagery. Similar is Andrei Orlov, who points to several texts with theophanic symbolism for intermediary figures that were "preparing a unique seedbed for the growth and development of early Christology."[188] In fact, Orlov surmises: "Earliest Christology thus emerges from this creative tension of the ocularcentric and aural theophanic molds in which the deity steadily abandons its corporeal profile in order to relieve the symbolic space for the new guardian, who from then on becomes the image and glory of the invisible God."[189]

(b) Principal angels.

Archangels stand at the top of the various hierarchies of angels (*1 En.* 6.7; *2 En.* 20.1; *3 En.* 14.1–5; 17.1–4; 4Q403 1 2.18–29). These are superlative heavenly powers archangels (Philo, *Conf.* 146; *Her.* 157; 1 Thess 4.16; Jude 9; *4 Ezra* 3.36). The various archangels are given labels such as "chief princes" (Dan 10.13), the "angel(s) of the presence" (*Jub.* 1.27, 29. 2.2; 18.9–12; 1QH 6.13; 1QSb 4.25), the "angel of his truth" (CD 3.24), and the "great angel" (CD 5.18; 1QM 13.10; 17.6). The most prominent principal angels in sources are named as Michael, Gabriel, Raphael, and Uriel/Sariel/Phanuel (Dan 8.16; 9.21; 10.13, 20–21; Tob 12.15; *1 En.* 9.1–2; 20.1–7; 40.1–10; 54.6; 71.8; 1QM 9.15–16; *Sib. Or.* 2.215; Jude 9; Rev 12.7; *4 Ezra* 4.1; 5.20). Michael can be described as "my mediator, my archistratig, Michael" (*2 En.* 33.10). Other notable angels are Melchizedek, who is probably not the Gen 14 character, but a name for a supreme divine being, "the highest angel in Qumran,"[190] who is given an important role in the Qumran sect's future deliverance (11QMelch 2.9–14). Melchizedek is prominent as he is the heavenly opponent of Belial, explicitly called a "god" (*elohim*), supreme over other divine beings, and has a special relationship to God.[191] There is Yahoel, whose name splices "Yahweh" and "Elohim," the mediator of the divine name, who appears in "a plethora of celestial and earthly offices, including the roles of a choirmaster, a heavenly priest, a revealer of secrets"

---

[188] Orlov, *Glory of the Invisible God*, 77.
[189] Orlov, *Glory of the Invisible God*, 190.
[190] Martin Hengel, *Der Sohn Gottes: Die Entstehung der Christologie und die jüdisch-hellenistische Religionsgeschichte* (2nd ed.; Tübingen: Mohr Siebeck, 1977), 126.
[191] Bühner, *Messianic High Christology*, 57–60.

(*Apoc. Ab.* 10.3–4, 8–9; 12.4; 16.2–4; 17.3–6).¹⁹² Metatron is the "capstone of vice-regent traditions";¹⁹³ his name means "little Yahweh" or "lesser Yahweh," and is perhaps derived by combining the Greek *meta* ("with") and *thronos* ("throne").¹⁹⁴ He was originally Enoch, then, after his translation into heaven, became Metatron. He is another mediator of the divine name, who attends the divine throne, and is even given his own throne of glory (*3 En.* 4.5; 7.1; 10.3–6; 12.1–5; 14.1–5; 16.1–2; *b.Ḥag.* 15a). A rabbi calls him "greater than all the princes, more exalted than all the angels, more beloved than all ministers, more honored than all the hosts, and elevated over all potentates in sovereignty, greatness, and glory" (*3 En.* 4.1–2).

Hurtado has argued that Christian devotion to Jesus was an "innovation" within Jewish monotheism and based on a "mutation" of a divine chief agent such as a principal angel. He detects an "unprecedented reshaping of monotheistic piety to include a second object of devotion alongside God, a figure seen in the position of God's chief agent, happening among a group that continued to consider itself firmly committed to 'one God.'"¹⁹⁵ The stimuli for this mutation was the memory of Jesus as "the eschatological spokesman of the final divine word," visions of Jesus "sharing the glory of God and participating so directly and fully in God's glory and majesty," and trying to remain within the "constraints" of Jewish monotheism.¹⁹⁶ In Hurtado's telling, at the earliest stage of the nascent church, among Aramaic-speaking Christians, there was experience and reflection of the risen Jesus that drew heavily upon the tradition of God's chief agent, a heavenly figure second only to God in authority and glory, and who could exercise a prominent role in God's creative and salvific actions. The result was a binitarian devotion to God and Jesus, not caused by borrowing from the smorgasbord of heroes and demigods of the Greco-Roman world or by long ideational development of Christology, but by a mutation of a divine chief agent within the aegis of Jewish monotheism.¹⁹⁷

(c) Angels and God's name and glory.

Angels are connected to God's name and glory in that they personify the tetragrammaton and are arraigned in divine glory.

---

¹⁹² Andrei A. Orlov, *Yahoel and Metatron: Aural Apocalypticism and the Origins of Jewish Mysticism* (TSAJ 69; Tübingen: Mohr Siebeck, 2017), 72.
¹⁹³ Heiser, *Angels*, 112, n. 90.
¹⁹⁴ See discussion in Orlov, *Yahoel and Metatron*, 164–65.
¹⁹⁵ Hurtado, *One God, One Lord*, 104.
¹⁹⁶ Hurtado, *One God, One Lord*, 119–29.
¹⁹⁷ Hurtado, *One God, One Lord*, 129–30.

Yahweh's "name" (*shem/onoma*) is significant as it can be a virtual synonym for Yahweh (Ps 20.21; Isa 30.27; 60.9; Tob 11.14; 14.8) and a way of referring to Yahweh's presence especially as related to the temple (Deut 12.2, 4–5, 11; 2 Sam 7.13; 1 Kgs 8.16; 2 Kgs 21.7; Jer 7.10–12). The divine name is embedded within, is carried by, or is even clothing over angels. In the Exodus narrative, the Lord declares that his angel will pardon transgression and should be obeyed because "my name is in him" (Exod 23.21). Hence Gieschen notes, "Exod 23.21 supports the deduction that this important aspect of God—the Divine Name—could be hypostatized as an angel."[198] The angel Metatron is called "The lesser YHWH" because "my name is in him" (*3 En.* 12.5), while Yahoel is one who mediates the "ineffable name" (*Apoc. Ab.* 10.3). Metatron and Yahoel are, says Orlov, "depicted as corporeal embodiments of the divine Name, whose functions include the protection and sustenance of the created order."[199]

Yahweh's glory often gets associated with angels, who share in the divine attribute of glory and even become a visual apparition of divine glory. In the Lucan infancy narrative, the appearance of the "angel of the Lord" included the resplendence of the "glory of the Lord" (Luke 2.9). Similarly, in the Matthean resurrection story, the angel's "appearance was like lightning, and his clothing white as snow" (Mat 28.3). Angels generally appear with dazzling visual splendor associated with heavenly and divine glory (2 Macc 3.24–25; *2 En.* 1.3–5; *Apoc. Ab.* 11.1–3; *Apoc. Zeph.* 6.11–13; *Barn.* 18.1). Angels are even called *doxas* for "glorious ones" (Exod 15.11 [LXX]; 1QH 10.8; 1QPs^{a}Zion 22.13; *2 En.* 22.7, 10; Jude 8; 2 Pet 2.10; *Ascen. Isa.* 9.33).

(d) The exaltation of angels.

Angels can be exalted within the divine council in contradistinction to rebellious angels and hostile gods.[200] Daniel's "one like a son of man" is an angelic-messianic figure who is given dominion, glory, and kingship over the world (Dan 7.13–14). Ben Sira has Wisdom acclaim her own glory in the council of the Most High (Sir 24.2). The Philonic Logos, God's firstborn and eldest angel, is elevated above the various angels to rule over them (*Conf.* 146). The Qumran War Scroll describes a scene after a great battle where God will "exalt the authority of Michael among the gods and the dominion of Israel among

---

[198] Charles Gieschen, *Angelomorphic Christology: Antecedents and Early Evidence* (AGAJU 42; Leiden: Brill, 1998), 77.

[199] Orlov, *Yahoel and Metatron*, 60.

[200] Emma Wasserman, *Apocalypse as Holy War: Divine Politics and Polemics in the Letters of Paul* (New Haven, Conn.: Yale University Press, 2018), 135–36.

all flesh" (1QM 17.7–8). Similarly, Qumran's Melchizedek midrash explicitly applies the position of Yahweh over the heavenly council in Pss 7.7–8 and 82.1 to the angelic Melchizedek (11QMelch 2.12–14). In Qumran's self-glorification hymn, the chief figure, whether angelic or human, is given a throne in the council of the "gods" (4Q491c 5).

(e) Angels and kings.

Attention should also be given to the intersection of Jewish messianology and angelology.[201] In several court scenes a supplicant lauds a monarch as one "like the angel of God" (2 Sam 14.17, 20; 19.27; Add Esth 15.13). The Israelite king in Isa 9.6 is called "Mighty God" (*el gibbor*) in Hebrew (Isa 9.5 [MT]), but "angel of the great counsel" (*megalēs boulēs angelos*)[202] in the Greek version (LXX), which marks a transition from a royal-salvific figure to an angelic figure.[203] A sizable number of scholars would argue that the "one like a son of man" in Dan 7.13–14 is an angelic figure, either "Michael" (cf. Dan 10.13, 21; 12.1), or "God's vice-regent" (cf. Dan 10.5–6; Ezek 1.26–28; *1 En.* 46.1–2).[204] There is a fascinating textual variant in Dan 7.13, where some Greek witnesses have the Son of Man coming not "towards" (*eōs*) the Ancient of Days but "as" (*ōs*) the Ancient of Days—either a scribal error or an acute theological judgment of the Son of Man as a second divine figure besides Yahweh.[205] At the same time, Daniel's Son

---

[201] See William Horbury, *Jewish Messianism and the Cult of Christ* (London: SCM Press, 1998), 119–27; Bühner, *Hohe Messianologie*, 197–273; Matthias Albani, "The 'One Like a Son of Man' (Dan 7:13) and the Royal Ideology," in *Enoch and Qumran Origins: New Light on a Forgotten Connection*, ed. Gabriele Boccaccini (Grand Rapids: Eerdmans, 2005), 47–53; and Markus Zehnder, "The Question of the 'Divine Status' of the Davidic Messiah," *BBR* 30 (2020): 485–514.

[202] I owe this insight to Dr. Michael Heiser (email, December 12, 2021). See discussion in Bühner, *Hohe Messianologie*, 199–206, and for patristic usage of Isa 9.5, see Hannah, *Michael and Christ*, 209–11. Another possibility is Mal 3.1, which was given messianic and angelic interpretation; see Bühner, *Hohe Messianologie*, 213–20.

[203] Bühner, *Hohe Messianologie*, 208.

[204] John J. Collins, *Daniel: A Commentary on the Book of Daniel* (Hermeneia; Minneapolis: Fortress, 1993), 318; Michael S. Heiser, *The Divine Council in Late Canonical and Non-canonical Second Temple Jewish Literature* (PhD diss., University of Wisconsin-Madison, 2004), § 7.4.

[205] Cf. Loren T. Stuckenbruck, "'One Like a Son of Man as the Ancient of Days' in the Old Greek Recension of Daniel 7, 13: Scribal Error or Theological Translation?" *ZNW* 86 (1995): 268–76; H. Daniel Zacharias, "Old Greek Daniel 7:13–14 and Matthew's Son of Man," *BBR* 21 (2011): 453–61; and Markus Zehnder, "Why the Danielic 'Son of Man' Is a Divine Being," *BBR* 24 (2014): 331–47. Cf Bühner (*Hohe Messianologie*, 325–26): "The Septuagint clearly expands the superhuman aspects of the messianic figure by drawing him

of Man received messianic interpretation in subsequent Jewish and Christian sources, often to narrate the heavenly origins of an earthly deliverer (e.g., *1 En.* 48.1–5; 4Q246 1–2; Mark 8.27–31; 14.62; John 1.51; 3.13; 12.34; *4 Ezra* 7.28–29; 12.31–32; 13.3; *Sib. Or.* 5.255).[206] The "one like a son of man" is a complex figure who is divine, angelic, royal, and represents the saints of the Most High over and against the pagan nations themselves signified by the various beasts. Taken together, these court scenes, Isa 9.6, and Dan 7.13–14 (LXX) are fascinating cases of the merging a royal/messianic figure with a principal angel in the Jewish interpretive tradition. As John Collins puts it: "Just as the king could be conceived as a god in pre-exilic Judah, so the messianic king could be conceived as an angelic being in the Hellenistic-Roman period."[207]

(f) Anthropophanic angels.

Angelic beings can be described in resplendent glory, but also in anthropological form as a "man." In Israel's sacred traditions, angels and even the angel of the Lord can take on human forms and sojourn on earth, sometimes incognito.[208] The most famous case is obviously Gen 6.1–4, with the story of the "sons of God" who descend to earth to copulate with the daughters of men, which exemplifies angels in an earthly existence (with its reception history in, e.g., *1 En.* 6–16). Another instance of angelic anthropomorphism is the three men who visited Abraham (Gen 18.1–19) and inspired the author of Hebrews to claim that people have "entertained angels without knowing it" (Heb 13.2). The angel of the Lord appeared to Manoah's wife, and she described her encounter with the angel as "a man of God came to me, and his appearance was like that of an angel" (Judg 13.6).

The angels of Ezekiel and Daniel are frequently described as a "man" or in "human likeness" (Ezek 1.26–28; 8.2; 9.2–3; Dan 10.5–6; 12.5–7). An angel

---

into a singular proximity to God and looking identical to God himself" ("Die Septuaginta erweitert dabei die übermenschlichen Aspekte der messianischen Gestalt noch deutlich, indem sie sie in singulärer Nähe zu und aussehensgleich mit Gott selbst zeichnet").

[206] Cf. William Horbury, "Messianic Associations of the Son of Man," *JTS* 36 (1985): 34–55; Michael F. Bird, *Are You the One Who Is to Come? The Historical Jesus and the Messianic Question* (Grand Rapids: Baker, 2009), 77–98; and Bühner, *Hohe Messianologie*, 107–97, who even says that the messianic interpretation of the Danielic Son of Man was "the predominant understanding" ("das vorherrschende Verständnis" [193]).

[207] John J. Collins, "Isaiah 8:23–9:6 and Its Greek Translation," in *Scripture in Transition: Essays on Septuagint, Hebrew Bible, and Dead Sea Scrolls in Honour of Raija Sollamo*, ed. Anssi Voitila and Jutta Jokiranta (JSJSup 126; Leiden: Brill, 2010), 218.

[208] Philo (*Gig.* 16) argues that souls, angels, and demons are basically the same thing, different in name only.

appeared as a "man who was standing among myrtle trees" in Zechariah's first vision (Zech 1.9, 11). Angels also appear as "a man with measuring line" and a "young man" in a subsequent vision (Zech 2.1–3). In *1 Enoch* angels can be likened to "flaming fire," yet have the power to transform into "human beings" (17.1). In the Hellenistic novella *Joseph and Aseneth*, Aseneth encounters "a man in every respect similar to Joseph . . . except that his face was like lightning, and his eyes like sunshine, and the hairs of his head like a flame of fire of a burning torch and hands and feet like iron shining forth from a fire, and sparks shot forth from his hands and feet" (*Jos. Asen.* 14.9). Similarly, in the *Apocalypse of Abraham*, the angel Yahoel visits Abraham "in the likeness of a man," yet the "appearance of his body was like sapphire, and the aspect of his face was like chrysolite, and the hair of his head like snow" (*Apoc. Ab.* 10.4; 11.2). Tobit and his son Tobias did not recognize the angel Raphael, who called himself "Azariah," and perceived him as only a "young man" (Tob 5.1–17).

The first-century CE *Prayer of Joseph* is premised on the idea that the patriarch Jacob was none other than the earthly manifestation of the "angel of Israel."[209] In fragment A (vv. 1–9) of the text, the angel Uriel tells Jacob that he is an angel in human form and then tries to wrestle Jacob for a superior position in the angelic hierarchy. In response, Jacob resists and asserts his superlative authority among the angels. The text uses several titles for Jacob (such as "an angel of God and a ruling spirit," "a man seeing God," "firstborn of every living thing," "archangel of the power of the Lord," "chief captain among the sons of God"), and Jacob is he who "tabernacled among men." In the contest, Jacob invokes God "by the indistinguishable name," indicating an element of dependency and inequality of power. Moreover, Origen (*Comm. Jo.* 2.25) cited *Pr. Jos.* frag A 1–9 to prove that John the Baptist surpassed the common nature of men as an angel who became human in order to witness to Jesus. In the resurrection narratives in the canonical Gospels, angels appear as a "young man" (Mark 16.5) or "two men in dazzling clothes" (Luke 24.4). These anthropomorphic angels demonstrate the compatibility of heavenly existence and human appearance.[210]

---

[209] Cf. Casey (*From Jewish Prophet*, 91): "This is a very elevated figure, and if we do not define incarnation so strictly as to include only fully divine beings who are born as people, this figure may be perceived as an incarnate angel during his earthly life." Though Casey wisely adds, "Fragmentary works of this kind must, however, be handled with great caution."

[210] See Kevin P. Sullivan, *Wrestling with Angels: A Study of the Relationship between Angels and Humans in Ancient Jewish Literature and the New Testament* (Leiden: Brill, 2004).

(g) Angelomorphic transformation.

A strand of Jewish tradition represents the dead as becoming angels or angel-like in their postmortem state. The notion of a glorified postmortem state where one shines like the stars of heaven (Dan 12.3; *4 Ezra* 7.97; *1 En.* 104.2) overlaps with descriptions of angels with resplendent and astral qualities (*Apoc. Zeph.* 6.11–12; *T. Ab.* 13.10) and even coheres with the exalted Jesus' self-description as a "morning star" according to John the Seer (Rev 22.16) or Ignatius' hymn to Jesus as "a star shone forth in heaven" (*Eph.* 19.2). Philo portrays Abraham as being added to the heavenly people of God, having received immortality and incorporeality, and "having become equal to the angels" (*Sacr.* 5). In the late first-century CE Jewish apocalypse *2 Baruch*, the risen righteous are transformed into the "splendor of angels," and "they will live in the heights of that world and they will be like the angels and be equal to the stars. And they will be changed into any shape which they wished, from beauty to loveliness, and from light to the splendor of glory" (*2 Bar* 51.5, 10). In another first-century CE apocalypse, *Apocalypse of Zephaniah*, Zephaniah undergoes a physical and noetic transformation: "I, myself, put on an angelic garment. I saw all of those angels praying. I, myself, prayed together with them, I knew their language, which they spoke with me" (*Apoc. Zeph.* 8.3–4). In the visionary section of the *Ascension of Isaiah* from the second century, an angel promises Isaiah that as he enters the upper levels of the heavens that he will receive a body "equal to the angels" (*Ascen. Isa.* 8.15).

In the Qumran community rule, the sons of light who heed the angel of truth will be transformed into an eternal blessed state with "a crown of glory with a robe of honor, resplendent forever and forever" (1QS 4.6–8). The *yaḥad* are to be "heirs in the legacy of the Holy Ones; with the angels he has united their assembly, a *yaḥad* society, they are an assembly built up for holiness, an eternal planting for all ages to come" (1QS 11.7–8). Just as the Qumranites believed that they had angels in their congregations (1QSa 2.8–9; 1QM 12.8), so too did they think that one day they would be part of an angelic congregation. In addition, in the visions of Amram, Amram makes a promise to his descendants that Aaron "will be [a mouth of] God, an angel of God" in his assistance rendered to Moses (4Q543 III 1.1; 4Q545 I 1.17) and a future member of the priestly line "shall be exalted as priest over all the children of the world" (4Q547 IV 6). Also, the self-glorification hymn includes a leader or representative of the community, who experiences something akin to an angelomorphic deification (4Q491c 12–20). This person is perhaps the Teacher of Righteousness or the eschatological Aaronic messiah.²¹¹ The language is genuinely astounding, as the figure claims that he is going to be elevated to a throne among the gods (*elim*), abide among the holy congregation, will be reckoned with the gods, and none of the kings of the earth will rival him in glory—and this last aspect echoes God's incomparability in Exod 15.11, Isa 44.7, and Ps 89.7 (4Q491c 8–13). In the words of Bühner: "The text certainly attests the exaltation and possibly also the apotheosis of a person who is exalted from earth to heaven, and in spatial coordinates sits among the angels, but probably also considers himself an angel. There he extols his own incomparability with words and phrases that express God's greatness and uniqueness in numerous texts drawn from the Hebrew Bible."²¹² The exaltation to a heavenly throne is merely an intensification of the fellowship that the sectarians claimed to already enjoy with the angels in the present, and the exaltation is also an anticipation of the reward of the righteous after death in the future.²¹³ The Qumran sectarians looked forward to their exaltation over their enemies and often described their vindication in angelic form and with divine status.

Turning to the New Testament, in Jesus' dispute with the Sadducees over the resurrection, he claimed that the dead are "like angels" (*hōs angeloi*; Mark 12.25; Matt 22.30) or, in Lucan language, "equals to angels" (*isangeloi*; Luke 20.36). Then, in Acts 12, when Peter escapes from prison, he goes to the house of Mary, the mother of John Mark, and knocks on the door. The enslaved girl Rhoda hears Peter's voice behind the door, and runs back and tells the others that Peter is outside the premises, but they do not believe her that it is Peter. They infer instead that "it must be his angel" (Acts 12.13–16). In other words,

---

²¹¹ Martin G. Abegg, "Who Ascended to Heaven? 4Q491, 4Q427 and the Teacher of Righteousness," in *Eschatology, Messianism and the Dead Sea Scrolls*, ed. C. A. Evans and P. W. Flint (Grand Rapids: Eerdmans, 1997), 72; and John J. Collins, *The Sceptre and the Star: The Messiahs of the Dead Sea Scrolls and Other Ancient Literature* (New York: Doubleday, 1995), 136–49.

²¹² Bühner, *Hohe Messianologie*, 262: "Dabei bezeugt der Text sicher die Erhöhung und evtl. auch die Apotheose eines Menschen, der von der Erde in den Himmel erhöht wird und sich mindestens in räumlicher Hinsicht bei den Engeln aufhält, sich wahrscheinlich aber auch selbst als Engel betrachtet. Dort preist er seine eigene Unvergleichlichkeit mit Worten und Wendungen, die in zahlreichen Texten der Hebräischen Bibel Gottes Größe und Einzigartigkeit ausdrücken." According to Laszlo Gallusz (*The Throne Motif in the Book of Revelation: Profiles from the History of Interpretation* [LNTS 487; London: T&T Clark, 2014], 73): "Such boasting by a human figure has no parallel, either in the Qumran library or in other Jewish literature. The writer not only claims the possession of his own heavenly throne, but even numbers himself among the gods. It seems that a kind of *apotheosis* appears here."

²¹³ Collins, *Sceptre and the Star*, 209.

they think that Peter is already dead, and the figure at the door must be his angelic doppelganger.

In later Enochic literature Enoch undergoes his own angelomorphic transformation. There is a heavenly metamorphosis of Enoch where his flesh melts away and his spirit is transformed, and he appears to take his place among the angels before the Head of Days (*1 En.* 71.11). In *2 Enoch*, Enoch ascends to the seventh heaven and is summoned before the "face of the Lord," whereupon he does "obeisance to the Lord" and experiences a transformation into a celestial being with a striking share in a conglomeration of divine characteristics (*2 En.* 22.1–3).[214] Enoch, speaking in the first person, reports:

> And the Lord, with his own mouth, said to me, "Be brave, Enoch! Don't be frightened! Stand up, and stand in front of my face forever." And Michael, the Lord's archistratig, lifted me up and brought me in front of the face of the Lord. And the Lord said to his servants, sound them out, "Let Enoch join in and stand in front of my face forever!" And the Lord's glorious ones did obeisance and said, "Let Enoch yield in accordance with your words, O Lord!" And the Lord said to Michael, "Go, and extract Enoch from [his] earthly clothing. And anoint him with my delightful oil, and put him in the clothes of my glory." And so Michael did, just as the Lord had said to me. He anointed me and he clothed me. And the appearance of that oil is greater than the greatest light, and its ointment is like sweet dew, and its fragrance myrrh; and it is like the rays of the glittering sun. And I looked at myself, and I had become like one of his glorious ones, and there was no observance difference. (*2 En.* 22.5–10 [J])

The mention of Enoch as standing in front of the Lord's face forever indicates a truly privileged position comparable to a principal angel such as Gabriel or Michael. In addition, the change of clothing (cf. Zech 3.1–5) and anointing with oil (cf. Lev 21.10; Sir 45.15) suggests a priestly vocation. Thereafter, Enoch is seated on the Lord's left next to Gabriel (*2 En.* 24.1). In the narrative of transformation, Enoch becomes a superhuman angelic priest.[215]

---

[214] Orlov, *Glory of the Invisible God*, 32.
[215] Charles A. Gieschen, "Enoch and Melchizedek: The Concern for Supra-human Priestly Mediators in 2 Enoch," in *New Perspectives on 2 Enoch: No Longer Slavonic Only*, ed. Andrei A. Orlov, Gabriele Boccaccini, and Jason M. Zurawski (Leiden: Brill, 2012), 379–82.

In *3 Enoch*, Rabbi Ishmael ascends to the heavens and meets the angel Metatron, the Prince of the Divine Presence, whom he discovers was originally the man Enoch (*3 En.* 4.3). Enoch had been taken up into heaven to serve the throne of glory day by day (*3 En.* 4.5; 6.1, 3, 7.1).

In Christian literature too, becoming an angel or angel-like was prevalent, especially in martyrologies, where martyrs were "inserted into the heavenly hierarchy alongside angels."[216] Stephen's martyrdom, recorded in Acts, begins with his arraignment before the Sanhedrin, where it is noted that "his face was like the face of an angel" (Acts 6.15). In the *Martyrdom of Polycarp*, the author lauds the martyrs, who despised the tortures of this world and by their fidelity to the Lord and endurance under suffering "were no longer humans but already angels" (*Mart. Pol.* 2.3). In the *Ascension of Isaiah*, the scriptural figures of Abel and Enoch are elevated to the seventh heaven, where they are "stripped of [their] robes of the flesh" and "they were like the angels who stand there in great glory" (*Ascen. Isa.* 9.9). Tertullian considered ascription of holiness to God in prayer as making people "candidates for angelhood," as angels ascribe holiness to God in his very presence (*Or.* 3). Or else angelification is the Latin version of theosis. To the docetism of Marcion, Tertullian replied: "He will one day form men into angels, who once formed angels into men" (*homines in angelos reformandi quandoque qui angelos in homines formarit aliquando*; *Marc.* 3.9.7). Origen, writing in the third century, referred to persons achieving "the rank of angels," even principalities, powers, and thrones (*Princ.* 1.6.2), and martyrs who become a "co-heir of Christ" are "equal to the angels" (*Mart.* 13). According to the *Apocalypse of Adam*, those who receive Adam's revelation to Seth come to resemble "the great eternal angels" far higher than the demiurge, who made the world (*Apoc. Adam* 64.14–19). In the fourth-century *Acts of Philip*, Philip prays, "Now then, my Lord Jesus Christ, make me worthy to meet you in the air, having forgiven me for the retribution which I visited upon my enemies. Transform the form of my body in angelic glory and give me rest in your bliss, and I will receive what was promised from you, what you promised to your saints, forever, amen" (*Acts Phil.* 38).

(h) Summary.

In sum, we have seen there are various aspects of ancient angelologies that provided fertile ground for christological origins and development. One could

---

[216] Candida R. Moss, *The Other Christs: Imitating Jesus in Ancient Christian Ideologies* (Oxford: Oxford University Press, 2012), 114.

connect Jesus with (1) the "angel of the Lord" and the second of "two powers in heaven"; (2) principal angels like Michael, Melchizedek, or Metatron; (3) the exaltation of principal angels within the divine council; (4) God's "name" and "glory" associated with angels; (5) royal leaders referred to as angels; (6) the capacity of angels to take on human appearance; and (7) the prospect of postmortem angelomorphic transformation.

(2) Jesus and the angels in Paul.

Did the apostle Paul think of Christ as an angel who became human and then returned to heaven? A minority of scholars have thought this the case.[217] When Paul referred to Christ as the "heavenly man" (*epaouranios*) in 1 Cor 15.48–49, it could imply that Christ was the heavenly archetype of Adam[218] or else a heavenly being akin to an angel. The sending of the Son (Rom 8.3; Gal 4.4) was perhaps the sending of an angelic son like the "sons of God" in the Hebrew Bible (Job 1.6; 2.1; 38.7; Ps 82.6; 89.6). Elsewhere, Paul praised the Galatians, who "welcomed me as an angel of God, as Christ Jesus" (Gal 4.14), and it is suggested that the association between receiving an angel and Christ is because Christ is a species of angel.[219] In addition, some attempt to read the Christ hymn of Phil 2.6–11 as narrating the story of the descent, anthropomorphic appearance, and super-exaltation of an angelic being to the upper echelons of the heavenly hierarchy.[220] In that case, the "hymn" is about a lowly god who has trailed downward to the chthonian regions, obtained death, and then by the power of the supreme god, been elevated within the pantheon, making the hymn a story about "the exalted and enthroned *deus descensus*."[221] Finally, much is often made of the fact

---

[217] Cf., e.g., Werner, *Formation of Christian Dogma*, 122–23; Horbury, *Jewish Messianism*, 113, 120; Gieschen, *Angelomorphic Christology*; Susan R. Garrett, *No Ordinary Angel: Celestial Spirits and Christian Claims* (New Haven, Conn.: Yale University Press, 2008); Ehrman, *How Jesus Became God*, 251–69; and Wasserman, *Apocalypse as Holy War*, 132–37.

[218] Cf. Philo, *Leg. all.* 1.31.

[219] Richard N. Longenecker, *The Christology of Early Jewish Christianity* (London: SCM Press, 1970), 31; Garrett, *No Ordinary Angel*, 11; and Ehrman, *How Jesus Became God*, 252–53.

[220] Horbury, *Jewish Messianism*, 113, 120; Ehrman, *How Jesus Became God*, 262–66; Wasserman, *Apocalypse as Holy War*, 132–35; and esp. James A. Sanders, "Dissenting Deities and Philippians 2:1–11," *JBL* 88 (1969): 279–90.

[221] Sanders, "Dissenting Deities," 282–83. Sanders writes: "He who did not attempt to set himself up as God's rival, and who in contrast to the dissenting angels was not motivated by *epitheia*, *kenodoxia*, and *harpagmos*, but only by *tapeinophrosynē*, is finally raised above them all so that they all must attend to the coronation by kneeling and acclaiming the humble one *kyrios*. The *theos tapeinos* has become *kyrios*" (286).

that Paul addresses Jesus as "God" (Rom 9.5) and applies prominent Yahweh texts to him to address him as "Lord" (e.g., Phil 2.11; 1 Cor 8.6). Yet calling an angel "Lord" (Zech 1.9; 4.4–5; *4 Ezra* 2.44; *Jos. Asen.* 17.10; Acts 10.3–5)[222] or "God" (Gen 31.11–13; Exod 3.1–22; Judg 13.22; *Jos. Asen.* 17.9; 4Q402 1 2.30–46; 11QMelch 2.10, 24–25) can be done without thinking twice. Even applying a Yahweh/Elohim texts to a heavenly figure is not without precedent (Micah 1.3–4; Ps 97.5 with *1 En.* 52.6; 53.7 // Ps 3.7; 58.6 with *1 En.* 46.4 // Isa 24.21–23 with *1 En.* 55.3–4 // Isa 52.7; 61.1–3; Ps 7.7–8; 82.1–2; with 11QMelch 2 // Exod 15.11; Isa 44.7; Ps 89.7 with 4Q491c 8–13 // Isa 66.20 with *Ps. Sol.* 17.31–32 and *4 Ezra* 13.12–13).[223]

Indirect evidence for a possible angel Christology from within the Pauline circle derives from the alleged "philosophy" behind the letter to the Colossians. The letter to the Colossians, whether authentically Pauline or post-Pauline, censures beliefs that include the "worship of angels" (Col 2.18) and perhaps even a demotion of Christ to merely an angelic mediator (Col 1.15–20; 2.8–9, 10, 15; 3.1). The caveat has to be that we do not know for certain whether there even was a Colossian "heresy," or if the letter's polemic is a generalized admonition against the sort of philosophies and religious devotion extant in central Asia Minor.[224] But if there was a particular philosophy that Paul and his coworkers were responding to in light of piecemeal reports, then it was probably a species of either Jewish mysticism[225] or perhaps something resembling the asceticism and angelology of the Therapeutae. I will reserve comment on the "worship of angels" for later, but the christological assertions of the epistle, especially Col 1.15–20, 2.9–10, 15, 20, and 3.1, heavily accent Christ's preeminence over heavenly intermediaries. Such assertions are arguably—on a mirror reading—intending to counter rival schemes where Christ is included but given only mundane status in a heavenly hierarchy. The Colossians, then, may have been puzzled by local Jewish teachers who were commending an ascetic and mystical form of Judaism: teachers who, rather than disparaging Christ, incorporated him into an existing hierarchy of powers, albeit with limited status. In response, Paul and his coworkers rework wisdom and royal traditions to place Jesus at the center of the cosmology and redemptive narratives that had been transmitted to the Colossians.

---

[222] Though an angel rejects the title "Lord" in *Ascen. Isa.* 8.4–5.
[223] Cf. discussion by Bauckham, *Jesus and the God of Israel*, 221–32.
[224] See Adam Copenhaver, *Reconstructing the Historical Background of Paul's Rhetoric in the Letter to the Colossians* (LNTS 585; London: T&T Clark, 2018).
[225] See Smith, *Heavenly Perspective*.

(3) Jesus and angels in post-70 writings.

(a) The canonical Gospels.

The Synoptic Gospels present several different ways in which angels were associated with Jesus' life and ministry. To begin with, concerning the birth and infancy narratives, Matthew has an "angel of the Lord" appear to Joseph in three dreams (Matt 1.20–24; 2:13, 19), while Luke names the angel Gabriel as visiting Zechariah and Mary (Luke 1.11–38) and describes an angelic visitation to the shepherds in Judea (Luke 2.9–20). Although later traditions will accent the role of the angel Gabriel in the birth story, there is little here to suggest an angelic figure impregnating Mary. Otherwise, Jesus remains quite distinct from the angels and even possesses a comprehensive authority over them. Angels are said to serve him (*diakoneō*) after his wilderness temptations (Mark 1.13/Matt 4.11; cf. Luke 22.43), he has authority to call upon the angels if he so wishes (Matt 4.6/Luke 4.10), and up to two legions of angels would come to his defense if he summoned them (Matt 26.53). The various sayings about the coming of the Son of Man describe the angels as his heavenly entourage (Matt 16.27/Mark 8.38/Luke 9.26; Matt 25.31; Luke 12.8–9), or else they are his agents of judgment for the wicked (Matt 13.41–42) or they rescue the elect (Mark 13.26–27/Matt 24.31). Apart from Mark 13.32 and Matt 24.36, where neither the Son of Man, nor the angels, but only the Father knows the timing of "that day," there is nothing to suggest that Jesus is on par with the angels. Finally, angels are prominent in the resurrection narratives (Mark 16.5; Matt 28.2, 5; Luke 24.23), but nothing can be taken to imply that Jesus somehow became an angel.

The angelological aspects of John's Christology are limited, but worth mentioning.[226] First, the Johannine Jesus as the divine Logos can be connected to Philo's depiction of the Logos as an archangel (*Conf.* 146). Second, Jesus' high priestly prayer appeals to "the name you have given me" (John 17.11–12). Here Jesus' "name" is indicative of his oneness with the Father and the oneness shared between the disciples and the Father through Jesus. Yet the possession of the divine name is somewhat analogous to how the divine name also indwells the exodus angel (Exod 23.20–21) and principal angels like Yahoel (*Apoc. Ab.* 10.3, 8–17) and Metatron (*3 En.* 12.5). Third, the identification of

---

[226] Cf. Gieschen, *Angelomorphic Christology*, 270–93, for the most concerted effort to detect angelomorphism in Johannine Christology. He concludes: "Although John never calls Jesus an angel, this analysis of evidence has demonstrated that angelomorphic terminology, traditions, and functions are an integral part of his Christology" (293).

Jesus with Jacob's ladder makes Jesus the pinnacle and portal of angelic visitations (John 1.51).

(b) The Epistle of Jude.

The Epistle of Jude is a letter of exhortation to Christian assemblies somewhere in the Hellenistic east, written principally to warn against certain intruders who are characterized by debauchery, the interpretation of dreams, a denial of Jesus Christ, and denunciation of angelic authorities (Jude 4–16).[227] Whereas much of the polemic against the intruders trades in stereotypical tropes to describe their godlessness; nonetheless, the allegation of rejecting lords and blaspheming glorious ones in vv. 8, 10 has a degree of specificity that is not stereotypical. This explains why the letter includes an unusual focus on angels compared to other New Testament writings. The intruders disparage angelic beings perhaps on account of a Hellenistic skepticism towards the invisible, because of ecstatic visionary experiences of the heavens with no angels, to denigrate the angels who gave the Torah, because of a prejudicial view of heavenly powers compared to Christ, to curse angels as wicked beings (4Q280 I 1–7),[228] or to invoke and manipulate angels through magical spells (*PGM* VII.795–85).[229]

Jude retorts: (1) "Jesus" himself was the angel of the exodus, thus, to disparage angels is to disparage the preexistent Jesus (Jude 5 alluding to Exod 23.20–23 and Num 14.26–38). (2) Angels are part and parcel of cosmic reality and redemptive history, as evil entered the world with evil angels and evil will finally be defeated at the judgment of the wicked angels; thus the intruders have abandoned Jewish theodicy and a theocentric heavenly hierarchy (Jude 6 alluding to *1 En.* 10.4–5, 11–15). (3) Those who denigrate angels will suffer the same fate as Sodom and Gomorrah, who tried to violate angels (Jude 7–8).[230] (4) Even the archangel Michael did not slander the Devil, the epitome of rebellious angels, but left judgment to God (Jude 9 alluding to Zech 3.2 and *Assumption of Moses* according to Clement of Alexandria, *frag.* 2 and Origen,

---

[227] Cf. Michael F. Bird and N. T. Wright, *The New Testament in Its World* (London: SPCK, 2019), 736–40.

[228] Cf. Klaus Berger, *Theologiegeschichte des Urchristentums* (Tübingen: Francke Verlag, 1994), 311: "Nobody has the right to curse spiritual powers based upon their own authority, even Michael only referred to the Lord in his dispute with the devil ('The Lord rebukes you')" ("Aus eigener Vollmacht hat niemand das Recht, Geistenmächte zu verfluchen, den selbst Michael hat im Streit mit dem Teufel nur auf den Herrn verwiesen ['Der Herr tadelt dich']").

[229] On Jude, the archangel Michael, and magical papyri, see esp. Rodolfo Gavan Estrada III, "Blaspheming Angels: The Presence of Magicians in Jude 8–10," *JETS* 63 (2020): 739–58.

[230] Cf. *T. Asher* 7.1: "Sodom which knew not the angels of the Lord, and perished forever."

Princ. 3.2.1). (5) These debauched dreamers and angel-deniers will ironically be judged when the Lord comes with his angels (Jude 14–15 quoting *1 En.* 1.9). Jude urges respect for angelic mediators as, dare I say, "guardians of the galaxy," the heavenly custodians of the cosmic order, and supernatural servants of the people of God. Jude, much like Justin, believes, "This God we do venerate and worship, and also the Son who came from him and taught us these things, and the company of other good angels who follow him and are like him, and also the prophetic spirit" (*1 Apol.* 6.2).

The author notably mentions how "Jesus once for all saved a people from Egypt and afterwards destroyed those who did not believe" (Jude 5). Here we must observe that there are significant textual variants in Jude at this point, as the earliest papyrus containing Jude has "God's Messiah" (*Theos Christos*) saved a people from Egypt (P^{72}), the majority of manuscripts read the "Lord" (*kyrios*; ℵ and many minuscules), while two prominent majuscules read "Jesus" (*Iēsous*; B A), with combinations of Lord, Jesus, God, and Christ in other witnesses. The evidence is thin and disputed, yet recent critical editions of the Greek New Testament have all favored "Jesus" (*Iēsous*) as the more original reading (ECM, NA²⁸, UBS⁵, SBLGNT, THGNT).[231] If "Jesus" is original in v. 5, then Jude would be explicitly identifying Jesus with the "angel of the Lord" in Exod 23.20–23 and be engaging in a typological argument similar to Paul's remark about Christ as rock that accompanied Israel in the wilderness (1 Cor 10.4). Of course, even if *kyrios* is original in v. 5, the description of Jesus as "master and lord" in v. 4 would permit a christological interpretation of *kyrios* in v. 5.

In this vein, Jarl E. Fossum believes that Jude, much like Justin some decades later, identified the pre-incarnate Jesus with the angel of the Lord, who, in Jewish tradition, was associated with the exodus, the punishment of the Israelites in the wilderness, the imprisonment of the fallen angels, and the destruction of Sodom and Gomorrah as we find in Jude 5–7.[232] Fossum concludes: "Jude 5 implies that the Son is modelled on an intermediary figure whose basic constituent is the Angel of the Lord."[233]

(c) The book of Hebrews.

The Epistle to the Hebrews engages in a christological discourse that stresses the Son's superiority to the angels in Heb 1.5–2.18. The contrast between the

---

[231] See discussion in Tommy Wasserman, *The Epistle of Jude: Its Text and Transmission* (CBNTS 43; Stockholm: Almqvist & Wiksell, 2006), 262–66, who favors *kyrios*.

[232] Jarl E. Fossum, "Kyrios Jesus as the Angel of the Lord in Jude 5–7," *NTS* 33 (1987): 226–43.

[233] Fossum, "Kyrios Jesus," 237. Cf. Hannah, *Michael and Christ*, 141.

Son and angels may be no more than rhetorical.²³⁴ However, it is also possible that, somewhat reminiscent of Colossians, the author accents the Son's superiority over angels precisely because some persons were identifying the Son as an angel or else putting him in competition with venerated angels. The argument for the Son's superiority to the angels runs thus: (1) God has never addressed any angel as his "Son" as per Ps 2.7 and 2 Sam 7.14 (1.5); (2) angels worship the Son as per Deut 32.43 (LXX) (1.6); (3) the Son makes angels to be ministering spirits, whereas the Son is a divine being as per Ps 104.4; 45.6–7 (Heb 1.7–9); (4) the Son is an eternal deity, with an everlasting reign, who participates in the work of creation as per Ps 102.25–27 (Heb 1.10–12); (5) God has never invited any angel to sit at his right hand until his enemies were subjugated as per Ps 110.1 (Heb 1.13); and (6) God has not subjected the world to come to angelic rule (Heb 2.5). True, this is hardly explicit evidence for an angel Christology or a rival angel veneration that the author is trying to refute. In addition, the reference to Pss 2, 8, 110, as well as mention of the Son's superiority to heavenly orders, are most likely part of prior tradition. Plus, the Son-angel contrast does not appear in the rest of the book. Even so, the author polemicizes against a *"Zeitgeist* in which fluid ideas about angels and preeminently heavenly figures, however metaphorically conceived, were perceived as threat to a belief in a surpassing exaltation of Christ."²³⁵ Or, he was responding to ideas that were "in the air," so to speak.²³⁶

(4) Revelation.

The book of Revelation is ground zero in discussions of Jesus as an angel or at least portrayed in angelomorphic imagery.

(a) The Old Testament background to Revelation's angelomorphic Christology.

What is striking to commentators is how Old Testament theophanies involving a humanlike figure and anthropomorphic descriptions of angels (Ezek 1.26–28; 8.1–4; Dan 7.13–14; 10.5–6) resemble the depiction of the exalted Jesus in the book of Revelation (Rev 1.13–16; 14.14–16; 19.11–16; while the angel in Rev 10.1–3 is portrayed like the exalted Jesus).²³⁷

---

[234] So Bauckham, *Jesus and the God of Israel*, 240–41; and Hurtado, *Lord Jesus Christ*, 499.

[235] Loren T. Stuckenbruck, *Angel Veneration and Christology: A Study in Early Judaism and in the Christology of the Apocalypse of John* (Waco, Tex.: Baylor University Press, 2017), 139.

[236] Hannah, *Michael and Christ*, 137–38.

[237] See esp. Christopher Rowland, *The Open Heaven: A Study of Apocalyptic Judaism and Early Christianity* (London: SPCK, 1982), 94–113; Stuckenbruck, *Angel Veneration*, 209–21; Carrell, *Jesus*, 24–52; Garrick V. Allen, "Son of God in the Book of Revelation and Apocalyptic

Ezek 1.26–28 (LXX)	Ezek 8.2–4 (LXX)	Dan 7.13–14 (LXX)	Dan 10.5–6 (LXX)
[26] There was a likeness of a chair upon it, and above the likeness of the chair was a likeness as the appearance of a man from above. [27] And I saw what looked like amber above from the appearance of the loins and from the appearance of the loins and further down I saw what looked like fire and its splendor around about. [28] As the appearance of a bow as in a cloud on a rainy day, such was the standing of the light from all around.	[2] And I looked, and look! A likeness of a man. There was fire from his loins and below, and from his loins above it was like the appearance of amber. [3] And a likeness of a hand stretched out and took up me by my head, and a spirit took me up me between the earth and sky, and it carried me into Jerusalem in a vision of God, onto the doorway of the gates looking into the north where there was the stone of the acquirer. [4] And look; the glory of the Lord God of Israel was there, just like the vision I saw in the plain.	[13] I continued to watch in a vision of the night, and behold, upon the clouds of heaven, a being like a son of mankind came, and the ancient of days was present, and his attendants were present with him. [14] Authority and royal honor was granted to him, and all the peoples of the earth according to races, and all honor will be directed to him, and his authority is an everlasting authority that will not be removed, and his kingdom is one that will not perish.	[5] And I raised my eyes and looked, and behold, there was a man clothed in fine linen and girded with fine linen on his loins and light gleamed from the midst of him. [6] And his mouth was like the sea, and his face was like an appearance of gleaming light, and his eyes were like torches of fire, and his arms and feet were like gleaming bronze, and the sound of his talking was like the sound of a roaring crowd.

Translations from LES.

Literature," in *Son of God: Divine Sonship in Jewish and Christian Antiquity*, ed. Garrick V. Allen, Kai Akagi, Paul Sloan, and Madhavi Nevader (University Park, Penn.: Eisenbrauns, 2019), 56–62.

Ezekiel's vision of God's throne-chariot is a highly descriptive account of God's mobile glory intended to be terrifying as much as awe-inspiring (Ezek 1.5–28). The vision is reminiscent of other theophanies (esp. Exod 3.2–15; 24.10, 17; Isa 6.1–4) and was to have a massive effect on the origins and development of Jewish *merkabah* mysticism in the future. What drives the chariot are the wings of the "four living creatures," who have "human form" (Ezek 1.5, 10), which intimates the human characteristic of angelic messengers (Ezek 9.2, 3, 11; 10.2, 6, 7) and the angelic qualities of the primal man (Ezek 28.13). At the climax of the vision in v. 26 is a description of a humanlike figure seated on a throne-like object[238] in the epicenter of God's glory. According to Susan Garrett, this human is "a mysterious and utterly awe-inspiring figure who seemed to represent God's very self—in human form."[239]

Ezekiel's vision of Israel's idolatry and sun-worship (Ezek 8.1–18) is facilitated by an angel in anthropophanic form with the Spirit of the Lord lifting Ezekiel up to heaven before "the glory of God of Israel" (Ezek 8.1–4). The angel is said to be "like" a "man"[240] who is arrayed in fire and bright splendor. Christopher Rowland has argued that the shift from Ezek 1.26–28 to 8.2 is very significant because the human form of God becomes separated from the divine throne-chariot and acts like a "quasi-angelic mediator" but also amounts to "the deity himself described in human form."[241]

Ezekiel's throne-chariot with a man upon it (Ezek 1.13, 16, 24, 26–28), the humanlike angel (Ezek 8.2), the priestlike angel dressed in linen (Ezekiel 9–10; cf. "linen" in Lev 6.10), and description of the primal man (Ezek 28.13) influenced the book of Daniel's angelology.

Daniel's third vision includes an angelic interpreter, "a man" dressed in light, precious metals, and fine materials. The "man" is reminiscent of Ezekiel's language for angels, and he explains to Daniel his vision about a great war (Dan 10.5–6; cf. 10.18; 12.5–7). The angel is sent by the angelic prince Michael, who himself is Israel's heavenly counterpart to the Princes of Persia

---

[238] The Hebrew *demût* and *ke-mărʾēh* and the Greek *homoiōma* indicate approximate resemblance.

[239] Garrett, *No Ordinary Angel*, 53.

[240] The MT reads *demût ke-mărʾēh ʾēš*, lit. "likeness and appearance of fire," but given the LXX reading of *homoiōma andros*, we can conjecture that *iš* ("man") was probably changed to *ēš* ("fire") to avoid divine anthropomorphism.

[241] Rowland, *Open Heaven*, 97–98. Hurtado (*One God, One Lord*, 78) thinks we should be more circumspect: "If the figure in Ezek. 8:2-4 is an angel, we know next to nothing about his status and role other than he acts as a messenger." Skeptical also is Bauckham, *Jesus and the God of Israel*, 160–61; and James D. G. Dunn, *Did the First Christians Worship Jesus? The New Testament Evidence* (London: SPCK, 2010), 70–71.

and Greece (Dan 10.11–21). The identity of the angel is not given, but it is not unreasonable to infer that the angel is Gabriel, who is mentioned earlier in Dan 8.16 and 9.21.

Daniel's first vision about the four beasts and arrogant horn climaxes in the description of God's heavenly court, where there are "thrones," including a throne of fiery flames with burning wheels for the Ancient of Days accompanied by his angels (Dan 7.9–10). After the beasts lose their dominion "one like a son of man" (Aram: *kĕbar ĕnāš*/Gk: *hōs huios anthrōpou*) approaches the Ancient of Days and is given everlasting dominion, glory, kingship, and all peoples, nations, and languages are said to serve him (Dan 7.13–14). In this throne-room scene we have a heavenly figure exalted by God and given God-like power and authority, yet without God's own uniqueness and sovereignty.[242] In light of the anthropophanic qualities of angels in Dan 8.15, 9.21, 10.5–6, and 12.5–7, the one like a son of man could be an angel.[243] That is supported further by the observation that Dan 7.13–14 was given an angelic interpretation in *1 Enoch*, where the Head of Days is accompanied by one "whose face was like the appearance of a man; and his face was full of graciousness like one of the holy angels" and he turns out to be the "son of man" (*1 En.* 46.1–2). Concerning the interpretation of the vision within Dan 7, Daniel is told that the destruction of the fourth beast and the many horns signifies how "The kingship and dominion and the greatness of the kingdoms under the whole heaven shall be given to the people of the holy ones of the Most High; their kingdom shall be an everlasting kingdom, and all dominions shall serve and obey them" (Dan 7.27; cf. vv. 18, 22). In which case, the investiture of the one like a son of man is the angelic rehearsal of the sovereignty of a restored Israel over her pagan oppressors. But it may be even more complex than that. The one like a son of man is a polyvalent symbol representing God, God's kingship against the reign of the beasts, and God's anointed king against the arrogant horn, combined with the role of angels as supernatural guardians and heavenly representatives of God's holy people.[244] The worship of the one like a son of man in Dan 7.14 is fitting for a being who embodies God's heavenly power and earthly

---

[242] Cf. Rowland, *Open Heaven*, 98; and Hurtado, *One God, One Lord*, 79.

[243] Werner, *Formation of Christian Dogma*, 120–25; and Collins, *Daniel*, 304–10, 318. But note Michael B. Shepherd's objection: "The great weakness of the angelic interpretation [of the Son of Man in Daniel 7] is that nowhere in the Hebrew canon do angels receive dominion and worship (Dan 7:14)" ("Daniel 7:13 and the New Testament Son of Man," *WTJ* 68 [2006]: 103). Thanks to Brandon Smith for alerting me to this quote.

[244] Bird, *Are You the One?* 83–87.

people. In addition, as we will see, Rev 1.13–16 is proof that the "one like a son of man" could be given a messianic interpretation with an angelic gloss.

(b) Rev 1.13–16.

> ¹³ [A]nd in the midst of the lampstands I saw one like the Son of Man, clothed with a long robe and with a golden sash across his chest. ¹⁴ His head and his hair were white as white wool, white as snow; his eyes were like a flame of fire, ¹⁵ his feet were like burnished bronze, refined as in a furnace, and his voice was like the sound of many waters. ¹⁶ In his right hand he held seven stars, and from his mouth came a sharp, two-edged sword, and his face was like the sun shining with full force.

The seer's first vision portrays Jesus standing among the "lampstands," symbolic for the seven churches of Asia Minor, indicating Jesus' presence with them (1.13). The Greek *homoion huion anthrōpou* ("one like a son of man") is anarthrous compared to the double articular *ho huios tou anthrōpou* ("*the* son of *the* man") of the Gospels and so indicates a reversion back to the Danielic form which is also anarthrous in the OG and Theodotian versions. The exalted Jesus functions here like an *angelus interpres* as he commissions John as a scribe and explains to him the meaning of the vision (Rev 1.19–20; cf. 4.1). But more than that, Jesus appears with divine qualities and angelic form in John's vision.

What is significant is that the appearance of the son of man assimilates features of Daniel's Ancient of Days and the angel on the bank of the Tigris River. The whiteness of the son of man's head and hair are drawn from the Ancient of Days (Dan 7.9; cf. *1 En.* 46.1),[245] while the description of his flaming eyes, bronze-like limbs, golden sash, and loud voice[246] reflects the angel (Dan 10.5–6 [OG/Theod.]). The seer's exalted Jesus so closely resembles the angel in Dan 10.5–6 that Hippolytus assumed that the angel was the pre-incarnate Jesus.[247] John's vision narrates Jesus as a divine being with a visible form interlacing theophanic and angelophanic qualities.

---

[245] Jesus' face "shining like the sun" in Rev 1.16 reflects *1 En.* 14.20, which describes the gown of the Great Glory as "shining more brightly than the sun."

[246] Ezek 1.24 and 43.2 refer to the sound of "mighty waters" similar to Rev 1.15.

[247] Hippolytus, *Dan.* frag. 2: 24–25. If the angel in Dan 10.5–6 is meant to be Gabriel (Dan 8.16; 9.21), then Adele Y. Collins ("The 'Son of Man' Tradition and the Book of Revelation," in *The Messiah: Developments in Early Judaism and Christianity*, ed. James H. Charlesworth [Philadelphia: Fortress, 1992], 558) infers: "the author of Revelation considered Gabriel to be God's principal angel and the risen Christ to be identified with Gabriel."

Various Jewish writings also draw on features from Daniel to describe angels. It is said of the angel Yahoel that the "appearance of his body was like sapphire, and the aspect of his face was like chrysolite, and the hair of his head like snow" (*Apoc. Ab.* 11.2). Aseneth encountered an angel similar to Josephus "except that his face was like lightning, and his eyes like sunshine, and the hairs of his head like a flame of fire of a burning torch, and hands and feet like iron shining forth from fire, and sporks shot forth from his hands and feet" (*Jos. Asen.* 14.9). Zephaniah thought he had met the "Lord almighty" in the form of a "great angel, Eremiel" with "his face shining like the rays of the sun in its glory since his face is like that which is perfected in its Glory. And he was girded as if a golden girdle were upon his breast. His feet were like bronze which is melted in fire" (*Apoc. Zeph.* 6.11–12). In an early medieval text, Metatron's description of the angelic host is that "every angel is as the Great Sea in height, and the appearance of their faces is like lightning; their eyes are like torches of fire; their arms and feet look like burnished bronze, and the roar of their voices when they speak is as the sound of a multitude" (*3 En.* 35.2).

In John's vision in Rev 1.13–16, Jesus has theophanic, angelophanic, and messianic[248] traits, which are indicative of other angelolophanies in Jewish literature.

(c) Rev 10.1–3.

> ¹ And I saw another mighty angel coming down from heaven, wrapped in a cloud, with a rainbow over his head; his face was like the sun, and his legs like pillars of fire. ² He held a little scroll open in his hand. Setting his right foot on the sea and his left foot on the land, ³ he gave a great shout, like a lion roaring. And when he shouted, the seven thunders sounded.

John sees "another mighty angel" descending from heaven, possessing "a little scroll" and a shout like seven peals of thunder (Rev 10.1–3). In v. 2 he is described as "wrapped in a cloud, with a rainbow over his head; his face was like the sun, and his legs like pillars of fire." This language is reminiscent of Jesus, who is "coming with clouds" (1.7), has feet glowing like bronze in a furnace (1.15), and has a sunlike shining face (1.16). Furthermore, rainbows are associated with the divine presence (Ezek 1.28; Rev 4.3) or divine favor in the case of Octavian, who was seen approaching Rome in what seemed like a rainbow crown on his head as a portent of his greatness (Vell. Pat. 2.59.6). According to G. K. Beale, "Although this heavenly being is called an 'angel,' he may be more than an angel, and, therefore, in a different class from the 'strong'

---

[248] The image of sword from/as mouth is used on royal figures in Isa 11.4 and 49.2, comparable with Rev 1.16; 2.16; 19.15, 21.

angels in 5:2 and 18:21." Moreover: "If he is an angel, he is an extraordinary one, since he is described in a majestic way, unlike any other angel in the book. He is given attributes that are given only to God in the OT or to God or Christ in Revelation."[249] Beale concludes that "Christ is presented [here] in the trappings of the OT Angel of the Lord."[250] This is a view shared by Victorinus, the third-century bishop of Pettau in Pannonia, who interpreted the "mighty angel" of Rev 10.1 as the exalted Jesus.[251]

What problematizes such an identification is that the mighty angel, despite his majestic appearance, has a very limited role as the carrier of the small scroll. There is no exercise of lordship and no association with a heavenly throne. The angel takes an oath to the living and enduring creator (Rev 10.5), which is odd if Jesus is himself the beginning of creation (Rev 3.14). In addition, John receives his instructions not from the mighty angel but from the divine voice from heaven (Rev 10.4, 8).[252] Even if the angel is not to be equated with the exalted Jesus, the angel is certainly Jesus-like and Jesus' angelic agent, perhaps an angel whom Jesus could call "my angel" (Rev 22.16).

(d) Rev 14.14–16.

> [14] Then I looked, and there was a white cloud, and seated on the cloud was one like the Son of Man, with a golden crown on his head, and a sharp sickle in his hand! [15] Another angel came out of the temple, calling with a loud voice to the one who sat on the cloud, "Use your sickle and reap, for the hour to reap has come, because the harvest of the earth is fully ripe." [16] So the one who sat on the cloud swung his sickle over the earth, and the earth was reaped.

The seer's sixth vision describes a scene of judgment where the judge is "one like a son of man sitting on the cloud," which is an allusion to Dan 7.13 and rehearses the description of Jesus coming with clouds from Rev 1.7. The "white cloud" is indicative of the divine presence, while "golden crown" is regal, and the "sharp sickle" signifies a harvest image for judgment (see Jer 50.16; Joel 3.13). There is no reason not to identify this son of man with the

---

[249] Greg K. Beale, *The Book of Revelation* (NIGTC; Grand Rapids: Eerdmans, 1999), 522. Cf. Robert H. Gundry, "Angelomorphic Christology in the Book of Revelation," in *The Old Is Better: New Testament Essays in Support of Traditional Interpretations* (WUNT 178; Tübingen: Mohr Siebeck, 2005), 377–98; and Gieschen, *Angelomorphic Christology*, 256–60.

[250] Beale, *Revelation*, 525.

[251] Gieschen, *Angelomorphic Christology*, 245.

[252] Stuckenbruck, *Angel Veneration*, 232.

exalted Jesus. Yet what intrigues interpreters is that four heavenly beings are mentioned in Rev 14.14–20.

After the description of the "son of man" on clouds in v. 14, there comes "another angel" in v. 15, who emerges from the heavenly temple and commands the one on the cloud to begin the harvest of judgment; the one on the clouds complies and begins swinging his sickle over the earth in v. 16. This can reasonably be taken to imply that the son of man is himself an angel and subordinate to the angel who tells him to begin the harvest of judgment.

The same scheme is repeated in Rev 14.17–20 but with two different angels. We see that "another angel" emerges from the heavenly temple with a sickle in v. 17, then "another angel" emerges from the heavenly altar to command the first angel to begin the harvest of judgment in v. 18, and the first angel complies and begins reaping with bloody effects in vv. 19–20.

On the premise that vv. 14–16 is duplicated in vv. 17–20, it would mean we have a double description of a two-angel task: angel-harvester and angel-commander. Further, the exalted Jesus is the angel-harvester subordinate to the angel-commander. The passage indicates that the exalted Jesus is temporarily separated from the divine throne and temporarily assumes angelic form and function. This is Christology shaped by angelology.[253]

(e) Rev 19.11–16.

> [11] Then I saw heaven opened, and there was a white horse! Its rider is called Faithful and True, and in righteousness he judges and makes war. [12] His eyes are like a flame of fire, and on his head are many diadems; and he has a name inscribed that no one knows but himself. [13] He is clothed in a robe dipped in blood, and his name is called The Word of God. [14] And the armies of heaven, wearing fine linen, white and pure, were following him on white horses. [15] From his mouth comes a sharp sword with which to strike down the nations, and he will rule them with a rod of iron; he will tread the wine press of the fury of the wrath of God the Almighty. [16] On his robe and on his thigh he has a name inscribed, "King of kings and Lord of lords."

---

[253] Carrell, *Jesus*, 194; Stuckenbruck, *Angel Veneration*, 244; and Gieschen, *Angelomorphic Christology*, 250–52. Matthias Reinhard Hoffmann (*The Destroyer and the Lamb: The Relationship between Angelomorphic and Lamb Christology in the Book of Revelation* [WUNT 2.203; Tübingen: Mohr Siebeck, 2005], 2) is correct that in Rev 14.14–15 "the distinction between Christ and angels is not always clear-cut, and sometimes angelic and christological categories cannot be differentiated."

The seer's depiction of the exalted Jesus' return in Rev 19.11–16 contains some tacit angelological elements. First, his eyes "like flame of fire" in Rev 19.12 recall 1.14 and 2.18, which are angelic qualities of resplendence. Second, Jesus leads the angels in Rev 19.14 in a similar way to how Michael rises to lead God's people in Dan 12.1 and how he led his angels against the dragon in Rev 12.7. In the very least, the role of Michael as angelic captain has been transferred to Jesus (see 1QM 9.15–16, 17.1–9).[254] Third, that Jesus has "a name inscribed that no one knows but himself" (Rev 19.12) could imply that Jesus is either a divine being (Gen 32.29) or else an angelic being (Judg 13.17).[255] The device of having a secret name parallels the Enochic Son of Man, who "was given a name, in the presence of the Lord of the Spirits, the Before Time; even before the creation of the sun and the moon, before the creation of the stars, he was given a name in the presence of the Lord of the Spirits" (*1 En.* 48.2–3) and later the angels "blessed, glorified, and extolled (the Lord) on account of the fact that the name of that (Son of) Man was revealed to them" (*1 En.* 69.27). Like other exalted heavenly figures, Jesus has a secret name that only God knows. Fourth, Jesus is called "The Word of God" (Rev 19.13), which, as we have seen, is an angelological title in Philo (*Leg. all.* 3.177; *Conf.* 146). In sum, Rev 19.11–16 presents Jesus as a warrior messiah and agent of judgment with angelic traits.

(5) Jesus and angels in second-century Christian literature.

Among the various Christian writings of the second century, in what would by later standards be judged to be both proto-orthodox and heterodox texts, there are consistent depictions of Jesus as either angel-like or an actual angel.

(a) *Ascension of Isaiah.*

The *Ascension of Isaiah* is a Christian revision of an earlier Jewish text, and its final form probably began to take shape in the earliest decades of the second century. Angels play a significant role in the text, especially in relation to its Christology. To begin with, the "Beloved"[256] (i.e., Jesus) is the counterpart to the "prince of this world, and his angels, and his authorities, and his powers" (*Ascen. Isa.* 1.3). In the vision section, the Beloved is a glorious being, who is worshipped by the deceased righteous such as Adam, Abel, and Seth, along with the angels in songs of praise even as the Beloved was "transformed and became like an angel" (*Ascen. Isa.* 9.27–32). The angelomorphic

---

[254] Gieschen, *Angelomorphic Christology*, 256; Carrell, *Jesus*, 209; Hannah, *Michael and Christ*, 148; and Hoffmann, *Destroyer and the Lamb*, 193–96.

[255] David E. Aune, *Revelation* (3 vols.; WBC; Dallas: Word, 1997), 3:1055.

[256] Cf. *Ascen. Isa.* 1.4, 5, 7, 13; 3.13, 17, 18; 4.3, 6, 9, 18, 21; 5.15; 7.17, 23; 8.18, 25; 9.12.

transformation of Jesus is not the basis for any ascribed divinity but indicates further his glory as a truly heavenly being. Parallel to the worship of Jesus is the worship of the Holy Spirit as a type of angel (*Ascen. Isa.* 9.33–36). Quite likely Jesus and the Holy Spirit are regarded as angelic equivalents to a cherubim and seraphim who attend to God (Irenaeus, *Epid.* 10; Hippolytus, *Ref.* 9.13.2–3; Origen, *Princ.* 1.3.4).[257]

When the "Lord Christ" is commissioned by the Father, he is told to take on the form of an angel after he passes through the lower five heavens in order to avoid being recognized by the angels, so that the angels will be caught by surprise when Jesus is recalled to heaven to judge the angels and gods of the world (*Ascen. Isa.* 10.7–16; cf. a similarly stealthy and polymorphic transformation in *Gos. Phil.* 57.32–58.10). Then, after Jesus leaves the seventh and sixth heavens, Isaiah's angelic guide announces that he will see "the transformation and descent of the Lord" (*Ascen. Isa.* 10.18). Interestingly, the angels of the sixth heaven praise and glorify Jesus, "for he had not been transformed into the form of the angels" (*Ascen. Isa.* 10.19); yet after entering the fifth heaven in angelic guise, they did not praise him, "for his form was like theirs" (*Ascen. Isa.* 10.20). The same is true for the lower heavens, and the firmament, where the angels did not praise him or recognize him, for he "made himself like the angels of the air" (*Ascen. Isa.* 10.30), though he takes on "the form of a man" (*Ascen. Isa.* 3.13; 9.13). After Jesus' birth, life, crucifixion, death, and resurrection, he is worshipped by the angels of the firmament, even by Satan, then by the angels of the various heavenly levels as he ascends towards the Father, and he is repeatedly said not to have been transformed into their angelic form (*Ascen. Isa.* 11.25–33). Later, after the anti-Christ is revealed, the Lord will return "with his angels and with the hosts of the saints from the seventh heaven," where Beliar will be dragged into hell (*Ascen. Isa.* 4.14).

According to the *Ascension of Isaiah*, Jesus is a glorious heavenly figure who takes on angelic form in order to disguise his earthward descent. Hence the exasperation of the angels: "How did our Lord remain hidden from us as he descended, and we did not notice?" (*Ascen. Isa.* 11.26).[258]

---

[257] Cf. Gieschen (*Angelomorphic Christology*, 244): "This abundant use of Jewish angelology is not for the purpose of undermining the divine status of either Christ or the Spirit. On the contrary, angelology was used to display dramatically the divinity of these two persons alongside God."

[258] From this Hannah (*Michael and Christ*, 199) rightly concludes: "Therefore, the *Ascension of Isaiah* does not contain an angel Christology: it does not assert, or even imply that Christ is an angel. At most it describes him disguising himself as an angel." However, I disagree with Hannah (218–19) that *Ascension of Isaiah* refutes or corrects an earlier angel Christology with an angelomorphic Christology.

Although worship and the greatest glory belong exclusively to "the Most High, the One who dwells in the upper world" (*Ascen. Isa.* 6.8–9; 7.37), Jesus is worshipped by angels before and after his descent-ascent (*Ascen. Isa.* 7.17, 23; 8.18; 9.27–32; 10.15, 19; 11.22–33). Isaiah's interpreting angel, though greater in glory that other angels, still acknowledges that Jesus is "greater" than himself (*Ascen. Isa.* 7.2, 7–8). Jesus is also considered more glorious than the angels as one "whose glory surpassed that of all" (*Ascen. Isa.* 9.27). Jesus is acclaimed as "Lord" (*Ascen. Isa.* 9.5; 10.7, 17; 11.24, 26) whereas Isaiah's angelic guide rejects the title "Lord" for himself (*Ascen. Isa.* 8.5). Jesus is "Lord of all the *glorious ones* [Latin: *gloriarum*] which you have seen" (*Ascen. Isa.* 9.32). Yet there is a type of subordination with the angelic Jesus and angel of the Holy Spirit worshipping the Great Glory (*Ascen. Isa.* 9.40). Also, Jesus is seated at the Great Glory's right hand and the Holy Spirit at the Great Glory's left hand (*Ascen. Isa.* 11.32–33). Nonetheless, the angelomorphic Christ is more closely aligned with the Most High than with the angels or with the gods of the world because he is worshipped by the angels.[259]

(b) *Shepherd of Hermas.*

The *Shepherd of Hermas* was an immensely popular Christian writing probably composed by an ex-slave in Rome in the 140s CE (*Herm.* 1.1). The document is predominantly paraenetic but does have an underlying Christology, albeit one that is difficult to explain let alone systematize because of the vagaries of the language within which the Christology is couched.[260] On the one hand, the Shepherd has composed a narrative in which "the Son of God preexists creation and appears prominently as a servant exalted for his fidelity, as joint heir with the Holy Spirit, as sustainer of the universe, and as inspector of the tower-church."[261] On the other hand, the Shepherd's Christology is often equated

---

[259] Richard Bauckham, "The Worship of Jesus in Apocalyptic Christianity," *NTS* 27 (1981): 322–41; republished as "The Worship of Jesus," in *The Climax of Prophecy: Studies on the Book of Revelation* (Edinburgh: T&T Clark, 1993), 147–48; and Carrell, *Jesus and the Angels*, 106.

[260] Jonathan Lookadoo (*The Shepherd of Hermas: A Literary, Historical, and Theological Handbook* [London: T&T Clark, 2021], 150) puts it well: "A coherent, systematic, and widely agreed upon approach to interpreting the Son's place in the *Shepherd* has proven difficult to come by." For a defense of the *Shepherd* as proto-trinitarian, see Michael J. Svigel, "Trinitarianism in *Didache, Barnabas*, and the *Shepherd*: Sketchy, Scant, or Scandalous?" *Perichoresis* 17 (2019): 30–35.

[261] Carolyn Osiek, *The Shepherd of Hermas* (Hermeneia; Minneapolis: Fortress, 1999), 36.

with an adoptionist Christology (58.1–59.8), thought to conflate the Son and the Spirit (28.1; 59.5; 78.1), or espouse a tacit angel Christology (89.7–8).[262]

Many angelic figures are mentioned; there is a hierarchy of angelic beings in operation, including the "great angel," the "glorious angel," the "angel of the Lord," the "angel of the spirit of prophecy," the "angel of righteousness," the "angel of iniquity," the "angel of repentance," and the "angel of affliction."[263] Some of these angels overlap; the shepherd is identified as the "angel of repentance," and others could be identified as a principal angel. The problem, as Jonathan Lookadoo points out, is that "there is a slippage in terminology when discussing otherworldly figures in the *Shepherd* that complicates precise identification of each figure."[264] For example, the six young men who carry the woman's chair and take the woman east are the "holy angels of God who were created first of all, to whom the Lord committed all his creation to increase and to build up, and to rule over all creation" (12.1). It is one of the young men who, acting as *angelus interpres*, explains to Hermas the meaning of the vision about the woman (8.1; 18.7–21.4). The angelic shepherd himself is sent to Hermas by the "most holy angel," "glorious angel," and "angel of the Lord" (25.1–2; 66.1–7; 111.1), and it is this superior angel who takes the shepherd away from Hermas at the end (114.4). Those who keep themselves from anger are "justified by the most holy angel" (33.7). In the parable of the vineyard, it is said that the servants of God each have their own Lord, who speaks in parables, and the "Lord" is potentially coordinate with the "holy angel" who strengthens them (57.3–4). In the parable of the tower and the virgins, the "glorious man" (*endoxos*) is the "Son of God," who is surrounded by six "glorious angels," and they together keep out of God's presence/the kingdom those who do not receive his name (89.7–8). Generally, the "angel of the Lord" is portrayed in such a way that he is capable of carrying christological freight (66.5; 67.2; 68.1). The imagery does not demand an angel

---

[262] I do not think the Shepherd's Christology is adoptionist (esp. in light of 89.2); it is more exemplarist and exaltationist. See Michael F. Bird, *Jesus the Eternal Son: Answering Adoptionist Christology* (Grand Rapids: Eerdmans, 2017), 107–12; Svigel, "Trinitarianism," 31–32; and Lookadoo, *Shepherd*, 152–55. Further, the occasional conflation of Son, Spirit, and church is, says Osiek, "not metaphysical but symbolic" (*Shepherd*, 35). Those who detect an angelomorphic Christology in the *Shepherd* include Martin Hengel, *Studies in Early Christology* (Edinburgh: T&T Clark, 1995), 221, 376; Gieschen, *Angelomorphic Christology*, 214–28; and Hannah, *Michael and Christ*, 187–92.

[263] Cf. survey in Gieschen, *Angelomorphic Christology*, 215–20; and Lookadoo, *Shepherd*, 102–3, 106–9.

[264] Lookadoo, *Shepherd*, 103.

Christology but certainly permits a principal angel to be identified with the Son of God.[265]

Elsewhere, however, the Son of God is distinguished from the angels. We read that the Son of God appointed angels to protect the people, and they are portrayed as a type of fence (58.2–3). It is claimed that the Son of God is not presented in the form of a slave, but in "great power and lordship" (59.1). God turned the vineyard over to the Son, who in turn placed angels over the vineyard, and "he is Lord of all the people, having received all power from his Father." The Lord appointed "his Son and the glorious angels as counsellors concerning the inheritance of slaves" (59.2–4). The apex of the author's Christology comes with the statement that "the Son of God is far older than all his creation, with the result that he was the Father's counsellor in his creation" (89.2) and that "all creation is sustained by the Son of God" (91.5), which is never attributed to any of the angels, but resembles the function of creatorhood (26.1).

In one instance, Michael is identified as "the great and glorious angel" who has "authority over this people and guides them"; yet he is immediately distinguished from the Son of God, since the Son of God is identified as the "law," and Michael puts the law into the hearts of those who believe (69.1–3). However, elsewhere it is the Son of God who is the giver of the law (59.3; 91.5). One solution is to argue for a conflation of Christ and Michael.[266] But this is unlikely precisely because Michael and the Son get distinguished in 69.2–3.[267] Even so, Michael and the Son of God do have overlapping functions in that both are invested with divine authority, they are glorious, they commission angels, they pronounce judgment on the faithful, and they deliver the sinful over to the angel of affliction.[268] Thus, we can legitimately say with Carrell that the Shepherd came "within a hair's breadth" of entertaining an "angel Christology not many decades after the composition of the Apocalypse."[269] The author assumes, then, an angelic hierarchy, with some angels superior to others, but we do not know for certain if the Son of God is supreme within the angelic

---

[265] Cf. Halvor Moxnes, "God and His Angel in the Shepherd of Hermas," *ST* 28 (1974): 49–56.

[266] Cf., e.g., Werner, *Formation of Christian Dogma*, 135; Jean Daniélou, *The Theology of Jewish Christianity* (2 vols.; London: Darton, Longman & Todd, 1964), 1:123–24; Segal, *Two Powers in Heaven*, 220; Gieschen, *Angelomorphic Christology*, 226; and Hannah, *Michael and Christ*, 187–88 (Hannah adds that if the Shepherd equates Michael and Christ, then such a position "remained a minority opinion in early Christianity" [170]).

[267] Similarly, Moxnes, "God and His Angel," 56; and Lookadoo, *Shepherd*, 158.

[268] Hannah, *Michael and Christ*, 187–88.

[269] Carrell, *Jesus*, 108.

hierarchy or if he somehow stands outside it and above it. In sum, the Shepherd engaged in a clumsy synthesis of angelological and christological motifs.

(c) *Epistula Apostolorum.*

The *Epistula Apostolorum* is presented as a letter from the apostles, whereas its contents are in fact an apocalyptic post-resurrection dialogue between the risen Jesus and the disciples dated to the third quarter of the second century.[270] The document arose in either Egypt or—and more likely—Asia Minor and was composed as an anti-Gnostic text given the denunciation of Simon Magus and Cerinthus (*Ep. Ap.* 1.2). In many ways, it is a typical piece of proto-orthodox Christology given its christological affirmations in a piece of quasi-creedal material (*Ep. Ap.* 3.1–15). The confession of faith summarizes the Synoptic infancy narratives and Johannine prologue with due emphasis on Jesus as "God," the demiurgical Word, divine Son, who is sovereign over angelic powers.[271] According to Francis Watson, the echoes of the Johannine prologue and the Lucan infancy narrative serve "to create a credal affirmation that anticipates the Nicene confession of the divine Son as the one who 'came down from heaven and became flesh by the Holy Spirit and Mary the virgin.'"[272]

Even with the rehearsal of Johannine Logos Christology (*Ep. Ap.* 3.5, 13; 18.1; 31.11; 39.12), there is a striking description of the Word's descent from heaven in angelic form (13.1–6), specifically taking the guise of the angel Gabriel (14.1–8).

> It came to pass that when I came from the Father of all and passed through the heavens, I put on the wisdom of the Father and clothed myself in the power of his might. I was in the heavens, and archangels and angels I passed in their likeness as though I were one of them. Among the powers and rulers and authorities I passed, having the wisdom of the one who sent me. And the commander of the angels is Michael, with Gabriel and Uriel and Raphael, and they followed me down to the fifth firmament, for they were thinking in their hearts that I was one of them—such was the power given me by the Father. And on that day I prepared the

---

[270] Clues for dating include (1) reference to the parousia occurring 120 years after Easter (*Ep. Ap.* 17.2); and (2) the mention of plagues which suggest proximity to the Antonine plagues (*Ep. Ap.* 17.2).

[271] Notable too is the linking together of the Johannine sent-Son and Father-Son perichoresis with the quality of pre-incarnate unbegottenness and incorporeality (*Ep. Ap.* 17.3–8; 21.2; 25.3; 31.11).

[272] Watson, *Apostolic Gospel*, 134.

archangels, in a voice of wonder, so that they might go in to the altar of the Father and serve and fulfil the ministry until I returned to him. This is what I did in the wisdom of the likeness, for I became all in all so that I might fulfil the will of the Father of glory who sent me and return to him. (*Ep. Ap.* 13.1–6)

> Then he answered and said to us, "Do you not remember that I told you a moment ago that I became an angel among angels and all in everything?"
> We said to him, "Yes, Lord."
> Then he answered and said to us, "When I took the form of the angel Gabriel, I appeared to Mary
> and I spoke with her. Her heart received me, she believed, sh[e mol]ded me, I entered into her, I
> became flesh. For I became my own servant in the appearance of the likeness of an angel. I will do
> likewise after I have returned to the Father." (*Ep. Ap.* 14.3–8)

The incarnational narrative is reminiscent, first, of the Son's incognito descent through the various tiers of the heavens in the form of an angel as found in the *Ascen. Isa.* 10.7–31. The key differences are that in *Ep. Ap.* 13–14 the descent is mentioned in the first person, the Son's adoption of angelic form temporarily deceives the archangels rather than the lower tiers of angels, and there is a single transformation into an angel rather than a series of transformations into different angelic forms. The notion of the Son "passing" angels and archons and changing form on his descent to earth had influence on subsequent tradition (*Disc. Seth* 56.21–57.7; *Pist. Soph.* 1.7–8).[273] Second, the coming of Jesus in the form of Gabriel to impregnate Mary reflects a tradition found in other sources. Among these are the teaching of the Marcosians according to Hippolytus, and two third-century texts, namely, the eighth book of the *Sibylline Oracles* and *Pistis Sophia*.[274]

[273] Watson, *Apostolic Gospel*, 136, n. 4.
[274] Several other documents accentuate the angelic role in Mary's pregnancy. In the *Protoevangelium of James* (late second century), Mary is said to conceive "a child from his Word" (*Proto-Ev. Jas* 11.2), and then later Joseph frets over what to do because the child inside Mary is "angelic" (*angelikon*; *Proto-Ev. Jas* 14.1). In the *Gospel of Pseudo-Matthew* (mid-seventh century), an angel of indescribable beauty enters Mary to make her pregnant, the virgins in her company are adamant that "no one but an angel of God has made her pregnant," and yet Joseph worries that it was not an angel, but someone disguised as an angel who seduced Mary (*Gos. Ps.-Matt* 9–10). Though eventually, in both cases, the Holy Spirit is invoked as the cause of the pregnancy (*Proto-Ev. Jas* 14.2; *Gos. Ps.-Matt* 11.1).

But concerning the creation of [Jesus], he [Marcos] expresses himself in this manner: The powers emanating from the second tetrad fashioned Jesus, who appeared on earth, and that the angel Gabriel filled the place of the Logos, and the Holy Spirit that of Zoe, and the Power of the Most High that of Anthropos, and the Virgin that of Ecclesia. Thus [in Marcos' system], this man [came] in accordance with the dispensation which transpired through Mary. The Father of all passed through the mother chosen through the Word by his knowledge. (Hippolytus, *Ref.* 6.51.1 [trans. MFB])

In the last times he changed the earth and, coming late as a new light, he rose from the womb of the Virgin Mary.
Coming from heaven, he put on a mortal form. First, then Gabriel was revealed in his strong and holy person. Second, the archangel also addressed the maiden in speech: "Receive God, Virgin, in your immaculate bosom."
Thus speaking, he breathed in the grace of God, even to one who was always a maiden. (*Sib. Or.* 8.456–61)

And when I entered the world, I came to the midst of the archons of the sphere, and I took the likeness of Gabriel, the angel of the aeons, and the archons of the of the aeons did not recognize me. But they thought that I was the Angel Gabriel. (*Pist. Soph.* 1.7.12)

Elsewhere, in a fourth-century text of dubious origins, the incarnation is connected to the archangel Michael, who is the divine power whom God entrusts to steward the impregnation of the divine Christ into Mary via a mysterious quickening in the so-called *Gospel according to the Hebrews* (cited in a Coptic text attributed to Ps.-Cyril of Jerusalem, *Disc. Theot.* 12a):

> It is written in the [Gospel] according to the Hebrews that when Christ wished to come upon the earth to men the Good Father called a mighty "power" in the heavens which was called "Michael" and committed

Christ to the care thereof. And the "power" came down into the world, and it was called Mary and [Christ] was in her womb for seven months.[275]

In the *Epistula Apostolorum*, the angelic descent of the divine Son and his taking the form of Gabriel is intended to fill in the narrative gap between John 1.1 (the Word's heavenly abode) and John 1.14/Luke 1.35–38 (the Word's incarnation). As Watson notes, "The likeness of an angel proves to be a transitional stage between disembodied divine sonship and human embodiment."[276] Even though the creedal section stated the Logos was joined to the flesh of Mary "through the Holy Spirit" (*Ep. Ap.* 3.13), the role of the Holy Spirit to "overshadow" (*episkiazō*) Mary (Luke 1.35) is eclipsed, replaced with a conflation of the Son with Gabriel, so that the conception of the divine son is via a mysterious christo-angelomorphic insemination.

The *Epistula Apostolorum* is a prime witness as to how an absolute divine Christology (see *Ep. Ap.* 22.1) could be easily married with an angelomorphic Christology without seeming contradictory.

(d) Justin Martyr.

The association of Jesus with angelic categories and the explicit identification of the Torah's "angel of the Lord" as christophanies of the pre-incarnate Jesus reaches a high point in Justin Martyr.[277]

First, Justin repeatedly calls Jesus an "angel" (*angelos*) and "captain" (*archistratēgos*) as a title beside "Apostle," "Son," "King," "Messiah," "Lord," "Logos," "Priest," "Power," "Man," "Glory," and "God." What is more, this is done in tandem with messianic exegesis, categories of begottenness, using a "fire from fire" analogy for a shared nature, and rejecting abscission and modalism (Justin, *Dial.* 34.2; 61.1; 86.3; 127.4; 128.1–4; *1 Apol.* 63.5, 14). The angel who appeared to Abraham is, for Justin, "another Lord and God who is subject to the maker of all things" (*Dial.* 56.4). Justin interprets the visible appearances of God as actual appearances of the pre-incarnate Jesus who is "both God, his Son, and Angel," who appeared in the burning bush to Moses, and was born of a virgin (*Dial.* 127.4). Jesus is the Logos who is God prior to the creation of the world and is

---

[275] Cited from Wilhelm Schneemelcher, *New Testament Apocrypha*, trans. R. McL. Wilson (2 vols.; rev. ed.; Cambridge: James Clark and Co., 1992), 1:177.

[276] Watson, *Apostolic Gospel*, 139.

[277] David Keck (*Angels and Angelology in the Middle Ages* [New York: Oxford University Press, 1998], 35) argues that in the early church, the identification of the angel of the Lord with Jesus "became an essential ingredient of anti-Jewish polemics."

called angel as the Father's messenger (*Dial.* 56.4, 10; 76.3; *1 Apol.* 63.5). Clearly for Justin, "angel" is not a diminished title, but is indicative of Jesus' heavenly status, revelatory function, and prior presence in Israel's sacred history.

Second, Justin's christological reading of Israel's sacred texts identifies Jesus with the "angel of the Lord." He writes that the angel of God who appeared to Moses as a flame of fire in a thorny bush (Exod 3.2, 6, 10) was "Jesus Christ, Son of God, apostle, and previously known as the Logos" (*1 Apol.* 63.7–10 [trans. MFB]). This appearance was not the Father, because Israel did not know Yahweh (Isa 1.3; 45.4) and no one knew the Father except the Son (Matt 11.27/ Luke 10.22). Furthermore, the Son is the Logos of God, also God, who took the form of fire and an incorporeal image, appeared to Moses and the other prophets, and now has been born of a virgin (*1 Apol.* 63.14–17). Whereas Trypho sees the burning bush as a "god" who is the "Angel of the Lord," Justin retorts that this "god" is none other than the "Lord" and "God" above whom there is no other, whom he yet identifies with the Son/Logos (*Dial.* 56, 59–61). Similarly, the angel who bears the divine name in Exod 23.20–21 is identified as Jesus, who was "declared mysteriously through Moses" (*Dial.* 75.1–2). Justin's typological and christological exegesis asserts that Jesus "is he who is called at one time the 'Angel of great counsel,' and a 'Man' by Ezekiel, and 'like the Son of man' by Daniel, and a 'Child' by Isaiah, and 'Christ' and 'God' to be worshipped by David, and 'Christ' and a 'Stone' by many, and 'Wisdom' by Solomon, and Joseph and Judah and a 'Star' by Moses, and the 'East' by Zechariah, and the 'Suffering One' and 'Jacob' and 'Israel' by Isaiah again, and a 'Rod,' and 'Flower,' and 'Corner-Stone,' and 'Son of God'" (*Dial.* 126.1). Justin is thus familiar with prior christological readings of the New Testament as well as Jewish traditions about a second divine figure alongside the creator-God.[278]

Third, Justin at points clearly accentuates Jesus' supremacy over the angels in function and form. Justin claims that Christians worship the true God, "also his Son who came from him and taught us these things, and the company of the other good angels who follow him and are like him" (*1 Apol.* 6.2).[279] He

---

[278] Oskar Skausaune, "The Development of Scriptural Interpretation in the Second and Third Centuries—Except Clement and Origen," in *Hebrew Bible/Old Testament: The History of Its Interpretation*, vol. 1: *From the Beginnings to the Middle Ages*, ed. Magne Sabe (Göttingen: Vandenhoeck & Ruprecht, 1997), 407–9. Cf. Garrett (*No Ordinary Angel*, 27): "when early Christian authors like Justin Martyr connected Jesus with God's word and that word, in turn, with the angel of the Lord, they were not inventing from scratch so much as adding a new layer to well-established ways of reading Scripture."

[279] Denis Minns and Paul Parvis (*Justin, Philosopher and Martyr: Apologies* [OECT; Oxford: Oxford University Press, 2009], 92, n. 2) state: "The Greek *allōn* does not necessarily imply that the Son is here ranked amongst the angels, although that is a natural

furthermore envisages Christ returning at the head of an angelic army (*1 Apol.* 51.8; 52.3; *Dial.* 31.1). Elsewhere, Christians are preserved from satanic temptations by "the Angel of God, i.e., the Power of God sent to us through Jesus Christ" (*Dial.* 116.1).

Fourth, there is an ontological likeness between Jesus and angels at a couple of points. While Justin can assert "we say that, in a special manner, not in the manner of an ordinary birth, he was born from God, as we said before, as Logos of God" (*tēn koinēn genesis gegennēsthai auto ek theou legomen logos theou*), this should be palatable to those who "say that Hermes is the angelic word of God" (*ton Hermēn logon ton para theou angelitikon legousin*). Justin thus analogizes the generation of the Logos with the messenger god/angelic logos Hermes (*1 Apol.* 22.2; cf. 21.1). Elsewhere, Justin anticipates those who say that angelic visitors, Logos, and the divine glory are generated, inferior expressions of the deity that spring forth from the deity. Angels are the obvious case in point; they are divine but not true deity. To which Justin retorts:

> But it is proved that there are angels who always exist, and are never reduced to that form out of which they sprang [*alla hoti men oun eisin angeloi kai aei menontes kai mē analuomenoi eis ekeino ex houper genonasis apodedeiktai*]. And that this power which the prophetic word calls God, as has been also amply demonstrated, and Angel, is not numbered [as different] in name only like the light of the sun but is indeed something numerically distinct, I have discussed briefly in what has gone before; when I asserted that this power was begotten from the Father, by His power and will, but not by abscission, as if the essence of the Father were divided; as all other things partitioned and divided are not the same after as before they were divided: and, for the sake of example, I took the case of fires kindled from a fire, which we see to be distinct from it, and yet that from which many can be kindled is by no means made less, but remains the same. (*Dial.* 128.4)

Justin distinguishes between the angels (note the plural) whose form is not inferior to the divine source from which they emerged and created angels, who are inferior and subordinate as servants. What other angels exist in this category we do not know! Jesus alone, or maybe Michael and Gabriel?

If one takes Justin's title "angel" in tandem with the language of "generation," with the analogies of light and fire, then "Nothing here suggests that Justin

---

reading.... But Justin normally uses the word we have translated as 'follow' in a moral sense. The likeness referred to here is presumably a moral likeness."

believed that ontologically Jesus Christ had the nature of an angel."[280] The problem is that Justin is not 100 percent consistent on this point, since he can speak of Jesus as an angel in titular sense, but implicitly within a class of angels (esp. *1 Apol.* 6.2; 22.2; *Dial.* 128.4), as one who is subordinate to the divine will (*Dial.* 56.11; 61.1; 113.4), worshipped in second place behind the Father (*1 Apol.* 13.3), while also part of God's divine being (*Dial.* 61.2–3; 128.3–4).

(e) Irenaeus.

Turning to Irenaeus, we encounter a second-century heresiologist and theologian who reasons through the Scriptures against "Gnostics" and represents a point of comparison and contrast with Justin's christological reading of the Scriptures. Irenaeus, like Justin, interprets scriptural theophanies christologically (*Haer.* 3.6.1–2; 4.10.1; *Epid.* 43–52). But unlike Justin, he does not use the title "angel," except in reference to Isa 9.6 LXX, and even then he accents the Son as "mighty God" (*Epid.* 55–56).

Irenaeus distinguishes the Son from angels by observing that God made the world by Word and Wisdom, not by angels (*Haer.* 4.20.1). The Lord Jesus is an intercessor different to both Moses and angels (*Epid.* 94). Salvation is wrought by God himself, not by an angel (*Haer.* 3.20.4; *Epid.* 88). However, Irenaeus can identify the Word and Wisdom of God with the angelic Cherubim and Seraphim (*Epid.* 10). Hannah points to a text of disputed authenticity, a Syrian and Armenian catena of Irenaeus, with a fragment from the so-called *On the Lord's Resurrection*, which states:

> He is all in all: Patriarch among the patriarch; Law in the laws; Chief Priests among priests; Ruler among kings; the Prophet among prophets; *the Angel among angels*; the Man among men; Son in the Father; God in God; King to all eternity. For it is he who sailed (in the ark) with Noah, and who guided Abraham; who was bound along with Isaac, and was a Wanderer with Jacob; the Shepherd of those who are saved, the Bridegroom on the Church; the Chief also of the cherubim, the Prince of angelic powers; God of God; Son of the Father; Jesus Christ; King forever and ever. Amen.[281]

While such a statement might not be from Irenaeus, it aligns well with a typological interpretation of the Jewish Scriptures by second-century theologians. Melito of Sardis, in the late second century, wrote similarly: "Jesus

---

[280] Carrell, *Jesus*, 99.
[281] Cited in Hannah, *Michael and Christ*, 208.

was patriarch among patriarchs, chief-priest among priests, a prophet among prophets, among the angels an archangel, a god in God."[282] Or else, in the Valentinian *Gospel of Philip* a similar statement can be found: "He [appeared to the] angels as an angel, and to men as a man" (*Gos. Phil.* 58.1–2). Of course, the argument here is typological, not ontological, or even functional as it pertains to Christology.

On the whole, it is impossible to align Irenaeus with an angel Christology. That is because Irenaeus' use of angelic language is rare, and he is strikingly clear that Son exists in unity with the Father, principally by sharing in the Father's eternality and life (*Haer.* 2.30.9; 4.4.2; 4.20.3). Irenaeus certainly reads the Scriptures christologically, making some tacit angel identifications, but without the cosmic hierarchy of Gnosticism or the subordinationism of Justin. As Hannah puts it, for Irenaeus, "Christ is an angel in that he is the messenger of the Father, but he also shares God's divinity and, thus, does not possess an angelic nature."[283]

(f) Clement of Alexandria.

Coming to the end of the second century, Clement of Alexandria (writing ca. 180–215 CE), represents a blend of the Word-angel analogies and typological exegeses of Scripture.

> For it is really the Lord [Jesus] that was the instructor of the ancient people by Moses; but he is the instructor of the new people by himself face to face. "For behold," he says to Moses, "My angel shall go before thee" [Exod 22.20] representing the evangelical and commanding power of the Word, but guarding the Lord's prerogative.... Formerly the older people had an old covenant, and the law disciplined the people with fear, and the Word was an angel; but to the fresh and new people has also been given a new covenant, and the Word has appeared, and fear is turned to love, and that mystic angel is born [as] Jesus. (*Paed.* 1.7)

Clement offers no reluctance, hint of embarrassment, or need for qualification in describing the Word as an angel who becomes Jesus.

(g) Christ as angel in proto-orthodox Christianity.

Despite the clear readiness to deploy angelic images, texts, and schemes to Jesus, there was a conscious resistance by some authors in regarding the pre-incarnate or exalted Jesus as merely an angel. We see that not only

---

[282] Melito, frag. 15.
[283] Hannah, *Michael and Christ*, 209.

in Colossians and Hebrews, but quite markedly in Tertullian, and quite aggressively in Athanasius.

Tertullian argued that the invisible and transcendent Father does not tread the earth, so that it was the Son of God who was revealed in Israel's history as part of an apprenticeship ahead of his incarnation: "It is the Son, therefore, who has been from the beginning administering judgment, throwing down the haughty tower, and dividing the tongues, punishing the whole world by the violence of waters, raining upon Sodom and Gomorrah fire and brimstone, as the Lord from the Lord" (*Prax.* 16). Tertullian knows of a heavenly monarchy over angelic beings (*Apol.* 24.2; *Prax.* 3), but he does not call the Son an angel. The reason is that in his work *On the Flesh of Christ*, Tertullian explicitly denies that the Son took on angelic form, polemicizing against the christological scheme of the Valentinians, Ebionites, and maybe the *Shepherd of Hermas*.[284] Tertullian asserts the Son did not become an angel because he is not in the business of delivering angels. While the Son can be called "the angel of the great counsel" (Isa 9.5 LXX), this is expressive of his mission, not his nature, which is unlike Gabriel or Michael (*Carne* 14.3). The Son is "truly God and Son of God" (*deus scilicet et dei filius*), who takes on human nature and is made lower than the angels (*Carne* 14.5).

Athanasius too argued vigorously against an angel Christology despite the obvious fact it had ample precedents in earlier Christian traditions. Arius was driven theologically to maintain the Father's monarchy against the perceived modalism of bishop Alexander and motivated locally by fragmentation within early fourth-century Alexandrian churches. Arius' *Thalia* makes no reference to the Son as an angel, majoring instead on the Son as God's wisdom, who was created in time, and as one begotten is inferior to the unbegotten, beginningless, and timeless begetter. However, from Athanasius' remarks, it is clear that Arius and later semi- and neo-Arian groups took the marginal category of "angel" and made it central to their christological exposition. "The Arians," argues David Keck, "had preferred the title of 'angel' for Christ because the term allowed them to reserve a special status for the figure of Jesus without actually linking him to the Godhead. Thus, Arian Christology has been called the final major attempt to construct an angel christology."[285] To which Athanasius argued that the Son did not become an angelic being because an angel cannot redeem a human being since an angel does not share the divine image

---

[284] That Tertullian mentions the view that "an angel was in him" resonates with the Ebionite view, while the mention of the "Lord of the vineyard" along with mention of a "Son," "laborers," and "servants" is a likely allusion to parable of the vineyard in *Herm.* 55.

[285] Keck, *Angels and Angelology*, 40.

(*Inc.* 13; 40). To say that the Son is "better than the angels" (Heb 1.4) is a contrast, not comparison; the Son does not share the nature of the angels (*Cont. Ar.* 1.55–56). The Son is worshipped, even by angels (Heb 1.6), who themselves do not receive worship (*Cont. Ar.* 2.23–24; *Syn.* 49).

At this point, we need to cast the net wider, look beyond proto-orthodox writers, and examine perspectives from "other" Christianities, where authors could make an angel Christology more than a typological insight, or a temporary disguise for the Word traveling through the heavens incognito, but the centerpiece of their Christology. For other Christian groups, viewing Christ as an angel or aeon was the proper expression of his divine self.[286] To these "other" Christianities we now turn.

(h) Jewish Christian groups.

In scholarship of early Christianity it has been customary to posit "Jewish Christian"[287] groups holding to either an adoptionist or an angelic Christology. In a previous work I have tried to dispel the assumption of primitive adoptionism,[288] but even the persistently recycled notion of Jewish Christian angel Christology deserves reevaluation. Looking at sources from Jude to John of Patmos to Justin Martyr, angelic categories are indeed present, but they are neither central nor distinctive of Jewish Christian Christology. The earliest Jewish Christian title we can excavate is *marêh* ("Lord"), not *malak* ("angel"), in our sources (1 Cor 16.22; Rev 22.20; Jude 4; *Did.* 10.6). In fact, the *Didachist* changes the well-known and celebrated liturgical formula "Hosanna to the Son of David" to "Hosanna to the God of David" in explicit relation to

---

[286] I am aware that "proto-orthodox" is a broad and malleable category, including writers who wrote things that by later standards were not regarded as orthodox (e.g., Justin); some authors truly skirt the proto-orthodox/heterodox divide (e.g., *Epistula Apostolorum* is seemingly anti-Gnostic even while its explanation of the incarnation can overlap with Gnostic schemes); and it was possible for groups of Valentinians, Sethians, Marcionites, and Jewish Christians to intersect at certain points (e.g., Valentinians could agree with the proto-orthodox in rejecting certain aspects of Marcionism). It is important to remember that when it comes to the unities and diversities of the second-century churches, we are not dealing with separate boxes, but a series of complex Venn diagrams. Even so, I find "proto-orthodox" a helpful albeit retrospective term for those writers who were *mostly* in agreement with the Christologies that would constitute the post-Nicene settlement.

[287] On the problems of defining Jewish Christianity, see James Carleton Paget, "The Definition of 'Jewish Christian/Jewish Christianity' in the History of Research," in *A History of Jewish Believers in Christ from Antiquity to the Present*, ed. Reidar Hvalvik and Oskar Skarsaune (Peabody, Mass.: Hendrickson, 2006), 22–52.

[288] Bird, *Jesus the Eternal Son*; cf. Matthew Bates, *The Birth of the Trinity* (Oxford: Oxford University Press, 2015), 76–79, 157–63.

Jesus (*Did.* 10.6). The purported low Christology of Jewish Christianity is an urban myth waiting to be debunked. Further, identifying Jesus with angelic figures from the Jewish Scriptures, with an angelic form, or with an angelic function, took place in Jewish and Gentile forms of Christianity (Jude 5; Rev 1.12–18; *Gos. Thom.* 13.2; *Ascen. Isa.* 10–11; *Herm.* 55–60; Justin, *Dial.* 55–56; *Ep. Ap.* 13–14).[289] If there was a center of gravity in Jewish Christianity, including the diverse forms that Justin encountered, it pertained to Jesus as crucified, the Messiah, judge, and arbiter of an everlasting kingdom (*Dial.* 46.1; 47.1–5; 48.4).[290] One could easily splice into that christological narrative an incognito angelic descent-ascent scheme, use titles like "Word" and "Law," pair the Son and Spirit with Cherubim and Seraphim, and identify the pre-incarnate Jesus with the angel of the Lord—and the Jewish Christian christological scheme would remain essentially proto-orthodox. But there were other Jewish Christian groups such as the Ebionites and Elkasaites, who were regarded by heresiologists as deviant for several reasons, including their Christology.

Irenaeus refers to the Ebionites as different from Cerinthus and Carpocrates in their belief that God, not angelic powers, made the world. But the Ebionites possess a *similar* view as Cerinthus and Carpocrates concerning the Lord (*ea autem quae sunt erga Dominum, [non] similiter, ut Cerinthus et Carpocrates opinantur*), whereby the "Christ" descended upon the man Jesus in the form of a dove and later departed from him prior to his crucifixion (*Haer.* 1.26.1–2). The problem is that the Latin witness to Irenaeus reads that the Ebionites' view of the Lord are *non similiter* ("not similar") to Cerinthus and Carpocrates, and most patristic scholars agree that the *non* is an error.[291] The rationale for

---

[289] It is possible that *T. Dan* 6.1–5 is a Jewish Christian text or a Christian revision of a Jewish text. The text describes the "angel who intercedes for you," who is a "mediator between God and men for the peace of Israel," and is an "angel of peace who strengthens Israel." But this angel is explicitly unequal to the Lord, and it could just as well describe the archangel Michael as per *T. Levi* 5.6 with the "angel who makes intercession." See similar descriptions of principal angels in *1 En.* 9.1–11; 40.6; 52.5; 53.4. Similarly, the *Testament of Solomon* is probably a first-century Jewish text that received a third-century Christian revision. At one point we read, "I [Solomon] said to him [demon], 'By what angel are you thwarted?' He said, 'By the one who is going to be born from a virgin and be crucified by the Jews'" (*T. Sol.* 22.20).

[290] According to John the Elder and Justin, the messiahship of Jesus is the primary marker of belonging and its denial the apex of apostasy; see 1 John 2.22; 5.1; Justin, *Dial.* 46.1; 47.4–5; 48.4.

[291] W. Wigan Harvey (*Sancti Irenaei episcopi Lugdunensis Libros quinque adversus haereses* [2 vols.; Cambridge: Cambridge University Press, 1857], 1:212–13) said: "*non* may have had its origin, by assimilation, from the preceding word; certainly it must be cancelled on the authority of the Hippolytan text. It spoils the sense; for in the first sentence it is shewn

rejecting the *non* is that if there were differences in Christology, why does Irenaeus not mention them, and why do later remarks about the Ebionites' Christology dependent upon Irenaeus continue to associate the Ebionites' view with Cerinthus and Carpocrates (Hippolytus; Epiphanius)? However, A. F. J. Klijn and G. J. Reinink argue that the *non* in *non similiter* might be authentic because, first, Irenaeus is more interested in theological aberrations than christological ones; and, second, Irenaeus' other statements about Ebionite Christology have nothing to do with possessionism or angels.[292] I would add, third, that Origen, who knew and met various Jewish Christians, never associates the Ebionites with Cerinthus or Carpocrates. Latin text aside, Irenaeus primarily posits the Ebionites believing that Jesus was the son of Joseph and Mary born by ordinary procreation, with no mention of Christ or an angel entering him (*Haer.* 3.21.1). Irenaeus infers on their part a denial that God became man, not an affirmation that Christ or an angel became human (*Haer.* 4.33.4; 5.1.3). This corresponds with information from Justin about Jewish Christians who believe that Jesus is the Messiah but claim that he was born of entirely human origin (*Dial.* 48.4; 49.1). Irenaeus does not unequivocally present the Ebionites as holding to a possessionist, adoptionist, or angel Christology, but to a purely human Jesus.[293]

Hippolytus closely follows Irenaeus in his account of the Ebionites. But Hippolytus clearly and unambiguously associates the Ebionites' Christology with that of Cerinthus and Carpocrates (*Ref.* 7.34.1–2 [cf. 10.22.1]: *ta de peri ton Christon homoiōs tō Kērinthō kai Karpokratei*). Hippolytus adds only reference to an exemplarist dimension whereby Jesus was justified on account of his virtuous life so that he received the name "Son of God" (*Ref.* 7.34.2).[294] Nothing about angels or even possessionism is stated, but emphasis again falls squarely on the Ebionites espousing a purely human Jesus.

Tertullian was the first to refer to "Ebion" (erroneously) as the person at the root of the Ebionite heresy (*Praescr.* 33). Much like Irenaeus, Tertullian

---

that the Ebionites disagreed with Cerinthus and Carpocrates as regards the creation; in the second, that they agreed with them as regards the birth of our Lord." Similarly, Oskar Skarsaune ("The Ebionites," in *A History of Jewish Believers in Christ from Antiquity to the Present*, ed. Reidar Hvalvik and Oskar Skarsaune [Peabody, Mass.: Hendrickson, 2006], 428) believes that if the Ebionites were not similar in their Christology to Cerinthus and Carpocrates, then Irenaeus would not mention the Ebionites as an appendix to the views of Cerinthus and Carpocrates.

[292] A. F. J. Klijn and G. J. Reinink, *Patristic Evidence for Jewish-Christian Sects* (Leiden: Brill, 1973), 19–20.

[293] Cf. similarly Origen, *Hom. Luc.* 17 (cited in Klijn and Reinink, *Patristic Evidence*, 126–27) and Eusebius, *Hist. eccl.* 3.27.2; 5.8.10; 6.17.

[294] Cf. Eusebius, *Hist. eccl.* 3.27.2; Epiphanius, *Pan.* 30.18.6.

(*Carne* 14.5) described Ebion(ites) as holding Jesus "to be a mere man" (*qui nudum hominem*) with the addition of being "nothing more than a descendant of David, and not also the [divine] Son of God" (*et tantum ex semine David, id est non et dei filium, constituit Iesum*). Thereafter, Tertullian states that Ebion regarded Jesus as "clearly some glorious prophet, as an angel was in him as said to be in Zechariah" (*plane prophetis aliquo gloriosiorem—ut ita in illo angelum fuisse dicatur quemadmodum in aliquo Zacharia*). The rationale being that Jesus, just like Zechariah (Zech 1.14: *ho angelos ho lalōn en moi* [LXX]), had his prophetic authority mediated from the angel within him. Unlike Klijn and Reinink, I do not think that Tertullian is speculating that it would have been convenient for Ebion to infer that Jesus had an angel in him; rather, this seems to be something that justified Jesus' superlative prophetic status in the eyes of (the) Ebion(ites).[295] In the Ebionite scheme, the angelic aspect is something of a prophetic spirit inhabiting Jesus, not really an angel Christology per se.

We now turn to the fifth-century author Epiphanius, who largely recycles earlier tradition about the Ebionites. However, he does add some new details, albeit much of it legendary embellishment or fanciful speculation. His main points about the Christology of Ebion and his followers are: (1) Jesus was a man born of natural procreation from Joseph and Mary; (2) the heavenly Christ descended into the man Jesus in the form of a dove; (3) others in the group say that Christ is a supreme heavenly lord who inhabited both Adam and the man Jesus; (4) Jesus became Son of God "by election after the Christ who came to him from on high in the form of a dove"; and (5) Christ was "not begotten of God the Father but created as one of the archangels, and that he is ruler both of angels and of all creatures of the Almighty" (*ou phaskousi de ek theou patros auton gegennēsthai alla kektisthai ōs hena tōn archangelōn*; Epiphanius, *Pan.* 20.30.2; 30.2.2; 30.3.3–6; 30.14.4; 30.16.3–4; 30.18.5–6). This reflects the same confusion we have seen since Irenaeus, namely, the Ebionites believed in a human Jesus, but if associated with Cerinthus or Carpocrates, then they (perhaps) believed in a possessionist, adoptionist, or angel Christology.[296]

In my estimation, the Ebionites should not be treated as the "poster boys" of angel Christology. More likely than not, they believed in a human Jesus born of ordinary procreation (Irenaeus; Tertullian; Hippolytus; Origen; Eusebius), they possibly conceived of Jesus as inhabited by a prophetic spirit, similar to the angel speaking within Zechariah (Tertullian), and they were—rightly

---

[295] Klijn and Reinink, *Patristic Evidence*, 21–22.
[296] Epiphanius (*Pan.* 20.30.1) likens the Ebionites to the Cerinthians and Nazoreans.

or wrongly—conflated with the possessionist Christologies of Cerinthus and Carpocrates (Irenaeus [?]; Hippolytus; Epiphanius).²⁹⁷

If our knowledge of the Ebionites is fragmentary and prejudiced by the negative opinions of the heresiologists, the same is doubly true for Elkasai and Elkasaites (Elchasaites).²⁹⁸ Hippolytus censures Pope Calixtus of Rome for leniency to heretics such Alcibiades, who received a sacred book (*Book of Elkasai*) that had been transmitted into Christian circles by a Jewish Christian named Elkasai, which he allegedly received from Sericans (i.e., northern Chinese) living in Parthia during Trajan's reign (Hippolytus, *Ref.* 9.13.1, 4; 9.16.4; Epiphanius, *Pan.* 19.1.4–5).²⁹⁹ The book contained, among other things, a second baptism ritual with invocations of angels for those who had committed mortal sins, even apostasy, after their first baptism (Hippolytus, *Ref.* 15.1–6; Eusebius, *Hist. eccl.* 6.38). Alcibiades, Hippolytus sarcastically quips, was "the most wondrous interpreter of the wretched Elkasai" because he delivers "the wondrous mysteries of Elkasai" to "his worthy disciples" (*Ref.* 9.15.2; 9.17.2). Those within the ranks of the Alcibiades-Elkasai circle advocated a Torah-observant way of life with male circumcision and, concerning Christ, said he "was a human being and was born just like everybody else" with the unique aspect that he had been born many times before in several incarnations (Hippolytus, *Ref.* 9.14.1). Elkasai's book was allegedly an oracle received from an angel of immense height (ninety-six miles high, in fact!), who was accompanied by a female of the same dimensions. Hippolytus records their view: "Now the male is the son of God, whereas the female is called 'Holy Spirit'" (Hippolytus, *Ref.* 9.13.2–3; cf. Epiphanius, *Pan.* 30.17.6–7).³⁰⁰

There is some very interesting information here. The notion of a human Jesus agrees with the Ebionite account, although a Pythagorean view of

---

²⁹⁷ The fact that Origen (*Cels.* 5.61), Eusebius (*Hist. eccl.* 3.27), and Jerome (*Ep.* 112.13.1–2) refer to Ebionites who believed in the virgin birth would suggest that "Ebionites" could be used as an unhelpful synonym for any Jewish Christian from the third century onwards.

²⁹⁸ Helpful here is Gerard P. Luttikhuizen, "Elchasaites and Their Book," in *A Companion to Second-Century Christian "Heretics*," ed. Antti Marjanen and Petri Luomanen (VigChrSup 76; Leiden: Brill, 2005), 335–64.

²⁹⁹ Eusebius quotes Origen saying that the Elchasaites believed the book fell from heaven (*Hist. eccl.* 6.38). Epiphanius (*Pan.* 19.1.4) says that Elchasai (or Elchai) claimed to have written the book under prophetic inspiration.

³⁰⁰ Alcibiades' book included baptism in the "name of the great and highest God and in the name of his Son, the great King" (Hippolytus, *Ref.* 15.1), and Elchasai confessed "Christ is the great King," although Epiphanius is unsure if he means the Lord Jesus Christ (*Pan.* 19.3.4).

reincarnation is novel, and perhaps even a smear.³⁰¹ The description of a massive angel can also be found in Jewish and Jewish Christian literature (*Herm.* 83.1; *Gos. Pet.* 39–40; *T. Reub.* 5.7; *2 En.* 1.4; 18.1; *3 En.* 9.1–5; *Acts John* 90), but this is the only place where Christ is identified as a gigantic angel. Likewise, pairing the Son and the Holy Spirit as companion angels marries together with what can be found in Irenaeus, *Epid.* 10, and *Ascen. Isa.* 9.33–36.

In sum, Elkasai was probably a Jewish Christian baptismal prophet in Parthia-Syria, ca. 117 CE, whose movement took shape in the aftermath of the upheaval caused by Trajan's invasion of Parthia, ca. 114–16 CE, and the travails it represented for Jews in Mesopotamia. The Elkasaites, self-described as "the Foreknowers" (*prognōstikoi*; Hippolytus, *Ref.* 9.14.2), believed a further Roman-Parthian conflict was looming, which would spill over into the angelic sphere among the "angels of impiety in the north [of the plain around the Tigris and Euphrates]" (Hippolytus, *Ref.* 9.16.4). The Elkasaites venerated a book about two angels, which was interpreted by some as referring to Christ and the Spirit, even while they concurrently taught a human Jesus. The Elkasaites had astrological, angelological, and numerological interests, they lived a Torah-obedient way of life, and they taught a second baptism for post-baptismal sins. The movement was indigenized in Rome via Alcibiades, who probably brought a copy of the *Book of Elkasai* to Rome after receiving it from a baptismal sect in Syria.

The proto-orthodox Jewish Christians were primarily messianic and no more or less angelic in their Christology than their Gentile counterparts like the Roman *Shepherd* or Justin Martyr. Among the Ebionites and Elkasaites, at least as the heresiologists report them, their main christological accent is upon Jesus the human prophet, perhaps joined with a few extra angelic traits, but not a Jesus who *is* an angel or who *becomes* an angel in any wildly innovative sense. Then again, all patristic statements about Ebionite and Elkasaite Christologies need an asterisk. By the time one gets to Epiphanius, most descriptions of them are exaggerated and blended with a hodgepodge of other allegedly deviant beliefs.³⁰²

---

³⁰¹ Epiphanius also attributes to the Ebionites the view of Christ experiencing several incarnations beginning with Adam (*Pan.* 20.30.2; 30.3.3, 5; 30.34.6; cf. Ps.-Clement, *Hom.* 3.17–28). A Pythagorean view of reincarnation may have been taught only by Alcibiades (Hippolytus), which has then been transferred to the Elkasaites and Ebionites by inference (Epiphanius). Alternatively, Luttikhuizen ("Elchasaites and Their Book," 353, 356–60) thinks that the many manifestations of Adam-Christ were part of a particular form of Jewish Christianity in western Syria that influenced the prophet Mani, the third-century founder of Manicheanism.

³⁰² Cf. Klijn and Reinink, *Patristic Evidence*, 67; and Hannah, *Michael and Christ*, 174–75.

(i) Jesus as angel among heterodox groups.

In the *Gospel of Thomas*, an esoteric text from the first quarter of the second century, the author at one place contrasts two proto-orthodox views of Jesus with his own view projected onto the lips of Thomas (*Gos. Thom.* 13.1–8). When Jesus asks his disciples whom he resembles (cf. Matt 16.13), Simon Peter answers that Jesus is a "righteous angel," Matthew replies that Jesus is a "wise philosopher," while Thomas responds by saying that Jesus' identity is completely mysterious and ineffable. Apart from calling Jesus "master," Thomas is said to be correct. After which, Thomas is rewarded by receiving a private audience with Jesus, who tells him "three words," which presumably sum up Jesus' contested identity, and Thomas cannot share it with the other two disciples as it would undoubtedly scandalize them.

What is interesting for our purposes is that Simon Peter and Matthew are probably regarded by the Thomasine author as representatives of the proto-orthodox churches. In the case of Simon Peter, he calls Jesus a "righteous angel" (ⲛ̄ⲟⲩⲁⲅ`ⲅⲉⲗⲟⲥ ⲛ̄ⲇⲓⲕⲁⲓⲟⲥ), in effect, "Jesus is a subordinate envoy who belongs to the creaturely realm."[303] Simon Peter's view is evidently trotted out only to be dismissed. Still, it is hard to determine whether the Thomasine author intends it as a smear against the sort of churches represented by Simon Peter, or whether he thinks it is genuinely indicative of what pro-Petrine churches truly believe about Jesus. It is not beyond the realm of possibility that *Thomas* attests the perception that proto-orthodox churches held to an angel Christology, all the more credible if the christological schemes of the *Ascension of Isaiah* or the *Epistula Apostolorum* are in mind as they derived from the same period.

As for the Christology of *Thomas*, the Thomasine Jesus is primarily a sage whose revelations impart an esoteric wisdom to followers (*Gos. Thom.* 5.1–2; 17.1; 62.1; 108.1–3). Jesus possesses some things from the Father (*Gos. Thom.* 61.3), he is a cause of division, and he is an agent of judgment (*Gos. Thom.* 10.1; 16.2; 82.1). At one place, Jesus is described as the universal light that permeates all things because he is one with all things: "I am the light who is above all things. I am the All. From me the All came forth, and the all reaches to me" (*Gos. Thom.* 77.1). Such a statement amounts to either a type of "panenchristism" (i.e., panentheistic Christology)[304] or else Jesus is "identified with the totality of the spiritual element of light wherever that

---

[303] Simon Gathercole, *The Gospel of Thomas: Introduction and Commentary* (TENT 11; Leiden: Brill, 2014), 262.

[304] Cf. *Gos. Phil.* 56.13–15: "Christ has everything in himself, whether man or angel or mystery, and the father."

element may reside."³⁰⁵ The Thomasine Jesus' eschatology is thoroughly realized and interiorized (*Gos. Thom.* 3.3; 51.1–2; 113.1–4). Salvation means several things, such as "not tasting death" (*Gos. Thom.* 1.1; 18.1–3; 19.4; 85.2; 111.2), "seeing/knowing the Father" (*Gos. Thom.* 3.4; 15.1; 27.2; 37.3; 59.1; 69.1; 105.1), entering the Father's kingdom (*Gos. Thom.* 22.1–7; 27.1; 49.1; 99.1–3), experiencing an end that rehearses the beginning (*Gos. Thom.* 18.1–3), and is summed up in the androgyne unity of the "female" with the "male," where the two become one (*Gos. Thom.* 11.4; 22.4–5; 30.2; 106.1; 114.1–3). April DeConick argues that in the earliest layer of the Thomasine tradition, "Jesus is God's Prophet who exclusively speaks God's truth. He also is understood to have been exalted to the status of a great Angel whose main role is that of the Judge, casting fire upon the earth. These descriptors are comparable to those commonly associated with early Christian Judaism from Jerusalem."³⁰⁶ While I am more circumspect as to how early the Thomasine tradition goes, nonetheless it envisages Jesus as a heavenly or even angelic figure of wisdom and agent of judgment.

The *Infancy Gospel of Thomas* is a second-century text, known to Irenaeus (*Haer.* 1.20.1) but difficult to place in either proto-orthodox or heterodox camps. It could be regarded as a kind of Christian "fan fiction" that tried to fill in the gaps about Jesus' childhood. One interesting vignette from it is when the local teacher Zacchaeus was astounded to the point of fear by Jesus' allegorical interpretation of the Greek alphabet, to the point that he begs Joseph to take the boy Jesus home, urging: "This child is not of this world; he can even tame fire. Maybe he was born before the world came into being. . . . What kind of great thing he could be—whether a divine being or an angel (*ē theos ē angelos*)—I do not know even what to say" (*Inf. Gos. Thom.* 7.2, 4).

For the Valentinians, Christology expressed itself in angelology, since the Savior's role required an angelic Christ, as well as a human Jesus.

Tertullian (*Carne* 14.1) probably had Valentinians in mind when he complained about those who said that Christ was clothed with the nature of an angel (*Sed et . . . angelum gestavit Christus*). That makes sense in that the Valentinians generally held to a possessionist Christology, where the man Jesus received Christ/Savior at his baptism. It was by means of the divine "Name" that "descended upon Jesus in the dove" that he became the agent of redemption and the human manifestation of the divine Savior (Clement of Alexandria,

---

³⁰⁵ Gathercole, *Gospel of Thomas*, 493–94.

³⁰⁶ April D. DeConick, *The Original Gospel of Thomas in Translation: With Commentary and New English Translation of the Complete Gospel* (LNTS 287; London: T&T Clark, 2006), 8.

Exc. 22.5–6; cf. Hippolytus, *Ref.* 10.13.3).³⁰⁷ It was also where the man Jesus was "begotten anew" and "redeemed" (*Gos. Phil.* 70.34–71.2) from the "deficiency" of the demiurge (*Exc.* 7). In other Valentinian schemes, Jesus is polymorphic and incognito in his coming, as in the case of a Valentinian interpretation of the transfiguration: "He appeared to [them all. He appeared] to the great as great. He [appeared] to the small as small. He [appeared to the] angels as an angel, and to men as a man. Because of this his word hid itself from everyone. Some indeed saw him, thinking that they were seeing themselves, but when he appeared to his disciples in glory on the mount he was not small. He became great, but he made the disciples great, that they might be able to see him in his greatness" (*Gos. Phil.* 57.32–58.10). Similarly, in another Valentinian account of the transfiguration (*Exc.* 4.1), "By reason of his great humility, the Lord did not appear as an angel, but as a man, . . . when he appeared in glory with the apostles on the mountain." The transfiguration was associated with a revelation of the angelic lord in human form.

To appreciate the Valentinian scheme, one must understand that for the Valentinians there was a rupture within the pleroma and there was a spiritual seed sown by Jesus but tragically trapped in the created order. Both were to be rescued by Christ "the angel of the pleroma" (*angelos ēn tou plērōmatos*), who would unite "males" (i.e., angels) with "females" (i.e., Valentinians; *Exc.* 21.3; 35.1; *Gos. Phil.* 58.10–14). This is why some Valentinians, when laying hands on someone, uttered the confessional formula "for the angelic redemption" (*eis lytrōsin angelikēn*; cf. *Tri. Trac.* 124.25–34; 125.19–20), with a view to being redeemed with the angels. In Valentinian perspective, Christian baptism celebrated reception of the same Name that the angels, even Jesus, received at their baptism. Baptism dispels the error and makes one become "equal to angels" (*isangeloi*) upon entering the pleroma (*Exc.* 22.3–5; cf. *Tri. Trac.* 132.14–27). According to Irenaeus, the Valentinians believed that Christ was the "very star of the pleroma and the perfect fruit of it," and he was protected by angels, who possessed "the same nature as himself" (*Haer.* 1.2.6). For Theodotus, the Logos is truly, or by "identity" (*tautotēs*),³⁰⁸ "God in God" (*theon en theō*), who is "unceasingly and undividedly one God" (*adiastatos*

---

³⁰⁷ On the angelic significance of the divine "Name" indwelling someone, see Exod 23.21 with "my name is in him [i.e., the angel]"; *Gos. Phil.* 54.4–10 with "One single name is not uttered in the world, the name which the father gave to the son; it is the name above all things: the name of the father. For the son would not become father unless he wore the name of the father"; and *Tri. Trac.* 56.35–38; 66.32, where the incomprehensible Father begets a "thought" who is "clothed with a single name."

³⁰⁸ GELS/BrillDAG.

ameristos heis theos), an angel, with a message from the ingenerate God (*Exc.* 8.1; 25.1). For the Valentinians, Christ the aeonic-generated Savior unites with fallen Sophia to create a conjunction where the spiritual ones (i.e., the Valentinians) are given as brides to the angels, after which comes a fiery purgation of the material world (Irenaeus, *Haer.* 1.7.1).[309]

The Valentinian Christology is not low; it is comprehensively cosmic! Christ is to redeem the spiritual expanse (i.e., the pleroma) by rescuing angels from the fall of Sophia and uniting the spiritual ones with the angelic realm to which they properly belong. Christ is from and for the angelic realm, and his deliverance of angelic orders will spill over into a redemption from the creation—a creation itself made by malevolent angels like the demiurge—in which humans tragically reside. We might sum up the Valentinian Christology this way: *Extra Christo Angelus non est salus* (Without Christ the angel there is no salvation).

Marcion's Christology is difficult to penetrate through our biased sources. It is more likely than not that Marcion's Jesus was in some sense docetic (Irenaeus, *Haer.* 4.33.2; Tertullian, *Marc.* 3.8.1), tangible but fleshless, with Jesus descending from the Good power in a body that was either comprised of cosmic elements (Hippolytus, *Ref.* 7.38.2–3; 10.19.3), or perhaps angelic substance (Tertullian, *Marc.* 3.9.1–7; *Carne* 6.9–11). Hippolytus wrote that Marcion's disciple Apelles multiplied Marcion's two divine principles into four. Apelles referred to these four principles not as "gods," but "angels." Christ, in Apelles' scheme, is a fifth god or angel (*Ref.* 10.19.1; 10.20.1).

Ps.-Cyprian was a late second- or early third-century author with ascetic and anti-Jewish tendencies. In *De Centesima Sexagesima Tricesima* (*Threefold Reward of the Martyrs*), the author identified Jesus as an angelic creature: "Christ . . . Son of God . . . was created by the divine mouth" (*Christus, cum sit dei filius atque diuino ore creatus; Centesima* 50); and "When the Lord created the seven principal angels from fire, he determined to make one of them his Son.[310] It is he who Isaiah declares to be the Lord Sabaoth. We see that there remained then six angels who had been created with the Son, whom the ascetics imitate" (angelos enim dominus cum ex igne principum numero vii crearet, ex his unum in filium sibi constituere. quem Isaias dominum Sabot [ut] praeconaret, disposuit. remansisse ergo repperimus sex quidem angelos

---

[309] Hannah, *Michael and Christ*, 180.

[310] The text includes an editorial gloss that smears the perspective of Ps.-Cyprian: "he says that the Son is a creature [which is] against the Catholic faith" (*creaturam filium dei dicit contra catholicam fidem*).

cum filio creatos, quos agonista imitator; *Centesima* 216–20).[311] According to Ps.-Cyprian, Jesus is an angelic creature and something of a first among equals beside the six other principal angels. Interestingly, Ps.-Cyprian seems to have known the *Shepherd of Hermas*, and it is possible that his identification of the Son of God beside the six holy angels is indebted to the Roman Shepherd, who said that angels "were created first of all" and who places the Son of God in proximity to six angels in his similitudes (*Herm.* 12.1; 58.3; 89.8).[312] Viewed this way, Ps.-Cyprian indicates an angel Christology as part of the reception history of Hermas and arguably prepares the way for some strands of Arian Christology.

(j) Angel veneration and worship of Jesus.

It is conceivable that further proof for angel Christology could be found in observing that Christ devotion was analogous to the "worship of angels" by Jews. If Jesus was comparable to or identifiable as an angel, then angel veneration has obvious currency for Christology. Horbury contends that "a cult of angels therefore accompanied the development of the cult of Christ."[313] Such a topic requires technical discussion on types of "worship," a survey of dozens of Jewish and Christian texts, comparison with patterns of devotion in early Christianity, and interaction with extensive secondary literature. I do not wish to insert a monograph at this point, but the topic obviously needs more than a footnote. Therefore, some brief comments and reliance on secondary literature will have to suffice, or else this section will become even painfully longer than it already is.

First, what do we mean by "worship" in the "worship of angels"?[314] Here it is helpful to note that worship can include practices of a cultus with temples and sacrifices, as well as various types of invocations and venerations in the form of thanksgivings, doxologies, prayers, and petitions. As such, I prefer the expansive definition of Hurtado: "I use the word 'worship' here to designate open, formal, public, and intentional actions of invocation, adoration, appeal,

---

[311] Cited in Hannah, *Michael and Christ*, 172.

[312] R. Reitzenstein, "Eine frühchristliche Schrift von der dreierlei Früchten des christlichen Lebens," *ZNW* 15 (1914): 76, 82; Lookadoo, *Shepherd*, 40, 45; and Hannah, *Michael and Christ*, 172.

[313] Horbury, *Jewish Messianism*, 121–22.

[314] Cf. BDAG, 882–83; LN 53.56; and Dunn, *Did the First Christians?*, 7–28. Notice should be given to Nathan MacDonald's caveat ("Monotheism," in *The World of the New Testament: Cultural, Social, and Historical Contexts*, ed. Joel B. Green and Lee Martin McDonald [Grand Rapids: Baker, 2013], 82): "The line between veneration and worship is notoriously thin, not only for modern scholarship, but also for ancient Jewish writers."

praise, and communion that characterized the corporate cultic gatherings of early Christian groups and that were clearly patterned after the sort of cultic devotional actions otherwise reserved for God in scrupulous Jewish monotheistic circles."[315] Second, did Jews really worship the angels? An exhaustive survey is impossible, but there are some materials that we can interrogate in want of an answer.

Jewish and Christian authors retained a very strong prohibition against the worship of "hosts" or "angels," which itself implies that people did, from time to time, for whatever reasons, engage in "worship" of angels in a way that allegedly contaminated a pure Yahweh devotion.[316] Paul makes one particularly pointed prohibition of angel worship in Col 2.18: "Do not let anyone disqualify you, insisting on self-abasement and worship of angels, dwelling on visions, puffed up without cause by a human way of thinking."[317] The question is whether the worship here pertains to the veneration of the angels themselves (objective genitive) or whether it pertains to worship that the angels themselves engage in (subjective genitive). There are examples of biblical and postbiblical acts of veneration directed at angels by Jewish worshippers, but there was also an abiding interest in the heavenly liturgy and worship offered by the angels themselves (e.g., 1QH 3.21–22; 4Q400–5). One can split the horns of the dilemma and say that interest in worship by the angels itself assumes that the angels have a liturgical vocation and access to God that is venerable![318]

In the book of Tobit, Tobit finds his son, and then prays, "Blessed be God, and blessed be his great name, and blessed be all his holy angels" (Tob 11.14). At Qumran, worshipping angels who engage in the heavenly liturgy are "honored in all the camps of the godlike beings and feared by those who direct human affairs" (4Q400 II 2). In an inscription on the island of Rheneia off the southwest coast of Asia Minor, dated to the first/second century BCE, there is an invocation with Jewish ambience: "O Lord who sees all things and angels of God, before whom all souls of this day humble themselves with a supplication,

---

[315] Larry Hurtado, *Ancient Jewish Monotheism and Early Christian Jesus-Devotion: The Context and Character of Christological Faith* (Waco, Tex.: Baylor University Press, 2017), 116, n. 4.

[316] See, e.g., Deut 4.19; 17.3; Jer 8.2; 19.13; Zeph 11.5; Rev 19.10; 22.9; Tob 12.16–22; *Ascen. Isa.* 7.2, 18–23; 8.1–10, 15; *Apoc. Ab.* 17.1–5; *Apoc. Zeph.* 6.11–15; *2 En.* 1.4–8; *3 En.* 1.7; 16.1–5; *b.Hull.* 40a; *b.Abod. Zar.* 42b; *t.Hull.* 2.6; Origen, *Cels.* 5.4–5. See Stuckenbruck, *Angel Veneration*, 103: "the intensity of the refusal [of angels to be worshipped] is hard to explain without positing some form of underlying venerative behavior which may have been deemed appropriate towards God's messengers, an attitude which at least the proponents themselves would probably not have considered to be destructive to a belief in one God."

[317] See Bird, *Colossians and Philemon*, 83–89 for discussion.

[318] Stuckenbruck, *Angel Veneration*, 117–19.

that you avenge the innocent blood and render account quickly."[319] The magical papyri are also filled with the invocation of angels from Jewish tradition, which belies Jewish influence.[320] The Enochic Son of Man/Chosen One is a heavenly, messianic, and angelic figure who receives worship from earthly kings (*1 En.* 48.5; 62.1–8). Persons can make personal pleas to angels about some matter (*T. Levi* 5.5; *4 Bar* 3.4). It is interesting too that in *Kerygma Petrou* (2) the Jews are accused of angel worship as a smear, while Origen exonerates Torah-observant Jews from Celsus' charge of angel worship (*Cels.* 5.5). What is more, even Justin Martyr can refer to Christians worshipping and praising God, the Son, the prophet Spirit, and "other good angels" (*1 Apol.* 6.2).

I surmise, prima facie, that among Second Temple Jews, veneration of angels as to Yahweh was taboo and not widely practiced. It appears that the veneration of angels was not undertaken with the same cultic veneration that was afforded to Yahweh in the Jerusalem cultus or celebrated in synagogal liturgies of the Jewish Diaspora. Hence no altar to Michael was erected inside or beside the Jerusalem temple, nor was a temple to Gabriel built by Jewish communities in Phrygia. Yet there were prayers, petitions, and blessings made to angels, largely in association with monotheistic worship, as Jewish worshippers sought angelic assistance for revenge and protection. Thus, even for Jewish monotheists, types of angel veneration were acceptable, even more so when the angels were thought of as God's healers, carriers of prayers, and intercessors (e.g., Tob 12.12, 15; *T. Levi* 3.5–7; 5.6; *T. Dan* 6.2; *1 En.* 9.3; 40.6; 47.1–2; 99.3; 104.1). Yet angel veneration was not "a regular part of ancient Jewish cultic practice" and enhanced rather than contaminated "vigorous and lively monotheistic piety."[321] Some Jewish and Christian authors were aware of the danger of angel veneration beside divine worship escalating into angel worship in isolation and independence from divine worship proper. Accordingly, the prohibitions of angel worship were an extension of prohibitions against idolatry and ruler worship, albeit rooted in a context where angels were especially revered and could conceivably be given over to deviant forms of devotion (see *3 En.* 16).[322] In the course of the second and third centuries, rabbinic authors become increasingly uncomfortable with popular forms of angelic veneration. In contrast, Christians become increasingly flexible in their adoration of angels, martyrs, and saints, and "angel worship" became an anti-Jewish slur. Angel veneration was not then necessarily a departure from monotheism, but it could certainly test its boundaries.

[319] Cited in Stuckenbruck, *Angel Veneration*, 183–84.
[320] Cf. Stuckenbruck, *Angel Veneration*, 188–200.
[321] Hurtado, *One God, One Lord*, 26, 28.
[322] Stuckenbruck, *Angel Veneration*, 87.

Third, was the worship of Jesus analogous to angel veneration or more approximate to divine worship? This a huge and diverse topic, and I can scarcely do justice to it in a brief section. All I can do is point to what I think are some important primary sources and refer to significant threads in secondary literature. Accordingly, I will have to be summative and point to other literature. To begin with, we have the following options to consider:

> *(1) God alone is worshipped in Judaism, and earliest Christianity was Jewish; therefore, Jesus was not worshipped.*[323]

For Maurice Casey, Jewish monotheism was strict and Jesus never received the type of worship normally associated with an absolute deity (i.e., sacrifices and temple). Further proof is the lack of dispute in the Pauline epistles concerning a possible breach of monotheism occasioned by the worship of Jesus.[324] The various prayers and hymns made to Jesus as well as invocations of Jesus' name are not tantamount to deification. Such practices indicate "that Jesus was viewed as a superior heavenly being and a central figure of identity and authority to whom the church was subject. However, it does not equate him with God, and its exact force could be differently perceived by different people."[325] Jesus was important in the worship of God, Casey argues, but not worshipped himself, not until such a time as the Pauline churches become sufficiently filled with Gentile adherents so that a dialectic of belief and experience led to the worship of Jesus. Thus, Paul's letters do not attest "the historical origins of the worship of Jesus, though some steps in that direction have been taken."[326]

Such a line of argument is interdicted, first, by observing how in the early church there were beliefs and devotional practices that included Jesus within the worship offered to Israel's one God, and they were treated as a breach of monotheism by some Jews. The persecution of the Judean churches by Saul of Tarsus (i.e., the pre-conversion Paul) were partly motivated by the perception of the churches as a rogue messianic cult with a transgressive veneration of Jesus beside or in association with Israel's one God.[327] The reason why Paul

---

[323] P. M. Casey, "Jewish Monotheism and Christological Developments in Christian Churches," in *The Jewish Roots of Christological Monotheism: Papers from the St. Andrews Conference on the Historical Origins of the Worship of Jesus*, ed. Carey C. Newman, James R. Davila, and Gladys S. Lewis (JSJSup 63; Leiden: Brill, 1999), 214-33; followed by Schrage, *Unterwegs zur Einheit und Einzigkeit Gottes*, 165-67.

[324] Casey, "Jewish Monotheism," 224-25.

[325] Casey, "Jewish Monotheism," 226.

[326] Casey, "Jewish Monotheism," 233.

[327] Cf. Hurtado, *Lord Jesus Christ*, 175-76; contested by Dunn, *Did the First Christians?* 113-16.

does not mention disputes over the worship of Jesus is because it was already accepted and practiced in Judean and Diasporan Christ-believing assemblies that Jesus was a subject of cultic worship.³²⁸ Second, looking beyond Paul's letters, the negative response of the high priest to the Synoptic Jesus' pronouncement of his position *sitting* at the right hand of the Power and *coming* with the clouds of heaven (Mark 14.62/Matt 26.64/Luke 22.69), as well as the Jerusalem crowd's violent reaction to Stephen's verbalizing his vision of the same thing (Acts 7.56-60), are indicative of an attribution to Jesus of a position and receipt of devotion that some Jews thought violated their monotheistic worship. In John's Gospel the divine nature and worship of Jesus was a major cause of the rupture between John's network of churches and synagogue communities (John 5.18, 23; 8.58-59; 10.33), and this continued into the time of Justin's Trypho (*Dial.* 38.1).

> *(2) Jesus was worshipped like an intermediary figure* but
> did not *receive cultic worship.*³²⁹
>
> *(3) Jesus was worshipped like an intermediary figure*
> and did *receive cultic worship.*³³⁰

There are a cluster of views that contend that Jesus was divine in the sense of an intermediary figure, but there is division as to whether the worship he received was a general veneration or genuinely cultlike.

There is the initial matter of the worship of intermediary figures such as angels. We have already touched upon the worship of angels by Jewish communities, but is that an analogy for the worship of Christ? To begin with, Jesus was not worshipped merely as a healer, avenger, and carrier of prayers, but in association with God the Father, with cultic elements, and in the context of his eschatological role and redemptive work. According to Stuckenbruck, while angel veneration is a useful analogue for early Jesus devotion insofar that it posits that "an independent figure coupled with an express retention of

---

³²⁸ Cf. Hurtado, *Lord Jesus Christ*, 165-67.

³²⁹ Dunn, *Theology of Paul*, 257-60; idem, *Did the First Christians?* and Collins and Collins, *King and Messiah*, 173-74, 211-13.

³³⁰ Bousset, *Kyrios Christos*, 129-52; Ernst Lohmeyer, *Christuskult und Kaiserkult* (Tübingen: Mohr Siebeck, 1919), 22-23; and Rudolf Bultmann (*Theology of the New Testament*, trans. K. Grobel [2 vols.; London: SCM Press, 1952-1955], 1:51) believed that the earliest Jerusalem churches did not cultically worship Jesus, whereas the Hellenistic church did cultically worship him as *kyrios*. The application of Old Testament *kyrios* language to Jesus in Antiochene Christianity was, for Bousset (147) "actually almost a deification of Jesus." On the failure to see the Jerusalem/Aramaic-speaking community engaging in cultic worship, see Hurtado, *One God, One Lord*, 105; and idem, *Lord Jesus Christ*, 135-37.

246 Jesus among the gods

a monotheistic framework is evident in some of the sources in which angels are honored alongside God as aligned yet subordinated beings," yet we are still "faced with a religio-historical discontinuity as to the kind and intensity of worship between angels and Christ."[331] That is to say, Jesus was worshipped, not as a subordinate angel, but alongside God the Father, and in conscious continuity with the worship of the one God of Israel's monotheistic tradition.

This brings us to the matter of the cultic worship of Jesus. According to David Aune: "Perhaps the single most important historical development within the early church was the rise of the cultic worship of the exalted Jesus within the primitive Palestinian church."[332] Yet this is disputed, as Dunn, for instance, thinks that

> Cultic worship of service (*latreuein, latreia*) as such is never offered to Christ, and other worship terms are used only in relation to God (including Acts 13.2?). In the case of the most common words of praise and thanksgiving (*eucharistein*), they too are never offered to Christ. More common is the giving of thanks to God for what Jesus has done. In all this we would have to speak of something like a reserve or caution in the language of worship insofar as it was used in reference to Jesus. The first answer to the question, "Did the first Christians worship Jesus?", would therefore seem to be "Generally no", or "only occasionally", or "only with some reserve."[333]

To be clear, by cultic worship, we mean "devotion offered in a liturgical setting and intended to represent, manifest, and reinforce the relationship of the devotee(s) to a deity."[334] The act of "calling on the name of the Lord" had cultic significance and is something of a smoking gun in terms of cultic devotion offered to the Lord Jesus (1 Cor 1.2; Rom 10.12–14; Acts 9.14, 21; *Herm.* 91.3).[335] That is even without considering cultic meals, hymns, prayers, and doxologies. Angels did not receive cultic worship in Judaism, but Jesus himself did!

Finally, one should not needlessly ambiguate "worship" to the point that we do not know whether Jesus was worshipped as a regal potentate, principal angel, or uncreated deity.[336] Yes, "worship" (*proskynesis/proskyneō*) was a broad

---

[331] Stuckenbruck, *Angel Veneration*, 272–73.
[332] David E. Aune, *Cultic Setting of Realized Eschatology in Early Christianity* (Leiden: Brill, 1972), 5.
[333] Dunn, *Did the First Christians?* 27–28.
[334] Hurtado, *Lord Jesus Christ*, 38, n. 36.
[335] Hurtado, *Lord Jesus Christ*, 198–206.
[336] Cf. Collins and Collins (*King and Messiah*, 174): "It is difficult to distinguish ancient texts and practices expressing political submission and respect, on the one

category including prostration, obeisance, and sacrifices, and could be offered to patrons, generals, kings, emperors, demigods, angels, and Olympian gods. However, I do not think ancient worshippers thought all things worshipped had the same status or there was no way to distinguish their status by types of worship. The exalted Jesus promised the Philadelphian believers that the local Jews would one day *proskyneō* at their feet (Rev 3.9), and there was the civic worship of the emperor (Rev 13.4, 8, 12), the worship of demons and idols (Rev 9.20), the worship of angels (Rev 19.10; 22.8–9), the worship of God Almighty (Rev 4.8–11; 7.11–12; 11.16–18; 14.7; 15.4; 19.4–8), the worship of God and the Lamb (Rev 5.9–14; 7.10; 15.3–4; 22.3). In the book of Revelation, God is worshipped as cosmic creator and the Lamb as cosmic redeemer—these are distinguishable from prostration, civic devotion, idolatry, and veneration of a heavenly figure. Furthermore, as early as Herodotus there were two different worships of Herakles depending on whether one thought he was an immortal or a hero (*Hist.* 2.44). The Arval Brothers, a college of male priests in Rome, offered sacrifices to the Olympian deities, the deceased, and living emperors, and the ranking of deities was based on the sacrifice offered.[337] There was a difference between the worship of Jupiter, Juno, and Julius Caesar and the type of sacrifice offered told you something about the status of the worshipped. For all the fuzziness of definitions of "worship," the practices themselves implied the status of the one worshipped.

The early church, with their prohibitions of angel worship and gag reflex at emperor worship, make it unlikely—though admittedly not impossible—for them to worship Jesus in the sense that he was a principal angel or earthly potentate. Whether the worship of Jesus automatically ranked him on the same level as God the Father should remain an open question. That said, Jesus is placed on par with the worship of God the Father in John 5.23, where people are called to "honor" the Son just as they "honor" the Father, and in Phil 2.9–11, where universal and cosmic obeisance attributed to Yahweh in Deutero-Isaiah is given to the Lord Jesus. However, merely appealing to the ambiguity of the term "worship," making angel veneration or ruler worship the first point of call to define the worship of Jesus, is needlessly obfuscating.

---

hand, from practices that we call religious, which express worship and devotion on the other."

[337] Ittai Gradel, *Emperor Worship and Roman Religion* (Oxford: Clarendon, 2002), 275–76; Michael Koortbojian, *The Divinization of Caesar and Augustus: Precedents, Consequences, Implications* (Cambridge: Cambridge University Press, 2013), 126; and John Scheid, "Hierarchy and Structure in Roman Polytheism: Roman Methods of Conceiving Action," in *Roman Religion*, ed. Clifford Ando (Edinburgh: Edinburgh University Press, 2003), 164–89.

(4) Jesus was worshipped alongside and in unity with Israel's God in cultic worship.[338]

I favor option 4 for the following reasons:

(a) Worship of the risen Jesus was part of the Easter experience of the disciples (Matt 28.9, 17; Luke 24.52).

(b) The early church engaged in messianic readings of the psalter in a way that celebrated in song Jesus as God's agent of deliverance, Jesus' lordship, and his abiding presence with the believing community (e.g., Heb 1.8–12; 2.12; *Did.* 10.6; Justin, *Dial.* 37–38; 63; 73–74; 126).[339]

(c) The devotional practices of the early church signified the inclusion of Jesus within divine worship. This is evident from the mentioning and venerating of Jesus in hymns (Phil 2.6–11; Eph 5.19; Rev 5.9–13; 7.15–17; 15.3–4; Pliny, *Ep.* 10.96.7; Ignatius, *Eph.* 4.1–2; Eusebius, *Hist. eccl.* 5.28.5–6; 7.30.10–11), cultic meals (1 Cor 10.21; 11.23–26; Jude 12; *Did.* 9.1–5), making Jesus the object of prayers (Acts 7.59; Rom 10.13; 1 Cor 1.2; 2 Cor 12.2–10; 1 Thess 3.11–13; 2 Thess 2.16–17; 3.5, 16; Ignatius, *Eph.* 20.1; *Rom.* 4.1; *Smyrn.* 4.1; *Acts Pet.* 20–21; 39), blessings (Rom 9.5; Ignatius, *Eph.* 1.3; *Mart. Pol.* 14.1), eschatological invocations (1 Cor 16.22; Rev 22.20; *Did.* 10.6), benedictions (2 Cor 13.14; *1 Clem.* 65.2), doxologies to God through Jesus (Rom 16.25; Heb 13.20–21; 1 Pet 4.11; Jude 25; *Did.* 9.4; *1 Clem.* 58.2; 61.3; 64.1; 65.2; *Barn.* 12.7; *Mart. Pol.* 14.3; 22.3; Justin *1 Apol.* 65.3), and doxologies to Jesus alone (2 Tim 4.18; 2 Pet 3.18; Rev 1.5–6; Ignatius, *Eph.* 2.2; *Smyrn.* 1.1; Melito, *Peri Pascha* 10, 45, 65, 105; *Acts John* 77; *Acts Paul and Thecla* 42; *Acts Pet.* 39).[340] Jesus' name is called upon akin to scriptural figures calling upon Yahweh (1 Cor 1.2; Rom 10.12–15; Acts 9.14, 21; 2 Tim 2.22; *Herm.* 91.3). There is also veneration of Jesus' "name" in baptism (Acts 2.38; 8.12, 16; 10.48; 19.5; 22.16) and invoking Jesus' name in healings (Acts 3.6, 16) and exorcisms (Acts 19.13–17). Taken collectively, what is offered here is more than obeisance to a king,

---

[338] Hurtado, *One God, One Lord*, 129; and Bauckham, *Jesus and the God of Israel*, 150–51.

[339] Martin Hengel, *Between Jesus and Paul* (London: SCM Press, 1983), 78–96.

[340] Bauckham (*Jesus and the God of Israel*, 132) says about the doxologies: "The attribution of doxologies to Christ is particularly clear evidence of unambiguously divine worship, i.e., worship that is appropriately offered only to the one God. Moreover, an unbroken tradition of use of christological doxologies can be traced from the New Testament through the whole ante-Nicene period."

more than panegyric poetry to a patron, more than homage to a hero; it exceeds veneration of a principal agent, and is proper worship to a true God.[341]

(d) The worship of Jesus in earliest Christian circles did not comprise a new cultus to an independent deity, but was always part of the worship of the one God of Israel.[342] Jesus did not displace the cult of Yahweh, but was the instrument or means of worship, praise, thanksgiving, and glory offered to Israel's God. Hence the ubiquitous language of worship to God "through Jesus" in prayers, thanksgivings, benedictions, and doxologies (i.e., no Jesus-olatry where Jesus substitutes for or surpasses God the Father)! Yet the inclusion of Jesus in the orbit of divine sovereignty, symbolized by his position beside God the Father upon the throne, entailed his fitness to receive divine worship, not in competition with God, but in association with the one God. Thus, the worship of God *through* Jesus very quickly began to entail the worship *of* Jesus as God as well.[343]

(e) The worship of Jesus also had the same exclusivity as cultic worship of Yahweh. We see that in the exclusivity of worship of God and Jesus to the exclusion of other worships (1 Thess 1.9-10; 1 Cor 10.14-22; 12.1-3). Or else, in the *Martyrdom of Polycarp*, we read, "They did not know that we will never be able either to abandon the Christ who suffered for the salvation of the whole world of those who are saved, the blameless on behalf of sinners, or to worship anyone else" (*Mart. Pol.* 17.2). A common refrain in the apocryphal Acts of the second and third centuries is mention of Jesus as "you [Jesus] are the only God and there is no other beside" (with variations in *Acts John* 77; *Acts Pet.* 21; 39; *Acts Thom.* 25; Eusebius, *Hist. eccl.* 7.11.5), which resembles the Deutero-Isaianic polemic against idol worship (Isa 43.11; 45.5, 11, 22; 46.9). According to Bauckham, what this makes clear is that "in the apocryphal Acts, where the worship of Jesus is so

---

[341] Cf. more fully, Hurtado, *One God, One Lord*, 105-9; and idem, *Lord Jesus Christ*, 134-53, 194-206.

[342] Hurtado, *One God, One Lord*, 104; idem, *Ancient Jewish Monotheism*, 101; and Bauckham, *Jesus and the God of Israel*, 142.

[343] On this point, I suspect that Dunn (*Did the First Christians?* 147-49), Larry Hurtado (*At the Origins of Christian Worship: The Context and Character of Earliest Christian Devotion* [Grand Rapids: Eerdmans, 1999], 103-6), and Bauckham (*Jesus and the God of Israel*, 141-42) might even agree!

prominent, it was conceived primarily in terms of Jewish monotheistic worship."³⁴⁴

(f) Jesus received worship in texts where the worship of angels was expressly forbidden (Rev 19.10; 22.9; *Ascen. Isa.* 7.2, 18–23; 8.1–10, 15).

(g) Jesus is said to receive worship from heavenly beings (Heb 1.6; *Ascen. Isa.* 10.15; 11.23–32; *Apoc. Jas.* 14.26–30) and from creation (Phil 2.10–11; Rev 5.12–14; Pol. *Phil.* 2.1). Meanwhile, Jesus himself is almost never³⁴⁵ listed as the subject who leads or gives worship to God the Father as part of a heavenly council, even though angels like Michael sometimes do.

(h) Jews like Trypho (*Dial.* 38.1), pagan authors like Pliny the Younger (*Ep.* 10.96), Lucian (*Pereg.* 13), Celsus (*Cels.* 8.12, 14), and Porphyry (Augustine, *Civ.* 19.23) recognized that Christians in the second century worshipped Jesus as a God, often mentioning hymnody.

I fully concede that there are rejoinders to these observations, and this is far from the end of the matter. The lingering issues for debate are the definition of cultic worship, evidence for the veneration of intermediary figures in ways that might be cultic or encroach upon divine worship, whether Jesus was worshipped beside God as a subordinate deity, and whether worship itself is a reliable index as to whether someone is a "true God." Scholars will no doubt continue to debate these matters in relation to ancient Jewish monotheism and the emergence of early Christian worship.

(6) Comparative analysis.

(a) The interface between angelology and Christology.

On the one hand, in the New Testament, Jesus is never *explicitly* identified as the angel of the Lord, as an angel in human form, or a human who became an angel.³⁴⁶ What is more, the tendency of the tradition as represented in the New Testament was to portray the exalted Jesus as above all angelic powers

---

³⁴⁴ Bauckham, *Jesus and the God of Israel*, 144 (141–46).

³⁴⁵ The exception is *Ascen. Isa.* 9.40.

³⁴⁶ Cf. esp. Barbel, *Christos Angelos*, 348, 352; Segal, *Two Powers in Heaven*, 205, 210, 219; Osborn, *Emergence of Christian Theology*, 179; Dunn, *Christology in the Making*, 155–56, 158–59, 161–62, Stuckenbruck, *Angel Veneration*, 138–39; Horbury, *Jewish Messianism*, 124; Hannah, *Michael and Christ*, 151–58, 161–62; Garrett, *No Ordinary Angel*, 57; Samuel Vollenweider, "Zwischen Monotheismus und Engelchristologie: Überlegungen zur Frühgeschichte des Christusglaubens," *ZTK* 99 [2002]: 37; and Bühner, *Messianic High Christology*, 173, 178–80.

and spiritual authorities, as served by angels, and thus sovereign over all tiers of angels too (Matt 16.27; Mark 1.13; 13.26–27; Phil 2.9–11; Rom 8.38–39; Col 1.16–17; 2.15, 20; Eph 1.20–22; 2 Thess 1.7; Heb 1.5–9; 2.5–9; 1 Pet 3.22; Rev 5.11–14). A similar phenomenon is attested in proto-orthodox texts where there are elaborations of Jesus as above rather than beside these angels (*1 Clem.* 36.2; *Mart. Pol.* 14.1; *Herm.* 59.2; *Ascen. Isa.* 4.14; 9.28; Irenaeus, *Haer.* 1.22.1; 3.11.1–2; 4.7.4; 5.18.1; *Epid.* 10; 40; 94; *Gos. Pet.* 39–40; Athenagoras, *Leg.* 10.2, 5; 24.2; *Diogn.* 7.2–4; Justin, *1 Apol.* 52.3; Tertullian, *Carne* 14.1–2; esp. Ps.-Clem. *Rec.* 1.45; 2.42; *Hom.* 18.4; Origen, *Cels.* 5.4–5).

On the other hand, angelology is already beginning to interface with Christology in the New Testament and with early post-apostolic authors. The Epistle of James is Christology-lite and could comport with any scheme that acclaims Jesus as "our glorious Lord Jesus Christ" (Jas 2.1). Jude has by far the most compatibility with angel Christology. That is apparent from Jude's mention of "Jesus" saving his people out of Egypt, which could equate Jesus with the "angel of the Lord" (Exod 23.20–23; Jude 5). Plus, the mention of the "archangel Michael" and Enoch's "holy ones" demonstrates Jude's acute interest in angels (*1 En.* 1.9; Jude 14–15). Jude also censures those who blaspheme "glorious ones," which might include Jesus (Jude 8). Furthermore, over time Jesus gradually acquired angelic characteristics (Rev 1.12–16; 14.14; *Ascen. Isa.* 9.30; *Herm.* 89.7–8), the title "angel" (Justin, *Dial.* 34.2; 61.1; 86.3; 127.4; 128.1; *1 Apol.* 63.5, 14), angelic texts like Exod 23.20 and Isa 9.5 (LXX) were repeatedly applied to the pre-incarnate Jesus (e.g., Justin, *Dial.* 75.1–2; 126.1; Irenaeus, *Epid.* 56; Clement of Alexandria, *Exc.* 43.2), Jesus and the Spirit were likened to two angels (*Ascen. Isa.* 9.27–36; Irenaeus, *Epid.* 10; Hippolytus, *Ref.* 9.13.2–3), and Jesus was portrayed as an angel who descended (incognito) to earth (*Ascen. Isa.* 10.7–31; *Ep. Ap.* 13.2–14.8; *Sib. Or.* 8.456–61; *Gos. Phil.* 57.32–58.10; *Pist. Soph.* 1.7.12; *Trim. Prot.* 49.11–20). There was a certain ambiguity between Michael and Christ at several points as to whether they overlap in roles or identity (e.g., Rev 12.7; 19.11–20; 20.1–2; *Herm.* 59.2–3; 69.3; 91.5; Justin, *Dial.* 61.1; 62.4–5). The Pseudo-Clementine *Recognitions*, datable to the second to fourth centuries, seamlessly combines a belief in Jesus as "an angel as chief of the angels" with a description of him as "the Son of God, and the beginning of all things" (Ps.-Clem. *Rec.* 1.45).

Thus, among writers we would retrospectively label as proto-orthodox, from John of Patmos to Clement of Alexandria, two things seem apparent: (1) there was little aversion to applying angelic categories to Jesus (a) as part of his prehistory with Israel in angelic theophanies, (b) as a way of describing his glorious form, or (c) as a way of explaining the descent of the Word to earth;

and (2) angelic categories were not invoked as the explanation for Jesus' mode of divinity, and angelic descriptions are regularly deployed beside analogies, scriptural citations, and reasonings to explain Jesus' share in the Father's own divinity. In sum, the utility of angelic imagery for Christ varied between Christian groups, but for the proto-orthodox, it is fair to say that Christ was Logos by nature and an angel by mission, appearance, or type (see Tertullian, *Carne* 14.1–2; Irenaeus, *Haer.* 3.16.3; Athanasius, *Cont. Ar.* 3.13–14; even some Valentinians such as Theodotus might accept such a formula, see *Exc.* 8.1; 25.1).[347] While there are undoubtedly exceptions to this rule (perhaps *Inf. Gos. Thom.* 7.4; *T. Sol.* 22.20), or ambiguities concerning the ontology in a Christ-angel amalgam, it generally holds true among the proto-orthodox.

Of course, there were other perspectives where angelology was more prominent in Christology. An angel Christology potentially cohered with the Colossian "philosophy," which preserved a place for Jesus by fitting him into an angelic hierarchy. The book of Hebrews executes a polemic against angels vis-à-vis the Son in its opening chapter, though it is impossible to determine whether this is a rhetorical comparison or a rejoinder to an actual angel Christology or perhaps even a retort to angel veneration.[348] The dominant image in Gnostic literature is Jesus as an angel or aeon (Clement of Alexandria, *Exc.* 35.1; Tertullian, *Carne* 14.1). Jesus was a "righteous angel" (*Gos. Thom.* 13.2), a thwarting angel (*T. Sol.* 22.20), or a mediating angel (*T. Dan* 6.5). Ps.-Cyprian (*Centesima* 50–54, 216–20) identified Jesus as an "archangel," or one of the "seven principal angels" who was promoted to be "Son of God" (also Ebionites, according to Epiphanius, *Pan.* 30.16.4). An angel Christology was curated into its mature form by the Libyan presbyter Arius, who saw angel Christology as a way of preserving the Father's monarchy and divine uniqueness while respecting the Son's heavenly origins. "The Arians," said Werner, by rehearsing angel Christology from the tradition, and by critiquing the Sabellian tendencies of their opponents, "set forth the essential and basic notion of the Angel-Christology in the precise dogmatic formulary, that the 'nature' (*physis*) of the heavenly Christ or the Son was the *physis*, the 'nature' of the angels."[349]

---

[347] Adolf von Harnack, *The History of Dogma* (Edinburgh: Williams & Norgate, 1894), 1:185, n. 3; Daniélou, *Jewish Christianity*, 1:118–19; and Hannah, *Michael and Christ*, 202, 215.

[348] Cf. Stuckenbruck (*Angel Veneration*, 203): "As the polemicizing statements in Colossians and Hebrews make clear, already within the first century some Christian writers considered angelological ideas and practices to be in conflict with Christ's soteriological and cosmological preeminence."

[349] Werner, *Formation of Christian Dogma*, 154.

As it goes, Christ was given the title "angel" right up until the fourth century.[350] It would appear that angelology shaped Christology in subsequent centuries in both proto-orthodox and heterodox circles.[351] It is the angelic features or angelic roles attributed to Jesus that provide the one point of christological unity between Jewish, Gentile, Gnostic, and Marcionite expressions of Christian faith. One can imagine an intricate Venn diagram displaying exegetical and theological agreements between the Valentinian Theodotus, the apologist Justin, the writings of Ps.-Cyprian, and the author of *Ascension of Isaiah* concerning Christ as an angelic figure. Confessing Christ as "the angel of the great counsel" (Isa 9.5) could function as a common creed between them, albeit a short-lived agreement once the statement was explained according to everyone's respective cosmological, protological, soteriological, and eschatological convictions. But angelological associations of Christ are ubiquitous in the second century. This falsifies, point-blank, Hengel's claim that "a real *angel christology* could only become significant right on the fringe of the Jewish-Christian sphere."[352]

What precipitated this angelizing of Jesus was probably several things: (1) Angels can be described with theophanic qualities; they can be described with "Lord" and "God" texts from Israel's sacred traditions; they were sometimes thought to be involved in the work of creation; they carry God's name and reflect his glory; they acted for Israel's deliverance in the exodus; they may have a heavenly throne and receive types of veneration; and they can appear in human form, or else humans become angels or angel-like postmortem. (2) The tradition of a principal angelic figure close to God was something of a ready-made analogue for Jesus to be divine in such a way as did not require abandoning Jewish monotheism. (3) The tradition of depicting Israel's rulers and eschatological deliverers as angelic beings also assisted in merging together messianic and supernatural motifs in early Christology. (4) If Daniel's "Son of Man" was an angel, and if "Son of Man" was among the earliest titles for Jesus (e.g., Mark 14.62; Acts 7.56; John 9.38), then it could explain why an angelomorphic or angel Christology arose very early. For a case in point, it explains why the "Son of Man" title for the exalted

---

[350] Grillmeier, *Christ in Christian Tradition*, 1:48; Daniélou, *Jewish Christianity*, 1:117; and Longenecker, *Christology of Early Jewish Christianity*, 26.

[351] Cf. Longenecker, *Christology of Early Jewish Christianity*, 27–28.

[352] Hengel, *Son of God*, 85 (italics original). Cf. Vollenweider ("Zwischen Monotheismus und Engelchristologie," 38), who says that angelomorphic Christology was a "marginal phenomenon" (*Randphänomen*) compared to Son of God, Son of Man, Logos, and Wisdom foci. In terms of preferred titles, that is certainly true for apostolic and some proto-orthodox Christianity. But Jesus-as-an-angel-as-messenger was still pertinent even if peripheral in some proto-orthodox schemes, and the angelic/aeonic Jesus was central in Gnostic Christianities.

Jesus in Revelation is accompanied with a description of him with angelic traits (Rev 1.13; 14.14). (5) The more Jesus' preexistence and heavenly origins were stressed, the easier or more natural it became to conceive of Jesus as an angelic figure. As such, an angel Christology arguably emerged due to its ability to attribute to Jesus a mode of divinity that was compatible with both messianism and monotheism.[353] Clearly, then, the origins, status, and proximity of Jesus to God developed in conversation with angelology.[354]

(b) Angel Christology and christological origins.

There is no doubt that angelomorphic Christologies (i.e., Jesus is angel-like in appearance), typological identification of the pre-incarnate Jesus as an angel (i.e., Jesus appeared as the "angel of the Lord" or is the messianic "angel of the great counsel"), and full-blown angel Christologies (i.e., Jesus-is-an-angel) began to arise no later than the end of the first century. However, was angel Christology the earliest Christology or the primary stimulus for identifying Jesus as a divine figure?[355] That is the point I would contest.

(1) The disparity of early Christology with principal angel figures.

Principal angels and archangels such as Michael and Metatron are salient in a heavenly hierarchy, but they do not seem to infringe against a strict

---

[353] Garrett (*No Ordinary Angel*, 26–27) notes: "Like Jesus—the incarnate word, in their view—the angel of the Lord represented God's meeting of finite and sinful human beings on a level they could manage."

[354] Moss, *Other Christs*, 117. Cf. Horbury (*Jewish Messianism*, 121–22): "A cult of angels therefore accompanied the development of the cult of Christ." Vollenweider ("Zwischen Monotheismus und Engelchristologie," 37): "The tendency to transfer angelic images and functions to Christ may have accompanied the development of Christology from the beginning" ("Die Tendenz, angelische Bilder und Funktionen auf Christus zu übertragen, durfte das Werden der Christologie von Anfang an begleitet haben").

[355] Cf. Werner, *Formation of Christian Dogma*, 120–61: "For Primitive Christianity, Christ was, in terms of late-Jewish apocalyptic, a being of the high celestial angel-world, who was created and chosen by God for the task of bringing in, at the end of the ages, against the daimonic-powers of the existing world, the new aeon of the Kingdom of God" (125). Garrett (*No Ordinary Angel*, 57): "traditions about angels lie at the heart of the earliest claims for Jesus as the preexistent and resurrected Lord." Cf. April D. DeConick, "How We Talk about Christology Matters," in *Israel's God and Rebecca's Children: Christology and Community in Early Judaism and Christianity*, ed. David B. Capes, April D. DeConick, Helen K. Bond, and Troy A. Miller (Waco, Tex.: Baylor University Press, 2007), 8–9. Contrasted with Vollenweider ("Zwischen Monotheismus und Engelchristologie," 37–38): "Only in the second and third centuries do we come across approaches to an angel Christology in the true sense, according to which Jesus Christ is the highest angel" ("Erst im zweiten und dritten Jahrhundert stoßen wir aber in stärkerem Ausmaß auf Ansätze zu einer Engelchristologie im eigentlichen Sinn, wonach es sich bei Jesus Christus um den höchsten Engel handelt").

monotheism, whereas early christological devotion and assertions did require a recasting of God's oneness, prerogatives, agency, and exclusive devotion in such a way that included Jesus within it. According to Samuel Vollenweider:

> The overall finding is fairly clear, even if around the edges of ancient Judaism occasional outliers can be discovered here and there. The position of angels and exalted patriarchs does not infringe upon God's uniqueness. The names of the angels are very clearly derivatives of the holy name of God. They are only involved in the royal rule of God over heaven and earth. They receive praise or veneration but only in a derivative form if at all. They do not participate in the act of creation. Their historical actions in favor of Israel are also completely overshadowed by God's reign.[356]

Vollenweider sees angels as providing a *preparatio christologie*[357] in the sense that Jesus shares in an analogous heavenly preexistence, human form, relationship to the divine name, and enthronement as do angels.[358]

Yet Vollenweider also contrasts angels with (a) the veneration of the name of Jesus and the relationship of God's fatherhood to divine sonship (e.g., Matt 28.19; Phil 2.9-11; Rom 10.13; Acts 4.12; John 17.26); (b) Jesus as mediator of creation (e.g., 1 Cor 8.6; Col 1.15-20; Heb 1.1-4; John 1.1-16; Rev 3.14); (c) Jesus' sovereignty over the cosmic powers (Col 1.13; Eph 1.20-22; 1 Pet 3.22; Matt 28.18) and his act of judging in God's stead (Matt 25.31; Rom 2.16; 2 Cor 5.10; Acts 10.42; 17.31; Ps.-Clem. *Rec.* 2.42); (d) God brings salvation and makes atonement through Jesus; (e) God and Jesus received cultic veneration in the form of prayers, invocations, and confessions to the point that God's *kyriosity* is mediated through Jesus (e.g., *1 Clem.* 59.2-61.3). Although angels can occasionally have a role in creation and judgment,[359] nonetheless

---

[356] Vollenweider, "Zwischen Monotheismus und Engelchristologie," 31: "Der Gesamtbefund ist ziemlich klar, auch wenn sich am Rand des antiken Judentums da und dort vereinzelt Gegenströmungen ausmachen lassen. Die Position von Engeln und erhöhten Patriarchen tangiert die Einzigkeit Gottes nicht. Die Namen der Engel sind überaus deutlich Derivate des heiligen Gottesnamens. An der Königsherrschaft Gottes über Himmel und Erde sind sie nur dienend beteiligt. Lobpreis bzw. Anbetung empfangen sie, wenn überhaupt, nur in abgeleiteter Form. An der Schöpfung wirken sie nicht mit; auch ihr geschichtliches Agieren zugunsten von Israel steht ganz im Schatten von Gottes Walten."

[357] This term *preparatio* is obviously theologically freighted and problematic in that it treats Christ devotion as a kind of telos that Jewish theology was heading towards.

[358] Vollenweider, "Zwischen Monotheismus und Engelchristologie," 34-38.

[359] Certain heterodox groups did attribute the creation of the world to the demiurge and/or his angels; see *Tri. Trac.* 105.1-2; 113.1; Irenaeus, *Haer.* 1.23.5; 1.26.1; Hippolytus, *Ref.* 10.21.1; Ps.-Tertullian, *Adv. omn. haer.* 3. On angels and judgment, angels frequently act as instruments of judgment, but less frequently do they act as the actual judges.

Vollenweider is generally right to conclude, "In all these points Jesus Christ shares in the privileges of the one God. Unlike the angelic princes, he belongs on the side of God, not on the side of creatures."³⁶⁰ Beyond that, Vollenweider sees three further reasons for an aversion towards angel Christology: (a) Jesus occupies both ends of the ontological spectrum, as creation-mediator and his full participation in human life, neither of which was fitting for an angel. (b) Very few appeals to Israel's sacred texts in the New Testament connect Jesus with the angels. (c) Jesus, unlike the myriad of angelic beings, does not stand before God's throne, but shares in God's oneness.³⁶¹

Regarding the possible "mutation" of principal angel traditions into early divine Christology, this has obvious utility for explaining the sudden emergence of a divine Christology, especially when christological exegeses of Dan 7.13 and Ps 110.1 are viewed synoptically with the depiction of other angelic figures like Qumran's Melchizedek and the Enochic Son of Man. Yet Hurtado's account of this mutation is not without its problems.

Against Hurtado's scheme, first, if divine Christology emerged as a mutation of a principal angel, then why is there no explicit formulation of an angel Christology in the earliest sources as one might expect? Second, if Jesus was included in divine worship alongside but subordinate to God the Father as a lesser being, one could legitimately infer that Jesus' divinity was honorific, he had a divine status as God's temple-sharer or throne-sharer, a well-known position in antiquity.³⁶² Yet the earliest Christians seem to have conceived of Jesus as divine in a stronger sense, whether we think in terms of a divine identity or even of a divine ontology. Third, we must countenance not merely angelic antecedents, but also theological, sapiential, messianic, and Adamic motifs that were weaved into early Christology as Jesus' divinity was resourced from multiple corners of Israel's sacred traditions.

(2) The inadequacy of divine Christology emerging from "two powers" angelologies.

Regarding the rabbinic "two powers in heaven" heresy, there are discernible analogues with early Christology, simply because both views are drinking from the same scriptural stream, so to speak, and dealing with intermediary figures in exalted positions. But there are factors that mitigate against seeing

---

³⁶⁰ Vollenweider, "Zwischen Monotheismus und Engelchristologie," 33–34 ("In all diesen Punkten gewinnt Jesus Christus Anteil an den Privilegien des einen Gottes. Anders als die Engelfursten gehört er auf die *Seite Gottes*, nicht auf die Seite der Kreaturen").

³⁶¹ Vollenweider, "Zwischen Monotheismus und Engelchristologie," 38–39.

³⁶² Cf. D. Clint Burnett, *Christ's Enthronement at God's Right Hand and Its Greco-Roman Cultural Context* (BZNW 242; Berlin: de Gruyter, 2021).

early Christology as necessarily a genetic ancestor or merely a variation of the two-powers perspective.

In favor of a relationship, we should admit that a second angelic power beside Yahweh or operating on Yahweh's behalf is common enough in Israel's Scriptures (Gen 31.13; Exod 3.1–14; 23.20–23; 24.9–11; Ezek 1.26–28; 8.2; Dan 7.9–14). Such texts inspired scriptural and post-scriptural exaltation of figures like Michael, Melchizedek, Metatron, and a Messiah. The more Jesus was likened to an angel, the more a second angelic "god" had capacity to explain the mode and manner of his divinity. In addition, Paul's splitting of the *shema* (Deut 6.4) between one God and one Lord in 1 Cor 8.6 resembles Philo's division of Israel's deity into the creative function of "God" and a ruling function as "Lord" (*Mos.* 2.99–100; *Abr.* 121), and the rabbis who hypostatized divine mercy (*Elohim*) and justice (Yahweh; *b.Ḥag.* 14a; *b.Sanh.* 38b), all of which constituted an interior bifurcation of the deity.[363] Further, the depiction of Jesus as seated at the right hand of God (Mark 14.62; Col 3.1; Eph 1.20; Heb 8.1; 12.2; *Ascen. Isa.* 10.14; 11.32–33; *1 Clem.* 36.5; *Barn.* 12.10; Pol. *Phil.* 2.1; Mark 16.19; *Ep. Ap.* 3.8; *Sib. Or.* 2.242–44; *Apoc. Jas.* 14.30–31; Justin, *1 Apol.* 45; *Dial.* 32) is expressing the exaltation of a figure that was regarded as blasphemous in later Jewish circles (Mark 14.63–64; Acts 7.56–60; *b.Ḥag.* 15a; *b.Sanh.* 38b; *3 En.* 16). It is very likely too that John the Evangelist's binitarianism and Justin's christological exegesis of the Greek Scriptures would be considered a variation of the two-powers heresy according to the later rabbis.[364]

In second- and third-century Christologies, proto-orthodox authors could deploy two-powers-like exegesis against Jewish and modalist detractors to justify a plurality within the Godhead, even as they criticized Gnostic teachers for pluralizing powers and positing a radical rupture within the Godhead.[365] The demiurgical creationism of several Gnostic systems was clearly in the mind of some Jewish authors when they spoke of a two-powers heresy.[366] Whereas Marcion's theology was dualistic with its two gods (Tertullian, *Marc.* 1.4, 15, 16), it was not based on an exegetical argument from the Jewish

---

[363] Logan A. Williams (*Love, Self-Gift, and the Incarnation: Christology and Ethics in Galatians, in the Context of Pauline Theology and Greco-Roman Philosophy* [PhD diss., Durham University, 2020], 47) notes: "The implication of distributing the divine titles in this way is not that there are multiple Gods—indeed, in the previous clause Paul distances himself from those who believe in 'many gods'—but rather that plurality exists within the one God, that the identity of the one God is fragmented, individuated, and inclusive of (at least) Jesus and the Father."

[364] Cf. Segal, *Two Powers in Heaven*, 213–17.

[365] Cf. Segal, *Two Powers in Heaven*, 220–33.

[366] Cf. Segal, *Two Powers in Heaven*, 244–59.

Scriptures as he repudiated the Jewish Scriptures in their entirety. Marcion's theology was reformulated by his disciple Apelles, who posited multiple deities: (1) one good God; (2) the Demiurge, who made the world; (3) an evil, fiery god who arose from creation and subjected humans to slavery through fleshly existence and the Torah; and (4) Christ as born from the one good deity as another god or a principal angel (Eusebius, *Hist. eccl.* 5.13.7; Hippolytus, *Ref.* 7.38; 10.20). Segal's conclusion seems to hold: the rabbinic two-powers heresy of the second century, which featured beliefs about humanlike or angelic figures in heaven, potentially had some degree of first-century forebears in Philo and early Christology.[367] There are, however, several considerations that give cause against a premature equation of early Christologies with the two-powers heresy.

First, it is one thing to map the developments of an angelic throne-epiphany from Ezekiel into Daniel and into later apocalypses, with a principal angel appointed as God's grand vizier, but whether this amounts to postulating a second power in heaven can be doubted. In all the literature cited, scriptural and Second Temple writings, Israel's one God remains the supreme figure of power and authority, who brooks no equals in the heavenly realm.[368] Even in Second Temple literature and beyond, references to an angelic grand vizier are sparse (see *Jos. Asen.* 14.8–9; 1QS 3.15–4.1; *3 En.* 16).[369] Belief in a principal angel was not a problem unless it was described in such a way as to infringe upon God's oneness and singular authority.[370] The bifurcation of deity into "God" and "Lord," "Father" and "Son," or "Mercy" and "Justice" that one finds in Philo, Paul, and the rabbis was not a pluralizing of deities but instead a pluralizing within the deity in order to retain monotheistic axioms. There was, therefore, no principal angel or anthropomorphic heavenly being entirely ripe and ready to be curated into a second deity without first reconfiguring Jewish monotheism. Thus, the shift from the Torah's "Angel of the Lord," to Ezekiel's throne-chariot, to Daniel's "one like a son of man," to Philo's "second god," to John's messianic Logos, to Marcion's two deities is not an inevitable progression towards a second divine power in heaven, but are contingent upon species

---

[367] Segal, *Two Powers in Heaven*, 260.

[368] Rowland, *Open Heaven*, 111; Maxwell J. Davidson, *Angels at Qumran: A Comparative Study of 1 Enoch 1–36 and 72–108 and Sectarian Writings from Qumran* (JSPSup 11; Sheffield: JSOT Press, 1992), 305–9; Wasserman, *Apocalypse as Holy War*, 107; and Benjamin D. Sommer, *The Bodies of God and the World of Ancient Israel* (New York: Cambridge University Press, 2009), 166.

[369] Bauckham, *Jesus and the God of Israel*, 160.

[370] Segal (*Two Powers in Heaven*, 187) is aware of this point.

of scriptural interpretation, religious experiences, cosmology, narratives, and philosophical hybridities.

Second, while Christian attributions of deity to Christ irrefutably fell under the aspersion of rabbinic heresiologists, Christianity itself was never specified as *the* two-powers heresy. Christian Christology and devotion instead were some of many deviations from true monotheism, and even then some Christologies were more condemnable than others (e.g., Ebionites, Modalists, Monarchians, and Adoptionists were less guilty of it).[371] Finally, Segal himself is rather circumspect about exactly how early the two-powers heresy is, finding antecedents rather than genuine advocates in the first century.[372] It is anachronistic to interpret Jewish and Christian documents from the first century as indicative of two-powers intermediary figures even if they anticipate them in some ways.[373] Thus, while early Christology became one of the two-powers heresies, we should question the notion that Christianity took up a preexisting second deity and spliced Christ into it.

(3) Paul's alleged angel Christology.

What about an angel Christology in Paul? As we have seen, an angel Christology plausibly aligns with the descent-ascent scheme of Phil 2.6–11, mention of Jesus as a heavenly man (1 Cor 15.48–49), the Galatians receiving Paul like an angel or like Christ (Gal 4.14), and the sending of the Son (Rom 8.3 and Gal. 4.4–5). All of this can be fitted with an angelic being who sojourned on earth as man and was subsequently exalted within a heavenly hierarchy. "As the Angel of the Lord," Ehrman claims for Paul, "Christ is a preexistent being who is divine; he can be called God; and he is God's manifestation on earth in human flesh."[374] Yet an angel Christology does not offer the most coherent way of articulating Paul's complete suite of christological convictions.

First, the main thrust in 1 Cor 15.48–49 is that Christ is the eschatological deliverer in heaven, that believers will one day be conformed to his image, and that he will return from heaven to establish God's kingdom. His heavenly residence does not entail an angelic identity.

---

[371] Segal, *Two Powers in Heaven*, 218.

[372] Segal (*Two Powers in Heaven*, 192) writes: "In spite of this early evidence of traditions about a principal angel or manlike figure, there is no way to document a *heresy* involving the divine name as a separate angelic hypostasis in first century dualistic contexts" (italics original).

[373] So too James F. McGrath, *The Only True God: Early Christian Monotheism in Its Jewish Context* (Urbana: University of Illinois Press, 2009), 95–96.

[374] Ehrman, *How Jesus Became God*, 253.

Second, equating Christ with an angel of God based on Gal 4.14 builds far too much on far too little.[375]

Third, what is predicated of Christ in Phil 2.6–11 in terms of his heavenly position as "equal with God,"[376] undergoing something closer to incarnation than merely angelic anthropophany,[377] and attaining super-exaltation is not truly paralleled in Jewish angelology. Qumran's Michael is the angelic representative of Israel, and his exaltation mirrors Israel's military supremacy over the nations, which does not resemble the Jesus of the Philippian Christ poem (1QM 17.7–8). In the midrashic text, Melchizedek remains Yahweh's agent against Belial, who is his true counterpart and carries out judgment on God's behalf (11QMelch 2.12–14).[378] While Melchizedek's name substitutes for the tetragram YHWH in Isa 61.1, yet the name Yahweh is not applied to Melchizedek the same way the poem applies *kyrios* from Isa 45.23–25 (LXX) to Jesus in Phil 2.10–11. The angel Yahoel from *Apoc. Ab.* 10, whose name is spliced from Yahweh and El and who appears to carry the divine name from Exod 23.21, remains himself a worshipping being who is not worshipped.[379] Even *Ascen. Isa.* 10, which depicts Jesus as taking on angelic form as he descends from the highest heaven to earth, and then being exalted over and worshipped by the angels and gods of the world when he is installed at the Most High's right hand, does not bear the marks of a promotion but merely a return to his prior state of glory—Jesus is worshipped before and after his descent and ascent (*Ascen. Isa.* 9.27–32; 10.15; 11.22–33). The Christ poem exceeds any notion of angelic exaltation by applying Isaianic language for Yahweh to Jesus in Phil 2.9–11, by identifying Jesus with the God who says, "I am God, and there is no other" (Isa 45.22), the God who expects universal obeisance and allegiance (Isa 45.23),

---

[375] Cf. Fee (*Pauline Christology*, 299–31), who rightly sees a progression of examples from an angel to Christ rather than an identification of Christ as an angel. Hannah (*Michael and Christ*, 155–56) says, "The grammar certainly permits this [i.e., Christ is an angel], but it is hardly compelling."

[376] That is assuming *res rapta* interpretation whereby "form of God" and "equality with God" are parallel and something already possessed.

[377] In Phil 2.7 the language of "emptied" (*ekenōsen*), "becoming" like human beings (*ginomai*) and "as a human being" (*hōs anthropos*) are indicative of ontological transformation, not merely outward appearance. Unlike the epiphanies of Olympian deities, Jesus' work is redemptive rather than rapacious, and there is stress on a change of status and state climaxing in "death on a cross" rather than on a temporary and mere outward appearance.

[378] One should note that in Jewish literature, Michael is the true adversary of Satan, e.g., Jude 9; Rev 12.7, *Life of Adam* 12–16; see Hannah, *Michael and Christ*, 41–42, 64–66, 127–30.

[379] Contra McGrath, *Only True God*, 49; and Casey, *From Jewish Prophet*, 113.

and the God who shares his glory with no other, who now shares it with Jesus (Isa 42.8).[380]

Sticking with Philippians, does Paul, or any Jewish author, say that any angel has his own "day" of judgment (Phil 1.6, 10; 2.16); is one whom people declare they are imprisoned for (1.13); is one proclaimed out of love (1.16); has a spirit who helps them (1.19); is exalted in their body (1.20); is whom they live for, participate in his sufferings, anticipate the power of his resurrection, and relish being with beyond death (1.21–23; 3.10); is whom they boast upon (1.26; 3.3); whom they consider gain and everything else loss (3.7–9); who made them his own (3.12); or "will transform the body of our humiliation that it may be conformed to the body of his glory" and who "by the power that also enables him to make all things subject to himself" (3.21)? This language of devotion is more appropriate for a Jewish author in his or her relation to Yahweh rather than to the angel of Yahweh, yet it describes Jesus.[381]

Fourth, the Pauline polemic against the Colossian philosophy, which placed Jesus within a hierarchy of angelic intermediaries proposed by teachers in Colossae, showcases a clear rejection of an angel Christology or any reduction of Jesus to a heavenly power. The Pauline retort is that Christ is the *archē*, not an angel; Christ is not an aeon within the *plērōma* but himself the bodily manifestation of the *plērōma*; Christ's supremacy, not his subordination, is accented; Christ does not struggle against the powers, as he has already vanquished them; Christ is no angelic vizier but God's co-enthroned vice-regent.[382]

Fifth, it would be straining some monotheistic sensibilities to include an angelic figure within the *shema* (Deut 6.5) as Paul does with Jesus Christ (1 Cor 8.6).[383] The knowledge of the one God over and against idols and in

---

[380] N. T. Wright, *Paul and the Faithfulness of God* (COQG 4; London: SPCK, 2014), 683; and Wesley Hill, *Paul and the Trinity: Persons, Relations, and the Pauline Letters* (Grand Rapids: Eerdmans, 2015), 92–95.

[381] Chris Tilling, "Misreading Paul's Christology: Problems with Ehrman's Exegesis," in *How God Became Jesus: The Real Origins of Belief in Jesus' Divine Nature*, ed. Michael F. Bird (Grand Rapids: Zondervan, 2014), 145–46.

[382] Cf. Bird, *Colossians and Philemon*, 47–59.

[383] Here I disagree with McGrath (*Only True God*, 39–44) that Paul includes Jesus alongside God as a deputy rather than beside God as an equal in the *shema*. Paul, like Philo (*Her.* 166; *Plant.* 86; *Somn.* 163; *Abr.* 121, 124; *Mos.* 2.99–100; *Spec. leg.* 1.30, 307), splits the creative and executive functions of Israel's one God, in Paul's case, between God the Father and the Lord Jesus Christ. Paul, it appears, can seamlessly relate Jesus Christ to God in terms of "subordination, coordination, and belonging" while declaring that Christ's "origin and essential being . . . belongs entirely on the side of God" (Udo Schnelle, *Apostle Paul: His Life and Theology* [Grand Rapids: Baker, 2005], 396–97). For Feldmeier and Spieckermann

distinction to the many gods and lords (1 Cor 8.1–5) includes the priority of "one God, the Father" as Creator along with "one Lord, Jesus Christ" as demiurge and deliverer (1 Cor 8.6). Importantly, Jesus is not a second god beside or below God the Father, but God's oneness (*eis*) is predicated of him as well as the exclusivity of Israel's devotion to the one God from the *shema*. In addition, this oneness operates only in the context of a God-Jesus unity as they are "for us."[384] Angels do not have a part in monotheistic confession, its exclusive devotion, and a mode of deliverance that puts the delivered in a relationship with them! Tilling's conclusion is apt: "There is no angel or intermediary being of any kind in any text that parallels the way Paul speaks of this Christ-relation. Rather the way Paul describes the relation between Christ and Christians is analogous only to the relation between Israel and YHWH."[385]

Sixth, and more pointedly, Paul habitually pairs God the Father with Jesus Christ his Son (1 Cor 1.3, 9; 8.6; 2 Cor 1.2–3; 11.31; Gal 1.1–3; 4.6; 1 Thess 1.1–3; 2 Thess 1.1–2). Further, angels are rarely mentioned and, if anything, they are Christ's attendants at his parousia (1 Thess 4.16; 2 Thess 1.7; cf. 1 Tim 5.21). Interesting too is how Paul conceives of the Father's love as operating in Christ above angels, rulers, and powers (Rom 8:38–39). In sum, Paul consistently places Christ beside God the Father, while nothing he says implies that Christ is merely first among equals in an angelic hierarchy.

(4) Jesus and angels in early Christian literature.

The Synoptic Gospels could potentially be read as containing an angel Christology *if* one emphasized those texts that speak of Jesus at the head of angelic orders as a kind of general of the angelic host (Matt 13.41–42; 24.31; 25.31; Mark 8.38; 13.26–27; Luke 12.8–9). One must accept the inherent ambiguity of speaking of Jesus/Son of Man and "his" angels, whether "his" means as per the same class, or as his subordinates.[386] What tells against Jesus as one among his

---

(*God Becoming Human*, 252): "With regard to Christ this means that precisely by submitting himself freely to the Father and letting God alone be God, he becomes completely one with the Father as the Son. This is why dominance and subordination are inadequate terms for the relationship between Father and Son. The relationship is determined by reciprocal sharing; and this is a biblical legacy."

[384] Samuel Vollenweider, "Vom israelitischen zum christologischen Monotheismus. Überlegungen zum Verhältnis zwischen dem Glauben an den einen Gott und dem Glauben an Jesus Christus," in *Antike und Urchristentum: Studien zur neutestamentlichen Theologie in ihren Kontexten und Rezeptionen* (WUNT 436; Tübingen: Mohr Siebeck, 2020), 130. Cf. Tilling, "Misreading Paul's Christology," 90–92, where he argues that Paul includes Christ in the same relational dynamic of love and knowledge as Israel had with Yahweh.

[385] Tilling, "Misreading Paul's Christology," 144.

[386] Cf. Justin, *1 Apol.* 6.1 for a similar problem.

angels is the way that the Synoptic Son of Man "coming" sayings rehearse Old Testament theophanies of God's own coming (e.g., Isa 40.10; 63.1–6; 66.15; Zech 9.14; 14.5) and in light of the *kyrios* passages found throughout which locate Jesus within the *kyriosity* of Israel's God (e.g., Mark 12.35–37; 14.62; Matt 24.37–42).[387] Plus, the shared ignorance of Jesus and the angels about the timing of "that day" (Mark 13.32/Matt 24.36) is an eschatological statement, not a christological one; it is meant to prompt readiness, not christological speculation about Jesus as an angel.

Matthew's statement that "when the Son of Man comes in his glory, and all the angels with him, then he will sit on the throne of his glory" to preside over a grand judgment (Matt 25.31) is analogous to *1 En.* 61.6–13, where the Lord of Spirits places the Chosen One on the throne of glory to judge the holy ones, climaxing in a heavenly anthem of praise for the Lord of Spirits. Or else, the Matthean scene resembles the archangel Michael, who has the angelic host under his command (Rev 12.7; 1QM 9.15; 18.7; *1 En.* 24.6; *2 En.* 22.6). As such, one could imagine the Matthean Son of Man as an archangel appointed to judge the nations as well as the Devil and his angels (Matt 25.41). Alternatively, the "coming" Son of Man statements in the Synoptics also put Jesus in a position analogous to the Enochic "Head of Days" who comes "with Michael and Raphael and Gabriel and Phanuel and thousands and tens of thousands of angels without number" to appoint Enoch as the Son of Man as narrated in *1 En.* 71.13. The Matthean statements about the Son of Man coming with the angels/holy ones puts Jesus in a place parallel to the Enochic "Lord of the Spirits," who comes with archangels in attendance. In sum, the Matthean Jesus partly resembles the Enochic Chosen One, who is enthroned and judges the angels, perhaps the archangel Michael, who leads the angelic host, but he also resembles the Enochic Head of Days/Lord of Spirits, who comes with angels to commission his servant.

The Fourth Gospel is not conducive to an angel Christology as Jesus is consistently portrayed as the eternal Son, personal and preexistent, who is divine in an absolute sense.[388] The mention of Jesus bearing the "name" the Father

---

[387] See Bird, *Jesus the Eternal Son*, 84–92; C. Kavin Rowe, *Early Narrative Christology: The Lord in the Gospel of Luke* (Berlin: de Gruyter, 2006); and David R. Bauer, *The Gospel of the Son of God: An Introduction to Matthew* (Downers Grove, Ill.: InterVarsity, 2019), 268–75.

[388] There is an exception to this! The *Prayer of Joseph* depicts Jacob as an "angel of God" who "tabernacled" among men (frag. A 4), and this text is known to us only through Origen (*Comm. Jo.* 2.25), who himself cites it to prove that John the Baptist was an angel who became human in order to witness to Jesus. Might the Johannine Jesus be interpreted this way? Possibly, but on the whole, John is not "fit" for an angel Christology due to other factors, as we have discussed.

has given him (John 17.11–12) is partly analogous to the angel of the exodus (Exod 23.20–21) and the angelic figures of Yahoel and Metatron (*Apoc. Ab.* 10.3, 8–17; *3 En.* 12.5), who have the divine name in them. However, the Johannine Jesus does not bear the divine name as a badge of divine authorization; rather, it is a mark of his special unity with God the Father. "The Fourth Gospel," argues Hannah, "seems to use the tradition about the angel of the Name, but transforms it to present Jesus as both the revealer of God and the Revelation of God—as well as expressing the Son's unity with the Father."[389]

Concerning the Epistle of Jude, the author is not necessarily "warding off an attack on the Angel-Christology."[390] True, irrespective of whether we read *Iēsous* or *kyrios* in Jude 5, it is possible to draw a link between Jesus and the angel of the Lord. However, while Jude and Justin identify Christ as the Angel of the Lord, it need not imply that Christ has an angelic nature.[391] Jude is principally attacking a disparagement of angels as guardians of cosmic order. Furthermore, while Jude's Christology probably includes a christophany similar to Justin's casting the pre-incarnate Jesus as angel of the Lord in Exod 23.20–23, Jude also exceeds that view: (a) Jesus Christ is "our only master and Lord," which constitutes superlative status and requires exclusive devotion (Jude 4; 25). (b) Jesus' sovereignty is underscored when Jude self-identifies as a "slave" of Jesus Christ while others deny Jesus' lordship (Jude 1; 4). (c) Jesus is perhaps the "Lord" who comes with his angels, given the general propensity of Christian authors to conflate scriptural theophany texts with Jesus' parousia (Jude 14–15).[392] (d) The functions of God and Jesus Christ are "interlaced"[393] concerning the preservation of the faithful with mercy to save them from judgment (Jude 1; 20–25). Jude's Jesus is no mere angel, but the eschatological Lord of divine mercy and judgment whose own work redounds to the glory of "the only God our Saviour" (Jude 25).

Hebrews could be read as confronting an angel Christology or a rival angel veneration, but this is unlikely. The Son's superiority to the angels does not reappear after Heb 1, and the comparison of Christ with Melchizedek in Heb 7 would seem to encourage rather than discourage the equation of Christ with a heavenly figure.[394] The author's point is probably the superiority of the Son

[389] Hannah, *Michael and Christ*, 146.
[390] Werner, *Formation of Christian Dogma*, 139.
[391] Hannah, *Michael and Christ*, 142.
[392] Richard J. Bauckham, *Jude, 2 Peter* (WBC; Waco, Tex.: Word, 1983), 96–97; and Jörg Frey, *The Letter of Jude and the Second Letter of Peter: A Theological Commentary* (Waco, Tex.: Baylor University Press, 2018), 118, 128.
[393] Frey, *Jude and the Second Letter of Peter*, 48.
[394] Hannah, *Michael and Christ*, 138.

and his salvation as opposed to the angels who gave the Torah to Israel (see Heb 2.2; Gal 3.19; Acts 7.38; *Jub.* 1.27–3.7).[395] That said, the author's polemics do perhaps offer a preventative inoculation against a demotion of the Son to angelic status, something comprehensible in the religious climate that the author and audience inhabited. What rules out an angel Christology by the author is how the Son is described as possessing a unique filial relationship to God with a messianic vocation, is worshipped by angels, participates in the act of creation and even in the creation of angels, shares in God's cosmic rule unlike angels, and condescends to full human life.[396] As Bauckham argues, the distinction between the Son and angels is ontological: "To be above the angels is to be God, to be below the angels is to be human. Above the angels, Jesus transcends all creation, sharing the divine identity as Creator and Ruler even of the angels. Below the angels, Jesus shares the common identity of earthly humans in birth, suffering, and death."[397] Added to that, the first instance of the reception of Heb 1 can be found in *1 Clem.* 36.1–6, where Clement cites Heb 1.5, 7, 13 to prove that the Son is "superior to angels" (*1 Clem.* 36.2).

John the Seer's apocalypse undoubtedly presents Jesus with angelic traits, but simultaneously locates Jesus within the orbit of God the Father's sovereignty, throne, glory, and worship—which is explicitly differentiated from angelic orders. Just like other post-70 CE Jewish apocalypses, there is a fusion of angelomorphic and messianic categories, designed to underscore how God's purposes are being effected by a messianic figure with heavenly qualities.[398]

The vision of the exalted Jesus in Rev 1.13–16 gives Jesus the form and function of an angel, or, more precisely, it resembles a theophanic angelophany developed in light of Dan 10.5–6.[399] The seer's depiction of the exalted Jesus is very comparable with the angel Yahoel in *Apoc. Ab.* 10–11 as both have authority over Hades and are described with white hair drawn from the Ancient of Days in Dan 7.9. Thus, Jesus can appear as a resplendent angel who commissions a human seer/scribe (Rev 1.13–15; 4.1), or an angelic agent of

---

[395] Hannah, *Michael and Christ*, 139.

[396] Contra Gieschen (*Angelomorphic Christology*, 295–303, 314), who makes tenuous links between angelic glory and the Son's radiance (Heb 1.3), the divine name in an angel and the Son's "word of power" (Heb 1.5), the title "firstborn" in light of Philo (Heb 1.6), and enthronement in light of *3 En.* 10–14 (Heb 1.13). Cf. similarly Rowland, *Open Heaven*, 112–13.

[397] Bauckham, *Jesus and the God of Israel*, 241; cf. Vollenweider ("Zwischen Monotheismus und Engelchristologie," 38) with Jesus on both ends of the ontological spectrum.

[398] Cf. Allen, "Son of God," 64–69.

[399] Contra Hannah (*Michael and Christ*, 153), who supposes that John portrays Jesus here with a "heavenly character" but not necessarily as an "angel."

judgment (Rev 14.14; 19.11–16),[400] and angels can also appear like Jesus (Rev 10.1–3). And yet, in the letters to the seven churches in Rev 2–3, Jesus has clear superiority over the angels, and his various sovereign attributes underscore his positional distinction from the angels (Rev 2.1, 8, 12, 18; 3.1, 7, 14).[401] Jesus' divine sonship is not derivative of angelic form, but based on the parameters of Ps 2 as one who shares in divine authority as messiah.[402] While Jesus may replace Michael as leader of the angelic host, the seer's vision of Jesus is far from Michael in a new guise,[403] but more akin to Yahweh, the divine warrior who treads with winepress of divine wrath (Isa 63.2–3) in Rev 19.15. In addition, the exalted Jesus is not called "angel" nor "sent" like an angel.[404] Instead, Jesus sends authoritative words to the angel of each of the seven churches (Rev. 2.1, 8, 12, 18; 3.1, 7), even his own angel to the churches (Rev 22.16), all indicative of his superiority over the angels.[405]

The seer's Jesus is more coordinate to than subordinate beneath the Lord God for several reasons.[406] The revelation given by the exalted Jesus is immediately parallel to the declarations of the "Lord God" (Rev 1.8) and the insights given by the Spirit's unction (Rev 1.11). Jesus shares the title "King of kings and Lord of lords" (Rev 17.14; 19.16) with Israel's God (Deut 10.17; Ezek 26.7; Dan 2.37; 4.37 [LXX]; Ezra 7.12; Ps 136.3; Sir 51.12; 2 Macc 13.4; 3 Macc 5.35; *1 En.* 9.4; 63.2; 84.2; 1QM 14.16). Furthermore, the Lord God is the *archē* and *telos* of all things (Rev 21.6), while Jesus too is the *archē tēs ktiseōs*, making

---

[400] Hoffmann (*Destroyer and the Lamb*, 123–28) connects Jesus with the "Destroyer angel" from Exod 12.23.

[401] Hurtado, *One God, One Lord*, 126; Stuckenbruck, *Angel Veneration*, 238–40; and Hoffmann, *Destroyer and the Lamb*, 213–15.

[402] Allen, "Son of God," 60–62.

[403] Cf. Hoffmann (*Destroyer and the Lamb*, 194): "One might certainly consider that Michael's role in the Apocalypse is a rather limited one: he is referred to by name only once and also the victory he achieves seems to be partial—Satan still has power (Apc 12:12) after the battle in heaven is won. By contrast, Christ's role is apparently far more important in Revelation. This is not only reflected by the greater number of references to Christ, but it is also given emphasis by characterising Christ's victory as a final one (Apc 19:11–20:10). It seems therefore that Christ's victory (by sacrificial death) is regarded as the crucial victory, which is mirrored by Michael's partial victory in heaven."

[404] Hannah, *Michael and Christ*, 151–55; Carrell, *Jesus*, 170; and Stuckenbruck, *Angel Veneration*, 208.

[405] Stuckenbruck, *Angel Veneration*, 233–39.

[406] Carrell, *Jesus*, 154, 219. Hoffmann (*Destroyer and the Lamb*, 252) notes: "As we have demonstrated, almost everywhere else [other than Rev 14.15] in the Apocalypse the author emphasises Christ's significance, his superiority over angels and his equal status with God. Accordingly, a single reference to a subordinate Christ can hardly be a major part of the author's Christology."

him somewhere between the source, beginning, and authority of creation (Rev 3.14; 22.13).[407] The title *archē* presages Jesus' "presence and power at creation [and] insinuate[s] his power and presence over the events of new creation."[408] Jesus, as the "I am, Alpha and Omega, Beginning and the End," shares in the divine side of Creator-creature distinction as well as participating in the eternality and comprehensive authority of God the Father (Rev 1.8, 17–18; 3.14; 21.6; 22.13; cf. Isa 44.6; 48.12).

In Rev 5, Jesus occupies a unique place on God's very own throne apart from the angels. The Lord God's throne was usually portrayed with a mixture of transcendent majesty, incomparable authority, and elevated inapproachability (Ps 47.1–9; Isa 6.1–5; Ezek 1.26–27; Dan 7.13–14; 11Q17 7.11; 4Q405 XX 2.6–11; XXIII 1.3; Rev 20.11; *4 Ezra* 7.33; *1 En.* 9.2–4; 14.18–22; 90.2; *2 En.* 20.3). It is from the divine throne that the Lord God exercises authority over heaven, earth, under the earth, and all that is in them, something true of no angel (Rev 5.3, 13; 20.11). The placement of the exalted Jesus beside God upon the heavenly throne is a profound statement of Jesus' *superlative* divine status (see Rev 3.21; 7.17; 22.3). This hymnic worship of the Lamb in 5.9–12 is not given to angels, but matches the worship given to the Lord God in Rev 4.8–11.[409]

It is true that picturing angelic beings on heavenly thrones was common enough in Israel's sacred literature (Ezek 1.26–28; Dan 7.9; 11Q17 5.8; Rev 4.4; 11.6; 20.4; *Apoc. Zeph.* A; *3 En.* 16; *Ascen. Isa.* 7.18–33; 8.7–10),[410] and there were types of angel veneration known to Christian authors (Col 2.18).[411] Yet there was a concern that an enthroned angel could potentially become a second deity and compromise monotheism. For example, in one strand of Jewish tradition, the angel Metatron was seated on a heavenly throne *like* the throne of glory (*3 En.* 10.1), which caused Rabbi Elisha ben Avuya (disrespectfully called "Aher" for "other") to wrongly believe that Metatron was a second power

---

[407] Contra Collins and Collins (*King and Messiah*, 194, 203), there is nothing here that makes Jesus a principal angel and God's first creature.

[408] Brandon D. Smith, *Vision of the Triune God: Reading Revelation through the Father, Son, and Holy Spirit* (PhD diss., Australian College of Theology, 2021), 155. Cf. Hoffmann (*Destroyer and the Lamb*, 163, n. 269) argues that *archē* in 3.14 functions similarly to *prōtotokos* in 1.5 so that "no subordinate, but rather an exalted status is implied here."

[409] Cf. worship of Jesus by angelic beings (Heb 1.6; Rev 5.9–14; *Ascen. Isa.* 10.15; 11.23–26; *Apoc. Jas.* 14.26–30) and all of creation (Phil 2.10–11; Rev 5.13–14; Pol. *Phil.* 2.1).

[410] There is also an order of angels called "thrones" (Col 1.16; *T. Levi* 3.8; *T. Adam* 4.8; *Ascen. Isa.* 7.21).

[411] The righteous also occupy thrones in the heavens but without infringing upon the sovereignty and worship of the one enthroned in the heavens (see *T. Abr.* 11.7–12 [A]; *Apoc. Mos.* 39.2–3; 1Q21 F 14; 4Q521 2 2.7; Matt 19.28/Luke 22.30; Rev 3.21; 20.4; *T. Job* 33.1–9; *1 En.* 108.12; *Ascen. Isa.* 9.24–25; 11.40; *Apoc. El.* 1.8; 4.27, 29).

in heaven, for which Metatron was scourged to remove any doubt about the heavenly hierarchy (*3 En.* 16.5; *b.Ḥag.* 15a). However, John's apocalypse shows no such aversion to the co-regency and worship of the exalted Jesus because, despite his angelomorphic traits, Jesus does not belong to the angelic orders. It is significant that the angels worship God (Rev 4.10; 7.11, 15; 11.16–17; 15.2–4; 19.4), but Jesus never worships God. Angels twice refuse to receive worship (Rev 19.10; 22.9), but Jesus is worshipped by John (Rev 1.17), by angels (Rev 5.12–14), and by a restored creation (Rev 22.1–4). Sarah Underwood Dixon observes, "The angel asserts that John must worship God alone, and the context makes clear that the worship of the exalted Christ is an appropriate and indeed required expression of his monotheistic devotion."[412] Or, as Steven Friesen puts it: "These three overlaid cadences—of recipient, worshipper, and action—draw together the One seated on the throne and the Lamb as the two beings uniquely worthy of worship. . . . In a [Jewish monotheistic] system that ought not to allow a second deity, Jesus was declared worthy of honors equal to God."[413] It is true that "worship" (Gk: *latreuō* and *proskynesis*) is a broad category, from honorific obeisance to cultic devotion. It is also true that hymns to gods and economia to kings were not distinguished in form, and the difference between them was blurry (Aelius Theon, *Progymn.* 109).[414] Nonetheless, the joint worship of the God and the Lamb in Rev 5.8–14 and 22.3, rehearsing the divine worship of the Lord God in 4.8–11, is inconceivable without a sense of divine unity with a shared purpose and comparative status.[415] There is no indication of the Lamb's promotion to the throne nor a potential rivalry with

---

[412] Sarah Underwood Dixon, "The Apocalypse of Zephaniah and Revelation 22:6–21: Angel Worship and Monotheistic Devotion," in *Reading Revelation in Context: John's Apocalypse and Second Temple Judaism*, ed. Ben C. Blackwell, John K. Goodrich, and Jason Maston (Grand Rapids: Zondervan, 2019), 180. Thanks to Brandon Smith for alerting me to this quotation.

[413] Steven J. Friesen, *Imperial Cults and the Apocalypse of John* (Oxford: Oxford University Press, 2001), 198.

[414] Cf. Matthew E. Gordley, *Teaching through Song in Antiquity* (WUNT 2.302; Tübingen: Mohr Siebeck, 2011), 123.

[415] Hurtado (*Lord Jesus Christ*, 592–93) comments: "In the religious values of this author [i.e., John the seer], it would be difficult to imagine a more direct and forceful way to express Jesus' divine status." Cf. Justin J. Schedtler ("Praising Christ the King: Royal Discourse and Ideology in Revelation 5," *NovT* 60 [2017]: 1–21): "The Lamb is honored with attributes—divine attributes—that function to highlight his unique status as God's chosen vicegerent. Some may go further than this to suggest that Jesus is thereby portrayed as a divine being. While there is room to debate the ontological nature of the Lamb in light of his portrayal as a king, the models from the Greek and Roman world suggest at the very least that the Lamb-as-King takes on the status greater than that of a mere mortal."

God. The Lamb properly belongs "upon" the throne with God and, in light of his paschal work, is a worthy recipient of divine worship.[416]

There is no doubt that in Revelation a speculative angelology has shaped a developing Christology (esp. Rev 1.13–16 and 14.14). Consequently, there is a clear angelomorphic Christology underlying in the seer's Christology. Even so, the coordination of the exalted Jesus and the Lord God, as well as the distinction between Jesus and the angels,[417] make an angel Christology impossible to plot within the apocalypse. John the Seer's Christology is an absolute divinity, not a subordinated divinity. The seer holds together Jesus' angelomorphism and equality with the Lord God to dually affirm Jesus' juridical function (angelomorphism) and his identity as Lord of the church (divine identity).[418] "Even if [angelic] polymorphism is involved," argues Smith, "John marries together his visionary experiences with a scripturally soaked imagination to communicate through marvel, metaphor, and midrash the Son's participation in what is uniquely true of YHWH while also underscoring his [Jesus'] divine commission from God and communion with his church."[419]

Jesus is divine in unity with the Father, evident by his place on the throne and reception of heavenly homage and earthly devotion. It is no exaggeration to say that the development of Christology from Nazareth to Nicaea only makes sense traveling via Patmos.[420]

(c) Other factors separating Christology from angelology.

Other considerations also exerted pressure away from an angelology as an explanatory paradigm for attributions of divinity to Jesus in a divine Christology. First, angelic orders are neither equals nor rivals to God, and this is salient for Christology. In Jewish cosmologies of God and angels, there is a distribution of power and authority in a heavenly hierarchy, which inevitably leads to the obvious question: Where does Jesus fit into it? We should begin with

---

[416] Cf. Schedtler, "Praising Christ the King," 21: "Whereas Alexander [the Great] and Julius Caesar received the title *deus invictus* on account of their success spilling the blood of their enemies, Jesus gained the throne through the shedding of his own blood. A conspicuous inversion of the popular royal ideology, Revelation's hymn makes clear that it is the conquered one who has become king."

[417] For instance, not even the "mighty angel" in Rev 5.1–3 is able to open the scroll, but the Lamb can in 5.5. Hoffmann, *Destroyer and the Lamb*, 114.

[418] Hoffmann, *Destroyer and the Lamb*, 249–50.

[419] Smith, *Vision of the Triune God*, 151.

[420] Origen, even with his subordinationist tendencies, can still offer a melange of Rev 1.8; 4.8; 21.6; and 22.13 to argue that "the omnipotence of Father and Son is one and the same, just as God and the Lord are one and the same with the Father" (*Princ.* 1.2.10). See Smith, *Vision of the Triune God*, 138–39.

the observation that in several Jewish writings, from the Hebrew Bible, to the composite *1 Enoch*, and to the Qumran scrolls, angels can be disobedient, rebellious, wicked, and destined for judgment. However, the angels are never portrayed as God's rival or God's equal; God is always superior to and sovereign over them.[421] Even Belial, the leader of angelic forces of evil, is God's creature, predestined for destruction (1QM 13.10–12). Belial's heavenly counterpart is more properly the "Prince of Light" (1QM 13.10), "Michael" (1QM 17.6), and "Melchizedek" (11Q13 2.11–14). In the Qumranic combat myth, God remains at a distance to both the good and evil angels as well as their minions. God is incomparably sovereign over the affairs of both kings and angels (1QM 12.7–10) and will defeat Belial (1QM 1.15; 17.4–6).[422] The outcome has been predetermined by God (1QM 18.9) to the point that Belial's defeat can already be celebrated (1QM 18.1–19.14). For all the talk of a "war in heaven" in apocalyptic literature (e.g., Rev 12.17) and its various narratives (1QM), there is no prospect that God's power hangs in the balance or that God could lose control of the heavenly council. God and the angels are in different leagues.[423]

What does this God-angel disparity mean for Christology? Well, it is comprehensible that one might think of Christ's subordination (1 Cor 15.23–28) and exaltation (Phil 2.9–11) as indicative of Christ's role as God's angelic agent in the purification and restoration of a chaotic universe, much akin to how Michael and Melchizedek function in Qumran.[424] For some Christologies, they narrated an angelic Christ who, through his earthly manifestation and subsequent exaltation, was promoted with divine honors to become "Son of God" (e.g., the Ebionites according to Epiphanius, *Pan.* 30.16.4).

However, in most apostolic and proto-orthodox writings, the spatial and doxological gap between God and Christ is—compared to the angels—acutely diminished. The dominating tendency was to integrate and equate God and Jesus more closely than ordinarily happened for angels in relation to God (see esp. New Testament epistolary openings [e.g., Gal 1.1–4] and doxologies [e.g.,

---

[421] Exod 15.11; Ps 86.8; 95.3; 96.4; 97.9; 135.5; Isa 36.18–20; Dan 2.47; *1 En.* 9.4; 1QHª; 15.26–33; 18.8–12.

[422] Davidson, *Angels at Qumran*, 307–8.

[423] Rowland, *Open Heaven*, 111; Davidson, *Angels at Qumran*, 305–9; and Wasserman, *Apocalypse as Holy War*, 107. Sommer (*Bodies of God*, 166) notes: "The divine retinue we know from the Hebrew Bible differs from those of Canaanite, Mesopotamian, and Greek literature, because lower beings never successfully or even realistically challenge Yhwh in the Hebrew Bible."

[424] Cf. Wasserman, *Apocalypse as Holy War*, 107–8.

Jude 25; *Barn.* 12.7]). The emphasis is upon God the Father and Christ the Son coordinated in purpose and even being, jointly sovereign over angelic orders (Mark 13.27; Matt 13.41; 16.27; 24.21; 2 Thess 1.7; Rev 3.5; 1 Tim 5.21; *Mart. Pol.* 14.1; Justin, *1 Apol.* 6.2). We see that in Christian claims that Christ shares the divine throne with God (Acts 2.33; 5.31; 7.55–56; Rom 8.34; Heb 1.8; 8.1; 12.2; Rev 3.21; 5.7, 13; 7.9–17; 12.5; 21.3–5; 22.3; Pol. *Phil.* 2.1), which angels cannot approach (*1 En.* 14.20–21; Rev 5.2–3), and he receives the worship (Rev 5.9–13) that angels refuse for themselves (Rev 19.10; 22.9). Christ is, then, aligned with God's creative and ruling powers, joined with God spatially and in worship, as God in relation to the church, and supreme over angels in a way that no ordinary angel ever is.[425] Christ is no aeonic rival or angelic vizier, but an expression of the true God. Thus, in light of the apostolic testimony of the New Testament, it is fitter to say that Christ is "equal to God" rather than "first among equals with the angels."

Second, Christ can be contrasted with the angels to the point that any resemblances are relativized in light of the stark difference. Now, I can easily imagine a Christian convert in Ephesus hearing Paul speak (50 CE), a candidate for baptism listening to a communal reading of the Gospel of Mark (75 CE), or a fruit seller in Rome watching Clement deliver a sermon on Ps 110 (95 CE), and come away thinking that Jesus is an angelic being. Persons initially conceived of Jesus based on their prior religious framework and exposure to Jewish texts and traditions, which had ample room for angelic entities. I have mapped out the various ways and many points at which Jesus was understood in angelic categories or identified as an angelic figure. But the similarities must be understood in relation to many and strong differences.

To underscore this point of difference, let me propose an experiment. Imagine if primitive Christology emerged as an angel Christology. What would an angel Christology look like in a confessional narrative? If an angel Christology had its own *regula fidei* (rule of faith) or *thalia* (festal poem), I would envisage it sounding something like this:

> In the beginning, God begat the Christ-angel as the firstborn of creation and the wisdom in creation, and through the Christ-angel he made all things in the heavens and on the earth, and the Christ-angel praised the Lord for his creation along with the holy angels. God's name was in the Christ-angel as the angel of the Lord who visited Abraham, Jacob, Moses, Gideon, and Daniel. The Christ-angel is the high-priest

---

[425] Cf. Bühner, *Hohe Messianologie*, 339–40; and Vollenweider, "Zwischen Monotheismus und Engelchristologie," 37.

Melchizedek who is king of righteousness, Christ is Michael who is the prince of Israel, and Christ is the son of man enthroned as the god of the ages. God sent the Christ-angel for the redemption of angels, and for the salvation of man. He came as an archangel to angels and as a man to men. The Christ-angel came as Gabriel to sow the spiritual seed into Mary. The Christ-angel become human so that humans could become angels. The flesh of the Christ-angel was crucified by Pontius Pilate, he died, was buried, and rose on the third day. The Christ-angel was super-exalted to become the archangel of the presence and placed above all thrones, authorities, dominions, and powers. The Christ-angel gives his spirit as Elijah gave his spirit to Elisha to those who hold to his testimony and trust in God. The Christ-angel will come again as the archangel Michael leading his angels to usher in the great day of judgment. This Lord God of creation and salvation we worship with his Christ-angel beside his throne.

If that scheme, or some variation thereof, was the *original* Christology, would it explain the contours of early Christology up to 100 CE? The preceding analysis would suggest a negative answer because Christ is not portrayed in such terms until much later.[426]

What is seldom acknowledged is that Christ does not act like an angel or undertake normal angelic occupations. As far as we know, in the first century, Christ is never coordinated with Michael, Gabriel, Sariel, Uriel, and Raphael (1QM 9.15; *1 En.* 40.9–10; *Sib. Or.* 2.215). Christ sends angelic messengers rather than being sent as an angelic messenger (Rev 2.1, 8, 12, 18; 3.7, 14; 4Q202 4 8–11; *T. Ab.* A 1.4–7). Christ never addressed God as "my Great One, the Lord Eternal" (4Q529 7). Christ never cooperated with others angels in his mediation of human petitions (*1 En.* 9.1–4). Christ is never appointed over a region (*1 En.* 20.1–5; *3 En.* 17.3). Christ never discusses the final judgment with other angels (*1 En.* 68.1–5). Christ does not present exalted patriarchs to the Lord (*2 En.* 22.1). Christ is never listed among those who "stand before" God (Rev 8.2; *1 En.* 40.1; *3 En.* 28.5, 8; 35.3; *2 Bar* 21.6; 48.10; *T. Ab.* A 7.11).[427] Christ does not give magical rings to people (*T. Sol.* 1.6). These differences

---

[426] Cf. Hengel (*Studies in Early Christology*, 171): "In the earliest period of Christianity an angel-Christology would have been an option given the Essene prefigurations and the manifold Jewish speculation about angels. The fact that in the immediate post-Easter period, that is, in a strict sense pre-Pauline time, no variant of an angel-Christology developed, can also be traced back to the very early influence of Ps. 8:7 (together with Ps. 110:1)."

[427] The exception is of course Acts 7.55–56. Luke himself normally portrays the ascended Jesus as "sitting" (Luke 20.42; 22.69; Acts 2.34). Hengel (*Studies in Early Christology*, 152)

should not be dismissed as contrastive pedantry but signify that Christ does not do what is normally attributed to angels. Added to that, if we appreciate the specificity of the incarnation as opposed to an angelic visitation, the emphasis on Christ as co-enthroned with God rather than depicted as a throne-room attendant, the identification of Christ as the mode of divine love as opposed to a messenger from above, and the absence of an angel-cult approximate to Christ devotion, then the difference between Christ and angels for some groups was one of kind not merely of degree.

Third, I would aver that it was a Pauline and Johannine synthesis in proto-orthodox churches that yielded a narrative and Christology that accented Christ as a divine being who was divine in the manner of God the Father and not divine in the mode of a supreme angel. For many groups, angelology could be a subsidiary motif in a christological scheme, but never the substructure of a divine Christology (this obviously depends about *who* and *when* we are talking about!). Paul professes that "God was in Christ reconciling the world to himself," not "God was in an angelic creature reconciling other creatures to himself" (2 Cor 5.19). The Pauline benediction in 2 Cor 13.14 would lose its rhetorical force if read as issuing the unmerited favor of an angel, the love of a supreme deity, and fellowship with a divine power. John's depiction of Jesus as the uncreated Logos through whom "all things" are made and as the Son who shares in the Father's own life and glory cannot be coherently sustained with an angel Christology (even though some tried!). Plus, Paul's soteriology with God's participation in humanity and human participation in God through Christ and the Spirit does not work with an angelic creature who is less god than God the Father. Paul, in his mystical dimension, treats union with Christ as a communion with God via the Spirit (Rom 8.9–11; 1 Cor 6.11; Phil 2.13–15; 3.9–11; Col 2.11–13; 3.3; Eph 2.19–22). Likewise, John the Evangelist envisages believers participating in the mutual indwelling between the Father and the Son (John 17.21). I know of no precedent or parallel for an angel as a conduit for a theotic communion as Paul and John imply.

It was the inadequacy of angel Christology to sustain accepted notions of incarnation, salvation, Spirit-giving, and worship that propelled figures such as Tertullian and eventually Athanasius to spurn angel Christologies in the varieties that they encountered. Therefore, as popular and persistent as angelomorphism, angelic functions, and angel Christology were in the early

---

thinks the standing posture of Jesus is the either a greeting for the martyr Stephen or a judgment on his enemies in the tradition of *As. Mos.* 10.3.

churches, their limitations became quickly apparent, and they were irreconcilable with the great church's gospel and worship.[428]

(d) Conclusion.

It is fair to say that an angel Christology is partly compatible with parts of the New Testament. In addition, para-apostolic and post-apostolic authors engaged in angelizing of Jesus to make him explainable or palatable in a wider religious environment. What is more, angelology clearly impacted Christology in varying degrees, with angelomorphic Christology (Jesus possessing the appearance of an angel), ascription of an angelic mission to Jesus (Jesus has the form and function of an angel in Israel's Scriptures), and angel Christology (Jesus is an angel). Angelic categories were applied to Jesus in the second half of the first century and developed thereafter, dominating in some sectors, becoming marginal in others. Even so, it is equally fair to say that an angel Christology does not explain the emergence of early divine Christology because it grates against discourses that had a propensity to connect Jesus primarily with God's identity and distinguished him from God's angelic servants. Among apostolic groups, Jesus' preexistence, person, power, and presence found their primary analogue with the God of Israel and only secondarily in relation to angelic intermediaries. In which case, for some groups, an angel Christology was either redundant, or else strenuously resisted as it removed Jesus from God's being, prerogatives, and worship. The primary rationale for a categorical separation was that Jesus, unlike the angels, shared God's side in the Creator-creature distinction, experienced a fully orbed human life, was worshipped beside God the Father, and held an unprecedented role in both creation and the eschatological drama of redemption.

Exalted Patriarchs

Another sense in which Jesus could be conceived of as divine is that of an exalted patriarch who undergoes a divine transformation and even receives worship. Hengel contended that the transformation of the risen Jesus' sonship from Davidic to eschatological in Rom 1.3–4 has its "nearest Jewish parallel" with "the exaltation, transformation and enthronement of the man Enoch."[429] Dunn believed that the heavenly assumptions of Elijah and Enoch with their angelic transformations, the godlike status attributed to Moses, even the worship of the divine image in Adam, as we find them in ancient sources, close the gulf between divine worship and the veneration of intermediate figures.

[428] Grillmeier, *Christ in Christian Tradition*, 1:53.
[429] Hengel, *Son of God*, 60.

"All this raises the possibility," Dunn wrote, "that even with the monotheistic Judaism of the first century the thought of a great human figure being exalted to heavenly status, and thus receiving the honour due to such a one, was not so far from being admissible."[430] It is worth surveying, then, the status and worship of figures such as Adam, Enoch, Jacob, Moses, and Elijah in literature and how they potentially overlap with early Christologies.

(1) Adam.

The story of the primeval couple in Gen 1–5 occupied many Jewish and Christian interpreters. Adam came to be associated with heavenly glory and a delegated divine rule over creation. Ben Sira makes a fleeting remark about how Adam was glorified "above every other created living being" (Sir 49.16). As for the reason for such glory, we must look to other Jewish authors. It may have to do with bearing the divine image (Gen 1.27–28; 4Q504 VIII 4–6), being given dominion over creation (Ps 8.3–8), being the heavenly man with a capacity for contemplation and virtue (Philo, *Leg. all.* 1.31–42; 2.4), having a gigantic physical form which itself is a mark of divinity (*Apoc. Ab.* 23.5), or his assigned position as a "second angel, honored and great and glorious" so that there was "nothing comparable to him on the earth" (*2 En.* 30.11–12 [J]). Or else the prelapsarian Edenic state in which Adam lived (*Apoc. Adam* 1.2), what the Qumran sectarians hoped to inherit as "the glory of Adam" (1QS 4.23; 1QH^a 4.15; CD-A 3.20; 4Q171 3.1–2), represents an incipient participation in the glory of God.[431]

At least one text, the *Testament of Adam*, probably a Jewish text given extensive Christian redaction, treats Adam's sin as wanting to be divine, and God offering to make him divine: "Adam, Adam do not fear. You wanted to be a god; I will make you a god, not right now, but after a space of many years. I am consigning you to death, and the maggot and the worm will eat your body" (*T. Adam* 3.2). God, speaking as the pre-incarnate Son, tells Adam:

> For your sake I will be born of the Virgin Mary. For your sake I will taste death and enter the house of the dead. For your sake I will make a new heaven, and I will be established over your posterity. And after three days, while I am in the tomb, I will raise up the body I received from you. And I will set you at the right hand of my divinity, and I will make you a god just like you wanted. And I will receive favor from God,

---

[430] Dunn, *Did the First Christians?* 88–89.
[431] Crispin H. T. Fletcher-Louis, *Jesus Monotheism*, vol. 1: *Christological Origins: The Emerging Consensus and Beyond* (Eugene, Ore.: Wipf & Stock, 2015), 251.

and I will restore to you and to your posterity that which is the justice of heaven. (*T. Adam* 3.3–4).

Here, being made a god is most likely Christian theosis (2 Pet 1.4), given the overtly Christian scheme of salvation with Adam's deliverance from *sheol* and entrance into heaven to worship God (*Ascen. Isa.* 9.28).

Adam also experienced a heavenly transportation, according to some authors. In *Life of Adam and Eve*, Adam is taken up by the archangel Michael in a chariot of wind and fire into the paradise of the righteous. There, God sentences Adam to death, Adam in turn pleads for mercy, God promises that his seed will not be abolished, Adam worships God, Michael then returns Adam to earth and escorts him out of paradise (*LAE* 25–29). In the parallel *Apocalypse of Moses*, proximate to his death, Adam's soul is carried up to heaven by angels, cleansed, and taken into the third paradise (*Apoc. Mos.* 37.1–6). Thereafter, Adam's body is interred in a tomb in the Edenic paradise with the promise of resurrection (*Apoc. Mos.* 38–42). In the *Testament of Abraham*, Adam is found in heaven "adorned in glory" seated on a throne before the gates of heaven, where he weeps over the damned and rejoices over the saved (*T. Ab.* 11.7–12). The later rabbis were also interested in Adam's redemption and heavenly exaltation as symbolized by descriptions of his being clothed in glorious garments.[432] The garments arguably represent a heavenly parallel to his initial post-fall covering (Gen 3.21) and a priestly garment of splendor (Exod 28.2, 40; Sir 50.11). "By the first century CE," observes Stephen Lambden, "Adam was, in certain Jewish circles, regarded as an exalted priestly figure and one initially in an elevated angelic state."[433]

Some of the texts cited above are either Christian or Christianized Jewish texts, but in any case, Jewish and Christian scribes depicted Adam with a pre-fall divine glory, angelic at least in the sense of being immortal, modeling a priestly and regal humanity that acted on behalf of God, and thereafter pardoned and taken up into a heavenly paradise. Importantly, these Adamic aspects were often amplified and applied to superhuman intermediary figures who recapture Adam's former glory and rehearse Adam's image-bearing role as the glorious priest-king of creation (see Ezek 1.26–28; Dan 7.9–14; 1 Cor 15.20–28, 45; *1 En.* 62.5; 69.29). It is notable too that the label "Son of Man"

---

[432] Robin Scroggs, *The Last Adam: A Study in Pauline Anthropology* (Philadelphia: Fortress, 1966), 38–58.

[433] Stephen N. Lambden, "From Fig Leaves to Fingernails: Some Notes on the Garments of Adam and Eve in the Hebrew Bible and Select Early Postbiblical Jewish Writings," in *A Walk in the Garden: Biblical, Iconographical and Literary Images of Eden*, ed. Paul Morris and Deborah Sawyer (Sheffield: JSOT Press, 1992), 81–82.

in its Hebrew, Aramaic, and Ethiopic forms can mean "Son of Adam," which means Adamic motifs are indelibly connected to certain intermediary figures in Jewish and Christian literature. Thus, Paul's Adam Christology and the Evangelists' account of the Son of Man did not emerge from a Gnostic *Urmensch*-redeemer myth, but grew from Jewish soil.[434]

Much has been especially made of a comparison between the worship of Christ and the worship offered to Adam in *LAE* 12–16 (ca. 110 BCE to 200 CE).[435] In the Latin narrative, Satan explains his expulsion from heaven as due to his refusal to worship the image of God in Adam. In the story, Satan rebuffs pressure from Michael to worship the image in Adam, saying, "Why do you compel me? I will not worship one inferior and subsequent to me. I am prior to him in creation; before he was made, I was already made. He ought to worship me" (*LAE* 14.3).[436] In the narrative, Adam and Eve are divinely manufactured idols that are fitting objects of angelic worship. Fletcher-Louis infers that "some Jews believed, in faithfulness to their reading of Gen 1, that the true humanity should be worshipped the way the pagans would worship an image (*tselem*) of a deity."[437] This opens a line of questioning in relation to the origins of Jesus devotion: "If this story is a pre-Christian anticipation of the worship of Jesus then it poses an important question for the nature of Christ devotion: namely, does the early Christian worship of the Lord Jesus Christ as one who belongs within the divine identity include, in any sense, the worship of the *human being* Jesus of Nazareth? If Jesus was considered a true Adam who recapitulated humanity's pre-fall identity then, at least in part, worship of him would surely be worship that reprised the angelic worship of Adam."[438]

(2) Enoch.

In scriptural tradition, Enoch was a son of Adam, who walked with God and was assumed into heaven (Gen 4.17–18; 5.18–24; 1QapGen 2.19–26; 5.3–4; *Jub.* 4.16–26). Various Jewish and Christian traditions made much of Enoch,

---

[434] Cf. Kim, *Origin of Paul's Gospel*, 162–92.

[435] See David Steenburg, "Worship of Adam and Christ as the Image of God," *JSNT* 39 (1990): 77–93; Chester, *Messiah and Exaltation*, 72–73, 113–15; Dunn, *Did the First Christians?* 88; and Fletcher-Louis, *Jesus Monotheism*, 1:256–92.

[436] Cf. *Apoc. Sedr.* 5.2: "You commanded your angels to worship Adam, but he who was first among the angels disobeyed your order and did not worship him; and so you banished him, because he transgressed your commandment and did not come forth (to worship) the creation of your hands."

[437] Fletcher-Louis, *Jesus Monotheism*, 1:291–92; cf. J. R. Daniel Kirk, *A Man Attested by God: The Human Jesus of the Synoptic Gospels* (Grand Rapids: Eerdmans, 2016), 74.

[438] Fletcher-Louis, *Jesus Monotheism*, 1:255 (italics original).

especially regarding his faithfulness, teachings, scribal activity, and heavenly assumption (Sir 44.16; 49.14; *Jub.* 4.21–25; Heb 11.5; Jude 14; *1 En.* 1.1–3; 14.8–23; 91.1–3; *1 Clem.* 9.3). Enoch is prominent in the Qumran scrolls as the scribe who interpreted the vision about the giants (4Q530 2.6–20). In the *Parables of Enoch* (*1 En.* 37–71), whose pre-70 CE date remains disputed, the Son of Man is a heavenly figure, who has preexistence before the foundation of the world (*1 En.* 48.2–3, 6–7), not merely ideal preexistence, but real preexistence as he is hidden (62.7).[439] The "Son of Man"[440] has the countenance of the holy angels (46.1) and is described as glorious and glorified (49.2, 51.3). He acts as an agent of revelation (46.3), he is a savior of the righteous (46.3; 48.4–7; 53.7; 62.14), judge of the wicked (46.4–8; 62.9; 63.11; 69.27–29), and even the judge of the angels (55.3–56.4; 61.8–9). He is given titles such as Messiah (48.10; 53.4), Chosen One (39.6; 40.5), and Righteous One (38.2; 40.5). Depending on one's interpretation of the epilogue of the Enochic parables, in the received form of the text, the Son of Man is an angelomorphized Enoch (*1 En.* 71.11, 14; cf. *2 En.* 22.8; *Ascen. Isa.* 9.9).[441]

Importantly, whereas the "throne of glory" is the unique seat of the Lord of Spirit's divine power (*1 En.* 47.3–4; 60.2; 71.7), the Enochic "Son of Man" is placed on the Lord of Spirit's "throne of glory" and there exercises divine functions of judgment and ruling (45.3; 51.3; 55.4; 61.8; 62.2–3, 5; 69.27, 29). The Son of Man receives obeisance from the wicked who prostrate themselves before him (48.5; 62.9), escalating up to a scene where they "bless and glorify and exalt him" (62.6). What is startling is that the Son of Man receives devotion and worship parallel to the worship of the Lord of Spirits, which means he receives a form of divine worship (39.12; 48.5; 61.9, 11, 12; 69.24). "He, in other words," says Ehrman, "is elevated to God's own status and functions

---

[439] Collins and Collins, *King and Messiah*, 89; and Bühner, *Hohe Messianologie*, 134–38.

[440] The Ethiopic terms are *walda sab'*, *walda be'esi*, and *walda 'egwala 'emaḥeyāw*; see George W. E. Nickelsburg and James C. VanderKam, *1 Enoch 2: A Commentary on the Book of 1 Enoch, Chapters 37–82* (Hermeneia; Minneapolis: Fortress, 2012), 114.

[441] *1 En.* 70–71 are very possibly additions by a Jewish redactor who tries to latently conflate Enoch (*1 En.* 14) with the Son of Man (Dan 7). Otherwise, there is little in the work to indicate that Enoch and the Son of Man are identical; the two figures are generally treated as separate throughout the work, though the Son of Man could be "the true heavenly counterpart of the prototypically righteous man Enoch, and that here in [*1 En.*] 71, Enoch finally becomes one with his heavenly double" (Chester, *Messiah and Exaltation*, 64). This would mesh with Andrei Orlov's account of a heavenly double—an angelic twin for an earthly figure as found in Iranian, Greco-Roman, Christian, Manichaean, Islamic, and Kabbalistic traditions (*The Greatest Mirror: Heavenly Counterparts in Jewish Pseudepigrapha* [New York: State University of New York Press, 2017]). See discussion in Collins and Collins, *King and Messiah*, 90–94.

as the divine being who carries out God's judgment on the earth. This is an exalted figure indeed, as exalted as one can possibly be without actually being the Lord God Almighty himself."[442]

The portrayal of the Enochic Son of Man as a being who preexisted creation, is predestined to greatness, is given a divine throne, has angelic traits and messianic titles, exercises judgment over kings and angels, and receives worship is very striking when placed in conversation with early Christology.[443]

On the one hand, the Enochic imagery is clearly indebted to Dan 7.9–14 with the "one like a son of man" given everlasting dominion and service from peoples from all nations and languages (esp. *1 En.* 46.1–8), and Christians may simply have shared in this tradition of applying Dan 7.9–14 to a divine agent and messianic figure (e.g., Mark 14.62).

On the other hand, there are striking similarities between the Enochic Son of Man and literary representations of Christ in the Matthean eschatological discourse in Matt 25.31–46 (esp. the motif of judgment), certain aspects of Paul's Christology (Messiah as heavenly, preexistent, enthroned, a judge, and worshipped), and the investiture and worship of the Lamb in Rev 5.9–14 (worship offered to a divine vice-regent). Importantly, what is only implied in Dan 7.13–14, namely, the enthronement and veneration of the "son of man," is simultaneously made explicit in the *Parables of Enoch* and early Christian messianic discourse. Plus, the Enochic parables and the canonical Gospels both provide a clear messianic interpretation of Daniel's son of man. The Son of Man title—implying certain function, identity, and vocation—in both discourses is deployed to link heavenly origins with a messianic status.[444]

Are these coincidences due to Christians drawing on the same pool of tradition or indicative of literary dependence? So close are some of the parallels in form and function that one has to wonder if the Enochic parables were known to Matthew, Paul, and John the Seer. Of course, it is not straightforward.[445]

---

[442] Ehrman, *How Jesus Became God*, 66; cf. Kirk (*Man Attested by God*, 152): "It is not merely that the son of man acts on God's behalf, but that this figure stands in the place of God both as executor of God's actions and as the recipient of what is due to God himself."

[443] Hengel (*Son of God*, 60) comments that the "nearest Jewish parallel" to Rom 1.3–4 is the "exaltation, transformation and enthronement of the man Enoch."

[444] Helge S. Kvanvig, "The Son of Man in the Parables of Enoch," in *Enoch and the Messiah Son of Man: Revisiting the Book of Parables*, ed. Gabriele Boccaccini (Grand Rapids: Eerdmans, 2007), 211–15.

[445] See discussion in Gabriele Boccaccini, ed., *Enoch and the Messiah Son of Man: Revisiting the Book of Parables* (Grand Rapids: Eerdmans, 2007); Darrell L. Bock and James H. Charlesworth, eds., *Parables of Enoch: A Paradigm Shift* (London: Bloomsbury, 2013); Loren T. Stuckenbruck and Gabriele Boccaccini, eds., *Enoch and the Synoptic Gospels:*

The differences are just as strong as the similarities. The Christian Son of Man texts tend to focus on Jesus' future "coming" (Mark 8.38–9.1; 14.62; 13.26; Matt 24.30, 37, 39, 44; Luke 12.40; 17.22), and they marry Jesus' "Son of Man" identity to his redemptive death (Mark 8.31; 9.31; 10.33, 45; Matt 17.12; Luke 24.7; John 3.14; 8.28; 12.34), neither of which parallels the Enochic Son of Man. Also, Jesus as the Son of Man is a historicization of the Danielic figure, whereas in the Enochic parables the Son of Man's role is projected into an eschatological future. That the Christian Son of Man tradition is independent of *1 Enoch* is not only plausible but more probable than not. If there is dependence perhaps it is the other way around, and the Enochic parables are a response to early Christology, with the parables presenting their own heavenly intermediary as a counterexample to Jewish Christian Christ devotion.

The evidence for an early dating of the *Parables of Enoch* is evenly balanced. On the one hand, the Enochic parables are not found in the Qumran scrolls, where other Enochic writings are extant; there are no quotations of the Enochic parables in the church fathers; and our manuscripts of the Enochic parables are preserved exclusively in Christian Ethiopic manuscripts of the late Middle Ages. But on the other hand, the *Parables of Enoch* can be reasonably located within the tumults of Herodian Judea as the response of the scribal class to social upheaval.[446] Plus, the Enochic parables do not seem to be a response to the crisis of 70 CE as *4 Ezra* clearly is (another apocalyptic text with its own mysterious Son of Man figure). Irrespective of whether we conceive of dependence, independence, or a confluence of shared traditions, the Enochic Son of Man is an indispensable figure in the study of Jewish intermediaries and early Christology.

(3) Moses.

Moses was likened to a god and considered a god and king of Israel in scriptural and Second Temple texts (see Exod 7.1, Philo, *Vit. Mos.* 1.155–58; *Somn.*

Reminiscences, Allusions, Intertextuality (Atlanta: SBL, 2016); James A. Waddell, *The Messiah: A Comparative Study of the Enochic Son of Man and the Pauline Kyrios* (London: T&T Clark, 2011); and Bruk Ayele Asale, *1 Enoch as Christian Scripture: A Study in the Reception and Appropriation of 1 Enoch in Jude and the Ethiopian Orthodox Tewahǝdo Canon* (Eugene, Ore.: Wipf & Stock, 2020), 68–70.

[446] There is a possible reference to the Parthian invasion of Judea in 40 BCE in *1 En.* 56.5–8 that we know about from Josephus, *War* 1.13.1–11; *Ant.* 14.13.3–14.6. Alternatively, *1 En.* 56.5–8 could be using the well-known tradition of eastern invaders who attempt to wage war against Israel in an eschatological battle (see Ezek 38–39; *Sib. Or.* 3.657–732; Rev 20.7–10; *4 Ezra* 13.5–11). See Ted Erho, "Historical-Allusional Dating and the Similitudes of Enoch," *JBL* 130 (2011): 493–511.

2.234–35; 4Q374 II 2.6). He is also depicted in an astounding dream sequence as seated on God's very own throne in *Ezekiel the Tragedian* (68–82). Josephus also refers to his assumption into heaven (*Ant.* 2.326). Samaritan traditions also describe Moses as an exalted heavenly scribe.[447] I have addressed Moses traditions at length in chapters 2 and 3 and will not retrace my steps. Suffice to say, Moses was reckoned as a god in a euergetic sense, and the dream sequence of *Ezekiel the Tragedian* is a figurative expression of Moses' divine favor and authority over Israel.

(4) Elijah.

In Jewish tradition, the prophet Elijah ascended to heaven in a whirlwind (2 Kgs 2.11; Sir 48.12; 1 Macc 2.58; *Liv. Pro.* 21.15; *Gk. Apoc. Ez.* 7.6), and he would one day return to herald the judgment of God (Mal 4.5; Mark 15.35–36; John 1.21; *Sib. Or.* 2.186–95). He is not normally associated with deification or divine worship in scriptural texts or Second Temple literature.

(5) Patriarchs in apostolic and post-apostolic authors.

Christian authors could incorporate types or scenes pertaining to patriarchs in their christological discourse, or else venerate the patriarchs as those already enjoying a heavenly state.

For the apostle Paul, Adam was the progenitor of humanity and the introducer of sin and death (Rom 5.12–14; 1 Cor 15.22), a typological anticipation of Christ (Rom 5.14), who, like Christ, is a federal representative of humanity (Rom 5.15–19). Paul's Adam is the protological man of dust/earth with a living soul contrasted with Christ who is the eschatological man of/from heaven with a living spirit (1 Cor 15.45–49). Adamic motifs are, to disputed degrees, interwoven into Phil 2.6–11 and combined with worship of Jesus. Luke can also designate Adam as "son of God" in a genealogical sense to anticipate the messianic sonship of Jesus (Luke 3.38). In the *Gospel of Thomas*, Adam was thought to have been a glorious primordial man: "Adam came from great power and great wealth, but he was not worthy of you. For had he been worthy, [he would] not [have tasted] death" (*Gos. Thom.* 85). The Sethian *Apocalypse of Adam* depicts Adam sharing in the glory of the aeons, who existed "like the great eternal angels" and who was loftier and mightier than the demiurge who created him (*Apoc. Adam* 1.1–3). In the Valentinian *Apocryphon of John*, Adam is formed in the likeness of the chief aeon with the assistance of lesser aeons who created Adam as "a power of light for us" (*Ap. John* 15.1–17.29) For

---

[447] Hengel, *Studies in Early Christology*, 200.

many authors of a Gnostic bent, Adam was the paradigm for all humans, who need to regain the glory of their primordial selves.[448]

Irenaeus focuses intently on the Adam-Christ contrast, with Christ as a recapitulation, perfection, and deification of Adamic humanity (*Haer.* 3.21.10–3.23.8; 5.1.2–3; 5.12.2–3; 5.14.1; 5.15.3–4; 5.16.1–3; 5.21.1–2; 5.23.2). A variant scheme occurs in the *Gospel of Philip*, where the purpose of Christ's advent was to reunite Adam and Eve, who were separated by the fall (*Gos. Phil.* 70.12–17), which is why they baptize in pairs (69.12), symbolizing their sacramental and marital union with each other and with Christ in the bridal chamber (70.18–22); this way, a person anticipates their ultimate union with the angelic realm (58.10–14).

The Evangelists depict Jesus as engaging in an Elijah-like prophetic ministry (Mark 6.15; Luke 4.25–26), John the Baptist was a typological Elijah who precedes Jesus (Mark 9.9–13), and glorified versions of Elijah and Moses appeared in the transfiguration scene (Mark 9.2–8). Irenaeus mentions the heavenly translations of Enoch and Elijah to show that their bodies were fit for heavenly existence (*Haer.* 5.5.1).

(6) Comparative analysis.

For the sake of brevity, I will focus on the relevance of Adam and Enoch for Christian discourse on the divinity and worship of Jesus.

(a) Adam.

Concerning the worship of Adam in comparison to Christ devotion, two erroneous lines of argumentation need to be interdicted. First, the absence of a "throne" and "all authority" in *LAE* 12–16 is moot because Christ is worshipped or acclaimed as divine in contexts where no throne or universal authority is mentioned.[449] Second, there is little point making a distinction between Adam created in/according to the divine image (Gen 1.28–29; Sir 17.3; Wis 2.23; *Jub.* 6.8; *Sib. Or.* 1.23; 3.8; *T. Naph.* 2.5) and Adam created as the image of God (1 Cor 11.7; *4 Ezra* 8.44; *2 Enoch* 30.10; *Sib. Or.* 8.403), because—either way—an image is by nature derivative of something else.[450]

A key observation is that Adam is not worshipped as a divine being, but it is the divine image in Adam that is worshipped by the angels. By specifying Adam's "countenance" (i.e., face) as the locus of the image, *LAE* 13.3 exhibits a physicalist understanding of the divine image (similar to other Jewish

---

[448] DeConick, *Gospel of Thomas*, 250.

[449] Contra Bauckham, *Jesus and the God of Israel*, 176, 204; with Chester, *Messiah and Exaltation*, 115; and Fletcher-Louis, *Jesus Monotheism*, 1:272.

[450] Contra Fletcher-Louis, *Jesus Monotheism*, 1:264–65.

literature, e.g., *2 En.* 44.1–3; *Sib. Or.* 1.22–24; 8.442–45; *T. Isaac* 6.33–7.1; *T. Naph.* 2.5).[451] It is because of a divine anthropology that a likeness of the divine image in humanity can be worshipped. Adam is the singularly approved icon of the divine being to be exhibited on earth and venerated in heaven. In fact, the Armenian text has God declare to the angels, "Come, bow down to the god whom I made."[452] Adam is not divine per se, then, but is a hypostatic icon of the divine being. A view which, says van Kooten, "if taken to extremes" entails that "humanity is to be worshipped" by angels.[453] Thus, the scene in *LAE* 12–16 is not about the worship of Adam as a being beside or slightly below God, but the establishment of Adam as a living icon through whom the angels worship the Lord God and express their subservience to humanity. What this means, as Orlov sums up, is that Adam is presented "not as the ultimate object of veneration but rather as a representation or an icon of the deity through whom the angels are able to worship God."[454]

This worship of the divine image in Adam does not amount to a divine status for Adam.[455] In the narrative, Adam and Satan are both "made" (*LAE* 14.3); they are creatures, so it is a question of relative priority and power of one to the other. Any status for Adam is, to use our earlier categories, relative rather than absolute. Michael does not invoke Adam's name as one would in a cultic setting; rather, Satan invokes Adam's name as the grounds for his opposition to bowing before a posterior and inferior being. The worship that Michael commands the angels to perform is directed to the divine image, and it is the act of prostration to an inferior that Satan and the rebellious angels refuse to perform. Satan's objection is not to an implied divine status that is idolatrously attributed to Adam; instead, the complaint is assigning him a servile status beneath Adam. That is because the worship directed towards Adam by the angels is like the worship of Adam offered by earthly creatures as their

---

[451] Steenburg, "Worship," 96–97.

[452] Cited from Fletcher-Louis, *Jesus Monotheism*, 1:285.

[453] George H. van Kooten, *Paul's Anthropology in Context: The Image of God, Assimilation to God, and Tripartite Man in Ancient Judaism, Ancient Philosophy and Early Christianity* (WUNT 232; Tübingen: Mohr Siebeck, 2008), 47.

[454] Andrei A. Orlov, *Dark Mirrors: Azazel and Satanael in Early Jewish Demonology* (Albany, N.Y.: State University of New York Press, 2014), 105. A similar analogy is Alexander the Great's worship by *proskynesis*, not of the high priest, but the divine name which the Jerusalem high priest had engraved on a golden plate he was wearing (Josephus, *Ant.* 11.331–35).

[455] Hurtado, *One God, One Lord*, x–xi; idem, *Lord Jesus Christ*, 39–40; Bauckham, *God of Israel*, 203–4; and Chris Tilling, *Paul's Divine Christology* (Grand Rapids: Eerdmans, 2012), 204–6.

natural governor and master according to Philo (*Opif.* 83). Or, for a better comparison, at Qumran, Adam and Eve are appointed "as rulers over all these things on the earth," and angels come "to serve Adam and to minister to him" (4Q381 I 6–11). Satan's objection is that he and the other angels are demoted to a rank beside mere beasts.[456]

In comparative perspective, *LAE* 12–16, when buttressed with 4Q381 I 6–11, is analogous to the Synoptic scene of Jesus in the wilderness, a preview of a restored creation, where the new Adam dwells harmoniously with the beasts while angels attend to him (Mark 1.13/Matt 4.11). Any similarities with the angelic worship of Jesus in Heb 1.6 and Rev 5.9–14 is only piecemeal, because both texts provide a far more intense association of Jesus with the divine eternity, majesty, sovereignty, and identity than anything attributed to Adam in *LAE* 12–16. This is underscored by the fact that Adam explicitly worships God as creator, as is fitting for a creature such as himself (*LAE* 26.1; 28.1–3; 29.1). This is proof of his intermediate status between God and the angels and no threat to God's singular, unique identity.[457] It seems unwise to treat *LAE* 12–16 as exhibiting or even preparing for the idea of a second figure worshipped beside God.[458]

More interesting is that there is a sense in which Jesus' exaltation is his apotheosis as the second/last Adam. Paul, using traditional material, narrates a transposition in the mode of Jesus' sonship from Davidic sonship to a cosmic, eschatological, and plenipotentiary sonship (Rom 1.3–4).[459] Similarly, Paul regards Jesus' earthly life and his messianic obedience unto death (Rom 5.14–19; Phil 2.8) as qualifying him to be the new/last Adam into whom he is transformed at his resurrection (1 Cor 15.45). Paul, and others beside him (see Heb 2.8–9), seem to have engaged in a christological reading of Ps 8.4–6 so that the risen and exalted Jesus is the new Adam who subdues all enemies and subordinates all things before himself (1 Cor 15.25–27; Phil 3.21).[460] In Paul's narration, Jesus shifts from solidarity with Adam in his human life, to undergoing a vicarious sacrificial death to undo Adam's disobedience and consequent

---

[456] Fletcher-Louis (*Jesus Monotheism*, 1:272–73) says that Adam's superiority to angels is not the point in *LAE* 12–16, but he proceeds to expound how the text implies Adam's position of universal and cosmic authority over creation, which is precisely how Adam's superiority is manifested.

[457] Andrei A. Orlov, *Demons of Change: Antagonism and Apotheosis in Jewish and Christian Apocalypticism* (Albany, N.Y.: State University of New York Press, 2020), 14; and Fletcher-Louis, *Jesus Monotheism*, 1:270.

[458] Hurtado, *Lord Jesus Christ*, 39.

[459] Bird, *Jesus the Eternal Son*, 11–24.

[460] Cf. esp. Irenaeus, *Haer.* 3.18.7; 5.1.3; 5.16.3.

death, to transformation into the new Adam at his resurrection, where he then reigns on behalf of God.⁴⁶¹

If an Adamic Christology was connected to the language of exaltation (Phil 2.9; Acts 2.33; 5.31) and ascension (Luke 24.51; Acts 1.9-11), it would be perfectly natural for ancient audiences familiar either with the *consecratio* of an *Urmensch* like Romulus (Cicero, *Rep.* 2.17-18; Plutarch, *Rom.* 28.1-3; Livy, *Hist.* 1.15.6; 16.1-8) or with the translation of Adam into heaven (*Apoc. Mos.* 37), to think of Jesus' exaltation as his apotheosis into the heavenly Adam (1 Cor 15.47-49). Two things, however, must be borne in mind. First, Paul combines his Adamic Christology with a divine status attributed to the preexistent Jesus as one who was already in the "form of God" and "equal to God" and who subsequently "becomes" human (Phil 2.6-7). This is more than a typological reading of Gen 1-3 concerning a human being whose earthly life stands in contrast to Adam and is thereafter exalted by God.⁴⁶² The Adamic

---

⁴⁶¹ Cf. Dunn, *Christology in the Making*, 107-13.

⁴⁶² Contra Dunn, *Christology in the Making*, 114-21; idem, *Theology of Paul*, 281-88; and Casey, *From Jewish Prophet*, 112-15. Bringing in an Adam via the mention of divine "form" is questionable because (1) the words "form" (*morphē*) and "image" (*eikōn*) are not strictly synonyms, proved by: (a) the Hebrew *tselem* used in Gen 1.27 does not oscillate in being translated as *morphē* and *eikōn* in the LXX, and (b) Paul uses the same two words differently in his letters; (2) "equality" (*iso*) and "likeness" (*homoiōma*) are not synonyms either, and it was Eve not Adam who wanted to be like God in Gen 3.5-6; (3) for Philo, humans do not resemble the divine form, so Philo would not equate it with the divine image in humans (*Opif.* 69; *Leg. all.* 1.37; *Sacr.* 95; *Plant.* 35; *Legat.* 110-11); and (4) the poem stresses Christ's origins, proximity, and parity with God, not with Adam. See Markus Bockmuehl, "'The Form of God' (Phil. 2:6): Variations on a Theme of Jewish Mysticism," *JTS* 48 (1997): 1-23; David Steenburg, "The Case against Synonymity of *Morphē* and *Eikōn*," *JSNT* 34 (1988): 77-86; Wright, *Climax of the Covenant*, 72; Fee, *Pauline Christology*, 377-79, 379n29, 522-23; Hurtado, *Lord Jesus Christ*, 121-23; and Ehrman, *How Jesus Became God*, 259-62. However, note discussion in Yongbom Lee, *The Son of Man as the Last Adam: The Early Church Tradition as a Source of Paul's Adam Christology* (Eugene, Ore.: Pickwick, 2012), 44-63, and Nicholas A. Meyer, *Adam's Dust and Adam's Glory in the Hodayot and the Letters of Paul: Rethinking Anthropogony and Theology* (NovTSup 168; Leiden: Brill, 2016), 147-62, who both favor an Adamic Christology for "form of God." There is also the excellent contribution of George H. van Kooten: "Image, Form and Transformation: A Semantic Taxonomy of Paul's 'Morphic' Language," in *Jesus, Paul and Early Christianity*, ed. Rieuwerd Buitenwerf, Harm W. Hollander, and Johannes Tromp (NovTSup 130; Leiden: Brill, 2008), 213-42. Kooten is correct that (1) *morphē* and *eikōn* do belong to the same semantic domain; (2) human beings are said to have been molded into the divine image/form in *Sib. Or.* 3.8-10; (3) for many Jewish and Christian authors, God's *morphē* is reflected, not in idols, but in the humans as God's *eikōn*. I think Kooten has shown that an image can reflect the divine form, not that they are synonymous. Also, Kooten is right that even if *morphē* and *eikōn* are parallel, they could be applied by Paul here to the preexistent Jesus so that

echoes, should readers detect them in Phil 2.6–11, are secondary to the metaphysics of messiahship concerning a heavenly figure who becomes human, serves in humiliation and degradation, and returns to heaven to receive divine homage. Second, Jesus is himself the agent of subjugation to whom enemies and heavenly powers submit. Whereas Ps 8.6 declares that God has put all things under humanity's dominion, Paul writes that God has put all things under Christ (1 Cor 15.28; Eph 1.21–22); it is Christ who subjugates all things to himself (1 Cor 15.24–25; Phil 3.21), and then hands the kingdom to the Father (1 Cor 15.24). The only thing not subjected to Christ is God the Father (1 Cor 15.27–28). Thus, exaltation is a sequel to incarnation, and Christ's exalted position is truly superlative.

(b) Enoch.

A comparison of the Enochic Son of Man and John the Seer's exalted Jesus provides the most salient example of how a christological discourse can resemble the narration of an intermediary figure from Jewish literature. These two figures constitute a natural albeit nutty instance of a Jewish parallel with an obvious relevance for divine Christology.[463] To recap, the Son of Man in the *Similitudes of Enoch* is a heavenly figure with an angelic appearance, identified as the "messiah," a redemptive agent who exercises judgment and receives worship from the inhabitants of the earth. It needs to be asked, then, is the divine status and worship of the Enochic Son of Man an analogue to the divine status and worship of Jesus in the early church, especially in comparison to Rev 5?

To begin with, we must note the debate over what kind of worship the Enochic Son of Man receives. Hurtado contended that there is no infringement upon divine worship in the Enochic parables concerning the Son of Man/Chosen One. He wrote: "The obeisance given to the Chosen One is that of conquered gentile rulers, not the gathered worship of believers (*1 Enoch* 55:4; 62:1–9). Moreover, and more crucially, there is no indication that these literary scenes produced or were accompanied by a devotional practice among

---

Jesus as the *morphē theou* is the "heavenly man" (1 Cor 15.47) and "image of God" (2 Cor 4.4; Col 1.15).

[463] Daniel Boyarin, "How Enoch Can Teach Us about Jesus," *EC* 2 (2011): 58–59; Benjamin E. Reynolds, "The Parables of Enoch and Revelation 1:1–20: Daniel's Son of Man," in *Reading Revelation in Context*, ed. Ben Blackwell, John Goodrich, and Jason Maston (Grand Rapids: Zondervan, 2019), 19–36; and Loren T. Stuckenbruck, "The Apocalypse of John, 1 Enoch, and the Question of Influence," in *Die Johannesapokalypse: Kontexte—Konzepte—Rezeption*, ed. J. Frey, J. Kelhoffer, and F. Tóth (WUNT 287; Tübingen: Mohr Siebeck, 2012), 190–234.

second-temple Jewish circles in which this Chosen One was a recipient of the sort of reverence given to Jesus in earliest Christian circles."[464] The scenes in *1 En.* 48.5 and 62.1–9 amount to "the eschatological acknowledgement of this figure as God's appointed one who will gather the elect and subdue the haughty kings and nations who have no acknowledged the true God and who have oppressed the Jewish righteous."[465] Tilling is similar: "The language in these passages [46.4–5; 48.5; 62.6–9], especially the first and last, sound very much like an earthly or military rout, the political submission of one king to another more mighty. . . . These Enochic passages likely do not portray the worship of the Son of Man in the way only God should be worshipped."[466] In contrast, Bauckham believes that while intermediary figures in Second Temple Judaism generally do not receive divine worship, the Enochic Son of Man is the exception that proves the rule.[467] The worship given to the Enochic Son of Man includes more than obeisance to a monarch because the placement of the Son of Man on the "throne of glory" is sufficient to establish his participation in the divine sovereignty and rightly elicits cultic worship by the kings and mighty ones, who see that he rules over all things. The Enochic Son of Man is, then, unique among exalted human or angelic figures in Second Temple Jewish literature by sitting on the divine throne, exercising divine functions, and receiving cultic worship.[468]

Collins and Collins are more circumspect: "Whether this obeisance [in *1 En.* 48.5] indicates divinity, or what degree of divinity, might be debated. . . . But he sits like the Lord on the throne of glory, and this surely bespeaks divine status in some sense, although it does not rule out the possibility that the figure in question is an exalted human being."[469] They detect a high grade of divinity attributed to the Enochic Son of Man, but just how high is somewhat ambiguous. Bühner contends that the Son of Man here is clearly a preexistent heavenly figure with

---

[464] Hurtado, *One God, One Lord*, 166.
[465] Hurtado, *Lord Jesus Christ*, 38–39.
[466] Tilling, *Paul's Divine Christology*, 215–16.
[467] Bauckham, *Jesus and the God of Israel*, 15–16. Chester (*Messiah and Exaltation*, 22–23) says that "to have even one such exception is potentially deeply damaging for the absolute distinction Bauckham wants to draw." Bühner (*Messianic High Christology*, 141) infers that "the Parables of Enoch are not the exception that proves the rule, but rather are an extreme example of a broader strand within Second Temple messianism." To be fair, Bauckham has changed his position in a forthcoming publication; closer to Hurtado and Tilling, he argues that the Enochic Son of Man receives obeisance on earth while the Head of Days receives cultic worship in heaven.
[468] Bauckham, *Jesus and the God of Israel*, 170–71.
[469] Collins and Collins, *King and Messiah*, 94.

theophanic qualities; what he receives may not necessarily be "liturgical performance," but it is certainly "divine veneration."[470]

Several things indicate the subordinated role granted to the Son of Man/Chosen One in the Enochic parables.

(1) The Head of Days/Lord of Spirits remains supreme on the throne of his glory (47.3; 60.2; 63.1–7) and the Son of Man's role is strictly judicial over earthly kings and to a lesser degree over rebellious angels.

(2) There is a large emphasis on the Son of Man/Chosen One as appointed and subservient to the Lord of Spirits (46.3; 48.2, 6, 10; 52.9; 61.8; 62.2).

(3) The Son of Man/Chosen One does not commit the sin of the angels or kings who "act as if they were like the Lord" (68.4–5).

(4) The Son of Man/Chosen One stands in the presence of the Lord of Spirits like an attending angelic courtier (49.2; cf. 60.2), who serves at the Lord of Spirit's "good pleasure" (49.4) and worships with the other angelic orders (61.8–11; 71.11–12).

(5) Even the judgment meted out by the Son of Man/Chosen One from his throne of glory against Azazel and all his host happens as part of the "wrath" of the Lord of Spirits and "in the name of the Lord of Spirits" (55.3–4).

(6) The Son of Man/Chosen One's power is not intrinsic, but based on receiving the "spirit of wisdom" (48.7; 49.3) and the "spirit of righteousness" (62.2) from the Lord of Spirits. He constantly acts "in the name of the Lord of Spirits" (48.7; 55.4; 61.13).

(7) The Lord of Spirits presides over an eschatological feast where the Son of Man/Chosen One and the righteous are together (62.14).

(8) The Son of Man/Chosen One is not equal to the "Lord of Spirits" as his throne of glory is the heavenly counterpart to the kings of the earth, who trusted and hoped in "our kingdom and throne of our glory" (62.9; 63.7).

(9) There is no sense in which the Son of Man/Chosen One impinges upon the authority of archangels such as Michael, Raphael, Gabriel, and Phanuel (40.9), who place rebellious angels into a type of celestial custody ahead of the day of judgment (54.6). The Son of Man's authority is perhaps parallel to theirs, or else limited to a judgment of wicked kings and rebellious angels.

---

[470] Bühner, *Hohe Messianologie*, 326 ("die wohl keinen liturgischen Vollzug erkennen, sich aber zumindest als gottgleiche Verehrung verstehen lässt").

(10) Even when kings bow down and worship the Son of Man/Chosen One, they still "glorify and bless and sing hymns to the name of the Lord of Spirits" (48.5). When the Chosen One takes his position on the throne of glory and metes out judgment, the holy ones "bless and glorify and exalt and sanctify the name of the Lord of Spirits" (61.9), and even the Chosen One joins the chorus of angelic praise (61.8–13).

Following Hurtado, the upshot is "not that the figure rivals God or becomes a second god but rather that he is seen as performing the eschatological functions associated with God and is therefore God's chief agent, linked with God's work to a specially intense degree," and "the description of Enoch as God's chief agent is an example of the ability of ancient Judaism to accommodate this or that figure in a position in God's rule like that of vizier of the royal court."[471]

If we compare the Enochic Son of Man with John the Seer's exalted Jesus, several similarities are evident:

(1) A description of a heavenly figure, prominent in an apocalypse, who acts on behalf of God, and exercises a judicial function (*1 En.* 62.3–5/Rev 6.15–16).

(2) Worship of God (*1 En.* 63.1–12/Rev 4.1–11) provides the backdrop to the worship of the Son of Man/Lamb (*1 En.* 48.5, 62.1–8/Rev 5.9–14).

(3) The Enochic Son of Man and exalted Jesus both receive blessings, doxologies, and prostration (*1 En.* 48.5; 61.7; 62.3, 6, 9/Rev 1.5–6; 5.12–13). Notably, the worship of the Son of Man/Lamb is closely associated with worship of the Lord of Spirits/God Almighty (*1 En.* 48.5/Rev 7.10; 15.3).

(4) The elect or righteous dine with Jesus/Son of Man (*1 En.* 62.14/Rev 3.20; 19.9).

(5) Placement of the Son of Man/Lamb upon a heavenly throne is a symbol of sharing in and exercising divine sovereignty (*1 En.* 45.3; 51.1; 55.4; 61.8; 62.2, 5; 69.26–29/Rev 3.21; 6.16; 22.1). The Enochic Son of Man "rules over all" (*1 En.* 62.6) as does the Lamb as "Lord of lords and King of kings" (Rev 17.14).

(6) Imagery for God's awesome power is applied to the Enochic Son of Man (mountains melt like wax before him; *1 En.* 1.6; 52.6, 53.7; Ps 97.5; Nah 1.5; Micah 1.3–4; Jdt 16.15; 4 Ezra 8.23; 13.4), just as

---

[471] Hurtado, *One God, One Lord*, 55–57.

scriptural imagery for Israel's Lord is repeatedly applied to Jesus (e.g., the Lord is a "faithful and true witness" in Jer 42.5, Ps 88.38 LXX, which is applied to Jesus twice in Rev 3.14, 19.11).

(7) The Enochic Son of Man and exalted Jesus are preexistent figures (*1 En.* 48.1–6; 62.7–8; Rev 3.14; 13.8).

(8) The Enochic Son of Man is likened to an angel (*1 En.* 46.1) and becomes an angel (*1 En.* 71.11), while the exalted Jesus is an angelomorphic figure (Rev 1.12–16).

(9) The Enochic Son of Man and exalted Jesus are both opposed to rebellious angels, idolatry, and arrogant kings.

Thus, the portrayal of the Son of Man/Chosen One in the *Parables of Enoch* places us "one step away from the formulation of early Christian speculation about Jesus of Nazareth,"[472] with the result that Enoch is "quite probably the most exalted heavenly mediator to be encountered in the Judaism of the Second Temple period apart, that is, from Jesus the Messiah of early Christianity."[473]

Be that as it may, there are some differences between the Enochic Son of Man and the exalted Jesus of John the Seer that stand out.

(1) The Enochic Son of Man is a heavenly counterpart to arrogant kings and their thrones of glory (*1 En.* 63.7), whereas the exalted Jesus is not a heavenly counterpart to the imperial cult.

(2) The worship of the Enochic Son of Man takes place on earth, while the worship of the exalted Jesus transpires in heaven.

(3) The Enochic Son of Man is consistently subordinated to God, whereas Jesus is subordinated in his angelic roles, but coordinate with God in other places (e.g., Rev 1.8; 21.6; 22.13). Whereas the Enoch Son of Man acts in the name of the Lord of Spirits (*1 En.* 48.7; 55.4; 61.13), Jesus does not act in God's name; moreover, Jesus commissions others to act for the sake of his name (Rev 2.3, 13; 3.8).

(4) The Enochic Son of Man's role is primarily judicial and secondarily salvific, whereas the exalted Jesus' roles are primarily salvific and secondarily judicial (Rev 19.11 is the only passage that explicitly speaks of judgment by the exalted Jesus, although it is arguably implied in

---

[472] George W. E. Nickelsburg, *Ancient Judaism and Christian Origins: Diversity, Continuity, and Transformation* (Minneapolis: Fortress, 2003), 107.

[473] Darrell Hannah, "The Elect Son of Man of the Parables of Enoch," in *"Who Is This Son of Man?": The Latest Scholarship on a Puzzling Expression of the Historical Jesus*, ed. Larry W. Hurtado and Paul L. Owen (LNTS 390; London: T&T Clark, 2011), 130.

Rev 14.14–16 depending on who the son of man with the crown and sickle is identified as).

(5) The Enochic Son of Man has no role in creation, whereas the exalted Jesus is considered the "beginning" of creation (Rev 3.14).

(6) The Enochic Son of Man does not command or send angels (Rev 2–3).

(7) The Enochic Son of Man does not enable creaturely participation in divine rule as the exalted Jesus does (Rev 1.6; 3.21; 5.10; 20.4–6; 22.5).[474]

(8) The human life of the Enochic Son of Man is immaterial in the narrative, yet crucial for the story of the exalted Jesus (Rev 1.5–7, 17–18; 5.9).

(9) The Enochic Son of Man's enthronement is projected into an eschatological future, whereas the exalted Jesus is enthroned as the reward for his sacrificial death.

(10) The Enochic Son of Man, unlike the exalted Jesus, is not worshipped by angels or creation (Rev 5.9–14).[475] The Son of Man does not receive hymnody, but the exalted Jesus does (Rev 5.9–14; 15.3–4), as does the Lord of Spirits (*1 En.* 48.5; 61.9–13) and Lord Almighty (Rev 4.8).

(11) The Enochic Son of Man joins the orders of angels in blessing and exalting the Lord of Spirits (*1 En.* 61.10–11), whereas the exalted Jesus never worships God.

(12) The Lord of Spirits and the Son of Man never share a throne, while in Revelation God and Jesus do (Rev. 3.21; 7.10, 17; 22.1–3).

---

[474] The participation of humans in divine rule is arguably a part of the democratization of the theocratic messianism in Dan 7.18, 27 and developed into 4Q174 3.18–19, 4Q246 2.1–10, and 4Q521 II 2.7.

[475] There is an ambiguity in *1 En.* 61.7 as to whether it is the Lord of Spirits or the Chosen One who is worshipped by the inhabitants of heaven. Nickelsburg and VanderKam (*1 Enoch*, 250) note: "It is uncertain to whom they are directing their multifaceted praise. One naturally thinks of the deity, who is explicitly the object of these verbs in vv. 9, 11–12, as well as in chap. 39. Dillmann suggests that the emphatic position of 'that one' hardly points to the deity, who is the natural object of such praise. He proposes, instead, that his praise is directed to the Chosen One, who, according to the very next verse, will be seated on the throne of God's glory and receive divine status and prerogatives. The suggestion is plausible in light of 62:6–7, where the kings and the mighty 'bless, glorify, and exalt' the Son of Man." I am grateful to Theron Clay Mock ("'New Testament Christology': A Critique of Larry Hurtado's Influence," unpublished paper presented at the Redescribing Christian Origins Seminar, Society of Biblical Literature [San Antonio, Tex., November 21, 2021], 51–52) for drawing my attention to this passage.

I surmise that the divine status and worship of the Enochic Son of Man is *more than* the Philadelphian Jews bowing down before the Philadelphian Christians in Rev 3.21 (contra Hurtado), but is *less than* the divine worship offered to the Lamb in Rev 5.9–14 (contra Bauckham).[476] Several factors contribute to a distinction in the status and worship of the two figures when put in juxtaposition.

To begin with, the Enochic Son of Man has a superlative status over the kings and inhabitants of the earth, but an ambiguous status in relation to the archangels. We do not know if he is higher or lower than Michael or Gabriel. The Son of Man appears to operate in a parallel jurisdiction to archangels, as neither among them nor above them. The Enochic Son of Man is principally a judge of angels (*1 En.* 55.4) and a heavenly plenipotentiary over earthly kings (*1 En.* 48.8; 53.5–7; 55.4), but his position in the heavenly hierarchy is unclear. In contrast, the exalted Jesus receives the worship of angels and angels do his bidding. The exalted Jesus overlaps somewhat with Michael, but Michael on the whole remains a peripheral character compared to Jesus in the apocalyptic saga that unfolds.

In addition, it appears that the worship scene in *1 En.* 48.1–9 is based on an interpretation of Isa 49, albeit spliced with the throne imagery of Dan 7.9–14. The Enochic Son of Man will be the "light of the nations" (*1 En.* 48.4), which is a clear allusion to Isa 49.6. Thereafter, the prostration of all the people of the earth before the Son of Man (*1 En.* 48.5) is reminiscent of the prostration of kings before the Isaianic servant: "Thus says the Lord, the Redeemer of Israel and his Holy One, to one deeply despised, abhorred by the nations, the slave of rulers, 'Kings shall see and stand up, princes, and they shall prostrate themselves, because of the Lord, who is faithful, the Holy One of Israel, who has chosen you'" (Isa 49.7). I submit that the Enochic Son of Man on the throne of glory marries together Isaiah's imagery of the prostration of kings before the Servant/Israel (Isa 45.14; 49.7, 23; 60.14) with Daniel's vision of one like a Son of Man receiving dominion, glory, and kingship (Dan 7.13–14) to indicate the vindication and sovereignty of God's people against the wicked kings of the earth.

It must be asked if the Enochic Son of Man's throne of glory is truly identical with the Lord of Spirit's throne of glory. There is a difference between God's "throne of glory" (Jer 14.21; 17.12; Wis 9.10; *4 Ezra* 8.21; *T. Levi* 5.1; 4Q405 XXIII 1.3; 11Q17 10.7; *1 En.* 9.4) and a "seat of honor" (1 Sam 2.8; Isa 22.23; Sir 7.4; 47.11; Luke 11.43), such as David's glorious

---

[476] We might say that the Enochic Son of Man receives either "obeisance premium" or "bronze-level divine worship." This is fairly close to what Richard Bauckham has argued in a forthcoming volume nominally titled *The Son of Man: Enoch and Jesus* (Grand Rapids: Eerdmans, forthcoming).

throne (Sir 47.11), the chair of privilege that Job enjoyed before his tragedy (*T. Job* 32–33), the throne promised to the descendants of Levi, who choose the path of wisdom (1Q21 F 14; 4Q213 I 1.19), and the "thrones of glory" promised to Christian martyrs in heaven (*Apoc. El.* 4.28; Rev 20.4). The postmortem Adam has a heavenly throne amid glory in heaven, but in no sense does it represent or compete with the divine throne (*T. Ab.* 11.5–12 [A]; *Apoc. Mos.* 39.2–3). Abel in heaven too has a terrifying throne with a resplendent appearance and renders judgments with angelic assistants (*T. Ab.* 12–13 [A]), but even his judgment is preliminary to a judgment by the tribes of Israel and by the Lord God (*T. Ab.* 13.4–8 [A]). It is because of the doxological disparity between God and others that Enoch/Metatron's throne in *3 Enoch* is said to be "a throne like the throne of glory" (*3 En.* 10.1). In rabbinic literature, it was inconceivable for the *kisse kabod* to be anything other than God's exclusive and unapproachable throne.[477] The same questions, of course, can be applied to descriptions of the exalted Jesus, especially when identified as the Son of Man with a glorious throne (see Matt 19.28; 25.31; Rev 3.21; 7.17; 22.3; *Apoc. Pet.* 6.1).

The worships of the Enochic Son of Man and the exalted Jesus may be no more than honorific homage offered to a messianic prince (1QSb 5.28; 4Q246 2.1) or to a supreme heavenly being like the veneration given to exalted patriarchs and angels (e.g., Tob 11.14; *LAE* 12–16; *Ezek. Trag.* 68–89; 4Q491c 5–6). God is honored by the honoring of his messiah, as his messiah, not as the high God. Perhaps in both cases the messianic worship is worship, but not divine worship—veneration of a penultimate and plenipotentiary figure, not the worship of God in his god-ness.[478] Alternatively, we may have in the accounts of the exalted Jesus and the Enochic Son of Man two examples in Jewish literature of a heavenly figure given unprecedented divine status and cultic worship.[479] Either way, the key differences are that the descriptions of Jesus bristle with divine filiality, functions, and form. The Enochic Son of Man does not share a throne with the Lord of Spirits as the exalted Jesus clearly does with the Lord Almighty. The exalted Jesus does not act in the name of the Lord, but others act for the sake of his name. The Seer's exalted Jesus participates more fully in God's absolute sovereignty insofar as he is associated with the origins of creation, the divine plan centers upon him, he is superior to angels, and there are more intertextual and intratextual associations between God and Jesus. Plus,

---

[477] Darrell D. Hannah, "The Throne of His Glory: The Divine Throne and Heavenly Mediators in Revelation and the Similitudes of Enoch," *ZNW* 94 (2003): 83.

[478] Mock, "'New Testament Christology,'" 65–66.

[479] See Bühner, *Messianic High Christology*, 123–42.

the worship of the Lamb is, to reiterate, far more than obeisance modeled on Isa 49.7 as it involves veneration by angels and creation.

Early patterns of Christian devotion may have venerated Jesus with a status more than or less than the Enochic Son of Man. Each liturgical episode needs to be compared in its own right. In the case of the book of Revelation, while the status and worship ascribed to Jesus undoubtedly mirrors the throne-sharing and judicial function of the Enochic Son of Man, it also exceeds it by making a closer and more coordinate connection between God Almighty and the Lamb in realm of creation, type of worship, and agency in deliverance. Whereas the Enochic Son of Man functionally *overlaps* with the Lord of Spirits, the Seer's exalted Jesus is *identified* with the Lord God's being as creator, ruler, and redeemer.[480]

(7) Conclusion.

Exalted patriarchs are important figures in Jewish and Christian texts. In the case of Adam and Enoch, we have two figures who are presented with a mixture of heavenly origins, heavenly translation, and heavenly worship by some authors. Yet, based on the preceding discussion, it is hard to detect in *LAE* 12–16 a true parallel between the worship of the divine image in Adam by angels with the patterns of Christ devotion that characterized early Christianity. That is because Adam is not treated as a divine being; rather, he is a fleshly icon of the divine image. Angels worship through him—not really to him, and angels express their subservience to him as heavenly servants of humanity. Even the Adamic motifs in Paul's Christology, though prominent at certain points, are quite muted. The Adamic elements in Paul's epistles are fairly mundane and present Jesus at most as the form of the preexistent Adam (Phil 2.6), the new Adam (1 Cor 15.22; Rom 5.12), and the eschatological Adam (1 Cor 15.45), but nothing like a deified Adam or deified as Adam.

The Enochic Son of Man of the parables is by far the most salient intermediary figure who can be paired with John the Seer's exalted Jesus. The two figures exhibit various parallels that demonstrate the exaltation and veneration of an intermediary figure beside God without ostensibly abandoning Jewish monotheism. This marks either two independent intermediary traditions in first-century Jewish sectarianism, or else, raises the prospect of a genetic relationship between Enochic and Jesuanic traditions in the first century. That said, I am also convinced that the Jesus of the book of Revelation exceeds the scale of divinity attributed to the Enochic Son of Man since the exalted Jesus more than overlaps with God's functions but is intensely identified with God.

[480] Bauckham, *Jesus and the God of Israel*, 232; and Fletcher-Louis, *Jesus Monotheism*, 1:185.

Ancient Ruler Cults

A further domain of comparison between early Christologies and their religious surroundings pertains to that of ancient ruler cults, especially the imperial cult. It can scarcely go unnoticed that hailing Jesus as Israel's anointed king—who is co-enthroned with God the Father, who is acclaimed as *theos*, *kyrios*, and *sōtēr*, who can be portrayed as high priest of a heavenly empire, who demands *pistis* of his followers, and who issues manifold blessings and benefactions to his subjects—has an uncanny resemblance to Near Eastern, Hellenistic, and Roman rulers and their pluriform cults. In an Oxyrhynchus papyrus fragment from Egypt or on an inscription on the side of a temple in Pergamum, one could easily scratch out the name "Caesar" and replace it with "Christ" in the divine accolades given to the emperor, and it would sound like ordinary christological discourse. Jesus was perhaps considered, imagined, or made divine in the same manner as the Seleucid ruler Antiochus IV, who was a divine *epiphaneia* (appearance), with a *theopatoros* (divine origin), and carried the divine *eikōn* (image); or like the deified Augustus with a string of temples, priesthoods, sacrifices, and associations in his honor; or the Sasanian *Shahanshah* Shapur I, who was the king of the kings of the Iranian plateau, and inscriptions told of his celestial origins and sonship from the divine king Papak—in which case, early Christology might simply be a Jewish messianic appropriation of the rhetoric and rituals of ancient ruler cults. Singing hymns to Christ as a god would not be much different from hymns sung to Augustus as equal to the Olympian deities, and confession of Jesus as lord is effectively the same as professing Nero as lord of the whole world.

The first programmatic comparison between early Christology and the Roman imperial cult was by Ernst Lohmeyer.[481] For Lohmeyer, the Roman imperial cult did not directly influence the Christ cult; rather, the imperial cult and Christ cult emerged from the same conceptual world. It was only in the post-apostolic age that there emerged "direct mutual influence" and "irreconcilable hostility" between the two cults. Christians like John the Seer pillaged imperial images and honors to underscore the ultimacy and supremacy of Jesus Christ. As a result, in the contest between the rival *kyrioi*, Jesus was later transformed by authors into the fulfilment of pagan longing for ultimate life and divine destiny. Then, with no disguise to his anti-Catholic polemics, Lohmeyer concluded that the real influence of the imperial cult comes when the Roman catholic church inherited and inhabited the administrative apparatus of the

---

[481] Lohmeyer, *Christuskult und Kaiserkult*.

empire and made Rome the epicenter of a world religion.[482] Martin Hengel did not envisage any initial influence of ruler cults on Christology, regarding it as "at best a negative stimulus, not a model" for Christology.[483] Similarly, Larry Hurtado was disinclined to detect influence from ruler cults on early Christology because, first, the "conviction that Jesus had been exalted to heavenly status and power arose among pious Jews, people not easily disposed to accepting the idea of the deification of humans." Second, Jesus' exaltation is of an altogether different character from pagan notions of apotheosis. Jesus is not portrayed as another god with a cultus of his own; rather, he aligned beside and associated with the one God of Israel.[484]

Others, however, are more sympathetic to a parallel and influence from ruler cults on early Christology. According to Wilhelm Bousset, Hellenistic Christianity in Antioch broke free from the constraint of Old Testament monotheism by its deification and cultic veneration of the Son. Irrespective of whether the mode of divinity was adoptionistic or pneumatic, Jesus was now the *kyrios* in the new cultus, which finds its closest parallel with ruler cults. Even so, Bousset acknowledged that it would be mistaken and hasty to posit a direct influence from the cult of the Caesars on the cult of Christ because *kyrios* language belongs in the broad Greek and Near Eastern setting of which the ruler cults were but one expression.[485]

William Horbury detected in the Israelite royal ideology of divine kingship and Jewish messianism ample precedents for early Christology.[486] The fact that psalms and hymns were addressed to Christ from apostolic times was a sure sign the Christ devotion was a "cult," given the practice of singing to and about a ruler-as-deity. The Christ cult began as a species of Jewish royal ideology since Israel's king was regarded as an object of pagan obeisance (Ps 2.12; 72.11), preexistent (Ps 109.3 [LXX]), and an angelic figure (Isa 9.5 LXX),

---

[482] Lohmeyer, *Christuskult und Kaiserkult*, 35–39: "direkten gegenseitigen Einwirkung" and "unversöhnliche Feindschaft" (38).

[483] Hengel, *Son of God*, 30.

[484] Hurtado, *One God, One Lord*, 102–3, 143–49.

[485] Bousset, *Kyrios Christos*, 138–52, 310–34.

[486] Horbury, *Jewish Messianism*; idem, *Messianism among Jews and Christians: Twelve Biblical and Historical Studies* (London: T&T Clark, 2003); idem, "Jewish and Christian Monotheism in the Herodian Age," in *Early Jewish and Christian Monotheism*, ed. Loren T. Stuckenbruck and Wendy E. S. North (London: T&T Clark, 2004), 15–44; idem, "Jewish Messianism and Early Christology," in *Contours of Christology in the New Testament*, ed. Richard N. Longenecker (Grand Rapids: Eerdmans, 2005), 3–24; and idem, review of *Lord Jesus Christ: Devotion to Jesus in Earliest Christianity*, by Larry W. Hurtado, *JTS* 56 (2005): 531–39.

who was supplemented with further heavenly power and divine prerogatives in later literature, even appearing with theophanic qualities (*1 En.* 52.6; *4 Ezra* 13.3–4). Hasmonean and Herodian rulers were afforded honorific language that edged into divine qualities, similar to that used during the Ptolemaic and Seleucid periods. According to Horbury: "The earliest Christian praise can then be located, despite its special features, within a continuum of Jewish praise which is related to contemporary ruler-cult and includes the theme of obeisance, *proskynesis*," and "Homage to the messiah was important in a Jewish messianism which formed a counterpart to gentile ruler-cult."[487]

Adela Collins also roots early Christology and the worship of Jesus in Jewish messianism and ancient ruler cults.[488] The Hebrew Bible and Septuagint implied the divinity of the ideal king, while the Dead Sea Scrolls and apocalyptic texts like *1 En.* 37–71 and *4 Ezra* implied the functional divinity of the Messiah. Given the presence of the Greco-Roman culture and religion in Palestine, including the imperial cult, Collins asserts that we "should take seriously the likelihood that non-Jewish Hellenistic and Roman traditions, as well as Jewish traditions, shaped the religious experiences, ideas and writings of especially the Greek-speaking Jewish followers of Jesus in the period immediately following his death."[489] As such, "The idea of the divinity of Christ, in a limited sense, did emerge early and have important precedents in biblical and Jewish traditions. But the successive reformulations and elaborations of this idea, and probably the earliest expression of it as well, surely owed a great deal to interaction with the influence of non-Jewish Greek and Roman ideas and practices, not least among them ruler-cults and imperial-cults."[490]

According to Ruben Bühner, Hellenistic ruler cults are the significant historical context in which the messianic discourses of early Judaism, with the notions of divine begetting and divine sonship, were applied to the eschatological figures. Irrespective of whatever derivation of these motifs had with ancient Egyptian and Israelite royal ideology, Jewish messianic discourse

---

[487] Horbury, *Jewish Messianism*, 127, 150.
[488] Adela Yarbro Collins, "The Worship of Jesus and the Imperial Cult," in *The Jewish Roots of Christological Monotheism: Papers from the St. Andrews Conference on the Historical Origins of the Worship of Jesus*, ed. Carey C. Newman, James R. Davila, and Gladys S. Lewis (JSJSup 63; Leiden: Brill, 1999), 234–57; idem, "Psalms, Philippians 2:6–11, and the Origins of Christology," *BibInt* 11 (2002): 361–72; and idem, "'How on Earth Did Jesus Become a God?': A Reply," in *Israel's God and Rebecca's Children: Christology and Community in Early Judaism and Christianity*, ed. David B. Capes, April D. DeConick, Helen K. Bond, and Troy A. Miller (Waco, Tex.: Baylor University Press, 2007), 55–66.
[489] Collins, "Worship of Jesus and the Imperial Cult," 242.
[490] Collins, "How on Earth," 66.

is only comprehensible in the historical context of Hellenistic ruler cults. Descriptions of the royal "Son of God" in various Jewish texts evidence the same dramatic synthesis of myth and metaphor that is detectable in Hellenistic ruler cults.[491]

Fletcher-Louis takes a mediating position, agreeing with Horbury that there were Jews in the Greco-Roman era who applied the divine honorific praise to human beings such as rulers and emperors. Furthermore, Christians inherited this tradition and utilized it themselves, particularly in their portrayal of Jesus as the true emperor, yielding a kind of "imperial Christology." But he agrees with Hurtado that the pattern of devotion that the early Christians applied to Jesus was more than obeisance, and he agrees with Bauckham that Jesus was fully included in the divine identity; both aspects were without precedent in the material examined by Horbury. According to Fletcher-Louis, the first Christians did not venerate or identify Jesus as a man with a godlike benefaction over them; rather, Jesus was more properly identified with and worshipped beside the one God who created the world. Jesus belonged to the divine orbit of Yahweh-Kyrios, within a divine identity, not on the plane of humans elevated to divine status.[492]

There is not any substantial debate about the relevance of ancient ruler cults for early Christology. The debate is whether that relevance pertains to influence, confluence, or polemic. If there was influence, then the issue is whether the primary drive was the Jewish tradition of ruler veneration or pagan expressions of imperial worship. We are asking, in effect, what do the *theotēs Sebastoi* ("divine emperors") have to do with the Lord Jesus Christ?

(1) Greco-Roman ruler cults.

According to Michael Peppard:

> I would argue that, of the gods in the Roman pantheon at the time of Jesus and his followers, the emperor is the most relevant for the study of early Christology more than Jupiter, more than Asclepius, more than Isis. Beyond the resonances of christological and imperial titles and the fact that the emperor was clearly acclaimed as a god while a living man, we can dwell on the utter ubiquity of the imperial presence and its diversity of expression. Imperial theology was manifest in the following ways: coins, temples, processions, statues, standards, milestones, priesthoods, sacrifices, compital altars, household shrines, battlefield rituals, legal proceedings, mealtime libations, feast days, birthdays, auspices,

---

[491] Bühner, *Hohe Messianologie*, 320–22, 330.
[492] Fletcher-Louis, *Jesus Monotheism*, 1:206–49.

augury, omens, games, eclogues, poetry, panegyric hymns, the job title of *sebastologos*, the retelling of oral stories about the emperor's mighty deeds and miracles, the papyri that record scripts for the divine election and liturgical acclamation of new emperors, and more. These are the things that Adolf Deissmann over a century ago encountered all over classical sources, which generated the research for his magnum opus *Licht vom Osten*. About the ubiquity of imperial ideology and emperor worship, Deissmann argued that the earliest Christians were not "going through the world with eyes closed, unaffected by what was moving hearts and minds in large cities at that time."[493]

Peppard is correct: imperial culture, cult, and consciousness inundated the agoras, shops, shrines, assemblies, and temples of antiquity—and the relevance for Christology cannot be understated, although how that relevance works out in terms of the origins of Christology and literary depictions of Christ are points of contention. Precisely why, we must ascertain: what do the *Christos* and *Sebastos* have in common and what separates them? In a previous chapter I offered a brief description of ancient ruler cults and their gradual evolution within the Roman empire. I also observed in a previous chapter that ruler cults were primarily a matter of euergetic divinity, honorific rather than ontological, depicting a human who had reached the triumphal precipice of human achievement, honor, and benefaction, albeit still situated below the rank of eternal and unbegotten deities. However, even then, there were tacit efforts to give ontological justification to the attribution of extraordinary divine honors, apotheosis being an obvious example, so that the subject of veneration was imagined as having changed physical form into an astral entity. Moving forward, I will sketch out relevant aspects of the imperial cults that can be contrasted and compared with early Christology.

(a) Hellenistic ruler cults.

Alexander the Great appears to have pursued greatness by his conquest to make himself greater than his father, Philip II, who was considered "equal to the gods" (*isotheoi*) by Greeks in Asia, and on par with his heroes Herakles and Achilles. When Alexander achieved this status, it seems that he was either presented with or courted his deification, perhaps under Egyptian influence after visiting the oracle of Ammon in the Egyptian desert, where he was allegedly greeted as the son of the god Ammon Re (whom the Greeks identified with

---

[493] Michael Peppard, "Son of God in Gentile Contexts," in *Son of God: Divine Sonship in Jewish and Christian Antiquity*, ed. Garrick V. Allen, Kai Akagi, Paul Sloan, and Madhavi Nevader (University Park, Penn.: Eisenbrauns, 2019), 143.

Zeus). Alexander consequently required those around him to venerate him as a god, and he controversially introduced the "barbarian" custom of prostration.[494] This was revolutionary because Macedonian kingship was not a divine institution; it was legitimated by the nobility and the populace, and it was not a divinely given office nor honored as a divine status, except outside of Macedon. In Greek culture of the fifth to fourth centuries, Greek heroes were honored as gods, and Greek generals such as the Spartan Lysander could be voted divine honors (Plutarch, *Lys.* 18.4). But neither Macedon nor Greece had a ruler cult approximate to Egypt or performed the type of rituals as were practiced at the Achaemenid court. Alexander's demand for prostration was accordingly contested as alien, impious, and self-aggrandizing, but it was nonetheless obeyed (see Plutarch, *Alex.* 54.1–55.1).

Alexander's demand for prostration was more than an effort to unify the Macedonian, Egyptian, and Persian realms with a shared religious devotion. It was more than "When in Persia, prostrate; when in Bactria, bow." Alexander introduced the custom because he wanted his Macedonian, Greek, Asian, Egyptian, and Persian subjects to regard him as truly divine, precisely what he had been claiming since his visit to the oracle of Ammon in Egypt. By the time Alexander reached India and up to his death, he began to cultivate—to a disputed degree, it should be said[495]—a cult complete with coinage, altars, statues, shrines, offerings, sacrifices, and a priesthood (Arrian, *Ann.* 4.10–12; 7.23.2; Plutarch, *Alex.* 27.8–28.6; 33.1; 74.2–3; Aelian, *Var. hist.* 2.19). Alexander cultivated the view of himself as the Pharaoh Amen-Ra, the son of Zeus, and Persian bearer of sacred fire. After his death, the cult of Alexander was centered in Alexandria; it persisted well into the Roman period, and undoubtedly influenced emperors from Augustus to Trajan.[496]

Ruler worship continued among the *Diadochi* (i.e., successors of Alexander) and their descendants, especially among the Ptolemaic and Seleucid dynasties, both of whom wrestled for control of Palestine over the next two centuries.

When Ptolemy I lifted the siege of Rhodes in 304 BCE, the citizens sent a delegation to the Ammonite priests of Siwah to inquire whether Ptolemy I should

---

[494] Cf. E. Badian, "Alexander the Great between Two Thrones and Heaven: Variations on an Old Theme," in *Subject and Ruler: The Cult of the Ruling Power in Classical Antiquity* (Ann Arbor: University of Michigan Press, 1996), 21–22.

[495] Cf. Joseph D. Fantin, *The Lord of the Entire World: Lord Jesus, a Challenge to Lord Caesar?* (NTM 31; Sheffield: Sheffield Phoenix, 2011), 104–5; and Badian, "Alexander the Great," 25–26.

[496] Cf. Fantin (*Lord of the Entire World*, 105): "It is with Alexander, whether while alive or after his death, that large-scale official ruler worship became part of the religious landscape of the part of the ancient world that would influence Roman emperor worship."

be honored as a god. The answer was affirmative, of course, and the title *Sōtēr* ("Savior") was granted to him and a shrine erected in his honor. Later, the island of Delos conferred on Ptolemy I the status of *isotheoi timai*, honors equal to the gods.[497] As things evolved, divine honors did not require great acts of liberation or conquest; instead, cultic honors were paid to the Egyptian king qua king, irrespective of any accomplishment, so that divinity was a characteristic of absolute monarchy.[498] The Alexandrian librarian Callimachus composed a *Hymn to Zeus*, which was also a veiled eulogy to Ptolemy II. Zeus' accession to the throne arose not by chance but by deeds of strength that are laid beside his throne. Zeus begat kings, and nothing is diviner than the kings of Zeus. Zeus bestowed greatness and riches on kings, but not equally, as Ptolemy II is a prime example of one who exceeded other kings (*Hymn. Jov.* 54–89). The hymn made the accession of Zeus a mythological topos for the accession of Ptolemy II and served to buttress the divine legitimacy of Ptolemy II.[499] As the Ptolemaic period progressed, Egyptian religion and Pharoanic devotion were merged with Hellenistic traditions in the religionizing of the Ptolemaic monarchs. The Ptolemies could be represented as Egyptian gods and have their statues erected in Egyptian temples, making them *synnaoi* ("temple-sharers") with the gods. By the late third century BCE an Egyptian festival to the *Theoi Euergetai* ("Divine Benefactors") had been established as well.[500] The Ptolemaic kings were given titles such as *Sōtēr* and *Epiphanes*; regarded as the image or son of Horus, the sun, or Isis and Osiris; associated with Zeus on coinage; and assimilated to gods like Dionysus. These identifications rested partly on the benefactions of kingship, partly from the place of Pharaoh in Egyptian religion, and partly in imitation of the cult of Alexander.

Among the Seleucids too, from Asia to Bactria, the monarch received divine honors and cultic worship. After his death, Seleukos I was worshipped as "Zeus Nikator." Following that, cultic worship of the Seleucid king began, and ruler worship was closely associated with the deities Zeus and Apollo.[501] Whereas Ptolemaic Egypt was a relatively homogenous realm with a single administration, the Seleucid empire was an amalgamation of heterogenous satrapies encompassing various ethnic groups and religions. It is therefore not surprising that Seleucid rulers sought to unify their diverse subjects by a ruler

---

[497] Collins and Collins, *King and Messiah*, 50.
[498] Duncan Fishwick, *The Imperial Cult in the Latin West* (3 vols.; Leiden: Brill, 1987–2004), 1:1.13.
[499] Gordley, *Teaching through Song*, 15–18.
[500] Günther Hölbl, *A History of Ptolemaic Empire* (London: Routledge, 2001), 105–12.
[501] Helmut Koester, *Introduction to the New Testament* (2 vols.; Berlin: de Gruyter, 1982–1987), 1:38–39.

cult. Antiochus I set up on the summit of Nemrud Dag a monument that heralded him as "The Great King Antiochos, the God, the Righteous One, the Divine Manifestation, Friend of the Romans, Friend of the Greeks, the Son of King Mithridates Kallinikos and of Laodike, the Brother-loving Goddess, the Daughter of King Antiochos Epiphanes, the Mother-loving, the Victorious." He wished his personal tomb to honor Persian and Greek customs even as he claims that his soul will soon be seated above the highest gods:

> I have taken forethought to lay the foundation of this sacred tomb, which is to be indestructible by the ravages of time, in closest proximity to the heavenly throne, wherein the fortunately preserved outer form of my person, preserved to ripe old age, shall, after the soul beloved by God has been sent to the heavenly thrones of Zeus Oromasdes, rest through immeasurable time, so I chose to make this holy place a common consecrated seat of all the gods; so that not only the heroic company of my ancestors, whom you behold before you, might be set up here by my pious devotion, but also that the divine representation of the manifest deities might be consecrated on the holy hill and that his place might likewise not be lacking in witness to my piety.

Antiochus I further claimed, "[I am to be] co-enthroned likewise among the deities who hear our prayers, I have consecrated the features of my own form, and have caused the ancient honor of great deities to become the coequal with a new Tyche." He endowed the temple with sufficient financial resources for "an unceasing cult and chosen priests arrayed in such vestments as are proper to the race of the Persians have I inaugurated, and I have dedicated the whole array and cult in a manner worthy of my fortune and the majesty of the gods."[502] Antiochus III issued an edict in 193–94 BCE that required a cult for the queen as well as the king and mandated its mention on all official documents (*OGIS* 224). The divine rhetoric was ratcheted up by Antiochus IV, who adopted the name *theos epiphanēs* ("appearance of a god"); though derided at the time—Polybius (26.1a) calls him *epimanēs* for "lunatic"—the name became standard thereafter for Seleucid rulers.[503]

(b) Roman imperial cults.

Roman ruler worship had precedents in hero cults that honored great figures, men as well as women, usually after their deaths, including warriors, healers,

---

[502] CIRM 32—Inscriptions on Throne-Backs, Nemrud Dag, https://www.tertullian.org/rpearse/mithras/display.php?page=cimrm32, accessed July 31, 2021.

[503] Fishwick, *Imperial Cult*, 1:1.16–17.

poets, city founders, even mythic figures like Herakles.[504] Romulus, the legendary founder of Rome, had his own hero cult, which was later married to the story of his deification (Livy, *Ab urbe cond.* 1.16; Cicero, *Nat. d.* 2.62). The Romulan narrative, plus escalating honors given to Roman generals in Italy and proconsuls in Asia, provide something of a *praeparatio* for the cult of the princeps. Nonetheless, ruler worship was primarily an eastern phenomenon based on Hellenistic ruler cults that were introduced into Roman civic religion with some resistance—so much so that divine honors for emperors received deliberate cultivation as well as careful moderation.

In the late republic, the Romans gradually began to apply divine honors to revered leaders such as Marius, Sulla, and especially to Julius Caesar. However, it was during the Augustan period that the imperial cult began to make strides as the civic religion of the empire. The introduction of the imperial cult in Rome was not without complications. Rome was supposed to have no king; thus, to worship one man as a deified king could prompt sneers and invite critique. There was also the danger of neglecting the traditional gods at the expense of the various cults and deities filtering in from the east. Accordingly, the imperial cult had to be wisely cultivated as well as politically managed, especially in Italy. Yet by the first century the various imperial cults (i.e., the diverse forms of veneration of living and deceased emperors), were among the most significant aspects of the Mediterranean religious landscape.

The Roman imperial cults included worship of deceased emperors and varying veneration of the living emperor.[505] Here it is useful to dispel older assumptions about the imperial cult.

First, we need to remember that the imperial cult was neither flattery nor pious pretense. The emperors, deceased and living, were real gods, real within the symbolic universe of the Roman imperium. The *divi* were a real source of benefaction and salvation and thus real gods for those who paid them homage.[506] The

---

[504] Cf. S. R. F. Price, *Rituals and Power: The Roman Imperial Cult in Asia Minor* (Cambridge: Cambridge University Press, 1984), 32–40.

[505] The various venerations of the emperor, often outside explicitly cultic acts, mean that the imperial cult needs to be either situated within a wider phenomenon of imperial ideology, or else, imperial cults need to be defined more broadly. See Christoph Heilig, *Hidden Criticism? The Methodology and Plausibility of the Search for a Counter-Imperial Subtext in Paul* (Minneapolis: Fortress, 2017), 81–82.

[506] Cf. Gradel, *Emperor Worship*, 270; Michael Peppard, *The Son of God in the Roman World: Divine Sonship in Its Social and Political Context* (Oxford: Oxford University Press, 2012), 35, 43–44; Fantin, *Lord of the Entire World*, 121; Horbury, *Jewish Messianism*, 69; Price, *Rituals and Power*, 15–19; and Stephen Mitchell, *Anatolia: Land, Men and Gods in Asia Minor* (2 vols.; Oxford: Clarendon, 1993), 1:103, 117.

emperor was a *praesens deus*, a god who was tangible, accessible, and present, as opposed to aloof, distant, or transcendent. "If divinity is revealed through effective presence and power," so argues Johnson, "then those who exercise imperial rule over the entire *oikoumenē* are truly *theoi phenomenoi* ('visible gods')."[507] We see this in a hymn honoring the Antigonid king Demetrius Poliorcetes in Athens at the end of the fourth century that even denigrates other gods in comparison to himself: "Welcome son of god, mightiest Poseidon, and of Aphrodite. The other gods are far away or do not have ears or do not exist or do not pay attention at all to us, but you we see present, not of wood or stone but real."[508] Notwithstanding the differences between Hellenistic ruler cults and the Roman imperial cults, the similarity is that the emperor was a divine power accessible in person and beneficial in practice. If religion is a response to disorder and chaos, then the emperor and his cult embodied law, life, peace, and prosperity.

After the turmoil of the first century BCE,[509] Augustus appeared to be "a savior who put an end to war and established all things," even a "god" whose advent "marked for the world the beginning of good tidings" (Priene Inscription). An elite woman in Cyzicus became an imperial priestess known for "displaying piety in all matters to the eternal house of Tiberius Sebastos Caesar the greatest of the gods and to his immortal rule" (*IGRR* 4.144).[510] Devotion to the emperor was devotion to the society he had created and from which people—obviously in variegated degrees—benefited.[511] To neglect, attack, or blaspheme the emperor was tantamount to an attack on the only force holding the powers of chaos and death at bay. Proof for the intensity of religious devotion to the emperor was the oft-zealous religious fervor that accompanied the veneration of the Roman emperor to the point that failure to worship the emperor could unleash state-sponsored and mob acts of fanatical violence, as the nascent Christian movement learned.[512]

---

[507] Luke Timothy Johnson, *Among the Gentiles: Greco-Roman Religion and Christianity* (New Haven, Conn.: Yale University Press, 2009), 37.

[508] *Mitteilungen des Deutschen Archäologischen Instituts. Athenische Abteilung* (De Gruyter), 6.253c–f, cited in Price, *Rituals and Power*, 38.

[509] One has to think of the situation at the end of the late first century BCE, when there had been economic exploitation in Asia by the *publicani*, the Mithridatic insurgency, a Parthian incursion into Syria and Judea, and four Roman civil wars (Marius vs. Sulla; Julius Caesar vs. Pompey; Octavian, Antony, and Lepidus vs. Brutus and Cassius; and Octavian vs. Anthony and Cleopatra).

[510] Cited from Price, *Rituals and Power*, 63–64.

[511] Karl Galinsky, "Continuity and Change: Religion in the Augustan Semi-century," in *A Companion to Roman Religion*, ed. Jörg Rüpke (Chichester, U.K.: Blackwell, 2007), 74, 80–81.

[512] Lohmeyer, *Christuskult und Kaiserkult*, 203.

Second, the imperial cults were not monolithic as they had various modes of expression, many outside the realm we would normally call "religion." The imperial cult's presence was felt in the sphere of individuals, provinces, cities, towns, temples, associations, the bureaucracy, and the military.[513] One can find inscriptions celebrating the birth and accession of the emperor, listing his various benefactions, and noting the divine honors granted to him by a city or province. Tacitus reports how all the elite Roman houses contained worshippers of Augustus (*Ann.* 1.73). In Italy, wealthy freedman formed societies of *Augustales*, a cult association from which its members engaged in public benefactions in Augustus' name.[514] Or else an association of cloth dyers would seek patronage of a priest of the local imperial cult to position themselves with the social networks of patronage and power.[515]

In the provinces, temples were erected for the emperor complete with a priesthood and calendar of events. Various festivals included the parading images of the emperor, songs about the emperor, and hymns to the emperor, and climaxed with sacrifices for the emperor.[516] Some of these festivals were for traditional gods into which the emperor was imported; other festivals were specifically for the emperor.[517] Municipal governments and associations venerated the emperor with inscriptions, shrines, libations, and sacrifices for his health, usually as thanksgiving for some type of benefaction like tax relief or security. Cities competed to host imperial temples, and elites jostled for positions with its priesthood. Shrines to the emperor could be placed within existing temples so as to embed imperial devotion within local deities, as was the case with the shrine to Augustus on the Athenian Acropolis or in the temple of Artemis in Ephesus. The emperor was included in the singing of traditional hymns to gods. Buildings were erected specially for the imperial cult, varyingly called *kaisereia* and *sebasteia*, where images of the emperor could be viewed, garlanded, and have petitions made to them.[518] In the army, at the center of every camp was the legion's standard, a golden eagle, the

---

[513] Cf. Christian Habicht, "Die augusteische Zeit und das Jahrhundert nach Christi Geburt," in *Le culte des souverains dans l'empire romain* (Geneva: Fondation Hardt, 1973), 41–88.

[514] Cf. Fishwick, *Imperial Cult*, 2:1.609–16.

[515] Harry O. Maier, *Picturing Paul in Empire: Imperial Image, Text and Persuasion in Colossians, Ephesians and the Pastoral Epistles* (London: Bloomsbury, 2013), 12, n. 47.

[516] Price, *Rituals and Power*, 104–5.

[517] Price, *Rituals and Power*, 3.

[518] Susanna McFadden, "Picturing Power in Late Roman Egypt: The Imperial Cult, Imperial Portraits, and a Visual Panegyric," in *Art of Empire: The Roman Frescoes and Imperial Cult Chamber in Luxor Temple*, ed. Michael Jones and Susanna McFadden (New Haven, Conn.: Yale University Press, 2015), 137.

treasury, and an image or bust of the emperor that oaths, vows, and offerings were either made to, or on behalf of, by the soldiery.[519] From Augustus to Marcus Aurelius, the emperor's image was enfaced all over the empire, in banks, booths, baths, gymnasia, graffiti, villas, shops, markets, grottos, taverns, porches, parades, festivals, and windows (see Nicolaus of Damascus, *FGH* 90 F 125; Philo, *Legat.* 149–51; Fronto, *Ep.* 4.12.4).[520] The mass media of coins, inscriptions, ubiquitous images, statues, festivals, games, temples, and networks manufactured liminal, subliminal, and even superliminal ways of Romanizing a populace around the figure of the emperor by concentrating on a supreme quasi-divine individual.

The emperor's veneration was a means of creating "imperial consciousness,"[521] that is, reinforcing social hierarchy while fostering loyalty. This was achieved by a generous benefaction and ritualized devotion that integrated imperial patrons with provincial supplicants. The result was a mutually reinforcing web of patronage and power laced with religious elements that was made effective by generously dispersing a currency of honor that anyone could purchase by a token act of piety.

The imperial cult became, then, a central sociopolitical and religious focus in the empire. It did this by marrying together princeps, polis, pantheon, and people, joining local cults with the goddess Roma and imperial *divi*, giving the Olympian deities an earthly embodiment, assimilating priestly and political offices, offering benefaction, and inviting supplication. According to Hans-Josef Klauck: "The emperor cult was not seen as an alternative to the inherited religions, but as a kind of superstructure which could be added onto the local cults. It functioned as a kind of institutional metonymy: it evoked the fact of Roman rule, gave an ideological foundation for it and furthered its social acceptability, at least for members of the leading classes to whom new and honourable careers as provincial priests of the emperor cult were offered."[522]

The following table demonstrates various forms of imperial devotion, both imposed top down and reciprocated from below, as it relates principally to Augustus.

---

[519] J. Helgeland, "Roman Army Religion," *ANRW* 2.16.2: 1476.

[520] See Paul Zanker, *The Power of Images in the Age of Augustus* (Ann Arbor: University of Michigan Press, 1988); and Maier, *Picturing Paul in Empire*.

[521] Oliver Stoll, *Excubatio ad Signa: Die Wache bei den Fahnen in der römischen Armee und andere Beiträge zur kulturgeschichtlichen und historischen Bedeutung eines militärischen Symbols* (St. Katharinen: Scripta Mercaturae, 1995), 36.

[522] Hans-Josef Klauck, "The Roman Empire," in *The Cambridge History of Christianity: Origins to Constantine*, ed. Margaret M. Mitchell and Frances M. Young (Cambridge: Cambridge University Press, 2006), 73.

Jesus and the "In-Betweeners"

Imperial Devotion	Commentary
The **name** Augustus had religious overtones.	According to Cassius Dio the honorific title "Augustus" implied that Octavian was "more than human, for all the most honored and sacred things are called *augusta*" (53.16.18).
Miracle stories were composed to the effect that Augustus was born of a supernatural conception: I have read the following story in the books of Asclepias of Mendes entitled *Theologumena*. When Atia had come in the middle of the night to the solemn service of Apollo, she had her litter set down in the temple and fell asleep, while the rest of the matrons also slept. On a sudden a serpent glided up to her and shortly went away. When she awoke, she purified herself, as if after the embraces of her husband, and at once there appeared on her body a mark in colours like a serpent, and she could never get rid of it; so that presently she ceased ever to go to the public baths. In the tenth month after that Augustus was born and was therefore regarded as the son of Apollo. Atia too, before she gave him birth, dreamed that her vitals were borne up to the stars and spread over the whole extent of land and sea, while Octavius dreamed that the sun rose from Atia's womb. (Suetonius, *Aug.* 94.4)	Suetonius initially writes about the birth of Octavius (i.e., Augustus) as the natural progeny of his parents (Suetonius, *Aug.* 1–6). Later, however, he reports a legendary tale about how his mother, Atia, was impregnated by the *genius* of the god Apollos as represented by a snake (see also Cassius Dio, *Hist. rom.* 45.1.1–5; Virgil, *Ecl.* 4). This is clearly modeled on the miraculous birth of Alexander the Great, whose mother Olympias, the night before her marriage to Philip II, allegedly dreamed that "a thunderbolt fell upon her body, which kindled a great fire." Also, a snake was once seen next to her as she slept and implied that she had had intercourse with a god. Olympias allegedly told Alexander the story of his divine origins, or alternatively, the story was concocted by Alexander himself, and Olympias resented being cast as Zeus' mistress (Plutarch, *Alex.* 2.2–3.4). The point of these stories is that Alexander and Augustus enjoy a divine destiny, possess a divine lineage, which means a divine status and even a divine nature.

Imperial Devotion	Commentary
There were also alleged **portents** of Augustus' greatness: When he was now a lad and was staying in Rome, Cicero dreamed that the boy had been let down from the sky by golden chains to the Capitol and had received a whip from Jupiter. He did not know who the boy was, but meeting him the next day on the Capitol itself, he recognized him and told the vision to the bystanders. Catulus, who had likewise never seen Octavius, thought in his sleep that all the noble boys had marched in a solemn procession to Jupiter on the Capitol, and in the course of the ceremony the god had cast what looked like an image of Rome into that boy's lap. Startled at this, he went up to the Capitol to offer prayers to the god, and finding there Octavius, who had gone up for some reason or other, he compared his appearance with the dream and convinced himself of the truth of the vision. (Cassius Dio, *Hist. rom.* 45.2.1–4).	Cassius Dio reports various dreams that the young Octavius was not only destined for greatness, but was destined so by the god Jupiter.

Imperial Devotion	Commentary
In **poetry**, Augustus was heralded by Virgil as "a god who wrought for us this peace—for a god he shall ever be to me; often shall a tender lamb from our folds stain his altar" (*Ecl.* 1.6–8). In Virgil's *Aeneid*, a civic epic meant to rival Homer's *Iliad* and *Odyssey*, he waxes about Augustus: "Here is Caesar and all of Julius' progeny, coming near the great dome of heaven. This man, this is he whom you have often heard promised, Augustus Caesar, born of the god, he will bring the golden age again to Latium, through the land reigned over by Saturn once upon a time, over the Garamants and Indians he will expand his rule; to the land beyond the stars, beyond the way of the year-long orbit and sun, where sky-carrying Atlas turns on his shoulder the vault fixed with glowing stars" (*Aen.* 6.789–98) (cited from Mark Reasoner, *Roman Imperial Texts: A Sourcebook* [Minneapolis: Fortress, 2013], 29). In a similar vein, Horace said of Augustus: "Thunder in heaven confirms our faith—Jove rules there; but here on earth Augustus shall be hailed as god also, when he makes new subjects of the Britons and the dour Parthians" (*Carm.* 3.5). Elsewhere, Horace depicts Augustus as Jupiter's second in command. After mention of Bacchus and Apollo as gods subordinate to the rule of Jupiter, Horace adds: "O father and defender of the human race [i.e., Jupiter], born of Saturn, to you by fate has been given the responsibility of mighty Caesar; may you reign, with Caesar second" (*Odes* 1.12.49–52) (cited from Reasoner, *Roman Imperial Texts*, 48–49).	This is certainly some of the most overt propaganda and literary sycophancy one can imagine. Horace's picture of Augustus as a kind of deputy of Jupiter resonates with Jesus as God the Father's plenipotentiary or vice-regent. The relationship of the emperor to Jupiter/Zeus was complex. On the one hand, coins show Zeus enthroned in his majesty while Trajan approaches him to pay homage. In other coins, Trajan is enthroned as Zeus, holding thunderbolt and lightning (Price, *Rituals and Power*, 158, 183).

Imperial Devotion	Commentary
Statues portrayed Augustus in the guise of Jupiter. According to Suetonius, Caligula attempted to take this further, by taking statues to the Greek gods and replacing their heads with his own bust (*Cal.* 22.2). A later sculpture presented Hadrian standing in the shape of Zeus/Jupiter, standing among the twelve gods like Zeus, even as he stood beside an image of Zeus/Jupiter (H. S. Vernsel, *Triumphus: An Inquiry into the Origin, Development and Meaning of the Roman Triumph* [Leiden: Brill, 1970], 69).	This is an instance of assimilating the emperor to a traditional deity, again, trying to balance the old deities with the living *sebastos*. According to Paul Zanker: "This does not mean of course, that Augustus' admirers genuinely equated him with Jupiter or that he felt himself to be a new Jupiter.... The comparison with Jupiter is rather an allegorical symbol of his rule, celebrating it as just, final, and all-embracing, like that of a supreme god. Augustus was the gods' representative on earth" (Zanker, *Power of Images*, 234).
Augustus **dressed** as Apollo at a dinner party: There was besides a private dinner of his, commonly called that of the "twelve gods," which was the subject of gossip. At this the guests appeared in the guise of gods and goddesses, while he himself was made up to represent Apollo, as was charged not merely in letters of Antony, who spitefully gives the names of all the guests.... The scandal of this banquet was the greater because of dearth and famine in the land at the time, and on the following day there was an outcry that the gods had eaten all the grain and that Caesar was in truth Apollo, but Apollo the Tormentor, a surname under which the god was worshipped in one part of the city. (Suetonius, *Aug.* 70.1–2)	While this dinner party and dress-up might seem like a bit of fun, for some it could convey a certain impiety. Philo certainly took issue with Caligula dressing and acting like the gods Mars, Mercury, Apollo, and Bacchus (*Legat.* 93–107). Otherwise, Augustus fostered connections between himself and Jupiter and Mars Ultor (Fishwick, *Imperial Cult*, 1:1.87–88). Note the comment of Fishwick: "A person who dresses up and plays the role of a god does so partly out of reverence, but also by way of self-comparison with the deity, whose powers and qualities he wishes to share or have reflected on himself; thus Alexander costumed himself as Hermes, Anthony as Dionysus, and Octavian as Apollo" (Fishwick, *Imperial Cult*, 1:1.30).

Imperial Devotion	Commentary
Temples to Augustus can be found in Asia Minor, Corinth, Vienna, Gaul, Spain, and Egypt. The temples were strategically located in prominent places in a city designed to be an integrating hub for cultic, commercial, judicial, and civil activities. Philo refers to the lavish splendor of the temple of Augustus in Alexandria: The whole inhabitable world voted him no less than honors equal to the Olympian gods. These are so well attested by temples, gateways, vestibules, porticoes, that every city which contains magnificent works new and old is surpassed in these by the beauty and magnitude of those appropriated to Caesar and particularly in our own Alexandria. For there is elsewhere no precinct like that which is called the Sebasteum, a temple to Caesar on shipboard, situated on an eminence, facing the harbors famed for their excellent moorage, huge and conspicuous, fitted on a scale not found elsewhere with dedicated offerings, around it a girdle of pictures and statues in silver and gold, forming a precinct of vast breadth, embellished with porticoes, libraries, chambers, groves, gateways, and wide open courts and everything which lavish expenditure could produce to beautify it. (Philo, *Legat.* 150–51)	In 29 BCE, Asian elites requested permission to grant divine honors to Augustus. He permitted the cities of Nicaea and Ephesus to build temples to Julius Caesar and to the goddess Roma for worship by Roman citizens. Greeks in Pergamon and Nicomedia were granted the same permission to build temples to Roma and Augustus. In other places, however, the imperial cult was imposed by the regime, notably in Lugdunum and Cologne, in order to create a culture of civic loyalty. (Price [*Rituals and Power*, 173] refers to the "interventions of Rome" and "constant and covert pressure exercised by Rome" for cities to engage in cultic practices of the emperor.) Proof that Augustus took the cult seriously comes from an amusing episode reported by Quintilian. The people of Tarraco in Spain built an altar to Augustus and a delegation informed Augustus that a palm tree had miraculously sprung out of it, to which Augustus sneered that they obviously didn't light fires on it very often then (Quintilian 6.3.77)! Imperial temples had priests and priestesses called *sebastophantēs/sebastophantis* (BrillDAG). There were also the *sebastologoi*, who were something like temple guardians (BrillDAG) or perhaps heralds of the emperor (Deissmann, *Light*, 348–49).

Imperial Devotion	Commentary
(continued) During the time of Caligula, a temple was built in his honor on Miletus with an inscription to its builders and curators, "the friends of the emperor" (*philosebastoi*): The temple officials who first curated his temple dedicated with their own money (the statue of) Emperor Gaius Caesar Germanicus son of Germanicus the divine Augustus, Gnaeus Vergilius Capito was high priest of the temple of Gaius Caesar in Miletus for the first time and high priest of Asia for the third time, and (under) Tiberius Iulius Menogenes, son of the nomothetes Demetrius high priest for the second time and the custodian of the temple at Miletus and Protomachus son of Glycon of Iulia the chief temple builder and *sebastoneoi* and *sebastologos*: Protomachus son of Glycon of Iulia (cited from Julia Margaret Tomas, *Variation in Representation through Architectural Benefaction under Roman Rule: Five Cases from the Province of Asia c. 40 B.C.–A.D. 68* [PhD diss., Durham University, 2020], 289–90).	

Imperial Devotion	Commentary
Sacrifices and petitions were often made for the emperor. An Egyptian papyrus witnesses to the cost of the sacrifices in the temple of Augustus, referring to the "sacrifices and libations offered on behalf of the god and lord emperor" (P. Oxy. 8.1143.4). After Augustus' victory over Antony and Cleopatra VII the senate decreed that libations should be poured out for him at all banquets (Cassius Dio 51.19.16). Otherwise, sacrifices could sometimes be offered to the emperor during games, festivals, or civic celebrations. Josephus records that "Gaius [Caligula] came out in a solemn manner, and offered sacrifice to Augustus Caesar, in whose honor, these games were celebrated" (Josephus, *Ant.* 19.87). An inscription from Smyrna states that "the whole world sacrifices and prays on behalf of the emperor's eternal duration and unconquered rule" (*IGRR* 4.1398) (cited from Price, *Rituals and Power*, 210). Aristides (*Or.* 26.32) says that with the very mention of the ruler's name everyone stands up and "praises and worships him and utters a twofold prayer, one on the ruler's behalf to the gods and one to the ruler himself about his own matters" (cited from Price, *Rituals and Power*, 232). The Calendar of Cumae contained a list of holidays, including January 16, where supplication was made to Augustus, and January 30 supplication was made to the imperium of Augustus (*CIL* 10.8375) (cited in Fishwick, *Imperial Cult*, 2:1.490).	It is notable that the sacrifices are sometimes offered "for" or "on behalf of" (*hyper*) the emperor. Sacrifices made for the emperor were for his health, prosperity, and victory. When sacrifices were made to the emperor, it was usually in association with a deified predecessor or in tandem with other gods. For instance, an inscription from Ancyra refers to "The Galatians who sacrificed to the divine Augustus and divine Roma" (*OGIS* 533). Sacrifices to a person were important as they designated the recipient a deity (Plutarch, *Lys.* 18; Cassius Dio 44.51.1; Appian, *Bell. civ.* 1.17). (Cf. discussion in Price, *Rituals and Power*, 210–20.)

Imperial Devotion	Commentary
Papyri often referred to the emperor in exalted and divine language (Fantin, *Lord of the Entire World*, 194). An Egyptian lawsuit is dated to the "seventh year of the lord [*tou kyriou*] Tiberius Claudius" ca. 49 CE (P. Oxy. 37.5–6).	Whereas Augustus (Suetonius, *Aug.* 53.1; Cassius Dio 55.12.2–3) and Tiberius (Tacitus, *Ann.* 2.87; Suetonius, *Tib.* 27; Cassius Dio 57.8.1–4) formally shunned the use of the titles *kyrios* and *dominus*, they were nevertheless used of them (P. Oxy. 1143.4; *OGIS* 606.1). The language of divinity and lordship would be increasingly used for later emperors such as Nero and Domitian. Domitian even wished to be addressed as "our lord and god" (Suetonius, *Dom.* 13). Domitian's "purported self-designation *dominus et deus* is less a new direction in imperial ideology as it is a tasteless violation of propriety" (David E. Aune, "The Influence of Roman Imperial Court Ceremonial on the Apocalypse of John," *BR* 28 [1983]: 20).
Hymns were sung to Augustus as a god and with the Olympian gods. After Augustus resolved a diplomatic conflict with the Parthians, concerning the recovery of Roman standards and establishing Armenia as a Roman client kingdom, the senate "arranged that his name should be included in their hymns equally with those of the gods" (Cassius Dio, *Hist. rom.* 51.20.1). Horace's *Odes* (esp. 4.5 and 4.15) are panegyrics to his greatness. Augustus' *Res Gestae* noted how his name was added into the "hymn of the Salii," a priestly college who sang songs to the deities in the *Carmen Saliare* (*RG* § 10.1). Philo refers to a trained chorus who sang paeans to Caligula, praising him particularly as Bacchus (Philo, *Legat.* 96).	Hymns could be sung to kings without implying their divinity. However, in this instance, it is significant that Augustus is the object of hymnody beside the Olympian gods.

Imperial Devotion	Commentary
Oaths of loyalty were sworn to the emperor by the army, governors, and leading citizens. An oath of loyalty to Augustus and his family for citizens in Paphlagonia in 3 BCE was administered in the local *Sebasteia* (Mitchell, *Anatolia*, 1:102). A group of citizens in Aritium in Lusitania 37 CE took an oath to Caligula with the words: "If I intentionally act or have acted falsely, then let Jupiter Optimus Maximus and the divine Augustus and all other undying gods make destitute country, safety, and everyone's fortune," and in the same year the people of Assus in Greece swore: "We swear by the Savior Zeus and the god Caesar Augustus and the Holy Maiden of our ancestors that we will aid Gaius Caesar Augustus and his entire household" (cited in Reasoner, *Roman Imperial Texts*, 212–14).	Oaths were sworn to the living emperor, calling upon deified emperors and other major deities as witnesses. Oaths were often made in the presence of an image of the emperor, or, in some cases, even in a temple to the foresaid emperor (i.e., Augustus).

Imperial Devotion	Commentary
Coins depicted Augustus with various degrees of status and relationship to the divine (http://numismatics.org/). These include: • Bust of Octavian with "divine son" (obverse) + bust of Julius Caesar with "the divine Julius" (reverse). 38 BCE. • Bust of Octavian with "Caesar the divine son" (obverse) + temple of Julius Caesar with a comet with "temple of the divine Julius" (reverse). 36 BCE. • Bust of goddess of Victory (obverse) + depiction of Octavian in the nude with foot on an orb with "Caesar the divine son" (reverse). 31–29 BCE.	Coins were the mass media of empire and so an emperor's achievements, relationship to the divine predecessor, family, and association with the gods were all presented.
A first-century BCE **inscription** from Mytilene honors the emperor Augustus with divine honors and offers to deify him further if any reasons can be found: "We reckon on his magnanimity to see that those who have attained celestial glory, and divine superiority and might, can never stand on the same level with what is humbler by both fortune and nature. However, if something more honoring should be discovered in the time to come, the city's willingness and piety will omit nothing that could contribute more effectively to his deification" (*OGIS* 456).	The inscription is notable because the city offers to increase the deification, i.e., the degree of divine honors granted to Augustus, should his accomplishments require it. This is proof of divinity, at one level, as a euergetic spectrum of power and benefaction.

Imperial Devotion	Commentary
In another **inscription** is a dedication to the well-being of Augustus on the island of Kea, in the city Ioulis, probably in a Sebasteion adjacent to the sanctuary of Apollos Pythios, dated to ca. 27 BCE to 14 CE (*SEG* 48-1129). It mentions the "Olympian deities" and the "Imperial deities" (i.e., Augustus and his wife Livia). Elsewhere, we read, "Since Emperor Caesar, son of god, god Sebastos, has by his benefactions to all men outdone even the Olympian gods" (*I. Olympia* 53) (cited in Price, *Rituals and Power*, 55).	The inscription is evidence precisely of how the Olympian gods and the emperors could be honored side by side in a noncompetitive way. Generally, the emperor did not transgress the honors of the Olympians; however, as you can see, there were some who could certainly flirt with putting the emperor on par with them, or even beyond them in his benefaction.
A further **inscription** from Pergamum refers to Augustus in divine terms: "Emperor Caesar, son of god, the god Augustus, of every land and sea the overseer" (*I. Pergamon* 381) (cited in Deissmann, *Light from the Ancient East*, 347).	Pergamum was the Mecca of imperial worship, and this inscription indicates enthusiasm for the emperor as a divine benefactor by Roman and non-Roman residents.

The emperor, as *pontifex maximus*, was the symbol of religious piety to the traditional deities and the preserver of the traditional religions. Augustus accordingly boasted that he was a member of all four priestly colleges (*RG* § 7.3), he restored temples, and he reinstituted neglected cults during his reign (*RG* § 19–21). At the same time, the emperor was increasingly the focus of religious attention,[523] chiefly in the assigning of divine honors to the living emperor, often followed with postmortem deification. The practice of imperial devotion "dovetailed with Hellenistic traditions of ruler cult in making the emperor the empire's one universal deity, a development which some have speculated may have helped facilitate the subsequent spread of monotheism."[524]

---

[523] Cf. Mary Beard, John North, and Simon Price, *Religions of Rome* (2 vols.; Cambridge: Cambridge University Press, 1998), 1:169.

[524] Trevor S. Luke, "Augustus," in *The Routledge Encyclopedia of Ancient Mediterranean Religions*, ed. Eric Orlin et al. (London: Routledge, 2016), 113.

(2) Israelite royal ideology, messianism, and ruler cults.

(a) Scriptural and Second Temple narrations of Israel's king.

The Israelite tradition, at the intersection of ancient Near Eastern cultures, developed its own royal ideology, which in turn evolved into multiple modes of messianic discourse during the Persian, Greek, and Roman periods.[525] There emerged within Israelite religion the idealization of various royal and priestly figures, who, in increasingly eschatologically focused roles, acted as divine agents, embodied divine power, were ascribed quasi-divine qualities, and sometimes received forms of veneration. This process is detectable already within the Hebrew Bible, but crystallizes in the Greek and Roman periods, that is, during periods of sociopolitical upheaval. It is possible, in a qualified sense, to speak of a Jewish messianic ruler cult that shaped early Christian conceptions of Jesus as a divine messianic king.

The Pentateuch celebrated the formation of the Israelite monarchy with its prophecies that "the scepter shall not depart from Judah, nor the ruler's staff from between his feet, until tribute comes to him; and the obedience of the peoples is his" (Gen 49.10), and "a star shall come out of Jacob, and a scepter shall rise out of Israel" (Num 24.17). The Israelite monarchy was given its distinctive charter in the Davidic covenant as narrated in 2 Sam 7.12–16, which focused on the Davidic dynasty as a manifestation of divine sonship and a promise of a never-ending kingdom. The royal ideology of the Davidic dynasty was intensified in many royal psalms (Ps 2; 45; 72; 89; 110; 132). In prophetic literature, during times of crisis, even when no Davidide was to be found, there was a hope for a future royal Davidic figure to arise in whom God would act to defeat Israel's and Judah's enemies (Isa 9.1–7; 11.1–4; Jer 22.4; 23.5–6; 30.9; 33.17–22; Ezek 34.22–24; 37.24–25; Amos 9.11–12; Hos 3.4–5; Micah 5.2). The Israelite king shares the divine throne, is given divine honorific titles, attains divine sonship, embodies and enacts God's power on earth, and holds back the chaotic forces of nature and nations.

One also finds simultaneous idealizations of another anointed figure, the priest, who could be considered a representative or embodiment of the divine realm (see Sir 50, *Arist.* 96–99, *Jub.* 31.14, Philo, *Fug.* 108; *T. Levi* 18.1–5). In the Persian era, Zerubbabel, the appointed governor, was of Davidic descent, and the high Priest, Joshua, was of Zadokite descent. These two figures were the "sons of oil" (Zech 4.12–14), and they began to rebuild Judean society amid idealized conceptions of priesthood and kingship. The offices of priest and ruler fostered expectation for a "diarchic restoration" of the Aaronic

---

[525] The preeminent discussions of this topic remain Horbury, *Jewish Messianism*; and Bühner, *Hohe Messianologie*.

priesthood and Davidic reign as implied in Haggai (1.12-14; 2.2-4, 20-23) and Zechariah (3.6-10; 4.2-6, 11-14) and became prominent in later messianic discourse. Qumran scrolls refer to the "the messiahs of Aaron and Israel" (CD 12.23-13.1; 14.19; 20.1), while coins minted under Simeon bar Kokhba carried the inscription "Simeon Prince of Israel," naming "Eleazar the Priest" on the obverse side.[526] The two anointed offices are combined in the case of Joshua son of Jehozadak (Zech 6.9-15).[527] This explains the assimilation of royal and priestly motifs, common too in Assyrian to Roman contexts, as well as in Jewish and Christian messianic texts.[528]

Disputes betide the very definition of messianism—whether one should focus on the presence of the term "anointed," examine wider literary functions, focus on idealized figures in certain social settings, or else identify messianism as a type of Mediterranean political discourse.[529] It is certainly true that prior to 70 CE one can hardly find any occurrence of the absolute term "the Messiah." Instead, the Hebrew, Aramaic, and Greek terms used for a messiah/anointed one are qualified with a genitive or possessive pronoun like "Messiah of Israel," "Messiah of Aaron," "Messiah of the Lord," or "his Messiah"—which means that the designation is always qualified rather than absolutized and no single meaning is ever assumed.[530] What is more, messianic figures could go by a variety of names other than "Messiah," including Son of David, Son of God, Son of Man, the Prophet, Elect/Chosen One, Prince, Branch, Root, Scepter, Star, Coming One, etc.[531] Consequently I prefer the definition of messianism given by John Collins, who proposes that a messianic figure is one who is "an agent of God in the end-time who is said somewhere in the literature to be anointed, but who is not necessarily called 'messiah' in every passage."[532] As such, in the Hebrew Bible there emerged an idealization of the Davidic dynasty

---

[526] Craig A. Evans, "Messianic Hopes and Messianic Figures in Late Antiquity," *JGRChJ* 3 (2006): 15-18.

[527] Collins, *Sceptre and the Star*, 31.

[528] Note too that Alexander the Great allegedly did obeisance to the divine name on the high priest's miter when entering the Jerusalem temple (Josephus, *Ant.* 11.331-39).

[529] See Matthew V. Novenson, *The Grammar of Messianism: An Ancient Jewish Political Idiom and Its Users* (Oxford: Oxford University Press, 2017), 272, who considers messianism "a regional-ethnic subset of ancient Mediterranean political discourse . . . [manifested as] a particularly Jewish and Christian way of talking about . . . who is and who should be in charge—about which Persians, Greeks, Romans, and others had their own ways of talking."

[530] Marinus de Jonge, "The Use of the Word 'Anointed' in the Time of Jesus," *NovT* 8 (1966): 133-34.

[531] Cf. Chester, *Messiah and Exaltation*, 204.

[532] John J. Collins, "'He Shall Not Judge by What His Eyes See': Messianic Authority in the Dead Sea Scrolls," *DSD* 2 (1995): 146; idem, *Sceptre and the Star*, 11-12, 17-18; cf. Bühner, *Messianic High Christology*, 6.

or something that we might call "proto-messianism,"[533] and the reception of such texts, when combined with experiences of oppression and eschatological hopes, crystallized into the messianism found in Jewish and Christian texts.[534]

In Jewish sacred traditions a consistent pattern emerges whereby God's kingly power and deliverance are to be manifested in an anointed Davidic king (see 2 Chr 13.8; Ps 2.1–12; Ps 110.1–7; Ezek 34.15, 23–24; *Sib. Or.* 3.48–49; *Ps. Sol.* 17.3–4, 21–46; Josephus, *Ant.* 4.297; 1QM 11.1–12; 4Q521 2.1–14; Luke 1.68–69; 19.44–45; *1 En.* 46.1–8; 48.10–49.4; 51.1–5; 61.1–13; 62.14; *4 Ezra* 13.25–50). This made the king/messiah somewhere between a human agent and a divine manifestation of Israel's national deity. True though it may be that some thought the messiah would be a blandly human figure (Justin, *Dial.* 49.1; Hippolytus, *Ref.* 9.30.7–8), such a view was not unanimous. In the Hebrew and Greek Scriptures, as well as in Second Temple Jewish texts, there are indications that royal and messianic figures were ascribed divine qualities, and they duly received forms of veneration on par with ancient ruler cults. The Israelite monarchy had rituals and rhetoric that could compete with Egyptian and Hellenistic ruler cults. This royal ideology provided the basis for the notion of a "divine" messiah, especially when situated in apocalyptic narratives featuring divine deliverance.

Ps 2 is a royal enthronement psalm celebrating the divine installment of Israel's king, who reigns and remains supreme over his vassals. The notion that the king was the son of a god was very common in the ancient Near East, and the language of begetting probably points to Egyptian influence.[535] The ceremony behind the psalm amounts to the king's divine election as conveyed through adoption into the Davidic line. The Israelite monarch was addressed as "Lord" (*adonai/kyrios*) by courtiers (Ps 110.1), and vassal rulers kissed his feet as an act of subjection (see Ps 72.11; 49.23, *Ps. Sol.* 17.32; *4 Ezra* 13.13 on prostration to Israel's ruler). While prostration was part of the worship of Yahweh (Gen 22.5 [LXX]; Deut 9.18, 25–26; 2 Esd 8.6; Sir 50.17, 21, 23; 2 Macc 3.15; 10.3–4; 13.12; 3 Macc 1.16), Israelite kings received obeisance from subjects (1 Sam 24.8; 28.14; 2 Sam 1.2; 9.6–8; 1 Kgs 1.16, 23, 31, 53; 1 Chr 21.21; 2 Chr 24.17), and there is one instance where the Judean king received obeisance beside Yahweh: "David said to the whole assembly, 'Bless the Lord your God.' And all the assembly blessed the Lord, the God of their ancestors, and

---

[533] Evans, "Messianic Hopes," 10; and Chester, *Messiah and Exaltation*, 229.

[534] Cf. survey in Bird, *Are You the One?* 31–62.

[535] Collins and Collins, *King and Messiah*, 10–15. Alternatively, Sam Janse (*"You Are My Son": The Reception History of Psalm 2 in Early Judaism and the Early Church* [CBET 51; Leuven: Peeters, 2009], 20–21, 30–31) sees a post-exilic setting due to the presence of Aramaisms and detects influence from Isa 11.10 and 49.1–6.

bowed their heads and prostrated themselves before the LORD and the king" (1 Chr 29.20). In later interpretation, Ps 2 was often combined with other texts like 2 Sam 7.12–16 and Ps 89, and contributed to Jewish and Christian messianic discourse (4Q174 3; *Ps. Sol.* 17.21–34; Mark 1.11; 9.7; Acts 13.17–47; Heb 1.5; 5.5; *1 Clem.* 36.4; 2 Pet 1.17).[536] In christological appropriations, the pagan nations may rage and howl, but Israel's God has acted in power, exalting his "son," promising to make his enemies his footstool and to give him an inheritance of nations.[537]

Ps 110 was highly significant for Jewish royal ideology. The text narrates Yahweh's invitation for the Davidic king, the courtier's "lord," to sit at his right hand, reflecting the ancient notion of throne sharing (Gk. *synthronos*). It should be observed that throne sharing can happen on a variety of levels.

First, among gods themselves.[538] Sophocles' Oedipus curses an enemy by appealing to the goddess "*Dikē* revealed long ago, [who] sits beside Zeus [*synedros Zēnos*], to share his throne through sanction of primordial laws" (*Oed. Col.* 1382). Similarly, in the *Orphic Hymns* 61.2, *Dikē* is eulogized as one "who sits upon the sacred throne of Zeus."[539] Lucian quotes a Sibylline oracle to the effect that Proteus will be "co-enthroned [*synthronos*] with Hephaestus and lord Herakles" (*Pereg.* 29)—interesting too because Philostratus described Apollonius of Tyana as an incarnation of Proteus and a "son of Zeus" (*Apol.* 1.4–6). It was also common to depict ancient deities seated with their wives on a *bisellium*, or double throne.[540]

Second, gods with kings. Most salient for this study is that in Egyptian iconography of the New Kingdom, the Pharaoh was portrayed as seated beside a god and his Nubian and Asiatic enemies were depicted as his footstool.[541] Philip II of Macedon included an image of himself among a procession of statues of twelve gods, which made him a "throne sharer" with the twelve deities,

---

[536] Janse, *"You Are My Son,"* 148.

[537] N. T. Wright, "Son of God and Christian Origins," in *Son of God: Divine Sonship in Jewish and Christian Antiquity*, ed. Garrick V. Allen, Kai Akagi, Paul Sloan, and Madhavi Nevader (University Park, Penn.: Eisenbrauns, 2019), 129–30.

[538] Following and augmenting Aune, *Revelation*, 1:262. But see Burnett, *Christ's Enthronement*, 94–110 for a fuller study.

[539] This dovetails with the Jewish tradition, which connects the divine throne and appointments to Israel's throne with righteousness; see, e.g., 1 Kgs 10.9; 2 Chr 9.8; Job 36.7; Ps 9.4; 45.6–7; 89.14; 97.2; Prov 16.12; 20.28; 25.5; Isa 9.7; 16.5.

[540] Christoph Markschies, "'Sessio ad dexteram': Bemerkungen zu einem altchristlichen Bekenntnismotiv in der christologischen Diskussion der altkirchlichen Theologen," in *Le Trône de Dieu*, ed. Marc Philonenko (WUNT 69; Tübingen: Mohr Siebeck, 1993), 260–65.

[541] Othmar Keel, *The Symbolism of the Biblical World* (Winona Lake, Ind.: Eisenbrauns, 1997), 253–55, 263.

according to Diodorus Siculus (16.91.1–16.95.1). The Persian king Darius said himself to be "King of kings and kinsmen of the gods, throne-sharer with the gods Mithras and the rising sun" (*Historia Alexandri Magni* 1.36.2).[542] In the same document, Alexander was considered Zeus' throne sharer after his victory over Darius, when he took possession of the Persian empire (*Historia Alexandri Magni* 2.22.9). Antiochus I claimed to be "co-enthroned likewise among the deities who hear our prayers" in his funeral inscription on Mount Nemrut. In the Roman era, the low-relief cameo *Gemma Augustea* depicts Augustus and the goddess *Roma* seated side by side on a single throne. Notably, *Roma* is seated at Augustus' right, effectively putting Augustus in the position of Jupiter. Meanwhile, *Oikoumene*, the female personification of the inhabited world, places a wreath on Augustus' head, and other gods such as Neptune and Gaia are seated around the periphery. Coinage from Philippi depicts a deified emperor (Julius Caesar or Augustus) on a dais with the living emperor (Augustus or Claudius), and the latter receives a crown from the former.[543]

Third, kings and heirs/vice-regents. A coin minted in Rome ca. 13 BCE depicts Augustus seated with his son-in-law Marcus Agrippa to indicate shared authority and his intention for succession.[544] In addition, somewhat blurring the second and third categories, a Roman coin ca. 55 CE depicts the divine Claudius seated at the right hand of the divine Augustus on a chariot pulled by four elephants.[545]

Ps 110 indicates that ancient Israelite religion shared this tradition of throne sharing between a deity and a monarch. The motif of throne sharing develops in the post-exilic and Second Temple eras. The Chronicler makes it clear that the throne of Israel's king is the throne of Yahweh. It is repeated that Solomon sits on the throne of the kingdom of Yahweh over Israel (1 Chr 28.5; 1 Chr 29.23; 2 Chr 9.8) to the point that the kingdom of Israel is coterminous with the kingdom of God (2 Chr 13.8).[546] The Enochic "Chosen One" is seated upon the Lord of Spirit's throne, and one can detect in this language a composite allusion to Dan 7.9–14 and Ps 110.1 in *1 En.* (51.3; 55.4; 61.8; 62.2).[547] In early Christianity, Ps 110 was the default text for explaining Jesus' exaltation

---

[542] Cited from Burnett, *Christ's Enthronement*, 100.

[543] Burnett, *Christ's Enthronement*, 133.

[544] "Augustus and Communicating the Succession," *Coins at Warwick* (blog), July 15, 2014, https://blogs.warwick.ac.uk/numismatics/entry/augustus_and_communicating/; and RIC I (second edition) Augustus 407, *Online Coins of the Roman Empire*, http://numismatics.org/ocre/id/ric.1(2).aug.407. Both sites accessed August 5, 2022.

[545] Gold Aureus of Nero, Rome, AD 55 1967.153.219, *Online Coins of the Roman Empire*, http://numismatics.org/collection/1967.153.219, accessed August 5, 2022.

[546] Aune, *Revelation*, 1:262.

[547] Hengel, *Studies in Early Christology*, 185.

and session at God's right hand.[548] Despite the paucity of messianic interpretations of Ps 110 in pre-70 CE texts,[549] "the best explanation for widespread use of Ps 110:1 in earliest Christianity is that because of royal and imperial temple and throne sharing the sharing of a god's temple and throne were cross-cultural rewards for pious, beneficent, and divinely approved rulers," says Burnett.[550]

Importantly, throne sharing implies co-rule, a form of vice-regency, so the king, co-enthroned with a deity, shares in the sovereignty of the deity. The position at a deity's right hand suggests not only a conferral of superlative honor, but a close association between the deity and his royal servant. The theological significance of throne sharing is the equality that it presumes between those who share such a throne.[551]

Consequently, Israel's king was not only enthroned by Yahweh (Ps 2.7; 89.20, 35–36; 132.11–12) but also was enthroned with Yahweh (Ps 80.1; 110.1). Accordingly, Pss 2 and 110, with the acclamation of the king as a divine son and co-enthroned "lord," the highest office humanly attainable, loomed large in early Christology and invited assimilation with other texts and traditions that would place Jesus beyond a human office and into the orbit of divine functions and nature. In addition, Ps 45 is a royal wedding psalm where the king is acclaimed with a divine title: "Your throne, O God, will last for ever and ever; a scepter of justice will be the scepter of your kingdom" (Ps 45.6), with a tacit echo of Gen 49.9–10 about Judah's scepter. In Isaiah, the coming Davidide is heralded as "Mighty God" (Heb) or "angel of the great counsel" (LXX) in Isa 9.6 (5).

Casting the king's origins back into a primordial history and among the stars of the heavens appears frequently in the literature. The Greek psalter presages the preexistence and heavenly origins of a messianic figure. In Psalm 72 (Heb)/71 (LXX) it is said in v. 17, "May his name endure forever, his fame continue as long as the sun" (Heb) and "Let his name be blessed forever. Before the sun his name will remain" (LXX). The Greek text provides an explicitly temporal sequence

---

[548] See Mark 12.35–37; 14.62; Acts 2.33–34; 5.21; 7.55–56; Rom 8.34; 1 Cor 15.25; Eph 1.20; Col 3.1; Heb 1.13; 8.1; 10.12; 12.2; 1 Pet 3.22; Rev 3.21; *1 Clem.* 36.5; Polycarp, *Phil.* 2.1; *Barn.* 12.10–11; *Sib. Or.* 2.241–45; *Ascen. Isa.* 10.14; 11.32; *Apoc. Pet.* 6.1; *Apoc. Jas.* 14.30–31; Clement of Alexandria, *Exc.* 62.1–2. In some cases, Christ is seated at the right hand of God's own throne (Rev 5.13; 7.9–10, 17; 12.5; 22.1–3; implicitly in Matt 19.28; 25.31; Heb 12.2; *Ep. Ap.* 3.8) or else on a throne to the right of God's own throne (1 Cor 15.23–28; Rev 3.21; *Ascen. Isa.* 11.32–33; Pol. *Phil.* 2.21; *Mart. Pol.* 21.1; *Apoc. Pet.* 6.1). See the helpful discussions in Burnett, *Christ's Enthronement*, 17–34; and Hannah, "Throne of His Glory," 74–81.

[549] Cf. *T. Job* 33.3; even the later *2 En.* 39.5.

[550] Burnett, *Christ's Enthronement*, 33.

[551] Aune, *Revelation*, 1:262.

so that the king's name exists "before" (*pro*) the sun. Added to that, in Ps 110 (Heb)/109 (LXX) v. 3, the ambiguity of the Hebrew (lit., from womb-dawn-dew-childhood) is translated into Greek as "from the womb, before the morning star, I begat you" with obvious influence from Ps 2.7 (begotten you) and perhaps from Isa 14.12 (morning star). Note too in Greek Micah that the coming Davidide's "entrance has its beginning from the days of the ages" (Micah 5.1 LXX).

The Enochic Son of Man was named by the Lord of Spirits "even before the sun and the constellations were created" (*1 En.* 48.3). In *4 Ezra*'s messianic vision, a "man" arises out of the sea, flies upon the clouds of heaven, and the earth trembles and melts at the sound of his voice (*4 Ezra* 13.1–3). In the interpretation of the vision, the man is described as "he whom the Most High has been keeping for many ages, who will himself deliver his creation; and he will direct those who are left" (*4 Ezra* 13.26). Book 5 of the *Sibylline Oracles*, probably second century, looks ahead to God sending a great king to destroy the vassals of Nero *redivivus* (*Sib. Or.* 5.108–10). This king is arguably depicted as "a great star" who comes from heaven to burn Babylon and Italy (*Sib. Or.* 5.158) and imagined as "a blessed man [who] came from the expanses of heaven with a scepter in his hands which God gave him" (*Sib. Or.* 5.414–15). There is a possible confluence of Ps 71.17 and 109.1–4 (LXX) upon the description of the eschatological high priest in the *Testament of Levi*: "The Lord will raise up a new priest to whom all the words of the Lord will be revealed. He shall effect the judgment of truth over the earth for many days. And his star shall rise in heaven like a king; kindling the light of knowledge as day is illumined by the sun. And he shall be extolled by the whole inhabited world. This one will shine forth like the sun in the earth; he shall take away all darkness from under heaven, and there shall be peace in all the earth" (*T. Levi* 18.1–4). Also, Justin retorted to Trypho concerning "Christ, Son of God, who was before the morning star and the moon, and submitted to become incarnate, and be born of this virgin of the family of David" (*Dial.* 45.4).

Simeon ben Kosiba's nickname "bar Kokhba," for "son of the star," was a patronymic play on words inspired by Num 24.17, "a star shall arise out of Jacob." Given that stars were associated with angelic entities as the "hosts of heaven" (Deut 4.19; 17.3; 1 Kgs 22.19; Isa 24.21–23), it is notable when Eusebius reports that Kokhba claimed to be a heavenly "luminary come down from heaven to shine upon those in distress" (Eusebius, *Hist. eccl.* 4.6.2).[552] The fact that a ruler in Num 24.17 LXX will "arise" (*anatellō*) seems to have given cause to identify the ruler as the "Dayspring" (*anatolē*) in several texts. In the Hebrew version of Zech 6.12, Joshua the

---

[552] Horbury, *Jewish Messianism*, 94.

high priest is called "Branch" (*tsemah*), while in the LXX he is called "Dayspring" (*anatolē*) and he arises (*anatellō*) to build the temple. The title *anatolē* is applied to Jesus in Zechariah's *Benedictus* as the "Dayspring/Dawn from on high will break upon us to give light to those who sit in darkness and in the shadow of death, to guide our feet into the way of peace" (Luke 1.78–79).[553]

Many descriptions of a messianic agent underscore divine attributes and a place in the heavenly realm. In a text from the Herodian era, the messianic lord subjugates Gentiles, cleanses Jerusalem, regathers the exiles, dispenses righteousness, and is the locus of divine glory (*Ps. Sol.* 17.30–32). Qumran's Melchizedek is lauded as a divine being who takes his place in the heavenly council, where he holds court in judgment with direct allusions to Ps 7.7–8; 82.1 (11QMelch 2.9–11). Similarly, the self-glorification hymn narrates a figure who claims to belong to a "mighty throne" among the "congregation of the gods (*elim*)," surpassing ancient kings and rulers (4Q491c 8–18). Such language of being seated or installed beside the gods deploys the language used for Greco-Roman rulers who were added to the Greek and Roman pantheons. Horace lyricized Augustus as "couched at ease" among the demigods Pollux and Hercules on "heaven's proud steep" (*Od.* 3.3.9–12). Suetonius wrote that Julius Caesar was "numbered among the gods, not only by a formal decree, but also in the conviction of the common people" (*Jul.* 88.1). At Qumran, then, one finds the "competitive emulation of the conventions of the pagan Ruler Cult."[554] Further evidence for the supernaturalizing of an ideal human deliverer is that Daniel's "one like a son of man" is an angelic or heavenly being, who represents God and God's reign among the saints of the Most High, and this figure was given a messianic interpretation in Jewish and Christian literature.[555] The heavenly origins, divine power, and supernatural traits of a messianic figure were certainly not uniform in Judaism, but they were ubiquitous in Jewish texts of the Second Temple and post-temple eras.

What is evident is that the language for Israel's monarch is often couched in divine election and royal majesty; he is the subject of divine throne sharing, addressed with honorific divine titles, lauded with metaphorical divine begetting, kings and nations prostrate before him, he can be attributed preexistence, and he can be likened to a heavenly object. The various psalms celebrate in song the king's election, enthronement, and rule in association with Yahweh. The king was venerated to the point of obeisance and revered as a divine son

---

[553] David Wenkel, *Jesus the Dayspring: The Sunrise and Visitation of Israel's Messiah* (NTM 43; Sheffield: Sheffield Phoenix, 2021), 1–9.

[554] Fletcher-Louis, *Jesus Monotheism*, 1:212.

[555] Cf. survey in Bird, *Are You the One?* 78–97.

as he embodied divine righteousness in his reign. Yet balancing the divine appointment and human veneration of kings was the Deuteronomistic history with its skepticism of kingship (e.g., 1 Sam 8) as well as the prophetic (e.g., Isa 14) and sapiential (Wis 14.15–17) critiques of royal pretentions to divinity. In addition, there is no evidence that Israel's king was ever the object of cultic devotion; rather, he was the object of cultic concern.[556] Israelite religion required obeying the king and offering prayers for the king, but not offering prayers to the king or sacrifices to the king. That is because, despite the rhetoric of divine titles, the king was a divinely elected ruler who embodied in himself the election of the Israelites; he had charge to execute righteousness in the land as Yahweh's representative. The king had responsibility for the operation of the Jerusalem cultus and to ensure Torah observance in the land. It is the place of the king within the cult and not as the cult that separates Israelite traditions from Greco-Roman ruler cults.

That qualification aside, the language of divine sonship and begetting is derivative of Egyptian ruler cults, various divine titles given to the king echo ancient Near Eastern royal honors, and co-enthronement with a deity is ubiquitous in antiquity for the divine power behind a king. The Israelite traditions share in the phenomenon of merging monarch, myth, and metaphor to bolster royal legitimacy. Furthermore, as we will soon see, Jewish messianic discourse developed simultaneously in proximity to, in opposition against, and in derivation from Greco-Roman ruler cults. This is quite evident the *Sibylline Oracles* with the designation of the messianic figure as "King of the Sun" (*Sib. Or.* 3.652–56), which matches Ptolemaic language for the Egyptian king (P. Rainer 19.813; Rosetta Stone 2.9).[557] The Israelite and Judean tradition of kingship emerges in the context of ancient ruler cults, which, as the background to early Christianity, exerts influence upon early Christology.

(b) Jewish resourcement of and resistance to ancient ruler cults during the Hasmonean and Herodian eras.

(1) Hasmonean and Herodian ruler veneration or ruler cult?

The Hasmoneans, despite expelling the Seleucids with their forced Hellenizing policies and imposition of impious ruler worship, exhibited their own forms of ruler devotion in an obvious appropriation of Hellenistic ruler cults.

---

[556] Ziony Zevit, "Israel's Royal Cult in the Ancient Near Eastern *Kulturkreis*," in *Text, Artifact, and Image*, ed. Gary M. Beckman and Theodore J. Lewis (Providence, R.I.: Brown Judaic Studies, 2006), 200.

[557] Horbury, *Jewish Messianism*, 128; and Bühner, *Hohe Messianologie*, 309–10, 320.

Judas Maccabaeus was eulogized as one like "a giant," and gigantism was a mark of deity (1 Macc 3.3-9),[558] while Simon Maccabaeus was praised for achieving what Micah (4.4) said Yahweh would do, allow people to sit safely under their own vines and fig trees, where nobody can make them afraid (1 Macc 14.4-15). In these laudatory poems, the encomiastic form and focus on the "glory" and "honor" of Hasmonean accomplishments are typical of the veneration of the very Hellenistic rulers against whom the Maccabean rebellion was launched (1 Macc 3.3; 14.4-5, 9-10, 21, 29, 35, 39). The language is striking precisely because it is without precedent in the scriptural tradition.[559] Further, the description of Judean priests electing Simon to be their leader and priest until a prophet arises is a creative merging of the "prince" of Gen 49.10, the priest-king Joshua from Zech 6.11-13, and the eschatological Mosaic prophet in Deut 18.15 (1 Macc 14.41). Later, Josephus would describe John Hyrcanus I with the *triplex munus* titles of king, priest, and prophet (*Ant.* 13.299-300; *War* 1.68-69). Evidently, in Hasmonean court ideology, there was a "messianic atmosphere" around the king, which would later be translated to Herod the Great and Simeon Bar Kokhba.[560]

We now come to Herod the Great, who attempted to vouchsafe his Jewish royal credentials by rebuilding the temple (Josephus, *War* 1.400) since it was the king or the messiah who would (re)build the temple (2 Sam 7.12-14; 1 Kgs 6-9; 1 Chr 29.1-20; 2 Chr 6.1-7.1; Zech 6.12-13; Tob 14.5; 4Q174 3.1-13; Mark 14.58; John 2.19). Herod's refurbishment of the temple made it a spectacular monument of grandeur that was remembered well into the rabbinic era. Samuel Rocca called Herod's temple "the greatest cultic *temenos* [sacred precinct] in the Classical World."[561] The proof that the temple buttressed Herod's royal legitimation is that the celebration of the temple's reconstruction fell on the annual celebration of Herod's accession (Josephus, *Ant.* 15.423), and Herod invoked his rebuilding of the temple when his Jewish piety was questioned (*Ant.* 17.161-62).

When Herod announced his plans for succession, he explicitly urged against giving his sons royal honors, while stating his desire to be hailed as "king and master of all" (*Ant.* 16.132-35; *War* 1.457-66). Herod wished to be known for his many benefactions (*Ant.* 16.140; 19.328; *War* 1.425-26), and

---

[558] M. David Litwa, *Iesus Deus: The Early Christian Depiction of Jesus as a Mediterranean God* (Minneapolis: Fortress, 2014), 169-70.
[559] Fletcher-Louis, *Jesus Monotheism*, 1:217-18.
[560] Horbury, *Jewish Messianism*, 133.
[561] Samuel Rocca, *Herod's Judaea: A Mediterranean State in the Classical World* (TSAJ 122; Tübingen: Mohr Siebeck, 2008), 281.

several inscriptions commemorate him as a benefactor in the cities of Jerusalem, Masada, Ashdod, Rome, Athens, Cos, Delos, and Siʻa.[562] More than that, one inscription lauds Herod as follows: "To king Herod, lord [*Basilei Heōdei kyriō*], Obiasath, son of Sardos, placed the statue at his own expense" (*OGIS* 415). The inscription was allegedly placed in front of a statue of Herod at "the temple of Baʻal Shamim" at Siʻa (i.e., Palmyra).[563] Similar language of lordship is also used for Herod Agrippa I (*OGIS* 418) and Herod Agrippa II (*OGIS* 423, 425, 426) in inscriptions.

When Herod Agrippa I visited Alexandria in Egypt, an Alexandrian mob seized, adorned, and mocked a mentally disturbed vagabond as Agrippa's stand-in, hailing him with the title *Marin*, "our Lord," as a mocking mimicry of Jewish adulation of Agrippa. *Mara*, Philo explained, is the Syro-Judean title for a *kyrios* (Philo, *Flacc.* 25–39), confirmed by its frequent usage in Nabatean inscriptions pertaining to the monarch.[564] Agrippa I was infamously involved in an incident at Caesarea where, after sponsoring games in Caligula's honor, he was acclaimed by the populace as a god and failed to moderate the enthusiasm of the crowd for his divine status. This act of impiety—which Luke discusses snidely and Josephus reservedly—caused his death soon after (Acts 12.20–23; Josephus, *Ant.* 19.343–50).

Otherwise, in terms of public displays of devotion to Judean rulers, there are several instances where Herodians received acclamations from the people (Gk. *euphēmia*). Herod's Hasmonean brother-in-law, Aristobulus, who served a short stint as high priest, was acclaimed in the temple during the Feast of Tabernacles, possibly inspiring Herod to have him drowned (Josephus, *Ant.* 15.51–57; *War* 1.437). After the death of Herod, his son Archelaus was enthroned and acclaimed in the temple (*Ant.* 17.200–12; *War* 2.1–3).

We can certainly speak of Judean ruler veneration, even the Gentile veneration of a Judean king, but I am unconvinced that we can speak of a Hasmonean or Herodian "cult" per se. Neither the Hasmoneans nor the Herodians were the subject of hymns, or were the object of prayers, or had temples built for them with sacrifices and a priesthood. There are no festivals parading their statues beside Yahweh or placing their image in the Jerusalem temple. We are a ways off from the Roman imperial cults of Pergamum or Tarraco. The Hasmoneans could be critiqued for usurping kingship and priesthood for

---

[562] Peter Richardson, *Herod: King of the Jews and Friend of the Romans* (Minneapolis: Fortress, 1999), 210.

[563] Richardson, *Herod*, 206–7; and D. Clint Burnett, *Studying the New Testament through Inscriptions* (Peabody, Mass.: Hendrickson, 2020), 70–71.

[564] Burnett, *Studying the New Testament*, 68–69.

themselves. Herod the Great was a benevolent benefactor, but also considered impious and tyrannical. Luke and Josephus concur that Herod Agrippa I should not have allowed the Phoenician populace to hail him with divine acclamations. Judean ruler veneration extolled rulers for their righteousness and benefactions, but expressions remained muted within the stern limits of a Jewish tradition that was highly allergic to the deification of monarchs.[565] Tacitus was correct; for the Jews, cultic worship "is not paid to their kings, nor is this honour given to the Caesars" (*Hist.* 5.5).

It is worth considering next the visible impact of the imperial cult in and around Palestine and its effect upon Jewish attitudes towards divine rulers.

(2) The introduction of the imperial cult into Herodian Judea.

First-century Judea and Galilee were literally surrounded by cities that housed imperial temples and altars, including those at Caesarea Maritima, Caesarea Philippi, Sebaste, the Decapolis, and in Petra. The imperial cult was part of the religious landscape of Syro-Palestine, the Trans-Jordan, and Arabia. But even then, imperial devotion was not something only on the geographical periphery of Galilee and Judea. These buildings were within *eretz Yisrael*, the historic boundaries of the land of Israel. The presence of imperial coins with their inscriptions, Roman legions with their standards, and non-Jews with their own religious practices show that imperial devotion penetrated the interior of Judea and Galilee. Even the Jerusalem cultus was not immune, as the offerings made twice daily *on behalf of* the emperor were a symbol of Jewish religious devotion *for* the emperor. While the imperial cult was not formally imposed in Judea, it was still informally present, and no less problematic at times. The result was a more restrictive interpretation of the Torah's ban on images (by zealous Judeans), a further restriction on Gentile proximity to the temple by the erection of the outer wall (by Herod to appease the zealous), the potential for the Jewish dispensation to abstain from emperor worship to be revoked (as Caligula intended), and a capacity to cause a confrontation with Rome by refusing to offer the daily sacrifices (as occurred in 66 CE). The imperial cult both encircled and penetrated Judea and Galilee, making it part of the sociopolitical realities of Jews and the early churches and something they had to negotiate.

Herod constructed cities, buildings, and monuments in honor of the imperial family, including Caesarea Maritima, Sebaste, the palaces Aggripaeum and Caesareum, and a tower at Caesarea Maritima named Drusium.[566] Herod built imperial temples to Augustus in Caesarea Maritima (Josephus, *War* 1.414; *Ant.*

---

[565] Cf. similarly Fletcher-Louis, *Jesus Monotheism*, 1:217–18.
[566] Richardson, *Herod*, 174–215.

15.339), Sebaste (*Ant.* 15.296–98; *War* 1.403), and Paneas (*War* 1.404–6; *Ant.* 15.363–64).[567] Such imperial buildings were a priority for Herod.[568] Josephus says that Herod did not build anything without thought of Caesar's honor, and he erected monuments to Caesar in several cities (*War* 1.407). Herod was keen to ingratiate himself to the Roman elites through these projects; in fact, any traveler arriving in Judea via the port of Caesarea Maritima would be instantly greeted by the sight of the temple to Augustus and Roma.[569] Even so, Herod wisely opted not to build any such temples in areas with a Jewish majority. Herod's aim, James S. McLaren suggests, was to create a kind of separate and parallel space for the cult of the emperor.[570] When slighted for this un-Jewish act, Herod protested that the imperial temples had been built out of obedience to Caesar, not out of his own convictions (*Ant.* 15.328–30). True, Herod did not willfully transgress Jewish scruples, but he certainly probed them and provoked a rancorous response. We see that in the golden eagle incident, when Herod erected a golden eagle over the gate of the temple, the eagle being a symbol for Roman power. Herod perhaps thought it innocuous as art, not something to be worshipped, and so unoffensive to Jewish sensibilities. Yet two popular teachers, probably Pharisees, stirred up their followers to pull the statue down as contrary to their ancestral laws about the prohibition of images of animals (Josephus, *Ant.* 17.149–155; *War* 1.648–55). All in all, Josephus considers that Herod's building projects were motivated more by the pursuit of his own honor rather than anybody else's, and the honors he offered to Caesar Augustus and Marcus Agrippa were foreign to the Jews, who preferred righteousness over glory (*Ant.* 16.157–58).

One must wonder why Herod, the supposed "King of the Jews," built imperial temples.[571] Afterall, the Jewish Scriptures are filled with stories of faithful Jews resisting ruler cults (e.g., Dan 2 and 6), and wisdom traditions warn against flattering rulers with images (Wis 14.17). The Maccabean uprising was

---

[567] Richardson, *Herod*, 194; and Rocca, *Herod's Judaea*, 315–19.

[568] Richardson, *Herod*, 184.

[569] James S. McLaren, "Jews and the Imperial Cult: From Augustus to Domitian," *JSNT* 27 (2005): 261.

[570] McLaren, "Jews and the Imperial Cult," 257.

[571] The rightful focus of Monika Bernett, "Der Kaiserkult in Judäa unter herodischer und römischer Herrschaft: Zu Herausbildung und Herausforderung neuer Konzepte jüdischer Herrschaftslegitimation," in *Jewish Identity in the Greco-Roman World*, ed. Jörg Frey, Daniel R. Schwartz, and Stephanie Gripentrog (AJEC 71; Leiden: Brill, 2007), 205–51 (esp. 213–14); and idem, *Der Kaiserkult in Judäa unter den Herodiern und Römern: Untersuchungen zur politischen und religiösen Geschichte Judäas von 30 v. bis 66 n. Chr.* (WUNT 2003; Tübingen: Mohr Siebeck, 2007).

waged precisely against the pagan religious monuments that Herod was erecting within *eretz Yisrael* and in cities that had significant Jewish populations. Previous scholarship regarded such projects as expressing a form of external devotion to the imperium and continuing a process of internal Judean Hellenization. But there may be more at play.[572]

After Octavius' victory over Antony and Cleopatra at Actium, Herod, a partisan of Antony, was in a precarious position, as was his kingdom. There was no prospect of Jewish independence (a return to the Hasmonean era), a mere treaty with Rome would not suffice (1 Macc 8), he did not want a military occupation and forced Hellenization (the policy of Antiochus IV), and he wanted to preserve the favorable treatment of Jews by previous Roman rulers (Julius Caesar and Mark Antony). Herod, in his reconciliation to Octavius, for the sake of his own self-preservation as much as to prevent the possible annexation of Judea into Syria, forged a solution that was novelty born of necessity. Herod pursued a grand strategy of embedding Judea and all the Jews into the edifice of Octavius' power to achieve a degree of autonomy within the aegis of imperial benefaction.[573] Herod was not alone in this endeavor, as there was something of a mad dash to set up the imperial cult in the domains of client kingdoms in the east (Suetonius, *Aug.* 60.1).[574] As a result, says Zanker, "The imperial cult rapidly became the most widespread of all cults."[575] Nevertheless, we can consider Herod's efforts a "work of messianic mediation" as he attempted to mediate Octavius' status as Savior and Redeemer of the whole world to the Jews of Judea and the Diaspora.[576] Herod would, in effect, Judaize the benefactions of Octavius and the reciprocation made to Octavius by showering Octavius with divine honors wherever practical while trying to protect Jewish spaces from the religious symbols of Roman hegemony as far as possible. This was a policy that was largely continued by successors in the Herodian dynasty.[577] I concur, then, with the judgment of Monika Bernett:

---

[572] Cf. McLaren, "Jews and the Imperial Cult," 260–61; and Bernett, "Der Kaiserkult in Judäa unter herodischer," 207.

[573] Bernett, "Der Kaiserkult in Judäa unter herodischer," 221.

[574] Cf. Mitchell, *Anatolia*, 1:100; and Andreas Kropp, "King-Caesar-God: Roman Imperial Cult among Near Eastern 'Client' Kings," in *Lokale Identität im Römischen Nahen Osten*, ed. Michael Blömer, Margherita Facella, and Engelbert Winter (Stuttgart: Franz Steiner, 2009), 99–150.

[575] Zanker, *Power of Images*, 297.

[576] Cf. Bernett, "Der Kaiserkult in Judäa unter herodischer," 208–9, n. 7, following the work of A. Schalit ("messianisches Vermittlungswerk").

[577] Cf., e.g., Herod Agrippa II, who enlarged Caesara Philippi and renamed it Neronias (Josephus, *Ant.* 20.211–12). Otherwise, see discussion in Bernett, "Der Kaiserkult in Judäa unter herodischer," 223–51.

The [introduction of the imperial] cult was neither vain flattery nor an excessive display of Herod's subservience to the Roman Caesar as is so often claimed. The contributions to the imperial cults (especially building city foundations) were rather part of a network of relationships that integrated many functions: a public response to the princeps' "benevolence," an affirmation of the relationship between the Roman center and the imperial periphery, demonstrable reciprocity, an announcement of favor by one who acted in the revered role of the ruling Euergeton, who can expect the friendship and the benevolence of the recipient.[578]

Herod's strategy was *regnum* and *religio* for *Realpolitik*. It was a careful balancing of imperial loyalty and Jewish integrity through simultaneous expressions of imperial and Jewish pieties. It was a working arrangement that (mostly!) maintained good order and kept good faith. The operating policy of various Augusti and Herodian rulers, as Philo makes clear, was to simultaneously honor the emperor while respecting Jewish customs concerning the temple (i.e., Jerusalem temple sacrifices would be made for the emperor but not to the emperor [*Legat.* 298, 301, 305, 309–10, 356, 364]). Augustus thus granted Jews the freedom to follow their customs in accordance with their ancestral traditions and without imperial interference (Philo, *Legat.* 155–57; Josephus, *Ant.* 16.162–65). Evidently, then, Herod the Great had been successful in his strategy, for, with few building projects and a few token gestures of devotion within the constraints of Jewish religious scruples, the Jews were relatively free in their worship in both Jerusalem and in the Diaspora.

However, the potential for the status quo to fall apart soon became apparent with the imposition of direct imperial rule in Judea after the dismissal of Herod's son Archelaus as ethnarch (6 CE), and again after the death of King Herod Agrippa I (44 CE). That is because direct imperial rule meant that the imperial apparatus and its religious paraphernalia formally penetrated Judea.[579] This led to a delicate situation that was often indelicately handled by parties. The many Roman prefects and procurators were wildly mixed

---

[578] Bernett, "Der Kaiserkult in Judäa unter herodischer," 227: "Der Kult war weder läßliche Schmeichelei noch übertriebenes Zeichen von Herodes' Unterwürfigkeit gegenüber dem römischen Kaiser, wie so oft behauptet wird. Die Kaiserkultakte (v. a. Baustiftungen, Stadtgründungen) waren vielmehr Teil eines Beziehungsgeflechtes, das viele Funktionen miteinander vereinte: eine öffentliche Antwort auf 'Wohltaten' des princeps, eine auf Reziprozität angelegte Beziehungsvergewisserung zwischen römischem Zentrum und Reichsperiphere, ein Bekanntmachen der Gunst, in der man stand sowie das Agieren in der geachteten Rolle des herrscherlichen Euergeten, der die Freundschaft und das Wohlwollen der Beschenkten erwarten darf."

[579] Bernett, "Der Kaiserkult in Judäa unter herodischer," 240.

in their dispositions towards the Jews and their competencies in addressing Jewish concerns. Even worse, many tended towards the incendiary, with dashes of incompetence and corruption. The best example of how volatile the situation was under direct Roman rule of Judea is the amusing story of how a fart literally started a riot at one Passover festival during the administration of the province by the procurator Cumanus ca. 48–52 CE. Things turned ugly when a Roman soldier standing on the porticoes around the temple "mooned" and expelled a rude sound at Jewish pilgrims entering the temple. This led to a response of rock throwing by pilgrims and then a violent melee breaking out in the temple precincts (Josephus, *War* 2.224–27; *Ant.* 20.105–12).

Some decades earlier, during the prefecture of Pontius Pilate (ca. 26/27–36/37 CE), two incidents took place that triggered a hostile reaction from local leaders. To begin with, Pilate brought Roman standards into Jerusalem, but had to back down after a mass protest (Josephus, *Ant.* 18.55–59; *War* 2.169–74). Then later, Pilate placed Roman votive shields, albeit without images, in the palace at Jerusalem, an act which annoyed the emperor Tiberius as much as it did the Judean leadership. Tiberius ordered the shields to be moved to the temple of Augustus in Caesarea Maritima (*Legat.* 299–306). For all the embedding of Jews and Judaism within the imperium, the symbols of Roman power and its imperial religion remained deeply resented in the Jewish homeland and had the capacity to trigger a volatile response.

Pilate found other ways to promote a pro-imperial agenda and to test the depth of Jewish resistance to imperial honors. The copper coins minted by Pontius Pilate show him deliberately using pagan iconography and testing the flexibility of Jewish scruples. His predecessors had minted coins with agricultural imagery, which could ambiguously be associated with pagan deities, like wine with Dionysus, but the engravings on the coins avoided anything explicitly associated with divine images or pagan religion. Yet Pilate minted coins carrying pagan religious utensils: the *lituus*, an "augury wand" used by Roman priests and vestals; and the *simpulum*, a "libation ladle" used by Roman priests. This was not unprecedented as there had been Roman coins previously minted with the *lituus* and *simpulum* together. The design of these coins was perhaps not intentionally offensive[580] or meant to provoke a hostile reaction; nonetheless, as Joan Taylor comments, "cultic items point to the cult in which they are used." Accordingly:

---

[580] Though Philo (*Legat.* 299) suggests that Pilate did try to irritate the Jewish population.

Pontius Pilate in his coinage honours the emperor Tiberius by celebrating his membership of two Roman priestly colleges in depicting Roman emblems symbolic of those colleges, but he also does more. It was the *pontifices* and *augures* who were the representatives of Roman religion in the two imperial cult temples of Caesarea Maritima and in Sebaste, located in the province he governed. The symbolism never points outside Roman cult to universal themes. The coins celebrate the religious roles of the emperor, and also the imperial cult, and Pilate does this in a province in which the institution of Roman religion is largely the preserve of the Roman administration and army, with its focus in the army barracks and in the temples of the imperial cult.[581]

Finally, the famous Pilate inscription testifies to the erection and dedication of a building called the Tiberium in honor of the emperor Tiberius. Although perhaps not a religious building, it would not have been religiously neutral, it probably had images or statues of the emperor within it, and it attests to devotion to the emperor in Caesarea Maritima.

(3) Jewish participation in the imperial cult.

Bernett is correct when she writes, "As a religious phenomenon, the Jews took the imperial cult more seriously than probably any other culture in the Roman Empire."[582] The imperial cult was part of the social, political, and religious fabric of Syro-Palestine including Judea and Galilee. But it had to be carefully negotiated, as the Judean leadership needed to be seen participating within the imperial system of divine honors even as they strove to preserve the integrity of their own ancestral tradition, which was not naturally conducive to pagan ruler worship.[583]

The Jews were embedded within the network of imperial devotion by tangibly contributing to divine honors for the emperor, but without compromising the aniconic worship of the Jews (see Exod 20.4; Lev 19.4; 26.1; Deut 4.23; 5.8; 7.25; 27.15; Wis 13.10–15.17; *Sib. Or.* 3.8–45; Philo, *Dec.* 66–76). The Jews

---

[581] Joan E. Taylor, "Pontius Pilate and the Imperial Cult in Roman Judaea," NTS 52 (2006): 563.

[582] Bernett, "Der Kaiserkult in Judäa unter herodischer," 210: "Als religiöses Phänomen nahmen die Juden den Kaiserkult so ernst wie vermutlich kaum eine andere Kultur im Römischen Reich, und zwar unabhängig davon."

[583] Cf. Horbury, *Jewish Messianism*, 74; McLaren, "Jews and the Imperial Cult," 257–78; Hans-Georg Gradl, "Kaisertum und Kaiserkult: Ein Vergleich zwischen Philos *Legatio ad Gaium* und der Offenbarung des Johannes," NTS 56 (2010): 116–38; and Bruce W. Winter, *Divine Honours for the Caesars: The First Christians' Responses* (Grand Rapids: Eerdmans, 2015), 94–123.

received in return a special dispensation of freedoms to follow their national customs in Judea and in the Diaspora. This was workable because, as Josephus points out, "Nothing in Mosaic traditions forbids honors to worthy men, only that they are not the same as honors given to God, honors which we freely offer to the emperor and to the people of Rome" (*Ag. Ap.* 2.76).

Besides the imperial temples built by the Herodians on the periphery of Jewish territory, the primary way that Jews demonstrated their loyalty to the imperium was through the Jerusalem cultus. Instead of offering sacrifices to the emperor, erecting an altar to the emperor in the temples, or setting up a Roman temple next to the Jerusalem temple, the Judean priesthood offered twice-daily sacrifices to Yahweh on behalf of the Roman emperor and the Roman people (Philo, *Legat.* 157, 232, 280, 317, 356; Josephus, *War* 2.197-98; *Ag. Ap.* 2.76-77). It was the refusal to offer this sacrifice that marked the beginning of the Judean rebellion against Rome in 66 CE (Josephus, *War* 2.409-19). Daniel Schwartz argues that the rejection of Gentile and imperial sacrifice (Josephus, *War* 2.414; 4QMMT B 1-3, 8-13) was premised on the logic of sacrifice whereby sacrifice could either remove a deficit (like sin) or else credit one's account before God (like merit). It may mean that some Jews objected to crediting the Roman account before God whereby the Jewish altar was being used for the benefit of pagans who competed with God for rule of his people and his land.[584]

There were several other acts in which Jews engaged to demonstrate loyalty to the regime and which often had a religious quality. This included acclamations of emperors upon their accession (Philo, *Legat.* 288, 299; Josephus, *War* 3.459; 4.417;7.126-29). There were Jewish loyalty oaths made to the emperor (Josephus, *Ant.* 17.42). Jewish elites could address the emperors as "master" and "lord" and use honorific divine titles like "savior" and "benefactor" (Philo, *Legat.* 22, 286, 290, 356; Josephus, *Ant.* 18.296; *War* 3.459; 7.71). In Alexandria, prayers houses contained shields, crowns, stelae, and inscriptions in homage to the emperor (Philo, *Flacc.* 48-50; *Legat.* 133). Prayers for the emperor can be found in Judean and Diasporan synagogues as attested by the presence of the inscription *pro salute Augusti* and variations.[585] Josephus also joined in the tradition of divine prophecy for an emperor's greatness when he said that an oracle about a world ruler who was prophesied to come from Judea pertained not to a Judean figure, but to Vespasian (Josephus, *War* 6.312-13).

---

[584] Daniel R. Schwartz, *Studies in the Jewish Background of Christianity* (Tübingen: Mohr Siebeck, 1992), 113-15.

[585] Pucci ben Zeev, *Jewish Rights in the Roman World: The Greek and Roman Documents Quoted by Josephus Flavius* (Tübingen: Mohr Siebeck, 1998), 477-78.

The most explicit pandering to the imperial regime is Philo's extraordinary panegyric to Augustus. Philo stresses Augustus' nonantagonistic attitude towards Jews who did not honor him with cultic sacrifices and his practice of *moderatio* concerning divine honors (*Legat.* 145–49). Yet Philo seems to support the fitness of cities regarding Augustus as equal to the Olympian gods:

> And yet if it was right to decree new and exceptional to anyone, he was the proper person to receive them. He was what we may call the source and fountain-head of the Augustan stock in general. He was also the first and the greatest and the common benefactor in that he displaced the rule of many and committed the ship of the commonwealth to be steered by a single pilot, that is himself, a marvelous master of the science of government. For there is justice in the saying: "It is not well that many lords should rule" since multiplicity of suffrages produces multiform evils. But besides all these the whole habitable world voted him no less than honors equal to those of the Olympian gods. (*Legat.* 149)

Philo is then quite comfortable treating Augustus as a superhuman being deserving of divine honors, and he praises him in a manner still congenial with the Torah's strictures (*Legat.* 143, 356; *Flacc.* 49).[586]

We may speak, then, of Jewish participation within the imperial cults of the Hellenistic east, albeit with certain conditions and distinctives.

(4) Jewish resistance to ruler cults.

Jewish resistance to ruler cults was native to its religious heritage and was constantly tested by unwise or provocative Roman leaders. We have to remember that the critique of the divine cult of rulers is ubiquitous through the Hebrew and Greek Bibles as well as in Second Temple Jewish literature.[587] Yahweh and his people, prophets, and princes have always stood against the idolatry, impurity, and impiety of the pagan nations with their kings, god-kings, and gods. Whether the Egyptian Pharaoh, the Babylonian conqueror Nebuchadnezzar, or the King of Tyre, the true and living God of the Israelites brooks no rivals and suffers no blasphemies even by mighty monarchs.[588] Indeed, divine ruler cults are attacked by a wide linguistic cross-section of Jewish texts in Aramaic

---

[586] M. David Litwa, *We Are Being Transformed: Deification in Paul's Soteriology* (Berlin: de Gruyter, 2012), 93.

[587] 2 Chr 24.17; Isa 14.13; Ezek 28.2; 29.3; Dan 3.1–30; 11.36–39; 2 Macc 9.8–12; Wis 7.1–6; 14.17–21; Jdt 3.8; 6.2–4; Sir 9.17–10.18; *Sib. Or.* 3.545–49; 5.33–55, 137–54, 214–21; Add Esth 3.3; Philo, *Legat.* 77–184; Josephus, *Ant.* 18.256–61; 19.4; *Ag. Ap.* 2.75–76

[588] Bird, *Jesus the Eternal Son*, 49–62; and idem, *An Anomalous Jew: Paul among Jews, Greeks, and Romans* (Grand Rapids: Eerdmans, 2016), 227–28.

(Daniel), Hebrew (Ben Sira), and Greek (Judith, Greek Esther, Wisdom of Solomon; 1–2 Maccabees).[589]

Jewish aniconic monolatry and its aversion to ruler worship meant that there were periodic conflicts between Jews and imperial authorities. Regional ethnic groups in Syro-Palestine knew that the Jews had specific scruples about "prostrations and foods" (3 Macc 3.7), which led eventually to the crisis of 167–64 BCE and Antiochus IV's desecration of the Jerusalem temple (1 Macc 1.20–26; 2 Macc 6.1–6). Tacitus noted that the Jews "set up no statues in their cities, still less in their temples; this flattery is not paid their kings, nor this honour given to the Caesars" (Tacitus, *Hist.* 5.5).

The Jews, of course, found ways to negotiate demands for emperor worship and to navigate their own traditions with its many cultic restrictions. There were ways of honoring the emperor without transgressing Jewish legal traditions. However, we might say that Jewish monuments to Caesar still had certain cracks that show that they could not carry the weight of devotion that some emperors and governors expected of their Jewish subjects.

Jewish reticence to *fully* participate in rituals of imperial honor came to a head when Caligula tried to impose the imperial cult in the Jerusalem temple (see Philo, *Legat.*; Josephus, *Ant.* 18.257–61; *War* 2.184–85). The Caligula-temple episode shows what happens when the irresistible force of imperial expectations for divine honors meets the immovable object of Jewish aniconic monolatry.

Sometime in 38/39 CE, a group of non-Jews in the coastal town of Jamnia, on the spur of the moment, set up an altar to Caligula. The Jewish majority of the town tore down the altar, and the non-Jews complained to a local governing official named Capiton. Capiton responded by writing to Caligula about the incident, and Caligula in turn ordered the erection of an even more ornate altar to be placed in the temple of Jerusalem (Philo, *Legat.* 199–203). Somewhat concurrently, tensions became inflamed in Alexandria between local Greeks and the Jewish minority over the Jewish refusal to pay full divine honors to the emperor. An anti-Jewish riot erupted where Jewish properties were looted, many Jews killed (*Legat.* 120–39), and a bronze statue of Caligula drawn by a four-horse chariot was erected in a Jewish prayer house (*Legat.* 134–37, 346). The Alexandrians wanted to turn the Jewish quarter of the city into an imperial precinct for the worship of the emperor (*Legat.* 137). In Rome, an Alexandrian delegation led by Apion arrived to denounce the Jews to Caligula, while a Jewish delegation from

---

[589] Horbury, *Jewish Messianism*, 74.

Alexandria led by Philo also arrived to state their case. The Jewish delegation was initially sidelined by Caligula and then when received was thoroughly reprimanded by him for their impious recalcitrance towards his cult (Josephus, *Ant.* 18.257–59; Philo, *Legat.* 178–96, 349–67). In sum:

- Caligula regarded his divine honors with tremendous import (Philo, *Legat.* 75–113, 162–64, 198, 201, 332, 338, 353, 357, 368; Josephus, *War* 2.184; *Ant.* 18.256; Suetonius, *Cal.* 21–22, 52; Cassius Dio 59.26.8–9), introducing prostration into Italy (*Legat.* 116; Cassius Dio 59.24.3–4)[590] and commissioning new temples (Cassius Dio 59.28.1).[591]

- Caligula was incensed by the neglect of imperial devotion by Jews in Alexandria (Philo, *Legat.*; Josephus, *Ant.* 18.257) and by the destruction of imperial altars by Jews in Jamnia (*Legat.* 199–203). He believed the sacking of Jewish prayer houses in Alexandria was done out of genuine devotion to himself (*Legat.* 164).

- Caligula was specifically dissatisfied with merely Jewish sacrifices *for* the emperor and required instead cultic sacrifices to the emperor (i.e., full-monty imperial cult [Philo, *Legat.* 162, 356–57]). Caligula, in Philo's narration, sounds like a spoiled child deprived of a trophy, as the Jews would sacrifice to another god for him, leading to his exasperated outburst, "What good is it then? For you have not sacrificed to me!" (*Legat.* 357).

- Caligula wanted to place his statue in the Jerusalem temple (Josephus, *War* 2.185; *Ant.* 18.261), renaming the temple "Zeus Epiphanes Neos known as Gaius" (Philo, *Legat.* 188, 346) and dedicating the temple to his own use (*Legat.* 198). This would effectively make Caligula a throne-sharer (*synnaos*) with Yahweh and assimilate him to Zeus/Jupiter as an epiphany of the supreme deity.

- The Jewish response was to emphasize Jewish devotion to the emperor in the form of being among the first to offer sacrifices for him (Philo, *Legat.* 232, 356) and the policy of previous Augusti in

---

[590] So did Nero allegedly: Tirades I of Armenia is reported to have said to Nero: "And I have come to thee, my god, to worship (*proskynesōn*) thee as I do Mithras. The destiny thou spinnest for me shall be mine; for thou art my Fortune and my Fate" (Cassius Dio 62.5.2).

[591] Cf. Fantin, *Lord of the Entire World*, 193–94; Reasoner, *Roman Imperial Texts*, 59–66; and Anthony Barrett, *Caligula: The Corruption of Power* (London: Routledge, 2000), 143–52.

respecting Jewish ancestral laws (Philo, *Legat*. 155–61; 298–320; Josephus, *Ant*. 16.162–65).

- After the intercession of Marcus Agrippa I, Caligula initially relented, and would only set up his statue in the Jerusalem temple if imperial altars in neighboring regions were interfered with. But Caligula then rescinded this concession and returned to his plan of placing his statue in the Jerusalem temple, only now one made of bronze, gilded with gold, and made in Rome (Philo, *Legat*. 334–38). He also ordered the seizure of all Jewish prayer houses in Alexandria and filled them with images and statues of himself as a foretaste of what he would do to the Jerusalem temple (*Legat*. 346).

- The Syrian legate, Petronius, was ordered to erect the statue by force, and a Jewish delegation persuaded him of what he already knew—that it was a bad idea that would lead to civil war. Petronius asked Caligula to consider his decision and was ordered to commit suicide for his disobedience. Fortunately for Petronius, the news of Caligula's death reached him before Caligula's order to commit suicide did (*Legat*. 207–60; Josephus, *Ant*. 18.261–309; *War* 2.184–203).

- After Caligula's assassination and with the accession of Claudius in Rome and Herod Agrippa I in Jerusalem, there were immediate decrees to respect the Jewish customs (see P. Lond. 1912, 70–104; Josephus, *Ant*. 19.278–306).[592] This was applicable to the new situation in the city of Dora, where local Greeks desecrated a synagogue by placing a statue of Claudius in it. By doing this, they were imitating what the Alexandrians had done to the Jewish prayer houses (Philo, *Legat*. 134–37, 346) and were hoping that a Jewish backlash would prompt the kind of response that Caligula had planned to make if imperial statues were assailed by Jewish radicals (Philo, *Legat*. 334). Notably, the imperial cult was used, in both Alexandria and Dora, as a weapon in interethnic conflict against local Jews.

The most palpable instances of Jewish rebellion against Roman rule in general and the imperial cult in particular were the rebellions of 66–70 and 132–35 CE, respectively. Jewish rebels from the first Judean rebellion, when captured and tortured, refused to call Caesar "lord" (*War* 7.418–19) and so anticipate the

---

[592] Cf. Bernett, "Der Kaiserkult in Judäa unter herodischer," 242–43.

later Christian refusal to address Caesar as a divine lord (*Mart. Pol.* 8.2; Tertullian, *Apol.* 33–34).

One could arguably regard the Pauline epistles, canonical Gospels, *4 Ezra*, *Parables of Enoch*, and the book of Revelation as carrying forms of Jewish protest against Roman religious hegemony, often invoking messianic scripts and mythological symbology, to hope for a world where Caesar is defeated and desecrated. These texts are not resistance literature in terms of Thomas Paine's *The Rights of Man* or Nikolai Chernyshevsky's *What Is to Be Done?* But they do collectively imagine divine retribution upon Rome and its religious edifices and look forward to a day of peace and prosperity for God's people. Apocalyptic texts are, by their subject matter and central concern, inherently anti-imperial. As Hans-Georg Gradl puts it:

> In contrast [to Philo], the early Jewish apocalypses share the radical political criticism and social repudiation of John the Seer. The power of the Roman state is repeatedly seen in the negative (*4 Ezra* 11.1–12.34; *2 Bar.* 35.1–40.4). No attempt is made to construct and protect Jewish identity through loyalty and integration with the empire. Rather, God brings retribution and implements justice (*Sib. Or.* 3.350–380; 4.145–148). The Roman Empire appears as a direct adversary of God (*Sib. Or.* 8.68–83) and is doomed. Here, the stabilisation and preservation of Jewish identity can only be achieved through a sharp demarcation from the social sphere and it takes place in a belief concerning an eschatological act brought about by God.[593]

Finally, we should consider the synagogue at Dura-Europos, which provides evidence for Jewish iconography with a tacit anti-imperial dimension. The iconographical representation of the tabernacle overlays Jewish iconography over Roman imperial temple imagery. There is a visual depiction of the prophet Elijah against the prophets of Baal from 1 Kgs 18.16–45, but the temple of the Philistine god Dagon is depicted with Roman imperial victories on its corners

---

[593] Gradl, "Kaisertum und Kaiserkult," 138: "Dagegen teilen die frühjüdischen Apokalypsen die radikale politische Kritik und gesellschaftliche Verweigerungshaltung des Sehers Johannes. Die römische Staatsmacht wird durchwegs negativ bewertet (4 Ezra 11.1–12.34; 2 Bar. 35.1–40.4). Entwicklung und Schutz der jüdischen Identität werden nicht durch eine loyal gestimmte Integrationshaltung zu erreichen versucht. Gott vollzieht die Vergeltung und schafft Gerechtigkeit (Sib. Or. 3.350–380; 4.145–148). Das römische Reich erscheint als direkter Gegenspieler Gottes (Sib. Or. 8.68–83) und ist dem Untergang geweiht. Abermals ist die Stabilisierung und Bewahrung jüdischer Identität nur durch die scharfe Abgrenzung von der Gesellschaft zu erreichen, die sich im Glauben an die von Gott herbeigeführte eschatologische Wende vollzieht."

and Greco-Roman nude figures on its doors. Thus, in effect, the imperial cult is simply the new Baal religion, a further enemy of God's people.[594]

(3) Ruler cults in early Christianity.

To state a simple thesis: *If* Jesus is the "Messiah," and *if* "Messiah" is a royal honorific title like "Sebastos" or "Epiphanes," and *if* "Messiah" was a Jewish expression of ancient Mediterranean political discourse,[595] and *if* Jesus was worshipped by the early church, *then* we are led to the inescapable conclusion early Christianity was a ruler cult . . . of sorts. Importantly, this does not require the "Gentilization" of Christianity. The scriptural roots of Jewish messianism in royal ideology, Daniel's Son of Man and its reception history, Jewish veneration of its own rulers as Yahweh's son and a heavenly lord, mean that ruler veneration can be considered indigenous to the Jewish tradition.[596]

However, in other respects, we may speak of direct Greco-Roman influence upon the messiah worship of early Christianity. Deissmann was right to say that the "New Testament is a book of the imperial age."[597] Early Christianity's usage of designations and imagery like "God and Savior," "Son of God," "Lord," "gospel," "peace and security," "triumph," "citizenship," and "presence" betray signs of Greco-Roman influence since this language is prevalent in socio-religio-political discourse. Now, to be sure, you can also find some Jewish equivalents: "Son of God" (2 Sam 7.12–16; Ps 2.7) and "gospel" (Isa 40.9; 41.27; 52.7; 61.1) are cases in point. However, Christian usage of these terms obviously resources Greco-Roman media, language, and traditions, and would inevitably resonate with auditors who inhabited Greco-Roman environs. Early christological discourse is simultaneously Septuagintal as it is imperial. We may say, with Harry O. Maier, that with regard to the apostle Paul, he is "heavily steeped in imperial language, metaphor and ideas" and engages in a type of "imperial hybridity" whereby imperial images are used and deployed for specifically Christian purposes.[598]

Many illustrations could be provided; perhaps the best one is the adjective *kyriakos*, which means generally "belonging to the Lord" or, more precisely,

---

[594] Maier, *Picturing Paul in Empire*, 11, n. 44.
[595] Obviously riffing off Matthew V. Novenson, *Christ among the Messiahs: Christ Language in Paul and Messiah Language in Ancient Judaism* (Oxford: Oxford University Press, 2016), and idem, *Grammar of Messianism*.
[596] This is largely the burden of Horbury, *Jewish Messianism*; and Bühner, *Hohe Messianologie*.
[597] Deissmann, *Light from the Ancient East*, 341.
[598] Maier, *Picturing Paul in Empire*, 6, 35–38.

"imperial."[599] Inscriptions and papyri show that *kyriakos* was used to indicate the "imperial treasury" and "imperial finances."[600] Christians used this language when referring to the "Lord's table" (1 Cor 11.20) and "Lord's day" (Rev 1.10; *Did.* 14.1; Ignatius, *Magn.* 9.1; *Gos. Pet.* 9.35; 12.50). In fact, "Lords' day" also seems to be parallel to "emperor's day" as attested on ostraca and papyri.[601] Deissmann's conclusion remains apt:

> The cult of Christ goes forth into the world of the Mediterranean and soon displays the endeavour to reserve for Christ the words already in use for worship in that world, words that had just been transferred to the deified emperors (or had perhaps even been newly invented in emperor worship). Thus there arises a *polemical parallelism* between the cult of the emperor and the cult of Christ, which makes itself felt where ancient words derived by Christianity from the treasury of the Septuagint and the Gospels happen to coincide with solemn concepts of the Imperial cult which sounded the same or similar.[602]

Deissmann's work is somewhat dated, and we can obviously contest exactly how polemical this parallelism is, whether profession of Jesus as Lord truly amounts to a "silent protest" against the emperor cult.[603] It suffices to note that the Roman imperial cult was the resident paradigm of royal and seemingly divine power and thus a paradigm or even an impetus for the messianic devotion. At the same time, and somewhat paradoxically, the Roman imperial cult was regarded as the summit of impiety, something to be satirized and sanitized by devotees to the one true God.

Unsurprisingly, then, there are several texts in the New Testament that show genuine analogies between ancient ruler cults and early christological discourse.

(a) 1 Cor 16.22.

> Let anyone be accursed who has no love for the Lord. Our Lord, come!
> (1 Cor 16.22)

Paul's closing peroration to 1 Corinthians includes a curse, an anathema, for those who do not love the Lord Jesus, as well as a prayerful petition to the

---

[599] BDAG, 576.
[600] Deissmann, *Light from the Ancient East*, 357–61.
[601] Deissmann, *Light from the Ancient East*, 359–60.
[602] Deissmann, *Light from the Ancient East*, 342 (italics added).
[603] Deissmann, *Light from the Ancient East*, 342, 359, 355. See my discussion of the counter-imperial Paul in Bird, *Anomalous Jew*, 205–55.

Lord Jesus for his return using the Aramaic formula *marana tha*, "our Lord come!"[604] The assonance of anathema and *marana tha* add emphasis and draw attention to the subject matter, namely, Jesus as one to be loved and Lord to be expected. Importantly, we have concrete proof here that Jesus was acclaimed as "Lord" in the earliest days of the Aramaic-speaking church without imagining that the title *kyrios* was first applied to Jesus in a Hellenistic setting, as Bousset and Bultmann wrongly supposed.[605]

Otherwise, the crux is what the identification of Jesus as "Lord" (Gk. *kyrios*; Aram. *marêh*) means with regard to Jesus' divine status (see Phil 2.9–11; 1 Cor 8.6; 12.3; Rom 10.8–9; Col 2.6). For many commentators, the identification of Jesus as Lord makes him far more than an earthly master; rather, it means that he participates in the lordship of the God of Israel. That is plausible because Jews, in sacred literature, inscriptions, texts, and papyri, often addressed God as *marêh* and *kyrios*, even as a translation of the divine name "YHWH."[606] Alternatively, Casey believed that confession of the risen Jesus as "Lord" indicated that "Jesus was viewed as a superior heavenly being, and a central figure of identity and authority to whom the church was subject," but it did not "equate him with God."[607]

In support of Casey's contention of identifying Jesus a lesser-divine lord, we should note that it is possible to locate *marêh* and *kyrios* in the context of Syro-Palestinian ruler veneration. There is ample evidence for the use of *kyrios* and *marêh* for non-divine figures, specifically Nabataean kings ("to Dusares the God and to our lord Aretas the king," i.e., Aretas IV [*CIS* 2.199]) and Herodian rulers (Philo, *Flacc*. 39; *OGIS* 415, 418, 423, 425, 426), who are designated as "lord" in numerous inscriptions in the southern Levant and Palestine.[608] The inscriptions demonstrate, says Burnett, that "those living in the southern Levant could distinguish between a human, non-divine *kyrios* who is king and a god *kyrios* who is divine."[609] Furthermore, *kyrios* can be correlated with *christos* as a royal title, to designate the "messianic lord," the "Lord's messiah," or "Messiah and Lord" (Lam 4.20 [LXX]; *Pss. Sol.* 17.32; 18.7; Luke 2.11; Acts

---

[604] While the grammar of the underlying Aramaic is ambiguous, I am assuming, in light of the parallel with Rev 22.20, that the verb *tha* is imperative. So too Joseph A. Fitzmyer, *A Wandering Aramean: Collected Aramaic Essays* (Missoula, Mont.: Scholars Press, 1979), 129.

[605] Cf. Bousset, *Kyrios Christos*, 126–29; and Bultmann, *Theology of the New Testament*, 1:124–25.

[606] Fitzmyer, *Wandering Aramean*, 115–42 (esp. 115–30).

[607] Casey, *From Jewish Prophet*, 110.

[608] Burnett, *Studying the New Testament*, 67–76.

[609] Burnett, *Studying the New Testament*, 74.

2.34–36; 4.26; *2 Clem.* 9.5; *Barn.* 12.10).[610] In other words, *kyrios* and *marêh* are not necessarily a divine title, but a designation for the royal lordship of a messianic agent.[611] Hengel recognized the priority and pressure that messianism exerted upon other christological titles, stating "in early Christianity there was no Kyrios-theology which was not dependent upon the messiahship of Jesus."[612] In which case, the titles *marêh* and *kyrios* could be expressing Jesus' messianic identity in heightened regal terminology, not equating Jesus with Israel's Lord.

It is certainly true, as Dunn comments, that Paul's "attribution of lordship to Jesus could not have been derived from or modelled on the cultic worship of his Hellenistic environment."[613] The appellation "Lord" had already been applied to Jesus by the primitive and pre-Pauline Aramaic-speaking churches of Palestine and only later was the title transmitted to the Greek-speaking churches by tradents such as Paul. However, we must countenance the possibility that Syro-Palestinian ruler cults with their veneration of monarchs as *marêh* influenced the form and grammar of primitive Christology.[614] Thus, the designation of Jesus as *marêh* does not necessitate that Jesus is part of a divine identity, or is even receiving divine worship. On a minimalist reading, Jesus is an exalted royal ruler, the *marêh mesiha*, who has been received into heaven.

(b) Phil 2.6–11.

There is considerable debate as to whether Phil 2.6–11[615] is a hymn or whether it is merely a form of poetic prose.[616] I remain uncommitted, but it is highly

[610] Cf. Bird, *Are You the One?* 54.

[611] Cf. Fitzmyer, *Wandering Aramean*, 131; Horbury, *Jewish Messianism*, 144–45; and Burnett, *Studying the New Testament*, 72–76.

[612] Martin Hengel, "Erwägungen zum Sprachgebrauch von *Christos* bei Paulus und in der 'vorpaulinischen' Überlieferung," in *Paul and Paulinism*, ed. M. D. Hooker and S. G. Wilson (London: SPCK, 1982), 154n54: "Es gab im Urchristentum keine Kyrios-Christologie, die unabhängig war von der Messianität Jesu."

[613] Dunn, *Theology of Paul*, 247.

[614] The point of Horbury, *Jewish Messianism*; and Zehnder, "Question of the 'Divine Status,'" 514.

[615] On the parity of Col 1.15–20 and imperial ideology, see Gordley, *Teaching through Song*, 298.

[616] Gordon D. Fee, "Philippians 2:5–11: Hymn or Exalted Pauline Prose?" *BBR* 2 (1992): 30–34; Joseph A. Marchal, "Expecting a Hymn, Encountering an Argument: Introducing the Rhetoric of Philippians and Pauline Interpretation," *Int* 61 (2007): 245–55; Michael Peppard, "'Poetry,' 'Hymns' and 'Traditional Material' in New Testament Epistles or How to Do Things with Indentations," *JSNT* 30 (2008): 322–27; Benjamin Edsall and Jennifer R. Strawbridge, "The Songs We Used to Sing? Hymn 'Traditions' and Reception in Pauline Letters," *JSNT* 37 (2015): 290–311; and Michael Wade Martin and Bryan A. Nash, "Philippians

plausible that Phil 2.6–11 is an anti-imperial poem,[617] perhaps a royal encomium[618] to Jesus that mirrors the hymns or paeans made to the emperor to laud his accomplishments and benefactions. If so, Paul would be assuming the mantle of a *christologos*, a herald of Christ, setting forth Christ's accomplishments over and against Caesar, something that would resonate in a Roman colony such as Philippi.[619] Extant evidence suggests that by the time of Paul's visit to Philippi, a Roman colony inhabited by Roman veterans and their descendants, cultic honors were paid to Augustus and his wife Livia, to Augustus' adopted sons Gaius and Lucius Caesar, and to Tiberius and Claudius in a temple in the Claudian forum.[620]

There are six aspects of Phil 2.6–11 that resonate with ancient ruler cults: sent by the gods, divine form, service without rapacity, equality with God, named after the gods, and apotheosis.

First, a ruler who is divinely sent and divinely sponsored. Both Alexander and Augustus could have their conception attributed to gods, the later obviously patterned after the former (Plutarch, *Alex.* 1–3; Cassius Dio, *Hist. rom.* 45.1.1–5). They also have their conquest, governance, and empire predestined by either divine providence or the divine pantheon (Plutarch, *Alex.* 1.8; Virgil, *Ecl.* 4; *Aen.* 1.257–96; Horace, *Od.* 1.4). Cicero described Pompey as one who was chosen and favored by the gods to end various wars (*De. Imp. Cn. P.* 42, 49). Similarly, Paul depicts Jesus as a divine Son, in the "form of God," who is "sent" (Rom 8.3; Gal 4.4) and "took on human likeness" and metamorphized into "human appearance" (Phil 2.6–7).

2:6–11 as Subversive *Hymnos*: A Study in the Light of Ancient Rhetorical Theory," *JTS* 66 (2015): 90–138.

[617] Cf. Mikael Tellbe, *Paul between Synagogue and State: Christians, Jews, and Civic Authorities in 1 Thessalonians, Romans, and Philippians* (ConBNT 34; Stockholm: Almqvist & Wiksell, 2001), 256–59; Erik M. Heen, "Phil 2:6–11 and Resistance to Local Timocratic Rule," in *Paul and the Roman Imperial Order*, ed. Richard A. Horsley (Harrisburg, Penn.: Trinity Press International, 2004), 125–53; Joseph H. Hellerman, *Reconstructing Honor in Roman Philippi: Carmen Christi as Cursus Podorum* (SNTSMS 132; Cambridge: Cambridge University Press, 2005), 129–56; Gordley, *New Testament Christological Hymns*, 104–10; and Fantin, *Lord of the Entire World*, 252–61.

[618] Samuel Vollenweider, "Politische Theologie im Philipperbrief?" in *Paulus und Johannes* (WUNT 198; Tübingen: Mohr Siebeck, 2006), 457–69; Joshua W. Jipp, *Christ Is King: Paul's Royal Ideology* (Minneapolis: Fortress, 2015), 127–35; and Collins, "Psalms, Philippians 2:6–11."

[619] Collins, "Psalms, Philippians 2:6–11," 371–72, but see reservations of Burnett, *Christ's Enthronement*, 121–22.

[620] Cf. Heen, "Phil 2:6–11," 134–35; and tables about inscriptions, coinage, and priesthoods compiled by Burnett, *Christ's Enthronement*, 129–35.

Second, as argued earlier, the "form of God" (*morphē theou*) is an outward display of a divine nature and status.[621] In other words, the form of God is a matter of both glorious radiance and divine reputation. Philo critiques Caligula's pretentious parading as Apollo as outlandish because Caligula proves by his behavior that he is no more than a counterfeit of the "divine form" (*theou morphē*; *Legat*. 110). Christ, in contrast, possessed the divine form, proving it by his act of self-giving service, even as a "slave" (*doulos*).

Third, there are motifs related to service and a lack of rapaciousness and self-aggrandizement attributed to Alexander and Augustus.

Plutarch declared how God sent Alexander's soul into the world, to bring law and reason, and his governance was without plundering or robbery (*Alex*. 1.8). Alexander "did not overrun Asia like a robber [*harpagma*] nor was he minded to tear and rend it, as if it were booty and plunder bestowed by unexpected good fortune, after the manner in which Hannibal later descended upon Italy, or as earlier the Treres descended upon Ionia and the Scythians upon Media." Instead, "Alexander desired to render all upon earth subject to one law of reason and one form of government and to reveal all men as one people, and to this purpose he made himself conform." Plutarch adds, "But if the deity that sent down Alexander's soul into this world of ours had not recalled him quickly, one law would govern all mankind, and they all would look toward one rule of justice as though toward a common source of light. But as it is, that part of the world which has not looked upon Alexander has remained without sunlight."

The *Res Gestae*, a public statement of Augustus' career of achievements, emphasizes at length Augustus' public service to Rome and its provinces, his refusal to seek honors for himself, and his willingness to turn down offices and honors. What stands out is what Augustus claims he did not do:

- "The dictatorship offered me by the people and the Roman Senate, in my absence and later when present, in the consulship of Marcus Marcellus and Lucius Arruntius I did not accept" (*RG* § 5).

- "The dictatorship, either yearly or for life, when offered to me, I did not accept" (*RG* § 5).

- "Whenever I was saluted as *imperator*, I did not accept the coronary gold, although the municipia and colonies voted it in the same kindly spirit as before" (*RG* § 21).

---

[621] I do not think we have to choose between "being" and "status" when, for instance, something like "glory" (i.e., *kabod* and *doxa*) implies a radiant physical state as much as the immense honor of the deity.

- "I took precedence of all in rank, but of power I possessed no more than those who were my colleagues in any magistracy" (*RG* § 34).

In addition, Philo's account of Moses as king of Israel notes that Moses did not exploit his people. In Philo's telling, Moses was appointed as king unlike those "who thrust themselves into positions of power by means of arms . . . but on account of his goodness and his nobility of conduct and the universal benevolence which he never failed to show" (*Mos.* 1.148). Or else, we might think of Caligula, who set up a cult for the living emperor at Miletus and two altars in Rome (Cassius Dio 59.28.1–2), and his enthusiasm for his divine status led him to despise the Jews for the failure to grant him follow divine honors in the Jerusalem cultus.[622] Caligula could be considered one who was *harpazein*, "snatching" with violence for more and more divine honors.[623]

It is not hard to see how these materials mesh with the narrative of Phil 2.6–11. Christ does not use equality with God as a license to engage in plunder and self-aggrandizing for divine honors; rather, in humility he serves humanity as a human. Similarly, the narratives of Alexander and Augustus—about heaven-sent beings marked out by unparalleled accomplishments, who do not engage in rapacious behavior, who serve others at their own expense, and who draw all people around themselves—fit snugly with the Christ hymn.

Fourth, to be considered equal to the gods was a divine honor for benefactors and rulers. One of the greatest honors a ruler could receive was to be heralded as *isotheos*, for "equal to the gods." Homer used *isotheoi* for persons who had godlike appearance, such as Euryalus and Telemachus (*Il.* 2.565; *Od.* 20.124). The first-century BCE historian Diodorus Siculus referred to certain men who were accounted worthy of divine honors: "For very great and most numerous deeds have been performed by the heroes and demi-gods and by good men, who, because of the benefits they conferred which have been shared by all men, have been honored by succeeding generations with sacrifices which in some cases are like those offered to the gods (*isotheos*), in other cases like such as are paid to heroes, and of one and all the appropriate praises have been sung by the voice of history for all time" (4.1.4). Diodorus refers to the Achaen general Philopoemen (29.17.18) and the Roman proconsul

---

[622] See Barrett, *Caligula*, 143–52.
[623] If that is the foil for Christ, then it renders moot whether divinity is a matter exploiting what one has (*res rapta*) or snatching after something one does not have (*res rapienda*), since Caligula was doing both and Christ does not follow that example.

Quintus Scaevola (37.5.1–37.6.1) as two men who were granted honors equal to the gods for their services.

Appian says that Caesar was the first of the Roman leaders to receive postmortem "honors equal to gods" (*Bell. civ.* 2.148). Philo eulogized Augustus with the fittingness of cities to grant him honors "equal to the Olympian gods [*isolympios*]" (*Legat.* 149), and Cassius Dio recorded how Roman senators voted that Augustus' name "should be listed, as equal to the gods [*isou tois theois*], in the hymns" (51.20.1). Another papyrus from the same era makes an equation of *isotheos* with *basileus* (Athen. 15.702a).[624] A second-century CE papyrus asks: "What is a god? Exercising power. What is a king? One who is equal to God" (P. Heid. 1716.5). This equality was not straightforward; it was honorific rather than actual, and it did not make a king or emperor truly equal to the Olympian gods. In practice or belief, the one heralded as *isotheos* was not truly *theos*.[625] That is because the position of the emperor between the gods and his people was not without ambiguity. As Price notes, "He was located in an ambivalent position, higher than mortals but not fully equal of the gods. The cult he received was described as *isotheoi timai*, and the *eusebeia* which the cult displayed was compatible with honours not fully divine."[626] Despite rhetoric and ritual, festivals and temples, Augustus and his successors were not fully equal to the traditional gods. But the emperor was likened to and visually displayed among the gods because he had a power that penetrated every aspect of the lives in people in the east and west.[627] What the emperor received in the imperial cult was "honours equivalent to those paid to the gods," comparable to but still distinguished from the cult of the gods, that is the meaning of *isotheoi timai*.[628]

In addition, in Jewish metrics of impiety, the claim to be "equal to God" was one of the most blasphemous things one could assert. God has no equal and brooks no rival, so any claim to equality with God is blasphemous (see Isa 40.25; 46.5). The Maccabean epitomist imagines Antiochus IV in his final

---

[624] Badian, "Alexander the Great," 15.

[625] Badian, "Alexander the Great," 15.

[626] S. R. F. Price, "Gods and Emperors: The Greek Language of the Roman Imperial Cult," *JHS* 104 (1984): 94.

[627] Zanker, *Power of Images*, 29; cf. Christian Habicht, *Divine Honors for Mortal Men in Greek City States: The Early Cases* (Ann Arbor: Michigan Classical Press, 2017), 141–44 concerning earlier Hellenistic ruler cults: "It is evident that the person in question is not a god like the Olympians in his worshippers' eyes, but rather is merely equated with them in terms of the honors he receives" (142).

[628] Price, "Gods and Emperors," 88.

throes from a torment of the bowels acknowledging, "It is right to be subject to God; mortals should not think that they are equal to God [*mē thnēton onta isothea phronein*]" (2 Macc 9.12). Philo, when not pandering to the Julio-Claudians, knows that assigning honors equal to God to wood and stone carvings is the summit of idolatry (*Dec.* 8–9). For Philo, only the mind that is atheistic and devoid of love would haughtily think itself equal with God (*Leg. all.* 1.149). The Jewish Sibyl attributes a claim to be equal with God to Nero *redivivus* (*Sib. Or.* 5.34; 12.86). Similarly, in the Fourth Gospel, the Judeans were seeking to kill Jesus, not only because he transgressed the sabbath but also because by claiming that God was his Father, he was "making himself equal with God" (*ison heauton poiōn tō theō*; John 5.18). I suspect that such a remark is a feature of Johannine irony; Jesus is equal to God as a son is equal to his father, but the Judeans wrongly think that Jesus is making himself a second and independent deity.

The honor of being equal to the gods was not taken lightly nor handed out freely. Such divine honors became the exclusive currency of devotion to the emperor and his family. The new political reality created by Augustus' supremacy made it perfectly clear to provincial and civic elites that only the emperor was *isotheoi timai*.[629] Even within the imperial family divine honors had to be safely deflected to the emperor alone, hence Tiberius' edict of 19 CE deprecating divine honors acclaimed to him, "for they are appropriate only to him who is actually the saviour and benefactor of the whole human race, my father."[630] Decades earlier Tiberius had stopped by Philippi when en route to Syria, and had lit "altars" erected by retired veterans (Suetonius, *Tib.* 14.3). Yet Paul, it seems, did not read the imperial *acta*, as he eulogizes Jesus as already in possession of *isotheoi timai*, making him, if not a usurpacious rival, then at least an alternative embodiment of divine power to the emperor. Following Erik Heen, it seems as if "the status claimed for the emperor (*to einai isa theō*) in the civic religions of the Greek cities of the East has been reassigned to Jesus in the early Christian hymn," and the "honor associated with the term in the public discourse is retained but redirected to one who is, from the perspective of the Pauline subaltern community, legitimately worthy of its claims."[631]

Fifth, apotheosis and exaltation to heaven are indicative of the imperial cults. According to John Reumann, "What, in their environment and thinking, stands behind the language of Phil 2,9–11? The most obvious analogy is the apotheosis

---

[629] Cf. Price, *Rituals and Power*, 49–51.
[630] Cited from Heen, "Phil 2:6–11," 145.
[631] Heen, "Phil 2:6–11," 149.

or deification of a hero, benefactor, or leader, as in the 'ruler cult.'"[632] As we saw above, the Roman ritual of *consecratio* or deification entailed the promotion of the princeps to a position among the divine pantheon and the conferral of the status of *divus*. Jesus may not have been elevated to the "halls of Jupiter" (Ovid, *Fasti* 3.697–710), to "heaven's proud steep" (Horace, *Od.* 2.3.10), or to "the glorious home of snowy Olympus" (*Hom. Hymn.* 15)—but he had been "super-exalted" (*hyperypsoō*) with incomparable honors to a heavenly position from which he exercises authority as the true cosmocrator appointed by God the Father.[633] Despite the insistence of many that God's exaltation of Jesus implies a subordination, even if theoretically true, that is simply beside the point here.[634] The issue is divine legitimacy, not intra-divine hierarchy. Moreover, as Peter Oakes suggests, Jesus is given divine legitimacy cast in the shape of an imperial mold. Jesus is not deified by the senate, the Roman people, his adopted heir, or a Greek city, nor does he acclaim himself as a god.[635] Instead, God confers on him a rank deserving of the reverence that God himself receives. God declares what is to be true of Jesus and how he is to be regarded with honors equal to himself. The basis of this super-exaltation is not military conquest or even *moderatio*, but on account of a mixture of self-emptying and sacrificial death; it is kenosis and crucifixion that makes Jesus worthy of divine honors. In receiving divine worship, "bowing," and "acclamation," acts that in imperial register acknowledge Jesus as the locus of divine power, Jesus is marked out as the imperial and celestial "Lord." In Paul's account, in God's messiah—in Jesus—Israel's long-awaited divine-human ruler had been revealed for the purpose of putting things to right, and he receives afterward the reverence fitting for his redemptive service.[636]

Sixth, to be given a divine name is also a mark of divine honor. There were various honorific names and titles for rulers in antiquity; *Augustus* and *Sebastos* are obvious imperial examples, but there are also divine titles such as *divus* and *filius divi*.[637] The Roman emperor was lauded as *dominus* and *kyrios*; however, we should not exaggerate the extent of usage, as the title *kyrios* turns up

---

[632] John Reumann, "Resurrection in Philippi and Paul's Letter(s) to the Philippians," in *Resurrection in the New Testament*, ed. R. Bieringer, V. Koperski, and B. Lataire (Leuven: University of Leuven Press, 2002), 420.

[633] Cf. *Odes Sol.* 41.12: "The man who humbled himself, but was exalted because of his own righteousness."

[634] Contra, e.g., McGrath, *Only True God*, 49–52; and Casey, *From Jewish Prophet*, 112–15.

[635] Peter Oakes, *Philippians: From People to Letter* (SNTSMS 110; Cambridge: Cambridge University Press, 2001), 151–60; and Burnett, *Christ's Enthronement*, 150.

[636] Fletcher-Louis, *Jesus Monotheism*, 1:213; and Oakes, *Philippians*, 170.

[637] Cf. Oakes, *Philippians*, 170–71.

in eastern inscriptions and papyri, proliferating mainly during Nero's reign (e.g., P. Lond. 280.6; P. Oxy. 37.5-7; Acts 25.26).[638] Also, if *kyrios* is intended as the divine name of Israel's God, Yahweh, then we may even have in Phil 2.9-11 an instance of royal theonymy whereby the name of a god is shared with a monarch, such as Horus, Zeus, or Jupiter. Honorific connections between Zeus/Jupiter and the Julio-Claudian and Flavian emperors were common.[639] The name sharing seemed to function as something like the deity appearing in the guise of the emperor, the deity as protector of the emperor, or the deity making the emperor his deputy. According to David Litwa: "The author of Phil. 2:6–11 knew, presumably, that those who bear a particular god's name also bear that god's status. Just as the emperors exercised world sovereignty as plenipotentiaries of Zeus, so the exalted Jesus obtained Yahweh's name as Yahweh's cosmic vice-regent. Such vice-regency implies a divine status, depicting Jesus in a divine status amounts to a deification."[640]

Putting this together, Phil 2.6–11 can be read as a royal encomium to "an imperial figure with universal authority,"[641] a heavenly being endowed with superlative status and rank as one already "equal with God" and possessing the "form of God."[642] Yet this Jesus did not consider exploiting his divine status for the purpose of plundering or self-promotion. To the contrary, Jesus was divinely sent for service, transforming himself into human likeness, in fact taking on the apron of a slave to the point of death, even death on a cross! Then, to reverse the punishment meted out against him by his foes and to reward his obedience, the true and living God exalted him, not merely to heaven, but over heaven, earth, and the underworld, by bestowing upon him the title *kyrios*, so that the inhabitants of every tier of the cosmos must do obeisance before him. The Philippian "Christ hymn," then, makes sense as a cultic hymn or encomium in the tradition of the imperial ruler cult. The Christ hymn would constitute a jarring juxtaposition with the panegyric poetry or hymns sung to the emperor during festivals and processions in the city of Philippi. While I do

---

[638] Fantin (*Lord of the Entire World*, 191) notes: "With the possible exception of Nero, the extant evidence for *kyrios* as a title for the Julio-Claudian Caesars is not extensive." Burnett (*Christ's Enthronement*, 123) is similar: "In actuality, kyrios was not a popular imperial title among Greeks for most of the Julio-Claudian period, being found sporadically in inscriptions and papyri and uncommon until the end of Nero's reign."

[639] Litwa, *Iesus Deus*, 181–214.

[640] Litwa, *Iesus Deus*, 212.

[641] Tellbe, *Paul between Synagogue and State*, 256.

[642] The anti-imperial reading does not require a *res rapienda* interpretation (Heen, "Phil 2:6–11," 138–39), as Hellerman (*Reconstructing Honor*, 166) adopts as *res rapta* interpretation.

not wish to apply the overused word "subversive,"[643] in Phil 2.6–11 it looks as if "Jesus, the *Kyrios* of the Christ-cult, and the Roman Caesar, the *Kyrios* of the Caesar-cult, are set in conscious opposition to each other."[644]

(c) Ascension as apotheosis.

The resurrection narratives broadly (Mark 16.1–8; Matt 28.1–20; Luke 24.1–49; John 1.1–29) and the ascension narratives specifically (Luke 24.50–53; Acts 1.9–11) stand in analogy with ancient descriptions of a person's apotheosis (i.e., deification).[645] Hengel admits a "certain formal analogy" between Matthew and Luke's risen Jesus and the apotheosis of Romulus and how ancient rulers could be considered hidden epiphanies of the gods.[646] That is because breaking free from the shackles of mortality into immortality was signified by crossing the boundary between heaven and earth. As a result, going to heaven entailed, in varied senses, becoming a god.[647]

Apotheosis was the posthumous transformation of the emperor from mere mortal into an astral entity, one seated among and as one of the gods.[648] The

---

[643] Perhaps the encomium was composed in Jewish Christian circles as a christological counterpoint to the divine pretentions of Caligula ca. 39–41 CE. See D. Karl Bornhäuser, *Jesus Imperator Mundi* (Gütersloh: C. Bertelsmann, 1938), 15–17; and David Seeley, "The Background of the Philippian Hymn (2:6–11)," *JHC* 1 (1994): 49–72. Oakes (*Philippians*, 131) acknowledges: "Comparison with Caligula would indeed have been a live issue in Paul's day, especially for a Jewish writer."

[644] Ernst Lohmeyer, *Kyrios Jesus: Eine Untersuchung zu Phil 2, 5–11* (Heidelberg: Winters, 1928), 60n1 (italics added): "Jesus, der Kyrios der Christuskultes, und der römische Cäser, der Kyrios des Kaiserkultes, in *besußten* Gegensatz einander gegenübergerstellt warden."

[645] Alan F. Segal, "Heavenly Ascent in Hellenistic Judaism, Early Christianity and Their Environment," *ANRW* 23.2: 1333–94; Laura J. Hunt, *Jesus Caesar: A Roman Reading of the Johannine Trial Narrative* (WUNT 2.5–6; Tübingen: Mohr Siebeck, 2019), 293–96; Wendy Cotter, "Greco-Roman Apotheosis Traditions and the Resurrection Appearances in Matthew," in *The Gospel of Matthew in Current Study*, ed. David E. Aune (Grand Rapids: Eerdmans, 2001), 127–53; Adela Yarbro Collins, "Traveling Up and Away: Journeys to the Upper and Outer Regions of the World," in *Greco-Roman Culture and the New Testament*, ed. David E. Aune and Frederick E. Brenk (Leiden: Brill, 2012), 135–66; A. W. Zwiep, "Assumptus est in caelum: Rapture and Heavenly Exaltation in Early Judaism and Luke-Acts," in *Auferstehung-Resurrection: Resurrection, Transfiguration and Exaltation in Old Testament, Ancient Judaism and Early Christianity*, ed. Friedrich Avemarie and Hermann Lichtenberger (WUNT 135; Tübingen: Mohr Siebeck, 2001), 323–50; and John Granger Cook, *Empty Tomb, Resurrection, Apotheosis* (WUNT 410; Tübingen: Mohr Siebeck, 2018), 621–22.

[646] Hengel, *Son of God*, 39.

[647] Segal, "Heavenly Ascent," 1382; Zwieg, "Assumptus," 334; Johnson, *Among the Gentiles*, 149–50; and Litwa, *Iesus Deus*, 174.

[648] Cf. survey in Cook, *Empty Tomb, Resurrection*, 413–54.

posthumous deification of an emperor had precedents in the Platonic notion of virtuous souls who returned to their original habitation within the stars; stories of Greek heroes and demigods such as Herakles, Dionysus, Castor and Pollux, and Asclepius, who were wafted up to heaven; the mythic Roman city founders of Romulus and Aeneas, who were also assumed and apotheosized; the cult of the dead with ancestor worship; Hellenistic ruler cults that Roman authorities encountered as they annexed the eastern Mediterranean; and practices of the late Roman republic, where there had been a gradual escalation of honors for general and rulers into the divine sphere. Cicero was a bellwether intellectual on evolving Roman attitudes towards deification, noting cynical responses to the politics and piety of divinization (Cotta in *Nat. d.*), but offering Hellenistic panegyrics to Pompey, Caesar, and Octavius. Cicero was in favor of apotheosis as an incentive for good rulers who have governed wisely and justly (Cicero, *Resp.* 6.13–16; *Leg.* 2.27–28; *Off.* 3.25). For Cicero, all souls are immortal, but virtuous ones, like noble rulers, may become divine.[649]

It was with Julius Caesar that a genuine innovation was introduced. Caesar cultivated a close association with the god Quirinus and arguably propagated an identification of Quirinus with the deified Romulus (Cicero, *Resp.* 2.20; Ovid, *Metamorph.* 14.827–28; Plutarch, *Rom.* 28.3; Dionysius Halicarnassus, *Ant. Rom.* 2.63.3). Caesar dressed like Romulus (Plutarch, *Rom.* 26.2; Cassius Dio 43.43.2; 46.6.1–4), he was a *flamen* ("priest") of the Quirinus cult, and he became temple-sharer with Quirinus when his statue was placed in Quirinus' temple (Cassius Dio 43.45.3; Cicero, *Att.* 290). After his assassination, the deceased dictator was transformed, deliberately reminiscent of Romulus, into an astral entity at the funeral ceremony, as signified by the sign of the appearance of a comet (Suetonius, *Jul.* 88). Thereafter, the apotheosis of deceased emperors became an intermittent norm, as Appian (*Bell. civ.* 2.148) states: "From this example [Octavius' deification of Julius Caesar] the Romans now pay like honors to each emperor at his death if he has not reigned in a tyrannical manner or made himself odious." The ritual was repeated for Augustus by Tiberius; it led the emperor Vespasian to memorably utter on his deathbed, "Oh dear, I think I'm becoming a god" (*uae, inquit, puto deus fio* [Suetonius, *Vesp.* 23.4]; *ephē theos ēdē ginomai* [Cassius Dio 66.17.3]); Cassius Dio provided an eyewitness account of the funeral rites for Pertinax in the late second century, including his apotheosis (75.4.2–5.5); and even Eusebius celebrated coinage commemorating Constantine's glorious ascension (*Vit. Const.* 4.73).

---

[649] See esp. Spencer Cole, *Cicero and the Rise of Deification at Rome* (Cambridge: Cambridge University Press, 2013), 185–98.

The Gospel accounts of the cosmic portents surrounding Jesus' death and resurrection (Mark 15.33, 38; Matt 27.51–53), his acclamation as "Son of God" (Mark 15.39) and "my Lord and my God" (John 20.28), the worship he receives (Matt 28.9, 17; Luke 24.52), claims that he holds all authority in heaven and on earth (Matt 28.18), his heavenly ascent (Luke 24.51; Acts 1.9–10), and position as a throne-sharer (Rev 5.6) all possess clear analogies with the artifacts, texts, and media that espouse imperial deification. Ovid's Caesar is snatched up to heaven by Vesta, even as the assassins plunged their dagger into him, and Caesar was taken to the "hall of Jupiter" (Ovid, *Fasti* 3.697–710). In *Metamorphoses* (15.745–870), Ovid waxes that the gods decreed that "Julius Caesar must change and be a god." Venus knew Caesar's fate and opined to the other gods about him; the gods in turn gave warnings and portents of the plot against Caesar. Jupiter consoled Venus that her son Caesar's time was up. Both she and Octavian would make him a deity, enable him to reach the heavens, and be worshipped in the temple therein. Caesar's soul must be transformed from his ill-fated body "to a starry light" so that a deified Julius would look down upon his people from his heavenly residence. Moreover, Caesar's greatest glory was his new son, Octavian, and his progeny's love would carry him afar, marked by a heavenly sign, a brightly flaming star. Later, Octavian, the August One, will himself ascend to heavenly dwellings to reside among his kindred stars. Although Jupiter reigns over the heavens, waters, and the underworld, Augustus now rules the lands, making Jupiter and Augustus both a father and a god. A day shall come when Augustus shall depart the earth that he now governs and ascend to heaven, carried to celestial heights by his people's prayers!

Whether it was through Latin poetry, a funeral rite for an emperor, a statue of Julius Caesar with a star over his crown, Julius Caesar's comet on a coin, the Antonine *consecratio* coins, or the reliefs showing an emperor carried to heaven, Romans and Greeks would have been reminded of imperial apotheosis when reading/hearing the resurrection and ascension narratives. Viewed through a "Roman encyclopedia," the crucifixion-resurrection-ascension narratives evoke imperial apotheosis.[650] As John G. Cook puts it: "The ascension of Jesus corresponds fairly closely with the translational narratives of paganism and Judaism and with the narratives of imperial apotheoses (*consecrationes*). Presumably those narratives rendered the ascension of Jesus more congenial for Mediterranean people."[651]

One could add that the tradition material pertaining to Jesus' exaltation can be understood as Christian acclamations of Jesus' *consecratio* or being

[650] Hunt, *Jesus Caesar*, 293–96.
[651] Cook, *Empty Tomb, Resurrection*, 623.

honored as a god by his followers and supplicants (Rom 1.3–4; Phil 2.6–11; Acts 2.14–26; 5.30–32). Such texts might remind readers of the depictions of imperial apotheosis on the Belvedere Altar, Titus' Arch, representation of Claudius taken to the gods on the back of an eagle, the column of Antoninus Pius, or, for that matter, the Grand Cameo of France.[652] Whatever differences there are between early Christology and the apotheoses of the Caesars, it is impossible to agree with Hengel that the christological discourse "completely transcend the possibilities of pagan—polytheistic apotheoses, whether those of the Roman Caesars, or an Alexander, or a Hercules."[653]

(d) Jesus as world conqueror.

Jesus was thought to be a world conqueror before whom all heavenly powers and earthly potentates would one day do obeisance. Jesus was, in some accounts, a messianic king who rivaled Caesar in the scales of absolute power.

Of course, Christian views of the empire are not so neat and tidy. The early Christians were hardly anti-imperial activists. Paul arguably urged the Christians in Rome not to imitate the anti-Roman and anti-Gentile sentiment that was simmering away in Judea (Rom 13.1–7). A similar urging of respect for imperial authority is apparent in Peter's epistle, with exhortations towards fearing God and honoring the emperor (1 Pet 2.12–17). Luke-Acts might have more than a hint of anti-imperialism even if it labors to show that Christians are not a threat to the social fabric. For Luke, Christians are upright citizens, something that would be clear if only magistrates and proconsuls gave them a fair hearing. It is Jewish communities, Luke complains, that stir up mobs and cause riots over disputes pertaining to their religion. It is true too that the Johannine Jesus can answer to Pilate, "My kingdom is not from this world. If my kingdom were from this world, my followers would be fighting to keep me from being handed over to the Jews. But as it is, my kingdom is not from here" (John 18.36). Along a similar line, Eusebius narrates an account from Hegesippus where the grand children of Jude, the Lord's brother, were summoned before emperor Domitian. They affirmed their Davidic lineage, but concerning Christ's kingdom, they saw it as future, spiritual, and no immediate threat to Domitian. "When they were asked concerning Christ and his kingdom, of what sort it was and where and when it was to appear," records Eusebius, "they

---

[652] Cf. Sarah Whittle, "'Declared to Be Son of God in Power': Romans 1:4 and the Iconography of Imperial Apotheosis," in *Son of God: Divine Sonship in Jewish and Christian Antiquity*, ed. Garrick V. Allen, Kai Akagi, Paul Sloan, and Madhavi Nevader (University Park, Penn.: Eisenbrauns, 2019), 158–70; Johnson, *Among the Gentiles*, 36; and Burnett, *Christ's Enthronement*, 135–40.

[653] Hengel, *Studies in Early Christology*, 373.

answered that it was not a temporal nor an earthly kingdom, but a heavenly and angelic one, which would appear at the end of the world, when he should come in glory to judge the living and the dead, and to give unto every one according to his works" (Eusebius, *Hist. eccl.* 3.19–20). Such remarks, rightly or wrongly, show that Luther's two-kingdoms theology had ample and early precedent. Tertullian can even complain that the emperor belongs more to Christians than anyone else, because they pray for him, not out of flattery, but believing his office is owed to the providence of the true and living God (*Apol.* 30–33). Christians can indeed make peace with Caesar.

At the same time, Christians also believed that when Christ put his foot down again upon the earth, all powers, from the Antonines to Zeus, were going to be subjected by God the Father to Jesus. Paul makes this clear on numerous points, drawing on Isa 11.10: "The root of Jesse shall come, the one who rises to rule the Gentiles; in him the Gentiles shall hope" (Rom 15.12). On more than one occasion, Paul can look at Christ's parousia as a moment when "he must reign until he has put all his enemies under his feet," including *Dios* as much as Death (1 Cor 15.25). Paul adds that the general resurrection will be manifested politically as a reordering power: "He will transform the body of our humiliation that it may be conformed to the body of his glory, by the power that also enables him to make all things subject to himself" (Phil 3.21). John the Seer claims he has seen behind the veil of the future, where Christ triumphs over the pagan monsters, and their systems of military power and economic exploitation are cast into oblivion (Rev 19.11–20.15). Turning to the second and third centuries, in the *Acts of Paul*, Nero's slave Patroclus is brought back to life by Paul, and when interviewed by Nero, Patroclus reports that Christ "destroys all kingdoms under heaven, and he alone shall reign in eternity, and there will be no kingdom which escapes him" (*Acts Paul* 11.2). Hippolytus too composed his own apocalyptic scheme that married Jewish messianic prophecies with apostolic instruction to imagine Christ setting aside the enemies of his church (*Christ and Anti-Christ*). Any peace with Caesar was only a temporary reprieve until Caesar was dethroned by Christ in the final denouement. Statues and coins portray Augustus with his foot on a globe; many Christians believed that one day that foot would be Jesus'.

Josephus referred to an "ambiguous oracle" about how a Judean ruler would arise to conquer the inhabited world (*War* 6.312–12)—an oracle which the Romans knew about full well and saw as partly responsible for Judean fanaticism for their liberation (Suetonius, *Vesp.* 4.5; Tacitus, *Hist.* 5.13). The early Christians, it has to be said, did not abandon such fanaticism for liberation from Roman hegemony; they merely had a different timetable and different scheme for its manifestation, divided up into Christ's first and second comings. Christian eschatologies cannot be reduced to spiritual niceties of immortal souls and angelic gardens in the hereafter, even if some veer in that direction in the post-Constantinian age. The book of Daniel as much as the Maccabean uprising show that resurrection and rebellion always went hand in hand. The eschatological narratives of the apostle Paul and John the Seer were variations of such a theme, not dancing to a different tune. Jewish hopes for a new Davidic kingdom with an earthly embodiment were modulated, not muted, by apostolic messianism. It is worth remembering that early Christian views of the future state did not imagine a heavenly utopia characterized by a kindly egalitarianism of equals; rather, the existing hierarchies of power and privilege were not going to be so much torn down as inverted. Thus, Christian worship of Jesus as the Messiah was the worship of "another king" besides and against Caesar, who would enact judgment, reward the faithful, make all things new, and turn the world upside down, so that the first would be last and the last would be first (Luke 13.30; Acts 17.6–7, 30–32).

(e) Jesus as triumphator.

Another aspect of imperial veneration that shaped early Christology is the depiction of Christ as a triumphator. The language of triumphing (*thriambeuō*) is found explicitly in Paul's letters (Col 2.15; 2 Cor 2.14; Rom 8.17), and "the one who is victorious" (*ho nikōnti*) is in John the Seer's apocalypse (Rev 2.7, 11, 17, 26; 3.5, 12, 21; 21.7). One could argue that John's language is more Persian/Parthian than Roman, as the title "king of kings" is equivalent to the Parthian title of *shahanshah* (Ezra 7.12; Dan 2.37; Rev 17.14; 19.16). Paul, however, is probably indebted to the tradition of a Roman triumph, even if he never saw one himself; the tradition was widely known in the Greco-Roman world.

The Roman triumph was an immense honor for a general, proconsul, or emperor to celebrate a major victory for the Roman people. It was a type of victory parade, but far more than what we might think of such a parade; it was meant to be a memorable spectacle, one of the highest honors the republic/empire could bestow upon a leading citizen. The triumph was filled with military regality, political propaganda, and divine symbols and rituals, with the triumphator dressed and acclaimed as Jupiter. Triumphs were much sought after and rarely awarded. The Roman triumph evolved over time, and we cannot refer to the triumph as a single thing, but as a fluid tradition of military celebration.[654]

---

[654] See Mary Beard, *The Roman Triumph* (Cambridge, Mass.: Belknap, 2007); and Markus Lau, *Der gekreuzigte Triumphator: Eine motivkritische Studie zum Markusevangelium* (Göttingen: Vandenhoeck & Ruprecht, 2019), 145–309.

When Paul describes himself as caught up in God's triumphal procession in Christ (2 Cor 2.14), he is deploying the image of the triumph to describe his own participation in the divine victory of Israel's God.[655]

The crucifixion narrative in the Gospel of Mark can be reasonably understood as a parody of a Roman triumphal procession.[656] To begin with, in the Marcan Gospel, the word "king" (*basileus*) occurs six times, always in contexts pertaining to confrontation with local rulers (Mark 6.14, 22, 25, 26, 27; 13.9). However, "king" occurs six times in Mark 15 and is used exclusively in relation to Jesus, and so accents the royal texture of the story (Mark 15.2, 9, 12, 18, 26, 32). It is ironic too that the Marcan Jesus proclaims the kingdom of God (Mark 1.15), yet the Gospel climaxes with a placard above the cross heralding the kingship of the crucified (Mark 15.26). Mark clearly weaves the kingdom and the cross together. More importantly, Mark portrays Jesus' humiliation and procession towards Golgotha as a mock triumph.[657] Amid Jesus' suffering and derision at the hands of the Romans, there is a strange blending of regal and triumphal imagery—dressed in purple, given a crown, hailed as a king by the praetorian guard, accompanied on a tour through the city, offered a drink of wine, a sacrifice offered, given acclamation as son of god—all this pertains to the "ritual movements, symbolic categories, and performative logic employed in the Roman triumph."[658] In Mark's telling, Jesus' passion was not the execution of a rebel, but a triumph and epiphany of Israel's Messiah. Thomas Schmidt summarizes the similarities this way:

> The Praetorians gather early in the morning to proclaim the triumphator. He is dressed in the triumphal garb, and a crown of laurel is placed on his

---

[655] See Christoph Heilig, *Paul's Triumph: Reassessing 2 Corinthians 2:14 in Its Literary and Historical Context* (Leuven: Peeters, 2017).

[656] Cf. Michael F. Bird, *Jesus Is the Christ: The Messianic Testimony of the Gospels* (Downers Grove, Ill.: InterVarsity, 2014), 39–43.

[657] Thomas E. Schmidt, "Mark 15.16–32: The Crucifixion Narrative and the Roman Triumphal Procession," *NTS* 41 (1995): 1–18. See also Peppard, *Son of God*, 130–31; and Adam Winn, *Reading Mark's Christology under Caesar: Jesus the Messiah and Roman Imperial Ideology* (Downers Grove, Ill.: InterVarsity, 2018), 157–62; and esp. Lau, *Der gekreuzigte Triumphator*, who shows that such allusions are not far-fetched.

[658] Allan T. Georgia, "Translating the Triumph: Reading Mark's Crucifixion Narrative against a Roman Ritual of Power," *JSNT* 36 (2013): 18: "Mark's narrative exhibits an eclectic bricolage of appropriated cultural and religious source material that borrows the *logic* of the Roman triumph, which paradigmatically imagined a republican, Roman general celebrating the defeat of a tyrannical, kingly adversary, in order to innovate an ingenious choreography for the procession of a victorious victim of Roman power, whose royal majesty is confirmed by his being made an ignominious spectacle" (18–19 [italics original]).

head. The soldiers then shout in acclamation of his Lordship and perform acts of homage to him. They accompany him from their camp through the streets of the city. The sacrificial victim is there in the procession, and alongside walks the official carrying the implement of his coming death. The procession ascends finally to the Place of the (Death's) Head, where the sacrifice is to take place. The triumphator is offered the ceremonial wine. He does not drink it, but it is poured out on the altar at the moment of sacrifice. Then, at the moment of being lifted up before the people, at the moment of the sacrifice, again the triumphator is acclaimed as Lord, and his vice-regents appear with him in confirmation of his glory. Following the lead of the soldiers, the people together with their leaders and the vice-regents themselves join in the acclamation. The epiphany is confirmed in portents by the gods: "Truly this man is the Son of God!"[659]

If Mark was written ca. 70 CE, perhaps in Rome, then the marvel and memory of Vespasian's and Titus' triumph for subjugating Judea would be an obvious analogue for readers of the Marcan passion narrative (see Josephus, *War* 7.118–62). The triumph was a spectacle of jarring juxtapositions—the absolute divine-like power of the triumphator in grandeur and fanfare contrasted with the abject weakness and defeat of the prisoners led out in the procession and executed at the climax. As Markus Lau notes, "Great power and absolute powerlessness are personified and presented in combination with each other in the triumph."[660] Yet Mark stunningly reverses the stakes so that the seemingly powerless one has all power, the mocked victim is the true victor, and the crucifixion is an enthronement. The point is, as Schmidt comments, "Mark designs this 'anti-triumph' to suggest that the seeming scandal of the cross is actually an exaltation of Christ."[661] Yet the christological significance is even more acute than crucifixion-as-exaltation; the acclamation of Jesus as the son of (a) god by the Roman centurion in Mark 15.39 applies to Jesus the honors normally given to an emperor who capitalized on his relationship to a deified predecessor. "In the end, Mark's view of divine sonship, which had been refracted throughout the gospel in the light of the Roman emperor, now shines through unmediated," comments Peppard. "It is Jesus who is the Roman world's 'son of God'—sorrowful as a Roman criminal, and powerful as a Roman emperor."[662]

---

[659] Schmidt, "Mark 15.16–32," 16.
[660] Lau, *Der gekreuzigte Triumphator*, 599 ("Größte Macht und absolute Ohnmacht werden im Triumph personifiziert und in Kombination miteinander präsentiert").
[661] Schmidt, "Mark 15.16–32," 1.
[662] Peppard, *Son of God*, 131.

(f) Homage to the Matthean Jesus.

The Matthean birth narrative includes the eastern magi arriving in Jerusalem to meet the newborn Judean king and to pay him *proskynesis* (Matt 2.2). Herod himself feigns a willingness to pay similar respects to the new king should the magi find him (Matt 2.8). This plays on the trope of foreign ambassadors or vassals coming to honor a king (see Josephus, *Ant.* 16.136–41; Cassius Dio, *Hist. rom.* 63.1–7; Suetonius, *Nero* 13). In the setting of Matthew's Gospel, *proskynesis* can be a form of reverential respect paid by a supplicant to a superior (Matt 4.9, 10; 20.20), but it is otherwise performed in a religious sense of the worship of a human invested with heavenly powers (Matt 14.33), or else the worship of a resurrected and "divine" person (Matt 28.9, 17, 20). In any case, Matthew depicts Jesus receiving the *proskynesis* of a divine king by the magi and his own disciples.

(g) Christian responses to and rehearsal of the imperial cult.

Roman emperors were known to Christians as the *Romanorum deus*, "the gods of the Romans" (Tertullian, *Apol.* 24.9). Christian aversion towards the emperor is captured by Luke, with his focus on Jesus as an alternative if not an outright rival to the emperor: "They," Paul and his coworkers in Thessalonica, "are all acting contrary to the decrees of the emperor, saying that there is another king named Jesus" (Acts 17.7). By Luke's day, the acclamation of Jesus as king could not be made without being perceived to be making an implicit sneer against the sovereignty of Caesar himself. True, Christians did not act like Jewish mobs and pull down statues of the emperor, nor were they forming secret cabals with disgruntled senators to do something about Domitian or Trajan. However, by 100 CE, Christians in Asia such as John the Seer considered the imperial cult to be the quintessence of idolatry and the material manifestation of a cosmic evil that had amassed against them. By 150 CE, Roman officials had cottoned on to using the imperial cult as the number one way to weed out Christians and the means to make a public spectacle of them.

As such, I think Deissmann's verdict is probably correct: "The deification of the Caesars was an abomination to Christianity from the beginning. It is very probable that this antipathy was inherited from monotheistic Judaism."[663] Christian antipathy towards most things imperial was inherited from a Jewish heritage with its contest of Yahweh against the gods and gag reflex at the notion of deified human rulers. But Christian anti-Caesarism was also developed out of a specific suite of christological commitments whereby the one true God

---

[663] Deissmann, *Light from the Ancient East*, 340.

had appointed one man, one king, and one lord to be the instrument through which the creation would be rescued from the anti-gods and malevolent lords who would themselves be subjugated by the Messiah. Unsurprisingly then, as I argued in an early chapter, Christians were militantly opposed to the worship of the emperor. Even Tertullian, who wants to imagine Tiberius asking the senate to deify Jesus, cannot bring himself to call Caesar lord and god in a religious sense (*Apol.* 4; 30–33).

Be that as it may, things are not so simple, as if Christology was merely the religious antithesis of Sebastology. While God had always put Pharaohs, kings, and emperors in their place, the Christian Son of David stood at odds with Caesar precisely because he was portrayed, well, a little bit like Caesar. For a case in point, Justin Martyr considered the deification of emperors to be a demonic impersonation of Christ's divinity, which of course admits a certain type of resemblance between the two divinities (*1 Apol.* 21.1–6), noticed as well by Celsus (Origen, *Cels.* 3.22). Similarly, Justin's Trypho pointed out the disparity between Jewish monotheism and the worship of Jesus, applying the same revulsion at emperor worship to Christ worship (*Dial.* 38.1; 49.1; 63.4–64.1). The aggravated denunciations of human deification by Justin, Athenagoras, Theophilus, and Minucius Felix were occasioned precisely because it was possible to explain Jesus' divinity in the categories of imperial deification.[664]

To be more specific, one could read Rev 5 as a kind of parody of Jupiter appointing the Roman emperor as his vice-regent, to be a throne-sharer with him. Roman art and coinage could posit a close relationship between Jupiter and the emperor, often showing them on shared thrones. The emperor could be, contingent upon interpretation, the envoy, embodiment, vice-regent, or agent of the high god—a scheme analogous with the portrayal of the exalted Jesus in John's apocalyptic narrative. Beyond that, the Seer's Christology parodies imperial devotion, in that (1) Jesus' association with God parallels the association made between an emperor and Olympian deities, and (2) Jesus, like Augustus, is portrayed as founder of a new type of cosmic order.[665]

In an influential article, David Aune shows the parallels between Rev 4–5 and the imperial court/cult. The operating premise is that in John's apocalypse Satan and Caesar, represented by the symbols of the Dragon and the Beast, are a diabolic duo who function as counterfeit counterparts to God and the Lamb.[666] Yet the language, symbols, and rituals of imperial veneration are nonetheless deployed by John to depict God and Jesus as the true embodiments of heavenly

---

[664] Cf. Maier, *Picturing Paul in Empire*, 5–6, against Hengel and Hurtado on this point.
[665] Friesen, *Imperial Cults*, 198.
[666] Aune, "Influence of Roman Imperial Court," 5.

power and dispensers of earthly justice for the faithful. The similarities pertain to (1) the role of God mirroring Zeus/Jupiter, because he passively hears petitions, enacting justice accordingly; (2) the appearance of God, Christ, and the elders reflecting the brightly colored clothing, laurel wreaths, and zodiac-inspired symbols that adorned emperors, lictors, and attendants, while the prostration of the elders also matches the prostration of visitors and supplicants to the emperor; (3) the function of the hymns and doxologies in the throne room of God and the Lamb echoing the hymns, acclamations, and encomiums made to the emperor—further, the praise delivered by those in heaven, on earth, and under earth parallels the senatorial, equestrian, and plebeian classes and so indicates a universal consensus of the divinities worthiness to be worshipped; and (4) God and the Lamb being described with honorific imperial titles and symbols—god, son of god, lord, savior, epiphany, imperator—which are also given to the emperors.[667] In effect, the Roman imperium and its emperor cult stood against the Lord God Almighty, *kyrios* Jesus, and the churches. By adopting the language of the imperial cult, John the Seer was pillaging the highest religious honors of the empire and applying them to Jesus.[668]

To cast the net wider than apostolic Christianity, Gnostic schemes do not overtly oppose the imperial cult, nor attempt to appropriate it for their Christology. Despite repeated claims to the contrary, there were actual Gnostic martyrs, which could conceivably yield opposition to imperial power and religion. Yet Gnostics did not explicitly voice an anti-imperial counter-Christology, most likely because the imperial cult belonged the cosmic order that they hoped to leave behind. The divine being was supreme in a realm and in a way that made all other religious claims redundant. The ultimate being in Valentinian thought had no rival and competitors: "The Monad is a monarchy with nothing above it. It is he who exists as God and Father of everything, the invisible One who is above everything, who exists as incorruption, which is in the pure light into which no eye can look. 'He is the invisible Spirit, of whom it is not right to think of him as a god, or something similar. For he is more than a god, since there is nothing above him, for no one lords it over him.'" (*Ap. John* 2.27–3.1).

Concerning Christology, Irenaeus claimed that Valentinians identified Jesus as a "Savior," while the title "Lord" was reserved for Sophia (Irenaeus, *Haer.* 1.1.3; 1.5.3). But other texts with likely Valentinian connections identify Jesus Christ as "the Lord of lords and King of the ages" (*Prayer of the Apostle Paul*, A12–14) and "our Savior, our Lord Jesus Christ" (*Treat. Res.* 43.36–37; 48.18–19; 50.1). In some schemes, the Logos appointed a Thought or Archon

---

[667] Aune, "Influence of Roman Imperial Court," 6–22.
[668] Lohmeyer, *Christuskult und Kaiserkult*, 35.

to rule over pleromatic orders with its own kings and lords in a way that mirrors the rule of the Roman emperor over the empire (*Tri. Trac.* 99.19–100.30). Further, knowledge of the Son enables the elect to abandon and even transcend the various heavenly and earthly lords whom they formerly worshipped.

> About the <one> who appeared in flesh, they believed without any doubt that he is the Son of the unknown God, who was not previously spoken of, and who could not be seen. They abandoned their gods whom they had previously worshipped, and the lords who are in heaven and on earth. Before he had taken them up, and while he was still a child, they testified that he had already begun to preach. And when he was in the tomb as a dead man the angels thought that he was alive, receiving life from the one who had died. They first desired their numerous services and wonders, which were in the temple on their behalf, to be performed continuously <as> the confession. That is, it can be done on their behalf through their approach to him. That preparation which they did not accept, they rejected, because of the one who had not been sent from that place, but they granted to Christ, of whom they thought that he exists in that place from which they had come along with him, a place of gods and lords whom they served, worshipped, and ministered to, in the names which they had received on loan.—They were given to the one who is designated by them properly. However, after his assumption, they had the experience to know that he is their Lord, over whom no one else is lord. They gave him their kingdoms; they rose from their thrones; they were kept from their crowns. He, however, revealed himself to them, for the reasons which we have already spoken of: their salvation and the return to a good thought until [. . .] companion and the angels [. . .], and the abundance of good which they did with it. Thus, they were entrusted with the services which benefit the elect, bringing their iniquity up to heaven. (*Tri. Trac.* 133.16–135.7)

The scheme described above could be considered a Valentinian answer to the same sorts of issues that Paul was wrestling with and working out in 1 Cor 8. What do we make of and do about the gods of this age, including but not limited to the imperial cult? The mythological motifs in Valentinian writings with their anti-cosmic ideology would entail that the imperial cult with its own lords belongs to the many errors behind the world that do not compete with the Monad or the Savior. The cult of the Sebastos is merely one of the many errors introduced by the Demiurge. Accordingly, the Christologies of Gnostics in general and Valentinians in particular had no reason to be explicitly anti-imperial because their Christ was supra-cosmic, rendering the imperial cults and their paraphernalia simply irrelevant because they were mired in flesh and tainted with ignorance.[669]

(4) Comparative analysis.

The points of contact between early Christology and ancient ruler cults, especially the imperial cult, can be granted. But what matters also is the degrees of similarity as well as the degrees of difference.

(a) Jesus devotion as ruler cult.

According to Michael Peppard: "The Roman emperor was the most well-known and powerful person in the first-century Mediterranean world, called 'god,' 'son of god,' 'savior,' and 'lord' in public texts in virtually every town, at the exact times and places of early christological development."[670] Also, as N. T. Wright observes, "In the Mediterranean world where Paul exercised his vocation as the apostle to the Gentiles, the pagans, the fastest growing religion was the Imperial cult, the worship of Caesar."[671] From what has been analyzed, it would seem that the early Christians did not shy away from appropriating and assimilating titles and tropes from the cult of divine rulers and apply them to Christ. There were patterns of worship known to them from Jewish traditions of royal ideology, messiahs with divine qualities, contemporary Hellenistic ruler cults, Judean ruler veneration of the Hasmoneans to the Herodians, and of course the Roman imperial cults of the Augustan age and thereafter.

The strongest arguments for ruler cults shaping Christology are (1) the honorific titles such as lord, savior, god, son of god, etc.; (2) 1 Cor 16.22 and its resonance with honorific language used for rulers in southern Syria and the Levant; (3) Phil 2.6–11, which reflects imperial devotion in several ways, not the least the honorific title *isotheoi timai*; (4) the resurrection and ascension of Jesus in the Gospels and Acts paralleling apotheosis and *consecratio* traditions; (5) the depiction of Jesus as conqueror of all powers and even arrayed in the imagery and symbols of a Roman triumph in his crucifixion; (6) Matthew's

---

[669] Michael A. Williams (*Rethinking "Gnosticism,"* 284n6) points out: "The essential absence of explicit evidence for any concrete 'gnostic' rejection of the imperial cult or the lack of any mention of the imperial cult in 'gnostic' texts, and, on the other hand, the well-known evidence that several such 'gnostics' in fact rejected the political deviance that would lead to martyrdom" indicates a lack of interest or need to critique the imperial cult."

[670] Peppard, "Son of God in Gentile Contexts," 136.

[671] N. T. Wright, "Paul and Caesar: A New Reading of Romans," in *Pauline Perspectives: Essays on Paul, 1978–2013* (London: SPCK, 2013), 239.

portrayal of Jesus as receiving the *proskynesis* fitting for an eastern divine king; and (7) the deliberate parody of the imperial cult in Rev 4–5 by John the Seer.

Given these similarities, one cannot regard the emperor cult from Augustus to Domitian as a negative stimulus for Jesus devotion unless one first acknowledges the parallels between the two worships and a shared language of veneration. The smoking gun here is that Christian denunciations of emperor worship and human deification were motivated in part by the similarities between an emperor's apotheosis and Jesus' exaltation.

We are led to the inescapable conclusion that ruler cults had a formative impact upon early Christology.[672] Ancient ruler cults were simultaneously resourced and rebutted in depictions of Jesus in Christian literature, increasingly so from the end of the first century. Christians imitated and parodied ruler cults with the venerative devotion offered to Jesus of Nazareth even as they viciously mocked the very concept of ruler worship and human deification.[673] How do we explain this disparity?

I would argue that this christological disparity—simultaneously rehearsing and rejecting ruler worship—was inherited from the Jewish context. Christians merely continued this tradition of Yahweh and his anointed king standing against the pagan nations with their divinized rulers by constructing their own apocalyptic narratives with Jesus at the center of God's actions and worship. Early Christology inherited from Judaism a conviction in God's unrivaled supremacy and the veneration of a Davidic ruler, an ideology which mirrored other ruler cults, even while it often polemicized against them. In turn, Christian discourses parodied and polemicized against the imperial cults and human deification by deliberately echoing some of their language. In which case, early Christians expressed their Jesus devotion with a simultaneous mix of derivation from, adaptation towards, and opposition against ruler cults. The derivation was on account of a cross-cultural lexicon of divine lordship and benefaction, the adaptation was undertaken in order to lodge a deliberate protest against competing ruler cults, and the opposition was because the mode of divinity attributed to Jesus was not deification, but incarnation—not a man made a god, but Israel's God become man. Where Christ was made to resemble the divine or deified Caesar, the intention was not to prop up a contested assertion of deity, but to make it clear that Caesar, the so-called *Deus Invictus*, would be made a footstool for Christ the *pantokrator*.

Hurtado finds the simultaneous repudiation of ruler worship and the rehearsal of ruler cults in early Christology to be inexplicable: "So how would

---

[672] Contra, e.g., Hengel, *Son of God*, 30.
[673] Rightly Bousset, *Kyrios Christos*, 310; and Horbury, *Jewish Messianism*, 118.

the avoidance of worshiping pagan deities and rulers dispose circles of Jewish Jesus-believers in Roman Palestine in the earliest period of the young Jesus-movement to appropriate the very ideas and practices that they regarded as repellent?"[674] To be blunt, probably in the same way that Philo commended the *proskynesis* offered to Joseph by his brothers and to the sons of the Hittites by Abraham (*Somn.* 2.80, 89–90; Gen 23.7, 12; 37.7), even as he remained highly allergic to any ruler seeking divine obeisance for themselves (*Somn.* 2.99–100), such as the demands of Caligula for *proskynesis* in Italy (*Legat.* 116). Similarly, in the book of Daniel, Daniel and his friends refuse to bow down and worship Nebuchadnezzar's image (Dan 3.1–18), even though the same book glowingly reports how "King Nebuchadnezzar fell on his face, worshiped Daniel, and commanded that a grain offering and incense be offered to him" (Dan 2.46; Josephus, *Ant.* 10.211–12). Or else, in *Jubilees*, there is an animated denunciation of idolatry by Abram (*Jub.* 12.1–9, 12–14; 20.7–8), while later the brief mention of the Egyptians being commanded to prostate themselves before Joseph in Gen 41.43 is expanded into a conventional Hellenistic acclamation of Joseph as "god, god, Mighty One of God" (*Jub.* 40.7). Christians too resourced their devotion from ancient ruler worship even as they found emperor worship and human deification to be impious travesties. Incongruent as it appears to us, it nonetheless happened, and here post-colonial criticism might prove to be a heuristic resource to explain the apparent inconsistency.[675]

Colonial powers frequently attempt to assimilate the colonized by compelling them to imitate their way of life, to bring them into sameness, while keeping them inferior and "other." In terms of Roman hegemony, this meant embedding Roman deities and the imperial cult beside the local cults and their civic expressions.[676] This forced the colonized both to worship like the Romans and give worship to the Romans: sameness and submission. However, the colonized can engage in subversive discourses and praxes against the colonizer by turning their own ideology, symbols, and stories against them. One can imagine this in something like Puerto Rican protestors chanting "Give me liberty or give me death" in opposition to US hegemony, Soviet dissidents writing Russian-style novels about Soviet gulags, or the leader of a Free Algerian movement imitating the dress and style of the president of France. One can imagine Judean zealots

---

[674] Hurtado, *One God, One Lord*, 145.

[675] Hurtado (*One God, One Lord*, 147) is aware of this from correspondence with Adela Collins, but fails to appreciate its significance. See also Peppard, *Son of God*, 123–24, 130–31, who also makes use of post-colonial criticism for the Christology of Mark.

[676] For example, Pisidian Antioch included a temple to Jupiter, Augustus, and the *genius* of the Roman colony. Burnett, *Christ's Enthronement*, 129.

toppling a statue of Caligula while yelling *sic semper tyrannis* ("always stick it to the tyrant" [allegedly uttered by Brutus on assassinating Julius Caesar]) or *heis koiranos estō, heis basileus epi poleōn kai anthrōpōn* ("let there be one lord and one king over the cities of all people" [a quotation from the *Iliad*]).[677] In the sociopolitical sphere, imitation can be an expression of either admiration or repudiation, and with a view to supplantation.

Similarly, Christian authors like Paul, Mark, and John the Seer, by constructing images of Jesus drawn from scriptural descriptions of Yahweh and the Davidic tradition, and by rehearsing language and images from imperial devotion, were identifying Jesus with God's sovereign power over and against the claims to divine legitimacy made by the Roman imperium. The barb in the rhetoric was that their Lord Jesus was not "made" but was "sent"; he "served" and "suffered," and was "exalted" to the highest position imaginable. Furthermore, it was the cross, a symbol of Roman power to terrorize subjects into submission, that became the representation of their resistance. The one true God's Son had suffered the most degrading and dehumanizing torture that the Romans could manufacture, yet God had reversed the death and disgrace they had inflicted, and God had installed his Son in the glory and greatness that the empire believed belonged to its own pantheon and princeps. The result of their subversive mimicry is, in effect: "Therefore, let Jupiter and the son of the divine Augustus know that this Jesus, whom they crucified, Israel's God has declared to be the Messiah and Lord by raising him from the dead and seating him at his right hand. Let everyone in heaven, on earth, and under the earth, bow down and call on him as Lord and Savior."

Hurtado argued that pagan ruler cults were unlikely to be the initial and formative force in the origins of Jesus devotion.[678] On this score, he was partly correct because, besides the impressions made by the historical Jesus, it was Easter and post-Easter religious experiences and their scriptural interpretation that were the most primitive and paramount factors shaping belief in Jesus' divinity and driving the emerging forms of Jesus devotion. Where Hurtado is wrong is that Ps 110.1 was the primary scriptural text used to explicate Jesus' divine status, and this royal psalm is connected to the veneration of Israel's monarch. Further, if the Israelite royal ideology as represented in Ps 110 is umbilically connected to ancient Near Eastern traditions of divine kings, then posing an absolute alternative between Jewish or pagan

---

[677] Which is not too far from what actually happened according to Josephus, *Ant.* 18.23; *War* 7.410.

[678] Hurtado, *One God, One Lord*, 147; contra Collins, "How on Earth," 66; and Horbury, *Jewish Messianism*, 119.

ruler cults is moot. Furthermore, Hurtado admitted that there was eventually influence from the emperor cult on christological discourses by the late first century and beyond.[679] This is not all that far from Collins, who herself posits religious experience and cultural experience of ruler-cult influence as two of the most formative factors in divine Christology.[680] The question is, how early was the resourcing of pagan ruler cults? The fact that Paul can speak of the "rulers of this age" who "crucified the Lord of glory" and "many gods and many lords" shows that the imperial cult was undoubtedly on his mind (1 Cor 2.6; 8.5), and he certainly portrays Jesus as the messianic king *destined* to rule over the nations (Rom 15.12; 1 Cor 15.24–28; Phil 3.21). Furthermore, looking at pre-Pauline tradition, the narration of Jesus as "equal with God" (Phil 2.6) certainly does resonate with various ruler cults, and even the title *marêh* (1 Cor 16.22) as applied to Jesus was perhaps not a parody of emperor worship but the veneration of the Herodian client rulers of Judea. In which case, it was very early![681]

(b) Jesus devotion as dissimilar to ruler cults.

Martin Hengel once asked:

> How did it come about that in the short space of less than twenty years the crucified Galilean Jew, Jesus of Nazareth, was elevated by his followers to a dignity which left every possible form of pagan-polytheistic apotheosis far behind? Pre-existence, Mediator of Creation and the revelation of his identity with the One God: this exceeds the possibilities of deification in a polytheistic pantheon; here we have a new *religions-geschichtliche* category before us that must be explained from the first Christian experience itself, or as the case may be, from its Jewish background.[682]

Hengel overstated his case on the lack of pagan, and specifically ruler cult, influences on early Christianity. However, he is partly right. The kerygmatic package of titles, roles, and functions attributed to Jesus—demiurgy, healing diseases, defeating demons, and deliverance from sin—does not parallel with imperial cults. When it comes to the differences between early Christology and ruler/imperial cults, we should take note of several things.

---

[679] Hurtado, *Lord Jesus Christ*, 74–77; idem, "Christ-Devotion in the First Two Centuries," in *Ancient Jewish Monotheism and Early Christian Jesus-Devotion: The Context and Character of Christological Faith* (Waco, Tex.: Baylor University Press, 2017), 24–25, 34–35.

[680] Collins, "Worship of Jesus and the Imperial Cult," 241; and Horbury, *Jewish Messianism*, 119.

[681] Cf. Horbury, *Jewish Messianism*, 119.

[682] Hengel, *Studies in Early Christology*, 383–84.

First, messianic discourse with its veneration of Jesus as Lord and Messiah remained steadfastly under the aegis of Jewish monotheism.[683] Christian worship of Jesus did not require the innovation of a Hellenistic setting or the influence of Hellenistic ruler cults in order to include Jesus within divine titles and worship. Rather, early Jesus devotion was a development within Jewish tradition with its exclusive worship of Yahweh and its veneration of an Israelite king who was varyingly associated with Yahweh's reign and power. Accordingly, early Jesus devotion was not expressed by the establishment of a new temple with its own cult to Jesus. The origins of Christian worship were not marked by the reverence to a new Mediterranean deity, but by the belief that the one God of Israel had appeared in fully human form, to serve, to suffer, and to be exalted. Early messianic discourse remained within the constraints of monotheism, that is, within the boundaries of belief in Israel's one God and God's oneness.[684]

Second, the primary species of ruler cult that influenced early Christology was Yahweh worship and the veneration of Israelite rulers.

To begin with, early Christology and Jesus devotion were principally shaped by Jewish conceptions of Yahweh as king who appoints human kings to rule over his people. Also, the Yahweh cult and the royal Davidic tradition had long been set against the pantheon and kings of the Near East. Yahweh was God of gods and King of kings over the Assyrians, Babylonians, Greeks, and Romans. It was thus in vain that the nations of the earth raged against the Lord and his anointed Davidic son (e.g., Ps 2.1–12; 89.1–52; Isa 9.1–16; 14.1–32; *Ps. Sol.* 17.1–46). Jewish literature of the Second Temple period intensified the conflict between Yahweh and other pagan kingdoms in various apocalypses with increased focus on royal and priestly intermediary figures who were divine agents, who appeared in divine power, and who received various forms of homage. Thus, already in ancient Israel the kingship of Yahweh and the election of the Davidic dynasty were oriented theologically and polemically against the ruler cults and deities of the surrounding nations even as they participated in comparative modes of royal ideology.

As such, while imperial influence makes itself felt fairly early, at least if Phil 2.6–11 is anything to go by, and Rev 5 proves it beyond all doubt, the initial impetus towards early Christology was Yahweh, who anointed Jesus as his son and appointed Jesus as Israel's *kyrios*, in other words, a messianic and

---

[683] Horbury, *Jewish Messianism*, 177; and Burnett, *Christ's Enthronement*, 8.
[684] Fletcher-Louis, *Jesus Monotheism*, 1:22.

post-Easter reading of Pss 2.7 and 110.1 (109.1 LXX).⁶⁸⁵ It was the cult of Yahweh and his kyriotic king that initially inspired the mode of divinity and patterns of devotion that sprouted with remarkable intensity in the earliest years of the Judean churches.⁶⁸⁶

Horbury is then partly correct to say that "the earliest Christian praise can then be located, despite its special features, within a continuum of Jewish praise which is related to contemporary ruler-cult and includes the theme of obeisance, *proskynesis*."⁶⁸⁷ The qualification we have to make is that the "special features" of Jesus devotion show that Jesus was venerated as more than an exemplary or exalted Judean king. The mere recognition of Jesus as Messiah and Lord would not necessarily evoke the unprecedented patterns of devotion that Jesus received in the forms of hymns, acclamations, and doxologies.⁶⁸⁸ A missing middle term is the identification of Jesus with God's own activity in the world as God's wisdom and word, in addition to influence from Jewish ruler veneration in the pattern of Ps 110.⁶⁸⁹ Early Christian worship of Jesus was not merely an intensification of ruler veneration, but a matter of Yahweh sharing with his messianic *kyrios* the worship that rightfully belonged to Yahweh alone.⁶⁹⁰ Phil 2.6–11 echoes Ps 110 (LXX) about David's *kyrios*, but it

---

⁶⁸⁵ Fitzmyer (*Wandering Aramean*, 118) is right to note that Hellenistic and imperial usage undoubtedly influenced New Testament usage of *kyrios*, but that does not explain the original application of the title to Jesus; nor is it the sole background to understand its meaning.

⁶⁸⁶ Cf. Hengel, *Studies in Early Christology*, 134; Larry W. Hurtado, "Two Case Studies in Earliest Christological Readings of Biblical Texts," in *All That the Prophets Have Declared: The Appropriation of Scripture in the Emergence of Christianity*, ed. Matthew R. Malcolm (London: Authentic Media, 2015), 5–14; idem, "Early Christological Interpretation," in *Ancient Jewish Monotheism and Early Christian Jesus-Devotion: The Context and Character of Christological Faith* (Waco, Tex.: Baylor University Press, 2017), 575–81; and Bauckham, *Jesus and the God of Israel*, 174–76.

⁶⁸⁷ Horbury, *Jewish Messianism*, 127.

⁶⁸⁸ Hurtado, *Lord Jesus Christ*, 149; and Fletcher-Louis, *Jesus Monotheism*, 1:219.

⁶⁸⁹ Cf. Dunn, *Christology in the Making*, 259; Tilling, *Paul's Divine Christology*, 231; and Fletcher-Louis, *Jesus Monotheism*, 1:247. Casey (*From Jewish Prophet*, 117) goes so far as to argue that "to understand the high position of Jesus in their compositions [Phil 2.6–11 and Col 1.15–20] we should look primarily to Adam and Wisdom speculation rather than to deification of people in the Greco-Roman world.... The assertion that Jesus was, for example, 'firstborn of all creation' (Col. 1.16), or even 'in the form of God' (Phil 2.6), was too remote in content from declarations of the deification of Heracles or Augustus to be perceived as pagan."

⁶⁹⁰ Larry W. Hurtado, *How on Earth Did Jesus Become God? Historical Questions about Earliest Devotion to Jesus* (Grand Rapids: Eerdmans, 2010), 22: "The fact is that we simply have no evidence that any other figure, whether human or angelic, ever featured in the

tangibly testifies to Jesus as *kyrios* along the lines of Isa 45.23. The worship of Jesus as "Lord" takes place, not as a subsidiary or secondary cult of a messianic king beside Yahweh worship, but in association with and as part of the worship of Israel's one God. We have here, as Wright memorably states: "A small step for the language; a giant leap for the theology. Jesus is not a 'second God': that would abrogate monotheism entirely. He is not a semi-divine intermediate figure. He is the one in whom the identity of Israel's God is revealed."[691]

Third, there are significant differences between Jesus' ascension/exaltation and the rituals associated with apotheosis. True, Jesus—like Romulus, Herakles, Asclepius, Julius Caesar, and Augustus—is transformed in his mode of existence, taken to heaven, designated as a god, and is thereafter given divine worship. But Jesus' deification, if that is the right term, is not depicted by a ritual where a wax image of the emperor is melted down while an eagle is released to soar above, to symbolize the transition from bodied mortality to disembodied immortality. Not only do the Evangelists have no such ritual, but also they emphasize instead the continuity between Jesus' earthly and resurrection body.[692] Neither is Jesus' heir or first disciple now designated as a son of God, who is duly sponsored by this newly installed heavenly patron. Rather, Jesus' resurrection marked out the beginning of the general resurrection, implying too Jesus' place as the firstborn of a new humanity. There is political significance here, yet not about a dynasty, legitimacy, succession, or adoption. Resurrection means that God has made the *messias designatus* the *messias sedet*, a new lord, a new son of God for Caesar to contend with; as the new Adam, the true human being is co-enthroned at the helm of the universe.[693] What this new lord asks for is not incense, fire, rams, or oaths, but *pistis*, covenantal faith and believing-allegiance.

Fourth, the Jesus cult, or more properly the cult of God and Jesus, lacks the addition of new names for Jesus as a way of sensationalizing his new status. Jesus is not called *theopatoros, neos theos, eleutherios,* or by honorific titles like "son of the Sun" as per ruler cults. Rather, the names that are lavished on Jesus are derived from scriptural testimony (see Justin, *Dial.* 34.2).

Fifth, concerning 1 Cor 16.22, one can see the attraction of regarding the title *marêh* as amounting to the veneration of Jesus as a royal heavenly figure

---

corporate and public devotional practice of Jewish circles in any way really comparable to the programmatic role of Jesus in early Christian circles."
[691] Wright, *Paul and the Faithfulness of God*, 666.
[692] Litwa, *Iesus Deus*, 170–73; and Cook, *Empty Tomb, Resurrection*, 454, 622.
[693] N. T. Wright, *Resurrection of the Son of God* (COGQ 2; London: SPCK, 2003), 243, 568–70, 656, 728–29; and idem, "Son of God," 133.

who yet remains far from the sphere of God's being and status. However, this conclusion is not preferable, and other factors suggest that Jesus' divinity is more intensely associated with Israel's God.

(a) In 1 Cor 16.22 we have a continuation of the pattern of Jesus devotion exhibited across the letter. The monotheistic confession of Deut 6.4, pertaining to Israel's one God and one Lord, was split by Paul in 1 Cor 8.6 to include *one God* the Father and the *one Lord* Jesus Christ. Then, in 1 Cor 16.22, the command to love God in Deut 6.5 is applied by Paul to the Lord Jesus. Such love has the character of covenant loyalty, and the absence of such love puts one under a covenant curse.[694] Paul binds Jesus to Israel's God in a matrix of divine worship (1 Cor 1.2; 11.26; 12.3), divine faithfulness (1 Cor 1.9; 10.13), divine oneness (1 Cor 6.4–5), enduring faith (1 Cor 2.5; 16.13), loving loyalty, and future hope (1 Cor 1.7–8; 12.3; 16.22). Thus, the identity of the Lord Jesus and the type of loyalty that is appropriate for him are determined by Israel's traditions of monotheistic devotion and obligations of covenantal loyalty to Yahweh.

(b) The application of lordship language to Jesus is made in a "cultic" setting, perhaps eucharistic (1 Cor 11.26; *Did.* 10.3), calling on Jesus as to a deity, indicating that Jesus is the object of divine worship.[695]

(c) The prayer to the Lord Jesus corresponds with other such prayers made to Jesus in the early church, notably Paul's prayer to the Lord for respite (2 Cor 12.8), Stephen's prayer for the Lord Jesus to receive his spirit (Acts 7.58), and Ignatius' assumption that the Ephesians prayed to Jesus for Ignatius to write to them (*Eph.* 20.1). Such prayers imply Jesus' bodily absence, his heavenly position, his capacity to hear prayers, and his willingness to answer prayers, that is, indications of a supermundane, personal, benevolent, and interactive deity. Beyond that, Paul's prayer in 1 Cor 16.22 evidences a sense of personal urgency and feverous passion for Jesus to return; as Tilling puts it, "having spoken a curse on all who do not love the Lord, his passion for the risen Lord expresses itself in this prayer, a prayer for the coming of the risen Lord himself."[696]

(d) The prayer-petition for Jesus to "come!" puts Jesus in the same position of the coming of the Lord God in judgment. The *marana tha* petition is analogous to texts that look forward to a divine theophany for the purpose of

---

[694] Jeffrey A. D. Weima, *Neglected Endings: The Significance of the Pauline Letter Closings* (JSNTSup 101; Sheffield: JSOT Press, 1994), 201–8. To be fair, Tilling (*Paul's Divine Christology*, 192) rightly notes that the LXX translates cursing language with *katara* rather than anathema, thus the covenantal echoes should not be overplayed.

[695] Hurtado, *Lord Jesus Christ*, 140–42; and Fletcher-Louis, *Jesus Monotheism*, 1:16, 24, 54.

[696] Tilling, *Paul's Divine Christology*, 193.

divine retribution (e.g., Ps 96.13; 98.9; Isa 66.15–16; Joel 2.1–3; Micah 1.1–8; Zech 14.1–5; Sir 21.5; *1 En.* 1.9). This was arguably the background from which Christians deployed the imagery of Jesus' "coming" in judgment (Acts 17.31; Rom 2.16; 1 Cor 4.4–5; 2 Cor 5.10; Jude 14–15; 2 Tim 4.1). The eschatological sense of *marana tha* is proved by the similar prayer language used by the apostle Paul and John the Seer for Jesus' return (1 Cor 11.26, 16.22 and Rev 22.20).[697] The prayer for Jesus to come is a prayer for the coming of God in judgment.

(e) It is a false alternative to imagine that Jesus was *marêh* as a royal figure rather than as a divine figure in a strong sense. The idea of Yahweh as king is basic to Jewish religion (e.g., Ps 10.16; 47.2; 97.1; Isa 43.15; 44.6).[698] Further, Ps 109.1–4 (LXX) acclaims Israel's king as a preexistent and priestly royal figure who is co-enthroned with Yahweh. Ps 109/110, then, marries together the royal and divine qualities of the messianic lord. If *marêh* has royal connotations, it is not because of Jesus was the ethnarch or ruler of Judea, but because he participates in the orbit of divine sovereignty, similar to how Jewish royal traditions associate Israel's king with Yahweh's rule. The titles *marêh* and *kyrios* might well enhance the messianic dimensions, but they are not restricted to them, and there are sufficient grounds for seeing such titles as appropriate for also signifying Jesus' incredible proximity to God's being, purpose, and identity.

Accordingly, Jesus as *marêh* is associated with Israel's monotheistic confession and covenantal loyalty, the object of personal prayer in a cultic setting, ascribed the theophanic role of God coming in judgment, and correlated with the kingship of Israel's God. Above all, these observations torpedo the older theories of Bousset and Bultmann that *kyrios* language was only applied to Jesus in a Hellenistic setting, such as Antioch, where early Christology was expressed in the idiom of ruler and mystery cults. That theory is sunk by the observation that 1 Cor 16.22 is an artifact that shows beyond doubt that the early Aramaic-speaking church venerated Jesus as Lord in the earliest stages of its existence, perhaps from the beginning.[699]

---

[697] Cf. Fitzmyer, *Wandering Aramean*, 129.

[698] Cf. Fitzmyer, *Wandering Aramean*, 132.

[699] See Cullmann, *Christology*, 199–214; C. F. D. Moule, *The Origins of Christology* (Cambridge: Cambridge University Press, 1977), 36–46, 149–50; Fitzmyer, *Wandering Aramean*, 117–27; Hurtado, *One God, One Lord*, 110–12; idem, *Lord Jesus Christ*, 21, 110, 140–42, 173–75, 617–18; Fee, *Pauline Christology*, 121–22; Bauckham, *Jesus and the God of Israel*, 128; David B. Capes, *The Divine Christ: Paul, the Lord Jesus, and the Scriptures of Israel* (ASBT; Grand Rapids: Baker, 2018), 27–31; Johnson, *Among the Gentiles*, 26–28; and Casey, *From Jewish Prophet*, 110, 132–33. Two ways to dismiss this text as evidence of early

Sixth, returning to Phil 2.6–11, yes, one can read this text as a counter-imperial Christology, with implicit parallels to and explicit parodies of veneration of the emperor. However, on the whole, the incarnational shape of the narrative cannot be derived exclusively from the influence of Hellenistic and imperial ruler cults.[700]

(a) The preexistence of Jesus in v. 6 is pronounced, more than an immortal soul destined for greatness or a man that the gods have intended to use to bring the toga-wearing Romans to the summit of supremacy. Jesus is personally preexistent, and, more stunningly, he seems to descend at his own initiative. He empties himself; he is not emptied onto the earth. The sense here is much like Justin Martyr: "Christ, the Son of God, who existed before the morning star and the moon, yet submitted to become Incarnate, and be born of this virgin of the family of David" (*Dial.* 45.4) or even akin to the Naassene Hymn, where Jesus pleads, "send me, Father! Bearing the seals I will descend; I will pass through all the Aeons; I will reveal all the mysteries and show the form of the gods" (15–19).[701]

(b) In v. 6 the clause *to einai isa theō* is tantamount to *isotheos* as both denote equality with God. In the realm of ruler cults, equality with the gods was honorific and did not eliminate the gap between a true god and a deified king. Furthermore, the equality was also ceremonial; it was exhibited in sacrifices and festivals, and it was less an idea than ritualized reverence. Yet what is notable in Phil 2.6 is that *to einai isa theō* ("equal with God") is parallel with *morphē theou* ("form of God"), which edges in an ontological direction so that divine equality is put on par with the display of divine glory.[702] Divine equality here is a matter of identity, not sacrificial offerings, sanctuaries, and festivals.[703] In effect, equality with God consists not of *harpagmos* but of *morphē theou*.[704] It is notable too that the status of being equal with God was not given to Jesus

---

divine Christology, unexplored as far as I am aware, would be: (1) to imagine that Paul reverted to his Aramaic register to find a word that rhymed with anathema, because wordplay is frequent in Paul's letters (e.g., Phlm 10–11); or (2) the possibility that *marana tha*, much like *Abba* (Mark 14.26; Rom 8.15; Gal 4.6), was part of Jesus' own style of prayer that Paul rehearses, and either Paul himself or someone else applied Jesus' own prayer to Jesus.

[700] Casey, *From Jewish Prophet*, 117; Wright, *Resurrection of the Son of God*, 728–29; idem, "Son of God," 133; and Fletcher-Louis, *Jesus Monotheism*, 1:216.

[701] Miroslav Marcovich, "The Naassene Psalm in Hippolytus," in *Studies in Graeco-Roman Religions and Gnosticism* (Leiden: Brill, 1988), 81.

[702] Cf., e.g., Wright, *Climax of the Covenant*, 83; Fee, *Pauline Christology*, 378; and Crispin H. T. Fletcher-Louis, "'The Being That Is in a Manner Equal with God' (Phil 2:6c): A Self-Transforming, Incarnational, Divine Ontology," *JTS* 96 (2020): 581–627.

[703] Cf. Fishwick, *Imperial Cult*, 1:1.21–31.

[704] Fee, *Pauline Christology*, 380.

by those bowing to him in vv. 9–11; rather, it is something that he begins with in v. 6, something that did not excuse him from service, but uniquely qualified him for his earthly mission.[705] Any supposed gap between God the Father and the Lord Jesus is narrowed by Jesus possessing the divine form and equality with God as well as receiving the divine name and devotion as fit for Israel's *kyrios*. Such language moves us beyond *Gleischsetzung* (comparability) and into *Verbindungsidentität* (shared identity).[706] Udo Schnelle rightly concludes that such language marks "the beginnings of thinking of God and Christ as equals."[707] In sum, Jesus and Augustus might both be *isotheos*; however, Paul would seem to be staking a claim that some *isotheoi* are more *iso* than others.

(c) While emperors can endure plots and military losses, not even Julius Caesar's assassination can be compared with the ignominy and scandal of Jesus' crucifixion in v. 8. If princeps was the highest rank in the empire, then a slave's torturous death, to be *crucifixus*, was the abject lowest. Yet the Father does not snatch away Jesus' soul before the first nail is driven into his body in the way that Vesta rescued Caesar's soul before the cabal of assassins could plunge their daggers into him (Ovid, *Fasti* 3.701–2).[708] No, Jesus participates in the lowest ebbs of degradation and death. This is startling because, as Sarah Whittle observes, "While demigods and Caesar could be raised to heaven, the idea of the resurrection of a *crucified one*—one clearly belonging to the category of those below representing lawlessness and chaos—was unthinkable."[709] Apotheosis was an elevation to heavenly heights and honors for one who had seen off all rivals and had ascended the summit of human accomplishment and done it supposedly without tyranny or avarice. Apotheosis recognized what was humanly true—a human had achieved incomparable and superlative honor. Yet Jesus' exaltation and enthronement takes one at the lowest rung of social hierarchy and puts them at the top as if, by some perverse logic— perverse to Roman aristocratic sensibility, that is—the last will be first and the first will be last.

(d) The exaltation of Jesus in vv. 9–11 is accented more than imperial deification. To begin with, Jesus is exalted by God and for his glory. Jesus is not exalted by senatorial decree, by the acclamation of a designated heir, or by

[705] Wright, *Climax of the Covenant*, 83–84; and Hill, *Paul and the Trinity*, 91–92.
[706] Contrasting Fitzmyer, *Wandering Aramean*, 130–31, with Rowe, *Early Narrative Christology*, 301.
[707] Schnelle, *Apostle Paul*, 396.
[708] Though later interpretations of Jesus' death would try to precisely get him out of crucifixion through a variety of docetic and place-switching devices; see Bird and Wright, *New Testament in Its World*, 791–95.
[709] Whittle, "Declared to Be Son," 161; cf. Burnett, *Christ's Enthronement*, 149–50.

popular sentiment—but by God the Father for his own glory. Augustus might have once reigned over land and sea and been accepted into Jupiter's halls. Augustus might have been sponsored by or even embodied Jupiter's power, but there was no sense in which the deified Augustus was presently invested with the type of sovereignty that Jupiter exercised (Ovid, *Met*. 15.858–70).[710] Further, in Homeric myth, Zeus, Poseidon, and Hades divided up the realms of heaven, sea, and underworld between them (*Il*. 15.185–95), while Plato describes how the gods distributed various allotments of the earth among themselves (Plato, *Crit*. 109b-c). Yet in Phi 2.9–11, Jesus is not merely exalted to heaven, not allotted a finite domain, but is enthroned over heaven, earth, and the underworld, presumably over kings, angels, shades, and powers.[711] Jesus is designated as the supreme authority over the entire three-tier realms beyond what even Augustus had and even what was allotted to Jupiter.

(e) For all the echoes and parallels with imperial veneration and apotheosis, the explicit intertext in vv. 9–11 that the hymn/poem draws on is from Isa 45.23 (LXX). While the title *kyrios* did not always feature as a translation of the divine name Yahweh and *kyrios* can function as a royal title, nonetheless the allusion to Isa 45.23 provides the context for the meaning of the name *kyrios* given to Jesus. While Litwa is perhaps correct to detect theonymy operating here, he is wrong to prefer imperial imagery over the Isaianic background.[712] If anything, we have a theonymic interpretation of Isa 45.22–25, where Israel's deity is called "God," "Savior," and "Lord." Sharing a divine title like *kyrios* is significant because imperial titles were not normally shared with junior family members—lest they decide to prosecute their ambitions before the living emperor had departed! True, Vespasian declared Titus to be *praenomen imperatoris*, and from the late second century the senior emperor could appoint a son or even a rival as a fellow Augusti.[713] But that was never true of the Julio-Claudians even when the heir apparent was tacitly nominated in coinage. The significance of this name sharing is, besides attesting the pre-Pauline cultic usage of the absolute title *kyrios* for Jesus, that it illustrates that Israel's God shares the divine name with Jesus and mandates the worship of him that was exclusively reserved for Yahweh.

Whatever imperial influences we can glean concerning Jesus' equality with God and possible apotheosis, they remain in the shadow of the kerygmatic narrative pertaining to Israel's preexistent messiah, who becomes human,

---

[710] Cf. Litwa, *Iesus Deus*, 212.
[711] Litwa, *Iesus Deus*, 178.
[712] Litwa, *Iesus Deus*, 210.
[713] Oakes, *Philippians*, 170.

is crucified, then exalted by God, which is then interpreted in light of the monotheistic rhetoric of Isa 45 so that the exalted Jesus is given the divine name *kyrios*, receives divine worship, and is sovereign over the tri-realm cosmos. This is more than Jesus "on the verge of deity" or a "monotheistic Christology"[714] but a proper "christological monotheism" whereby Israel's God is known, named, and worshipped in light of the story of Jesus.[715]

Seventh, revisiting Rev 4–5, there is more going on here besides the Lord God/Jesus mirroring the Jupiter-emperor relationship. In Rev 4, God's throne is portrayed as not merely a snapshot of a heavenly liturgy, but the very center of the universe.[716] Then, in Rev 5, the location of the exalted Jesus with God upon the divine throne is combined with his receipt of divine worship, which is a profound statement of Jesus' *superlative* divine status.[717] The Greek of Rev 5.6 is indeed ambiguous (*in mesō tou thronou*) whether the Lamb stands "between the throne" (NRSV; NASB; CEB; CSB) or "in the middle of the throne" (NJB; NIV; NET; BDAG), or whether the scene is one of "enthronement" or "investiture."[718] That Jesus stands in the midst of God's throne in Rev 5.6 seems preferable in light of Rev 7.17, where it is said, "the Lamb at the center of the throne will be their shepherd."[719] As such, Jesus is more than a Davidic Messiah being given an earthly throne (4Q161 frgs. 8–10, 23), more than one seated

---

[714] Casey, *From Jewish Prophet*, 116; and McGrath, *Only True God*, 44.

[715] With, e.g., Bauckham, *Jesus and the God of Israel*, 197–210; and Capes, *Divine Christ*, 122–23, 146–48.

[716] Gallusz, *Throne Motif*, 331.

[717] Cf. Gieschen, *Angelomorphic Christology*, 93–94; Bauckham, *Jesus and the God of Israel*, 165n35, 172–81; and Hoffmann, *Destroyer and the Lamb*, 167: "Within many passages of the Apocalypse the elements of praises and doxologies given to God and the Lamb correspond well with each other and therefore indicate equality between God and Lamb rather than ascribing subordinate tendencies to the Lamb." Hannah ("Throne of His Glory," 71): "It is then surely significant that John asserts that the divine throne belongs to Christ, as well as to his Father. To be sure, Christ's right to the throne of God appears to be a consequence of his victory over death (3,21) and not, or at least not necessarily, a consequence of his eternal divinity. Nonetheless, the right is real and one which no creature in all of creation shares, at least not before the eschatological victory (cf. 3,21 with 6,9–11 and 20,4–5). . . . There can be no doubt that John has placed Christ on the divine side of the chasm between divinity and creation. By placing Christ on the throne he indicates both his authority to rule (cf. 20,4), as well as his right to receive cultic veneration, for the throne is the heavenly parallel of the earthly ark of the covenant and the throne room is the holy of holies of the heavenly sanctuary."

[718] Cf. discussion in Hoffmann, *Destroyer and the Lamb*, 134–38; Aune, *Revelation*, 1:332–38; and Gallusz, *Throne Motif*, 153–58.

[719] On Christ sitting on God's throne in Rev 5.6, see Hannah, "Throne of His Glory," 68–71; and Gallusz, *Throne Motif*, 153–58.

among or over the heavenly council (4Q491c 5; 11QMelch 2.10–11), but is located upon the Lord God's throne, which is why there is repeated mention of God's throne and the Lamb (Rev 7.9–10, 17; 22.1, 3) and even worship is directed towards "the one seated on the throne and to the Lamb!" (Rev 5.13).[720] That is highly significant, as Jonathan Knight notes: "Two beings, one throne means one shared authority and as close as possible union as it is possible to achieve."[721] Jesus thus shares in the tradition of *synthronos*, or throne sharing with a deity, indicative of one's piety or a reward for one's reign.[722] Jesus' position with God upon the throne becomes a *leitmotif*, beginning with the exalted Jesus promising the Laodiceans, "To the one who conquers I will give a place with me on my throne, just as I myself conquered and sat down with my Father on his throne" (Rev 3.21). Later, the messianic child is taken "to God and to his throne" (Rev 12.5). The Lamb is enthroned in the context of a historical plan for redemption (Rev 5.6), as an anchor of hope for a future salvation (Rev 7.17), while being associated with consummation and new creation (Rev 22.1, 3), and as he stands in opposition to the Satan and his imperial surrogates (Rev 2.13; 13.2).[723] The enthronement of Jesus surpasses what is normally attributed to the emperors beside Jupiter due to the cosmic splendor, heavenly liturgy, eschatological scope, and salvific import attributed Jesus' position with God on the throne.[724]

(c) Conclusion

Hurtado and Collins agree that religious experience and cultural factors shaped early Christology. They understand "cultural factors" to include ruler cults, especially the Roman imperial cult. Hurtado admitted that imperial influences became a palpable influence on literary representations of Christology at least towards the end of the first century, whereas Collins thinks that such influence is

---

[720] Cf. worship of Jesus by angelic beings (Heb 1.6; Rev 5.9–14; *Ascen. Isa.* 10.15; 11.23–26; *Apoc. Jas.* 14.26–30) and all of creation (Phil 2.10–11; Rev 5.13–14; Pol. *Phil.* 2.1).

[721] Jonathan Knight, "The Enthroned Christ of Revelation 5:6 and the Development of Christian Theology," in *Studies in the Book of Revelation*, ed. Stephen Moyise (Edinburgh: T&T Clark, 2001), 47.

[722] Cf. Burnett, *Christ's Enthronement*, 94–110.

[723] Gallusz, *Throne Motif*, 331.

[724] Friesen (*Imperial Cults*, 198) is correct to say that "John did not attempt to work out the relationship between the Lamb and the One on the throne through discussions of ontology or through abstract reasoning. His vision report works through the logic of worship and of apocalyptic symbol." Be that as it may, I would add that worship implies an ontology; worship is directed to the one who "is, was, and is to come," which are states of being (Rev 1.4, 8; 4.8); and apocalypticism trades in divine metaphysics in the mode of metaphor, marvel, and mystery.

much earlier, as early as the 50s CE, as evidenced by Phil 2.6–11. I am inclined to agree with Collins against Hurtado, but in a very qualified sense.

Ruler cults were a significant sociopolitical and religious factor of the ancient Near East, Second Temple Judaism, and Greco-Roman period. They were part of the world behind the New Testament, the world inhabited by apostolic Christianity, and ruler cults came in for specific treatment in proto-orthodox Christianity. The Jewish world participated in these cults of rulers, albeit as constrained by the specificities of the Yahweh cult, so that Israel's king, though venerated, never attained the same cultic or honorific status that the monarch held in other kingdoms. Accordingly, it was Jewish ruler veneration, particularly as represented in the Greek Psalter, with influence drawn too from messianic traditions, that was the single most formative influence upon the textualization of the religious experience of the first Christians about the identity of Jesus and his relationship to Israel's Lord. In other words, Ps 109/110 was the primary way hermeneuts of apostolic Christianity made sense of the experience of Jesus and the status that he now occupied.[725] This was partly at parity with Judean ruler veneration by resembling the honorific titles that were given to the Hasmonean and Herodian rulers (as Horbury notes).

However, this does not mean that early Christology was merely replacing Herod's name in an inscription with Jesus', or that the early Christians surreptitiously replaced the head of Augustus with the head of Jesus on a statue of the emperor. Jesus devotion was not born on the Palatine hill, and it radically exceeded scriptural patterns and first-century expressions of Judean ruler veneration. The chief differences are that royal ideology was married to a kerygmatic narrative of Jesus' passion, resurrection, and exaltation (Acts 2.36), identifying Jesus with the coming of God in judgment (1 Cor 16.22), splicing together ruler cult tropes of *isotheoi timai* with Isaianic imagery (Phil 2.6–11), and parodying the imperial cult in conjunction with Jewish throne-sharing traditions (Rev 5.1–14). In patterns of Jesus devotion, Jesus receives more than ruler veneration, but worship appropriate for Israel's God because he is intensely identified with Israel's God.

In summary, while ruler cults were generative for early Christology and Jesus devotion, they were not the determinative factor for species of early Christology that placed Jesus in distinct proximity to God's being, sovereignty, identity, and worship.

---

[725] Cf. Hengel (*Studies in Early Christology*, 221): "The enthronement of Jesus, the crucified Messiah, as the 'Son' with the Father 'through the resurrection from the dead' belongs to the oldest message which all of the missionaries proclaimed in common."

Conclusion

The preceding analysis has demonstrated that Jesus was portrayed in apostolic, proto-orthodox, heterodox, and other writings with a likeness to a variety of intermediary figures. In some cases, this resemblance was an ancillary feature added to Jesus' divine nature. In other cases, the resemblance constituted the basis for his divine nature. To illustrate, the difference is between Jesus as a divine being with angelic qualities, in contrast to Jesus as inhabited by an angel or explicitly identified as an angel as the explanation for his divine nature. It is indisputable that Christian authors and their readers had these intermediary figures in mind when they conceived of Jesus in terms of his transcending the heaven-earth divide, his preexistence and heavenly origins, his embodiment of divine power, his representing the climax of God's self-revelation, his exaltation to heaven, and his sharing in divine functions and prerogatives. Yet no single intermediary figure explains the totality of the christological discourses and their attribution of divine roles, titles, and nature to Jesus.[726] That is true for canonical and noncanonical texts, proto-orthodox and heterodox Christianities, in the first and second centuries. Moreover, for every similarity we find, whether in demiurgical figures, wisdom traditions, principal angels, exalted patriarchs, or ruler cults, it is never complete, and must be balanced with some degree of differentiation between these intermediary figures and the portrayals of Jesus. In other words, intermediary figures are relevant for how Christian authors conceived of Jesus as divine and a divine agent, but they are insufficient to explain why divinity was attributed to Jesus at all, and why that divinity was attributed in ways that were sometimes unusually intense. Whatever similarities there are, the differences are often stark and pertain to how Jesus is associated with the one God, made the object of divine worship, and shares in the divine nature of God the Father. To this subject of differences we now turn.

---

[726] Cf. similarly Timo Eskola, *Messiah and the Throne* (WUNT 2.142; Tübingen: Mohr Siebeck, 2001), 383; and Bühner, *Hohe Messianologie*, 339.

5
Setting Jesus apart from Demiurges, Deities, Daemons, and Divi

> The identity of Jesus of Nazareth was central to the early church's self-understanding and appropriation of its Jewish heritage.
>
> George W. E. Nickelsburg

> Incarnation is what keeps Christianity, in this sense—the biblical sense—Jewish.
>
> Paula Fredriksen

> I used to think that becoming incarnate was impossible for God. But recently I have come to the conclusion that it is unjewish to say that this is something the God of the Bible cannot do, that he cannot come that close.
>
> Pinchas Lapide

> On the level of the history of religions, we see that this préexistent Logos, i.e., the préexistent Logos upon which the Fourth Gospel is founded, in every sense, is a Jewish Logos, and the continuity of Johannine religion with the Judaism of its day is assured.
>
> Daniel Boyarin

> It was not the transformation of a Jewish prophet into a pagan God, . . . but the transformation of a Jewish prophet and messianic claimant into a Jewish God.
>
> Gabriele Boccaccini

> Incarnation is an important perception of God in the Jewish-Christian tradition. The incarnation is God's definitive act of love on the part of the God who has created for himself, in his own creation, an opposite number without whom he does not wish to be God.
>
> Reinhard Feldmeier and Hermann Spieckermann

> The presence of God and of God-as-Jesus on earth is nothing more than a particular form of this old idea of multiple embodiment, and hence no more offensive to a monotheistic theology than J and E sections of the Pentateuch.
>
> Benjamin Sommer

Introduction

In the previous chapters I noted the similarities and differences between portrayals of Jesus and various intermediary figures, such as the demiurge, Logos, Wisdom, principal angels, exalted patriarchs, and deified rulers. The similarities are undeniable, as are the differences. Yet the question is, so what? Well, two things stand out.

First, the similarities mean that Jesus was in many respects a Greco-Roman deity, a comparable and comprehensible divine being of antiquity.[1] Thus, Litwa is correct to state that "early Christians imagined and depicted Jesus with some of the basic traits common to other Mediterranean divinities and deified men."[2] Accordingly, when Pauline, Johannine, Ignatian, or Justinian Christology is viewed synoptically beside the intermediary figures of Plato, Philo, and Plutarch, we are dealing with a parallel religious conceptuality of deity and divine agency. The fact that Jesus was described as an unbegotten and uncreated god is proof that Jesus was considered a divine being in the strongest Greco-Roman sense imaginable. By virtue of this context, we should naturally expect that "the treatment of 'divine' human beings in the wider Gentile world *do* offer likely precedents for

---

[1] Cf. Frances M. Young ("Prelude," in *The Cambridge History of Christianity: Origins to Constantine*, ed. Margaret M. Mitchell and Frances M. Young [Cambridge: Cambridge University Press, 2006], 13): "That Christians prayed to Christ as to a god is clear, and also undeniable is assimilation to the cultic language and imagery of the religious world around them."

[2] M. David Litwa, *Iesus Deus: The Early Christian Depiction of Jesus as a Mediterranean God* (Minneapolis: Fortress, 2014), 215.

some aspects of the worship of Jesus and his inclusion within the divine identity."[3]

Second, the differences mean that Jesus was distinguished from each of the intermediary figures that we have analyzed. Jesus' preexistence, earthly life, crucifixion, resurrection, exaltation, and divine status sometimes get described as divine in ways that depart from other intermediary figures, beginning in apostolic Christianity and developing further in both proto-orthodox and heterodox circles. In other words, Jesus could be deliberately portrayed like a demiurge, Wisdom, an angel, an exalted patriarch, or a deified ruler, but there was simultaneously a consciousness, varying in degrees across the literature, that Jesus was somehow different from these intermediary figures. Or, as Timo Eskola concludes, "The interpretation of early Jewish Christian Christology is not dependent on typological explanation, even though it does have some evident typological features."[4] As such, no single intermediary figure can be regarded as a progenitor of early Christology, just as no single intermediary figure can be considered the hermeneutic key explaining the development of early Christology. Early Christologies have unique mutations and hybridities in their account of Jesus as a divine agent who is simultaneously and varyingly identified with the one God of Israel's monotheistic worship.

In what follows I will explore the significance of the differences with a view to demonstrating that early Christologies were conspicuously divergent from the sundry intermediary figures of Greco-Roman antiquity. Those differences are sometimes of *degree*, other times of *genus*, and the distinctiveness of early Christologies is indebted to Jewish precursors and their evolution within a wider Hellenistic context. In other words, although early Christologies were not nakedly unique from intermediate figures of antiquity, they are principally innovations within a Jewish divine discourse and its encounter with Mediterranean and ancient Near Eastern religions.

Contrastive Early High Christology

Amid all the similarities of Jesus with intermediary figures, there are several crucial distinctives that stand out.

First, the kerygmatic aggregate—where Christians proclaimed and praised Jesus as the preexistent, humanized, prophet of the God's kingdom, who was

---

[3] Crispin H. T. Fletcher-Louis, *Jesus Monotheism*, vol. 1: *Christological Origins: The Emerging Consensus and Beyond* (Eugene, Ore.: Wipf & Stock, 2015), 248 (italics original).

[4] Timo Eskola, *Messiah and the Throne* (WUNT 2.142; Tübingen: Mohr Siebeck, 2001), 389.

crucified, risen, and exalted as Lord and Messiah, associated too with God's identity and purposes, by using an eclectic blend of images drawn from the Jewish sacred traditions and Greco-Roman tropes—attests a form of divine intermediary hybridity that is genuinely remarkable. Whether expressed in Jewish or Hellenistic schemes, a crucified and exalted messiah was peculiar to the point of scandal if it is meant to describe the mode of God's action and very presence. But beyond that, the various representations of Jesus derived from Jewish and Greco-Roman traditions, while not remotely unique if taken individually, are simply unprecedented when collated together. A divine agent as concurrently a crucified martyr, personified Wisdom, demiurge, animated prophet, Messiah, rabbi, angel, Word, and imperial counterpart is not exactly a common pattern. This kerygmatic compilation is significant in at least two ways. To begin with, according to Eskola, "The first Christian theologians had connected traditions that did not yet belong together in Second Temple Judaism."[5] On top of that, to quote Chester, "What is utterly outstanding, then, is that a humiliated, crucified figure of the immediate past is acclaimed, at a very early stage, as the companion of God's throne, thus set in the supreme place in heaven, and ascribed the most intimate possible communion with God."[6] The eclectic accumulation and integration of types, titles, and tropes for a divine agent, who is simultaneously identified with Israel's one God in an unusually intense manner, is what is distinctive in Christian literary representations of their proclamation and praise of Jesus.[7]

[5] Eskola, *Messiah and the Throne*, 383.
[6] Andrew Chester, *Messiah and Exaltation* (WUNT 207; Tübingen: Mohr Siebeck, 2007), 37.
[7] Cf. Charles Moule (*The Origins of Christology* [Cambridge: Cambridge University Press, 1977], 150–51): "Yes, he did recall recognizable categories—but in a highly distinctive and startling new manner. In the first place, when he was presented as an anointed one—'Messiah' or 'Christ'—it was in an almost unrecognizable paradoxical guise. Who had ever before heard of a crucified Messiah? Some pre-Christian Jews, it appears, had daringly thought of a suffering Messiah—even a martyred Messiah; but never one martyred with this degree of ignominy. And, second, the other most remarkable feature of the Christians' presentation was that not only was Jesus claimed to be an anointed one, but also a whole welter of other figures converged upon him—figures both for individuals saviours and also for the realization of the true destiny of Israel as a whole. As far as I know, this is unparalleled in the whole of ancient Jewish literature." Martin Hengel (*The Son of God: The Origin of Christology and the History of Jewish Hellenistic Religion* [Minneapolis: Fortress, 1976], 1): "The confession that depicts this executed man as a pre-existent divine figure who becomes man and humbles himself to a slave's death is, as far as I can see, without analogy in the ancient world." Maurice Casey (*From Jewish Prophet to Gentile God* [Louisville, Ky.: Westminster John Knox, 1991], 81): "If we look at New Testament Christology as a whole, many aspects of Christ's finished work have no parallel. Moreover, to find all these parallels, we have

Second, schemes where Jesus is identified with the creative action of God, either as mediator of creation or as cocreator with God the Father, which separate God from creation, signify a distinctly Jewish metric for divinity and denote an intense association of Jesus with Israel's God.[8] Theologians like Irenaeus certainly hardened the God/Christ and creation divide, but Irenaeus was not wildly innovating here and was working with earlier texts and traditions from Jewish and Christian corpora. Of course, it is certainly true that not all christological schemes posited Jesus as the mediator of creation. Many Gnostics did not attribute a demiurgical function to Jesus, except perhaps as the curator of the pleroma. The many exaltationist and adoptionist Christologies could see Jesus as a human being promoted to divinity within the created order and make him a deified human. Nonetheless, the identification of Jesus as the mediator of creation is incredibly significant. Greco-Roman philosophers could speak of a divine creator, yet the supreme gods, Zeus and Jupiter, were not ordinarily attributed a creative function; they were progeny of the old

---

had to look at several Jewish figures, and it may be asserted that Jesus is quite remarkably unique, since he has taken up all these different figures into himself." Larry Hurtado (*One God, One Lord: Early Christian Devotion and Ancient Jewish Monotheism* [3rd ed.; London: T&T Clark, 2015], 21): "This placing of Jesus at the center of virtually all aspects of God's activity, this rather comprehensive way in which Jesus functions as God's chief agent, is not fully paralleled in the roles assigned to other chief agent figures in the Jewish literature of the early Greco-Roman period." Chester (*Messiah and Exaltation*, 80–81): "Christ is seen as seated in the heavenly world and set at the right hand of God; he is also seen as having the form of image of God. Indeed, he is portrayed as having himself the very name of God, and is given elevated titles, such as Lord and Son of God, otherwise. Thus also he becomes the object of prayer and worship, and has scriptural texts applied to him and used of him that originally and in themselves refer to God. All this seems, and indeed is, astounding. In its cumulative and concentrated effect, if not in every single facet, it certainly goes beyond anything we find in the Jewish sources." Chris Tilling (*Paul's Divine Christology* [Grand Rapids: Eerdmans, 2012], 240): "While some figures share one or two identifying features, (e.g., some are worshipped, some are exaltedly described as pre-existent to creation, others are described as sitting on God's throne, Melchizedek was called 'god,' Metatron was called the 'little YHWH,' the 'heavenly' Enoch was called up by Noah, the Son of Man was associated with ultimate goals, etc.), the complete pattern remains descriptive of the God-relation alone." Ruben A. Bühner (*Hohe Messianologie: Übermenschliche Aspekte eschatologischer Heilsgestalten im Frühjudentum* [WUNT 2.523; Tübingen: Mohr Siebeck, 2020], 339): "A further distinction between early Jewish discourses on eschatological saving figures and New Testament high Christology, does not consist of individual aspects and motifs, but in their sum" ("Ein weiterer bemerkenswerter Unterschied zwischen frühjüdischen Diskursen über eschatologische Heilsgestalten und der neutestamentlichen Hoch-christologie besteht nicht in einzelnen Aspekten und Motiven, sondern in deren Summe").

[8] See esp. Richard Bauckham, *Jesus and the God of Israel* (Milton Keynes, U.K.: Paternoster, 2008), 19, 26–30.

gods, Kronos and Saturn. The Olympian gods were not creators of the world as much as the most powerful forces permeating the world. While very few intermediary figures were attributed a demiurgical role or a mediating function in creation, it was not unprecedented. Wisdom and angels were sometimes given creative role, as was Plato's demiurge with the young gods and Philo's Logos. Even the Babylonian deity Marduk is among divine beings who create. Yet even these creator-gods and demiurgical figures are themselves created beings, and that is the difference. To attribute a creative function to Christ would not itself make him species unique or require his promotion within a divine hierarchy. However, when Christ is considered eternal, placed above angels and powers, and attributed a creative function, that is the telling point. Thus, when the early Christians confessed Jesus as the one by or through whom "all things" were made (1 Cor 8.6; Col 1.15–18; Heb 1.2; *Odes Sol.* 16.19; John 1.3; Rev 3.14; *Keryg. Pet.* 2; *Herm.* 3.4; 91.5; *Diogn.* 7.2; Justin, *2 Apol.* 6.3; Irenaeus, *Haer.* 4.11.1), with absolute preexistence and even eternality (John 1.1–2; 17.5; Pol. *Phil.* 14.3; *Diogn.* 11.5), and differentiated him from and above intermediary figures (*1 Clem.* 36.2; *Mart. Pol.* 14.1; *Herm.* 59.2; *Ascen. Isa.* 4.14; 9.28; Irenaeus, *Haer.* 1.22.1; 3.11.1–2; 4.7.4; 5.18.1; *Epid.* 10; 40; 94; *Gos. Pet.* 39–40; Athenagoras, *Leg.* 10.2, 5; 24.2; *Diogn.* 7.2–4; Justin, *1 Apol.* 52.3; Tertullian, *Carne* 14.1–2; Ps.-Clem. *Rec..* 1.45; 2.42; *Hom.* 18.4; Origen, *Cels.* 5.4–5), they were placing him on the side of the uncreated creating God in distinction from created creator-deities and their creation.

Again, what is telling is that this is all being said within the auspices of scripturally rooted monotheism. As early as Paul (1 Cor 8.6) we see that Christ as a creator-deity does not threaten the divinity of God the Father, as if Christ were a rival and rebellious sub-deity; in fact, the language from Deut 6.4 shows that Christ shares more of the Father's divine identity as an uncreated creator.[9] In addition, the opening stichs of the Johannine prologue depict the Logos as the creative instrument of the one, true, uncreated Creator, and presages the Logos' participation in God's own being (John 1.1–3). Now, as I have stated, some intermediary figures could have relative preexistence and a creative mediating function attributed to them (e.g., Wisdom, Philo's Logos, sometimes angels), but it is only with Jesus that we find absolute preexistence, eternality, and a creative mediating function.[10] Jesus' eternality and his role as mediator of creation implied that he was an "uncreated" God, and that is what makes representations of Jesus stand out among creator-deities and other intermediary figures

---

[9] M. David Litwa, *We Are Being Transformed: Deification in Paul's Soteriology* (Berlin: de Gruyter, 2012), 272, n. 35.

[10] Bühner, *Hohe Messianologie*, 323, 333.

who pull levers in the creative work. In the words of Bühner, "the notion of any kind of participation in creation or a creative mediation cannot be proven for any eschatological salvation figure independent of the early Jesus movement,"[11] and "the specifically Johannine conception of Christ's preexistence actually serves the purpose of describing the Logos, or Christ, as participating in the essence of the one God of Israel and thus attests a divinity that exceeds that of other Jewish mediator figures."[12]

Third, in addition to resembling the intermediary figures of antiquity, Jesus also resembles the God above the intermediary figures of antiquity. Chris Tilling points out how the Yahweh-Israel relation of Jewish sacred literature mirrors the Christ-believer relation in 1 Corinthians. Also, Jesus, as the "Lord of Glory," bears a closer resemblance to *1 Enoch*'s "Lord of Spirits" than to *1 Enoch*'s "Son of Man."[13] Or else, in Phil 2.6–11, for all the parallels with Adam, Wisdom, or imperial apotheosis, Paul casts the exalted Jesus in the likeness of Deutero-Isaiah's *kyrios*. Now, to be sure, one can find God-language applied to various intermediary figures, 4Q491c and 11QMelch are obvious examples, and the Yahoel appears to bear the divine name. However, the application of the title *kyrios*, not merely as a royal title, but as a representation of the divine name, and a signifier of the superlative sovereignty of Israel's God, applied to a human figure, is without precise parallel.[14] Even Bousset, who believed that the impetus for applying the title *kyrios* to Jesus came from Hellenistic ruler cults, recognized that the content of Jesus as *kyrios* was shaped by Jewish tradition of Yahweh's exclusive worship: "The spirit of unconquerable and stalwart Old Testament monotheism is transferred to the Kyrios worship and the Kyrios faith!"[15]

---

[11] Bühner, *Hohe Messianologie*, 323: "Auch die Vorstellung einer wie auch immer gearteten Mitwirkung an der Schöpfung oder einer Schöpfungsmittlerschaft lässt sich für keine eschatologische Heilsgestalt unabhängig von der frühen Jesusbewegung nachweisen."

[12] Ruben A. Bühner, "Die theologischen Implikationen der Präexistenzchristologie in Joh 1,1–3," in *Perspektiven zur Präexistenz im Frühjudentum und frühen Christentum*, ed. Jörg Frey, Friederike Kunath, and Jens Schröter (Tübingen: Mohr Siebeck, 2021), 186: "die spezifisch johanneische Konzeption von Christi Präexistenz in der Tat diesem Zweck dient, den Logos, bzw. Christus, als an dem Wesen des einen Gottes Israels partizipierend zu beschreiben und ihm damit eine Göttlichkeit bescheinigt, die jene aller anderen jüdischen Mittlerwesen übersteigt."

[13] Tilling, *Paul's Divine Christology*, 228–29; and James A. Waddell, *The Messiah: A Comparative Study of the Enochic Son of Man and the Pauline Kyrios* (London: T&T Clark, 2011), 178–86.

[14] Bauckham, *Jesus and the God of Israel*, 221–32.

[15] Wilhelm Bousset, *Kyrios Christos* (Waco, Tex.: Baylor University Press, 2013 [1970]), 151.

Mapping parallels between Jesus and intermediary figures, useful as they are, perhaps exposes our bias, as we casually assumed that the cause and comparison of Jesus' divine status exists from these intermediary figures. But what if we have been looking in the wrong place? What if the most appropriate analogue for Jesus' divinity is not any single one of the exalted humans or intermediate heavenly powers, but the God who resides above the powers? Is Jesus like the Enochic Lord of Spirits *or* the Enochic Son of Man? Is Jesus parallel to Wisdom or like the Most High God of the Wisdom of Solomon and Ben Sira? Is Jesus like Yahoel or like the God who sends Yahoel to Abraham? I suspect the answer is, "a bit of both," but rarely does a study of parallels and comparative intermediaries take into account literary representations of God beside a study of intermediary figures.[16]

Fourth, a further element that appears to be without precise parallel—though, as with any negative claim, I cannot absolutely guarantee this—is Jesus as giver of the Spirit. The notion of Jesus as Spirit-dispenser is found in Paul (Gal 3.14; Phil 1.19; Rom 8.2, 9–11), Luke (Luke 3.16; Acts 2.38), and John (John 15.26; 20.2). This resembles Greco-Roman religion in that a deity can give power to a person for certain deeds, as in the case with ecstatic utterances, dreams, healings, military prowess, or even moral transformation.[17] Also, in Stoicism, God is Logos, cosmic word and reason, an intelligent fiery force of *pneuma* that penetrates the entire cosmos (Tertullian, *Apol.* 21.10–11; Origen, *Cels.* 6.71; Aetius 1.6.1). Notable the Platonic dialectic between the demiurge and the World-Soul is telescoped by Stoics into a divinely immanent *pneuma*, a divine rational being that orders all things even as it is married in various ways to all matter. This *pneuma* is not just an instrument of God, but it is God blended with the material world.[18] Yet an intermediary agent who bestows God's Spirit upon others does not have any parallel with Greek heroes, angelic beings, Wisdom, or exalted humans as far as I am aware. A "most high god" endows devotees with divine energy: Dios provides *dynamis*, the Stoic God unites everything with *pneuma*, Yahweh pours out *ruach*, and Jesus bestows the *paraclete*. As Spirit-giver, Jesus is more like a high god than an intermediary. Furthermore, Jesus' giving of the Spirit posits him doing what only Yahweh does according to the Jewish Scriptures, since Yahweh promises to dispense his Spirit in full and fresh

---

[16] The closest one comes, I think, is Larry J. Kreitzer, *Jesus and God in Paul's Eschatology* (Sheffield: Sheffield Academic Press, 1987), but even that book is limited to Paul's eschatological narrative and assumes an ontological vs. functional Christology dichotomy.

[17] Cf. Luke Timothy Johnson, *Among the Gentiles: Greco-Roman Religion and Christianity* (New Haven, Conn.: Yale University Press, 2009), 134–35.

[18] Adam Drozdek, *Greek Philosophers as Theologians: The Divine Arche* (London: Routledge, 2016), 234.

ways (Ps 104.30; Isa 44.3; Ezek 39.29; Joel 2.29–29; Acts 2.17–18). Christian discourse of *hagion pneuma* was genuinely novel. For a start, there was the synthesis of divine power, presence, and personage that was infused into the believer, a divine inhabitation of the God within the person. On top of that, there is the extraordinary association of *pneuma* with eschatology, cosmology, anthropology, and ethics. Jesus' giving of divine *pneuma* yielded a new age, a new creation, a new humanity, a new covenant, and a new moral disposition.[19]

Fifth, something must be said too of the intensity of the affection for Christ. Paul clearly stands out as one considering all things loss for the sake of Christ and his death as gain if it means joining Christ (Phil 1.21; 3.8). Or else, there is an expectation of love for Jesus with a steadfast devotion that abandons all other relationships and pursuits (John 21.15–17). Religious devotion and affection for a deity were far from unknown in antiquity. Aristides' intense devotion for Asclepius is an obvious example from the second century CE. Christians similarly believed that God and Christ loved them in an immeasurable way, for which they could never repay (Rom 5.8; 8.35–39; Eph 5.2; 1 John 3.16; 4.19; Rev 1.5; *1 Clem.* 49.5–6; *Barn.* 1.1; *Diogn.* 9.2). They reciprocated divine charity with their own rituals, prayers, and hymns, but also with an intense love for the God and Christ who first love them. The pathos of affection can be illustrated in a fifth-century Syrian hymn:

> Jesus is mine and I am his. He has desired me;
> He has clothed himself in me, I am clothed in him;
> With the kisses of his mouth has he kissed me
> And brought me to his Bridal chamber on high.[20]

Yet the sense of identification with Christ and experience of the love of Christ does not have a clear analogue with figures like the Enochic Son of Man, Qumran's Melchizedek, the archangels Michael or Yahoel, exalted patriarchs like Jacob, figures such as Herakles, or a deified emperor. That is not to say that such figures did not receive devotion, nor that they were not esteemed in some respects, but Christians had an exceedingly acute affection for and identification with Christ that does not neatly correspond with devotion to other intermediary figures as far as I am aware.

Sixth, early Christology needs to be situated in terms of the incipient trinitarianism of early Christianity. Now, I am very cognizant of the fact that the mere mention of the "Trinity" at this juncture will prompt looks of eye-rolling

---

[19] Johnson, *Among the Gentiles*, 134–45.
[20] Cited in Sebastian Brock, "Syriac Tradition," in *Jesus in History, Thought, and Culture: An Encyclopedia*, ed. Leslie Houlden (2 vols.; Santa Barbara, Calif.: ABC Clio, 2003), 1:827.

contempt by historians of religion, who will judge me guilty of anachronism and doing that dubious, dreaded, and dark art of theology—for the worst insult a historian of religion can level at another is call them a "theologian"! But I ask for eyes to remain unrolled and derisive expressions to remain unuttered at least until I am given a preliminary hearing. It should not be controversial to state that early christological discourses as presented in the New Testament and beyond were expressed among descriptions of the operation of the triadic characters of God the Father, the messianic Son, and the Holy Spirit. Whether one refers to the baptism of Jesus (Matt 3.16–17), the Matthean baptismal formulae (Matt 28.19; *Did.* 7.1–4), Paul's account of his proclamation (1 Cor 2.1–5), Paul's famous benediction (2 Cor 13.14), the Johannine Jesus' high priestly prayer (John 17.1–26), or Ignatius' exhortation (*Phld.* 4.2), we are confronted with a portrait of Christ in relation to God the Father and the Holy Spirit. What is more, if the nature of these persons and the relations between these persons are a matter of concerted reflection, then christological discourse is inevitably brought into conversation with theology proper and pneumatology. The true historian of Christian religion will have to admit that mapping the origins of early Christology with its diversities and developments cannot be abstracted from the church's broader divine discourse that quickly transformed into conversations about God's unity and tripartite economy. What became the Trinity was not a series of proof-texts, but a mixture of hermeneutics, worship culture, and philosophical exploration. The Trinity was partly an analytical interrogation of Scripture, partly the search for coherences in syntheses of Scripture, partly an experiment in developing a lexicon for liturgies of worship, and partly a quest for philosophical coherence in conceptuality and grammar.

Christian accounts of God provided the parameters and paradigm for the development of its Christologies. We can detect elements of christological conflict in the first century (2 Cor 11.4; 1 John 2.22, 4.2-3; 2 John 7), and by the first quarter of the fourth century underlying christological debates came to a dramatic confrontation in the east (e.g., bishop Alexander vs. presbyter Arius). Even so, Paul and John, the two most formative theologians for proto-orthodox and heterodox Christianities, for all their christocentrism, were both highly theocentric thinkers. In addition, by the second century, the primary matters of philosophical contention were on the nature and being of God, for which christological disputes were largely ancillary. Justin, Irenaeus, and Marcion were discoursing mainly about God in light of preferred scriptural syntheses and diverse appropriations of Platonic thought. That is to say that early Christology and Jesus devotion were distinct in the fact that they emerged in the context of Christianized discussions about the nature of deity. Early Christology, then, must be understood as more than a new ruler cult and more than an acute angelology emerging from within the Jewish religion. Early Christology is more than the story of how Christ came to be a member of the Christian version of Capitoline Triad (i.e., Jupiter, Juno, Minerva). What needs to be grasped is that early Christology was distinct because it was part of a religious and philosophical revolution at the crossroads of Jewish monotheism and Middle Platonism that eventually evolved into the Christian doctrine of a triune God.

Thus, we can speak of the distinctiveness of early Christology in light of (1) the sum of kerygmatic titles and functions attributed to Jesus as the crucified and risen Messiah who is viewed as God's principal agent and as an expression of God's very self; (2) the postulation of Jesus as belonging to the Creator side of the Creator-creature distinction with the implication of his functional and ontic differentiation from intermediaries; (3) the ways in which Jesus resembled God rather than God's heavenly and earthly agents in literary representations; (4) the manner in which Jesus is depicted as the dispenser of the Spirit, which is, as far as we know, was a role for high gods and not intermediary figures; (5) the intensity of affection for Jesus Christ; and (6) the nesting of early Christology within the incipient trinitarianism of the early church.

These distinctive aspects are, in general, derived from Jewish specificities. The vast majority of distinctive points find their most natural analogue with Jewish messianism and its attribution of superhuman traits to a Messiah and Jewish wisdom traditions with their account of Wisdom or the Logos as plenipotentiary intermediary. Digging down deeper, we could say that only the God of Israel can have a crucified Messiah who is raised and exalted to his right hand. Only the God of Israel can invite a Son to cocreate with him. Only the God of Israel can share his divine name with the messianic lord. Only the God of Israel gives the Spirit to renew Israel, make people alive, raise the dead, and rescue creation. Only the Jewish religion with its account of monotheism and divine agency could transform into an incipient trinitarianism. In other words, Jesus could not be the type of divinity he was considered to be without the Jewish texts and traditions in which his divinity was articulated. There is no pagan version of 1 Cor 8.6. Further, while John 1.1–3 makes perfect sense within Stoicism or within Hellenistic Judaism, John 1.14 and 18 do not without a mutation of monotheism and messianism into the forms that they took in early Christianity.

Let me back up and offer an important qualification. The deity of Jesus is not contingent upon its uniqueness or distinctiveness. We need to avoid the specious reasoning that runs: Jesus shares in a special form or function that only applies to Yahweh, a form or function that has no parallel with Greco-Roman religion, therefore, Jesus is fully divine.[21] This is not my argument because I have precisely argued that Jesus is similar to Jewish and Greco-Roman intermediaries in many ways and his divinity is no worse for it. Jesus was depicted as divine in various modes in the manifold Christianities from Paul to Arius. The burden of my song is three things: (1) Jesus was often treated as more than an intermediary, closer to an absolute deity, whether as unbegotten and eternal or as a true and living God; (2) there are dissimilarities with intermediary figures, even a distinctiveness in places, largely derived from a Jewish context where Jesus is identified as being under, beside, and united with Israel's God in extraordinarily intense ways; and (3) early Christology appears to have been resourced from within Jewish tradition and yet also intentionally constructed to resonate with wider Hellenistic traditions.

Almost half a century ago, Charlie Moule asked whether presentations of Jesus fitted with varied and wide-ranging expectations of intermediary figures, or whether Jesus was completely distinctive. His answer was a paradoxical yes to both questions. Jesus was described in "recognizable categories—but in a highly distinctive and startling new manner."[22] The *novum* was a Messiah crucified into ignominy and a convergence of roles and titles never seen before. I believe this study has vindicated that claim and extended it by showing precisely how portrayals of Jesus rehearsed these intermediary figures and in what ways Jesus was made distinct from them.

In summary, Jesus was not a new Mediterranean god who had been hived off from the Yahweh cult, given a garb borrowed from Asclepius or Zeus, and had an independent cult established for him. Rather, Jesus was a Jewish deity; more precisely, he was considered an embodiment and expression of the God of Israel's person and power who was described with diverse Jewish traditions and Greco-Roman tropes. In christological narrations, Jesus was divine in many senses, including Jewish ways of describing God's being and identity, whether as a divine hypostasis or analogous to heavenly and earthly agents, and sometimes too evidencing derivation from Greco-Roman figures, who were part of the atmosphere of antiquity. What is more, the appropriation of

---

[21] Well noted by Theron Clay Mock III, "'New Testament Christology': A Critique of Larry Hurtado's Influence," unpublished paper presented at the Redescribing Christian Origins Seminar, Society of Biblical Literature (San Antonio, Tex., November 21, 2021), 66.

[22] Moule, *Origins*, 150–51.

Jewish and Greco-Roman imagery was often expressed in such a way that the lines between God and the messianic son became blurry. The net effect was that we have a distinctive transformation of Jewish and Hellenistic notions of divinity when it came to explicating Jesus as a divine being in association with the God of Israel.[23]

If I may push back on "new old *religionsgeschichtliche Schule*," I am all in favor of removing the artificial divide between Jewish and Greco-Roman influences upon Christology, but not if it means surrendering textual realities to ostentatious parallelomania. I would aver that "meaning" is a matter of context, content, and reception. We need to discern the appropriate historical and literary contexts that clarify the substance, form, and function of a text with contextual plausibility determined by availability to authors/readers and resonance with a text's contents. Certainly, the experience of first-century imperial media will be far more available, relatable, and plausible for understanding a text like Luke-Acts than mapping correspondences with Mandaean literature from fourth-century Iran. At the same time, an explicit allusion in a text to a passage from the book of Genesis will ordinarily carry more weight than possible resonances with Roman coinage in Africa and Pythagorean philosophers unless a missing middle term turns up. We need to undertake parallel comparisons within the constraints of textual phenomenon and explanatory of power.

Litwa writes, "In Christian writings—indeed, in the person of Jesus himself—the theology of the Greeks and Romans did not die. In Christ, it rose again."[24] That would be unobjectionable if it were not for omitting that "Christ" is a unique Jewish title and that resurrection is intended in a distinctive Jewish sense of eschatological restoration. So, I would prefer to say that when the time had fully come, the God of Israel sent his preexistent Son, to recapitulate Adam, to sum up Israel in his own person, to be the royal and eschatological Davidide; who became a Galilean prophet proclaiming the *malkutha di elaha*, whose miraculous deeds made him comparable to Elijah and the assorted *theios anēr* of antiquity, who died like a Roman slave; was raised by the power that the Maccabean martyrs longed for, was arrayed in a glory like the archangel Michael, was seated on a bisellium reminiscent of Jupiter and Augustus, and was heralded by a cohort of devotees learned in the lore of Moses and Plato, so that the pagans of antiquity would make

---

[23] Cf. Eskola, *Messiah and the Throne*, 390; and Chester, *Messiah and Exaltation*, 119–20.

[24] Litwa, *Iesus Deus*, 223.

acclamation to the Jews, "Truly, your God is God of gods and Lord of kings" (Dan 2.47) and then sing "a hymn to Christ as a god" (Pliny, *Ep.* 10.96).

Jesus as a Jewish God among the Greco-Roman Gods?

Does my thesis of casting Jesus as a Jewish deity in the Greco-Roman world reiterate the Hellenism vs. Judaism dichotomy, deploy Hellenistic Judaism as a convenient buffer zone between Christianity and "paganism," or amount to an apologetic strategy for Christ's uniqueness? No, I do not think so. The reasons are that, first, intermediation is more of a Jewish concern than a Greco-Roman one. Second, Judaism is distinguishable from Hellenism even as they overlap and coalesce. Third, absolute uniqueness of Christ as a divine figure is a mirage, but relative uniqueness is a valid conclusion about early christological discourses.

Intermediation as a Distinctly Jewish Problem

The focus on intermediation, while not unique to Judaism, is nonetheless characteristic of ancient Judaism because of the intense significance that it holds eschatological hopes.

Paula Fredriksen chides those in the "early high Christology club" who believe that "Christianity burst fully-formed from Jewish foreheads unsullied by messy ideas of divine intermediation."[25] True, no "religion" in the ancient East and in classical antiquity emerged without beings, persons, and institutions that mediated the divine world to human beings.[26] Accordingly, one can find in Platonic philosophy a question of how the invisible and immaterial deity contacts and acts in the terrestrial order, for which the daemons, demiurge, World-Soul, and young gods were the answer.[27] In addition, the various heroes and immortals were useful semi-divine figures that explained the transactions between the heavens and the world in Greco-Roman thought.

---

[25] Paula Fredriksen, "How High Can Early Christology Be?" in *Monotheism and Christology in Greco-Roman Antiquity*, ed. Matthew V. Novenson (Leiden: Brill, 2020), 304.

[26] Reinhard Feldmeier and Hermann Spieckermann, *God Becoming Human: Incarnation in the Christian Bible* (Waco, Tex.: Baylor University Press, 2021), 31.

[27] Plato (*Symp.* 202d–203a) recounts how "the whole *daimonia*" is a sphere that "exists between the mortal and immortal" where "power" consists of "Interpreting and transporting human things to the gods and divine things to men; entreaties and sacrifices from below, and ordinances and requitals from above: being midway between, it makes each to supplement the other, so that the whole is combined in one. Through it are conveyed all divination and priestcraft concerning sacrifice and ritual and incantations, and all soothsaying and sorcery." Philo translates the Greek notion of *daimōn* into the scriptural category of *angeloi*, who are "mediating and intercessory words" (*mesitais kai diaitētais logois*; *Somn.* 1.141–42).

However, it is fair to say that Greco-Roman religion and philosophy were not preoccupied with divine intermediaries to the same degree as Jewish authors. In Greco-Roman religion, apart from the odd mythical incident with a god engaging in rapine or the occasional appearance, there was little interest in divine "intervention, inspiration, or incubation." Instead, human-divine transactions transpired principally through "ritualized exchange and the interpretation of signs."[28]

In other words, while Greco-Roman religion had demiurges, daemons, demigods, and divi, it was the family, city, and provincial cults that did the heavy lifting in terms of divine transactions and mediation. This perhaps explains why there was no need for a Greco-Roman version of Daniel's Son of Man. If you are sick, go the temple of Asclepius. If you are concerned about a business deal, consult an augur. If you are at war, make a sacrifice to Mars. If you win the war, thank Mars for victory, praise the princeps as "Lord and Savior," and grant him divine honors. But nobody—as far as I know—was expecting the Roman people to be vindicated against the Goths and Parthians by the mysterious enthronement of a heavenly being who represents them and who symbolizes a victorious divine rout against the blasphemies of an arrogant Near Eastern ruler with impious enthusiasm for their own deification.[29]

In Jewish "theology," by contrast, God's holiness, glory, and transcendence were acutely problematic if one posited such a God as covenantally bound to a people, a communicative deity giving a Torah and concerned with the preservation and salvation of a specific people. It was not just the spatial and ontological gap between the God of heaven and human subjects that needed to be traversed; there was a sacred history and prophetic hope that seemed to require divine intervention in the future. But how? Jewish texts opine the need for a human "mediator" (Heb. *mēlîṣ* [Job 33.23]/Gk. *mesitēs* [Job 9.33 LXX]) largely in light of the failure of kings and priests to deliver them or to receive divine favor (Isa 43.27; 1QH 10.12–19; Gal 3.19–20). Jewish authors thereafter looked to one or more heavenly beings sent by God for the intermediation and intervention expected of a God who was in covenant with them.[30] Accordingly,

---

[28] Mary Beard, John North, and Simon Price, *Religions of Rome* (2 vols.; Cambridge: Cambridge University Press, 1998), 1:31–32.

[29] To pre-empt a possible response, I have my doubts about how concrete the parallels are between the Danielic, Enochic, and Johannine Son of Man and the *Sebastoi* of the imperial cults because the various Sons of Man represent a nation in a position of disempowerment and subjection.

[30] Cf. 1QH 14.12–13, which contrasts the failure of a "mediator between your holy ones" with the "angels of presence"; *T. Dan* 6.5: "Draw near to God and to the angel who intercedes for you, because he is the mediator between God and men for the peace of Israel"; and

Christian beliefs of divine intermediation, though not wholly removed from Greco-Roman notions of intermediation—demiurgy and the Logos being obvious examples—find their primary impetus in the Jewish cosmos. For in such a cosmos, with its monarchical monotheism, Yahweh presides over the heavenly hosts, commands angels, exalts patriarchs, sends prophets, and anoints priests and kings to make good on his promises that he is "mighty to save" (Isa 63.1). Christians inherited their focus on intermediation from Judaism and Christian accounts of Christ and the Spirit as divine intermediaries are indelibly tethered to Jewish narratives, hopes, and categories that feature intermediaries.

The Christian focus on Christ as not merely one intermediary, but as *the* mediator, God's final envoy, or God's definitive self-expression, is an appropriation of Jewish views of the divine nature, prophetic scripts, and apocalyptic agents. While Christian notions of Christ's mediatorship undoubtedly have analogues in the Greco-Roman world, their primary impetus derives from the Jewish context with a specific concern on intermediation and several specific modes of divine intermediation.

Early Christology between Judaism and Hellenism

The primary backdrop for plotting the sudden emergence of Jesus devotion/early Christology has to be its first-century Jewish literary context, religious milieu, and socio-cultural setting. Of course, ancient Judaism was embedded in the Hellenistic macro-culture of the eastern Mediterranean, the early church was a Greek-speaking religious movement, literary parallels between Jesus and Greco-Roman religious figures are not exactly hard to find, and so Hellenistic influence cannot be siloed from early Christianity. Yet I am convinced that Judaism and Hellenism are distinct entities and early Christology was primarily, not exclusively, shaped by its Jewish context at least in its embryonic stages.[31] This is obviously a controversial thesis, especially given recent analyses that tend to flatten out the distinctions between Judaism and Hellenism, thus I will expound my view in a "yes, however" fashion.

---

2 En. 33.10: "I will give [to] you, Enoch, my mediator, my archistratig, Michael." It is interesting that Paul contrasts the role of angels with Moses as a "mediator" in giving Torah in Gal 3.19–20 and casts aspersions on any event that requires mediation because "God is one."

[31] Larry Hurtado ("The New *religionsgeschichtliche Schule* at Thirty," in *Monotheism and Christology in Greco-Roman Antiquity*, ed. Matthew V. Novenson [Leiden: Brill, 2020], 7–31) points out that one needs to distinguish two different tasks: (1) mapping the parallels between Greco-Roman texts and literary depictions of Christ in the New Testament; and (2) explaining the impetus for the eruption of Jesus devotion/Christology in Judea in the second quarter of the first century.

Yes, the whole eastern Mediterranean was Hellenized in that it was pervaded by Greek language and culture, at least at the levels of political elites, the merchant class, and scribes, in urban environs, and in the military.

However, the diffusion of Hellenism must be qualified. We need to get away from the tacit assumption of many New Testament scholars that everybody from Athens to Armenia spoke Greek, read Homer, and wondered when the latest oracle from Delphi was going to arrive. The Roman east remained multilingual and multicultural. Hellenization was a process that varied in intensity and depth of penetration over the centuries. The Hellenization of Palestine and Mesopotamia in the fourth century BCE was different from the second century CE. In addition, Hellenization was not merely a top-down imposition of Greek culture on a subjugated people, but included a more dynamic interplay of influence and confluence. Hellenization was a "process of selection, adoption, and adaptation" as it brought resident cultures into new expressions.[32] The "Hellenization" of a region also met with the "Orientalization" of Greekness.[33] Hellenistic influence was uneven and sketchy. Each region maintained its indigenous traditions, distinctive histories, relative circumstances, and localized color. Thus, Hellenism did not overpower or evaporate local culture; sometimes its penetration was shallow, and where it took root, it was given to all sorts of hybridities—points rarely appreciated as scholarship often situates individuals within a Hellenistic meta-culture with little regard for regional peculiarities. Scholarship rattles on about Paul as a citizen of Rome, a Jew by birth and religion, and a Greek by culture, but typically underestimates how his local culture in Cilicia shaped him too.[34] Furthermore, even with Hellenization, local languages still dominated in most places, whether Aramaic, Thracian, or Phrygian.[35] Even where Greek was spoken, it varied markedly in both dialect and register.[36] For all we know, when Paul's letter to the Galatians was read, it might have required a translator for much of the congregation!

---

[32] Lee I. Levine, *Judaism and Hellenism in Antiquity: Conflict or Confluence?* (Peabody, Mass.: Hendrickson, 1998), 19.

[33] Levine, *Judaism and Hellenism*, 19–20.

[34] Cf. rightly Dale B. Martin, "Paul and the Judaism/Hellenism Dichotomy: Toward a Social History of the Question," in *Paul beyond the Judaism/Hellenism Divide*, ed. Troels Engberg-Pedersen (Louisville, Ky.: Westminster John Knox, 2001), 30.

[35] Cf. the centurion's surprise at Paul's ability to speak Greek in Acts 21.37.

[36] See esp. Rick Strelan, "'We Hear Them Telling in Our Own Tongues the Mighty Works of God' (Acts 2:11)," *NeoT* 40 (2006): 295–319; and idem, "The Languages of the Lycus Valley," in *Colossae in Space and Time: Linking to an Ancient City*, ed. Alan H. Cadwallader and Michael Trainor (Gottingen: Vandenhoeck & Ruprecht, 2011), 77–103.

Yes, all Judaism in the first century *in varying degrees* was Hellenistic Judaism, embedded within the religion and theologies of the eastern Mediterranean.[37] Thus, the Judaism that shaped Christianity had been interacting with Hellenism for some three hundred years prior to Christianity. Indeed, in the second century, while rabbinic Judaism leaned away from Hellenism, Christianity leaned deeper into it.[38]

However, Hellenization was an ongoing process, varied and uneven across the centuries, whether in Judea or the Diaspora. Most of the Hellenization of Judea and Galilee occurred not under Alexander or the Diadochoi but under the Romans, accelerated in the post-70 and 135 CE periods.[39] Hellenism penetrated the Jewish homeland in patchy ways depending on locale, time, and class.[40] Thus, as Mark Chancey notes, "All Judaism was Hellenistic Judaism, but not all Judaism was affected by Hellenism in the same ways or to the same extent."[41] One cannot imagine that Galilee and Judea were just as Hellenized as everywhere because, in reality, no place was like everywhere.[42] Where and when Hellenism took root, it did not replace Jewish culture as much as it brought Jewish culture into new local expressions from religion to architecture. Hellenism could be hybridized with a mixture of Jewish resistance and assimilation.[43] While we need to avoid essentializing Judaism and Hellenism,

---

Also, S. R. F. Price, *Rituals and Power: The Roman Imperial Cult in Asia Minor* (Cambridge: Cambridge University Press, 1984), 91–93.

[37] Martin Hengel, *Judaism and Hellenism: Studies in the Encounter in Palestine during the Early Hellenistic Period* (2 vols.; Philadelphia: Fortress, 1974). But see the pushback from Louis H. Feldman, "How Much Hellenism in Jewish Palestine?" *Hebrew Union College Annual* 57 (1986): 83–111.

[38] Johnson, *Among the Gentiles*, 131.

[39] Mark A. Chancey, *Greco-Roman Culture and the Galilee of Jesus* (SNTSMS 134; Cambridge: Cambridge University Press, 2005), 225.

[40] Chancey (*Greco-Roman Culture*, 221) says about the Hellenization of Galilee: "By Jesus' time, the region's encounter with Hellenism was over three centuries old. Despite occasional scholarly claims to the contrary, however, the penetration of Greek culture does not seem to have been especially deep, at least in respect to the spheres of culture we have considered."

[41] Chancey, *Greco-Roman Culture*, 225. Cf. Philip S. Alexander ("Hellenism and Hellenization as Problematic Historiographical Categories," in *Paul beyond the Judaism/Hellenism Divide*, ed. Troels Engberg-Pedersen [Louisville, Ky.: Westminster John Knox, 2001], 72): "In short, the effects of Hellenization in the Transjordan may appear impressive and significant, but they may on closer inspection amount in cultural and historical terms to much less than we might at first suppose."

[42] Chancey, *Greco-Roman Culture*, 225.

[43] I am reluctant to use the word "syncretism" because of its negative connotations, and because it assumes that cultures are homogenous and undiluted from each other and that one culture contaminates another culture in a one-dimensional and detrimental way. In

we still need to appreciate their distinct cultures in light of concrete phenomena such as language, literature, customs, kinship, cultus, worship, local histories, and institutions.[44]

Yes, the Judaism and Hellenism divide has served numerous furtive ideological functions. We must be alert to the danger that Judaism and Hellenism are reduced to nothing more than a background and foreground upon which the uniqueness of Christianity and its Christology leaps forth. In addition, the Judaism vs. Hellenism divide has functioned as a cipher for particularism and universalism; a symbol of nationalism and cosmopolitanism; a contrast of religion and reason; or a juxtaposition of Scripture with paganization.[45] Accordingly, a case can be made that, when setting things Hellenistic and Jewish side-by-side, one should think of comparisons rather than contrasts, similarity rather than juxtaposition, or search for analogy over antagonism.[46]

However, while the boundary between Judaism and Hellenism was porous and overlapping, they were still two distinct things. We know there were differences because Roman authors like Tacitus tell us of those differences as it pertains to worship and customs. The very word *Ioudaismos* developed its currency precisely in opposition to *Hellenismos* as two conflicting ways of life (2 Macc 2.21; 8.1; 14.38; 4 Macc 4.26). Paul regarded *Ioudaismos* as equivalent to the separatism and anti-Gentile ethos of Judean Pharisaism (Gal 1.13–14). Jewish authors wrote biting critiques of Greco-Roman religion and urged separation from Greeks because the two "isms" could be mutually antagonistic and because many Jews wanted to harden the differences (Wis 13–15; *Ep. Arist.* 128–71; *Jub.* 22.16). Even within the Diaspora there were different strategies for negotiating one's Hellenistic surroundings ranging from apostasy into Hellenism (e.g., Tiberius Alexander) to embittered resistance against Hellenism (e.g., tearing down statues of Caligula in Jamnia). The Jewish/Hellenistic binary was accented in early Christianity by dividing the world into "Jews" and "Greeks" (Gal 3.28; 1 Cor 10.32; Rom 10.12; Acts 19.10, 17; *Diogn.* 1.1; 5.17; Tertullian, *Praescr.* 7; Eusebius, *Praep. ev.* 1.5.16). This division is more than contrasting views of worship,[47] but sets up a disparity between divergent *ethnoi* separated by their ancestral customs and way of life. The Judaism of the Mediterranean basin was neither a

---

reality, ancient cultures clashed and coalesced all the time, in ways that often enhanced and enriched an existing culture.

[44] Cf. Alexander, "Hellenism and Hellenization," 79.
[45] Martin, "Paul and the Judaism/Hellenism Dichotomy," 30, 58–59.
[46] Alexander, "Hellenism and Hellenization," 79.
[47] Contra Martin, "Paul and the Judaism/Hellenism Dichotomy," 32.

Jewish ghetto nor dissolved into its Hellenistic environs. The cultures of the Greco-Roman basis and Near East were a series of interlocking petri dishes; however, that does not mean that every dish had the same bacteria and grew the same culture. This means that the Judaism of the Hellenistic period was not merely Hellenism without a foreskin.

Yes, Christians were truly embedded in the Greco-Roman world, and they evidence knowledge of its cultures, religions, and many literary forms. Christianity drew directly and powerfully from Greco-Roman culture just as it did from Jewish culture. Greco-Roman influence increased over time—this need not be construed as Harnack's "acute Hellenization"—but second- and third-century Christianities became increasingly imbibed with a Hellenistic ethos.[48]

However, concerning the most formative textual influences on the early church, the Greek Scriptures (i.e., Septuagint) and wider Jewish textual traditions are paramount. Piles of parallels made from Greco-Roman literature, though often illuminating, can never overpower the avalanche of citation and allusions to the Greek Scriptures that the New Testament authors and early Christian writers overwhelmingly deploy. Homer, Hesiod, or Herodotus are useful background resources in many instances, but probably not as much as Hosea, Habakkuk, or Qumran's *Hodayot* when it comes to understanding the piety of Jewish Christians. For all the discussion of the Platonism and rhetorical tropes of the book of Hebrews, twenty-five percent of the book's content consists of quotations from the Greek Scriptures.[49]

Early Christologies were telling a very Jewish story about how Israel's one true and living God spoke in his Son, whom he promised beforehand through his prophets in the holy Scriptures, a Son born of a woman, born under the Torah, the Word made flesh, descended from the seed of David, in order to redeem those who were under the law, became a servant of the circumcised on behalf of the truth of God in order that he might confirm the God's promises given to the patriarchs. This Jesus was a man attested by God and by miracles, wonders, and signs, which he did by God's power. He was sent to the people of Israel, announcing the gospel of peace, beginning in Galilee and throughout the province of Judea, with the Holy Spirit and in great power. Then he humbled himself, and, for the joy set before him, he became obedient to the point of death—even death on a cross. Indeed, before everyone's eyes Jesus was publicly crucified by the rulers of this age. The Messiah, the paschal lamb,

---

[48] Johnson, *Among the Gentiles*, 131.
[49] Cf. Mogens Müller, *The First Bible of the Church: A Plea for the Septuagint* (JSOTSup 206; Sheffield: Sheffield Academic Press, 2006).

had been sacrificed, crucified for sins in accordance with the Scriptures. He was buried, he was raised on the third day in accordance with the Scriptures, and after that he appeared to Cephas, then to the twelve. Then he appeared to more than five hundred brothers and sisters at one time, most of whom are still alive, though some have died. Then he appeared to James, then to all the apostles. God made this Jesus, whom Pilate handed over to be crucified, Messiah and Lord. God highly exalted him to his right hand and gave him the name that is above every name, so that at the name of Jesus every knee should bow, in heaven and on earth and under the earth, and every tongue should confess that Jesus Christ is Lord, to the glory of God the Father. And now the faithful wait for his Son from heaven, whom he raised from the dead—Jesus, who rescues believers from the wrath that is coming. Such a story as I have laid out only makes sense in light of the Jewish scriptural narrative and the diverse ways it was explained and explored in the first century. The stories about Christ were cut from Jewish cloth even if some Greco-Roman symbols and stitching have been added to the tapestry for extra effect.

To distill my perspective to its basic claims I would assert that Christianity grew from within the Judaism of the Greco-Roman world. It was not strictly a two-stage development, as if the church was initially Jewish in ethos and only later and gradually became influenced by the Greco-Roman world (although there is some truth to that generalization!). The reason is that Greek speakers were part of the church from the very beginning, thus so was Hellenism (see Acts 6.1–16). The earliest Christian assemblies were concurrently Jewish and Hellenistic. The challenge is to identify and explain which parts of Jewish and Greek tradition are being resourced and rehearsed in a given instance.[50] What I am trying to add is that in the construction of the churches' christological edifices Jewish traditions do seem to provide something of scaffolding and adhesive for the brickwork even if a few of the supporting beams have been especially imported from Rome and Athens. What shaped the titles given to Jesus and the narratives drawn around him were religious experiences explained through scriptural imagery, leading to discrete types of christological discourses. Those discourses, when mapped to their point of origin, betray influence from Jewish fixtures such as creational monotheism, Israel's election, scriptural modes of intermediation, and apocalyptic eschatology.

---

[50] Wayne A. Meeks, "Judaism, Hellenism, and the Birth of Christianity," in *Paul beyond the Judaism/Hellenism Divide*, ed. Troels Engberg-Pedersen (Louisville, Ky.: Westminster John Knox, 2001), 26.

Of course, if one wants to dissent from this thesis, and abandon the Jewish-heavy influence on primitive Christology in favor of a model front-loaded with Greco-Roman materials, I suggest a slight pause and uttering the phrases "Gnostic Redeemer Myth," "Cynic Jesus," and "divine man Christology" as a salutary reminder of what happens when Greco-Roman religions become the primary matrix for telling the story of early Christianity. Greco-Roman religion is indelibly relevant for any reconstruction of Christian origins, but the Judaism of the Hellenistic world is the primary impetus for plotting the christological claims of early Christianity.

Let it be known that it is not an either-or equation of Judaism or Hellenism.[51] While the center of gravity lies with the Jewish tradition for the origins of Christology, Greco-Roman concepts were interwoven into early Christianity, not despite its Hellenistic Judaism, but precisely through it. Early Christology should be located—much like the church at Dura-Europos—between a synagogue and a Mithraeum,[52] even if the church is several yards closer to the synagogue. So, if you are looking at the divine exaltation of a crucified messiah, the deaths of Socrates and Leonidas are interesting comparisons, as is the apotheosis of Herakles and Augustus; they might even have been evoked in the minds of some readers/auditors of Christian texts. Yet we are kidding ourselves if we think that they have the same relevance as Deut 21.23, Ps 2.7, 110.1, Dan 7.13, or Isa 53.11–12 for the formulation and explication of early Christology. Similarly, Justin can try to plot the parity of Moses, Jesus, and Plato; he can compare Christianity to mystery cults, and liken Jesus to Hermes. But Justin's primary matrix remains the Greek Scriptures and the Synoptic Gospels. Or else, Cassius Dio's account of Septimius Severus' deification of Pertinax makes for excellent reading, but one cannot help but think that exaltation stories from Genesis, Daniel, *1 Enoch*, and Qumran are far more likely to resonate with narrations about Jesus' exaltation by Paul, Luke, and John.[53]

---

[51] Paul was clearly a Greek speaker and thinker, aware of Greco-Roman literature (1 Cor 15.33; Acts 17.28–29; Titus 1.12), shaped by Greek cosmologies and anthropologies (1 Cor 15.35–50), and who echoed Stoic ethics (Phil 4.11). John's Logos is impossible without Middle Platonic ideas of intermediaries (John 1.1). 2 Peter refers to the destiny of being cast into Tartarus, the Greek underworld (2 Pet 2.4). Key terms used by the early church, like "gospel," "lord," and "savior," can only be understood in light of Greco-Roman usage.

[52] Johnson, *Among the Gentiles*, 22.

[53] In Peppard's latest offering, I detect sympathy with this very point, the priority of Jewish scriptural texts for Christology, but not to the exclusion of Greco-Roman sources and artifacts, not least the imperial cult. See Michael Peppard, "Son of God in Gentile Contexts," in *Son of God: Divine Sonship in Jewish and Christian Antiquity*, ed. Garrick V. Allen, Kai Akagi, Paul Sloan, and Madhavi Nevader (University Park, Penn.: Eisenbrauns, 2019), 154–57.

Now, to be fair, Michael Peppard has a point, that scholars routinely and wrongly ignore imperial inscriptions that could be found in every major town in the first century and yet gush over a Jewish text like *3 Enoch* which postdates the New Testament by some centuries when it comes to Christology.[54] Hopefully this study has shown that such a point is well made and taken seriously. However, to switch things around, Peppard himself diminishes, without fully rejecting, the concrete allusions to Ps 2.7 and Isa 42.1 in the Marcan baptismal story (Mark 1.9-11). Peppard prefers instead to favor how a Roman reader would understand the baptismal imagery as an imperial adoption, the Spirit as *genius* and *numen*, and the dove as an omen indicative of a transmission of power.[55] On the whole, his conclusion is quite sound: "In the end, Mark's view of divine sonship, which had been refracted throughout the gospel in the light of the Roman emperor, now shines through unmediated. It is Jesus who is the Roman world's 'son of God'—sorrowful as a Roman criminal, and powerful as a Roman emperor."[56] The problem is not what Peppard affirms, but what he correlates (potential resonances with literary purpose)[57] and prioritizes (Roman cultural matrix over scriptural intertextuality) for grasping Mark's Christology.[58] I have my reservations on this construction.

First, that Roman readers/auditors of Mark's Gospel *might* have understood the baptism story in light of imperial adoptive sonship is plausibly established by Peppard. But he mistakenly attempts to align a possible resonance among a cluster of readers with Mark's intentionality, and that is where he runs amiss. I am unpersuaded as to the merit of making resonances by a hypothetical reader the controlling premise for grasping Mark's authorial intent, elevating such a hypothetical resonance over Mark's intertextual deployment of the Greek Scriptures, putting potential resonances above an authorial design to shape how a "Marcan community" regarded Jesus, neglecting Mark's wider christological claims, or overlooking Matthean and Lucan redaction of Mark's baptismal episode. I cannot help but think that projected reader-response resonances, while useful to a point, do not carry the same weight as readings of a text that account for the author's enacted intentionality, a text's internal coherences, explicit intertextuality, direct appeals to nonliterary media and cultural

---

[54] Peppard, "Son of God in Gentile Contexts," 136-37.
[55] Michael Peppard, *The Son of God in the Roman World: Divine Sonship in Its Social and Political Context* (Oxford: Oxford University Press, 2012), 86-131 (esp. 95-96).
[56] Peppard, *Son of God*, 131.
[57] Hurtado, "New *religionsgeschichtliche Schule*," 28.
[58] Cf. Michael F. Bird, *Jesus the Eternal Son: Answering Adoptionist Christology* (Grand Rapids: Eerdmans, 2017), 71-76; and Matthew Bates, *The Birth of the Trinity* (Oxford: Oxford University Press, 2015), 78n72.

scripts, the effect intended upon implied readers, and the interpretations of real readers in the history of reception. Many imagined readings are possible and illuminating—reading Paul's letter to the Romans in Pompeii comes to mind[59]—but not all resonances are equal, and possible resonances should not trump concrete textual phenomenon.

Second, Peppard's preferencing of particular literary parallels and a possible way of reading Mark requires a migration away from the Jewish encyclopedia as a matrix for understanding Mark and entails replacing it with a Roman encyclopedia as Mark's principal context. Peppard's insights as to how Mark could resonate with Roman readers need not be denied; in fact, its utility is enhanced if Mark is assigned a Roman provenance, and if one intuits a counter-imperial edge to the Marcan narrative. I am happy to integrate Peppard's proposals about connotations of Roman adoptive imagery into a comprehensive account of Marcan Christology, but without sidelining the scriptural intertexts about divine sonship, without discounting Mark's *kyrios* Christology, and without glossing over the implied and real readers of the text. I infer from Mark 1.1–15 that Mark's Gospel is a Jewish messianic biography that tells the story of Jesus for Greco-Roman readers. It is a Greek composition immersed in Jewish sacred literature and cultural location with a view to heralding a crucified Messiah for audiences composed of Jews, Greeks, and Romans. It could potentially resonate a certain way with audiences who witnessed Titus' triumph along the Via Sacra, but it explicitly sets forth its own story in light of the scenes and scripts drawn principally from the Psalms and Isaiah. Roman emperors and their imprint upon the landscape loom behind the story, but the God of Israel, his scriptural promises, the realities of first-century Judea, and Jesus of Nazareth dominate the characters and scenery within it. The protagonists, plot, and places are not ciphers for extra discerning readers to evoke Roman media and tropes outside the story. Rather—let the reader understand—Mark's Gospel really is a story about Israel's God and Jesus the crucified Messiah written up in light of the Jewish Scriptures and Jewish apocalyptic imagery.

Is this to make Hellenistic Judaism a buffer state between Christianity and paganism, like the Kingdom of Siam between English Burma and French Indochina in the early twentieth century? Not in the slightest! Christianity expresses the cosmological, theological, and cultic realities of the Greco-Roman world, but with Judaism of the Hellenistic period as the primary lens and conduit for it. On the one hand, Hellenistic Judaism inoculated early

---

[59] Peter Oakes, *Reading Romans in Pompeii: Paul's Letter at Ground Level* (Minneapolis: Fortress, 2013).

Christianity from certain aspects of Greco-Roman religious culture (e.g., polytheism, iconic worship, deification, etc.). On the other hand, Hellenistic Judaism itself expresses ancient and widespread convictions about gods and cultus and transmits these convictions to early Christian as its own progeny (e.g., demiurgy, ideas of "true deity," views of the afterlife, etc.). Furthermore, one need not deny that from time to time certain things could be spliced directly into Christianity from Stoic ethics, to Middle Platonic cosmology, to household codes, and more. Or else, you can sometimes end up with strange paradoxical features where, for instance, Christians imitate the rhetoric of the ruler cultus (e.g., Jesus is Lord and Savior) even as they emulate Jewish critiques of ruler worship (e.g., emperor worship is a farce). Thus, early Christianity is a child of its Jewish parental religion and bears an overwhelming family resemblance in its constitution. The two qualifications are, first, even these Jewish parents are not unrelated to the wider family of ancient religion; and second, as Christianity entered its adolescence and maturity, it came to resist, negotiate, absorb, and then transform the religion of antiquity in ways that could either intensify its Jewish pedigree (e.g., iconoclasm) or else abandon its Jewish heritage (the *verus Israel* tradition).

The Hellenism/Judaism dichotomy is unhelpful, but so is flattening out the distinctive features of ancient Judaism with its common theology, set of practices, literary traditions, and group identity that were often expressed in opposition to Hellenism. The interface of Hellenism and Judaism was diverse in its historical and local expressions, but heightened interactions often led to the erection and policing of group boundaries between Jews and Greeks. In this context, early Christology emerged from a Judaism within Hellenism, evidenced by the complex blend of assimilation and resistance to Hellenistic forms that has been mapped out in this study. Hellenism, then, cannot be reduced to a purely negative stimulus for early Christology, just as much as Hellenism cannot be made the primary backdrop with Jewish religious culture swept to one side.[60]

Let me add as well that this is not a "low" vs. "high" Christology debate in terms of the nature and intensity of Jesus' divinity.[61] Some scholars write as if

[60] Helpful on this topic of Hellenism and Judaism is Joseph D. Fantin, *The Lord of the Entire World: Lord Jesus, a Challenge to Lord Caesar?* (NTM 31; Sheffield: Sheffield Phoenix, 2011), 54–76.

[61] To be honest, there is no real rhyme or reason as to why one Christology is "high" and another is "low." The various Christologies of the early church really are just different ways of conceiving Jesus as divine, a divine agent, human, and immortal. If "divinity" is the measure for "high" Christology, then surely docetism and modalism are infinitely higher than Pauline, Synoptic, or Johannine Christologies. Or else, if the Gospel of John is the

positing a Jewish context amounts to a high Christology and positing a Greco-Roman context amounts to a low Christology.⁶² One could construct a Christology in very Jewish categories, using Prov 8.22–23 about Wisdom as a divine creature, appeal to the divine Name inhabiting Jesus as it did for the angel of the Lord in Exod 23.20–21, focus on the prophetic life of Jesus, and see his promotion to divine sonship at his resurrection. Such views were expressed in the church of the first two centuries and yield a Jesus who is divine but less divine than God the Father. Or else, one could construct a Christology in Greco-Roman coordinates, focusing on a Jesus who was so divine that he was scarcely human, use religious categories like "unbegotten" or "true God" to describe Jesus as divine, resource the rhetoric of ruler cults for Jesus' equality, sonship, and lordship, and even philosophize over words like *ousia* or *homoousios* to make strong affirmations of divinity. Such views were also expressed in the early church to make Jesus divine in the strongest senses imaginable, even to the point of pressing into modalism.⁶³

Let me stress too that finding the primacy in Jewish literature and religion for Christology is not an apologetic strategy despite the ad nauseam degree to which this charge has been elevated since J. Z. Smith's famous monograph. Tying early Christology to its Jewish roots and only secondarily to its wider Greco-Roman environs is not a tactic from apologetics.com but comes from a tracing of the intertextual references from Matthew to Irenaeus and then examining the internal dynamics of christological discourse.⁶⁴ James Dunn

---

watermark for high Christology, then it is a low mark compared to the Christologies of the *Gospel of Thomas*, Valentinians, or Sabellians, who identify Jesus with the heavenly or fatherly standard of divinity. Also, the assumption that Christology evolved from "low" to "high" is likewise fallacious, for whatever metrics one applies, the Christologies of the second century do not amount to incremental growth in divine-ness, but zig and zag like stock in a tumultuous period of trading.

⁶² Cf. similarly on this point, N. T. Wright's reflections on scholarly attitudes towards Jewish and pagan sources for Christology, "Son of God and Christian Origins," in *Son of God: Divine Sonship in Jewish and Christian Antiquity*, ed. Garrick V. Allen, Kai Akagi, Paul Sloan, and Madhavi Nevader (University Park, Penn.: Eisenbrauns, 2019), 118–24. Wright thinks Hengel's preference for Jewish sources and dismissal of pagan ones might derive in part from a "Two-Kingdoms" theology (124).

⁶³ Cf. Wesley Hill, *Paul and the Trinity: Persons, Relations, and the Pauline Letters* (Grand Rapids: Eerdmans, 2015), 23–25; and April D. DeConick, "How We Talk about Christology Matters," in *Israel's God and Rebecca's Children: Christology and Community in Early Judaism and Christianity*, ed. David B. Capes, April D. DeConick, Helen K. Bond, and Troy A. Miller (Waco, Tex.: Baylor University Press, 2007), 1–2.

⁶⁴ Funnily enough, William Horbury (*Jewish Messianism and the Cult of Christ* [London: SCM Press, 1998], 117) points out that Friedrich Engels, no orthodox Christian,

and Maurice Casey rooted early Christology primarily in Jewish types and tropes related to Adam and Wisdom traditions, with Jesus only properly or fully divine in the Gospel of John, proof that a primary Jewish backdrop is no sure path to early high Christology.

To be clear, Jewish and Greco-Roman literature, religion, and traditions are relevant for how the early churches constructed their divine Christologies. Preferencing Jewish or Greco-Roman categories does not pre-empt the question of *if* or *whether* Jesus was divine, as if the answer is only positive or negative. Rather, the questions are, *in what sense* is Jesus divine and *how closely* is his divinity related to the divinity of God the Father? Further, what are the categories, cosmologies, cults, myths, metaphors, texts, types, rhetoric, rituals, pieties, practices, names, and narratives that the early church used to proclaim and praise Jesus as a divine being? My point is, once we have examined the early christological discourses in all their diversities, once when we have laid out the texts, and described early Christian devotional practices, then it appears to me that Jewish texts and traditions *normally* have the primacy for the construction of a divine Christology, even if that does not exclude a significant place for Greco-Roman influences. In other words: precise Septuagintal intertextuality > broad Greco-Roman parallels.[65] As Horbury put it: "In the end, whatever use may be made of arguments about origins in defending or attacking Christianity, the continuities between early Christian and Jewish literature remain so prominent as to demand inquiry into the possible Jewish origins of Christian customs and tenets."[66]

In sum, Hellenistic Judaism is, in one sense, an inoculation against Greco-Roman religion insofar that early Christianity participates in Jewish distinctiveness and its allergy to certain aspects of Greco-Roman religious cultures. But on the other hand, Hellenistic Judaism is also a conduit by which Greco-Roman religion is transmitted into Christianity as the apostolic and post-apostolic generations were immersed in the religious atmosphere of antiquity. Hence my overall thesis: Jesus is a Jewish deity of the Greco-Roman world. Jesus sits among the gods of antiquity, and he can sometimes be mistaken for a Hermes or a Serapis; but his likeness to more than any

---

identified Philo as the real father of Christianity and underlined the influence of the book of Enoch on early Christianity.

[65] For example, Litwa (*Iesus Deus*, 192–94, 210) marginalizes the significance of the echo of Ps 110.1 and the clear allusion to Ps 45.23 in Phil 2.6–11 in favor of Greco-Roman notions of theonymy as the main explanatory tool.

[66] Horbury, *Jewish Messianism*, 117; similarly Ruben Bühner, *Messianic High Christology: New Testament Variants of Second Temple Judaism* (Waco, Tex.: Baylor University Press, 2021), 185.

other is to the God of Abraham, Isaac, and Jacob, at least as he was believed upon and worshipped by Christians in the Roman east in the first two centuries. Jesus is a Jewish Mediterranean deity, or Jesus is identifiable with the Jewish God as expressed in the forms and tropes of eastern Mediterranean religion. Jewish literature and religion are the primary coordinates for mapping the origins of Christology, but, like many maps, the borders between adjacent regions are ambiguous and contested.[67]

Anyone who knows me knows that I am naturally reluctant to be needlessly provocative. Yet one must inquire about implicit or unstated agendas by scholars and collaborations who attempt to cast Christianity as a Greco-Roman religion to the neglect of its Jewish roots. My suspicion is that the de-Judaizing of Christian origins can sometimes betray the inclinations of scholars who wish to pursue certain political and cultural agendas about the meaning of Christianity and its place in the world. From the colonialist and secular "comparative religion," to the embarrassments of the "Gnostic Redeemer Myth," the concerted effort to displace Christianity from its Jewish environs is not a value-neutral act. In other words, sometimes the debates about Jewish and Greco-Roman religious parallels in a Christian text are not actually about finding the source or most salient parallel to a Christian text; rather, it might actually be about attitudes to piety, politics, and pluralism! Hurtado is even more forthright: "This program of portraying early Christianity as decisively shaped by non-Jewish forces involved an over-simplification of ancient Jewish tradition, an overt anti-Jewish attitude [by early twentieth-century German scholars], and a cultural and theological agenda shaping the historical analysis."[68]

The Quest(ion) of Christ's Uniqueness

Many ancient Christians believed that the one true living God had revealed himself definitively and specially in Christ Jesus, who, in some accounts, was far more than a prophet or a heavenly figure, but was more like God's final envoy (Heb 1.1–4).[69] Christ was, on such a scheme, the "one intermediary

---

[67] In this sense, I would identify myself as someone from the *schule* of Martin Hengel, who has been informed and corrected by the works of Luke Timothy Johnson.

[68] Hurtado, "New *religionsgeschichtliche Schule*," 31; idem, *One God, One Lord*, 7–9, 140–41; and Andrew Chester, "High Christology: Whence, When and Why?" *EC* 2 (2011): 22–50.

[69] Cf. Marinus de Jonge, *Christology in Context: The Earliest Christian Responses to Jesus* (Philadelphia: Westminster, 1988), 212; and idem, *God's Final Envoy: Early Christology and Jesus' Own View of His Mission* (Grand Rapids: Eerdmans, 1998), 10: "Characteristic of early Christian views about Jesus is the conviction that Jesus was not just a prophet, but the last

between God and humanity" (1 Tim 2.5 [NET]), and not any intermediary power, but an unusually powerful one at the right hand of God "with angels and authorities and powers subject to him" (1 Pet 3.22 [NET]). What are we to make of such claims considering the preceding study, where ample similarities and parallels between Christ and intermediary figures have been demonstrated? Does this make Jesus unique or set apart in Christian imagination? The answer is more than a little complicated.

First, uniqueness is an ambiguous term. Unique in relation to what? Unique to what extent? Does unique mean absolutely dissimilar or relatively dissimilar?

If uniqueness requires absolute dissimilarity, then the many Christs of early Christianity are never going to be unique in comparison to any religion with an intermediary figure. I mean, given the ubiquity of religion in human societies, given the roughly relatable ways humans have for talking about deities and spirits, it would be entirely unsurprising that there would be similarities between Christ and Mayan deities or between Christ and Chinese spirits. All the more so when it comes to Judaism, the religion of Jesus and the apostles, and Greco-Roman religions, since Hellenistic culture was the backdrop for the expansion of early Christianity. Whatever place in world religions one looks at, similarities between Christ and intermediary figures would be inevitable on some metrics. Absolute uniqueness, then, is a dead end and an apologetic sleight of hand.

But if uniqueness can be relative, then we are on firmer ground. The diverse portraits of Christ should not be haphazardly lumped into the category of "ideal hero figures." If attempting to prove the pure and unadulterated uniqueness of Christ is futile as it is inaccurate, equally tendentious is trying to flatten out the distinctives of early Christologies in favor of some trans-cultural or inter-religious epiphenomenon. It can lead to, "Jesus is just X with a minor wardrobe change," a view no less dogmatic and ideologically driven than that of the most ardent Christian apologist! Yes, Christ is comparable with the Stoic Logos, the archangel Michael, the deified Augustus, and other intermediaries. However, as we have seen, there are always dissimilarities that accompany genuine parallels. Philo, John, and Justin exhibit genuine creativity in how they

and *final* envoy of the God of Israel, and that he was a righteous person and a martyr whose death and vindication brought a decisive and *definitive* turn in the history of humanity. To put it differently: with him the time of the end had already begun. Jesus was an eschatological figure who had inaugurated the new era in God's dealings with Israel and the world. This notion is not inherent in the notion of the resurrection of a martyr, neither is it connected with any of the Jewish models of interpretation used to explain Jesus' suffering and death. Our conclusion has to be that already before Jesus' death his followers must have believed that he was the herald and inaugurator of God's reign" (italics original).

marry the Logos tradition to the Jewish Scriptures. In addition, Jewish ruler cults venerated their kings, but not to the extent that Antiochus I or Augustus were acclaimed by their subjects. Or else, concepts of apotheosis and deification are easily aligned with Jesus' resurrection and ascension. But Christian accounts of incarnation and exaltation had to negotiate monotheism, which does not map onto Greco-Roman sensitivities. Those dissimilarities are important because they exhibit variations driven by local, historical, and experiential factors that are often non-repeatable, sometimes culture-specific, and occasionally without true analogy. Thus, while claims to uniqueness should be met with cold derision, we should acknowledge that Christian accounts of its central figure had their own specificities that underpinned distinctive claims.

Second, absolute uniqueness is a hermeneutical and missiological impossibility. The only Christian theologian who postulated a truly unique Christ as far as I can tell was Marcion, for whom Christ was the salvific agent of an alien God. Marcion's Jesus does not arrive as prophesied and promised in the Jewish Scriptures; rather, he is inimitable and an original. Uniqueness is obviously easy to establish if there is no typology or prophecy paving the way for a divine agent and the narrower one's job description the narrower the range of parallels that can be drawn. In direct contrast, Justin had a divine Christology, subordinationist in parts, but otherwise Jesus was explicitly put into ontological parity with God the Father. Yet even Justin knows that Jesus resembles Herakles and Mercury, even if he fumbles over the reasons why. For the most part, apostolic and post-apostolic authors chose to describe Jesus in light of traditions that made Jesus' identity, work, and relationship to the Father comprehensible. In effect, Jesus (the unfamiliar one) was proclaimed and explained in light of what was familiar (Logos, Adam, angels, exalted patriarchs, Wisdom, and messiah). A totally unique Jesus would have been a missiological impossibility to proclaim for the early church. The many parallels between Christ and the divine intermediaries of antiquity are not proof of a Christianity contaminated by paganism, but point to the enduring capacity of Christian proclamation to speak within as much as against the religious cultures of antiquity.

In my estimation, animated insistence of Christian uniqueness among ancient religions by the apologist is hardly different from the aggravated denials by the comparative religion academic who insists that Christianity is most certainly not unique. Both are dogmatism and tribalism because something *else*, some other *claim* is at stake. Christianity, in most of its forms, never claimed to be unprecedent and original, but a revelation or evolution within a Jewish religion negotiating its way in the Greco-Roman world. Yet Christians, whether by eccentricity or eclecticism, stood out; we know this because pagan authors from Pliny to Porphyry share with us their disgust and derision at this new superstitious sect with its atheism and misanthropy that had blown in from the east. Furthermore, I cannot imagine how Christianity, without some *novum*, would ever have had the Christian revolution that absorbed and transformed the western and eastern Roman empire in the way that it did.

In sum, the early Christian views of Christ are, in the qualified senses I have laid out, "unique," by which I mean neither unprecedented nor incomparable, but distinctive and characteristic. There were specific generative experiences, peculiarities of persons, special socio-religious hybridities, and particularities of intertextuality that fostered the narration of a figure, partly derivative of intermediary figures in Judaism and Hellenism, but with points of variation that made Christ exceptional among the gods of antiquity. Rather than pursue Christ's absolute uniqueness among intermediary figures, a dead end, we do better to map out how early christological discourses make Christ intelligible to ancient peoples in light of their resident religious traditions. Such a study as I have undertaken has intended to show that Christ was portrayed in a creative mix of reworking cultural ideas about God and divine intermediaries while imaginatively adapting them in fresh, startingly, and often innovative ways. By the time one reaches proto-orthodox Christianity, the core conviction that the divine had come near was not remotely unusual, but it was distinctive in its specificities: The one true God sends his preexistent Son, known by the titles Messiah, Lord, and God, to be crucified, then raises him up by his Spirit, and exalts him to his right hand, to one day conquer the nations (Rom 1.3–4; 4.25; 8.3, 11, 34; 9.1–5; 10.13; 15.12). The crucified Galilean prophet Jesus was "Immanuel, God with us" (Matt 1.23); the Middle Platonic Logos was "made flesh" in Jesus the son of Joseph from Nazareth (John 1.14, 45); and Jesus was begotten in his humanity and unbegotten in his divinity (Ignatius, *Eph.* 7.2). These are views which many found believable—even more than that, as fundamental to their existence.

Bibliography

Primary Sources

(1) Holy Scripture

Elliger, K., and W. Rudolph, eds. *Biblia Hebraica Stuttgartensia*. Stuttgart: Württembergische Bibelanstalt Stuttgart, 1968–1976.

Rahlfs, Alfred, and Robert Hanhart, eds. *Septuaginta*. Stuttgart: Deutsche Bibelgesellschaft, 2006.

Penner, Ken M., ed. *The Lexham English Septuagint*. Bellingham, Wash.: Lexham, 2019.

Pietersma, Albert, and Benjamin G. Wright, eds. *A New English Translation of the Septuagint*. Oxford: Oxford University Press, 2007.

Nestle, Eberhard, Erwin Nestle, Kurt Aland, and Barbara Aland, eds. *Novum Testamentum Graece*. 28th ed. Stuttgart: Deutsche Bibelgesellschaft, 2012.

Holmes, Michael W., ed. *The Greek New Testament: SBL Edition*. Atlanta: SBL, 2010.

(2) Jewish Writings

Charlesworth, James H., ed. *The Old Testament Pseudepigrapha*. 2 vols. ABRL. New York: Doubleday, 1983–1985.

Colson, F. H., G. H. Whitaker, J. W. Earp, and R. Marcus, trans. *Philo*. 12 vols. LCL. Cambridge, Mass.: Harvard University Press, 1929–1953.

Nickelsburg, George W. E., and James C. VanderKam, trans. *1 Enoch*. 2 vols. Hermeneia. Minneapolis: Fortress, 2012.

Thackeray, H. St. J., R. Marcus, A. Wikgren, and L. H. Feldman, trans. *Josephus*. 9 vols. LCL. Cambridge, Mass.: Harvard University Press, 1926–1965.

Wise, Michael, Martin Abegg, and Edward Cook, trans. *The Dead Sea Scrolls: A New Translation*. San Francisco: HarperSanFrancisco, 1996.

(3) Christian Writings

Behr, John, trans. *On the Apostolic Preaching: St Irenaeus of Lyon*. Crestwood, N.Y.: St. Vladimir's Seminary Press, 1997.

Casey, R. P., ed. and trans. *The Excerpta ex Theodoto of Clement of Alexandria*. London: Christophers, 1934.

Ehrman, Bart D., and Zlatko Pleše. *The Apocryphal Gospels: Texts and Translations*. Oxford: Oxford University Press, 2011.

Elliott, J. K. *The Apocryphal New Testament*. Oxford: Oxford University Press, 1993.

Evans, Ernest, ed. and trans. *De carne Christi liber: Tertullian's Treatise on the Incarnation*. London: SPCK, 1956.

Falls, Thomas B., trans. *Dialogue with Trypho*. Revised by Thomas P. Halton. Edited by Michael Sussler. Washington, D.C.: Catholic University of America Press, 2003.

Grant, Robert M. *Theophilus of Antioch: Ad Autolycum*. OECT. Oxford: Clarendon, 1970.

Gregory, Andrew, ed. *The Gospel according to the Hebrews and the Gospel of the Ebionites*. OECGT. Oxford: Oxford University Press, 2017.

Harvey, W. Wigan, ed. *Sancti Irenaei episcopi Lugdunensis Libros quinque adversus haereses*. 2 vols. Cambridge: Cambridge University Press, 1857.

Holmes, Michael W., ed. and trans. *The Apostolic Fathers: Greek Texts and English Translations*. 3rd ed. Grand Rapids: Baker, 2007. All citations of the *Shepherd of Hermas* refer to this volume.

Layton, Bentley, trans. *The Gnostic Scriptures: A New Translation with Annotations and Introductions*. New Haven, Conn.: Yale University Press, 1995.

Litwa, M. David, trans. *Refutation of All Heresies*. Atlanta: SBL, 2016.

Marcovich, Miroslav, ed. *Hippolytus Refutatio Omnium Haeresium*. PTS 25. Berlin: de Gruyter, 1986.

Minns, Denis, and Paul Parvis, ed. and trans. *Justin, Philosopher and Martyr: Apologies*. OECT. Oxford: Oxford University Press, 2009.

Opitz, H.-G., ed. *Athanasius' Werke*, vol. 3, bk. 1, *Urkunden zur Geschichte des arianischen Streites, 318–328*. Berlin: de Gruyter, 1934.

Quispel, Gilles, ed. and trans. *Lettre à Flora*. Paris: Cerf, 1966.

Reitzenstein, R. "Eine frühchristliche Schrift von der dreierlei Früchten des christlichen Lebens." *ZNW* 15 (1914): 60–88.

Robinson, James M., ed. *The Nag Hammadi Library*. 3rd ed. San Francisco: HarperSanFrancisco, 1988.

Schmidt, Carl, ed. *Pistis Sophia*. Translated by Violet Macdermot. Leiden: Brill, 1978.

Schneemelcher, Wilhelm, ed. *New Testament Apocrypha*. Translated by R. McL. Wilson. 2 vols. Rev. ed. Cambridge: James Clark and Co., 1992.

Schoedel, William R., ed. and trans. *Athenagoras: Legatio and De Resurrectione*. OECT. Oxford: Clarendon, 1972.

Stewart, Alistair C., trans. *On Pascha: With the Fragments of Melito and Other Material Related to the Quartodecimans*. 2nd ed. Crestwood, N.Y.: St. Vladimir's Seminary Press, 2016.
Watson, Francis. *An Apostolic Gospel: The "Epistula Apostolorum" in Literary Context*. SNTS 179. Cambridge: Cambridge University Press, 2021.

(4) Greco-Roman Writings

Babbit, F. C., trans. *Plutarch's Moralia V*. LCL. Cambridge, Mass.: Harvard University Press, 1936.
Bury, R. G., trans. *Plato: Timaeus, Critias, Cleitophon, Menexenus, Epistles*. LCL. Cambridge, Mass.: Harvard University Press, 1929.
Chinnock, Edward J., trans. *Arrian's Anabasis of Alexander*. New York: G. Bell & Sons, 1893.
Thom, Johan C. *Cleanthes' Hymn to Zeus: Text, Translation, and Commentary*. Tübingen: Mohr Siebeck, 2005.
Goldberg, Sander M., and Gesine Manuwald, trans. *Fragmentary Republican Latin*. Vol. 1: *Ennius, Testimonia, Epic Fragments*. Cambridge, Mass.: Harvard University Press, 2018.

Secondary Literature

Abegg, Martin G. "Who Ascended to Heaven? 4Q491, 4Q427 and the Teacher of Righteousness." Pages 61–73 in *Eschatology, Messianism and the Dead Sea Scrolls*. Edited by C. A. Evans and P. W. Flint. Grand Rapids: Eerdmans, 1997.
Akerman, Susan. *Under Every Green Tree: Popular Religion in Sixth-Century Judah*. Winona Lake, Ind.: Eisenbrauns, 2001.
Albani, Matthias. "The 'One Like a Son of Man' (Dan 7:13) and the Royal Ideology." Pages 47–53 in *Enoch and Qumran Origins: New Light on a Forgotten Connection*. Edited by Gabriele Boccaccini. Grand Rapids: Eerdmans, 2005.
Alexander, Philip S. "Hellenism and Hellenization as Problematic Historiographical Categories." Pages 63–80 in *Paul beyond the Judaism/Hellenism Divide*. Edited by Troels Engberg-Pedersen. Louisville, Ky.: Westminster John Knox, 2001.
Allen, Garrick V. "Son of God in the Book of Revelation and Apocalyptic Literature." Pages 53–71 in *Son of God: Divine Sonship in Jewish and Christian Antiquity*. Edited by Garrick V. Allen, Kai Akagi, Paul Sloan, and Madhavi Nevader. University Park, Penn.: Eisenbrauns, 2019.
Allison, Dale C. *Constructing Jesus: Memory, Imagination, and History*. Grand Rapids: Baker, 2010.
Anderson, James S. *Monotheism and Yahweh's Appropriation of Baal*. London: T&T Clark, 2015.
Anderson, Paul. *The Riddles of the Fourth Gospel*. Minneapolis: Fortress, 2011.
Argyle, A. W. "Philo and the Fourth Gospel." *ExpT* 63 (1951–1952): 385–86.

Asale, Bruk Ayele. *1 Enoch as Christian Scripture: A Study in the Reception and Appropriation of 1 Enoch in Jude and the Ethiopian Orthodox Tewahǝdo Canon*. Eugene, Ore.: Wipf & Stock, 2020.
Assman, Jan. *Exodus: Die Revolution der Alten Welt*. Munich: C. H. Beck, 2015.
———. "Monotheism and Polytheism." Pages 17–31 in *Religions of the Ancient World: A Guide*. Edited by Sarah Illes Johnston. Cambridge, Mass.: Belknap, 2004.
Athanassiadi, Polymnia, and Michael Frede, eds. *Pagan Monotheism in Late Antiquity*. Oxford: Clarendon, 2008.
Atkins, Christopher S. "Rethinking John 1:1: The Word Was Godward." *NovT* 63 (2021): 44–62.
Attridge, Harold W. *Essays on John and Hebrews*. Grand Rapids: Baker, 2010.
———. *History, Theology and Narrative Rhetoric in the Fourth Gospel*. Milwaukee, Wis.: Marquette University Press, 2019.
———. "Stoic and Platonic Reflections on Naming in Early Christian Circles: Or, What's in a Name?" Pages 277–95 in *From Stoicism to Platonism: The Development of Philosophy, 100 BCE–100 CE*. Edited by Troels Engberg-Pedersen. Cambridge: Cambridge University Press, 2017.
Aune, David E. *Cultic Setting of Realized Eschatology in Early Christianity*. Leiden: Brill, 1972.
———. "The Influence of Roman Imperial Court Ceremonial on the Apocalypse of John." *BR* 28 (1983): 5–26.
———. *Revelation*. 3 vols. WBC. Dallas: Word, 1997.
Ayres, Lewis. *Nicaea and Its Legacy: An Approach to Fourth-Century Trinitarian Theology*. Oxford: Oxford University Press, 2004.
———. "Scripture in Trinitarian Controversies." Pages 439–54 in *The Oxford Handbook of Early Christian Biblical Interpretation*. Edited by Paul M. Blowers and Peter W. Martens. Oxford: Oxford University Press, 2019.
Badian, E. "Alexander the Great between Two Thrones and Heaven: Variations on an Old Theme." Pages 11–26 in *Subject and Ruler: The Cult of the Ruling Power in Classical Antiquity*. Ann Arbor: University of Michigan Press, 1996.
Barbel, Joseph. *Christos Angelos: Die Anschauung von Christus als Bote und Engel in der gelehrten und volkstümlichen Literatur des christlichen Altertums: Zugleich ein Beitrag zur Geschichte des Ursprungs und der Fortdauer des Arianismus*. Bonn: Hanstein, 1964.
Barclay, John M. G. *Jews in the Ancient Mediterranean Diaspora: From Alexander to Trajan (323 BCE—117 CE)*. Edinburgh: T&T Clark, 1996.
———. *Paul: A Very Brief History*. London: SPCK, 2018.
Barnard, L. W. *Justin Martyr: His Life and Thought*. Cambridge: Cambridge University Press, 1967.
Barrett, Anthony. *Caligula: The Corruption of Power*. London: Routledge, 2000.
Barrett, C. K. *The Gospel according to St. John*. 2nd ed. London: SPCK, 1978.
Bates, Matthew. *The Birth of the Trinity*. Oxford: Oxford University Press, 2015.

Bauckham, Richard. *Jesus and the God of Israel*. Milton Keynes, U.K.: Paternoster, 2008.

———. "Jesus, Worship of." *ABD* 3:812–19. Edited by David Noel Freedman. New York: Doubleday, 1992.

———. *Jude, 2 Peter*. WBC. Waco, Tex.: Word, 1983.

———. "Monotheism and Christology in the Gospel of John." Pages 148–66 in *Contours of Christology in the New Testament*. Edited by Richard N. Longenecker. Grand Rapids: Eerdmans, 2005.

———. "The 'Most High' God and the Nature of Early Jewish Monotheism." Pages 39–53 in *Israel's God and Rebecca's Children: Christology and Community in Early Judaism and Christianity*. Edited by David B. Capes, April D. DeConick, Helen K. Bond, and Troy A. Miller. Waco, Tex.: Baylor University Press, 2007.

———. "The Worship of Jesus." Pages 118–49 in *The Climax of Prophecy: Studies on the Book of Revelation*. Edinburgh: T&T Clark, 1993.

———. "The Worship of Jesus in Apocalyptic Christianity." *NTS* 27 (1981): 322–41.

Bauer, David R. *The Gospel of the Son of God: An Introduction to Matthew*. Downers Grove, Ill.: InterVarsity, 2019.

Beale, Greg K. *The Book of Revelation*. NIGTC. Grand Rapids: Eerdmans, 1999.

Beard, Mary. *The Roman Triumph*. Cambridge, Mass.: Belknap, 2007.

Beard, Mary, John North, and Simon Price. *Religions of Rome*. 2 vols. Cambridge: Cambridge University Press, 1998.

Beetham, Christopher A. *Echoes of Scripture in the Letters of Paul to the Colossians*. BIS 96. Leiden: Brill, 2008.

Berger, Klaus. *Theologiegeschichte des Urchristentums*. Tübingen: Francke Verlag, 1994.

Bernett, Monika. *Der Kaiserkult in Judäa unter den Herodiern und Römern: Untersuchungen zur politischen und religiösen Geschichte Judäas von 30 v. bis 66 n. Chr.* WUNT 203. Tübingen: Mohr Siebeck, 2007.

———. "Der Kaiserkult in Judäa unter herodischer und römischer Herrschaft: Zu Herausbildung und Herausforderung neuer Konzepte jüdischer Herrschaftslegitimation." Pages 205–51 in *Jewish Identity in the Greco-Roman World*. Edited by Jörg Frey, Daniel R. Schwartz, and Stephanie Gripentrog. AJEC 71. Leiden: Brill, 2007.

Bird, Michael F. *An Anomalous Jew: Paul among Jews, Greeks, and Romans*. Grand Rapids: Eerdmans, 2016.

———. *Are You the One Who Is to Come? The Historical Jesus and the Messianic Question*. Grand Rapids: Baker, 2009.

———. *Colossians and Philemon*. NCCS. Eugene, Ore.: Cascade, 2009.

———. *Crossing over Sea and Land: Jewish Missionary Activity in the Second Temple Period*. Peabody, Mass.: Hendrickson, 2010.

———. "Of Gods, Angels, and Men." Pages 22–44 in *How God Became Jesus: The Real Origins of Belief in Jesus' Divine Nature*. Edited by Michael F. Bird. Grand Rapids: Zondervan, 2014.

———. *Jesus the Eternal Son: Answering Adoptionist Christology*. Grand Rapids: Eerdmans, 2017.

———. *Jesus Is the Christ: The Messianic Testimony of the Gospels*. Downers Grove, Ill.: InterVarsity, 2014.

———. *Romans*. SGBC. Grand Rapids: Zondervan, 2016.

Bird, Michael F., and Kirsten Mackerras. "The Epistle to Diognetus and the Fragment of Quadratus." Pages 309–31 in *The Cambridge Companion to the Apostolic Fathers*. Edited by Michael F. Bird and Scott Harrower. Cambridge: Cambridge University Press, 2021.

Bird, Michael F., and N. T. Wright. *The New Testament in Its World*. London: SPCK, 2019.

Boccaccini, Gabriele, ed. *Enoch and the Messiah Son of Man: Revisiting the Book of Parables*. Grand Rapids: Eerdmans, 2007.

———. "From Jewish Prophet to Jewish God." Pages 335–57 in *Reading the Gospel of John's Christology as Jewish Messianism*. Edited by Benjamin Reynolds and Gabriele Boccaccini. AJEC 106. Leiden: Brill, 2018.

———. "How Jesus Became Uncreated." Pages 185–208 in *Sibyls, Scriptures, and Scrolls*, vol. 1. Edited by Joel Baden, Hindy Nayman, and Eibert Tigchelaar. 2 vols. JSPSup 175. Leiden: Brill, 2016.

Bock, Darrell L., and James H. Charlesworth, eds. *Parables of Enoch: A Paradigm Shift*. London: Bloomsbury, 2013.

Bockmuehl, Markus. "'The Form of God' (Phil. 2:6): Variations on a Theme of Jewish Mysticism." *JTS* 48 (1997): 1–23.

———. "The Idea of Creation out of Nothing: From Qumran to *Genesis Rabbah*." Pages 17–31 in *Visualising Jews through the Ages: Literary and Material Representation of Jewishness and Judaism*. Edited by Hannah Ewence and Helen Spurling. New York: Routledge, 2015.

Bornhäuser, D. Karl. *Jesus Imperator Mundi*. Gütersloh: C. Bertelsmann, 1938.

Bousset, Wilhelm. *Kyrios Christos*. Waco, Tex.: Baylor University Press, 2013. Original translation 1970.

Boyarin, Daniel. "Enoch, Ezra, and the Jewishness of 'High Christology.'" Pages 337–61 in *Fourth Ezra and Second Baruch: Reconstruction after the Fall*. Edited by Matthias Henze and Gabriele Boccaccini. JSJSup 164. Leiden: Brill, 2013.

———. "The Gospel of the *Memra*: Jewish Binitarianism and the Prologue to John." *HTR* 94 (2001): 243–84.

———. "How Enoch Can Teach Us about Jesus." *EC* 2 (2011): 51–76.

———. *The Jewish Gospels: The Story of the Jewish Christ*. New York: New Press, 2013.

Brent, Allen. "Ignatius and Polycarp: The Transformation of New Testament Traditions in the Context of Mystery Cults." Pages 325–49 in *The New Testament and the Apostolic Fathers*, vol. 2. Edited by Andrew Gregory and Christopher Tuckett. 2 vols. Oxford: Oxford University Press, 2006.

Brock, Sebastian. "Syriac Tradition." Pages 1:824–29 in *Jesus in History, Thought, and Culture: An Encyclopedia*. Edited by Leslie Houlden. 2 vols. Santa Barbara, Calif.: ABC Clio, 2003.

Brown, Raymond E. *Introduction to New Testament Christology*. New York: Paulist, 1994.

Bühner, Ruben A. "Die theologischen Implikationen der Präexistenzchristologie in Joh 1,1–3." Pages 185–208 in *Perspektiven zur Präexistenz im Frühjudentum und frühen Christentum*, ed. Jörg Frey, Friederike Kunath, and Jens Schröter. Tübingen: Mohr Siebeck, 2021.

———. *Hohe Messianologie: Übermenschliche Aspekte eschatologischer Heilsgestalten im Frühjudentum*. WUNT 2.523. Tübingen: Mohr Siebeck, 2020.

———. *Messianic High Christology: New Testament Variants of Second Temple Judaism*. Waco, Tex.: Baylor University Press, 2021.

Bultmann, Rudolf. *The Gospel of John: A Commentary*. Philadelphia: Westminster, 1971.

———. *Theology of the New Testament*. 2 vols. Translated by K. Grobel. London: SCM Press, 1952–1955.

Burnett, D. Clint. *Christ's Enthronement at God's Right Hand and Its Greco-Roman Cultural Context*. BZNW 242. Berlin: de Gruyter, 2021.

———. *Studying the New Testament through Inscriptions*. Peabody, Mass.: Hendrickson, 2020.

Capes, David B. *The Divine Christ: Paul, the Lord Jesus, and the Scriptures of Israel*. ASBT. Grand Rapids: Baker, 2018.

Carrell, Peter R. *Jesus and the Angels: Angelology and the Christology of the Apocalypse of John*. SNTSMS 95. Cambridge: Cambridge University Press, 1997.

Carter, Craig A. *Interpreting Scripture with the Great Tradition*. Grand Rapids: Baker, 2018.

Casey, P. M. *From Jewish Prophet to Gentile God*. Louisville, Ky.: Westminster John Knox, 1991.

———. "Monotheism, Worship and Christological Developments in the Pauline Churches." Pages 214–33 in *The Jewish Roots of Christological Monotheism: Papers from the St. Andrews Conference on the Historical Origins of the Worship of Jesus*. Edited by Carey C. Newman, James R. Davila, and Gladys S. Lewis. JSJSup 63. Leiden: Brill, 1999.

Chancey, Mark A. *Greco-Roman Culture and the Galilee of Jesus*. SNTSMS 134. Cambridge: Cambridge University Press, 2005.

Chaniotis, Angela. "The Divinity of Hellenistic Rulers." Pages 431–45 in *A Companion to the Hellenistic World*. Edited by A. Erskine. Oxford: Blackwell, 2003.

Charlesworth, M. P. "Einige Beobachtungen zum Herrscherkult, besonders in Rom." Pages 163–200 in *Römischer Kaiserkult*. Edited by Antonie Wlosok. Darmstadt: Wissenschaftliche Buchgesellschaft, 1978.

Chester, Andrew. "High Christology—Whence, When and Why?" *EC* 2 (2011): 22–50.

———. *Messiah and Exaltation*. WUNT 207. Tübingen: Mohr Siebeck, 2007.

Childs, Brevard S. *Exodus: A Commentary*. OTL. London: SCM Press, 1974.

Clark, David J. "Linguistic and Cultural Influences on Interpretation in Bible Translations." Pages 200–213 in *The Oxford Handbook on the Reception History of the Bible*. Edited by Michael Lieb, Emma Mason, and Jonathan Roberts. Oxford: Oxford University Press, 2011.

Clauss, Manfred. *Kaiser und Gott: Herrscherkult im römischen Reich*. Berlin: K. G. Saur, 1999.

Cohen, Shaye J. D. *From the Maccabees to the Mishnah*. Philadelphia: Westminster, 1987.

Cole, Spencer. *Cicero and the Rise of Deification at Rome*. Cambridge: Cambridge University Press, 2013.

Collins, Adela Yarbro. "'How on Earth Did Jesus Become a God?': A Reply." Pages 55–66 in *Israel's God and Rebecca's Children: Christology and Community in Early Judaism and Christianity*. Edited by David B. Capes, April D. DeConick, Helen K. Bond, and Troy A. Miller. Waco, Tex.: Baylor University Press, 2007.

———. "Mark and His Readers: The Son of God among Greeks and Romans." *HTR* 93 (2000): 85–100.

———. "Mark and His Readers: The Son of God among Jews." *HTR* 92 (1999): 393–408.

———. "Psalms, Philippians 2:6–11, and the Origins of Christology." *BibInt* 11 (2002): 361–72.

———. "The 'Son of Man' Tradition and the Book of Revelation." Pages 536–68 in *The Messiah: Developments in Early Judaism and Christianity*. Edited by James H. Charlesworth. Philadelphia: Fortress, 1992.

———. "Traveling Up and Away: Journeys to the Upper and Outer Regions of the World." Pages 135–66 in *Greco-Roman Culture and the New Testament*. Edited by David E. Aune and Frederick E. Brenk. Leiden: Brill, 2012.

———. "The Worship of Jesus and the Imperial Cult." Pages 234–57 in *The Jewish Roots of Christological Monotheism: Papers from the St. Andrews Conference on the Historical Origins of the Worship of Jesus*. Edited by Carey C. Newman, James R. Davila, and Gladys S. Lewis. JSJSup 63. Leiden: Brill, 1999.

Collins, Adela Yarbro, and John J. Collins. *King and Messiah as Son of God: Divine, Human, and Angelic Messianic Figures in Biblical and Related Literature*. Grand Rapids: Eerdmans, 2008.

Collins, John J. *Daniel: A Commentary on the Book of Daniel*. Hermeneia. Minneapolis: Fortress, 1993.

———. "'He Shall Not Judge by What His Eyes See': Messianic Authority in the Dead Sea Scrolls." *DSD* 2 (1995): 145–64.

———. "Isaiah 8:23–9:6 and Its Greek Translation." Pages 205–21 in *Scripture in Transition: Essays on Septuagint, Hebrew Bible, and Dead Sea Scrolls in Honour of Raija Sollamo*. Edited by Anssi Voitila and Jutta Jokiranta. JSJSup 126. Leiden: Brill, 2010.

———. "Jewish Monotheism and Christian Theology." Pages 81–105 in *Aspects of Monotheism: How God Is One*. Edited by Hershel Shanks and Jack Meinhardt. Washington, D.C.: Biblical Archaeological Society, 1997.

———. *Jewish Wisdom in the Hellenistic Age*. OTL. Philadelphia: Westminster John Knox, 1997.

———. "Judaism as *Praeparatio Evangelica* in the Work of Martin Hengel." *RelSRev* 15 (1989): 226–28.

———. *The Sceptre and the Star: The Messiahs of the Dead Sea Scrolls and Other Ancient Literature*. New York: Doubleday, 1995.

———. "A Throne in the Heavens: Apotheosis in Pre-Christian Judaism." Pages 43–58 in *Death, Ecstasy, and Otherworldly Journeys*. Edited by John J. Collins and Michael Fishbane. Albany, N.Y.: State University of New York Press, 1995.

Cook, John Granger. *Empty Tomb, Resurrection, Apotheosis*. WUNT 410. Tübingen: Mohr Siebeck, 2018.

Copenhaver, Adam. *Reconstructing the Historical Background of Paul's Rhetoric in the Letter to the Colossians*. LNTS 585. London: T&T Clark, 2018.

Cotter, Wendy. "Greco-Roman Apotheosis Traditions and the Resurrection Appearances in Matthew." Pages 127–53 in *The Gospel of Matthew in Current Study*. Edited by David E. Aune. Grand Rapids: Eerdmans, 2001.

Cover, Michael B. "The Death of Tragedy: The Form of God in Euripides's *Bacchae* and Paul's *Carmen Christi*." *HTR* 111 (2018): 66–89.

Cox, Ronald. *By the Same Word: Creation and Salvation in Hellenistic Judaism and Early Christianity*. Berlin: de Gruyter, 1997.

Croy, N. Clayton. "A God by Any Other Name: Polyonymy in Greco-Roman Antiquity and Early Christianity." *BBR* 24 (2014): 27–43.

Cullmann, Oscar. *The Christology of the New Testament*. 2nd ed. London: SCM Press, 1963.

Dahl, Nils A. "Christ, Creation, and the Church." Pages 422–43 in *The Background of the New Testament and Its Eschatology*. Edited by William D. Davies and David Daube. Cambridge: Cambridge University Press, 1954.

———. *Jesus the Christ: The Historical Origins of Christological Doctrine*. Minneapolis: Fortress, 1991.

Daniélou, Jean. *The Theology of Jewish Christianity*. 2 vols. London: Darton, Longman & Todd, 1964.

Davidson, Maxwell J. *Angels at Qumran: A Comparative Study of 1 Enoch 1–36 and 72–108 and Sectarian Writings from Qumran*. JSPSup 11. Sheffield: JSOT Press, 1992.

Davies, W. D. *Paul and Rabbinic Judaism*. Philadelphia: Fortress, 1980.

DeConick, April D. "How We Talk about Christology Matters." Pages 1–23 in *Israel's God and Rebecca's Children: Christology and Community in Early Judaism and Christianity*. Edited by David B. Capes, April D. DeConick, Helen K. Bond, and Troy A. Miller. Waco, Tex.: Baylor University Press, 2007.

———. "The One God Is No Simple Matter." Pages 263–92 in *Monotheism and Christology in Greco-Roman Antiquity*. Edited by Matthew V. Novenson. Leiden: Brill, 2020.

———. *The Original Gospel of Thomas in Translation: With Commentary and New English Translation of the Complete Gospel*. LNTS 287. London: T&T Clark, 2006.

Deissmann, Gustav Adolf. *Light from the Ancient East: The New Testament Illustrated by Recently Discovered Texts of the Graeco-Roman World*. Grand Rapids: Baker, 1965.

de Jáuregui, Miguel Herrero. *Orphism and Christianity in Late Antiquity*. Berlin: de Gruyter, 2010.

de Jonge, Marinus. *Christology in Context: The Earliest Christian Responses to Jesus*. Philadelphia: Westminster, 1988.

———. *God's Final Envoy: Early Christology and Jesus' Own View of His Mission*. Grand Rapids: Eerdmans, 1998.

———. "The Use of the Word 'Anointed' in the Time of Jesus." *NovT* 8 (1966): 132–48.

Dever, William G. *Did God Have a Wife? Archaeology and Folk Religion in Ancient Israel*. Grand Rapids: Eerdmans, 2005.

Dixon, Sarah Underwood. "The Apocalypse of Zephaniah and Revelation 22:6–21: Angel Worship and Monotheistic Devotion." Pages 175–82 in *Reading Revelation in Context: John's Apocalypse and Second Temple Judaism*. Edited by Ben C. Blackwell, John K. Goodrich, and Jason Maston. Grand Rapids: Zondervan, 2019.

Dodd, C. H. *The Interpretation of the Fourth Gospel*. Cambridge: Cambridge University Press, 1963.

Drozdek, Adam. *Greek Philosophers as Theologians: The Divine Arche*. London: Routledge, 2016.

Dunn, James D. G. *Christology in the Making: A New Testament Inquiry into the Origins of the Doctrine of the Incarnation*. 2nd ed. Grand Rapids: Eerdmans, 1989.

———. *Did the First Christians Worship Jesus? The New Testament Evidence*. London: SPCK, 2010.

———. *Theology of Paul the Apostle*. Edinburgh: T&T Clark, 1998.

Edsall, Benjamin, and Jennifer R. Strawbridge. "The Songs We Used to Sing? Hymn 'Traditions' and Reception in Pauline Letters." *JSNT* 37 (2015): 290–311.

Edwards, Mark J. "Justin's Logos and the Word of God." *JECS* 3 (1995): 261–80.

Ehrman, Bart D. *How Jesus Became God: The Exaltation of a Jewish Preacher from Galilee*. New York: HarperOne, 2014.

Endo, Masanobu. *Creation and Christology: A Study of the Johannine Prologue in Light of Early Jewish Creation Accounts*. WUNT 2.146. Tübingen: Mohr Siebeck, 2002.

Engberg-Pedersen, Troels. *John and Philosophy: A New Reading of the Fourth Gospel*. Oxford: Oxford University Press, 2017.

———. "Logos and Pneuma in the Fourth Gospel." Pages 27–48 in *Greco-Roman Culture and the New Testament*. Edited by David E. Aune and Frederick E. Brenk. Leiden: Brill, 2012.

Erho, Ted. "Historical-Allusional Dating and the Similitudes of Enoch." *JBL* 130 (2011): 493–511.

Eskola, Timo. *Messiah and the Throne*. WUNT 2.142. Tübingen: Mohr Siebeck, 2001.

Estrada, Rodolfo Gavan, III. "Blaspheming Angels: The Presence of Magicians in Jude 8–10." *JETS* 63 (2020): 739–58.

Evans, Craig A. "Messianic Hopes and Messianic Figures in Late Antiquity." *JGRChJ* 3 (2006): 9–40.

———. "On the Prologue of John and the Trimorphic Protennoia." *NTS* 27 (1981): 395–401.

———. *Word and Glory: On the Exegetical and Theological Background of John's Prologue*. JSNTSup 89. Sheffield: JSOT Press, 1993.

Fantin, Joseph D. *The Lord of the Entire World: Lord Jesus, a Challenge to Lord Caesar?* NTM 31. Sheffield: Sheffield Phoenix, 2011.

Fee, Gordon D. *Pauline Christology: An Exegetical-Theological Study*. Peabody, Mass.: Hendrickson, 2007.

———. "Philippians 2:5–11: Hymn or Exalted Pauline Prose?" *BBR* 2 (1992): 30–34.

Feldman, Louis H. "How Much Hellenism in Jewish Palestine?" *Hebrew Union College Annual* 57 (1986): 83–111.

Feldmeier, Reinhard, and Hermann Spieckermann. *God Becoming Human: Incarnation in the Christian Bible*. Waco, Tex.: Baylor University Press, 2021.

Ferrari, Franco. "Der Gott Plutarchs und der Gott Platons." Pages 13–24 in *Gott und die Götter bei Plutarch: Götterbilder—Gottesbilder—Weltbilder*. Edited by Rainer Hirsch-Luipold. RVV 54. Berlin: de Gruyter, 2005.

Feuillet, André. *Le Christ, sagesse de Dieu: d'après les épitres pauliniennes*. Paris: Lecoffre, 1966.

Fishwick, Duncan. *The Imperial Cult in the Latin West*. 3 vols. Leiden: Brill, 1987–2004.

Fitzmyer, Joseph A. *A Wandering Aramean: Collected Aramaic Essays*. Missoula, Mont.: Scholars Press, 1979.

Fletcher-Louis, Crispin H. T. "'The Being That Is in a Manner Equal with God' (Phil 2:6c): A Self-Transforming, Incarnational, Divine Ontology." *JTS* 96 (2020): 581–627.

———. *Jesus Monotheism*. Vol. 1: *Christological Origins: The Emerging Consensus and Beyond*. Eugene, Ore.: Wipf & Stock, 2015.

Fossum, Jarl E. "Kyrios Jesus as the Angel of the Lord in Jude 5–7." *NTS* 33 (1987): 226–43.

———. "The New Religionsgeschichtliche Schule: The Quest for Jewish Christology." Pages 638–46 in *SBL Seminar Papers 1991*. Edited by Eugene H. Lovering. Atlanta: Scholars Press, 1991.

Foster, Paul. "The Epistles of Ignatius of Antioch and the Writings That Later Formed the New Testament." Pages 159–86 in *The New Testament and the Apostolic Fathers*, vol. 1. Edited by Andrew Gregory and Christopher Tuckett. 2 vols. Oxford: Oxford University Press, 2006.

Frede, Michael. "The Case for Pagan Monotheism." Pages 53–81 in *One God: Pagan Monotheism in the Roman Empire*. Edited by Stephen Mitchell and Peter van Nuffelen. Cambridge: Cambridge University Press, 2010.

Fredriksen, Paula. "How High Can Early Christology Be?" Pages 293–319 in *Monotheism and Christology in Greco-Roman Antiquity*. Edited by Matthew V. Novenson. Leiden: Brill, 2020.

———. "Mandatory Retirement: Ideas in the Study of Christian Origins Whose Time Has Come to Go." Pages 25–38 in *Israel's God and Rebecca's Children: Christology and Community in Early Judaism and Christianity*. Edited by David B. Capes, April D. DeConick, Helen K. Bond, and Troy A. Miller. Waco, Tex.: Baylor University Press, 2007.

———. "What Does Jesus Have to Do with Christ? What Does Knowledge Have to Do with Faith? What Does History Have to Do with Theology?" Pages 3–17 in *Christology: Memory, Inquiry, Practice*. Edited by A. M. Clifford and A. J. Godzieba. Maryknoll, N.Y.: Orbis, 2003.

Frey, Jörg. "Between Jewish Monotheism and Proto-trinitarian Tradition Relations: The Making and Character of Johannine Christology." Pages 189–221 in *Monotheism and Christology in Greco-Roman Antiquity*. Edited by Matthew V. Novenson. Leiden: Brill, 2020.

———. "Between Torah and Stoa: How Could Readers Have Understood the Johannine Logos?" Pages 189–234 in *The Prologue of the Gospel of John*. Edited by Jan G. van der Watt, R. Alan Culpepper, and Udo Schnelle. WUNT 359. Tübingen: Mohr Siebeck, 2016.

———. "Eine neue religionsgeschichtliche Perspektive: Larry W. Hurtados *Lord Jesus Christ* und die Herausbildung der frühen Christologie." Pages 117–70 in *Reflections on the Early Christian History of Religion—Erwägungen zur frühchristlichen Religionsgeschichte*. Edited by Cilliers Breytenbach and Jörg Frey. AJEC 81. Leiden: Brill, 2013.

———. "The Incarnation of the Logos and the Dwelling of God in Jesus Christ." Pages 261–84 in *The Glory of the Crucified One: Christology and Theology in the Gospel of John*. Waco, Tex.: Baylor University Press, 2018.

———. "The Johannine Logos and the Reference to the Creation of the World in Its Second Century Receptions." Pages 221–44 in *Les Judaïsmes dans tours leurs états aux Ier-IIIe siècles (les Judéens des synagogues, les chrétiens et les rabbins)*. Edited by C. Clivaz. Turnhout: Brepols, 2015.

———. *The Letter of Jude and the Second Letter of Peter: A Theological Commentary*. Waco, Tex.: Baylor University Press, 2018.

———. "Review of *John and Philosophy*, by Troels Engberg-Pedersen." *EC* 10 (2019): 225–36.

Friesen, Steven J. *Imperial Cults and the Apocalypse of John*. Oxford: Oxford University Press, 2001.
———. *Twice Neokoros: Ephesus, Asia, and the Cult of the Imperial Family*. Leiden: Brill, 1993.
Fürst, Alfons. "Pagan und christlicher 'Monotheismus': Zur Hermeneutik eines antiken Diskurses." *JAC* 51 (2008): 5–24.
Galinsky, Karl. "Continuity and Change: Religion in the Augustan Semi-century." In *A Companion to Roman Religion*. Edited by Jörg Rüpke. Chichester, U.K.: Blackwell, 2007.
Gallusz, Laszlo. *The Throne Motif in the Book of Revelation: Profiles from the History of Interpretation*. LNTS 487. London: T&T Clark, 2014.
Garrett, Susan R. *No Ordinary Angel: Celestial Spirits and Christian Claims*. New Haven, Conn.: Yale University Press, 2008.
Gathercole, Simon J. *The Gospel of Thomas: Introduction and Commentary*. TENT 11. Leiden: Brill, 2014.
———. *The Pre-existent Son: Recovering the Christologies of Matthew, Mark, and Luke*. Grand Rapids: Eerdmans, 2006.
Georgia, Allan T. "Translating the Triumph: Reading Mark's Crucifixion Narrative against a Roman Ritual of Power." *JSNT* 36 (2013): 17–38.
Gese, Harmut. *Essays on Biblical Theology*. Minneapolis: Augsburg, 1981.
Gieschen, Charles. *Angelomorphic Christology: Antecedents and Early Evidence*. AGAJU 42. Leiden: Brill, 1998.
———. "The Divine Name in the Ante-Nicene Christology." *VC* 57 (2003): 115–58.
———. "Enoch and Melchizedek: The Concern for Supra-human Priestly Mediators in 2 Enoch." Pages 369–86 in *New Perspectives on 2 Enoch: No Longer Slavonic Only*. Edited by Andrei A. Orlov, Gabriele Boccaccini, and Jason M. Zurawski. Leiden: Brill, 2012.
Gnuse, Robert K. *No Other Gods: Emergent Monotheism in Israel*. JSOTSup 242. Sheffield: Sheffield Academic Press, 1997.
Gordley, Matthew E. *New Testament Christological Hymns: Exploring Texts, Contexts, and Significance*. Downers Grove, Ill.: InterVarsity, 2018.
———. *Teaching through Song in Antiquity*. WUNT 2.302. Tübingen: Mohr Siebeck, 2011.
Gradel, Ittai. *Emperor Worship and Roman Religion*. Oxford: Clarendon, 2002.
Gradl, Hans-Georg. "Kaisertum und Kaiserkult: Ein Vergleich zwischen Philos *Legatio ad Gaium* und der Offenbarung des Johannes." *NTS* 56 (2010): 116–38.
Grillmeier, Aloys. *Christ in Christian Tradition*. 2 vols. 2nd ed. London: Mowbrays, 1975.
Grindheim, Sigurd. "Eternal Generation of the Son in Heb 1,5." *Bib* 102 (2021): 97–105.
———. *God's Equal: What Can We Know about Jesus' Self-Understanding in the Synoptic Gospels?* LNTS 446. London: T&T Clark, 2011.
Gruning, Herb. *How in the World Does God Act?* Lanham, Md.: University of America Press, 2000.

Gundry, Robert H. "Angelomorphic Christology in the Book of Revelation." Pages 377–98 in *The Old Is Better: New Testament Essays in Support of Traditional Interpretations*. WUNT 178. Tübingen: Mohr Siebeck, 2005.

———. *Jesus the Word according to John the Sectarian: A Paleofundamentalist Manifesto for Contemporary Evangelicalism, Especially Its Elites, in North America*. Grand Rapids: Eerdmans, 2002.

Habets, Myk. *The Anointed Son: A Trinitarian Spirit Christology*. Eugene, Ore.: Pickwick, 2010.

Habicht, Christian. "Die augusteische Zeit und das Jahrhundert nach Christi Geburt." Pages 41–99 in *Le culte des souverains dans l'empire romain*. Geneva: Fondation Hardt, 1973.

———. *Divine Honors for Mortal Men in Greek City States: The Early Cases*. Ann Arbor: Michigan Classical Press, 2017.

Hägg, Henny Fiskå. *Clement of Alexandria and the Beginnings of Christian Apophaticism*. OECS. Oxford: Oxford University Press, 2006.

Hamerton-Kelly, R. G. *Pre-existence, Wisdom, and the Son of Man: A Study in the Idea of Pre-existence in the New Testament*. Cambridge: Cambridge University Press, 1973.

Hannah, Darrell D. "The Elect Son of Man of the Parables of Enoch." Pages 130–58 in *"Who Is This Son of Man?": The Latest Scholarship on a Puzzling Expression of the Historical Jesus*. Edited by Larry W. Hurtado and Paul L. Owen. LNTS 390. London: T&T Clark, 2011.

———. *Michael and Christ: Michael Traditions and Angel Christology in Early Christianity*. WUNT 2.109. Tübingen: Mohr Siebeck, 1999.

———. "The Throne of His Glory: The Divine Throne and Heavenly Mediators in Revelation and the Similitudes of Enoch." *ZNW* 94 (2003): 68–96.

Hanson, R. P. C. *The Search for the Christian Doctrine of God*. Edinburgh: T&T Clark, 1988.

Harnack, Adolf von. *The History of Dogma*. Vol. 1. Edinburgh: Williams & Norgate, 1894.

Harris, J. R. *The Origin of the Prologue to St. John's Gospel*. Cambridge: Cambridge University Press, 1917.

Hayman, Peter. "Monotheism—A Misused Word in Jewish Studies?" *JJS* 42 (1991): 1–15.

Hays, Richard B. *Reading Backwards: Figural Christology and the Fourfold Gospel Witness*. Waco, Tex.: Baylor University Press, 2014.

Heen, Erik M. "Phil 2:6–11 and Resistance to Local Timocratic Rule." Pages 125–53 in *Paul and the Roman Imperial Order*. Edited by Richard A. Horsley. Harrisburg, Penn.: Trinity Press International, 2004.

Heilig, Christoph. *Hidden Criticism? The Methodology and Plausibility of the Search for a Counter-Imperial Subtext in Paul*. Minneapolis: Fortress, 2017.

———. *Paul's Triumph: Reassessing 2 Corinthians 2:14 in Its Literary and Historical Context*. Leuven: Peeters, 2017.

Heiser, Michael S. *Angels: What the Bible Really Says about God's Heavenly Host*. Bellingham, Wash.: Lexham, 2018.

———. *The Divine Council in Late Canonical and Non-canonical Second Temple Jewish Literature*. PhD dissertation. University of Wisconsin-Madison, 2004.

———. "Monotheism, Polytheism, Monolatry, or Henotheism? Toward an Understanding of Divine Plurality in the Hebrew Bible." *BBR* 18 (2008): 1–30.

Helgeland, J. "Roman Army Religion." *ANRW* 2.16.2: 1470–505. Edited by Wolfgang Haase. Berlin: de Gruyter, 1978.

Hellerman, Joseph H. *Reconstructing Honor in Roman Philippi: Carmen Christi as Cursus Podorum*. SNTSMS 132. Cambridge: Cambridge University Press, 2005.

———. "Μορφῇ θεοῦ as a Signifier of Social Status in Philippians 2:6." *JETS* 52 (2009): 779–97.

Hengel, Martin. *Between Jesus and Paul*. London: SCM Press, 1983.

———. *Der Sohn Gottes: Die Entstehung der Christologie und die jüdisch-hellenistische Religionsgeschichte*. 2nd ed. Tübingen: Mohr Siebeck, 1977.

———. "Erwägungen zum Sprachgebrauch von *Christos* bei Paulus und in der 'vorpaulinischen' Überlieferung." Pages 135–59 in *Paul and Paulinism*. Edited by M. D. Hooker and S. G. Wilson. London: SPCK, 1982.

———. *The Johannine Question*. London: SCM Press, 1989.

———. *Judaism and Hellenism: Studies in the Encounter in Palestine during the Early Hellenistic Period*. 2 vols. Philadelphia: Fortress, 1974.

———. *The Son of God: The Origin of Christology and the History of Jewish Hellenistic Religion*. Minneapolis: Fortress, 1976.

———. *Studies in Early Christology*. Edinburgh: T&T Clark, 1995.

Henrichs-Tarasenkova, Nina. *Luke's Christology of Divine Identity*. LNTS 542. London: T&T Clark, 2016.

Herbener, Jens-André P. "On the Term 'Monotheism.'" *Numen* 60 (2013): 616–48.

Hill, Charles E. "The *Epistula Apostolorum*: An Asian Tract from the Time of Polycarp." *JECS* 7 (1999): 1–53.

———. *The Johannine Corpus in the Early Church*. Oxford: Oxford University Press, 2004.

Hill, Wesley. *Paul and the Trinity: Persons, Relations, and the Pauline Letters*. Grand Rapids: Eerdmans, 2015.

Hillar, Marian. *From Logos to Trinity: The Evolution of Religious Belief from Pythagoras to Tertullian*. Cambridge: Cambridge University Press, 2012.

Hoffmann, Matthias Reinhard. *The Destroyer and the Lamb: The Relationship between Angelomorphic and Lamb Christology in the Book of Revelation*. WUNT 2.203. Tübingen: Mohr Siebeck, 2005.

Hofius, Otfried. "Christus als Schöpfungsmittler und Erlösungsmittler: Das Bekenntnis 1Kor 8,6 im Kontext der paulinischen Theologie." Pages 47–58 in *Paulinische Christologie: Exegetische Beiträge*. Edited by Udo Schnelle and Thomas Söding. Göttingen: Vandenhoeck & Ruprecht, 2000.

Hölbl, Günther. *A History of Ptolemaic Empire*. London: Routledge, 2001.

Holladay, Carl R. *Theios Aner in Hellenistic Judaism*. Missoula, Mont.: Scholars Press, 1977.

Holmes, Stephen R. *The Quest for the Trinity: The Doctrine of God in Scripture, History, and Modernity*. Downers Grove, Ill.: InterVarsity, 2012.

Horbury, William. "Jewish and Christian Monotheism in the Herodian Age." Pages 15–44 in *Early Jewish and Christian Monotheism*, edited by Loren T. Stuckenbruck and Wendy E. S. North. London: T&T Clark, 2004.

———. "Jewish Messianism and Early Christology." Pages 3–24 in *Contours of Christology in the New Testament*. Edited by Richard N. Longenecker. Grand Rapids: Eerdmans, 2005.

———. *Jewish Messianism and the Cult of Christ*. London: SCM Press, 1998.

———. "Messianic Associations of the Son of Man." *JTS* 36 (1985): 34–55.

———. *Messianism among Jews and Christians: Twelve Biblical and Historical Studies*. London: T&T Clark, 2003.

———. Review of *Lord Jesus Christ: Devotion to Jesus in Earliest Christianity*, by Larry W. Hurtado. *JTS* 56 (2005): 531–39.

Hunsinger, George. *Philippians*. BTCB. Grand Rapids: Brazos, 2020.

Hunt, Laura J. *Jesus Caesar: A Roman Reading of the Johannine Trial Narrative*. WUNT 2.5-6. Tübingen: Mohr Siebeck, 2019.

Hurtado, Larry. *Ancient Jewish Monotheism and Early Christian Jesus-Devotion: The Context and Character of Christological Faith*. Waco, Tex.: Baylor University Press, 2017.

———. "'Ancient Jewish Monotheism' in the Hellenistic and Roman Periods." *Journal of Ancient Judaism* 4 (2013): 379–400.

———. *At the Origins of Christian Worship: The Context and Character of Earliest Christian Devotion*. Grand Rapids: Eerdmans, 1999.

———. "Chronology and Ontology." *Larry Hurtado's Blog*. September 26, 2016. https://larryhurtado.wordpress.com/2016/09/26/chronology-and-ontology/. Accessed June 1, 2020.

———. *How on Earth Did Jesus Become God? Historical Questions about Earliest Devotion to Jesus*. Grand Rapids: Eerdmans, 2010.

———. "Interactive Diversity: A Proposed Model of Christian Origins." *JTS* 64 (2013): 445–62.

———. *Lord Jesus Christ: Devotion to Jesus in Earliest Christianity*. Grand Rapids: Eerdmans, 2003.

———. "Monotheism." Pages 961–64 in *The Eerdmans Dictionary of Early Judaism*. Edited by John J. Collins and Daniel C. Harlow. Grand Rapids: Eerdmans, 2010.

———. "Monotheism, Principal Angels, and the Background of Christology." Pages 546–64 in *The Oxford Handbook of the Dead Sea Scrolls*. Edited by Timothy H. Lim and John J. Collins. Oxford: Oxford University Press, 2010.

———. "The New *religionsgeschichtliche Schule* at Thirty." Pages 7–31 in *Monotheism and Christology in Greco-Roman Antiquity*. Edited by Matthew V. Novenson. Leiden: Brill, 2020.

———. "Observations on the 'Monotheism' Affirmed in the New Testament." Pages 50–68 in *The Bible and Early Trinitarian Theology*. Edited by Christopher A. Beeley and Mark E. Weedman. Washington, D.C.: Catholic University of America Press, 2018.

———. *One God, One Lord: Early Christian Devotion and Ancient Jewish Monotheism*. 3rd ed. London: T&T Clark, 2015.

———. "Two Case Studies in Earliest Christological Readings of Biblical Texts." Pages 3–23 in *All That the Prophets Have Declared: The Appropriation of Scripture in the Emergence of Christianity*. Edited by Matthew R. Malcolm. London: Authentic Media, 2015.

Janse, Sam. *"You Are My Son": The Reception History of Psalm 2 in Early Judaism and the Early Church*. CBET 51. Leuven: Peeters, 2009.

Jefford, Clayton N., ed. *The* Epistle to Diognetus *(with the* Fragment of Quadratus*): Introduction, Text, and Commentary*. OAF. Oxford: Oxford University Press, 2013.

Jensen, Robin M. "The Emperor Cult and Christian Iconography." Pages 153–71 in *Rome and Religion: A Cross-Disciplinary Dialogue on the Imperial Cult*. Edited by Jeffrey Brodd and Jonathan L. Reed. Atlanta: SBL, 2011.

Jipp, Joshua W. *Christ Is King: Paul's Royal Ideology*. Minneapolis: Fortress, 2015.

Johnson, Luke Timothy. *Among the Gentiles: Greco-Roman Religion and Christianity*. New Haven, Conn.: Yale University Press, 2009.

———. Review of Richard H. Bell, *No One Seeks for God: An Exegetical and Theological Study of Romans 1:18–3:20*. *RBL* (1999).

Johnson, Peter C. *The Gospel of Truth: Christology, Deification and the Kingdom of God*. PhD dissertation. University of New England, 2015.

Kaiser, Christopher B. *Seeing the Lord's Glory: Kyriocentric Visions and the Dilemma of Early Christology*. Minneapolis: Fortress, 2014.

Keck, David. *Angels and Angelology in the Middle Ages*. New York: Oxford University Press, 1998.

Keel, Othmar. *The Symbolism of the Biblical World*. Winona Lake, Ind.: Eisenbrauns, 1997.

Keener, Craig S. *The Gospel of John*. 2 vols. Grand Rapids: Baker, 2010.

Kerkeslager, Allen. "Jewish Pilgrimage and Jewish Identity in Hellenistic and Early Roman Egypt." Pages 99–228 in *Pilgrimage and Holy Space in Late Antique Egypt*. Edited by David Frankfurter. Leiden: Brill, 1998.

Kim, Kyu Seop. *The Firstborn Son in Ancient Judaism and Early Christianity: A Study of Primogeniture and Christology*. BIS 171. Leiden: Brill, 2019.

Kim, Seyoon. *The Origin of Paul's Gospel*. Eugene, Ore.: Wipf & Stock, 2007.

Kindt, Julia. "The Story of Theology and the Theology of the Story." Pages 12–34 in *Theologies of Ancient Greek Religion*. Edited by Esther Eidinow, Julia Kindt, and Robin Osborne. Cambridge: Cambridge University Press, 2016.

King, Charles. "The Organization of Roman Religious Beliefs." *Classical Antiquity* 22 (2003): 275–31.

Kirk, J. R. Daniel. *A Man Attested by God: The Human Jesus of the Synoptic Gospels*. Grand Rapids: Eerdmans, 2016.

Klauck, Hans-Josef. "Das Sendschreiben nach Pergamon und der Kaiserkult in der Johannes Offenbarung." *Bib* 73 (1992): 153–82.

———. *Religious Context of Early Christianity: A Guide to Graeco-Roman Religions*. Edinburgh: T&T Clark, 2000.

———. "The Roman Empire." Pages 69–83 in *The Cambridge History of Christianity: Origins to Constantine*. Edited by Margaret M. Mitchell and Frances M. Young. Cambridge: Cambridge University Press, 2006.

Klijn, A. F. J., and G. J. Reinink. *Patristic Evidence for Jewish-Christian Sects*. Leiden: Brill, 1973.

Knight, Jonathan. "The Enthroned Christ of Revelation 5:6 and the Development of Christian Theology." Pages 43–50 in *Studies in the Book of Revelation*. Edited by Stephen Moyise. Edinburgh: T&T Clark, 2001.

Koester, Craig R. *The Dwelling of God: The Tabernacle in the Old Testament, Intertestamental Jewish Literature, and the New Testament*. Washington, D.C.: Catholic Biblical Association of America, 1989.

Koester, Helmut. *Introduction to the New Testament*. 2 vols. Berlin: de Gruyter, 1982–1987.

Koortbojian, Michael. *The Divinization of Caesar and Augustus: Precedents, Consequences, Implications*. Cambridge: Cambridge University Press, 2013.

Kranz, Walther. "Der Logos Heraklits und der Logos des Johannes." *Rheinisches Museum für Philologie* 93 (1950): 81–95.

Kratz, Reinhard G., and Hermann Spieckermann, eds. *Götterbilder, Gottesbilder, Weltbilder: Polytheismus and Monotheismus in der Welt der Antike*. Tübingen: Mohr Siebeck, 2006.

Krebernick, Manfred, and Jürgen van Oorschot, eds. *Polytheismus und Monotheismus in den Religionen des Vorderen Orients*. Münster: Ugarit-Verlag, 2002.

Kreitzer, Larry J. *Jesus and God in Paul's Eschatology*. Sheffield: Sheffield Academic Press, 1987.

Kropp, Andreas. "King-Caesar-God: Roman Imperial Cult among Near Eastern 'Client' Kings." Pages 99–150 in *Lokale Identität im Römischen Nahen Osten*. Edited by Michael Blömer, Margherita Facella, and Engelbert Winter. Stuttgart: Franz Steiner, 2009.

Kunath, Friederike. *Die Präexistenz Jesu im Johannesevangelium: Struktur und Theologie eines johanneischen Motivs*. BZNW 212. Berlin: de Gruyter, 2016.

Kvanvig, Helge S. "The Son of Man in the Parables of Enoch." Pages 179–215 in *Enoch and the Messiah Son of Man: Revisiting the Book of Parables*. Edited by Gabriele Boccaccini. Grand Rapids: Eerdmans, 2007.

Lambden, Stephen N. "From Fig Leaves to Fingernails: Some Notes on the Garments of Adam and Eve in the Hebrew Bible and Select Early Postbiblical Jewish Writings." Pages 74–90 in *A Walk in the Garden: Biblical, Iconographical and Literary Images of Eden*. Edited by Paul Morris and Deborah Sawyer. Sheffield: JSOT Press, 1992.

Lamp, Jeffrey S. "Wisdom in Col 1:15–20: Contribution and Significance." *JETS* 41 (1998): 45–53.

Lang, Bernhard. "The Yahweh-Alone Movement and the Making of Jewish Monotheism." Pages 13–59 in *Monotheism and the Prophetic Minority: An Essay in Biblical History and Sociology*. Sheffield: Almond, 1983.

———. "Zur Entstehung des biblischen Monotheismus." *ThQS* 166 (1985): 135–42.

Lattke, Michael. *The Odes of Solomon*. Hermeneia. Minneapolis: Fortress, 2009.

Lau, Markus. *Der gekreuzigte Triumphator: Eine motivkritische Studie zum Markusevangelium*. Göttingen: Vandenhoeck & Ruprecht, 2019.

Lee, Aquila H. I. *From Messiah to Preexistent Son: Jesus' Self-Consciousness and Early Christian Exegesis of Messianic Psalms*. Eugene, Ore.: Wipf & Stock, 2005.

Lee, Max J. *Moral Transformation in Greco-Roman Philosophy of Mind*. WUNT 2.515. Tübingen: Mohr Siebeck, 2020.

Lee, Yongbom. *The Son of Man as the Last Adam: The Early Church Tradition as a Source of Paul's Adam Christology*. Eugene, Ore.: Pickwick, 2012.

Leim, Joshua. "Theological Hermeneutics, Exegesis, and J. R. Daniel Kirk's *A Man Attested by God*." *JTI* 15 (2021): 22–43.

Leonhardt-Balzer, Jutta. "Der Logos und die Schöpfung: Streiflichter bei Philo (Op. 20–5) und im Johannesprolog (Joh 1:1–18)." Pages 295–319 in *Kontexte des Johannesevangeliums: Das vierte Evangelium in religions- und traditionsgeschichtlicher Perspektive*. Edited by Jörg Frey and Udo Schnelle. WUNT 175. Tübingen: Mohr Siebeck, 2004.

Levene, D. S. "Defining the Divine in Rome." *TAPhA* 142 (2012): 41–81.

Levine, Lee I. *Judaism and Hellenism in Antiquity: Conflict or Confluence?* Peabody, Mass.: Hendrickson, 1998.

Lienhard, J. T., and R. J. Rombs, eds. *Exodus, Leviticus, Numbers, Deuteronomy*. ACCS. Downers Grove, Ill.: InterVarsity, 2001.

Lierman, John. *The New Testament Moses: Christian Perceptions of Moses and Israel in the Setting of Jewish Religion*. WUNT 2.173. Tübingen: Mohr Siebeck, 2004.

Lieu, Judith M. *Marcion and the Making of a Heretic: God and Scripture in the Second Century*. Cambridge: Cambridge University Press, 2015.

Lin, Yii-Jan. *The Erotic Life of Manuscripts: New Testament Textual Criticism and the Biological Sciences*. New York: Oxford University Press, 2016.

Litwa, M. David. *Iesus Deus: The Early Christian Depiction of Jesus as a Mediterranean God*. Minneapolis: Fortress, 2014.

———. *We Are Being Transformed: Deification in Paul's Soteriology*. Berlin: de Gruyter, 2012.

Loader, William. "Wisdom and Logos Traditions in Judaism and John's Christology." Pages 303–34 in *Reading the Gospel of John's Christology as Jewish Messianism*. Edited by Benjamin Reynolds and Gabriele Boccaccini. AJEC 106. Leiden: Brill, 2018.

Lohmeyer, Ernst. *Christuskult und Kaiserkult*. Tübingen: Mohr Siebeck, 1919.

———. *Kyrios Jesus: Eine Untersuchung zu Phil 2, 5–11*. Heidelberg: Winters, 1928.

Loke, Andrew Ter Ern. *The Origin of Divine Christology*. SNTSMS 169. Cambridge: Cambridge University Press, 2017.
Longenecker, Richard N. *The Christology of Early Jewish Christianity*. London: SCM Press, 1970.
Lookadoo, Jonathan. *The Shepherd of Hermas: A Literary, Historical, and Theological Handbook*. London: T&T Clark, 2021.
Lorenz, Rudolf. *Arius Judaizans? Untersuchungen zur dogmengeschichtlichen Einordnung des Arius*. Göttingen: Vandenhoeck & Ruprecht, 1980.
Ludwig, Theodore. "Monotheism." Pages 6155–63 in *The Encyclopedia of Religion*, vol. 9. Edited by Lindsay Jones. 15 vols. Detroit: MacMillan, 2005.
Luke, Trevor S. "Augustus." Pages 112–14 in *The Routledge Encyclopedia of Ancient Mediterranean Religions*. Edited by Eric Orlin et al. London: Routledge, 2016.
Luttikhuizen, Gerard P. "Elchasaites and Their Book." Pages 335–64 in *A Companion to Second-Century Christian "Heretics."* Edited by Antti Marjanen and Petri Luomanen. VigChrSup 76. Leiden: Brill, 2005.
Lynch, Matthew J. "Mapping Monotheism: Modes of Monotheistic Rhetoric in the Hebrew Bible." *VT* 64 (2014): 47–68.
Macaskill, Grant. *Revealed Wisdom and Inaugurated Eschatology in Ancient Judaism and Early Christianity*. Leiden: Brill, 2007.
MacDonald, Nathan. *Deuteronomy and the Meaning of "Monotheism."* FZAT 2.1. Tübingen: Mohr Siebeck, 2012.
———. "Monotheism." Pages 77–84 in *The World of the New Testament: Cultural, Social, and Historical Contexts*. Edited by Joel B. Green and Lee Martin McDonald. Grand Rapids: Baker, 2013.
MacMullen, Ramsay. *Paganism in the Roman Empire*. New Haven, Conn.: Yale University Press, 1981.
MacRae, George W. "The Jewish Background of the Gnostic Sophia Myth." *NovT* 12 (1970): 86–101.
Maier, Harry O. *Picturing Paul in Empire: Imperial Image, Text and Persuasion in Colossians, Ephesians and the Pastoral Epistles*. London: Bloomsbury, 2013.
Malone, Andrew. *Knowing Jesus in the Old Testament? A Fresh Look at Christophanies*. Nottingham, U.K.: InterVarsity, 2015.
Marchal, Joseph A. "Expecting a Hymn, Encountering an Argument: Introducing the Rhetoric of Philippians and Pauline Interpretation." *Int* 61 (2007): 245–55.
Marcovich, Miroslav. "The Naassene Psalm in Hippolytus." Pages 80–88 in *Studies in Graeco-Roman Religions and Gnosticism*. Leiden: Brill, 1988.
Markschies, Christoph. "Gnosis/Gnostizismus." Pages 1045–49 in *RGG*, vol. 3. Tübingen: Mohr Siebeck, 2000.
———. "'Sessio ad dexteram': Bemerkungen zu einem altchristlichen Bekenntnismotiv in der christologischen Diskussion der altkirchlichen Theologen." Pages 252–317 in *Le Trône de Dieu*. Edited by Marc Philonenko. WUNT 69. Tübingen: Mohr Siebeck, 1993.

Martin, Dale B. "Paul and the Judaism/Hellenism Dichotomy: Toward a Social History of the Question." Pages 29–61 in *Paul beyond the Judaism/Hellenism Divide*. Edited by Troels Engberg-Pedersen. Louisville, Ky.: Westminster John Knox, 2001.

Martin, Michael Wade, and Bryan A. Nash. "Philippians 2:6–11 as Subversive *Hymnos*: A Study in the Light of Ancient Rhetorical Theory." *JTS* 66 (2015): 90–138.

Mauser, Ulrich. "One God and Trinitarian Language in the Letters of Paul." *HBT* 20 (1998): 99–108.

McDonough, Sean M. *Christ as Creator: Origins of a New Testament Doctrine*. Oxford: Oxford University Press, 2009.

McFadden, Susanna. "Picturing Power in Late Roman Egypt: The Imperial Cult, Imperial Portraits, and a Visual Panegyric." Pages 135–53 in *Art of Empire: The Roman Frescoes and Imperial Cult Chamber in Luxor Temple*. Edited by Michael Jones and Susanna McFadden. New Haven, Conn.: Yale University Press, 2015.

McGrath, James F. *The Only True God: Early Christian Monotheism in Its Jewish Context*. Urbana: University of Illinois Press, 2009.

McHugh, John. *John 1–4*. ICC. London: Bloomsbury, 2014.

McLaren, James S. "Jews and the Imperial Cult: From Augustus to Domitian." *JSNT* 27 (2005): 257–78.

Meeks, Wayne A. "The Divine Agent and His Counterfeit in Philo and the Fourth Gospel." Pages 43–67 in *Aspects of Religious Propaganda in Judaism and Early Christianity*. Edited by Elisabeth Schüssler Fiorenza. Notre Dame, Ind.: University of Notre Dame Press, 1976.

———. "Judaism, Hellenism, and the Birth of Christianity." Pages 17–27 in *Paul beyond the Judaism/Hellenism Divide*. Edited by Troels Engberg-Pedersen. Louisville, Ky.: Westminster John Knox, 2001.

———. *The Prophet-King: Moses Traditions and the Johannine Christology*. NovTSup 14. Leiden: Brill, 1967.

Meyer, Nicholas A. *Adam's Dust and Adam's Glory in the Hodayot and the Letters of Paul: Rethinking Anthropogony and Theology*. NovTSup 168. Leiden: Brill, 2016.

Miller, Ed L. "The Logos of Heraclitus: Updating the Report." *HTR* 74 (1980): 161–76.

Mitchell, Stephen. *Anatolia: Land, Men and Gods in Asia Minor*. 2 vols. Oxford: Clarendon, 1993.

Mitchell, Stephen, and Peter van Nuffelen, eds. *Monotheism between Pagans and Christians in Late Antiquity*. Leuven: Peeters, 2010.

———, eds. *One God: Pagan Monotheism in the Roman Empire*. Cambridge: Cambridge University Press, 2010.

Mock, Theron Clay, III. "'New Testament Christology': A Critique of Larry Hurtado's Influence." Unpublished paper presented at the Redescribing Christian Origins Seminar, Society of Biblical Literature. San Antonio, Tex., November 21, 2021.

Momigliano, Arnaldo. *On Pagans, Jews, and Christians*. Middletown, Conn.: Wesleyan University Press, 1987.

Moss, Candida R. *The Other Christs: Imitating Jesus in Ancient Christian Ideologies*. Oxford: Oxford University Press, 2012.

Moule, C. F. D. "The Borderlands of Ontology in the New Testament." In *The Philosophical Frontiers of Christian Theology*, ed. Brian Hebblethwaite and Stewart Sutherland, 1–11. Cambridge: Cambridge University Press, 1977.

———. *The Origins of Christology*. Cambridge: Cambridge University Press, 1977.

Moxnes, Halvor. "God and His Angel in the Shepherd of Hermas." *ST* 28 (1974): 49–56.

Müller, Mogens. *The First Bible of the Church: A Plea for the Septuagint*. JSOTSup 206. Sheffield: Sheffield Academic Press, 2006.

Murphy, Roland E. "The Personification of Wisdom." Pages 222–33 in *Wisdom in Ancient Israel*. Edited by John Day. Cambridge: Cambridge University Press, 1995.

Murray, John C. *The Problem of God: Yesterday and Today*. New Haven, Conn.: Yale University Press, 1964.

Mutschler, Bernhard. *Das Corpus Johanneum bei Irenäus von Lyon: Studien und Kommentar zum dritten Buch von Adversus Haereses*. Tübingen: Mohr Siebeck, 2006.

———. *Irenäus als johanneischer Theologe: Studien zur Schriftauslegung bei Irenäus von Lyon*. Tübingen: Mohr Siebeck, 2004.

———. "John and His Gospel in the Mirror of Irenaeus of Lyons: Perspectives of Recent Research." Pages 319–43 in *The Legacy of John: Second-Century Reception of the Fourth Gospel*. Edited by Tuomas Rasimus. NovTSup 132. Leiden: Brill, 2010.

Neyrey, Jerome H. *Render to God: New Testament Understandings of the Divine*. Minneapolis: Fortress, 2004.

Nickelsburg, George W. E. *Ancient Judaism and Christian Origins: Diversity, Continuity, and Transformation*. Minneapolis: Fortress, 2003.

Nickelsburg, George W. E., and James C. VanderKam. *1 Enoch 2: A Commentary on the Book of 1 Enoch, Chapters 37–82*. Hermeneia. Minneapolis: Fortress, 2012.

Nilsson, M. P. "The High God and the Mediator." *HTR* 56 (1963): 101–20.

Nock, A. D. *Cambridge History: 10, Augustan Empire 44 B.C.–A.D. 70*. Edited by F. E. Adcock, J. B. Bury, M. P. Charlesworth, N. H. Baynes, and S. A. Cook. Cambridge: Cambridge University Press, 1934.

Norden, Eduard. *Agnostos Theos: Untersuchungen zur Formengeschichte religiöser Rede*. Leipzig: Teubner, 1923.

Novenson, Matthew V. *Christ among the Messiahs: Christ Language in Paul and Messiah Language in Ancient Judaism*. Oxford: Oxford University Press, 2012.

———. *The Grammar of Messianism: An Ancient Jewish Political Idiom and Its Users*. Oxford: Oxford University Press, 2017.

———. "Introduction." Pages 1–31 in *Monotheism and Christology in Greco-Roman Antiquity*. Edited by Matthew V. Novenson. Leiden: Brill, 2020.

———. "A Novel Argument for the Divinity of Christ in Paul." *ExpT* 124 (2013): 619.
Oakes, Peter. *Philippians: From People to Letter.* SNTSMS 110. Cambridge: Cambridge University Press, 2001.
———. *Reading Romans in Pompeii: Paul's Letter at Ground Level.* Minneapolis: Fortress, 2013.
O'Brien, Carl Séan. *The Demiurge in Ancient Thought: Secondary Gods and Divine Mediators.* Cambridge: Cambridge University Press, 2015.
O'Donnell, James J. *Pagans: The End of Traditional Religion and the Rise of Christianity.* New York: Ecco, 2016.
Opsomer, Jan. "Demiurges in Early Imperial Platonism." Pages 51–99 in *Gott und die Götter bei Plutarch: Götterbilder—Gottesbilder—Weltbilder.* Edited by Rainer Hirsch-Luipold. RVV 54. Berlin: de Gruyter, 2005.
Orlov, Andrei A. *Dark Mirrors: Azazel and Satanael in Early Jewish Demonology.* Albany, N.Y.: State University of New York Press, 2014.
———. *Demons of Change: Antagonism and Apotheosis in Jewish and Christian Apocalypticism.* Albany, N.Y.: State University of New York Press, 2020.
———. *The Enoch-Metatron Tradition.* TSAJ 107. Tübingen: Mohr Siebeck, 2005.
———. *The Glory of the Invisible God: Two Powers in Heaven and Early Christology.* London: T&T Clark, 2019.
———. *The Greatest Mirror: Heavenly Counterparts in Jewish Pseudepigrapha.* New York: State University of New York Press, 2017.
———. *Yahoel and Metatron: Aural Apocalypticism and the Origins of Jewish Mysticism.* TSAJ 69. Tübingen: Mohr Siebeck, 2017.
Osborn, Eric F. *The Emergence of Christian Theology.* Cambridge: Cambridge University Press, 1993.
———. *Irenaeus of Lyons.* Cambridge: Cambridge University Press, 2001.
———. *Justin Martyr.* BZHT 47. Tübingen: Mohr Siebeck, 1973.
Osiek, Carolyn. *Philippians, Philemon.* Nashville: Abingdon, 2000.
———. *The Shepherd of Hermas.* Hermeneia. Minneapolis: Fortress, 1999.
Pagels, Elaine. *The Johannine Gospel in Gnostic Exegesis: Heracleon's Commentary on John.* SBLMS 17. Nashville: Abingdon, 1973.
Paget, James Carleton. "The Definition of 'Jewish Christian/Jewish Christianity' in the History of Research." Pages 22–52 in *A History of Jewish Believers in Christ from Antiquity to the Present.* Edited by Reidar Hvalvik and Oskar Skarsaune. Peabody, Mass.: Hendrickson, 2006.
Peppard, Michael. "'Poetry,' 'Hymns' and 'Traditional Material' in New Testament Epistles or How to Do Things with Indentations." *JSNT* 30 (2008): 322–27.
———. "Son of God in Gentile Contexts." Pages 135–57 in *Son of God: Divine Sonship in Jewish and Christian Antiquity.* Edited by Garrick V. Allen, Kai Akagi, Paul Sloan, and Madhavi Nevader. University Park, Penn.: Eisenbrauns, 2019.
———. *The Son of God in the Roman World: Divine Sonship in Its Social and Political Context.* Oxford: Oxford University Press, 2012.

———. *The World's Oldest Church: Bible, Art and Ritual and Dura-Europos, Syria.* New Haven, Conn.: Yale University Press, 2016.
Pierce, Madison N. "Hebrews 1 and the Son Begotten 'Today.'" Pages 117–31 in *Retrieving Eternal Generation.* Edited by F. Sanders and S. R. Swain. Grand Rapids: Zondervan, 2017.
Poirier, Paul-Hubert. "The *Trimorphic Protennoia* (NHC XIII,I) and the Johannine Prologue: A Reconsideration." Pages 93–103 in *The Legacy of John: Second-Century Reception of the Fourth Gospel.* Edited by Tuomas Rasimus. NovTSup 132. Leiden: Brill, 2010.
Porter, Barbara N., ed. *One God or Many? Concepts of Divinity in the Ancient World.* Chebeague, Maine: Casco Bay Assyriological Institute, 2000.
Price, S. R. F. "Gods and Emperors: The Greek Language of the Roman Imperial Cult." *JHS* 104 (1984): 79–95.
———. *Rituals and Power: The Roman Imperial Cult in Asia Minor.* Cambridge: Cambridge University Press, 1984.
Putthoff, Tyson L. *God and Humans in the Ancient Near East.* Cambridge: Cambridge University Press, 2020.
Rasimus, Tuomas, ed. *The Legacy of John: Second-Century Reception of the Fourth Gospel.* NovTSup 132. Leiden: Brill, 2010.
———. "Ptolemaeus and the Valentinian Exegesis of John's Prologue." Pages 145–71 in *The Legacy of John: Second-Century Reception of the Fourth Gospel.* Edited by Tuomas Rasimus. NovTSup 132. Leiden: Brill, 2010.
Reasoner, Mark. *Roman Imperial Texts: A Sourcebook.* Minneapolis: Fortress, 2013.
Reinhartz, Adele. "'And the Word Was God': John's Christology and Jesus' Discourse in Jewish Context." Pages 69–91 in *Reading the Gospel of John's Christology as Jewish Messianism.* Edited by Benjamin Reynolds and Gabriele Boccaccini. AJEC 106. Leiden: Brill, 2018.
Reiterer, Friedrich V., Tobias Nicklas, and Karin Schöpflin, eds. *Angels: The Concept of Celestial Beings: Origins, Development and Reception.* Berlin: de Gruyter, 2007.
Reumann, John. "Resurrection in Philippi and Paul's Letter(s) to the Philippians." Pages 407–22 in *Resurrection in the New Testament.* Edited by R. Bieringer, V. Koperski, and B. Lataire. Leuven: University of Leuven Press, 2002.
Reynolds, Benjamin E. "Logos." Pages 523–26 in *Dictionary of Jesus and the Gospels.* Edited by J. B. Green, J. K. Brown, and N. Perrin. Downers Grove, Ill.: InterVarsity, 2013.
———. "The Parables of Enoch and Revelation 1:1–20: Daniel's Son of Man." Pages 19–36 in *Reading Revelation in Context.* Edited by Ben Blackwell, John Goodrich, and Jason Maston. Grand Rapids: Zondervan, 2019.
Richardson, Peter. *Herod: King of the Jews and Friend of the Romans.* Minneapolis: Fortress, 1999.
Rives, James B. *Religion in the Roman Empire.* Oxford: Blackwell, 2007.
Robinson, James. "Sethians and Johannine Thought: The Trimorphic Protennoia and the Prologue of the Gospel of John." Pages 643–62 in *The Rediscovery of Gnosticism: Proceedings of the International Conference on Gnosticism at Yale,*

New Haven, Connecticut, March 28–31, 1978, vol. 2: *Sethian Gnosticism*. Edited by Bentley Layton. Leiden: Brill, 1981.

Rocca, Samuel. *Herod's Judaea: A Mediterranean State in the Classical World*. TSAJ 122. Tübingen: Mohr Siebeck, 2008.

Römer, Thomas. "From the Call of Moses to the Parting of the Sea: Reflections on the Priestly Version of the Exodus Narrative." Pages 121–50 in *The Book of Exodus: Composition, Reception, and Interpretation*. Edited by Thomas Dozeman, Craig A. Evans, and Joel N. Lohr. Leiden: Brill, 2014.

Rowe, C. Kavin. *Early Narrative Christology: The Lord in the Gospel of Luke*. Berlin: de Gruyter, 2006.

Rowland, Christopher. *The Open Heaven: A Study of Apocalyptic Judaism and Early Christianity*. London: SPCK, 1982.

Rubin, Benjamin B. *(Re)presenting Empire: The Roman Imperial Cult in Asia Minor, 31 BC–AD 68*. PhD dissertation. University of Michigan, 2008.

Runia, David T. "God and Man in Philo of Alexandria," *JTS* 39 (1988): 48–75.

———. "Logos." Pages 525–31 in *Dictionary of Deities and Demons in the Bible*. Edited by Karel van der Toorn, Bob Becking, and Pieter W. van der Horst. Grand Rapids: Eerdmans, 1999.

———. *Philo of Alexandria and the* Timaeus *of Plato*. Leiden: Brill, 1986.

———. "Philo, *Quaestiones in Genesim* 2.62 and the Problem of Deutero-theology." Pages 259–69 in *Armenian, Hittite and Indo-European Studies*. Edited by U. Bläsing, J. Dum-Tragut, and T. M. van Lint. Leuven: Peeters, 2019.

Sanders, James A. "Dissenting Deities and Philippians 2:1–11." *JBL* 88 (1969): 279–90.

Sanders, Joseph N. *The Fourth Gospel in the Early Church: Its Origin and Influence on Christian Theology up to Irenaeus*. Cambridge: Cambridge University Press, 1943.

Schaper, Joachim. *Media and Monotheism: Presence, Representation, and Abstraction in Ancient Judah*. ORA 33. Tübingen: Mohr Siebeck, 2019.

Schedtler, Justin J. "Praising Christ the King: Royal Discourse and Ideology in Revelation 5." *NovT* 60 (2017): 1–21.

Scheid, John. "Hierarchy and Structure in Roman Polytheism: Roman Methods of Conceiving Action." Pages 164–89 in *Roman Religion*. Edited by Clifford Ando. Edinburgh: Edinburgh University Press, 2003.

Schimanowski, Gottfried. *Weisheit und Messias. Die jüdischen Voraussetzungen der urchristlichen Präexistenzchristologie*. WUNT 2.17. Tübingen: Mohr Siebeck, 1985.

Schmidt, Thomas E. "Mark 15.16–32: The Crucifixion Narrative and the Roman Triumphal Procession." *NTS* 41 (1995): 1–18.

Schmidt, Werner H. *The Faith of the Old Testament*. Oxford: Blackwell, 1983.

Schnabel, Eckhard. *Law and Wisdom from Ben Sira to Paul*. WUNT 2.16. Tübingen: Mohr Siebeck, 1985.

Schnelle, Udo. *Apostle Paul: His Life and Theology*. Grand Rapids: Baker, 2005.

———. "Philosophische Interpretation des Johannesevangeliums: Voraussetzungen, Methoden und Perspektiven." Pages 159–87 in *The Prologue of the Gospel of John: Its Literary, Theological, and Philosophical Contexts.* Edited by Jan G. van der Watt, R. Alan Culpepper, and Udo Schnelle. WUNT 359. Tübingen: Mohr Siebeck, 2016.

Schrage, Wolfgang. *Unterwegs zur Einheit und Einzigkeit Gottes: Zum "Monotheismus" des Paulus and seiner alttestamentlich-frühjüdischen Tradition.* Neukirchen-Vluyn: Neukirchener, 2002.

Schröter, Jens, Reimund Bieringer, Joseph Verheyden, and Ines Jäger, eds. *Docetism in the Early Church.* Tübingen: Mohr Siebeck, 2018.

Schüssler Fiorenza, Elisabeth. "Wisdom Mythology and the Christological Hymns of the New Testament." Pages 17–41 in *Aspects of Wisdom in Judaism and Early Christianity.* Edited by Robert L. Wilken. Notre Dame, Ind.: University of Notre Dame Press, 1975.

Schwartz, Daniel R. *Studies in the Jewish Background of Christianity.* Tübingen: Mohr Siebeck, 1992.

Scroggs, Robin. *The Last Adam: A Study in Pauline Anthropology.* Philadelphia: Fortress, 1966.

Seeley, David. "The Background of the Philippian Hymn (2:6–11)." *JHC* 1 (1994): 49–72.

Segal, Alan F. "Heavenly Ascent in Hellenistic Judaism, Early Christianity and Their Environment." *ANRW* 23.2: 1333–94. Edited by Wolfgang Haase. Berlin: de Gruyter, 1980.

———. *Two Powers in Heaven: Early Rabbinic Reports about Christianity and Gnosticism.* Leiden: Brill, 1977.

Shepherd, Michael B. "Daniel 7:13 and the New Testament Son of Man." *WTJ* 68 (2006): 99–111.

Siegert, Folker. "Der Logos, 'älterer Sohn' des Schöpfers und 'zweiter Gott': Philons Logos und der Johannesprolog." Pages 277–93 in *Kontexte des Johannesevangeliums: Das vierte Evangelium in religions- und traditionsgeschichtlicher Perspektive.* Edited by Jörg Frey and Udo Schnelle. WUNT 175. Tübingen: Mohr Siebeck, 2004.

Skarsaune, Oskar. "The Development of Scriptural Interpretation in the Second and Third Centuries—Except Clement and Origen." Pages 373–442 in *Hebrew Bible/Old Testament: The History of Its Interpretation*, vol. 1: *From the Beginnings to the Middle Ages.* Edited by Magne Sabe. Göttingen: Vandenhoeck & Ruprecht, 1997.

———. "The Ebionites." Pages 419–62 in *A History of Jewish Believers in Christ from Antiquity to the Present.* Edited by Reidar Hvalvik and Oskar Skarsaune. Peabody, Mass.: Hendrickson, 2006.

———. "Is Christianity Monotheistic? Patristic Perspectives on a Jewish/Christian Debate." *Patristic Studies* 29 (1997): 340–63.

Smith, Brandon D. *Vision of the Triune God: Reading Revelation through the Father, Son, and Holy Spirit.* PhD dissertation. Australian College of Theology, 2021.

———. "What Christ Does, God Does: Surveying Recent Scholarship on Christological Monotheism." *CBR* 17 (2019): 184–208.
Smith, Ian K. *Heavenly Perspective: A Study of the Apostle Paul's Response to a Jewish Mystical Movement at Colossae*. LNTS 326. London: T&T Clark, 2006.
Smith, Mark S. *The Origins of Biblical Monotheism: Israel's Polytheistic Background and the Ugaritic Texts*. Oxford: Oxford University Press, 2001.
Sommer, Benjamin D. *The Bodies of God and the World of Ancient Israel*. New York: Cambridge University Press, 2009.
Steenburg, David. "The Case against Synonymity of *Morphē* and *Eikōn*." *JSNT* 34 (1988): 77–86.
———. "Worship of Adam and Christ as the Image of God." *JSNT* 39 (1990): 77–93.
Sterling, Gregory. "Prepositional Metaphysics in Jewish Wisdom Speculation and Early Christian Liturgical Texts." *Studio Philonica Annual* 9 (1997): 219–38.
Stoll, Oliver. *Excubatio ad Signa: Die Wache bei den Fahnen in der römischen Armee und andere Beiträge zur kulturgeschichtlichen und historischen Bedeutung eines militärischen Symbols*. St. Katharinen: Scripta Mercaturae, 1995.
Strelan, Rick. "The Languages of the Lycus Valley." Pages 77–103 in *Colossae in Space and Time: Linking to an Ancient City*. Edited by Alan H. Cadwallader and Michael Trainor. Gottingen: Vandenhoeck & Ruprecht, 2011.
———. "'We Hear Them Telling in Our Own Tongues the Mighty Works of God' (Acts 2:11)." *NeoT* 40 (2006): 295–319.
Stroumsa, Gedaliahu. "Form(s) of God: Some Notes on Metatron and Christ." *HTR* 76 (1983): 269–88.
Stuckenbruck, Loren T. *Angel Veneration and Christology: A Study in Early Judaism and in the Christology of the Apocalypse of John*. Waco, Tex.: Baylor University Press, 2017.
———. "The Apocalypse of John, 1 Enoch, and the Question of Influence." Pages 190–234 in *Die Johannesapokalypse: Kontexte—Konzepte—Rezeption*. Edited by J. Frey, J. Kelhoffer, and F. Tóth. WUNT 287. Tübingen: Mohr Siebeck, 2012.
———. "'One Like a Son of Man as the Ancient of Days' in the Old Greek Recension of Daniel 7, 13: Scribal Error or Theological Translation?" *ZNW* 86 (1995): 268–76.
Stuckenbruck, Loren T., and Gabriele Boccaccini, eds. *Enoch and the Synoptic Gospels: Reminiscences, Allusions, Intertextuality*. Atlanta: SBL, 2016.
Sullivan, Kevin P. *Wrestling with Angels: A Study of the Relationship between Angels and Humans in Ancient Jewish Literature and the New Testament*. Leiden: Brill, 2004.
Svigel, Michael J. "Trinitarianism in *Didache*, *Barnabas*, and the *Shepherd*: Sketchy, Scant, or Scandalous?" *Perichoresis* 17 (2019): 23–40.
Talbert, Charles H. "The Concept of Immortals in Mediterranean Antiquity." *JBL* 94 (1975): 419–36.
———. *The Development of Christology during the First Hundred Years: And Other Essays on Early Christology*. Leiden: Brill, 2011.

———. "The Myth of a Descending-Ascending Redeemer in Mediterranean Antiquity." *NTS* 22 (1976): 418–40.

Taylor, Joan E. "Pontius Pilate and the Imperial Cult in Roman Judaea." *NTS* 52 (2006): 552–82.

Taylor, Lily Ross. *The Divinity of the Roman Emperor*. New York: Arno, 1975.

Teixidor, Javier. *The Pagan God: Popular Religion in the Graeco-Roman Near East*. Princeton, N.J.: Princeton University Press, 1977.

Tellbe, Mikael. *Paul between Synagogue and State: Christians, Jews, and Civic Authorities in 1 Thessalonians, Romans, and Philippians*. ConBNT 34. Stockholm: Almqvist & Wiksell, 2001.

Theobald, Michael. *Das Evangelium nach Johannes: Kapital 1–12*. Regensburg: Friedrich Pustet, 2009.

———. *Fleischwerdung des Logos: Studien zum Verhältnis des Johannes prologus zum Corpus des Evangeliums and zu 1 Joh*. Münster: Ascendorff, 1988.

Thompson, Marianne Meye. *The God of the Gospel of John*. Grand Rapids: Eerdmans, 2001.

Tilling, Chris. "Misreading Paul's Christology: Problems with Ehrman's Exegesis." Pages 134–50 in *How God Became Jesus: The Real Origins of Belief in Jesus' Divine Nature*. Edited by Michael F. Bird. Grand Rapids: Zondervan, 2014.

———. *Paul's Divine Christology*. Grand Rapids: Eerdmans, 2012.

Tobin, Thomas H. "Logos." *ABD* 4:348–56. Edited by David Noel Freedman. New York: Doubleday, 1992.

———. "Logos." Pages 894–96 in *The Eerdmans Dictionary of Early Judaism*. Edited by John J. Collins and Daniel C. Harlow. Grand Rapids: Eerdmans, 2010.

———. "The Prologue of John in Hellenistic Jewish Speculation." *CBQ* 52 (1990): 252–69.

Tomas, Julia Margaret. *Variation in Representation through Architectural Benefaction under Roman Rule: Five Cases from the Province of Asia c. 40 B.C.–A.D. 68*. PhD dissertation. Durham University, 2020.

Toom, Tarmo. *Classical Trinitarian Theology: A Textbook*. London: T&T Clark, 2007.

Toynbee, J. M. C. "Ruler-Apotheosis in Ancient Rome." *Numismatics Chronicle* 7 (1947): 126–27.

Turner, John D. "The Johannine Legacy: The Gospel and *Apocryphon* of John." Pages 105–44 in *The Legacy of John: Second-Century Reception of the Fourth Gospel*. Edited by Tuomas Rasimus. NovTSup 132. Leiden: Brill, 2010.

van der Horst, Pieter W. "Moses' Throne Vision in Ezekiel the Dramatist." *JJS* 34 (1983): 21–29.

van der Watt, Jan G., R. Alan Culpepper, and Udo Schnelle, eds. *The Prologue of the Gospel of John: Its Literary, Theological, and Philosophical Contexts*. WUNT 359. Tübingen: Mohr Siebeck, 2016.

van Kooten, George H. "Image, Form and Transformation. A Semantic Taxonomy of Paul's 'Morphic' Language." Pages 213–42 in *Jesus, Paul and Early Christianity*. Edited by Rieuwerd Buitenwerf, Harm W. Hollander, and Johannes Tromp. NovTSup 130. Leiden: Brill, 2008.

———. "The Last Days of Socrates and Christ: *Euthyphro, Apology, Crito,* and *Phaedo* Read in Counterpoint with John's Gospel." Pages 219–43 in *Religiophilosophical Discourses in the Mediterranean World: From Plato, through Jesus, to Late Antiquity*. Edited by Anders Klostergaard Petersen and George van Kooten. Leiden: Brill, 2017.

———. *Paul's Anthropology in Context: The Image of God, Assimilation to God, and Tripartite Man in Ancient Judaism, Ancient Philosophy and Early Christianity*. WUNT 232. Tübingen: Mohr Siebeck, 2008.

———. "The Sign of Socrates, the Sign of Apollo, and the Signs of Christ: Hiding and Sharing Religious Knowledge in the Gospel of John; A Contrapuntal Reading of John's Gospel and Plato's Dialogues." Pages 145–70 in *Sharing and Hiding Religious Knowledge in Early Judaism, Christianity, and Islam*. Edited by M. Popovic, L. R. Lanzillotta, and C. Wilde. Berlin: de Gruyter, 2018.

Van Riel, Gerd. "Theology and Religiosity in the Greek Pagan Tradition." Pages 93–118 in *The Origins of New Testament Theology*. Edited by Rainer Hirsch-Luipold and Robert Matthew Calhoun. WUNT 440. Tübingen: Mohr Siebeck, 2020.

van Roon, Aart. "The Relationship between Christ and the Wisdom of God according to Paul." *NovT* 16 (1974): 207–39.

Vermes, Geza. *Christian Beginnings: From Nazareth to Nicaea*. New Haven, Conn.: Yale University Press, 2012.

Vernsel, H. S. *Triumphus: An Inquiry into the Origin, Development and Meaning of the Roman Triumph*. Leiden: Brill, 1970.

Vollenweider, Samuel. "Politische Theologie im Philipperbrief?" Pages 457–69 in *Paulus und Johannes*. WUNT 198. Tübingen: Mohr Siebeck, 2006.

———. "Vom israelitischen zum christologischen Monotheismus. Überlegungen zum Verhältnis zwischen dem Glauben an den einen Gott und dem Glauben an Jesus Christus." Pages 123–33 in *Antike und Urchristentum: Studien zur neutestamentlichen Theologie in ihren Kontexten und Rezeptionen*. WUNT 436. Tübingen: Mohr Siebeck, 2020.

———. "Zwischen Monotheismus und Engelchristologie: Überlegungen zur Frühgeschichte des Christusglaubens." *ZTK* 99 (2002): 21–44.

Waddell, James A. *The Messiah: A Comparative Study of the Enochic Son of Man and the Pauline Kyrios*. London: T&T Clark, 2011.

Wasserman, Emma. *Apocalypse as Holy War: Divine Politics and Polemics in the Letters of Paul*. New Haven, Conn.: Yale University Press, 2018.

Wasserman, Tommy. *The Epistle of Jude: Its Text and Transmission*. CBNTS 43. Stockholm: Almqvist & Wiksell, 2006.

Weima, Jeffrey A. D. *Neglected Endings: The Significance of the Pauline Letter Closings*. JSNTSup 101. Sheffield: JSOT Press, 1994.

Weiss, H.-F. *Untersuchungen zur Kosmologie des hellenistischen und palästinischen Judentums*. Berlin: Akademie Verlag, 1966.

Wenkel, David. *Jesus the Dayspring: The Sunrise and Visitation of Israel's Messiah*. NTM 43. Sheffield: Sheffield Phoenix, 2021.

Werner, Martin. *The Formation of Christian Dogma.* Boston: Beacon, 1965.
White, John L. *The Apostle of God: Paul and the Promise of Abraham.* Peabody, Mass.: Hendrickson, 1999.
Whittle, Sarah. "'Declared to Be Son of God in Power': Romans 1:4 and the Iconography of Imperial Apotheosis." Pages 158–70 in *Son of God: Divine Sonship in Jewish and Christian Antiquity.* Edited by Garrick V. Allen, Kai Akagi, Paul Sloan, and Madhavi Nevader. University Park, Penn.: Eisenbrauns, 2019.
Williams, Logan A. *Love, Self-Gift, and the Incarnation: Christology and Ethics in Galatians, in the Context of Pauline Theology and Greco-Roman Philosophy.* PhD dissertation. Durham University, 2020.
Williams, Michael A. *Rethinking "Gnosticism": An Argument for Dismantling a Dubious Category.* Princeton, N.J.: Princeton University Press, 1999.
Wilson, Robert McL. "Philo and the Fourth Gospel." *ExpT* 65 (1953–1954): 47–49.
Wilson, Stephen G. *Leaving the Fold: Apostates and Defectors in Antiquity.* Minneapolis: Fortress, 2004.
Windisch, Hans. "Die göttliche Weisheit der Juden und die paulinische Christologie." Pages 220–34 in *Neutestamentliche Studien.* Edited by Adolf Deissmann. Leipzig: Hinrichs, 1914.
Winn, Adam. *Reading Mark's Christology under Caesar: Jesus the Messiah and Roman Imperial Ideology.* Downers Grove, Ill.: InterVarsity, 2018.
Winter, Bruce W. *Divine Honours for the Caesars: The First Christians' Responses.* Grand Rapids: Eerdmans, 2015.
Witherington, Ben. *Jesus the Sage: The Pilgrimage of Wisdom.* Minneapolis: Fortress, 1994.
Wright, Archie T. "Angels." Pages 328–31 in *The Eerdmans Dictionary of Early Judaism.* Edited by John J. Collins and Daniel C. Harlow. Grand Rapids: Eerdmans, 2010.
———. *The Origin of Evil Spirits.* Tübingen: Mohr Siebeck, 2005.
Wright, N. T. *The Climax of the Covenant: Christ and the Law in Pauline Theology.* Edinburgh: T&T Clark, 1991.
———. *The New Testament and the People of God.* COQG 1. London: SPCK, 1992.
———. "Paul and Caesar: A New Reading of Romans." Pages 237–54 in *Pauline Perspectives: Essays on Paul, 1978–2013.* London: SPCK, 2013.
———. *Paul and the Faithfulness of God.* COQG 4. London: SPCK, 2014.
———. *Resurrection of the Son of God.* COQG 2. London: SPCK, 2003.
———. "Son of God and Christian Origins." Pages 118–34 in *Son of God: Divine Sonship in Jewish and Christian Antiquity.* Edited by Garrick V. Allen, Kai Akagi, Paul Sloan, and Madhavi Nevader. University Park, Penn.: Eisenbrauns, 2019.
Yeago, David S. "The New Testament and the Nicene Dogma: A Contribution to the Recovery of Theological Exegesis." *STR* 45 (2002): 379–80.
Young, Frances M. "Monotheism and Christology." Pages 452–69 in *The Cambridge History of Christianity: Origins to Constantine.* Edited by Margaret M. Mitchell and Frances M. Young. Cambridge: Cambridge University Press, 2006.

———. "Prelude." Pages 1–34 in *The Cambridge History of Christianity: Origins to Constantine*. Edited by Margaret M. Mitchell and Frances M. Young. Cambridge: Cambridge University Press, 2006.

———. "Two Roots or a Tangled Mess?" Pages 87–121 in *The Myth of God Incarnate*. Edited by John Hick. Philadelphia: Westminster, 1977.

Zacharias, H. Daniel. "Old Greek Daniel 7:13–14 and Matthew's Son of Man." *BBR* 21 (2011): 453–61.

Zanker, Paul. *The Power of Images in the Age of Augustus*. Ann Arbor: University of Michigan Press, 1988.

Zeev, Pucci ben. *Jewish Rights in the Roman World: The Greek and Roman Documents Quoted by Josephus Flavius*. Tübingen: Mohr Siebeck, 1998.

Zehnder, Markus. "The Question of the 'Divine Status' of the Davidic Messiah." *BBR* 30 (2020): 485–514.

———. "Why the Danielic 'Son of Man' Is a Divine Being." *BBR* 24 (2014): 331–47.

Zeller, Dieter. "Die Menschwerdung des Sohnes Gottes im Neuen Testament und die antike Religionsgeschichichte." Pages 141–76 in *Menschwerdung Gottes—Vergöttlichung von Menschen*. Göttingen: Vandenhoeck & Ruprecht, 1988.

———. "New Testament Christology in Its Hellenistic Reception." *NTS* 46 (2001): 312–33.

Zelyck, Lorne R. *John among the Other Gospels: The Reception of the Fourth Gospel in the Extra-canonical Gospels*. WUNT 2.347. Tübingen: Mohr Siebeck, 2013.

Zevit, Ziony. "Israel's Royal Cult in the Ancient Near Eastern *Kulturkreis*." Pages 189–200 in *Text, Artifact, and Image*. Edited by Gary M. Beckman and Theodore J. Lewis. Providence, R.I.: Brown Judaic Studies, 2006.

Zwiep, A. W. "Assumptus est in caelum: Rapture and Heavenly Exaltation in Early Judaism and Luke-Acts." Pages 323–50 in *Auferstehung-Resurrection: Resurrection, Transfiguration and Exaltation in Old Testament, Ancient Judaism and Early Christianity*. Edited by Friedrich Avemarie and Hermann Lichtenberger. WUNT 135. Tübingen: Mohr Siebeck, 2001.

Index of Modern Authors

Abegg, Martin G., 201n211
Akerman, Susan, 25n37
Albani, Matthias, 197n201
Alexander, Philip S., 398n41, 399n44, 399n46
Allen, Garrick V., 209–10n237, 265n398, 266n402, 299n493, 321n537, 355n652, 402n53, 406n62
Anderson, James S., 25n36
Anderson, Paul, 137n51
Argyle, A. W., 164n126
Asale, Bruk Ayele, 279–80n445
Assman, Jan, 25n38, 49n22
Athanassiadi, Polymnia, 23–24n34
Atkins, Christopher S., 163, 163n124
Attridge, Harold W., 64n63, 69, 69n76, 165n127, 167n130, 169n136
Aune, David E., 17–18n16, 64n64, 65nn67–68, 217n255, 246, 246n332, 314, 321n538, 322n546, 323n551, 352n645, 361, 361–62nn666–67, 377n718
Ayres, Lewis, 43n5, 62n56

Badian, E., 18n17, 300nn494–95, 348nn624–25
Barbel, Joseph, 179n158, 250n346
Barclay, John M. G., 33n64, 82–83n119
Barnard, L. W., 151n96
Barrett, Anthony, 338n591, 347n622
Barrett, C. K., 82–83n119, 121n19, 127–28n30, 132n38

Bates, Matthew, 95n17, 95n19, 231n288, 403n58
Bauckham, Richard, 3, 12n3, 27–28nn48–49, 30n56, 32n63, 42, 42n3, 52n28, 60n43, 61n51, 62–63nn57–58, 64n63, 70n78, 79n112, 93–97, 93–94nn9–16, 96n20, 97n22, 105–6, 105–6nn58–60, 107, 135–36n47, 143–44, 144n75, 170n139, 175n148, 179n159, 205n223, 209n234, 211n241, 219n259, 248n338, 248n340, 249–50nn342–44, 252–53nn349–50, 258n369, 264n392, 265, 265n397, 282n449, 283n455, 287–88, 287nn467–68, 292n476, 294n480, 298, 370n686, 373–74n699, 377n715, 377n717, 385n8, 387n14
Bauer, David R., 263n387
Beale, Greg K., 65n69, 214–15, 215nn249–50
Beard, Mary, 15n6, 18n18, 19n21, 54n29, 74n88, 317n523, 357n654, 395n28
Beetham, Christopher A., 179n157
Berger, Klaus, 207n228
Bernett, Monika, 20n27, 330n571, 331–32, 331n576, 332nn578–79, 334, 334n582, 339n592
Bieringer, Reimund, 68n74, 350n632
Bird, Michael F., 21n28, 33n64, 54n29, 57n37, 68n74, 81n118, 117–18n8, 153n9, 178–79nn156–57, 198n206, 207n227, 212n244, 220n262, 231n288, 242n117,

446 Index of Modern Authors

261nn381–82, 263n387, 284n459, 325n555, 336n588, 342n603, 344n610, 358n656, 375n708, 403n58
Blömer, Michael, 20n27, 331n574
Boccaccini, Gabriele, 12n3, 30n56, 45–46, 45–46nn10–11, 46n11, 70, 70n79, 117n6, 139n55, 143n72, 170nn139–40, 181n167, 197n201, 202n215, 279–80nn444–45, 381
Bock, Darrell L., 279–80n445
Bockmuehl, Markus, 29n53, 61n51, 285–86n462
Bornhäuser, D. Karl, 352n643
Bousset, Wilhelm, 16n10, 133n41, 141n65, 151n95, 162n121, 245n330, 296, 296n485, 343, 343n605, 365n673, 373, 387, 387n15
Boyarin, Daniel, 103, 103n47, 117n6, 132n40, 169n137, 286n463, 381
Brenk, Frederick E., 64n64, 352n645
Brent, Allen, 146, 146n81
Brock, Sebastian, 389n20
Brown, J. K., 129n31
Brown, Raymond E., 38n79
Bühner, Ruben A., 12n3, 33–34, 34n67, 37n78, 46n12, 63–64, 64n62, 93n9, 114n90, 116n4, 117n7, 138n52, 140, 140nn60–61, 143n72, 170n139, 194n191, 197nn201–3, 197–98n205–6, 201, 201n212, 250n346, 271n425, 278n439, 287–88, 287n467, 288n470, 293n479, 297nn297–98, 298n491, 318n525, 319n532, 326n557, 341n596, 380n726, 384–85n7, 386–87nn10–12, 387, 407n66
Bultmann, Rudolf, 87, 89, 124n22, 127–28n30, 139, 139nn55–56, 140n62, 245n330, 343, 343n605, 373
Burnett, D. Clint, 256n362, 321n538, 322nn542–43, 323, 323n548, 323n550, 328nn563–64, 343–44, 343nn608–9, 344n611, 345nn619–20, 350n635, 351n638, 355n652, 366n676, 369n683, 375n709, 378n722

Capes, David B., 3, 11n2, 26–27n45, 60n43, 60n46, 93n9, 109n69, 254n355, 297n488, 373–74n699, 377n715, 406n63
Carrell, Peter R., 135–36n47, 168n135, 209–10n237, 216–17nn253–54, 219n259, 221–22, 221n269, 228n280, 266n404, 266n406
Carter, Craig A., 38–39n81
Casey, Maurice, 10n1, 16n10, 38–39n81, 101–3nn39–46, 101–4, 104n50, 106n61, 136–37nn47–48, 199n209, 244, 244nn323–26, 260n379, 285–86n462, 343, 343n607, 350n634, 370n689, 373–74nn699–700, 377n714, 384–85n7, 407
Chancey, Mark A., 398–99, 398nn39–42
Chaniotis, Angela, 18n17
Charlesworth, James H., 213n247, 279–80n445
Charlesworth, M. P., 54n30, 70n80
Chester, Andrew, 1n1, 42nn2–3, 62n55, 67n71, 96n20, 107–8nn65–68, 107–9, 114n89, 117–18n8, 137n49, 277n435, 278n441, 282n449, 287n467, 319n531, 320n533, 384, 384n6, 384–85n7, 393n23, 408n68
Childs, Brevard S., 35n70
Clark, David J., 34n69
Clauss, Manfred, 15, 15nn6–7, 72n87
Cohen, Shaye J. D., 27nn47–48
Cole, Spencer, 18n18, 19n22, 54n29, 353n649
Collins, Adela Yarbro, 3–4, 12n3, 17–18n16, 38n79, 60, 60n46, 109–11nn69–82, 109–12, 140n62, 213n247, 245n329, 246–47n336, 267n407, 278n439, 278n441, 287, 287n469, 297, 297nn488–90, 301n497, 320n535, 345nn618–19, 352n645, 366n675, 367n678, 368, 368n680, 378–79
Collins, John J., 12–13n4, 33n64, 34n68, 38n79, 80n113, 100–101n35, 109n71, 110nn74–75, 111nn79–82, 117–18n8, 129n31, 140n62, 175n149, 190n182, 197n204, 198, 198n207, 201n211, 201n213, 212n243, 245n329, 246–47n336, 267n407, 278n439, 278n441, 287, 287n469, 301n497, 319, 319n527, 319n532, 320n535
Cook, John G., 352n645, 352n648, 354, 354n651, 371n692
Cook, S. A., 54n30
Copenhaver, Adam, 205n224
Cotter, Wendy, 352n645
Cover, Michael B., 162n122
Cox, Ronald, 21n30
Croy, N. Clayton, 23–24n34
Cullmann, Oscar, 38n79, 139n55, 139n57, 373–74n699

Culpepper, R. Alan, 22n31, 64–65n66, 116n3, 129n35, 137n51
Dahl, Nils A., 117–18n8, 140n59
Daniélou, Jean, 221n266, 252n347, 253n350
Davidson, Maxwell J., 258n368, 270nn422–23
Davies, W. D., 140n59, 185, 185n173
de Jáuregui, Miguel Herrero, 118–19, 119n9
de Jonge, Marinus, 23n33, 60n44, 82–83n119
DeConick, April D., 11–12nn2–3, 26–27n45, 32n63, 60n43, 60n46, 109n69, 238, 238n306, 254n355, 282n488, 297n488, 406n63
Deissmann, Gustav Adolf, 177n154, 299, 311, 317, 341–42, 341n597, 342nn600–603, 360–61, 360n663
Dever, William G., 25n37
Dixon, Sarah Underwood, 268–69, 268n412
Dodd, C. H., 133n41, 139n55, 142n69, 163n123, 164n126, 181n167
Drozdek, Adam, 388n18
Dunn, James D. G., 10n1, 12n3, 89nn89–93, 90–92nn1–6, 95n17, 106n61, 133n41, 135–36n47, 138n52, 163, 163n125, 169n137, 170n140, 175n148, 175nn150–51, 177n154, 178, 180n165, 211n241, 241n314, 244n327, 245n329, 246, 246n333, 249n343, 250n346, 274–75, 275n430, 277n435, 285–86nn461–62, 344, 344n613, 370n689, 406–7

Edsall, Benjamin, 344–45n116
Edwards, Mark J., 155n102
Ehrman, Bart D., 12n3, 15n6, 43–44n6, 117–18n8, 204n217, 204nn219–20, 259, 259n374, 278–79, 279n442, 285–86n462
Eidinow, Esther, 46–47n14
Endo, Masanobu, 121n18, 133n41, 138–39nn54–55, 165n128
Engberg-Pedersen, Troels, 64, 64nn64–65, 165n127, 397n34, 398n41, 401n50
Erho, Ted, 280n446
Eskola, Timo, 37n78, 380n726, 383, 383–84nn4–5, 384, 393n23
Estrada, Rodolfo Gavan, III, 207n229

Evans, Craig A., 35n71, 133n41, 155n104, 156n107, 164n126, 169n137, 181n167, 201n211, 319n526, 320n533

Facella, Margherita, 20n27, 331n574
Fantin, Joseph D., 18n17, 19n23, 21n28, 45n8, 70n77, 75, 75nn89–90, 76n99, 300nn495–96, 303n506, 314, 338n591, 345n617, 351n638, 405n60
Fee, Gordon D., 60n47, 177–78nn154–55, 179n157, 260n375, 285–86n462, 344–45n616, 373–74n699, 374n702, 374n704
Feldman, Louis H., 398n37
Feldmeier, Reinhard, 141n63, 141n67, 261–62n383, 382, 394n26
Ferrari, Franco, 121, 121n16
Feuillet, André, 177n154
Fishwick, Duncan, 15n6, 20n24, 74n88, 301n498, 302n503, 305n514, 310, 313, 374n703
Fitzmyer, Joseph A., 343n604, 343n606, 344n611, 370n685, 373nn697–99, 375n706
Fletcher-Louis, Crispin H. T., 1n1, 3, 60n47, 95n18, 275n431, 277, 277n435, 277nn437–38, 282nn449–50, 283n452, 284nn456–57, 294n480, 298, 298n492, 325n554, 327n559, 329n565, 350n636, 369n684, 370nn688–89, 372n695, 374n700, 374n702, 383n3
Flint, P. W., 201n211
Fossum, Jarl E., 3n3, 208, 208nn232–33
Foster, Paul, 146n81
Frede, Michael, 23–24n34, 46–47n14
Fredriksen, Paula, 15n6, 26–27n45, 29n53, 43–44n6, 70n77, 84n120, 381, 394–95, 394n25
Frey, Jörg, 1n1, 3n3, 12–13n4, 20n27, 63, 63–64nn59–63, 64–65nn65–66, 116n3, 127–28n30, 129nn31–32, 133n41, 138n52, 140n60, 140n62, 144n76, 144n77, 150n91, 152, 152n98, 162–63nn122–23, 167n131, 167–68n133, 169–70nn137–39, 184n171, 187, 187n177, 264nn392–93, 286n463, 330n571, 387n12
Friesen, Steven J., 75n92, 268–69, 268n413, 361n665, 378n724
Fürst, Alfons, 23n34

Gallusz, Laszlo, 201n212, 377n716, 377nn718–19, 378n723
Garrett, Susan R., 204n217, 204n219, 211, 211n239, 226n278, 250n346, 254n353, 254n355
Gathercole, Simon J., 93n9, 176n253, 237n303, 238n305
Georgia, Allan T., 358n658
Gese, Harmut, 181n167
Gieschen, Charles, 12n3, 190, 190n181, 196, 196n198, 202n215, 204n217, 206n226, 215n249, 215n251, 216–17nn253–54, 218n257, 220nn262–63, 221n266, 265n396, 377n717
Gnuse, Robert K., 25n37
Gordley, Matthew E., 181n166, 268n414, 301n499, 344n615, 345n617
Gradel, Ittai, 15n6, 15n8, 18nn18–19, 20n25, 45n8, 49n21, 49n23, 56, 56n35, 71n82, 74–75nn88–90, 75nn92–93, 76n95, 77n103, 247n337, 303n506
Gradl, Hans-Georg, 334n583, 340, 340n593
Green, Joel B., 129n31, 241n314
Grillmeier, Aloys, 139n56, 141nn64–66, 151n96, 253n350, 274n428
Grindheim, Sigurd, 62–63n58, 117–18n8
Gripentrog, Stephanie, 20n27
Gruning, Herb, 120n12
Gundry, Robert H., 139n55, 215n249

Habets, Myk, 64n65
Habicht, Christian, 48n20, 71n81, 75n91, 305n513, 348n627
Hamerton-Kelly, R. G., 178n155
Hannah, Darrell D., 133, 133n42, 197n202, 208n233, 209n236, 217n254, 218n258, 220n262, 221n266, 221n268, 228, 228n281, 229, 229n283, 236n302, 240n309, 241nn311–12, 250n346, 252n347, 260n375, 260n378, 264, 264nn389, 264n391, 264–65nn394–95, 265n399, 266n404, 290n473, 293n477, 323n548, 377n717, 377n719
Hanson, R. P. C. (Richard P. C.), 12, 12–13n4, 38–39n81, 43n5
Harnack, Adolf von, 124n22, 252n347, 400
Harris, J. R., 181n167

Hayman, Peter, 26–27n45
Hays, Richard B., 93n9
Heen, Erik M., 71n81, 345n617, 345n620, 349, 349nn630–31, 351n642
Heilig, Christoph, 56n34, 303n505, 358n655
Heiser, Michael S., 26–27n45, 28n49, 189n179, 195n193, 197n202, 197n204
Helgeland, J., 306n519
Hellerman, Joseph H., 60n47, 345n617, 351n642
Hengel, Martin, 3, 16n9, 17n11, 61n51, 87, 89, 99, 99–101nn28–38, 100, 101, 138n52, 141n64, 144n77, 150n91, 156n108, 162n122, 171n142, 175n151, 180n165, 194n190, 220n262, 248n339, 253, 253n352, 272–73nn426–27, 274, 274n429, 279n443, 281n447, 296, 296n483, 322n547, 344, 344n612, 352, 352n646, 355, 355n653, 361n664, 365n672, 368, 368n682, 370n686, 379n725, 384–85n7, 398n37, 406n62, 408n67
Henrichs-Tarasenkova, Nina, 93n9
Herbener, Jens-André P., 26–27n45
Hill, Charles E., 144n77, 147n83, 150n91, 158n113
Hill, Wesley, 11n2, 82–83n119, 261n380, 375n705, 406n63
Hillar, Marian, 135–36n47
Hoffmann, Matthias Reinhard, 12n3, 216–17nn253–54, 266nn400–401, 266n403, 266n406, 267n408, 269nn417–18, 377nn717–18
Hofius, Otfried, 62n53
Hölbl, Günther, 301n500
Holladay, Carl R., 79n108
Holmes, Stephen R., 43n5
Hooker, M. D., 344n612
Horbury, William, 3, 15n6, 17–18n16, 43–44n6, 54n29, 54n31, 197n201, 198n206, 204n217, 204n220, 241, 241n313, 250n346, 254n354, 296, 296–97nn486–87, 297, 298, 303n506, 318n525, 324n552, 326n557, 327n560, 334n583, 337n589, 341n596, 344n611, 344n614, 365n673, 367n678, 368nn680–81, 369n683, 370, 370n687, 379, 406–7n64, 407, 407n66
Hunsinger, George, 61n51
Hunt, Laura J., 352n645, 354n650
Hurtado, Larry, 1n1, 3, 3n3, 12–13n4,

16n9, 23–24n34, 30n56, 31n58, 33n65, 42, 42n2, 79n109, 92n7, 97n22, 103n48, 104, 104–5nn51–57, 105, 106, 106n60, 106n64, 107, 108, 117–18n8, 133n41, 135n46, 135–36n47, 175n148, 195, 195nn195–97, 209n234, 211–12nn241–42, 241, 242n315, 243n321, 244–45nn327–28, 245n330, 246nn334–35, 248n338, 249nn341–43, 256, 266n401, 268n415, 283n455, 284n458, 285–86n462, 286, 287nn464–65, 287n467, 289, 289n471, 290n473, 291n475, 292, 296, 296n484, 296n486, 298, 361n664, 365, 366nn674–75, 367–68, 367–68nn678–79, 370n686, 370n688, 370–71n690, 372n695, 373n699, 378–79, 384–85n7, 392n21, 396n31, 403n57, 408, 408n68
Hvalvik, Reidar, 231n287, 232–33n291

Jäger, Ines, 68n74
Janse, Sam, 320–21nn535–36
Jefford, Clayton N., 50n24
Jensen, Robin M., 17n14
Jipp, Joshua W., 345n618
Johnson, Luke Timothy, 3–4, 4n5, 100–101n35, 304, 304n507, 352n647, 355n652, 373–74n699, 388n17, 389n19, 398n38, 400n48, 402n52, 408n67
Johnson, Peter C., 149nn88–89

Kaiser, Christopher B., 12–13n4
Keck, David, 225n277, 230–31, 230n285
Keel, Othmar, 321n541
Keener, Craig S., 132n39, 133n41, 139n55, 181n167, 184, 184n172, 185, 185n174
Kerkeslager, Allen, 106n62
Kim, Kyu Seop, 179n157
Kim, Seyoon, 171n142, 180n165, 277n434
Kindt, Julia, 46–47n14
King, Charles, 46–47n14, 124n22
Kirk, J. R. Daniel, 80n113, 95n18, 277n437, 279n442
Klauck, Hans-Josef, 17–18nn16–17, 306, 306n522
Klijn, A. F. J., 233–34, 233nn292–93, 234n295, 236n302
Knight, Jonathan, 378, 378n721
Koester, Craig R., 142n70
Koester, Helmut, 301n501
Koortbojian, Michael, 18n18, 47n17, 54n29, 72n87, 75–76, 75–76nn94–95, 247n337
Kranz, Walther, 160n118

Kratz, Reinhard G., 23n34
Krebernick, Manfred, 23n34
Kreitzer, Larry J., 82–83n119, 115–16, 115–16nn1–2, 388n16
Kropp, Andreas, 20n27, 331n574
Kunath, Friederike, 64n62, 139, 139n58, 140n60, 387n12
Kvanvig, Helge S., 279n444

Lambden, Stephen N., 276, 276n433
Lamp, Jeffrey S., 179n157
Lang, Bernhard, 25n37
Lattke, Michael, 146n82
Lau, Markus, 357n654, 358n657, 359, 359n660
Lee, Aquila H. I., 135–36n47, 170–71nn141–42, 175n148, 175n150
Lee, Max J., 120n11
Lee, Yongbom, 285–86n462
Leim, Joshua, 80n113
Leonhardt-Balzer, Jutta, 167nn131–32, 168n134
Levene, D. S., 46–47n14, 48n19, 49, 49n23, 59n42
Levine, Lee I., 397nn32–33
Lienhard, J. T., 80nn114–15
Lierman, John, 79n107
Lieu, Judith M., 127n28
Lin, Yii-Jan, 116n5
Litwa, M. David, 3–4, 3n2, 4n4, 16n10, 32n63, 54n32, 59n41, 72n84, 100–101n35, 327n558, 336n586, 351, 351nn639–40, 352n647, 371n692, 376, 376nn710–12, 382, 382n2, 386n9, 393, 393n24, 407n65
Loader, William, 181n167
Lohmeyer, Ernst, 17–18n16, 245n330, 295–96, 295–96nn481–82, 304n512, 352n644, 362n668
Loke, Andrew Ter Ern, 60n47, 62n55, 117–18n8
Longenecker, Richard N., 144n75, 204n219, 253nn350–51, 296n486
Lookadoo, Jonathan, 219n260, 220–21, 220–21nn262–64, 221n267, 241n312
Lorenz, Rudolf, 179n158
Ludwig, Theodore, 32n63
Luke, Trevor S., 317n524
Luttikhuizen, Gerard P., 235n298, 236n301
Lynch, Matthew J., 26n41, 30n54, 31n61

Macaskill, Grant, 176n253
MacDonald, Nathan, 24n35, 25n38, 26n42, 241n314
Mackerras, Kirsten, 153n9
MacMullen, Ramsay, 12n3, 15nn6–7, 17n13, 23n34, 26n44
MacRae, George W., 183n169
Maier, Harry O., 305n515, 306n520, 341, 341n594, 341n598, 361n664
Malone, Andrew, 189n180
Marchal, Joseph A., 344–45n616
Marcovich, Miroslav, 374n701
Markschies, Christoph, 124n22, 321n540
Martin, Dale B., 397n34, 399n45, 399n47
Martin, Michael Wade, 60n47, 344–45n116
Mauser, Ulrich, 38n79
McDonald, Lee Martin, 241n314
McDonough, Sean M., 132n40, 177n154, 179n157
McFadden, Susanna, 305n518
McGrath, James F., 31n59, 33, 33n66, 106n61, 259n373, 260n379, 261n383, 350n634, 377n714
McHugh, John, 163n123, 169n137
McLaren, James S., 330, 330nn569–70, 331n572, 334n583
Meeks, Wayne A., 36n75, 79, 79n111, 401n50
Meyer, Nicholas A., 285–86n462
Miller, Ed L., 161n119
Miller, Troy A., 11–12nn2–3, 26–27n45, 60n43, 60n46, 109n69, 254n355, 297n488, 406n63
Mitchell, Margaret M., 67n72, 306n522, 382n1
Mitchell, Stephen, 23–24n34, 46–47n14, 303n506, 315, 331n574
Mock, Theron Clay, III, 106n64, 291n475, 293n478, 392n21
Momigliano, Arnaldo, 30n55
Moss, Candida R., 203n216, 254n354
Moule, C. F. D., 39n82, 62n57, 373–74n699, 384–85n7, 392, 392n22
Moxnes, Halvor, 221n265, 221n267
Müller, Mogens, 400n49
Murphy, Roland E., 175n147
Murray, John C., 43n5
Mutschler, Bernhard, 144n77, 158nn113–14, 160nn115–16

Nash, Bryan A., 60n47, 344–45n116
Neyrey, Jerome H., 43–44n6, 51, 51nn26–27, 62n57
Nickelsburg, George W. E., 278n440, 290n472, 291n475, 381
Nicklas, Tobias, 189n179
Nilsson, M. P., 23n34
Nock, A. D., 54, 54n30
Norden, Eduard, 143n74
North, John, 15n6, 18n18, 54n29, 74n88, 317n523, 395n28
North, Wendy E. S., 296n486
Novenson, Matthew V., 1n1, 3n3, 12–13n4, 26–27n45, 32n63, 43–44n6, 63n59, 98n27, 138n52, 319n529, 341n595, 394n25, 396n31

O'Donnell, James J., 30n55
Opsomer, Jan, 121n17
Orlov, Andrei A., 36n76, 190n184, 191n187, 194, 194nn188–89, 195n192, 195n194, 196, 196n199, 202nn214–15, 278n441, 283, 283n454, 284n457
Osborn, Eric F., 22, 22n32, 148n85, 151, 151n95, 158n112, 250n346
Osborne, Robin, 46–47n14
Osiek, Carolyn, 219n261, 220n262

Pagels, Elaine, 155n103
Paget, James Carleton, 231n287
Peppard, Michael, 3–4, 15n6, 41, 41n1, 47, 47n15, 70n77, 72n85, 75n89, 81, 81nn117–18, 298–99, 299n493, 303n506, 344–45n616, 358n657, 359, 359n662, 364, 364n670, 366n675, 402nn53–56, 403–4
Pierce, Madison N., 62–63n58
Poirier, Paul-Hubert, 155n104, 157n110
Porter, Barbara N., 23n34
Price, S. R. F. (Simon R. F.), 12n3, 15n6, 18n18, 20n26, 46n13, 47n16, 54n29, 54n31, 56n34, 71n83, 74n88, 75n92, 76, 76n96, 76n98, 77, 77n102, 303n504, 303n506, 304n508, 304n510, 305nn516–17, 309, 311, 313, 317, 317n523, 348, 348n626, 348–49nn628–29, 395n28, 397–98n36
Putthoff, Tyson L., 18n17, 48n18, 55n33

Rasimus, Tuomas, 127n29, 144n77, 149nn86–87, 155n104, 157n109, 158n114
Reasoner, Mark, 309, 315, 338n591

Reinhartz, Adele, 139n55, 143n71
Reinink, G. J., 233–34, 233nn292–93, 234n295, 236n302
Reiterer, Friedrich V., 189n179
Reitzenstein, R., 241n312
Reumann, John, 349–50, 350n632
Reynolds, Benjamin E., 30n56, 46n11, 129n31, 139n55, 143n72, 181n167, 286n463
Richardson, Peter, 328nn562–63, 329–30nn566–68
Rives, James B., 46–47n14, 49n22, 77n101
Robinson, James, 156n106
Rocca, Samuel, 20n27, 327, 327n561, 330n567
Rombs, R. J., 80nn114–15
Römer, Thomas, 35n71
Rowe, C. Kavin, 61n50, 263n387, 375n706
Rowland, Christopher, 209n237, 211, 211–12nn241–42, 258n368, 265n396, 270n423
Rubin, Benjamin B., 19n20
Runia, David T., 78nn104–6, 79nn110–11, 121n18, 129n31, 129nn33–34, 131n37, 135–36nn46–48

Sanders, E., 62–63n58
Sanders, James A., 204nn220–21
Sanders, Joseph N., 144nn77–78
Schaper, Joachim, 27n46
Schedtler, Justin J., 268–69nn415–16
Scheid, John, 76n95, 76n97, 247n337
Schimanowski, Gottfried, 140n59
Schmidt, Thomas E., 358–59, 358n657, 359n659, 359n661
Schmidt, Werner H., 31n61
Schnabel, Eckhard, 61n52, 177n154, 180n163, 180n165
Schneemelcher, Wilhelm, 225n275
Schnelle, Udo, 22n31, 60, 60n45, 62nn53–54, 64–65n66, 116n3, 129, 129n35, 137n51, 138, 138n53, 167n131, 167–68n133, 261n383, 375, 375n707
Schöpflin, Karin, 189n179
Schrage, Wolfgang, 39n83, 180n161, 244n323
Schröter, Jens, 64n62, 68n74, 140n60, 387n12
Schüsser Fiorenza, Elizabeth, 17, 17n15, 79n111

Schwartz, Daniel R., 20n27, 335, 335n584
Scroggs, Robin, 276n432
Seeley, David, 352n643
Segal, Alan F., 190, 190–91nn184–86, 194, 221n266, 250n346, 257–58nn364–67, 258, 258–59nn370–72, 259, 352n645, 352n647
Shepherd, Michael B., 212n243
Siegert, Folker, 167–68n133
Skarsaune, Oskar, 58n39, 231n287, 232–33n291
Smith, Brandon D., 1n1, 114n89, 267n408, 269, 269nn419–20
Smith, Ian K., 180n164, 205n225
Smith, J. Z., 406
Smith, Mark S., 25n37
Sommer, Benjamin D., 25n37, 27n48, 30nn54–56, 258n368, 270n423, 382
Spieckermann, Hermann, 23n34, 141n63, 141n67, 261–62n383, 382, 394n26
Steenburg, David, 277n435, 283n451, 285–86n462
Sterling, Gregory, 21n29
Stoll, Oliver, 306n521
Strawbridge, Jennifer R., 344–45n116
Strelan, Rick, 397–98n36
Stroumsa, Gedaliahu, 190n183
Stuckenbruck, Loren T., 197–98n205, 209n235, 209–10n237, 215–16nn252–53, 242n315, 242–43nn318–20, 243n322, 245–46, 246n331, 250n346, 252n348, 266n401, 266nn404–5, 279–80n445, 286n463, 296n486
Sullivan, Kevin P., 199n210
Svigel, Michael J., 219n260, 220n262

Talbert, Charles H., 23n33, 43–44n6, 62n57, 117–18n8, 156n108
Taylor, Joan E., 333–34, 334n581
Taylor, Lily Ross, 74n88
Teixidor, Javier, 23n34
Tellbe, Mikael, 345n617, 351n641
Theobald, Michael, 141n68, 186n175
Thompson, Marianne Meye, 12n3, 81n116
Tilling, Chris, 38n79, 42n4, 97–99, 97–98nn23–26, 102n44, 261n381, 262, 262nn384–85, 283n455, 287, 287nn466–67, 370n689, 372, 372n694, 372n696, 384–85n7, 387, 387n13
Tobin, Thomas H., 129n31, 133n43, 137n50, 138n52, 144n78

Tomas, Julia Margaret, 312
Toom, Tarmo, 52n28, 154n100
Toynbee, J. M. C., 15, 15n6
Turner, John D., 157n109

van der Horst, Pieter W., 36n74, 129n31
van der Watt, Jan G., 22n31, 64–65n66, 116n3, 129n35, 137n51
van Kooten, George H., 16, 17nn11–12, 283, 283n453, 285–86n462
van Nuffelen, Peter, 23–24n34, 46–47n14
van Oorschot, Jürgen, 23n34
Van Riel, Gerd, 47n14
van Roon, Aart, 177n154
VanderKam, James C., 278n440, 291n475
Verheyden, Joseph, 68n74
Vermes, Geza, 38n79
Vernsel, H. S., 310
Vollenweider, Samuel, 28n50, 37n77, 39n83, 82–83n119, 95n19, 250n346, 253n352, 254–56, 254–55nn354–56, 255n358, 256nn360–61, 262n384, 265n387, 271n425, 345n618

Wasserman, Emma, 15n6, 112–13, 112–13nn83–88, 196n200, 204n217, 204n220, 258n368, 270nn423–24
Wasserman, Tommy, 208n231
Watson, F., 147
Weima, Jeffrey A. D., 372n694
Weiss, H.-F., 135–36n47
Wenkel, David, 325n553
Werner, Martin, 179n158, 204n217, 212n243, 221n266, 252, 252n349, 254n355, 264n390
White, John L., 72, 72n86
Whittle, Sarah, 355n652, 375, 375n709
Williams, Logan A., 257n363
Williams, Michael A., 124n22, 125n26, 364n669
Wilson, Robert McL., 164n126, 225n275
Wilson, Stephen G., 106n63, 344n612
Windisch, Hans, 177n154
Winn, Adam, 358n657
Winter, Bruce W., 334n583
Winter, Engelbert, 20n27, 331n574
Witherington, Ben, 176, 176n152
Wright, Archie T., 188n178, 190n182
Wright, N. T., 3, 9, 12n3, 24n35, 27n47, 30n56, 31n59, 45n9, 61n49, 68n74, 82–83n119, 93n9, 175n148, 179n157, 187n176, 207n227, 261n380, 285–86n462, 321n537, 364, 364n671, 371, 371n691, 371n693, 374n700, 374n702, 375n705, 375n708, 406n62

Yeago, David S., 61n51
Young, Frances M., 67n72, 117–18n8, 306n522, 382n1

Zacharias, H. Daniel, 197–98n205
Zanker, Paul, 306n520, 310, 331, 331n575, 348n627
Zeev, Pucci ben, 335n585
Zehnder, Markus, 197n201, 197–98n205, 344n614
Zeller, Dieter, 16n10, 81n118
Zelyck, Lorne R., 144n77
Zevit, Ziony, 326n556
Zwiep, A. W., 352n645

Index of Ancient Authors

Aelius Aristides, 16
Aelius Theon, 268
Appian, 19n22, 348, 353
Apuleius, 174
Aristides, 52–53, 58, 123, 145n79, 313, 389
Aristotle, 31n57, 42n3, 71, 148, 155
Arius, 65–66n70, 93, 179–80, 230–31, 252, 390
Arnobius, 16
Arrian, 18, 55, 300
Asclepias of Mendes, 307
Athanasius, 21, 29n53, 38–39n81, 62, 65–66n70, 67, 83, 230, 252, 273
Athenagoras, 14, 26n43, 28–29n52, 53, 58, 64, 66–67, 81, 83, 84n120, 119n10, 123, 128, 132, 143n74, 149, 151–52, 154, 169, 182, 251, 361, 386
Augustine, 49n22, 59, 118, 161, 250
Aulus Gellius, 19n22

Basil of Caesarea, 61n51, 118

Callimachus, 301
Cassius Dio, 18, 18n19, 20, 48, 57n38, 72, 72n87, 73, 74, 307, 308, 313, 314, 338, 338n590, 345, 347, 348, 353, 360, 402
Cicero, 18n19, 19n22, 31n57, 44, 55, 57, 71, 72n87, 74, 142, 285, 303, 308, 353
Cleanthes, 17, 129–31, 162
Clement of Alexandria, 21, 22, 26n43, 53, 55, 61n51, 65, 66, 68, 126, 128, 148–49, 148n84, 160, 207, 229, 238–39, 251, 252, 323n548

Clement of Rome, 52, 122–23
Cyril of Alexandria, 59

Diodorus Siculus, 44, 322, 347
Diogenes Laertius, 51, 129, 131
Dionysius Halicarnassus, 353

Epiphanius, 233, 233n294, 234, 234n296, 235, 235–36nn299–301, 236, 252, 270
Euripides, 162n122
Eusebius, 9, 36, 65–66n70, 124n22, 233nn293–94, 234, 235, 235n297, 235n299, 248, 249, 258, 324, 353, 355, 356, 399
Ezekiel the Tragedian, 36, 80, 281, 293

Fronto, 306

Heraclitus, 14, 17, 21, 129, 160–62, 170
Herodotus, 44, 45n7, 247
Hippolytus, 64n65, 65, 127, 148n84, 153, 157n111, 213, 213n247, 218, 223, 224, 233, 234, 235, 235–36nn300–301, 236, 239, 240, 251, 255n359, 258, 320, 356
Homer, 54, 309, 347
Horace, 48, 72–73, 309, 314, 325, 345, 350

Ignatius, 10, 32n62, 64, 65, 65–66n70, 68, 145–46, 146n81, 148, 200, 248, 342, 372, 390, 411
Irenaeus, 26n43, 29n53, 53, 62, 65–68, 68n75, 84n120, 119n10, 123, 124nn22–24, 125–27, 127n29, 132, 143n74, 146n80, 148n84, 149, 155, 155n101, 158–60, 169,

453

182–85, 218, 228–29, 232–36, 232–33n291, 238–40, 251–52, 255n359, 282, 284n460, 362–63, 385–86, 390, 406

Jerome, 80n115, 235n297
John of Damascus, 80n115
Josephus, 28, 29n53, 30, 31n60, 35, 52, 57, 60, 65, 77, 122n20, 143n73, 176, 188, 214, 280n446, 281, 283n454, 313, 319n528, 320, 327–30, 331n577, 332–33, 335, 336n587, 337–39, 356, 359–60, 366, 367n677
Justin Martyr, 10, 16, 21, 26n43, 29n53, 31n60, 32, 53, 56n36, 58, 58n39, 60–62, 64, 64n65, 65–66n70, 66, 81, 83, 84n120, 92, 93, 117, 119n10, 122, 128, 132, 143nn73–74, 145, 148–51, 150nn91–92, 150–51nn94–97, 154, 155n102, 157, 161, 162n121, 165, 169, 182, 184, 185, 208, 225–29, 226–27nn128–29, 231–33, 231n286, 232n290, 236, 243, 245, 248, 251, 253, 257, 262n386, 264, 271, 320, 324, 361, 371, 374, 382, 386, 390, 402, 409, 410

Lactantius, 28–29n52
Livy, 18n19, 19n22, 285, 303
Lucian, 14, 176, 250, 321

Melito of Sardis, 9, 153, 228–29, 229n282, 248
Minucius Felix, 26n43, 58, 62, 81, 119n10, 131, 182, 361

Nicolaus of Damascus, 306

Origen, 4, 11, 21, 22, 26n43, 32, 59, 65, 66, 68n73, 81, 83, 123, 125, 137n49, 143n74, 148, 148n84, 157, 159, 165, 169, 181n168, 199, 203, 207, 218, 226n278, 233–34, 233n293, 235n297, 235n299, 242n316, 243, 251, 263n388, 269n420, 361, 386, 388
Ovid, 48, 74, 77, 350, 353, 354, 375, 376

Philo of Alexandria, 2, 21, 28, 28–29nn52–53, 30–31, 31n57, 31n60, 35, 35n73, 50n25, 51, 52, 56n36, 57, 57–58nn38–39, 58, 60–62, 65, 70, 73, 78, 79, 82, 90, 92, 96, 96n21, 102, 112, 115, 121–22, 121n19, 124n23, 128, 132–37, 135–37nn47–49, 141, 143n73, 148, 150n91, 161, 161n120, 164–70, 166n129, 172n145, 174–75, 179, 183–85, 187, 189–92, 194, 198n208, 200, 204n218, 206, 217, 257, 258, 261–62n383, 265n396, 275, 280, 284, 285–86n462, 306, 310–11, 314, 318, 328, 332, 333n580, 334–40, 336n587, 343, 346–49, 366, 382, 386, 394n27, 406–7n64, 409
Plato, 14, 17, 21, 44, 46–47n14, 50n25, 53, 65, 119–21, 120n11, 122, 124, 124n24, 131, 148, 151, 155, 376, 386, 394n27
Plautus, 77
Pliny the Elder, 46–47n14, 48, 71
Pliny the Younger, 10, 74, 76, 248, 250, 394
Plotinus, 124nn22–23
Plutarch, 2, 9, 14, 15, 18, 19nn21–22, 41, 44, 45, 48, 49, 51, 55–57, 58n40, 60n48, 127n27, 131, 162, 174, 285, 300, 307, 313, 345, 346, 353
Porphyry, 16, 17, 250
Pseudo-Clement, 29n53, 65–66n70, 127, 236n301, 251–, 255, 386
Pseudo-Cyprian, 240–41, 240n310, 252, 253
Pseudo-Cyril, 224
Pseudo-Philo, 35, 188
Pseudo-Plato, 14
Pseudo-Tertullian, 255n349
Ptolemy, 53, 96n21, 115, 126, 127, 127n29, 148n84

Quintilian, 45, 74, 311

Seneca, 21, 56–57, 56n35, 74
Strobaeus, 17, 130
Suetonius, 18, 18n19, 19, 31n57, 48, 57, 57n38, 58, 72, 72n87, 73, 307, 310, 314, 325, 331, 338, 349, 353, 356, 360

Tacitus, 19n22, 20, 31n60, 32, 41, 47, 74, 305, 314, 329, 337, 356, 399
Tatian, 58, 66, 123, 143n74, 148, 157–58, 169
Tertullian, 14, 22, 26n43, 53, 59, 68, 125, 127, 135–37n47, 157, 182, 203, 230, 230n284, 233, 234, 238, 240, 251, 252, 257, 273, 340, 356, 360, 361, 386, 388, 399
Theophilus of Antioch, 29n53, 53, 58, 64, 81, 119n10, 123, 132, 143n74, 148, 149, 152–53, 154, 169, 182, 361

Varro, 49n22, 59
Virgil, 48, 72, 73, 307, 309, 345

Index of Ancient Sources

SCRIPTURE

OLD TESTAMENT
Genesis

1–5	275
1–3	285
1–2	118
1	118, 186, 187, 277
1.1–2	29n53
1.1	118, 122, 137, 142, 152, 179, 187
1.1 [LXX]	148
1.3	131
1.6	131
1.9	131
1.11	131
1.14	131
1.20	131
1.24	131
1.26–28	187
1.26	131
1.27–28	275
1.27	61, 166
1.27 [LXX]	285–86n462
1.28–29	282
2	118
3.5–6	285–86n462
3.8	132
3.21	276
4.17–18	277
5.18–24	277
5.24	112
6.1–4	198
6.2	188
6.4	188
9.6 [LXX]	134
14	194
16.7–13	189
18.1–19	198
18.1	164
19.24 [LXX]	151n97
21.17–18	189
22.5 [LXX]	320
23.7	366
23.12	366
31.11–13	205
31.13	189, 191, 257
32.29	217
37.7	366
37.9–10	79
41.43	366
48.14–16	189
49.9–10	323
49.9	111
49.10	318, 327

Exodus

3.1–22	205
3.1–14	257
3.2–15	211
3.2	226
3.6	189, 226
3.10	226
3.14–16	28
3.14	140
4.16	34
4.22–23	180
7.1	34, 34n69, 35, 35n73, 78, 79, 34, 280
8.10	28n51
8.19	35
12.12	26n39
12.23	266n400
14.19	189
15.11	26n39, 28n51, 29n53, 30, 201, 205, 270n421
15.11 [LXX]	196
18.11	26n39
20.2–3	31n60
20.2	28
20.4	334
20.11	28–29n52, 29n53, 143n74
23.13	31n60
23.20–23	189, 207, 208, 251, 257, 264
23.20–21	166, 206, 226, 264, 406
23.20	93, 251
23.21	191, 196, 239n307, 260
23.24	31n60
23.32	31n60
24.9–11	257
24.10–11	190, 191
24.10	211
24.17	211
25.8	184
28.2	276
28.40	276
29.46	184
32.34	189
33.2–3	189
33.9	142
34.14	31n60
40.34–35	172
40.34	142

455

Leviticus

6.10	211
16.17 [LXX]	134, 166
18.5	178
19.4	334
21.10	202
26.1	334

Numbers

14.26–38	207
16.48	79
18.11	31
20.16	189
24.17	318
24.17 [LXX]	324

Deuteronomy

3.24	28n51
4.19–20	188
4.19	324
4.23	334
4.35	26n40, 28n51
4.39	26n40, 28n51
5.5	115
5.5 [LXX]	166
5.6	28
5.7	31n60
5.8	334
6.4	10, 28, 28n51, 257, 372, 386
6.5	261, 372
6.13–14	31n60
7.3–4	31n60
7.9	26n40
7.25	334
8.19–20	31n60
9.4	178
9.18	320
9.25–26	320
10.17	26n39, 32, 266
11.16	31n60
11.28	31n60
12.2	196
12.4–5	196
12.11	196
13.1–15	31n60
14.1	136, 165
17.2–6	31n60
17.3	188, 242n316, 324
18.15	327
18.20	31n60
21.23	402
27.15	334
28.14	31n60
28.26	31n60
30.12–14	178
30.12–13	178
30.17–18	31n60
31.18–20	31n60
32	26n42
32.2–3	189
32.8	26n39, 188
32.17	31
32.21	31
32.37–39	31
32.39	28n51
32.43	26n39
32.43 [LXX]	209, 188n178
33.3	26n39
33.26–29	33
33.26–27	28n51
33.27	26n39

Joshua

22.22	26n39

Judges

2.1	189
6.22	189
9.22–23	188
13.1–22	189
13.6	198
13.17	217
13.22	189, 205

1 Samuel

1.3	26n39
2.2	28n51
2.8	292
8	326
24.8	320
28.14	320

2 Samuel

1.2	320
7.12–16	318, 321, 341
7.12–14	327
7.13	196
7.14	209
7.22	28n51
14.17	197
14.20	197
19.27	197

1 Kings

1.16	320
1.23	320
1.31	320
1.53	320
2.11–12	112
4.29	173
5.12	173
6–9	327
8.6	28n51
8.16	196
8.60	26n40
10.9	321n539
11.19–23	188
18.16–45	340
18.19	24
22.19–23	26n39
22.19	188, 189, 324

2 Kings

2.11	281
17.16	24, 188
21.3–5	188
21.3	24
21.7	196
23.4	24, 188

1 Chronicles

21.16	189
21.21	320
28.5	322
29.1–20	327
29.20	321
29.23	322

2 Chronicles

6.1–7.1	327
9.8	321n539, 322
13.8	320, 322
24.17	57n37, 320, 336n587

Ezra

7.12	266, 357

Nehemiah

9.6	26n39, 28, 28–29n52, 29n53, 143n74, 88, 188n178

Esther

15.13	197

Job

1.6	26n39, 188, 204
1.6 [LXX]	188n178
2.1	188, 204
2.1 [LXX]	188n178
5.1	189
9.33 [LXX]	395
15.15	189
28	171, 172, 174
28.12–28	173
28.27–28	171
33.23	395
36.7	321n539
38.5–7	189
38.7	26n39, 29n53, 188, 204
38.7 [LXX]	188n178

Psalms

2	91, 209, 266, 318, 320, 321, 323
2.1–12	320, 369
2.4	275
2.7	209, 323, 324, 341, 370, 402, 403
2.8–9	111
2.12	296
3.7	205
7.7–8	197, 205, 325
8	91, 209
8.3–8	275
8.4–6	284
8.4	96
8.5–6	112
8.6	286
8.6 [LXX]	188n178
8.7	272n426

9.4	321n539	97.2	321n539	8.35	185
10.16	373	97.5	205, 289	9.3–5	176
20.21	196	97.7	26n39	16.12	321n539
22.18	26n39	97.9	26n39, 270n421	20.28	321n539
23.10 [LXX]	26n39	98.9	373	25.5	321n539
24.10	26n39	102.25–27	209	30	178
29.1–3	26n39	103.19–22	26n39	30.4–5	173
29.1	26n39, 188	104.4	209	30.4	178
33.2	158	104.24	179, 184	Ecclesiastes	
33.6	132, 142, 150n92, 187	104.30	389	5.6	192
		107.20	132	Isaiah	
45	318, 323	109	373, 379	1.3	226
45.6–7	151, 209, 321n539	109.1–4 [LXX]	324, 373	1.24	26n39
		109.1 [LXX]	370	6.1–5	267
45.6	77, 323	109.3 [LXX]	296	6.1–4	211
45.7	78	110	91, 209, 271, 318, 321, 322, 323, 367, 373, 379	9.1–16	369
45.23	407n65			9.1–7	318
47.1–9	267			9.5	197, 197n202, 253
47.2	373	110 [Heb.]	370	9.5 [LXX]	230, 251, 296, 323
47.8	26n39	110.1–7	320		
58.6	205	110.1	83, 110, 116, 151, 185, 209, 256, 272n426, 320, 322, 323, 367, 402, 407n65	9.5 [MT]	197
68	25			9.6	78, 93, 198
71.17	324			9.6 [LXX]	197, 228, 323
72	318, 323			9.7	321n539
72.11	296, 320	110.1 [Heb.]	370	9.8	132
72.17	323	110.3 [Heb.]	324	10.23–24	78
79.5 [LXX]	26n39	115.15	28–29n52	11.1–4	318
79.8 [LXX]	26n39	132	318	11.4	214n248
79.15 [LXX]	26n39	132.11–12	323	11.10	320n535, 356
79.20 [LXX]	26n9	135.5	26n39, 270n421	14	326
80.1	323	136.2	26n39	14.1–32	369
82.1–2	205	136.3	266	14.12	324
82.1	26n39, 78, 197, 325	137.1 [LXX]	188n178	14.13	57n37, 336n587
		138.1	26n39	16.5	321n539
82.6	78, 188, 204	147.15	132	22.23	292
82.8	26n39	147.18	132	24.21–23	205, 324
84.7	26n39	148.1–13	29n53	24.21	26n39, 188
86.8	26n39, 28n51, 270n421	148.1–5	29n53, 143n74	30.27	196
		148.2	29n53	36.18–20	270n421
88.38 [LXX]	290	Proverbs		37.16	29n53
89	25, 318, 321	1.20–33	171	40	25
89.1–52	369	2.6	173	40.9	341
89.5–8	26n39, 29n53	3.18–20	171	40.10	263
89.5–7	189	3.19	171n144, 174, 179, 184, 187	40.18–20	31n60
89.5	189			40.25	348
89.6–8	28n51	8	184	40.28	28–29n52
89.6	204	8.1–11	171	41.6	65
89.7	26n39, 188, 201, 205	8.12–21	171	41.21–24	31n60
		8.22–31	96, 109, 171	41.27	341
89.14	321n539	8.22–30	174	42.1	403
89.20	323	8.22–23	93, 93n8, 132, 142, 161, 174, 179, 181, 182, 183, 406	42.8	261
89.27	180			43–46	28n51
89.35–36	323			43.11	249
95.3	26n39, 29n53, 270n421			43.15	373
		8.22	83, 152, 170n139, 179, 187	43.27	395
95.3–4	28n51			44.3	389
96.4–5	28–29n52	8.25	184	44.6	26n40, 31n60, 65, 267, 373
96.4	270n421	8.27	183		
96.7 [LXX]	188n178	8.30	132, 174, 179, 183	44.7	201, 205
96.13	373	8.32–36	171	44.8	26n40
97.1	373				

44.24	28–29n52, 29n53, 143n73, 180	Lamentations				278n441
		4.20 [LXX]	343	7.9–14	257, 276, 279, 292, 322
45	377	Ezekiel			
45.4	226	1.5–28	211	7.9–10	190, 192, 212
45.5	26n40, 249	1.5	211	7.9	191, 192, 213, 265, 267
45.7	127	1.10	211		
45.11	249	1.13	211	7.13–14	196, 197, 209, 212, 267, 279, 292
45.6	26n40	1.16	211		
45.14	26n40, 292	1.24	211, 213n246	7.13–14 [LXX]	198, 210
45.18	26n40	1.26–28	111, 191, 192, 197, 198, 209, 211, 257, 267, 276	7.13	33, 110, 116, 191, 197, 215, 256, 402
45.20–21	31n60				
45.22–25	376			7.14	212, 212n243
45.22	26n40, 249, 260	1.26–28 [LXX]	210	7.18	212, 291n474
		1.26–27	267	7.22	212
45.23–25 [LXX]	260	1.28	214	7.27	212, 291n474
45.23	10, 61, 101n44, 112, 113, 260, 371	5.8	33	8.15	212
		8.1–18	211	8.16	194, 212
45.23 [LXX]	376	8.1–4	209, 211	9.21	194, 212, 213n247
46.5–7	31n60	8.2–4 [LXX]	210, 211n241	10.2–9	92
46.5	348			10.5–9	111
46.9	26n40, 249	8.2	111, 198, 211, 257	10.5–6	145, 197, 198, 209, 211, 212, 213, 213n247, 265
48.12	65, 267	9–10	211		
49	292	9.2–3	198		
49.1–6	320n535	9.2	211	10.5–6 [LXX]	210
49.2	214n248	9.3	211	10.11–21	212
49.6	292	9.11	211	10.13	188, 194, 197
49.7	292, 294	10.2	211	10.18	211
49.23	292	10.6	211	10.20–21	194
52.7	205, 341	10.7	211	10.21	197
53.8	159	21.3	33	11.36–39	57n37, 336n587
53.11–12	402	26.7	266		
55.10–11	132	28.2	57n37, 336n587	12.1	197, 217
60.9	196	28.13	211	12.3	200
60.14	292	28.26	211	12.5–7	198, 211, 212
61.1–3	205	29.3	57n37, 336n587	Hosea	
61.1	260, 341	34.15	320	3.4–5	318
63.1–6	263	34.22–24	318	Joel	
63.1	396	34.23–24	320	2.1–3	373
63.2–3	266	37.24–25	318	2.27	28n51
66.1–2	180	37.27	142	2.29–29	389
66.15–16	373	38–39	280n446	3.13	215
66.15	263	39.29	389	3.17	142, 184
66.18–19	33	43.2	213n246	Amos	
66.20	205	Daniel		9.11–12	318
Jeremiah		1.17	173	Micah	
7.10–12	196	2	330	1.1–8	373
8.2	242n316	2.37	266, 357	1.3–4	205, 289
10.10	28n51	2.46	366	5.1 [LXX]	324
10.11	28–29n52	2.47	26n39, 270n421, 394	5.2	318
10.12	184			Habakkuk	
14.21	292	3.1–30	57n37, 336n587	1.5	289
17.12	292			3.5 [LXX]	132
19.13	242n316	3.1–18	366	Zephaniah	
22.4	318	4.13	189	11.5	242n316
23.5–6	318	4.17	189	Haggai	
30.9	318	4.23	189	1.12–14	319
33.17–22	318	4.35	26n39, 188	2.2–4	319
42.5	290	4.37 [LXX]	266	2.20–23	319
50.16	215	6	330	Zechariah	
51.15	184	7	212, 212n243,	1.9	199, 205

1.11	199	7.22	97, 171n144,	21.5	373		
1.14	234		179, 181, 184	21.11	172		
2.1–3	199	7.23–24	173	24	161, 173		
2.10	184	7.25–26	97, 173,	24.1–23	142, 172, 174		
2.14–15 [LXX]	142		179, 183	24.1–2	172		
2.14 [LXX]	234	7.25	181, 185	24.2	96, 196		
3.1–5	202	7.26	61, 111,	24.3	96, 172,		
3.2	207		132, 179, 187		179, 181, 183		
3.6–10	319	7.27–28	186	24.4	97, 185		
4.2–6	319	7.29–30	185	24.6	97		
4.4–5	205	7.29	132	24.8–10	172, 173, 187		
4.11–14	319	8.1	173	24.8–9	96		
4.12–14	318	8.3–4	173, 183	24.8	132, 180, 181, 184		
6.9–15	319	8.3	181	24.9	172, 179, 181, 183		
6.11–13	327	8.4–6	179, 184	24.10–12	97		
6.12–13	327	8.4	174	24.16	172		
6.12	134, 324–25	8.6	132, 171n144, 181	24.17	185		
6.12 [LXX]	325	8.13	185	24.19–22	176		
9.14	263	8.19–20	173n146	24.19–21	171		
14.1–5	373	8.21	173	24.22	171		
14.5	189, 263	9.1–10	179	24.23	97, 172, 185		
Malachi		9.1–4	173, 184–85	24.28	173, 181		
3.1	197n202	9.1–2	132, 171n144,	34.8	172, 185		
4.5	281		181, 184	36.5	28n51		
		9.1	132, 181	36.17	180		
Apocrypha		9.2	97	39.1	172		
2 Esdras		9.4	97, 185	39.6	172, 173		
11.1–12.34	340n593	9.9	132, 183, 185	39.8	185		
Tobit		9.10	97, 181, 185, 292	42.15	132		
5.1–17	199	9.15	142	42.21	143n73		
11.14	196, 242, 293	9.18	172	42.31	29n53		
12.12	243	10.8	173	43.26	132, 135, 179		
12.15	194, 243	11.17	173n146	43.33	173		
12.16–22	31n60,	12.1	173	44–50	98		
	242n316	12.13	28n51	44.16	112, 278		
13.1–5	33	13–15	399	45.2–3	35		
14.5	327	13.10–15.17	334	45.15	202		
14.8	196	14.15–17	326	47.11	292, 293		
Judith		14.17–21	57n37,	48.12	281		
3.8	57n37, 336n587		336n587	49.14	112, 278		
6.2–4	57n37, 336n587	14.17	330	49.16	275		
16.15	289	18.14–16	132	50	318		
Additions to Esther		18.15–16	173	50.11	276		
3.3	336n587	18.15	132, 185, 187	50.17	320		
13.12–14	31n60	Sirach		50.21	320		
15.13	197	Prologue 1	185	50.23	320		
Wisdom		1.1	172, 173, 181, 183	51.12	266		
1.6–7	179	1.4	172, 179, 181, 183	51.17	173		
1.7	173	1.10	181, 184	51.23–27	176		
2.23–34	112	1.26	185	Baruch			
2.23	282	4.11	171	3	178		
3.4	173n146	4.12–13	171	3.9–4.4	172, 174		
6.18–19	173n146	4.12	111, 132	3.9	171, 185		
6.22	172, 181, 183	4.24	172, 185	3.10–14	171		
6.24	172	6.37	185	3.12	181		
7.1–6	57n37,	7.4	292	3.14–23	173		
	336n587	9.17–10.18	336n587	3.29–31	174		
7.10	111	15.1	172, 185	3.29–30	178, 181		
7.22–8.1	109	17.3	282	3.36–37	173, 187		
7.22–24	172	19.20	172, 185	3.37–4.1	172		

460   Index of Ancient Sources

3.37	181, 184	11.16–17	176	9.9–13	282		
3.38	172	11.19	176	9.31	280		
4.1–2	185	11.27	69, 226	9.35	176		
4.1	185	11.28–30	176	10.25	176		
Prayer of Azariah		12.42	176	10.29	32n62		
22	28n51	13.41–42	206, 262	10.31	176		
37	29n53	13.41	271	10.33	280		
Prayer of Manasseh		14.33	360	10.45	280		
15	188	16.13	237	11.24	176		
1 Maccabees		16.27	206, 251, 271	12.25	201		
1.20–26	337	17.12	280	12.29	28		
2.58	112, 281	19.28	267n411, 293, 323n548	12.35–37	263, 323n548		
3.3–9	327			13.9	358		
3.3	327	20.20	360	13.26–27	110, 206, 251, 262		
4.4	327	21.22	176				
8	331	22.30	201	13.26	280		
14.4–15	327	23.34	176	13.27	271		
14.4–5	327	24.21	271	13.32	206, 263		
14.9–10	327	24.30	280	14.26	373–74n699		
14.21	327	24.31	206, 262	14.58	327		
14.29	327	24.36	206, 263	14.62	198, 245, 253, 257, 263, 279, 280, 323n548		
14.35	327	24.37–42	263				
14.39	327	24.37	280				
14.41	327	24.39	280	14.63–64	257		
2 Maccabees		24.44	280	15	358		
1.24–25	28n51	25.31–46	279	15.2	358		
2.21	399	25.31	206, 255, 262, 263, 293, 323n548	15.9	358		
3.15	320			15.12	358		
3.24–25	196	25.41	263	15.18	358		
6.1–6	337	26.53	206	15.26	358		
7.28–29	28n51	26.64	245	15.32	358		
8.1	399	27.51–53	354	15.33	354		
9.5–12	57n37	28.1–20	352	15.35–36	281		
9.8–12	336n587	28.2	206	15.38	354		
9.12	110, 112, 349	28.3	196	15.39	110, 354, 359		
10.3–4	320	28.5	206	16.1–8	352		
13.4	266	28.9	248, 354, 360	16.5	199, 206		
14.38	399	28.17	248, 354, 360	16.19	257		
3 Maccabees		28.18	255, 354	Luke			
1.16	320	28.19	255, 390	1.11–38	206		
2.2–3	29n53	28.20	360	1.35–38	225		
3.7	337	Mark		1.35	225		
5.35	266	1.1–15	139, 404	1.68–69	320		
4 Maccabees		1.9–11	403	1.78–79	325		
4.26	399	1.11	321	2.9–20	206		
		1.13	206, 251, 284	2.9	196		
NEW TESTAMENT		1.15	358	2.11	21, 343		
Matthew		6.14	358	3.16	388		
1.20–24	206	6.15	282	3.38	281		
1.23	411	6.22	358	4.10	206		
2.2	360	6.25	358	4.25–26	282		
2.8	360	6.26	358	6.43	127		
2.13	206	6.27	358	7.32	176		
2.19	206	6.45–53	10	7.35	176		
3.16–17	390	8.27–31	198	9.26	206		
4.6	206	8.31	280	10.21–22	176		
4.9	360	8.38–9.1	280	10.22	69, 226		
4.10	360	8.38	206, 262	11.43	292		
4.11	206, 284	9.2–8	282	11.49	176		
11.15–30	176	9.7	321	12.8–9	206, 262		

Index of Ancient Sources   461

12.40	280		169, 181, 183,	14–16	64n65
13.30	357		184, 186, 391	14.1–5	141
17.22	280	1.21	281	14.3	181
19.44–45	320	1.26–30	64n65	14.6	138, 166
20.36	201	1.30	140	14.7–10	184
20.42	272–73n427	1.32–34	64n65	14.8–11	63, 141
22.30	267n411	1.45	63, 142, 411	14.10	152
22.43	206	1.50–51	63	14.20	63, 141
22.69	73n427, 245	1.51	63, 140, 198, 207	14.28	141, 168
24.1–49	352	2.19	327	15.15	63, 69
24.4	199	3.5	149n90	15.26	388
24.7	280	3.11–13	138	16.24	176
24.23	206	3.13	63, 140,	16.27–28	140
24.50–53	352		166, 181, 198	16.28	146
24.51	285, 354	3.14	280	17.1–26	390
24.52	248, 354	3.16	63, 112, 141, 184	17.3	32n62, 63, 166
John		3.18	69, 112, 141, 184	17.4–8	139
1	186, 186n175	3.31	140	17.4–5	63
1.1–29	352	3.35	181	17.4	139, 164
1.1–18	163	4.5	142	17.5	63, 140,
1.1–16	255	4.24	52		181, 183, 386
1.1–5	137, 138, 142, 148	4.42	63, 141	17.6	63, 69
1.1–3	67, 139, 140, 142,	5.1	145	17.11–12	69, 206, 264
	148, 150n92, 153,	5.18	10, 63, 141, 168,	17.11	63, 141, 146
	160, 181, 386, 391		245, 349	17.18	140
1.1–2	10, 63, 127–28n30,	5.20	181	17.20–23	141
	140, 164, 183, 386	5.22	141	17.21–23	63, 141
1.1	83, 141n64, 143,	5.23	10, 63, 141, 245, 247	17.21–22	146
	146, 148, 149, 157,	5.24	63	17.21	273
	162, 164, 165, 184,	5.26	63, 164	17.24	63, 140, 141,
	185, 187, 225, 402n51	5.27	141		146, 181, 183
1.2	152	5.30	141	17.26	63, 69, 139,
1.3	21, 29n53, 60, 63,	5.34	63		141, 255
	67n71, 119n10, 126,	5.36–37	63	18.36	355
	127–28n30, 143,	5.37–38	138	20.2	388
	146, 149, 157, 158,	5.44	32n62	20.17	63, 181
	160, 165, 184, 386	6.32–58	140	20.28	10, 63, 165,
1.4–9	138	6.33	63		184, 354
1.4–5	185, 188	6.38	63	20.31	139
1.4	165	6.42	142	21.15–17	389
1.5	149	6.62	140	Acts	
1.9	149	8.16–18	63	1.9–11	285, 352
1.10–11	174, 181	8.23	140	1.9–10	354
1.10	21, 142	8.28	280	2.14–26	355
1.11–13	185	8.29	141	2.17–18	389
1.12–13	166	8.42	140	2.33–34	323n548
1.12	69	8.56–58	164	2.33	271, 285
1.14–18	185	8.58–59	245	2.34–36	343–44
1.14	10, 63, 137, 141,	8.58	140, 141, 164, 184	2.34	272–73n427
	141n64, 142, 143,	9.38	63, 253	2.36	379
	145, 146, 149, 155,	10.30	63, 112, 141,	2.38	69, 248, 388
	158, 160, 166, 168,		141n64,	3.6	248
	169n137, 181,		146, 152, 168	3.16	248
	184, 185, 187, 188,	10.33–34	63, 141	4.12	255
	225, 391, 411	10.33	245	4.24	28–29n52
1.15	140	10.36	141	4.26	344
1.16	188	10.38	63, 141	4.36	103
1.18	17, 52, 63, 112,	12.34	198, 280	5.21	323n548
	138, 139, 141, 142,	12.47	63, 141	5.30–32	355
	159, 160, 164, 166,	13.16–20	141	5.31	271, 285

462 Index of Ancient Sources

6.1–16	401	8.3	146, 170, 183, 184, 186, 204, 259, 345, 411	10.21	248
6.15	203			10.32	399
7.38	265			11.7	282
7.55–56	271, 272–73n427, 323n548	8.9–11	273, 388	11.12	21
		8.11	411	11.20	342
7.56–60	245, 257	8.15	373–74n699	11.23–26	248
7.56	253	8.17	357	11.26	372, 373
7.58	372	8.29	185	12.1–3	249
7.59	248	8.34	271, 323n548, 411	12.3	343, 372
8.12	248	8.35–39	389	15.20–28	276
8.16	248	8.38–39	251, 262	15.22	281, 294
9.14	246, 248	8.38	26	15.23–28	112, 113, 270, 323n548
9.21	246, 248	9.1–5	411		
10.3–5	205	9.5	10, 205, 248	15.24–28	368
10.25–26	31n60	10.5–8	178	15.24–25	286
10.42	255	10.8–9	343	15.24	286
10.48	248	10.12–15	248	15.25–27	284
11.22–25	103	10.12–14	246	15.25	95, 356
12	201	10.12	399	15.27–28	286
12.13–16	201	10.13	248, 255, 411	15.28	286
12.20–23	58, 77, 328	11.36	21, 60, 67n71	15.33	402n51
13–15	103	13.1–7	355	15.35–50	402n51
13.2	246	15.12	356, 368, 411	15.45–49	281
13.17–47	321	16.25	248	15.45	276, 284, 294
14.11–15	31n60	16.27	32n62	15.47–49	185, 285
14.11–12	16	1 Corinthians		15.47	285–86n462
14.15	28–29n52, 52	1–2	186	15.48–49	204, 259
15.37–39	103	1.2	246, 248, 372	15.48	189
17.6–7	357	1.3	262	16.13	372
17.7	360	1.7–8	372	16.22	231, 248, 342–44, 364, 368, 371, 372, 373, 379
17.24–25	52	1.9	262, 372		
17.24	28–29n52	1.18–21	177		
17.28–29	402n51	1.24	177	2 Corinthians	
17.30–32	357	1.30	177, 177n154	1.2–3	262
17.31	255, 373	2.1–10	177	2.14	357, 358
19.5	248	2.1–5	390	3	185
19.10	399	2.5	372	4.4–6	109, 184, 185
19.13–17	248	2.6–7	177	4.4	26, 61, 184, 285–86n462
19.17	399	2.6	368		
21.37	397n35	2.8	26, 111	5.4	142
22.16	248	4.4–5	373	5.10	255, 373
25.26	110, 351	6.4–5	372	5.19	170, 273
Romans		6.11	69, 273	6.16	60
1.3–4	274, 279n443, 284, 355, 411	8	363	8.9	183
		8.1–5	262	11.4	390
1.18–25	28–29n52	8.4–6	10, 32n62	11.31	262
1.20	52	8.4	60	12.2–10	248
1.24	60	8.5–6	25n38, 109	12.8	372
2.16	255, 373	8.5	26, 368	13.14	248, 273, 390
3.30	28, 32n62	8.6	21, 53, 60, 67, 67n71, 70n79, 119n10, 177n154, 183, 184, 205, 255, 257, 261, 262, 343, 372, 386, 391	Galatians	
4.17	29n53			1.1–4	270
4.25	411			1.1–3	262
5.8	389			1.13–14	399
5.12–14	281			2.1–10	103
5.12	294	9.6	103	2.1	103
5.14–19	284	10.4	208	2.12–14	103
5.14	281	10.13	372	3.14	388
5.15–19	281	10.14–22	249	3.19–20	395, 395–96n30
8.2	388	10.20	60	3.19	265

3.20	28, 32n62	3.21	261, 284, 286, 356, 368	2 Timothy	
3.28	399			2.12	96
4.4–5	183, 186, 259	4.11	402n51	2.22	248
4.4	170, 204, 345	Colossians		4.1	373
4.6	262, 373–74n699	1.5	209	4.18	248
4.8	60	1.6	209	Titus	
4.14	204, 259, 260	1.13	255	1.12	402n51
Ephesians		1.15–20	21, 67, 177n154, 178, 186, 205, 255, 344n615, 370n689	2.13	10
1.20–22	251, 255			Philemon	
1.20	257, 323n548			10–11	373–74n699
1.21–22	286			Hebrews	
2.19–22	273	1.15–18	119n10, 184, 386	1–2	62, 92
4.6	32n62			1	264, 265
5.1	50n25	1.15–17	183	1.1–14	62
5.2	389	1.15–16	178, 179, 179n157	1.1–4	67, 255, 408
5.19	248			1.2–3	60
6.12	26	1.15	61, 83, 93, 150n91, 161, 167, 184, 185, 285–86n462	1.2	21, 62, 67n71, 119n10, 184, 386
Philippians				1.3	62, 112, 135, 170, 184, 265n396
1.6	261	1.16–17	60, 251		
1.10	261	1.16	26, 9n53, 67n71, 267n410, 18, 370n689	1.4	231
1.13	261			1.5–2.18	208
1.16	261			1.5–9	251
1.19	261, 388	1.17	135	1.5	62, 265, 265n396, 321
1.20	261	1.18	148		
1.21–23	261	1.19	180	1.6	231, 250, 265n396, 267n409, 284, 378n720
1.21	389	2.6	343		
1.26	261	2.8–9	205		
2	349	2.9–10	205	1.7–9	209
2.5–11	70n79, 177n154	2.9	62	1.7	29n53, 265
2.6–11	61, 101n44, 110, 113, 204, 248, 259, 260, 281, 286, 344–45, 347, 351–52, 355, 364, 369, 370, 370n689, 374, 379, 387, 407n65	2.10	205	1.8–12	62, 248
		2.11–13	273	1.8	62, 271
		2.15	26, 205, 251, 357	1.10–12	209
		2.18	31n60, 92, 205, 242, 267	1.13	209, 265, 265n396, 323n548
2.6–9	112	2.20	205, 251	1.14	188
2.6–7	183, 186, 285, 345	3.1	205, 257, 323n548	2.2	265
2.6	60, 61n51, 112, 113, 294, 368, 370n689, 374, 375	3.3	273	2.5–9	251
		3.16	132	2.5	209
2.7	16, 146, 184, 260n377	1 Thessalonians		2.8–9	284
2.8	284, 375	1.1–3	262	2.10	21, 60, 67, 67n71
2.9–11	10, 67, 106, 247, 251, 255, 260, 270, 343, 349, 351, 375, 376	1.9–10	249	2.12	248
		1.9	52, 60	3.12	52
		3.11–13	248	4.14	62
		3.13	189	5.5	62, 321
2.9	285	4.16–17	110	7	264
2.10–11	69, 250, 260, 267n409, 378n720	4.16	194, 262	7.3	62
		2 Thessalonians		7.28	62
2.11	205	1.1–2	262	8.1	257, 271, 323n548
2.13–15	273	1.7	251, 262, 271	10.12	323n548
2.16	261	2.16–17	248	11.3	29n53
3.3	261	3.5	248	11.5	112, 278
3.7–9	261	3.16	248	11.10	122
3.8	389	1 Timothy		12.2	257, 271, 323n548
3.9–11	273	1.17	60	12.22	52
3.10	261	2.5	32n62, 409	13.2	198
3.12	261	3.16	184	13.8	62
3.20	21	5.21	262, 271	13.20–21	248

James
1.17	29n53, 143n74
2.1	251
2.19	32n62

1 Peter
2.12–17	355
3.22	251, 255, 323n548, 409
4.11	248

2 Peter
1.4	276
1.11	21
1.13	142
1.14	142
1.17	321
2.4	402n51
2.10	196
2.20	21
3.2	21
3.18	21, 248

1 John
1.1–4	145
2.2	145
2.22	232n290, 390
3.16	389
3.23	69
4.2–3	68, 145, 390
4.12	52
4.19	389
5.1	232n290
5.20	62, 112

2 John
7	68, 145, 390

3 John
11	52

Jude
1	264
4–16	207
4	208, 231, 264
5–7	208
5	207, 208, 232, 251, 264
6	207
7–8	207
8	196, 207, 251
9	194, 207, 260n378
10	207
12	248
14–15	208, 251, 264, 373
14	189, 278
20–25	264
25	32n62, 248, 264

Revelation
1.4	188, 378n724
1.5–7	291
1.5–6	248, 289
1.5	267n408, 389
1.6	96, 291
1.7	214, 215
1.8	65, 111, 266, 267, 269n420, 290, 378n724
1.10	342
1.11	266
1.12–20	92
1.12–18	232
1.12–16	145, 148, 251, 290
1.13–16	111, 209, 213–14, 265, 269
1.13–15	265
1.13	213, 254
1.14	217
1.15	213n246, 214
1.16	213n245, 214, 214n248
1.17–18	267, 291
1.17	65, 111, 268
1.19–20	213
2–3	266, 291
2.1	266, 272
2.3	290
2.7	357
2.8	266, 272
2.11	357
2.12	266, 272
2.13	20, 290, 378
2.16	214n248
2.17	357
2.18	217, 266, 272
2.26	357
3.1	266
3.5	271, 357
3.7	266, 272
3.8	290
3.9	247
3.12	357
3.14	148, 184, 215, 255, 266, 267, 267n408, 272, 290, 291, 386
3.20	289
3.21	185, 267, 267n411, 271, 289, 291, 292, 293, 323n548, 357, 377n717, 378
4–5	361, 365, 377
4	377
4.1–11	289
4.1	213, 265
4.3	214
4.4	267
4.8–11	247, 267, 268
4.8	269n420, 291, 378n724
4.10	268
5	267, 286, 361, 369, 377
5.1–14	26n43, 67, 106, 145, 379
5.1–3	269n417
5.2–3	271
5.2	215
5.3	267
5.5	111, 269n417
5.6	185, 354, 377, 377n719, 378
5.7	271
5.8–14	268
5.9–14	247, 267n409, 279, 284, 289, 291, 292, 378n720
5.9–13	248, 271
5.9–12	267
5.9	291
5.10	96, 291
5.11–14	251
5.12–14	250, 268
5.12–13	289
5.13–14	267n409, 378n720
5.13	267, 271, 323n548, 378
6.9–11	377n717
6.15–16	289
6.16	289
7.9–17	271
7.9–10	323n548, 378
7.10	247, 289, 291
7.11–12	247
7.11	268
7.15–17	248
7.15	268
7.17	185, 267, 291, 293, 323n548, 377, 378
8.2	272
9.11	188
9.20	247
10.1–3	209, 214–15, 266
10.1	215
10.2	214
10.4	215
10.5	215
10.6	29n53, 143n74
10.8	215
11.6	267
11.15	95
11.16–18	247
11.16–17	268
11.17	95
12.5	111, 271, 323n548, 378
12.7	194, 217, 251, 260n378, 263
12.12	266n403
12.17	270
13.2	378
13.4	247
13.8	247, 290
13.12	247

Index of Ancient Sources   465

14.7	28–29n52, 247	22.16	200, 215, 266	46.1	213, 290
14.9–10	21	22.20	231, 248, 343n604, 373	46.4	205
14.14–20	216			47.1–2	243
14.14–16	209, 215–16			47.3–4	278
14.14–15	216n253			48.1–9	292
14.14	216, 251, 254, 266, 269	**PSEUDEPIGRAPHA**		48.1–6	290
				48.1–5	198
14.15	216, 266n406	*2 Baruch*		48.2–3	110, 217, 278
14.16	216	21.4	29n53	48.3	324
14.17–20	216	21.6	272	48.4	292
14.17	216	35.1–40.4	340, 340n593	48.5	243, 287, 289, 291, 292
14.18	216	48.10	272		
14.19–20	216	51.5	200	48.6–7	278
15.2–4	268	51.10	200	48.6	110
15.3–4	247, 248, 291	*4 Baruch*		48.7	290
15.3	289	3.4	243	48.8	292
15.4	247			48.10–49.4	320
17.14	266, 289, 357	*1 Enoch*		49.1–4	176
18.21	215	1.1–3	278	51.1–5	320
19.4–8	247	1.3–8	33	51.1	289
19.4	268	1.6	289	51.3	176
19.6	95	1.9	208, 251, 373	52.5	232n289
19.9	289	6.7	194	52.6	205, 289, 297
19.10	31n60, 92, 242n316, 247, 250, 268, 271	6–16	189, 198	53.4	232n289
		9.1–11	232n289	53.5–7	292
		9.1–4	272	53.7	205, 289
19.11–20.15	356	9.1–2	194	54.6	194
19.11–20.10	266n403	9.2–4	267	55	286
19.11–20	251	9.3	243	55.3–4	205
19.11–16	209, 216–17, 266	9.4–5	29n53	55.4	289, 290, 292
		9.4	266, 270n421, 292	56.5–8	280n446
19.11	290	9.5	29n53, 180	60.2	278
19.12	217	10.4–5	207	61.1–13	320
19.13	145, 217	10.11–15	207	61.6–13	263
19.14	217	14	278n441	61.7	289, 291n475
19.15	214n248, 266	14.8–23	278	61.8	289
19.16	266, 357	14.18–22	267	61.9–13	291
19.21	214n248	14.20–21	271	61.10–11	291
20.1–2	251	14.20	213n245	61.13	290
20.4–6	96, 291	15.6–11	188	62.1–8	243, 289
20.4–5	377n717	20.1–7	194	62.2	289
20.4	267, 267n411, 293, 377n717	20.1–5	272	62.3–5	289
		22.14	111	62.3	289
20.7–10	280n446	24.6	263	62.5	276, 289
20.11	267	25.3	111	62.6	289
21.3–5	271	25.7	111	62.7–8	290
21.6	65, 111, 266, 267, 269n420, 290	27.3	111	62.9	289
		27.5	111	62.14	289, 320
21.7	357	36.4	111	63.1–12	289
22.1–4	268	37–71	278, 297	63.2	111, 266
22.1–3	291, 323n548	40.1–10	194	63.7	290
22.1	289, 378	40.1	272	68.1–5	272
22.3	185, 247, 267, 268, 271, 293, 378	40.6	232n289, 243	69.26–29	289
		40.9–10	272	69.27	217
22.5	96, 291	42	187	69.29	276
22.8–9	31n60, 247	42.1–3	173	70–71	278n441
22.9	92, 242n316, 250, 268, 271	42.2	132, 181, 184, 185	71.7	278
		45.3	289	71.8	194
22.13	65, 111, 267, 269n420, 290	46.1–8	279, 320	71.11	202, 278, 290
		46.1–2	197, 212	71.13	263

466 Index of Ancient Sources

71.14	278	16.1–2	195	37.1–6	276
83.8	111	16.5	268	38–42	276
84.2–3	97, 173	17.1–4	194	39.2–3	267n411, 293
84.2	266	17.3	272		
84.3–4	185	28.5	272	*Apocalypse of Sedrach*	
90.2	267	28.8	272	5.2	277n4360
91.1–3	278	35.2	214	*Apocalypse of Zephaniah*	
99.3	243	35.3	272	6.11–15	31n60,
104.1	243	*4 Ezra*			242n316
104.2	200	2.44	205	6.11–13	196
108.12	267n411	3.4	29n53, 143n73	6.11–12	200, 214
2 Enoch		3.36	194	8.3–4	200
1.3–5	196	4.1	194		
1.4–8	242n316	5.20	194	*Ascension of Isaiah*	
1.4	236	6.6	29n53, 143n73	1.3	217
2.2	31n60	6.38	29n53, 132	1.4	217n256
18.1–9	189	7.28–29	198	1.5	217n256
18.1	236	7.33	267	1.7	217n256
20.1	194	7.97	200	1.13	217n256
20.3	267	8.21	292	3.13	217n256, 218
22.1–3	202	8.23	289	3.17	217n256
22.1	272	8.44	282	3.18	217n256
22.5–10 [J]	202	11.1–12.34	340,	4.3	217n256
22.6	263		340n593	4.6	217n256
22.7	196	12.31–32	198	4.9	217n256
22.8	278	13.1–3	324	4.14	218, 251, 386
22.10	196	13.3–4	297	4.18	217n256
24.1	202	13.3	198	4.21	217n256
24.2	29n53	13.4	289	5.15	217n256
29.1–3	29n53	13.5–11	280n446	6.8–9	219
30.10	282	13.12–13	205	7.2	219, 242n316, 250
30.11–12 [J]	275	13.13	320	7.7–8	219
33.4	28n51, 29n53, 132, 143n73, 174	13.25–50	320	7.8–23	250
		13.26	324	7.17	217n256, 219
33.10	194, 395–96n30	*Apocalypse of Abraham*		7.18–33	267
39.5	323n549	10–11	265	7.18–23	242n316
44.1–3	283	10	260	7.21–23	31n60
3 Enoch		10.3–4	195	7.21	267n410
1.7	242n316	10.3	196, 206, 264	7.23	217n256, 219
4.1–2	195	10.4	199	7.37	219
4.1	29n53	10.8–17	206, 264	8.1–10	242n316, 250
4.3	203	10.8–9	195	8.4–5	205n222
4.5	195, 203	11.1–3	196	8.5	31n60, 219
6.1	203	11.2	199, 214	8.7–10	267
6.3	203	12.4	195	8.15	200, 242n316, 250
7.1	195, 203	16.2–4	195	8.18	217n256, 219
9.1–5	236	17.1–5	242n316	8.25	217n256
10–14 [Heb. 1.13]	265n396	17.3–6	195	9.5	219
10.1	267, 293	17.8–11	52	9.9	203, 278
10.3–6	195	23.5	275	9.12	217n256
12.1–5	195	*Apocalypse of Adam*		9.13	218
12.5	196, 206, 264	1.1–3	281	9.24–25	267n411
14.1–5	194, 195	1.2	275	9.27–36	251
16	191, 243, 257, 258, 267	64.14–19	203	9.27–32	217, 219, 260
		Apocalypse of Moses		9.27	219
16.1–5	31n60, 242n316	37	285	9.28	251, 276, 386
				9.30	251

9.32	219	5.1	189	17.31–32	205	
9.33–36	218, 236	6.8	282	17.32	320, 343	
9.33	196	12.1–9	366	18.7	343	
9.40	219, 250n345	12.12–14	366			
10–11	26n43, 232	12.19–20	25n28	Pseudo-Philo		
10	260	18.9–12	194	Liber Antiquitatum Biblicarum		
10.7–31	223, 251	20.7–8	366	3.1	188	
10.7–16	218	22.16	399	6.4	28	
10.7	219	31.14	318	9.13	35	
10.14	257, 323n548	36.7	143			
10.15	219, 250, 260, 267n409, 378n720	40.7	366	Sibylline Oracles		
		Letter of Aristeas (Ep. Arist.)		Prologue 94–98	52	
10.17	219	128–71	399	1.19	132	
10.18	218	132	32	1.22–24	283	
10.19	218, 219	134–39	31n60	1.23	282	
10.20	218	139	32	2.186–95	281	
10.30	218			2.215	194, 272	
11.22–33	219, 260	Life of Adam and Eve		2.241–45	323n548	
11.23–32	250	12–16	260n378, 277, 282, 283, 284, 284n456, 293, 294	2.242–44	257	
11.23–26	267n409, 378n720			3.8–45	334	
				3.8–10	285–86n462	
11.24	219	13.3	282	3.8	282	
11.25–33	218	14.3	277, 283	3.11–16	28	
11.26	218, 219	25–29	276	3.20	132	
11.32–33	219, 257, 323n548	26.1	284	3.48–49	320	
		28.1–3	284	3.350–380	340	
11.32	323n548	29.1	284	3.545–49	57n37, 336n587	
11.40	267n411	Lives of the Prophets				
Assumption of Moses		21.15	281	3.652–56	326	
10.3	272–73n427	Odes of Solomon		3.657–732	280n446	
				4.145–148	340	
Ezekiel the Tragedian (Exagōgē)		7.4	146	5.33–55	57n37, 336n587	
		12.10	146	5.34	349	
68–89	293	16.18	29n53, 143n74, 146	5.108–10	324	
85–89	80			5.137–54	57n37, 336n587	
68–82	36, 281	16.19	146, 184, 386	5.158	324	
		17.17	146	5.214–21	57n37, 336n587	
Greek Apocalypse of Ezra		19.1–11	146	5.255	198	
7.6	281	24.1	146	5.414–15	324	
Joseph and Aseneth		29.6	146	8.68–83	340	
11.7–9	31n60	36.3–4	146	8.249–50	10	
14.8–9	258	39.11	146	8.375–76	65	
14.9	199, 214	41.12–13	146	8.403	282	
17.9	205	41.12	350n633	8.429–30	53	
17.10	205	41.15	146	8.442–45	283	
18.11	180	Parables of Enoch	279–80, 290	8.445–46	157n111	
21.4	180			8.456–61	224, 251	
Jubilees				8.469–73	157n111	
1.17	142	Prayer of Joseph		12.86	349	
1.27–3.7	265	frag. A 1–9	199			
1.27	194	frag. A 4	142, 263n388	Similitudes of Enoch	286	
1.29	194			Testament of Abraham		
2.2	28–29n52, 29n53, 194	Psalms of Solomon		1.4–7 [A]	272	
		17.1–46	369	7.11 [A]	272	
2.3	29n53	17.3–4	320	11.5–12 [A]	293	
4.15	189	17.21–46	320	11.7–12	276	
4.16–26	277	17.21–34	321	11.7–12 [A]	267n411	
4.21–25	278	17.30–32	325	12–13 [A]	293	

Index of Ancient Sources

13.4–8 [A]	293	9.14	184	3.1–13	327
13.10	200	9.20	29n53, 143	3.18–19	291n474
Testament of Adam		15.26–33	28–29n52, 29–30, 270n421	4Q185	
3.2	275			I–II 1.13–2.8	171
3.3–4	276	18.8–12	28–29n52, 30, 270n421	4Q201	
4.8	267n410			1	189
Testament of Asher		1QM		4Q202	
7.1	207n230	1.15	270	4 8–11	272
Testament of Dan		9.15–16	194, 217	4Q204	
6.1–5	232n289	9.15	263, 272	1	189
6.2	243	11.1–12	320	4Q212	
6.5	252, 395–96n30	12.7–10	270	3	189
		12.8	200		
Testament of Isaac		13.2	188	4Q213	
6.33–7.1	283	13.9–13	29n53	I 1.19	293
Testament of Job		13.10–12	270	4Q246	
32–33	293	13.10	194, 270	1–2	198
33.1–9	267n411	13.11–12	188	2.1–10	291n474
33.3	323n549	14.10	188	2.1	293
		14.16	266		
Testament of Levi		17.1–9	217	4Q266	
3.5–7	243	17.4–6	270	2.2	189
3.8	267n410	17.6	194, 270	4Q280	
5.1	292	17.7–8	197, 260	I 1–7	207
5.5	243	18.1–19.14	270		
5.6	232n289, 243	18.7	263	4Q374	
18.1–5	318	18.9	270	II 2.6	35, 281
18.1–4	324	1QPs^{a}Zion		4Q381	
Testament of Moses		22.13	196	I 3	132
1.14	35			I 6–11	284
11.16	35	1QS			
		3.13–26	29n53	4Q400	
Testament of Naphtali		3.15–4.1	258	II 2	242
2.5	282, 283	3.15–16	29n53		
		3.18–19	188	4Q402	
Testament of Reuben		3.25	188	1 2.30–46	205
5.7	236	4.6–8	200		
		4.23	275	4Q403	
Testament of Solomon		11.7–8	200	1 2.18–29	194
1.6	272	11.11	29n53, 143	I 1.35	29n53, 187
22.20	232n289, 252	11.17–18	29n53	4Q405	
		1QSa		XX 2.6–11	267
DEAD SEA SCROLLS		2.8–9	200	XXIII 1.3	267, 292
1QapGen		1QSb		4Q415	
2.19–26	277	4.25	194	IX 5–11	179, 184
5.3–4	277	5.28	293	4Q422	
1QH		4Q21		I 1.6	187
3.21–23	188	F 14	267	4Q491c	
3.21–22	242			5–6	293
6.13	194	4Q161		5	197, 378
10.8	196	frg. 23	377	8–18	325
10.12–19	395	frgs. 8–10	377	8–13	201, 205
11.13	188	4Q171		12–20	200
14.12–13	395–96n30	3.1–2	275	4Q504	
1QH^a		4Q174		VIII 4–6	275
4.15	275	3	321	4Q521	
9.7	184				

II.1–14	320	15a	191, 192, 195, 257, 268	10.1	237
II 2.7	267n411, 291n474			11.4	238
4Q529		b.Sanhedrin		13.1–8	237
7	272	38b	257	13.2	232, 252
		b.Abodah Zarah		15.1	238
4Q530		42b	242n316	16.2	237
2.6–20	278	b.Hullin		17.1	237
4Q543		40a	242n316	18.1–3	238
III 1.1	200	Tosefta		19.4	238
4Q545		t.Hullin		22.1–7	238
I 1.17	200	2.6	242n316	22.4–5	238
4Q547				27.1	238
IV 6	200			27.2	238
4QMMT		**NAG HAMMADI**		28	148
B 1–3	335	**WRITINGS**		30.2	238
B 8–13	335			37.3	238
11Q5		Apocalypse of James		49.1	238
26 14	179	14.26–30	250, 267n409, 378n720	51.1–2	238
26.12	29n53			59.1	238
XXVI 14	184	14.30–31	257, 323n548	61.3	237
11Q13				62.1	237
2.11–14	270	Apocalypse of Peter		69.1	238
11Q17		6.1	293, 323n548	77.1	237
5.8	267	Apocryphon of John		82.1	237
7.11	267	2.27–4.10	53	85	281
10.7	292	2.27–3.1	362	85.2	238
11Q19–20		6.10–8.28	69	99.1–3	238
29.7–8	142	7.27–29	69	105.1	238
11QMelch		7.30–8.27	126	106.1	238
2	205	9.25–19.33	125	108.1–3	237
2.9–14	194	9.25–10.7	183	111.2	238
2.9–11	325	11.15–22	125	113.1–4	238
2.10–11	378	15.1–17.29	281	114.1–3	238
2.10	113, 205	24.8–25	125	Gospel of Truth	
2.12–14	197, 260	24.12	125	16.31–17.4	149
2.24–25	205	30.11–31.31	125	17.1–37	125
Damascus Document (CD)		Gospel of the Egyptians		17.5–20	125
3.20	275	58.25–59.9	29n53, 125	17.37–18.19	125
3.24	194	Gospel of Philip		18.11–21	149
5.18	194	54.4–10	239n307	18.32–19.10	26n43
12.2–3	188	54.5–10	69	19.7–10	26n43
12.23–13.1	319	56.13–15	237n304	23.19–24.10	149
14.19	319	57.32–58.10	218, 239, 251	23.33–24.2	149
20.1	319			24.9–14	146
		58.1–2	229	24.28–25.2	125
		58.10–14	239	26.4–7	149
		58.33	148	30.24–26	69
RABBINIC		60.12	183	30.27–31	149
LITERATURE		70.12–17	282	30.32–31.12	149
		70.34–71.2	239	31.4–6	149
Babylonian Talmud		Gospel of Thomas		31.5–6	149
b.Berakhot		1.1	238	37.1–38.6	149
32b	29n53	3.3	238	37.20–24	149
b.Hagigah		3.4	238	37.21	143n74
14a	29n53, 192, 257	5.1–2	237	38.7–39.28	149
				38.7–14	69
				38.33–36	53
				40.26	69
				41.15–42.10	26n43

470 Index of Ancient Sources

Prayer of the Apostle Paul
  A12–14 362

Second Discourse of
Great Seth
  56.21–57.7 223

Treatise on the Resurrection
  43.36–37 362
  48.18–19 362
  50.1 362

Trimorphic Protennoia
  35.1–6 155
  35.12–13 155
  35.33–34 155
  36.5 155
  37.4–20 155
  37.4–5 155
  37.7–8 155
  37.13–14 155
  38.7–12 126
  38.12–13 155
  38.22–23 155
  39.6 155
  39.12–13 155
  40.29–41.1 155
  41.16 155
  46.5–6 155
  46.10 155
  46.14–16 155
  46.24–25 155
  46.30 155
  47.13–18 155
  47.14–18 156
  47.15–16 155
  47.15 155
  49.11–20 251

Tripartite Tractate
  51.6–57.8 54
  56.23–24 69
  56.35–38 239n307
  57.19–22 69
  58.7–8 69
  63.30–35 26n43
  66.32 239n307
  80.30–81.7 125
  99.19–100.30 363
  100.19–35 125
  104.30–106.5 125
  105.1–3 26n43
  105.1–2 255n359
  105.19 125
  105.29–35 125
  108.13–138.27 125
  113.1 255n359
  124.25–34 239
  125.19–20 239
  132.14–27 239
  133.16–135.7 363

NEW TESTAMENT APOCRYPHA

Acts of John
  77 248, 249
  90 236

Acts of Paul
  11.2 356

Acts of Paul and Thecla
  42 248

Acts of Peter
  20–21 248
  21 249
  39 248, 249

Acts of Philip
  38 203

Acts of Thomas
  25 249

Apocalypse of Elijah
  1.8 267n411
  4.27 267n411
  4.28 293
  4.29 267n411

Apocalypse of John
  3–14 26n43
  10.20–12.13 124n23
  11.20–22 29n53
  13.5–13 26n43, 29n53
  19.2–3 124n23
  31.3–4 156n105

Book of Elkasai 236

Epistula Apostolorum
  1.2 147, 222
  3.1–15 147, 222
  3.5 222
  3.8 257, 323n548
  3.13 222, 225
  7.1–4 147
  13–14 223, 232
  13.1–6 223
  13.1–2 148
  13.1 182
  13.2–14.8 251
  14.3–8 223
  14.6 [Eth.] 147
  17.2 222n270
  17.3–8 222n271
  17.4 147
  17.8 147
  18.1 222
  19.16 147
  21.2 66, 222n271
  22.1 225
  25.3 222n271
  31.11 222, 222n271
  39.12 147, 222

Gospel of Judas
  44.4 183

Gospel of Peter
  9.35 342
  12.50 342
  39–40 236, 251, 386

Gospel of Pseudo-Matthew
  9–10 223n274
  11.1 223n274

Infancy Gospel of Thomas
  7.2 238
  7.4 238, 252

Kerygma Petrou
  1 157n111, 185
  2 5, 119n10, 143n74, 184, 386

Naassene Hymn 374

Pistis Sophia
  1.7–8 223
  1.7.12 224, 251

Protoevangelium of James
  11.2 223n274
  14.1 223n274
  14.2 223n274

PATRISTIC AUTHORS

1 Clement
  9.3 278
  20.11 122
  26.1 122
  33.2 122
  35.3 122
  36.1–6 265
  36.2 251, 265, 386
  36.4 321
  36.5 257, 323n548
  38.3 122
  43.6 32n62, 52
  46.6 32n62
  49.5–6 389
  58.2 248
  59.2–61.3 255
  59.2 122
  61.3 248
  64.1 248
  65.2 248

Index of Ancient Sources   471

2 Clement
1.1	10
9.5	64n65, 145, 344

Ambrose
On the Christian Faith
5.1.23	35n72

Aristides
Apology
1	32, 53
2 [Syr.]	145n79
7	58
15 [Gk.]	123

Arnobius
Adversus gentes
1.38	16

Athanasius
De synodis
47	65–66n70
49	231

Incarnation
13	231
16.1	62
40	231
45.4	62
47.3	62
55.5	62

Oratio contra Arianos
1.9	67
1.55–56	231
2.21	29n53
2.23–24	231
3.13–14	252

Athenagoras
Legatio pro Christianis
4.1	53
4.2	119n10, 143n74, 151
5.2	28–29n52
6.2	53, 119n10, 123, 143n74, 151, 152
10.1–2	53
10.1	119n10, 151, 152
10.2	64, 66, 143n74, 152, 251, 386
10.3–4	132, 152
10.3	64
10.5	14, 26n43, 64, 66, 119n10, 151, 152, 251, 386
12.3	152
15.1–16.4	53
15.1	152
18.1–19.3	66, 152
18.2	119n10, 151
24.2–5	152
24.2	64, 66, 152, 251, 386
27.1–30.6	152
30.3	58

Augustine
Confessions
7.9.13	161

De civitate Dei
4.27	49n22
6.5	49n22
6.6–7	59
6.12	49n22
10.29	161
19.23	250

The Literal Meaning of Genesis
	118

Basil of Caesarea
Adversus Eunomium
I.18	61n51

Clement of Alexandria
Eclogae Propheticae
4.1	148

Cyril of Alexandria
Fragments
190	59

Didache
7.1–4	390
9.1–5	248
9.4	248
10.3	372
10.6	231, 232, 248
14.1	342

Epistle of Barnabas
1.1	389
5.10–11	145
6.14	145, 184
12.7	180n162, 248, 271
12.10–11	323n548
12.10	257, 344
18.1	196

Epistle to Diognetus
1.1	399
5.17	399
6.8	142
7.2–4	50, 67, 251, 386
7.2	119n10, 123, 135, 143n74, 153, 184, 386
7.3–5	154
8.7	123
9.2	389
10.2	184
10.5–6	50
11.2	154
11.3	154
11.4–5	154
11.5	67, 386
11.7–9	154
12.9	154

Eusebius
De vita Constantini
4.73	353

Historia ecclesiastica
3.19–20	356
3.27	235n297
3.27.2	233nn293–294
4.6.2	324
5.8.10	233n293
5.13.7	258
5.28.5–6	9, 248
6.17	233n293
6.38	235, 235n299
7.11.5	249
7.30.10–11	248

Praeparatio evangelica
1.5.16	399
9.27.6	36

Hippolytus
Commentary on Daniel
frag. 2: 24–25	213n247

Contra Noetum
16	157n111

Refutatio Omnium Haeresium
6.35	64n65
6.42.2	148n84
6.51.1	224
7.29–30	127
7.34.1–2	233
7.34.2	233
7.38	258
7.38.2–3	240
9.13.1	235
9.13.2–3	218, 235, 251
9.13.4	235
9.14.1	235
9.14.2	236
9.15.2	235
9.16.4	235, 236
9.17.2	235
9.30.7–8	320
10.13.3	239
10.19.1	240
10.19.3	240
10.20	258
10.20.1	240
10.21.1	255n359
10.22.1	233
15.1–6	235
15.1	235n300
19.6	65

472 Index of Ancient Sources

Ignatius
  Epistle to Polycarp
    3.2   65, 145
    8.3   10, 145
  Epistle to the Ephesians
    1.3   248
    2.2   248
    3.2   64, 145
    4.1–2   248
    7.2   10, 65, 145, 411
    18.2   145
    19.2   200
    20.1   248, 372
  Epistle to the Magnesians
    7.2   146
    8.2   32n62, 146
    9.1   342
  Epistle to the Philadelphians
    4.2   390
  Epistle to the Romans
    3.3   145
    4.1   248
  Epistle to the Smyrnaeans
    1.1   145, 248
    2.1   68
    3.1–3   68
    4.1   248
    4.2   68
    5.2   68
    7.1   68
    12.2   68
  Epistle to the Trallians
    10.1   68

Irenaeus
  Adversus haereses
    1.1.1   68, 149
    1.1.3   362
    1.2.1–6   149
    1.2.2–5   183
    1.2.5–6   68
    1.2.5   149
    1.2.6   26n43, 239
    1.4.5   126
    1.5.1–6   125
    1.5.1–2   126
    1.5.3–4   29n53
    1.5.3   184, 362
    1.7.1   240
    1.8.5   126, 148n84, 149
    1.10.3   123
    1.11.1–5   124n23
    1.11.1   146n80, 148n84, 149
    1.12.1–4   148n84
    1.15.5   123
    1.16.3   123
    1.18.1   149
    1.20.1   124n23, 238
    1.22.1   67, 119n10, 123, 155n101, 158, 251, 386
    1.23.5   255n359
    1.24.1   68
    1.24.2   68
    1.25.1   158
    1.26.1–2   232
    1.26.1   68, 125, 158, 255n359
    1.27.2   125
    1.29.1–4   155
    1.29.4   183
    1.30.1–14   183
    1.30.2   183
    1.30.6   29n53, 125
    1.30.12   183
    1.30.13   68
    2.1.1   123, 125
    2.1.2   123
    2.13.2–8   159
    2.28.4–5   159
    2.30.9   229
    3.3.3   123
    3.6.1–2   228
    3.6.5   26n43
    3.7.1   123
    3.8.1   62
    3.9.3   68
    3.10.3   29n53
    3.11.1–6   160
    3.11.1–2   67, 127n29, 143n74, 158, 251, 386
    3.11.3   158
    3.11.6   159
    3.11.7   68
    3.11.8   119n10, 158, 159
    3.11.9   68n75
    3.16.2   158
    3.16.3   252
    3.16.8   123, 124n23
    3.18.3   124n23
    3.18.7   284n460
    3.19.1–20.2   160
    3.19.1–3   66, 67
    3.19.1   158, 159
    3.19.3   158
    3.20.4   228
    3.21.1   158, 233
    3.21.9   158
    3.21.10–3.23.8   282
    3.21.10   143n74, 158
    3.24.2   124n23
    3.25.3   127
    3.25.5   65, 124n24
    4.2.2   229
    4.6.2   158
    4.6.7   67, 159
    4.7.4   67, 158, 251, 386
    4.10.1   228
    4.11.1   158, 184, 386
    4.20.1–7   160
    4.20.1–6   182
    4.20.1–5   158
    4.20.1–4   119n10
    4.20.1   53, 62, 132, 228
    4.20.2   158
    4.20.3   229
    4.20.5   158
    4.20.6–7   159
    4.20.7   159
    4.22.1–23.2   158
    4.24.1   158
    4.33.2   240
    4.33.4   233
    4.34.4   185
    4.38.3   123
    5.1.2–3   282
    5.1.3   233, 284n460
    5.5.1   282
    5.12.2–3   282
    5.14.1   282
    5.15.3–4   282
    5.16.1–3   282
    5.16.3   284n460
    5.17.1   123
    5.18.1   67, 125, 251, 386
    5.18.2–3   158
    5.21.1–2   282
    5.23.2   282
  Demonstration of the Apostolic Preaching
    31   158
    37   158
    39   158
    84   158
    94   158
  Epideixis
    4   53, 123
    5   123, 158, 160
    6   53
    8   29n53
    9   26n43
    10   158, 159, 160, 218, 228, 236, 251, 386
    30–31   158
    31   159
    40   251, 386
    43–66   158
    43–52   228
    43   143n74, 158
    47   67, 159, 160
    52–53   159
    52   160
    55–56   228
    56   251

Index of Ancient Sources   473

88	228	59.1	123	57–60	151
94	228, 251, 386	59.5	150	59–61	226
99	123	60.7	150, 151	60.5	151n97
Jerome		61.4–5	149n90	61.1–3	150
Epistulae		62.3–4	151	61.1	64, 148, 150, 151, 225, 228, 251
112.13.1–2	235n297	63.4	150	61.2–3	228
Homilies on the Psalms		63.5	225, 226, 251	61.2	66, 151
14	80n115	63.7–10	226	61.3	182
John Chrysostom		63.7–8	151	62.1–4	150
Migne, *Patrologiae Cursus,*		63.10	150	62.4–5	251
series Graeca (PG)		63.14–17	226	62.4	148, 184
61.38–42	59n41	63.14	225, 251	63–70	150
61.697	59n41	63.15	150, 185	63	248
John of Damascus		63.16	150	63.4–64.1	361
De fide orthodoxa		63.17	151	63.5	10
4.15	80n115	64.5	16, 150	68.1	58n39
		65.3	248	69.1–3	16
Justin Martyr		66.2	150	69.3	58
1 Apology		*2 Apology*		73–74	248
5.4	150	5.1	53	75.1–2	226, 251
6.1	53, 62, 262n386	6.3	119n10, 150, 184, 386	76.3	226
6.2	92, 150, 208, 226, 228, 243, 271	6.9	143n74	84.2	150
8.2	122	7.1	161	86.3	225, 251
9.1	61	10.1	150	87.2	150
10.6	150	10.3	150	100.2	150
12.7	184	10.8	150	113.4	228
13.3–4	150, 151	13.3–6	150	116.1	227
13.3	62, 150, 228	13.4	150	126	248
13.4	53	*Dialogue with Trypho*		126.1	150, 226, 251
14.1	65–66n70	5.4	53, 151	127.4	151, 225, 251
14.2	53	11.4	185	127.5	151n97
21.1–22.3	16	24.1	185	128.1–4	225
21.1–6	81, 361	31.1	227	128.1	10, 150, 251
21.1–2	150	32	257	128.2	150
21.1	150, 184, 227	34.2	225, 251, 371	128.3–4	66, 151, 228
21.2	162n121	37–38	248	128.3	29n53
21.3	58	38.1	150, 245, 250, 361	128.4	151, 157, 227, 228
21.4	56n36	43.1	185	129.1	151n97
22.1–2	150	45.4	150, 324, 374	129.3–5	182
22.2	150, 184, 227, 228	46.1	232, 232n290	129.3–4	132
23.2	150	47.1–5	232	129.3	150, 151
25	53	47.4–5	232n290	129.4	151
29.4	58	48.1	150	*Martyrdom of Polycarp*	
32.10–33.9	150	48.4	232, 232n290, 233	2.3	203
32.10	150	49.1	233, 320, 361	8.2	340
33.6	64n65, 185	55–56	232	14.1	248, 251, 271, 386
36.1	150	55.1–2	31n60	14.3	248
44.10	150	55.1	151	17.2	249
45	257	55.2	32, 62	19.2	21
46.1–6	150	56	226	20.2	145n79
46.2	150, 185	56.2	26n43	21.1	323n548
46.3	161	56.3	29n53, 122n20, 143n73	22.3	248
46.5	64n65, 150	56.4	151, 165, 225, 226	**Origen**	
51.8	227	56.10	226	*Against Celsus*	
52.3	227, 251, 386	56.11	151, 228	1.23–24	32
53.2	150	56.14	151	2.31	68n73
53.6	62	56.17	151	3.22	59, 81, 361
		56.23	151n97	4.14	169

4.18	68n73, 169	2.42	29n53, 251,	24.9	360
5.4–5	242n316,		255, 386	30–33	356, 361
	251, 386			33–34	340

4.18 68n73, 169
5.4–5 242n316, 251, 386
5.5 243
5.39 165, 181n168
5.61 235n297
6.15 65
6.17 66
6.34 137n49
6.60 123
6.61 165
6.71 388
7.57 165
8.12 10, 250
8.14 250
8.35 26n43

Commentary on the Gospel of John
1.19 148
1.110–11 123
2.8 125, 143n74, 148n84
2.25 199, 263n388

Dialogue with Heraclides
1 11

Exhortation to Martyrdom
13 203

Homilies on Genesis
1.1 148

Homilies on Luke
17 233n293

On First Principles
1.2.6 137n49
1.2.10 269n420
1.3.4 218
1.6.2 203
3.2.1 207–8

Peter Chrysologus
Sermon
43 80n114

Polycarp
Epistle to the Philippians
1.1 21
2.1 250, 257, 267n409, 271, 323n548, 378n720
2.21 323n548
14.3 386

Pseudo-Clement
Homilies
3.17–28 236n301
3.38 127
16.15–16 65–66n70
18.4 251, 386
Recognitions
1.45 386, 251

2.42 29n53, 251, 255, 386

Pseudo-Cyprian
De centesima sexagesima tricesima
50–54 252
50 240
216–20 241, 252

Pseudo-Cyril
Discourse on the Theotokos
12a 224

Pseudo-Tertullian
Adversus omnes haereses
3 255n359

Shepherd of Hermas
1.1 219
3.4 119n10, 182, 184, 386
12.1 29n53, 241
26.1 29n53
55–60 232
55 230n284
58.3 29n53, 241
59.2–3 251
59.2 251, 386
69.2 185
69.3 251
83.1 236
89.2 145n79
89.7–8 251
89.8 241
91.3 248
91.5 119n10, 135, 184, 251, 386

Tertullian
Adversus Marcionem
1.2–2.1 127
1.2 125
1.4 257
1.15 257
1.16 257
2.1 127
3.8.1 240
3.9.1–7 240
3.9.7 203
Adversus Praxean
3 26n43, 230
6–7 182
8 157
16 230
Apologeticus pro Christianis
4 361
21.10–11 388
24 53
24.2 14, 26n43, 230

24.9 360
30–33 356, 361
33–34 340
De carne Christi
6.9–11 240
14.1–2 251, 252, 386
14.1 238, 252
14.3 230
14.5 230, 234
24 68
De oratione
3 203
De praescriptione haereticorum
7 399
33 233
De spectaculis
30 59

Theophilus of Antioch
Autolycus
1.4 53
1.7 119n10, 182
1.11 58
2.10 64, 119n10, 143n74, 152, 182
2.13 29n53, 148
2.15 132, 182
2.20 148
2.22 64, 119n10, 153
2.34 123

GRECO-ROMAN AUTHORS

Aelian
Varia historia
2.19 300

Aelius Aristides
Orations
26.32 313
37 16

Aelius Theon
Progymnasmata
109 268

Appian
Bella civilia
1.17 313
2.106 72n87
2.148 19n22, 348, 353

Apuleius
Metamorphoses
11.5 174

Index of Ancient Sources 475

Aristotle
  Metaphysics
    12.1076a.3   31n57
    1013a   148
  Politics
    3.13   71
  Rhetoric
    1.5.9   71
Arius
  Letter to Eusebius of
    Nicomedia
    1.6   65–66n70
  Thalia   65–66n70
Arrian
  Anabasis
    4.10–12   18, 300
    4.11.1–4   55
    7.23.2   18, 300
Asclepias of Mendes
  Theologumena   307
Augustus Caesar
  Res gestae (RG)
    § 5   345
    § 7   76
    § 7.3   317
    § 10.1   314
    § 19–21   317
    § 21   345
    § 34   347
Aulus Gellius
  Noctes atticae
    6.1.6   19n22
Callimachus
  Hymn to Zeus
    54–89   301
Cassius Dio
  Historia Romana
    1.1–2.4   48
    43.14.6   72n87
    43.43.2   353
    43.45.3   72n87, 353
    44.4.4–5   72n87
    44.11.3   18n19
    44.51.1   313
    45.1.1–5   307, 345
    45.2.1–4   308
    46.6.1–4   353
    51.19.16   313
    51.20.1   73, 314
    51.20.6–8   20, 73
    51.20.6   72
    55.12.2–3   314
    56.41.9   74
    56.46   73

    57.8.1–4   314
    59.7.1   57n38
    59.24.3–4   338
    59.26.8–9   338
    59.28.1–2   347
    59.28.1   20, 338
    62.5.2   338n590
    63.1–7   360
    66.17.3   353
    68.29.1–30.1   18
Cicero
  Ad Atticum
    16.15.13   74
    290   353
  De divinatione
    1.88   44
  De haruspicum responsis
    2.20   353
    6.13–16   353
  De imperio Cn. Pompei /
    Pro Lege manilia 19n22
    42   345
    49   345
  De legibus
    2.19   44
    2.27–28   19n22, 353
  De natura deorum
    1.18   142
    1.119   55
    2.2   31n57
    2.62   19n22, 44, 71, 303
    3.39–50   55
    3.49   44
  De officiis
    3.25   353
  De republica
    2.17–18   285
  Philippics
    2.34   18n19
    2.110   72n87
    3.5   18n19
  Pro Marcello   19n22
Cleanthes
  Hymn to Zeus   17, 129–30, 162
Corpus hermeticum
    frag. 24.3   77
Excerpta ex Theodoto
    4.1   239
    6.1–4   148n84, 149
    7   239
    7.3–4   68
    8.1   68, 240, 252
    8.2   184
    17.4   68
    19.1   148n84, 149

    21.3   239
    22.3–5   239
    22.5–6   239
    23.1   149
    25.1   240, 252
    35.1   239, 252
    43.2   251
    45.1–3   126
    45.3   148n84
    47.1–2   126
    62.1–2   323n548
  Paedagogus
    1.7   229
  Protrepticus
    1   61n51, 123
    2.24.3   55
    6   53
    7   160
    10   66
    110   160
    117   53
  Stromata
    2.22   65
    5.14.125   26n43
    7.1   148
Diodorus Siculus
  Library
    3.9.1   44
    4.1.4   347
    6.1.2   44
    16.91.1–16.95.1 322
    37.5.1–37.6.1   348
Diogenes Laertius
  Lives of the Philosophers
    7.1.137   51
    7.134   129
    7.135–36   131
    7.136   129
    9.1.1   129
Dionysius Halicarnassus
  Antiquitates Romanae
    2.63.3   353
Epiphanius
  Panarion
    19.1.4–5   235
    19.1.4   235n299
    19.3.4   235n300
    20.30.1   234n296
    20.30.2   234, 236n301
    30.2.2   234
    30.3.3–6   234
    30.3.3   236n301
    30.3.5   236n301
    30.14.4   234
    30.16.3–4   234

476 Index of Ancient Sources

30.16.4	252, 270	1.155	28, 30	2.184–203	339
30.17.6–7	235	2.326	281	2.184–85	337
30.18.5–6	234	3.91	28, 31n60	2.184	338
30.18.6	233n294	4.201	28	2.185	338
30.34.6	236n301	4.297	320	2.197–98	335
		4.326	35	2.224–27	333
		5.112	28	2.409–19	335
		8.280	65	2.414	335
		10.211–12	366	3.459	335
		11.331–35	283n454	4.417	335
		11.331–39	319n528	6.312–13	335
		13.299–300	327	6.312–12	356
		14.13.3–14.6	280n446	7.71	335
		15.51–57	328	7.118–62	359
		15.296–98	330	7.410	367n677
		15.328–30	330	7.418–19	339
		15.339	329–30		
		15.363–64	330		
		15.423	327		28–29n52
		16.132–35	327		
		16.136–41	360		
		16.157–58	330		
		16.162–65	332, 339		
		17.42	335	1.15.6	285
		17.149–155	330	1.16	19n22, 303
		17.161–62	327	1.53	18n19
		17.200–212	328	16.1–8	285
		18.23	367n677		
		18.55–59	333		
		18.63	176		
		18.256–61	57, 336n587	13	176, 250
		18.256	338	13	176, 250
		18.257–61	337	29	321
		18.257–59	338		
		18.257	338	14	14
		18.261–309	339		
		18.261	338		
		18.296	335		
		19.4	57, 336n587	8	9
		19.87	313	10	248
		19.278–306	339	45	248
		19.343–50	77, 328	65	248
		20.105–12	333	105	248
		20.211–12	331n577	frag. 15	229n282

Euripides
  Bacchae
    1–5 162n122

Fronto
  Epistulae
    4.12.4 306

Heraclitus
  Allegoriae
    28.2 17
    55.1 17
    72.4–5 17

Herodotus
  Histories
    2.44 44, 45n7, 247

Homer
  Iliad 309, 367
    2.204–5 31n57
    2.565 347
    5.440–42 54
    15.185–95 376
  Odyssey 309
    20.124 347

Horace
  Carmen Saeculare
    1.2.1–46 48, 73
    3.5 73, 309
  Homeric Hymns
    15 350
  Odes
    1.4 345
    1.12.49–52 309
    2.3.10 350
    3.3.9–12 325
    4.5 314
    4.15 314

Josephus
  Against Apion
    2.75–76 57, 336n587
    2.76–77 335
    2.76 335
    2.167 52
    2.190–91 60
    2.190 65
    2.192 29n53, 122n20, 143n73
    2.248 60
  Antiquities
    1.73 188
    1.155–56 31n60

Jewish War
    1.13.1–11 280n446
    1.68–69 327
    1.400 327
    1.403 330
    1.404–6 330
    1.407 330
    1.414 329
    1.425–26 327
    1.437 328
    1.457–66 327
    1.648–55 330
    2.1–3 328
    2.145 36
    2.169–74 333

Lactantius
  The Divine Institutes
    1.5.18 28–29n52

Livy
  History of Rome (Ab urbe condita)

Lucian
  De morte Peregrini
  Vitarum auctio

Melito of Sardis
  Peri Pascha

Minucius Felix
  Octavius
    18 26n43, 119n10, 182
    19 131
    23 59
    26 62
    29 59

Orphic Hymns
  32.1 16
  61.2 321

Ovid
  Fasti
    3.697–710 350, 354
    3.701–2 375

Index of Ancient Sources   477

Metamorphoses		66–76	334	69	58n39, 168,
14.123–39	77	81	31		285–86n462
14.284–85	48	111	50n25	72–76	122
14.827–28	353	*De ebrietate*		74	122n20
15.745–870	354	30–31	174, 184	83	284
15.745–50	74	31	174	100	52, 122
15.844–48	48	45	32	139	166n129
15.858–70	376	61	174	170–72	31n57
Pausanias		*De fuga et inventione*		170–71	28–29n52
Description of Greece		5	136, 148	*De plantatione*	
2.20.1	45n7	50–51	179	8–10	135
Philo		68–70	31n57	18	179
De Abrahamo		70	122	35	285–86n462
29	161n120	95	96, 121,	86	261–62n383
51	190		135, 165, 182	93	65
70–71	164	97	165, 174	*De posteritate Caini*	
83	161n120	101	96, 134,	16–20	135
121	96, 121, 135,		136, 164, 168	28	35
	165, 182, 257,	103	96, 121, 135, 165, 182	66	52
	261–62n383	108–9	174, 182	136–38	174
124	261–62n383	108	134, 136,	136	174
143–45	31n57		166, 318	138	174
143	31, 122	109	174, 179, 184	160–61	35n73
De agricultura		112	135	183	31
51	136, 185	191	161n120	*De sacrificiis Abelis et Caini*	
De cherubim		*De gigantibus*		5	200
27–29	135	16	198n208	8–10	35
35	136	*De Iosepho*		8–9	35n73
36	96	254	52	8	121, 135,
44	51	*De migratione Abrahami*			135n44, 165
49	174	6	122, 135n44, 165	9–10	56n36, 78
124–27	21	84	35n73	60	31, 31n57
125	122	130	172n145	64	174
126–27	121	174	190	65	133
127	135, 135n44, 165	*De mutatione nominum*		95	285–86n462
De confusione linguarum		16–17	164	*De somniis*	
41	136, 164	19	35n73	1.18	166
60–63	134	22	28n52, 31	1.51	166
61–63	179	87	148	1.65–69	135, 166
62–63	185	125–29	35n73	1.70	31n57
146–47	136, 166	129	50n25, 70	1.75	134
146–67	179	137	174	1.141–42	394n27
146	96, 136, 148,	181	79, 168	1.215	96, 134, 136,
	166, 185, 194,	208	161n120		166, 168,
	196, 206, 217	*De opificio mundi*			185
147	134, 166	7	122n20	1.227–39	31n57
170–75	31n57	10	121	1.227–37	191
170	28–29n52, 31n57,	20	165	1.229–30	136, 164
	112, 122n20, 168	23	29n53, 122n20,	1.229	52
171	122		143n73	1.230	136
175	122	24–25	134, 166	1.234–49	122
179–81	31n57	24	165	1.238–39	136
De decalogo		29–31	134	1.239	148, 166
8–9	349	29	122n20	1.241	135, 136, 185
41	52	30	165	2.80	366
52–65	31n60	33	165	2.89–90	366
65	28, 31, 31n57	36	134	2.99–100	366
		46	92	2.130	57
				2.188–89	134

2.189	35n73	77–184	336n587	356–57	338
2.234–35	79, 280–81	77	57	356	332, 335, 336, 338
2.242–45	174	80	61	357	338
2.242	174	91	56n36	364	332
3.13	166	93–118	57n38	366	52
8.19	166	93–107	310	368	338
14.6	166	95	61		
14.7–9	166	96	314	*Legum allegoriae*	
15.5	166	97	61	1.18	122n20
16.3	166	110–11	61, 285–86n462	1.31–42	275
17.24	166	110	57, 345	1.31	204n218
163	261–62n383	112	57	1.37	285–86n462

De specialibus legibus

		114	57	1.40–41	35n73
1.13–20	122	115	28–29n52, 57	1.41	21, 122
1.13–19	31n57	116	31n60, 338, 366	1.43	174, 179, 184
1.30	261–62n383	118	57, 58, 168	1.49	31n57
1.81	122, 135, 135n44, 165	120–39	337	1.65	174, 185
		133	335	1.105–8	161
1.277	174	134–37	337, 339	1.149	349
1.307	261–62n383	137	337	2.1	31n57
1.329	121	143–53	58	2.3	122n20
2.166	51	143	336	2.4	275
4.75	174	145–49	336	2.49	174

De virtutibus

		149–51	306	2.68	52
62	179	149	73, 336, 348	2.86–87	174
65	31n57, 57	150–51	311	2.87	174
168	50n25	155–61	339	3.3	174
172	31n57, 57	155–57	332	3.46	174
		157	335	3.52	174

De vita contemplativa

		162–64	338	3.82	28–29n52
6	58	162	338	3.96	122, 135, 135n44, 165, 166

De vita Mosis

		164	338		
1.27	35	178–96	338	3.177	148, 217
1.66–67	191	188	338	3.207	122
1.100	122n20	198	338		
1.148	347	199–203	337, 338	*Quaestiones et solutiones in Exodum*	
1.155–58	35, 280	201	338		
1.156	78	207–60	339	2.6	35n73
1.167	191	232	335, 338	2.13	166, 168, 190
2.99–100	96, 121, 135, 65, 182, 192, 257, 261–62n383	278	57n38	2.62	96, 121, 135, 165, 182
		280	335	2.68	31n57, 121, 124n23, 135, 165, 166, 168, 182
		286	335		
		288	335		
2.100	28–29n52, 31	290	335	68	96
2.127–29	134	298–320	339	*Quaestiones et solutiones in Genesim*	
2.127	161n120	298	332		
2.171	52	299–306	333	1.4	166
2.205	31	299	333n580, 335	1.58	21

In Flaccum

		301	332	2.16	96, 121, 135, 165, 182
25–39	328	305	332		
39	343	309–10	332	2.62	62, 134, 136, 165, 166, 168, 191, 192
48–50	335	317	335		
49	336	332	338	4.97	179, 185

Legatio ad Gaium

		334–38	339	*Quis rerum divinarum heres sit*	
6	31n57, 122	334	339		
10.2	152	338	338	1	194
10.5	152	346	337, 338, 339	53	174
22	335	347	52	119	135n44, 161n120, 165
24.2	152, 182	349–67	338		
75–113	338	353	338		

Index of Ancient Sources   479

133–43	121	40d–41b	120	*Life of Antony*	
156	121	41c	120	60.3	19n21
157	190, 194	42d–43a	120	75.4	19n21
165–66	165	68e–69d	120	*Life of Caius Gracchus*	
166	96, 121, 135, 168, 182, 261–62n383	Plautus		18	19n22
187	135	*Asinaria*		*Life of Lysander*	
199	174, 179, 184	712–13	77	18	313
205–6	62, 96, 137, 166	Pliny the Elder		18.4	300
205	136, 148	*Natural History*		*Life of Marius*	
206	31n57, 168	2.14	71	27.5	19n22
213–14	161	2.26	46–47n14	*Life of Pelopidas*	
230–35	134	2.93–94	48	16.5	45
235–36	96	Pliny the Younger		*Life of Pompey*	
Quod deterius potiori insidiari soleat		*Epistulae*		27	41
39	161n120	10.96	250, 394	*Life of Romulus*	
54	174, 179, 184	10.96.7	248	26.2	353
83	134	10.97.6	10	28.1–3	285
115–17	174	*Panegyricus*		28.3	353
117	174	1	76	28.8	48, 56
161–62	78	4	76	*Life of Titus Flaminius*	
Quod Deus sit immutabilis		11.2	74	16.3–4	19n22
83	96	52.6	76	*Moralia*	
110	31n57	Plotinus		601A	14
138	166	*Enneads*		*On Superstition*	
182	148	II 9 [33] 6.29–31	124n23	13	55
Quod omnis probus liber sit		Plutarch		*Stoic Republic*	
42–44	56n36	*Amatorius*		1052A	44
43	78	18	49	Porphyry	
Philostratus		18.12	55	*On Statues (Agalm.)*	
Life of Apollonius of Tyana		*De defectu oraculorum*		8.103–6	17
1.4–6	321	10	15	Pseudo-Plato	
Plato		11	14	*Epinomus*	
Cratylus		*De laude*		984d–985c	14
407e–408b	131	12	56	Ptolemy	
Crito		*Isis and Osiris*		*Letter to Flora*	
109b	376	2	9	33.3.5–6	127n29
De legibus		21	51	33.3.6	126, 127, 143n74, 148n84
4.715e	65	24	56	33.7.4	115, 126, 148n84
4.717a–b	14	25	14	33.7.5–7	96n21
Phaedo		26	58n40	33.7.5	126
252de	50n25	27	15	33.7.6–7	126
Republic		46	127n27	33.7.6	53, 126
2.378d–e	46–47n14	53	60n48, 174	Quintilian	
4.493d	46	54	131	*Institutio Oratoria*	
6.509b	44	67	131	3.7.9	45
427c	17	70	55	6.3.77	74, 311
202d–203a	394n27	*Life of Alexander*		Quintus Curtius Rufus	
202e	14	1–3	345	*Historia Alexandri Magni*	
Timaeus		1.8	345	1.36.2	322
27c–34b	124	2.2–3.4	307	2.22.9	322
28a–e	124	2.2–3.9	48	Seneca	
28a–c	120	27.8–28.6	18, 300	*Apocolocyntosis*	
29b	120	33.1	18, 300	9	56
30b	120	54.1–55.1	18, 300		
35a–b	120	74.2–3	18, 300		

De clementia
1.10.3   74
Epistulae
65.7–10   21
Sophocles
Oedipus at Colonus
1382   321
Strobaeus
Anthology
1.1.12   130
Eclogues
1.1.12   17
Suetonius
Augustus
1–6   307
18.1   18
51.1   73
53.1   314
60.1   331
70.1–2   310
94.4–6   73
94.4   48, 73, 307
Caligula
21–22   338
22   31n57, 57
22.2   310
52   57n38, 338
Claudius
11.1–12.1   58
12.1   19
Domitian
13   314
Julius Caesar
7.1–2   18
76.1–3   72
76.1   72n87
79.2   18n19
84.2   72
88   48, 353
88.1   325
Nero
13   360
Tiberius
14.3   349
26.1   19
27   314
Vespasian
4.5   356
23.4   353
Tacitus
Annals
1.10.6   74
1.73   20, 305
2.87   314
4.38.1   41, 47

4.55   20
4.56.1   19n22
Histories
5.3   31n60, 32
5.5   329, 337
5.13   356
Tatian
Oratio
4   157
5   66, 123, 148, 157, 158
7   123, 158
10.3   58
19   143n74, 157, 158
Varro
*Antiquitates rerum
   divinarum*   49n22
Velleius Paterculus
History of Rome
2.126.1   47
Virgil
Aeneid
1.257–96   345
6.789–98   309
Eclogues
1.6–8   72, 309
4   48, 307, 345
4.1–10   48, 73

PAPYRI

Athen.
15.702a   348
Derveni papyrus   65
Papyri Graecae Magicae
VII.795–85   207
P. Egerton
2   145
P. Heidelberg
1716.5   72, 348
P. London
280.6   351
P. London 1912
46–51   19
70–104   339
P. Oxyrhynchus
8.1143.4   313
37.5–7   351
37.5–6   314
840   145
1143.4   20, 314
1453.10–11   48, 72

P. Rainer
19.813   326

INSCRIPTIONS AND ARCHAEOLOGICAL MATERIALS

*Corpus Inscriptionum
Latinarum (CIL)*
10.3757   20n25
10.8375   313
*Corpus Inscriptionum
Semiticarum (CIS)*
2.199   343
*Die Fragmente der
griechischen Historiker
(FGH)*
90 F 125   306
*Inscriptiones Graecae ad
Res Romanas Pertinentes
(IGRR)*
4.18   76
4.144   304
4.145   20
4.975   72
4.1398   313
I. Olympia
53   73, 317
I. Pergamon
381   317
*Orientis Graeci Inscriptiones
Selecta (OGIS)*
224   302
332   76n100
415   328, 343
418   328, 343
423   328, 343
425   328, 343
426   328, 343
456   73, 316
533   313
606.1   314
655.1–2   48
Rosetta Stone
2.9   326
*Sylloge Inscriptionum
Graecarum (SIG)*
747   44

www.ingramcontent.com/pod-product-compliance
Lightning Source LLC
Chambersburg PA
CBHW021813300426
44114CB00009BA/154